VICKERS
AIRCRAFT
SINCE 1908

Wellington Is of 149 Squadron 'showing the flag' over the centre of Paris on Bastille Day, 14 July, 1939; Les Invalides appears at the bottom of the picture. (*Charles E. Brown photo.*)

VICKERS
AIRCRAFT
SINCE 1908

C. F. ANDREWS

FUNK & WAGNALLS
New York

To the pilots who first flew
the aircraft mentioned herein

CONTENTS

FOREWORD

Many of the leading characters whose work is recorded in this book have passed on. It is a book that could have been written with greater facility a decade or more ago, for many of the records so essential to compile a definitive technical history of this sort proved difficult to find. How grateful the author would have been to have put questions to Rex Pierson on so many of the perplexing and sometimes contradictory facts which were uncovered in the arduous research involved in writing the story of Vickers aircraft. Alas, Pierson died before retirement. So the facts have been pieced together painstakingly by a small band of devoted enthusiasts, all with expertise and experience of the specialist business of designing and making aircraft.

When the book was first mooted all that could be found was a collection of general arrangement drawings—many reproduced in these pages in simplified form. Little difficulty was encountered, of course, with the period since the end of the second world war, as the great success of the Viscount, for example, has been well chronicled by aeronautical writers, fed by factual information from the publicity offices at Weybridge and Vickers House. Much of the earlier backroom story, however, remained very much a closed book, presumably because Vickers were concerned mainly with military contracts subject to security restrictions prevailing at the time.

Fortuitously the records kept over the years in so immaculate a fashion by the late W. H. (Sammy) Seabrook, technical assistant to Rex Pierson, have survived, and the few files not found were like pieces missing from a jig-saw puzzle; bits which had to be provided by circumstantial evidence. An excellent framework was available to the author in the form of H. E. Scrope's unpublished thesis *Golden Wings*, compiled to aid J. D. Scott in his most able chronicle of the Vickers enterprise, in its many branches, entitled *Vickers—A History*. C. H. Barnes gave his usual unselfish assistance and the work of Jack Bruce also was of great help in regard to first world war aircraft.

On this basic structure the detailed story was filled in, with facts and data gleaned from researches involving many hundreds of man-hours of spare time on the part of my voluntary assistants and myself. My hope is that the reader will find the end product acceptable.

I must thank in particular Eric Morgan for his collation and compilation of the statistics in this book, especially in the Appendices. James Goulding, I feel sure, enjoyed unravelling the complexities of Virginia and Victoria development, and the result will I know please Rex King, former Editor of *Flight*, who begged me some years ago to sort them out. I was relieved of a heavy burden when Bill Cox, at one time of R. J. Mitchell's design staff at Supermarine, voluntarily undertook to search through scores of files to reveal at long last the inner story of Wellington development in all its varying rôles. Alas he, too, has now passed on—a great loss to aeronautical history, for his work in this field was unfinished.

As regards the drawings, I would have been lost without some professional assistance from Ted Shreeve, Norman Jackman, Jeff Booth and Mrs Carnell and her staff of lady tracers, and to all these I again render thanks. I must also pay tribute to Peter Osman for acting as chief detective in spotting differences of factual opinion between the various parts of the book. As an inspector in the works assembly at Weybridge, he knew where to look, and his unfortunate incapacity to do active work gave him the opportunity and time to take a long, hard look at the whole canvas. The final presentation of the drawings has been in the capable hands of L. E. Bradford and the multiplicity of illustrations, collected from diverse sources over a long period, has been amplified by much assistance from the Weybridge and Vickers House photographic departments.

In a work of this kind it is manifestly impossible to credit all those kind people who have contributed in one way or another by drawing on their memories or searching through their precious personal archives. In this category I am especially grateful to Bob Handasyde, bearer of a name well known in aeronautics half a century ago—that of his father—and to former Vickers service engineers who are mentioned in the text. From them so much has been learned of what went on in that closed shop known between the wars as Martlesham Heath.

It has been a privilege for me to accept all this invaluable assistance and that of many others who cannot be mentioned for want of space. Finally, I feel an obligation to Norman Barfield, of Weybridge publicity, for so kindly agreeing to read the whole of the text for technical authenticity, in which capacity he must have few rivals, particularly where Weybridge aircraft are concerned.

C. F. A.

Weybridge, 1 *October*, 1968

Introduction

The great armament firm Vickers, Sons and Maxim * Limited became interested in aircraft as soon as their military potential was appreciated. This was in the period just after the turn of the twentieth century when powered balloons, or dirigibles as they were called, were successfully navigated through the air and when the Wright brothers had shown that powered flight with a man-controlled heavier-than-air machine was a reality.

Vickers' interest crystallised in 1908, when they undertook to construct a large airship of the rigid type for the Admiralty. The British naval authorities were alarmed at the progress being made by the German Zeppelin airships, particularly in their application to naval reconnaisance.

This Vickers' naval airship, facetiously called the *Mayfly*, was not a success, and on its trials at Barrow suffered structural failure when being brought out of its shed for flight. However, this setback made no difference to Vickers' attitude to aviation, and in the same year as the disaster, 1911, the Company established an aviation department to design and construct aeroplanes and, a little later, started a flying school at Brooklands, scene of a great deal of the early British pioneering effort in aviation.

A small part of Vickers' works at Erith in Kent was allocated to aircraft construction, and an aircraft drawing office was established at Vickers House in Broadway, Westminster. A licence to manufacture and sell aeroplanes and engines of French R.E.P. design was negotiated with Robert Esnault Pelterie of Billancourt, Seine, largely on the recommendation of Capt (later Major) Herbert F. Wood, formerly of the 12th Lancers and a pioneer aviator trained at the Bristol School of Flying, Brooklands. A favourable report had been made to Vickers on the R.E.P. designs by Capt Murray Sueter, RN, who as Admiralty Inspecting Captain of Airships was overseeing the construction of the airship No. 1 at Barrow, in a similar capacity to an R.T.O. (resident technical officer) today. He not only confirmed that the two types of R.E.P. aeroplanes considered were outstanding examples of French design but also suggested to Vickers that the Admiralty might want British-built naval aeroplanes.

This was wishful thinking as, in response to a serious presentation from Vickers of the case for a naval aeroplane, the Admiralty declared that they did not propose to acquire aeroplanes for naval service. In spite of this

---

* A note on the individual pioneering work of Sir Hiram Maxim in aviation is included in the Appendices.

1

Major Herbert F. Wood, creator of Vickers Aviation (on left) and Sir George R. Edwards, C.B.E., consolidator of the enterprise in more recent days.

rebuff, Vickers went ahead by buying a French-built R.E.P. monoplane for demonstration and an R.E.P. rear fuselage. The latter was converted into the first Vickers aeroplane, known as No. 1 monoplane. This redesign was done mainly by Archibald R. Low, engaged as a designer draughtsman by Vickers along with George H. Challenger, an engineer, and Leslie F. Macdonald, a pilot, from the British and Colonial Aeroplane Co. Later Howard Flanders also joined the team from Brooklands, where he had been constructing aeroplanes of his own design.

The essential features of the R.E.P. were a steel-tube structure and a form of pilot control which in broad principle remains today and embodied the single control-column. Subsequently the subject of much litigation, this control system later cost Vickers some £40,000 (with other contractual liabilities), but Pelterie, its inventor, was not so fortunate with claims on other constructors for alleged infringements of his patents.

Vickers No. 2 monoplane was sold for the 1912 Australian Antarctic expedition, and its type successors were usefully employed in Vickers' Flying School. This, like other flying schools at Brooklands, was also instructing with pusher biplanes of the Farman genus, a modified version very similar to the Bristol Boxkite. The immediate advantages of the pusher aeroplane for carrying a nose-mounted machine-gun must have occurred to Vickers' design office quite early. An extraordinary series of project designs emerged from the aviation department at this time, including a whole range of proposals for the German Government, none of which ever materialised, as war overtook the schemes in 1914.

In common with other aircraft concerns just before the first world war, Vickers had been allocated contracts by the War Office or Admiralty (who had by then changed their attitude) for military or naval aircraft. Vickers' orders were for the B.E.2 and B.E.2a to the design of the Royal Aircraft Factory at Farnborough, and were made at Erith, Kent. A summary of

2

Vickers production up to 1918 (end of the first world war) is given in the appendices. In this it will be noticed that after Weybridge works were established at Brooklands in 1915 large numbers of Government-designed aircraft were produced there.

Meanwhile, in the aircraft design office, which had been located at Vickers' Crayford works since August 1914, together with most of the aircraft production, R. K. Pierson, a former engineering apprentice of Vickers and a qualified pilot, had been appointed chief designer, a position he was destined to hold for 28 years. His first solo task was to redesign the Barnwell Bullet single-seat scout.

Following the pattern of the aircraft industry at that time, Vickers produced a large number of designs to cater for the primary requirements of the air services. Few of these experimental types gained an official order, as none was particularly successful when submitted to flight test at the Central Flying School, Upavon, or later at the Aeroplane Experimental Establishment, Martlesham Heath.

In July 1917 Vickers were asked by the Air Board to design a long-range bomber using Hispano Suiza engines. Pierson had previously designed a small twin-engined biplane, the F.B.8 of equal span, as a development of Howard Flanders' F.B.7 of unequal span. The F.B.8 was a fighting aeroplane following ideas current in 1915 and 1916 and had little more in combat capability than contemporary single-engined two-seat fighters. Although it was abandoned, the experience proved useful in designing the new bomber to meet the Air Board specification, the main provision of which was to carry a respectable bomb load to Berlin and then to return to base in Northern France or East Anglia.

Staff of Vickers Flying School at Brooklands, pre-first world war, posing in front of Vickers-REP Monoplane; under propeller boss, R. H. Barnwell, chief instructor, also with cap, Archie Knight, assistant instructor.

3

The Vickers prototype bomber, F.B.27, with Hispano Suiza engines, was flown by Capt Gordon Bell on 30 November, 1917, Vickers' former chief test pilot, Harold Barnwell, having been killed the previous August while testing the prototype F.B.26 pusher fighter. Later adopting the Rolls-Royce Eagle as its standard engine, the production F.B.27A was designated the Vimy, a name which has gone down into aeronautical history. This aeroplane, the first to make a non-stop Atlantic crossing, established Pierson in the front rank of designers. The Armistice of 11 November, 1918, intervened to prevent the Vimy going operational in the first world war.

Cancellation of war contracts after the Armistice led to retrenchment in the young aircraft industry, with disastrous results for many of the companies which had sprung up during the war. After considering Crayford as a peacetime aircraft production works, Vickers decided to concentrate solely at Weybridge, and the design office was moved there from Imperial Court, Knightsbridge, where it had been since 1916.

The design staff was drastically reduced in numbers and was hived off into Pinewood House, where Percy Maxwell-Muller, the works manager, had lived during the war, but was later brought within the Weybridge works confines. Muller had followed F. T. Hearle (later of de Havillands) in that position, with Archibald Knight, who had been an instructor in Vickers' flying school, as his assistant. Later their titles were raised to works superintendent and works manager respectively.

The Weybridge factory remained under the control of the aviation department of Vickers Ltd, which department had as its manager Capt Peter Dyke Acland, who had succeeded Major Wood. The latter had succumbed to the influenza epidemic in December 1918. Major Wood undoubtedly had been the creator of Vickers aviation, notably in his close association with French constructors and aircraft contracts, leading to the rapid expansion of Vickers' enterprise in this field.

Thus after the first world war a new horizon confronted the aircraft industry, and for the first time a gap appeared between potential production and orders for aircraft. Vickers aviation attempted diversification on a small scale with non-aviation products, but gradually reverted to full-scale aircraft production by 1924. By then the works were fully occupied with Vimys, Vernons and Viking amphibians and were about to embark on the long series of Virginia bombers and Victoria bomber-transports, both types extending into numerous variants.

R. K. Pierson had channelled his post-war ideas in two directions, the development of the large twin-engined long-range load carrier and of the single-engined amphibian flying-boat. The former was triggered off by the success of the Vimy and the latter by the winning of the 1920 Air Ministry competition for amphibians by the Vickers Viking III. A close runner-up in this competition was the entry from the Supermarine Aviation Company, which in 1928 became a subsidiary of Vickers.

At this stage it is appropriate to indicate that already Vickers' aircraft design was developing into distinct families, as shown in the accompanying genealogical tree. The succeeding chapters deal with individual types, as developments from earlier aircraft of similar configuration and character-istics, on this basis. From this analysis emerge two main lines of develop-ment. One is the evolution of transport aircraft, from the Vimy to VC10, and the other is the preoccupation of Vickers with military aeroplanes, from the Gunbus through the Wellington to the Valiant and the ill-fated TSR2. Pierson was always striving to find a peg to hang his military hat on, and his successors followed his example.

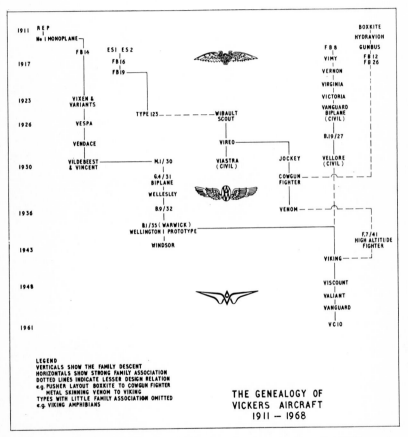

THE GENEALOGY OF
VICKERS AIRCRAFT
1911 — 1968

LEGEND
VERTICALS SHOW THE FAMILY DESCENT
HORIZONTALS SHOW STRONG FAMILY ASSOCIATION
DOTTED LINES INDICATE LESSER DESIGN RELATION
e.g. PUSHER LAYOUT BOXKITE TO COWGUN FIGHTER
METAL SKINNING VENOM TO VIKING
TYPES WITH LITTLE FAMILY ASSOCIATION OMITTED
e.g. VIKING AMPHIBIANS

Another family of aircraft developed with some success by Vickers was in the single-engined tractor biplane class, from the F.B.14 of 1916 to the Vincent which saw service in the earlier years of the second world war. Pierson's efforts to produce a single-seat fighter never quite achieved a winner, although no doubt he was inspired by his first introduction in that field with his redesign of the Barnwell Bullet and the massive production of the S.E.5a by Vickers in the first world war.

5

In one class Vickers were always in the front rank, that of the long-range load carrier for military use. Following the Vimy bomber and its transport version, the Vernon, a larger design of similar configuration was evolved and appeared in operational service in 1924 as the Virginia. In the Virginia, the standard night-bomber of the Royal Air Force up to the middle 1930s, the more powerful Napier Lion engines replaced the Rolls-Royce Eagles of the Vimy and Vernon. The bomber-transport version of the Virginia was the Victoria, also used operationally for many years. It incorporated the same wing structure and engine mountings with the fat-bodied fuselage then becoming a regular feature of Vickers transport aircraft.

Jack Alcock and Arthur Whitten Brown in Newfoundland before their historic first direct flight across the Atlantic in a Vimy, 14 and 15 June, 1919.

No doubt the epic flights of Vimys in 1919 and 1920 contributed to the selection of the type for military requirements. The supreme effort of Alcock and Brown, in their first direct crossing of the Atlantic in June 1919, is now regarded as one of the outstanding events of aviation history. Of equal value technically, the flight of Ross Smith and Keith Smith from England to Australia in a Vimy late in the same year was a pointer to the future, when prepared airfields would be established, with all the aids to navigation and ground control that exist today. Similarly, the valiant attempts of Van Ryneveld and Quintin Brand, as well as of Cockerell and Broome, to reach the Cape in Vimys emphasised the critical influence of high temperatures and altitudes on engine performance and reliability. Today, Africa is a recognised proving ground for modern aeroplanes undergoing tropical condition certification.

The Vimy, quite apart from the fame accruing from its great flights in the immediate period after the first world war, was notable in civil air transport. Soon after the Armistice Capt Acland and R. K. Pierson began to think about peacetime aviation. Their deliberations led to three ideas for the short-term development of civil aircraft. The first was a conversion of the Vimy for commercial flying, named appropriately the Vimy Commercial. With the same wing and tail structure and basic rear fuselage, a new forebody was designed in wooden monocoque form, with a large oval cross-section which accommodated an unobstructed cabin remarkably like that of a modern transport aeroplane. In only one respect was this aeroplane before its time. Civil aviation hardly developed so rapidly in the early 1920s to justify Vickers' hopes that many of the lost war contracts for Vimys could be regained. However, the Vimy Commercial may be regarded as the 'true father of all airliners', as described by Oliver Stewart, a well-informed aeronautical writer.

Tommy Broome (*left*) and Stan Cockerell before the start of their attempt to fly to the Cape in Vickers Vimy Commercial G-EAAV in 1920.

The second project started by Pierson at the same time as the Vimy Commercial—at the end of 1918—was for a single-engined amphibian flying-boat. The paucity and poor quality of aerodromes throughout the world at that time was evident, and an amphibian aeroplane would be able to use land or water bases with equal facility. The theoretical advantage of stretches of water, such as harbours, creeks, estuaries and inland lakes, seemed attractive to Pierson, and he called his amphibian the Viking, after the seafaring explorers who sallied forth from Scandinavian fjords in olden times. As recorded later, the Vickers Viking did achieve a measure of success, but again not quite matching up to the optimistic forecasts of potential sales.

The third project, of 1919, was the most ambitious of all. Designs were prepared for a giant long-range flying-boat, called the Vigilant, to be powered by eight Rolls-Royce Condor engines in coupled pairs. The Vigilant ultimately went the way of so many ambitious and expensive projects; it fell under the Government economy 'axe' of 1922 and support was withdrawn. The design anticipated the Dornier Do X by some years and multi-engined trans-oceanic airliners by many more.

E. R. C. 'Tiny' Scholefield, chief test pilot of Vickers from 1926 to 1928, engaged in his pastime, motor racing at Brooklands.

Pierson was never noted for aesthetic lines in his designs, but surely his next effort, a single-engined short-haul airliner called the Vulcan, was the most ungainly of all. It was not easy to fly, probably because of the excessive side area of the Commercial-type body. Inevitably it was dubbed the *Flying Pig* by Instone Air Line staff. Sad to tell, expected demand failed once more to materialise, and redundant Vulcan bodies later made a funeral pyre in the middle of Brooklands.

Sales of Vimy Commercials were more successful, on paper at least, and the Chinese were persuaded to buy 40 of them, the ultimate fate of which is uncertain, although indicated by Cecil Lewis in his delightful last chapter of *Sagittarius Rising*. With these Commercials went also a small number of VIM* (Vickers Instructional Machine) and rebuilt Avro 504K trainers. The VIM was a converted F.E.2d with a redesigned dual-control nacelle.

In parallel with the development of the larger twin-engined bombers and commercial aeroplanes and of the Viking amphibians, Vickers produced a series of metal-framed single-engined military biplanes. These were lineal descendants of the wartime F.B.14, the only outstanding characteristic of which had been its steel-tube airframe members. The strength of this basic structure had been statically proved at Farnborough in 1917. This led to the continuance of the structural theory in the Vixen of 1923 and its derivatives. One of these, the Venture, won the Air Ministry competition in 1923 for a two-seat fighter-reconnaissance aeroplane, and six were ordered for the Royal Air Force.

Some success also was achieved abroad with this family, Chile buying

* See page 476.

8

19 Vixen Vs in 1925, and Portugal 14 Valparaisos with a licence to build others. In 1928 two Valparaisos made a long-distance flight to and around the Portuguese colonies in Africa, at that time a considerable achievement in tropical and equatorial conditions. Contributing to this success was the Napier Lion engine, which was then at the peak of its performance and reliability.

In the same family can be included the later and larger Vespa, which, powered by the Bristol Jupiter, offered a general-purpose military aeroplane in what today would be called the STOL class—with high lift for operation in and out of cramped airfields. Here again limited success was obtained, with sales to Ireland and Bolivia. In 1932 a specially converted Vespa with a Bristol Pegasus S3 engine took the World Height Record at 43,976 ft, piloted by Capt Cyril Uwins of the Bristol Aeroplane Company.

In 1925 Vickers formed a separate company to exploit in its designs the patents in metal construction of Michel Wibault, a French aeronautical engineer, thus following the traditions originally established with the R.E.P. patents. This simple construction promoted torsional rigidity in a cantilever wing and followed the lead set by Junkers as far back as the first world war. While this was only a tentative approach to all-metal construction, the availability of duralumin light alloy, then Vickers' proprietary, and the knowledge gained, bore fruit later on when complete metal structures were adopted by Vickers.

Types which employed Wibault construction were the Wibault Scout for Chile, the Vireo experimental fleet fighter and the Viastra; the Vellore and Vellox civil transport aeroplanes used certain Wibault features, such

After capturing the world altitude record in September 1932 the leading people concerned were photographed in front of the Vickers Vespa with special Bristol Pegasus 'S' engine: left to right, H. W. R. Fedden (later Sir Roy Fedden), chief engineer and engine designer, Bristol Aeroplane Co; Capt Cyril Uwins, chief pilot to Bristol Aeroplane Co; and, on right, R. K. Pierson, designer of the Vespa.

as corrugated fuselage panels, while the Jockey single-seat fighter of 1929 was basically developed on Wibault structural methods.

In 1928 national reorganisation in the engineering industry led to a merger of the heavy engineering interests of Vickers and Armstrong Whitworth in a new company called Vickers-Armstrongs Ltd. Because Sir W. G. Armstrong Whitworth Aircraft Ltd were not included in this merger, endless confusion has since been caused regarding aircraft company identification.

Another aspect of reorganisation which was to have a profound influence on Vickers' aviation interests was the acquisition at the same time of the Supermarine Aviation works of Southampton. From then on the two former rivals went forward in a mutual aid pact, both in design and production. An immediate result of the coupling of these two companies was the construction at Woolston, Southampton, of the Vickers Viastra IIs for West Australian Airways and of wing structures for the Air Ministry Vildebeest contracts. Supermarine also built the special Viastra for official journeys of the then Prince of Wales, while Weybridge designed and made the wings of the Southampton X three-engined flying-boat, a Supermarine design.

The Weybridge works were reconstructed at this time, with greatly increased floor space, and kept busy with Air Ministry orders for Armstrong Whitworth Siskins and, later, Hawker Harts and Hart Trainers, additional to Vickers' own designs.

Over the course of time Vickers had also developed a large range of specialised aircraft accessories and were bulk suppliers to the rest of the British aircraft industry and to overseas customers. Tommy Duncan was Vickers' accessory designer, and the range included oleo-pneumatic undercarriages, fuel pumps and cocks, Vickers-Potts oil-coolers, Vickers-Reid blind flying instruments, Vickers-Davis navigation lights and a host of VGS (Vickers general stores) parts in addition to AGS (aircraft general stores) fittings as already standardised since the first world war. From this branch of Vickers aviation developed much of the aircraft ancillary industry that exists today. The originators had by force of circumstances to drop much of this enterprise, when massive orders for complete aircraft began to flow in under the Royal Air Force expansion scheme of 1935, except for complete undercarriages, which on Vickers aircraft have always been of Vickers design.

Before the RAF expansion scheme Vickers had continued to explore the slender civil market as then existing, and two quite promising designs were produced, one a development of the other. These were the Vellore and Vellox. The Vellore first appeared as a single-engined biplane for the Air Ministry; later a twin-engined model was built and made an appearance in the 1930 King's Cup Air Race and was the last complete aeroplane ever made at the Crayford works of Vickers. The refined Vellox was added to Imperial Airways fleet.

On the military side Vickers made two attempts to win the competition

10

for a heavy bomber to replace the Virginia. The designs were a twin-engined biplane, known after its specification number as the 19/27 Bomber, and a four-engined private-venture biplane of similar configuration but of larger scale, known simply as Type 163. Neither was accepted, and the small official contract went elsewhere, in the middle of yet another cycle of disarmament retrenchment. However, the rise of Hitler soon altered the situation, and the re-armament forced upon the Government of the day by events beyond its control put Vickers aviation into the expansion scheme of the Royal Air Force.

On 1 January, 1930, an event of some influence on later technical history occurred at Weybridge; B. N. Wallis was appointed Chief Designer (Structures) after the winding up of the design of the Vickers airship R.100. Wallis had been a Vickers' engineer since before the first world war, but is best known today as Sir Barnes Wallis, designer of the Dam-buster bomb and, more recently, for his researches into variable-geometry aircraft.

As chief structures designer, Wallis initiated a programme of research into the improvement of strength/weight ratios in airframes, for which his design experience in the light-alloy framework for R.100 had been a good introduction. When he eventually evolved his geodetic system of stress-balancing members he was not, as is commonly held, repeating something that was done in the airship but was attempting to abolish main members by developing the lattice-work netting of the airship ballonets as itself the main structure, on great-circle principles. In this connection, it should be noted that despite progress by way of the Junkers/Wibault system towards stressed-skin construction, this was still in its infancy in Britain at that time; fabric was still the conventional covering, and remained so in Vickers' designs later than most, because of Wallis geodetics.

In 1930 a specification, M.1/30, was issued for a torpedo-bomber for operation from aircraft carriers. An attempt was made by Wallis to intro-duce weight saving in the structure by special lightweight screwed attach-ments for the tubular members, and by drastically reducing the secondary structure. Unfortunately the specification had overdone the weight-saving requirement, and the aeroplane broke up during a test flight by Capt J. ('Mutt') Summers with J. Radcliffe as his flight test observer. Both landed safely by parachute. From the laconic entry in Mutt's log regarding the termination of this flight, it may be assumed that his oral comments were unprintable! In his 22 years as Vickers' chief test pilot, Summers made the first flights of some 30 prototypes, but this was probably his most embar-rassing moment.

Then came the issue of specification G.4/31 for a general-purpose aero-plane. Wallis had been experimenting with a geodetic wing for the Viastra, and Vickers G.4/31 biplane incorporated a geodetic fuselage. However, in a private-venture monoplane of high aspect ratio to the same specifica-tion, Weybridge went the whole way and applied the new Wallis system to the complete airframe. There was such an improvement of performance

Visit of MPs to Weybridge works in 1935 during the Wellesley biplane versus monoplane controversy—on extreme right is B. N. Wallis, later Sir Barnes Wallis; on extreme left, Capt Broome; in front row with cigarette, Sir Robert McLean; on his right, P. Maxwell-Muller; third from right, Mutt Summers; and fifth from right, R. K. Pierson.

that the Air Ministry had really no alternative but to order this G.4/31 monoplane, subsequently named the Wellesley, in place of the biplane.

Although the Wellesley was intended for general-purpose operation, its range and payload were attractive in the bomber rôle, and it became the equipment of several squadrons of the RAF. In November 1937 a specially formed Long Range Flight of the RAF captured the World Distance Record with Wellesleys, modified to take a high-compression Pegasus engine with economical cruise characteristics, and with long-range tankage.

As a bomber the Wellesley was fitted with external bomb-pods slung under the wings to avoid breaking the geodetic great circles of its slender fuselage. The same problem cropped up later when a second geodetic type was designed to specification B. 9/32 as a medium bomber. Eventually this was solved, and the Wellington, as the type was finally named, became the mainstay of Bomber Command in the critical first years of the second world war. Whether the legendary resistance to battle damage of the *Wimpey*, as the Wellington was affectionately dubbed, has been coloured by process of time is a moot point; however, many senior officers of the Royal Air Force attributed their continued existence to the ability of the surviving geodetic members of their Wellington to hang together during the limp home after damaging action.

Parallel with the complete redesign of the B.9/32 into the Wellington I was the design of a heavy bomber, also twin-engined, to specification B.1/35, later called the Warwick. In fact, the larger aircraft structure was drawn first, and this accounts for the fuselage and wings of the Wellington having a section of fuselage and inner panels of the wings missing in the station numbering.

While the Wellington was going from strength to strength and was to serve throughout the war in almost every rôle possible for a twin-engined aeroplane, the Warwick was bedevilled by the slow development of the high-power, multi-cylinder engines around which it was designed.

Brought up on more conventional methods, Maxwell-Muller and Knight shied at geodetics and retired in 1936, after long and hard service at Weybridge. They had been primarily responsible for keeping Vickers in aircraft production during the lean years and deserve full recognition, as business was down to the bone on more occasions than they cared to remember, attributable to the vacillations of the official procurement policy of successive governments.

In their stead, Trevor Westbrook was brought back from the Supermarine works, where he had been deputy superintendent since the takeover by Vickers, and his drive eventually succeeded in getting the geodetic airframe concept through on the shop floor. Special rolling and forming machines were evolved to produce the curved members, and similar machinery has been in use ever since for airframe components of Vickers aircraft up to the VC10.

Before leaving the Wellington story to its appropriate chapter, mention must be made of the shadow factories built under Government sponsorship at Chester and Blackpool, a wise move, justified later in view of the bombing of Weybridge works, at Brooklands, early in September 1940. This enemy action seriously reduced Wellington production capacity until it was restored by a vast dispersal scheme of small production units around the Weybridge district.

Meanwhile Pierson unsuccessfully tendered for a four-engined bomber to specification B.12/36, but the Supermarine works of Vickers gained a

Visit of H.M. King George VI and Queen Elizabeth to Vickers-Armstrong's factory at Chester to see wartime Wellington production; with His Majesty is B. A. Duncan, general manager (Chester), with Her Majesty is H. Kilner, managing director aviation division (later Sir Hew Kilner) and on extreme right is R. P. H. Yapp, commercial manager, V-A Chester factory and later managing director Vickers Ltd.

development contract for two prototypes. By a trick of fate, the two partly built Supermarine B.12/36 airframes were wrapped round the girders at the Itchen works, Southampton, during another enemy air raid in the month following the bombing of Brooklands. So Supermarines went on with the Spitfire, and Weybridge, Chester and Blackpool continued with the Wellington and its many variants.

At this time Pierson once again revived his giant aeroplane concept and submitted a scheme for a Wallis geodetic six-engined bomber with a 20-ton bomb load. In vain did he try to convince the Air Ministry that a seven-member aircrew was better than 48 (equivalent of a squadron of Wellingtons) and that six engines with about half the aggregate structure weight were better than 24. The official argument, no doubt, was that one bomber was much more vulnerable than a squadron of them, some of which should get through the defences. One more unsuccessful attempt was made later in the war to promote a scheme for a very large bomber (not the Windsor), so the VC10 remains, in fact, the largest aeroplane ever turned out from the Vickers stable, although things might have been otherwise.

However, a four-engined heavy bomber, the B.3/42 Windsor, was designed and produced in three prototypes with progressive development, the third carrying remotely controlled cannon armament in engine nacelle barbettes. With the higher speeds then prevailing, some difficulty was encountered with fabric billowing, and a new pattern of material was evolved embodying a metal-mesh interweave.

Destined for the Pacific theatre of war, the Windsor never saw service. The contract for the Windsor was whittled down to a small batch with Rolls-Royce Griffon piston engines or, later, Clyde propeller-turbines. Even this contract was cancelled, which was unfortunate, as the ultimate development of Wallis geodetics never materialised and the early experience that might have accrued from operating propeller-turbines was lost.

After the war was over, Vickers were quickly off the mark and produced the first post-war civil airliner, the VC1 Viking. Early production used geodetic wing and tail structures with a metal monocoque fuselage embodying an unpressurised cabin. Later production at last adopted stressed-skin construction throughout.* Vikings became the mainstay of British European Airways in its formative years and rendered reliable service, as they did to airlines throughout the world.

Then came the VC2 Viscount, the first civil aeroplane with propeller-turbine power to go into production. So much has been written about this phenomenally successful type that only the basic facts need be introduced here. Designed by Vickers in association with the aviation authorities requirements codified by the Brabazon Committee for post-war civil aircraft, the VC2 was an orthodox aeroplane of light-alloy stressed-skin construction with a single-spar wing. Although inevitably outmoded by the passage of time, the airframe has stood up to millions of passenger

* This, however, had been previously used in the Vickers F.7/41 high-altitude experimental fighter of 1942.

14

flying hours without disclosing any major defects such as regrettably beset one or two of the other Brabazon types.

Likewise, the Viscount's Dart turbine was designed to the latest thermodynamic and mechanical theories of its day. It set the seal on the gas-turbine as the ideal prime-mover for subsonic air transport and was one of those aero-engine winners that crop up from time to time, particularly in the history of Rolls-Royce.

A triumvirate of Vickers chief test pilots; in order of succession, Mutt Summers in centre, Jock Bryce on left and Brian Trubshaw on right, photographed by Charles Brown beside the prototype Viscount.

To go back to 1935, just before Trevor Westbrook took over Wellington production, another personality unobtrusively arrived at Weybridge, who was to play the most significant part in the subsequent history of Vickers aircraft. This was G. R. Edwards, who entered the design office in that year and was destined, as Sir George Edwards, to hold the executive reins of the British Aircraft Corporation, formed to merge the aviation interests of Vickers, English Electric and Bristol.

How the VC2 Viscount project popped in and out of the official pigeon-hole is told later, but one thing is certain. With a less forceful character than Edwards in charge of its development design it might still be there. The aircraft industry, and Vickers in particular, is noted for throwing up such hardy spirits when most needed. Sir George Edwards was the champion of the gas-turbine airliner, and the Viscount will rank as one of the milestones of world aviation.

Meanwhile, military variants of the civil Viking were produced for the Royal Air Force. The Valetta (the original spelling of the place name) was a general-purpose version for transport, Army co-operation and crew training. For the last-named rôle, its successor the Varsity was an extensive redesign including a nosewheel undercarriage.

15

Next complete design from Vickers was the first of the new generation of jet bombers for the Royal Air Force, the B.9/48 Valiant. Three years of design and construction resulted in the first flight of the prototype in May 1951, a remarkable achievement in the latter days of complexity, especially as the Valiant was designed with virtually all-electric services. It went into operational service in 1955, its straightforward configuration, internally as well as externally, accelerating its appearance in the RAF. Extensive sub-contracting speeded the rate of production, and the last of the 104 Valiants was delivered in the autumn of 1958.

At the same time, Vickers were producing, with the substantial aid of their Hurn factory near Bournemouth, a steady flow of Viscounts at a peak rate of three a week for the civil market, including a large number for export. Almost from the beginning, one of the outstanding characteristics of Vickers' production has been the turning out—simultaneously—of aircraft of widely differing specifications. The earlier experience of constructing Siskins, Harts, Vildebeests and so on alongside larger aircraft such as the Virginia and Victoria was an experience which was to influence later generations.

In 1953 British European Airways began to think in terms of a Viscount replacement. The Corporation had achieved considerable success in operating the Viscount, and its ideas eventually crystallised into the larger second-generation turbo-prop airliner, the Vanguard. With high-density seating and high-volumetric underfloor capacity for freight, the Vanguard seemed to be the ideal express air coach when projected, but the rapid development of the pure-jet transport mitigated against large sales. The travelling public's ready acceptance of jet travel was unforeseen in 1953.

This was to be no better illustrated than in the four-jet VC10 designed to a requirement of BOAC. The great popularity of this British big jet, which appeared somewhat belatedly because of the Government cancellation of the Vickers V1000 project to a parallel requirement, was because it provided the ultimate in high-speed comfortable air travel. The VC10 was the last aircraft entirely designed and constructed by Vickers and completed over half a century of steady and continuous progress in aviation, as traced in the pages of this book.

16

Mayfly undergoing preliminary mooring trials in Cavendish Dock, Barrow. Comparison with the picture on page 20 reveals that the considerable structural changes made after these trials involved a transposition of the fore and aft engines and propellers.

Vickers Airships

As recorded in the Introduction, Vickers' first interests in aviation came through the airship. The success of Count von Zeppelin in Germany with the development of the rigid type prior to the first world war had led Britain's defence authorities, particularly the Admiralty, to do some hard thinking about the military potentialities of aircraft in general and of the airship in particular. The airship had one great advantage over the fixed-wing aeroplane of the day, and that was endurance, which meant radius of action. At that time there was only a small margin in favour of the aeroplane in speed, but the airship, which generated its lift from the differential weights of the hydrogen-filled gasbags and the volume of air they displaced, could soar above the ceilings of heavier-than-air craft. Because of its capacity to stay aloft for long periods and to reach useful operational heights, the airship was regarded as a practical proposition for long-range reconnaisance. It was these capabilities that had attracted the attention of the German naval command.

On the other hand, the British strategists saw the airship more as a bomb carrier for attacks on docks, shipping and military installations. The progress being made in Germany with rigid airships led the Admiralty to propose in July 1908 that the Royal Navy should build a large airship to test its usefulness. The idea originated in a memorandum to Admiral

17

Fisher, the First Sea Lord, from Capt R. H. S. Bacon, who in 1900 had supervised the introduction of submarines to the Royal Navy. Among the recommendations in this document was the suggestion to place an order with Vickers, Sons and Maxim (later Vickers Ltd) for a rigid type airship, the Company having been closely associated with the Navy in the supply of warships and ordnance.

Approved by the Admiralty, the proposals were submitted to the Cabinet at an opportune time, for it had become known that Germany had allocated large amounts of national finance for airship development following the promise of the rigid types. The Prime Minister of the day, H. H. Asquith, was himself well aware of the value airships could have for the Navy. Treasury sanction having been obtained in principle, the matter then went forward to the sub-committee on air navigation of the Committee of Imperial Defence. The full Committee accepted the proposals in February 1909, and Vickers were offered £30,000 for a complete airship.

Largely as a result of the researches of Dr Robin Higham for his book *The British Rigid Airship 1908–1931*, much more is known today of the design and construction of the Vickers-built HMA No. 1, an enterprise that ended in failure from a number of complementary causes. Design was started late in 1908 and continued into 1909 by a consortium of naval officers and Vickers engineers at Barrow naval construction yard. There was little technical knowledge available, and what there was consisted of submarine experience and sparse information obtained from Germany. Construction began in 1909, and to accommodate the airship, with a length of 512 ft and a beam of 48 ft, Vickers also started the construction of a shed in the Cavendish Dock, as the ship was to float on boat-like gondolas, thus following the lead set by the early Zeppelins with their floating shed on Lake Constance.

In view of the dearth of design and constructional knowledge at that time, the subsequent changes and delays were obviously inevitable and hardly justified the opprobrious nickname *Mayfly* which was to be attached to HMA No. 1. In fact, the design conception was remarkable and, had the project been proceeded with even after the break-up of the ship at its launching, subsequent events, such as the battle against the U-boats in the first world war, might have taken a different turn. *Mayfly* sadly set the pattern for many similar cancellations in British aeronautics in later times.

During the design of the airship, duralumin became available, and the use of this original light alloy, a German invention, promoted a 100 per cent increase in structure strength, with consequent improvement in pay-load and range. Vickers obtained all proprietary rights in the new metal, and it is interesting to note that the first duralumin Zeppelin did not fly until four years later.

Construction of the airship proceeded during 1910 along trial-and-error lines, which included many modifications of the skeleton structure and control surfaces and a considerable amount of research into the material

H.M.A. No. 1 *Mayfly* approaching completion in its shed at Barrow, 1911.

for the gasbags and outer cover. The rubber companies co-operated in the development of the gasbags, which were layers of cotton and rubber; the cover was of silk, treated with a waterproofing and protective substance known as Ioco. Most of the fabrication of the gasbags, the cover and the control-surface covering was done by Short Brothers, who already had considerable aeronautical experience. The two cars or gondolas, which were shaped like small boats because they had to float, were made from a material called Consuta, a copper-sewn mahogany planking, devised by S. E. Saunders of Cowes (later Saunders-Roe). The gondolas carried a 160 hp Wolseley engine in each, with the forward engine driving two four-bladed propellers and the rear engine a single two-bladed propeller.

At the end of September 1910 the naval airship crew left Portsmouth for Barrow in HMS *Hermione*, a light cruiser, under conditions of great secrecy, which also permeated the proceedings in the airship shed. This crew trained inside the shed in uncomfortable conditions throughout the following winter, and on 13 February, 1911, the shed trials of *Mayfly* were made in the presence of the Advisory Committee for Aeronautics, including Capt Murray F. Sueter, then Inspecting Captain of Aircraft, Capt Bacon by that time having retired.

On 22 May the airship was moved out of the shed to undergo mooring trials from a 38 ft mast erected on a pontoon in the Cavendish Dock. She stayed out for two nights and withstood winds of up to 45 mph. For all her impressive appearance, silver on top and yellow underneath, it was clear that when fully loaded she was too heavy by some three tons, and drastic modifications had to be made. A proposal was even made to insert another bay giving an extra 40,000 cu ft of lift, but this was not carried out, partly because of the limiting shed dimensions. Considerable structural alterations were undertaken involving the keel, the cars and the gasbag suspension, and the deletion of a lot of handling equipment derived from traditional naval practice. It was planned originally even to carry an anchor!

By 22 September all the alterations were completed and *Mayfly* was inflated in 10½ hours, weighed and trimmed. Two days later she was eased out of the shed, but just as she was almost clear she was struck by a squall which laid her over on to her beam ends. What happened after that is conjectural (as the official report has been lost) but the fact remains that *Mayfly* broke in two, the damage being aggravated by the jackstay on the top of the ship holding fast and ripping out several frames. The crippled ship was returned to her shed to await the traditional 'inquest' or Court of Inquiry.

By that time Winston Churchill had become First Lord of the Admiralty, and he and the Secretary for War attended the first sitting of the Court

The moment of truth—the structure of *Mayfly* just beginning to break up as the airship was being brought out of its shed at Barrow on 24 September, 1911, when it was struck by a sudden gust. Distortion of the airframe can be seen just forward of the port rear propeller. (*Royal Aeronautical Society photo.*)

Mayfly after collapse of structure.

aboard *Hermione*. Churchill refused to allow the minutes or findings to be published; it was known he was not a protagonist of airships, as became evident later. The cost of the HMA No. 1 programme was estimated to have more than doubled the £30,000 originally allocated, and thus *Mayfly* again set a pattern for the future. But a great deal of knowledge had been gained and, as Dr Higham rightly says, she was not a dead loss.

HMA NO. 9. After the failure of *Mayfly*, Vickers' airship department was disbanded; but it was reconstituted early in 1913 at the request of the Admiralty to undertake the design and construction of a new rigid, HMA No. 9. This department at Barrow lasted for eight years, and in that time produced three rigids, three Parseval-type large non-rigids, a number of the SS Blimp-type non-rigids, kite balloons and airship equipment.

Design started on No. 9 in April 1913 under H. B. Pratt (engaged from S. E. Saunders of Cowes), who had criticised the design of *Mayfly* and had predicted the accident. He took with him an apprentice named B. N. Wallis, who is mentioned later in this book many times and whose name was eventually to become known all over the world.* The order for No. 9 was placed in June 1913.

There were the inevitable delays in design and construction. This airship was also intended to be experimental to give the Admiralty and the Defence Committee data upon which to assess the operation and value of this type of aircraft. No. 9 was ready for erection when war broke out on 4 August, 1914. The old *Mayfly* shed in Cavendish Dock had been superseded by a new establishment on Walney Island, west of Barrow, for Vickers' airship works.

No. 9 then became the subject of a stop–go policy which was the forerunner of many later vacillations in British aviation policy. In December

---

* Previously Pratt had been employed by Vickers on the design staff of *Mayfly*, and Wallis had been apprenticed to J. Samuel White of Cowes, shipbuilders.

1914 two of the Sea Lords of the Admiralty pronounced against spending more money on airships, and Churchill, as First Lord, concurred. On 12 March, 1915, he ordered No. 9's cancellation. Two months later Churchill left the Admiralty, and in June the airship policy was reversed, which meant that Vickers' personnel had to be recalled and the Walney Island base reconditioned.

Construction of No. 9 dragged on until late in 1916, constant delays being caused by major changes in design and by problems in materials and methods. Although Vickers had the experience of *Mayfly* to help, knowledge of German progress with airship development was still scarce, with the exception of the Zeppelin ZIV, which force-landed on a French airfield in April 1913 and was examined in detail by French technicians while the crew were being entertained.

H.M.A. No. 9 in flight showing multiple horizontal control surfaces.

No. 9 was designed from the beginning for the training of crews for later airships. For this reason it was essential that she should be able to withstand heavy handling and at the same time be easy to manoeuvre. Again duralumin was used, with steel strengthening. The airship was 530 ft in length, with a capacity of 880,000 cu ft and a designed gross lift of 26·5 tons. Power was supplied by four 180 hp Wolseley-Maybach engines; the forward motors were equipped with Vickers patent swivelling gear to enable the thrust direction of the propellers to be changed, even at full power, from ahead to astern, up or down or any intermediate direction, an ability of great assistance in manoeuvring the airship near the ground. To reduce the permeability of the envelope to hydrogen, the rubber-proofed cotton fabric had for the first time an inner layer of gold-beater's skin, an innovation which proved very satisfactory in practice.

No. 9 first flew on 16 November, 1916, the first British rigid to fly, but she was unable to lift her specified disposable weight of 3·1 tons. Two of her four 180 hp Wolseley-Maybach engines were taken out and replaced by one 250 hp Maybach recovered from the crashed German Zeppelin L.33. Modification and the removal of the propeller swivelling gear enabled the ship to lift 3·8 tons, and she was accepted on 4 April, 1917. On trials,

H.M.A. No. 23 in flight showing development of single control surfaces.

No. 9 reached a speed of 45 mph and was used for mooring trials and training, based on Howden airship station in Yorkshire. Damaged in a storm, she was broken up in 1918. The estimated cost of the airship, with its shed, was between £120,000 and £150,000.

NOS. 23 AND 26. When the Admiralty had approved the completion of No. 9 on 19 June, 1915, it was proposed at the same time that Vickers be asked to build a sister ship, and in the following August this was approved. The new design was to be known as the '23' class, this being its number in the consecutive order of Royal Navy airships, including the Farnborough Army airships which had been taken over for naval use.

Three '23' class airships were ordered in October 1915 to a modified No. 9 design but slightly longer and with more fullness at bow and stern.

R.26 in flight showing close affinity to the 23 class. (*IWM photo.*)

No. 23 was made by Vickers at Barrow, No. 24 by Beardmore on the Clyde and No. 25 by Armstrong Whitworth near Selby in Yorkshire, all to Vickers' design. A further five airships were ordered in January 1916, only the first of which was built by Vickers to the original design, the other four being of an improved class known as the '23X' and built by Beardmore and Armstrong Whitworth. The Vickers design was the first British airship to bear the prefix R with its number, 26, to signify rigid.

Control car of R.26—details of interest include swivelling propellers and air pressure ducting. (*IWM photo.*)

No. 23 and R.26 were delivered by Vickers in October 1917 and March 1918 respectively and were used for patrols over the North Sea and for training. When No. 23 was taken out of service in 1918 static tests were made with two Sopwith Camels slung underneath, the idea being to launch them in the air for independent sorties. This experiment was continued in 1925 with R.33. With the length increased by five feet compared with that of No. 9, No. 23 and R.26 had their capacity raised by 70,000 cu ft. Four Rolls-Royce Eagle I engines each of 250 hp provided the power, one in the front car driving two swivelling propellers, two in the midships car and the fourth in the rear car. The speed was about 52 mph. Following the lead of Vickers airships Nos. 1 and 9, the structure of these two later types was largely of duralumin.

R.80. Plans for producing rigid airships at a much greater rate for naval reconnaisance and anti-submarine patrols were thrown out of gear in September 1916 when a brand-new Zeppelin, L.33, was captured almost intact on the Essex coast after being shot down by gunfire. Examination of this German airship disclosed such an advanced state of design and per-

R.80 showing Wallis' ultimate development of streamline shape.

formance compared to British practice that a halt was called in the building programme.

Two new British ships were authorised in November 1916 which were copies of L.33. These were R.33 and R.34, built by Armstrong Whitworth and Beardmore respectively. Vickers meanwhile were left with no complete airship to build, as their shed at Walney Island was too small for the intended R.37, also in the new '33' class, therefore they suggested that they should design and build the largest possible ship in the space available. This proposal was accepted, and an order for R.80 was placed in November 1917.

R.80 was designed by B. N. Wallis within the dimensional limits set by the shed at Walney Island, and he evolved a beautiful streamline shape, rejecting in the process the Zalm shape and NPL (National Physical Laboratory) research results. In consequence, the R.80 was calculated to have considerably reduced drag compared with that of its predecessors,

Interior of control car of R.80 disclosing marine-type engine telegraphs and helm.

25

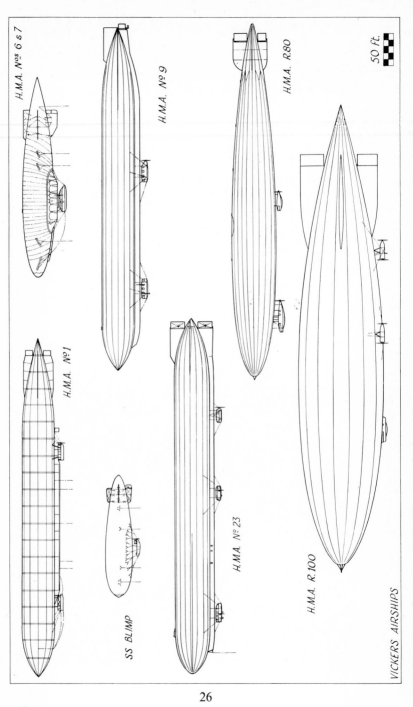

H.M.A. Nos 6 & 7

H.M.A. Nº 9

H.M.A. R.80

H.M.A. Nº 1

SS BLIMP

H.M.A. Nº 23

H.M.A. R.100

VICKERS AIRSHIPS

50 ft.

especially No. 23 of the same length but of smaller beam. The result was a most significant advance in performance, for with four 230 hp Wolseley-Maybach engines, R.80 had a range of nearly 4,000 miles at 65 mph or 6,400 miles at 50 mph. It was well armed, with a quick-firing two-pounder gun and Lewis guns in tactical positions, and eight 230-lb bombs could be stowed horizontally in the keel. The disposable load of the R.80 was 17·8 tons.

In spite of the promise of her configuration, which should have been used as a flying scale-model for the R.100 and R.101, R.80 flew for only 75 hours before she was scrapped in 1924. This was a decision taken by a Labour Government to avoid a challenge from private enterprise, as R.80 was costing less to maintain than the bigger ships designed by the official Naval Constructors' team and, with one exception, was in better condition. Politically the evidence was inconvenient.* In consequence, proposals by Vickers to initiate civil air transport services with R.80 fell on deaf ears.

NON-RIGIDS. During the first world war it was not only with rigid airships that Vickers were engaged; towards the end of 1912 the Admiralty placed an order through Vickers for a non-rigid airship of the Parseval type, at that time a successful German design. In fulfilment of this contract, on 25 November, 1912, Vickers entered into a licence agreement with

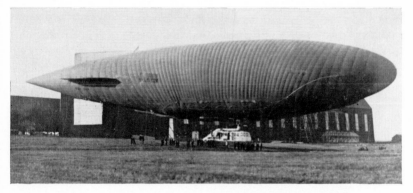

Vickers-built Parseval non-rigid airship on an East Coast station during the first world war. (*IWM photo.*)

Luft-Fahrzeug Gesellschaft, the owners of the Parseval patents, under which Vickers received a full set of drawings for the airship P.L.18, which was built at the Parseval works at Bitterfeld and delivered to the Admiralty at Farnborough in June 1913.

In July 1913 Winston Churchill, the then First Lord, approved a programme which included the purchase of a Parseval airship, the P.5, from Germany (in the event, made by Vickers at Barrow) and the manufacture

---

* *The British Rigid Airship 1908–1931*, R. Higham.

of two more, the P.6 and P.7, by Vickers at Barrow. The envelopes for the last two were also to be made in Germany. During the following November Vickers, through Luft-Fahrzeug, obtained in addition the exclusive rights, free of royalties, from Motorenbau Gesellschaft for Maybach engines on the payment of 120,000 marks and an order for 20 engines.

Construction of the P.5, P.6 and P.7 progressed at Barrow during the early part of the war, but great difficulty was experienced with the German-designed car structure and transmission gear. Eventually the whole of the transmission gear was scrapped and a new type of swivelling propeller equipment was designed and fitted by Vickers. All this work held up the completion of the three airships, and it was not until December 1917 that they all completed their flight trials.

Although these airships were considerably smaller than the rigids, they were large for their type, being some 312 ft in length and with a capacity of 364,000 cu ft. Each was fitted with two Maybach engines mounted side-by-side in a duralumin car; the bottom of this car was made seaworthy to enable alightings to be made on water. The P.5, P.6 and P.7 had a top speed of 42·5 mph, and at their economical cruising speed of 28 mph they had an endurance of 70 hours and a range of 1,950 miles. They were used primarily for patrol duties off the East Coast over the North Sea.

Smaller than these were the SS (Sea Scout) type known as Blimps, and a number was constructed at Barrow. The Blimps had a capacity of 70,000 cu ft and a length of 144 ft, and were operated by a crew of two, who sat in a B.E. type aeroplane fuselage which was suspended by wire ropes attached to the envelope. Blimps had a 1,000 mile range at 35 mph and,

A typical Blimp, at an East Coast station, with its adapted early B.E.2c fuselage serving as control car.

powered by an 80 hp Renault or similar engine, their top speed was approximately 45 mph. They carried out many patrols along the East Coast and in the Mediterranean.

The envelopes for these and many of the gasbags for the rigid airships were made first at Barrow and later at a special works opened in ballrooms in the Palace and Derby Castle grounds at Douglas, Isle of Man. Barrow also manufactured a total of 26 kite balloons.

Before the war much of the fabric used in airship work was imported from the Continent, but the Vickers subsidiary, Ioco Rubber and Waterproofing Co Ltd (today Vickers Ltd Ioco), took over the manufacture of suitable material and by 1918 had produced over 2,500,000 yards.

The last airship built at Barrow was a small non-rigid reconnaissance type for the Japanese Government. It made its first flight on 27 April, 1921, and after successful tests in the Barrow district was dismantled and delivered to Japan by sea.

In addition to actual airship construction work, Vickers engaged in much research in connection with the mooring of both rigid and non-rigid airships. The first Vickers mast was for the *Mayfly* in 1911 and was built on a pontoon secured to a concrete pillar sunk in the Cavendish Dock. The pontoon was free to swing round the pillar so that the airship rode nose to wind with its cars floating on the water. Attached to this mast, the *Mayfly* successfully rode a wind strength of 36 mph gusting up to 45 mph. Experimental work during and after the war resulted in airships being able to ride out much greater wind strengths.

R.100. After the end of the war in 1918 various schemes were put forward for using the airship for long-distance air transport. It had the advantage of being able to remain aloft for at least 24 hours, could hover and operate safely in most conditions of bad visibility, things that no heavier-than-air craft could do at that time. It was the only possible long-range aircraft capable of carrying a reasonable payload of passengers or freight. The attraction of the airship persisted for a number of years in Britain and for even longer in America and Germany. With today's knowledge of meteorology, with better materials and new forms of propulsion and more adequate supplies of helium, many of the vulnerable features of the airship might disappear, factors which led to the abandoning of this type of aircraft and to the Vickers R.100 being the last British rigid airship.

While R.80 was still operational, Vickers were advocating the establishment of a transatlantic airship service and produced designs and estimates to support the proposition, but, in a period of rehabilitation and retrenchment, little interest was aroused. Not until they later put forward a scheme, devised by Cmdr C. D. Burney, for a private passenger service by airship to India and Australia, was any official enthusiasm kindled. The Burney scheme proposed the taking over of all Government airship material and bases by a company financed by Vickers and the Shell Petroleum Group and with an annual Government subsidy. Although the need for Empire

R.100, G-FAAV, jettisoning water ballast.

air communications was appreciated by the Government of the day, it could not agree to all the somewhat involved terms of the scheme.

While negotiations were still proceeding, Vickers, in conjunction with Cmdr Burney, formed a subsidiary, the Airship Guarantee Company. In the following year, 1924, the Labour Government launched their own Empire communications scheme for an airship service to India and Canada, their guiding light being Brig-Gen Lord Thomson of Cardington, a soldier turned politician and an air enthusiast, who was appointed Air Minister. To implement the official scheme, two airships were ordered, R.100 from the Airship Guarantee Company and R.101 from the Royal Airship Works at Cardington, near Bedford. Thus arose a rivalry between the private-enterprise design and the official design, which repeated in a way past errors made when the Royal Aircraft Factory was competing with private industry. The story is best read in Dr Higham's book; here it must be confined to that of Vickers' R.100, designed by B. N. Wallis with a team which included N. S. Norway* as his chief calculator, and Maj P. L. Teed, an eminent metallurgist.

The contract for the construction of R.100 was awarded on 22 October, 1924, and the fixed price was £350,000, with a penalty clause of £1,000 for each half mph below the specified maximum speed of 70 mph. The contract also stipulated an obligation for a flight to India and back, later

* Later to become notable as Nevil Shute, the novelist.

altered to Canada and back. Design began at Vickers House in 1924, was continued at Crayford and finally transferred with the construction to the disused RNAS station at Howden in Yorkshire, an establishment purchased by the Airship Guarantee Company for £61,000.

Every effort was made to build the airship as cheaply and simply as possible. The hull was a 16-sided polygon 709 ft in length with a beam of 133 ft, and of a streamline shape believed to have the lowest resistance of any at that time. Wallis introduced several novel features into the structure, such as the lift being taken at the main joints only, and a system of wire-mesh netting to contain the gasbags and prevent them from pressing on the longitudinal girders. This secondary netting was to give Wallis the germ of the idea for his geodetic structure for aeroplanes. There were 15 gasbags of three-ply material composed of one layer of cotton lined with two layers of gold-beater's skin made in Germany because of non-availability in Britain.

To reduce resistance as much as possible, the passenger accommodation was arranged within the lower hull in three decks, the lowest being occupied by the crew. The dining saloon seated 56 and was on the centre deck, with a viewing promenade 40 ft long on either side. From the saloon a divided staircase led up to a gallery lounge. The cabins, with accommodation for 100 passengers, were of two-berth and four-berth type, located on the middle and upper decks.

R.100 under construction in its shed at Howden, Yorkshire.

Power was supplied by six 670 hp Rolls-Royce Condor IIIB engines mounted in tandem in three cars and driving three tractor and three pusher two-bladed propellers with reverse gear to each rear engine. Originally it was intended to install experimental kerosene-hydrogen engines, but the final choice of well-tried aeroplane engines proved to be wise in view of subsequent events with R.101.

R.100 first flew on 16 December, 1929, commanded by Maj G. H. Scott, and arrived at Cardington about two hours later. From that base it carried out air tests, including an endurance flight of 54 hours mostly in fog. On speed tests a maximum of 81 mph was recorded, well above the specification. The flight to Canada and back was duly completed during July and August 1930, the outward flight time being 78 hours against the prevailing headwinds, and homeward bound 58 hours. Nevil Shute, having become the assistant designer of the R.100, took part in this flight and dramatically tells the story of it in his book *Slide Rule*.

Dining saloon of R.100 with Nevil Shute on stairs to promenade deck.

The only incident of note during the journey was the damage to two of the stabilising fins of R.100 during a brief but violent thunderstorm when flying up the St Lawrence estuary. Fabric covering was ripped in several places, a 15 ft hole appeared and repairs had to be made by the crew while in flight, but the most significant feature of the incident was the proof obtained of the capacity of the structure to withstand the severe stresses set up by the rolling, pitching and hunting of the ship in conditions of severe turbulence.

The structural strength of R.100, despite the simplicity of the design, led to unfavourable criticisms of the strength of the complex structure of R.101, the competitive ship, particularly after the latter had suffered its tragic disaster in the following October. The Government airship was highly experimental and contained many novel features, including diesel

A recent picture of Sir Barnes Wallis, a leading figure in the design of Vickers airships. On his right is a photograph of the Mohne Dam, breached by his spinning bombs.

engines, but the actual cause of the fatal accident at the start of its projected journey to India was never properly established.

With the loss of R.101 and with it a number of the protagonists of the Empire communications programme, including the Air Minister, Lord Thomson and Sir Sefton Brancker, Director of Civil Aviation, the whole airship scheme came to an end. R.100 was taken out of commission, eventually literally steam-rollered and committed to the scrap dealer's yard, and Vickers were still owed some of its cost, the official contention being that the airship had never been accepted!

So Vickers, having lost money over their participation in airship construction over the whole period, were left with the distinction of having built the first British rigid airship and the last.

AIRSHIPS DESIGNED AND BUILT BY VICKERS 1908–1929

Type	Length (ft)	Beam (ft)	Gas volume (cu ft)	Gross lift (tons)	Engines	Total bhp	Max. speed (mph)	Date completed
H.M.A. No. 1	512	48	663,000	20 (estimated)	2 Wolseley	320	40	1911
H.M.A. No. 9	530	53	880,000	26·5	3 Wolseley-Maybach	610 *	45	1917 *
H.M.A. No. 23	535	53	950,000	28·5	4 R-R Eagle I	1,000	52	1917
R.26	535	53	950,000	28·5	4 R-R Eagle I	1,000	52	1918
R.80	534	70	1,250,000	37·5	4 Wolseley-Maybach	920	65	1920
R.100	709	133	5,200,000	156	6 R-R Condor III	4,020	81	1929
NON-RIGIDS								
P.5	312	51	364,000	11	2 Maybach	360	42·5	1917
P.6	312	51	364,000	11	2 Maybach	360	42·5	1917
P.7	312	51	364,000	11	2 Maybach	360	42·5	1918
SS Blimps	144	28	70,000	2·1	1 Renault	80	45	—

* No. 9 was originally completed in 1916 with four engines of 720 total bhp.

Vickers first aeroplane, the No. 1 monoplane, before its first flight at Joyce Green, Dartford, July 1911.

The Early Monoplanes

Vickers, Sons and Maxim presented a strong case to the Admiralty on 3 January, 1911, offering to supply one Pelterie-type monoplane for £1,500. They stressed the point that the framework of the proposed machine, except the wings, was of steel, with a possible substitution of duralumin in later models. In reply, the Admiralty expressed disinterest, and consequently no order materialised. This approach was of some historical significance, for it presaged the adherence of Vickers to advanced structural philosophies and to metal construction in particular. At that time there were few metal aeroplanes.

The metal-tube airframe was indeed the only outstanding characteristic of the early Vickers monoplanes. Beyond the fact that they were quite strong for the performance then prevailing, they had little else to commend them. They were heavy for the limited power of the standard R.E.P. engine, and attempts were made to improve their power/weight ratio by using Gnome or other engines of greater power. The small margin between flying and stalling speeds made them tricky to fly, especially with the lack of power and the absence of inherent stability, the problems of which had still to be solved at that time.

Those were the pioneering days. The hardy aviators who took to the air in flying machines had perforce to learn the hard way. The Vickers monoplanes, with their steel-tube fuselages, were capable of absorbing rougher usage than contemporary wooden aircraft. With their rigid airframes they were also more easily transported, whereas wooden aircraft were easily damaged in transit.

34

No. 1 monoplane was part Pelterie (rear fuselage), but the rest was of Vickers construction. Comparing the standard R.E.P with Vickers' first effort, various small modifications appear to have been made. One of the difficulties encountered in building French aircraft under licence was the conversion of metric mensuration into feet and inches, consequently most of the original drawings had to be redrawn to British practice, although it is true that certain constructors, like Bristol and Martin-Handasyde, adopted the metric system throughout their original designs.

The first monoplane was built in the Erith works of Vickers, Sons and Maxim and not at Barrow-in-Furness as was suggested in the proposals to the Admiralty. H. F. Field was works foreman in charge, and he controlled a small number of workers detailed from general engineering jobs and having no previous experience in aircraft construction. This was a situation that was to reappear later on a much greater scale in aeronautical history, especially in the two world wars.

No. 1 monoplane showing fan-type REP engine and typical REP fuselage of steel-tube construction.

Capt Herbert F. Wood, who had been appointed manager of Vickers' aviation department on 28 March, 1911, made the first flight from a new private aerodrome established by Vickers at Joyce Green, near Dartford, Kent, and adjacent to the Long Reach Tavern by the River Thames. All Vickers' experimental test flying was made from this site right up to the Vimy Commercial of 1919. However, soon after this first flight in July 1911, the No. 1 monoplane was taken to Brooklands and flown there.

Early in 1912 the Vickers Flying School was established at Brooklands in sheds near the Byfleet banking, where later the final erecting shops of Hawker Aircraft Ltd were situated. After the successful trials of No. 1 monoplane, more were developed from the basic design and gave good service in the Vickers School as instructional machines.

No. 1 was written off in a crash. No. 2 was sold to Dr (later Sir) Douglas Mawson for the 1912 Australian Antarctic expedition, but crashed on a trial flight in October 1911 at Adelaide; without its wings it was taken with the expedition as a tractor sledge, but the extreme cold solidified the lubricating oil and the engine seized, so the vehicle never served any

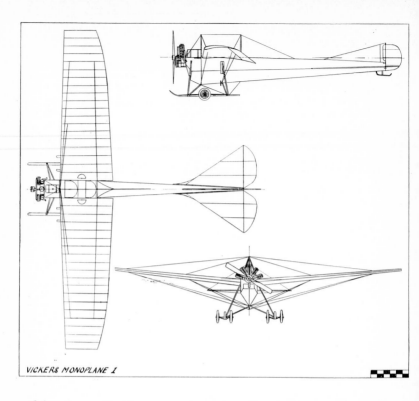

VICKERS MONOPLANE I

useful purpose. However, as a pioneering winterisation test, the steel-tube fuselage stood up so well that in recent years, according to report, its remains have been observed at Cape Denison, the Antarctic base of the expedition.

The first five Vickers monoplanes were shoulder-wing aeroplanes carrying a pilot and passenger (or pupil). The fuselages were of steel tubing with welded and bolted tubular end-fittings at the joints, braced with piano wire and covered with fabric. According to Archie Knight, then an instructor at the School, doping was done by any agent that would tighten up the fabric, various concoctions being tried until the advent of acetate dopes as developed by Dr J. E. Ramsbottom of the Royal Aircraft Factory and by various companies in the paint trade.

The undercarriages of the first Vickers monoplanes had dual wooden skids and four wheels sprung by elastic cord on a lever system at the top of the legs. As was common at the time, lateral control was by wing warping. Various engines and propellers were experimented with, but usually Vickers-built R.E.P. five-cylinder fan radials with air cooling were fitted, reputed to be of 60 hp each. Maximum speed attained was around 56 mph and the empty weight about 1,000 lb. No. 5 monoplane was deeper bodied, which gave the crew more protection from the elements, and

36

No. 2 monoplane at Brooklands in 1911—the primitive giraffe-type servicing steps are interesting.

various small geometrical changes were made between the individual aircraft, including fin and stabiliser configuration.

Extensive redesign was introduced in the No. 6 monoplane, built at Erith in June 1912 for the Military Aeroplane Trials Competition, held on Salisbury Plain that year by the War Office. In the No. 6 the wing span was reduced and the undercarriage simplified by the adoption of a two-wheel arrangement with one central skid. Crew seating was side by side, which led to the unofficial designation of the monoplane as the *Vickers Sociable*. One of the requirements of the Competition was that both members of the crew should be provided with the best possible view of the ground in a forward arc, as the aeroplane was regarded then mainly as an instrument for supporting reconnaissance by cavalry.

No. 6 was powered by a 70 hp Viale seven-cylinder air-cooled radial engine, but this proved too unreliable to give the aeroplane a reasonable chance in the Competition, in which it was flown by L. F. Macdonald, Vickers' pilot. From this type a two-seat biplane was developed and test flown from Joyce Green in December 1912. It was in this aircraft that Macdonald, with his mechanic H. England, crashed in the Thames on 13 January, 1913, both occupants being drowned. The accident was attributed to failure of the 70 hp Gnome rotary engine, which type of engine had previously replaced the Viale in No. 6. No photographs or drawings have survived of this biplane conversion.

Nos. 3 and 5 monoplanes taxying at Brooklands—No. 5 has the deeper body—No. 4 closely resembled No. 3.

Vickers No. 6 monoplane with Viale engine at the War Office Military Aeroplane Trials in 1912 at Larkhill, Salisbury Plain. (*Flight photo.*)

In No. 7 monoplane, Vickers' designers reverted to the earlier and larger layouts with tandem seating, a two-skid four-wheel undercarriage and a 100 hp Gnome rotary engine as power unit. No. 8, the last of the early monoplanes built, reverted to the configuration of No. 6, with a 70 hp or 80 hp Gnome rotary engine as power. It was displayed at the Fourth International Aero Show at Olympia in February 1913. At the next Aero Show, also at Olympia in 1914, Vickers showed a two-seat scout biplane of wooden construction which was obviously a development of the earlier biplane of 1913. Here again few details were released, except that its estimated speed was 100 mph. Presumably this design was dropped in favour of the development of the Vickers Gunbus, which had become a priority for active service.

The following extract is taken from *Flight* for February 1913, and is a description of the typical construction of the Vickers monoplanes, couched in the terminology of the period. It refers to No. 8 as exhibited in the Aero Show of that year.

'The 80 hp Vickers Two-seater Monoplane—This monoplane is of the

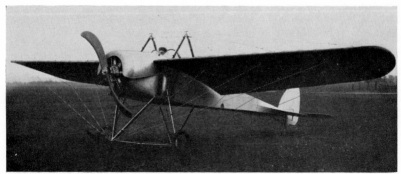

No. 6 monoplane re-engined with a 70 hp Gnome and with a Levasseur-type propeller.

Three-quarter front view of No. 7 monoplane with three-bladed propeller.

same type as the one which, fitted with a 70 hp stationary Viale motor, put up such praiseworthy flights at the time of the Military Aeroplane Competitions in August last. The identical machine shown, driven by a 70 hp Gnome motor, has done upwards of 500 miles in the air at the Vickers private flying ground at Erith, piloted by the late Mr Leslie Macdonald and by their present pilot instructor, Mr Barnwell.

'Its body is an all-steel structure, built lattice-girder fashion, with light tubular longitudinals and tubular cross members. They are assembled by means of welded steel sockets, the joints being afterwards sweated together and pinned. At the front end the four longitudinals meet in a flat upright plate, which serves as one of the mounting plates of the motor. Further support for the motor is provided by a stout flanged plate arranged some little distance behind the front cap. Seats are provided for the pilot and passenger side by side, and there are transparent wind shields fitted in front of them, so that they may suffer no inconvenience from the propeller draught. So carefully has this been carried out that when the machine is

Side view of No. 7 disclosing reversion to the elaborate well-sprung four-wheel undercarriage of Nos. 1 to 5.

flying the occupants can detect scarcely any wind at all. Dual control is fitted. The seats are arranged well forward in the body, so that the occupants have a good clear view over the leading edge of the wings. To still further increase their range of vision, Cellon windows are let into the sides of the body. An interesting fitting in the cockpit is a Clift anti-drift compass, which is mounted over a hole in the floor and by which the machine may be kept on a true course in a side wind.

No. 8 monoplane in Vickers Erith works, showing balanced elevators and sociable side-by-side seating first exploited in No. 6.

'The landing chassis is of the central skid and double wheel type. Two Vs of stout steel tube support the body from a long ash skid, which is curved up in front and which is armoured by the application of Duralumin sheeting. Two axles, carrying the rolling wheels, extend on either side of the skid. Landing shocks are absorbed by elastic springs in tension.

'The wings are built about two tubular steel spars cored with wood. Over them the ash ribs are loosely fitted in such a manner that continual warping of the wings does not tend to weaken them in any way. On the under side of the wings three stranded steel cables proceed to each spar, and these take the main lift. In a similar manner the wings are braced from above to a cabane above the pilot's cockpit.

'The tail is formed by the splaying out of the body at the rear to give a fixed stabilising surface behind which are hinged the two lifting flaps. On this monoplane, as distinct from the one that flew in connection with the Military Competitions at Salisbury, a vertical fin is fitted, which precedes an unbalanced directional rudder. A small steel skid protects the tail unit, but it is probable that it very seldom comes into play, for most of the weight of the tail on landing is taken by the backward laminated extension of the main landing skid.

'Fitted with an engine of 70 hp this monoplane shows a speed of 63 mph, and is capable of climbing with the useful load aboard of pilot, passenger, and sufficient fuel for a $3\frac{1}{2}$-hours' flight at the rate of 250 ft per minute. With an 80 hp Gnome motor installed, the machine has been timed to attain and maintain a speed of over 70 mph.'

The early Vickers monoplanes, supported by three Vickers Boxkites of Farman biplane genus, earned their keep despite the hazards of their low-powered engines of dubious reliability and the local physical obstructions to low-altitude flying at Brooklands in the wooded uplands of nearby St George's Hill and Weybridge Heath. There was also the notorious sewage farm, located inside the motor-racing track towards the railway embankment, ready to receive into its sticky mire the unwary flier in trouble on take-off or approach. The monoplanes competed in the popular flying meetings held at Brooklands in pre-1914 days and were always prominent in the handicap races flown on a circuit out to Coxes Lock Mill, near Addlestone, and back. Those halcyon afternoons of real peacetime aeronautics are fast fading from living memory.

No. 8 monoplane packed for field transport on trailer and complete with ground crew in Napier car.

Vickers Flying School at Brooklands trained 77 pupils between 1912 and 1914, the second highest of all the civilian schools in the country, and was only bettered by the Bristol School, who also trained most of their pupils at Brooklands. From January to August 1914, when Vickers School closed down because of the outbreak of war, it produced 36 pilots with aviators' certificates—popularly known as flying tickets. This was the record for the country, and the list of Vickers pupils contained names of pilots who achieved fame later on. The work of the pre-1914 civilian flying schools contributed much to the air services by way of trained pilots in the critical early period of the first world war.

Meanwhile Vickers went on with their development of metallised airframes as pioneered by the R.E.P. type monoplanes and with the evolution of a gun-carrying pusher biplane as well as various attempts to find a satisfactory alternative engine to the ubiquitous Gnome.

Monoplanes Nos. 1–7

	Nos 1, 2 and 3	No. 6	No. 7
Accommodation:	Pilot and passenger	Pilot and passenger	Pilot and passenger
Engine:	60 hp R.E.P.*	70 hp Viale†	100 hp Gnome
Span:	47 ft 6 in	35 ft	34 ft 6 in
Length:	36 ft 5 in	—	25 ft
Wing Area:	290 sq ft	220 sq ft	220 sq ft
Empty Weight:	1,000 lb	—	730 lb
Gross Weight:	—	—	1,200 lb
Max Speed at Ground Level:	56 mph	63 mph	70 mph
Range:			350 miles

* Changed to 60 hp Vickers-REP on No. 2.
† Changed to 70 hp Gnome rotary.

The Evolution of the Gunbus

At first the only types of instructional aeroplanes used by Vickers Flying School were the various Vickers monoplanes. Towards the end of 1912, however, three Farman-type biplanes were purchased for pupil training from Vickers' next-door neighbours at Brooklands, Hewlett and Blondeau. With some reconstruction these biplanes became known as Vickers Boxkites and were numbered 19, 20 and 21.* In December 1913 an equal-span version of the Vickers Boxkite appeared, with a primitive enclosed nacelle to afford the instructor and pupil some protection from the wind. They sat side by side in staggered seats, and the odd-looking structure which resulted from this arrangement led to the aeroplane becoming known as the *Pumpkin*, bearing the Vickers number 26. A 50 hp Vickers-Boucier static radial engine was fitted, but this was eventually replaced by the 70 hp Gnome.

Among the designs emerging from Vickers' drawing office at that time from which an attempt was made at actual construction was No. 14, known as the *Hydravion*, presumably because it was intended for operation off land or water. Duralumin floats for the *Hydravion* were made at Vickers' Dartford works and were tested for corrosion in the adjacent River

* See Vickers Type List in Appendices for explanatory note.

Vickers 1914 tractor scout biplane, a clean design, but abandoned in favour of Gunbus development.

Darent. According to records held by Vickers House, the whole machine was intended to be made at Dartford, although there is some doubt about this, since the factory there was concerned with explosives and projectiles; most early Vickers aircraft were, in fact, constructed at Erith.

The *Hydravion* was a large biplane designed on Farman lines, with the 100 hp Gnome engine mounted at the back of the nacelle and driving a pusher propeller, the tail being supported on outrigger booms. A pilot and three passengers were carried. One version was made—the seaplane, according to Vickers House—and as this crashed on an early test flight no photographs have been located. The estimated maximum speed was 51½ mph and the stalling speed 32 mph.

Further developments of the *Hydravion* included one designated No. 14B. This was projected with two 100 hp Gnome engines, buried in the fuselage, driving tractor propellers through shafts and gearing, with provision for the disengagement of one or other engine, the remaining one still driving both propellers. There was a crew of three, and a 37-mm semi-automatic cannon, with a magazine of 50 shells, was to be mounted in the nose.

From this 14B and other designs on the same lines it may be concluded that Vickers were thinking in terms of a pusher aeroplane with offensive capability. The linking of their interests in armaments and aviation achieved practical recognition on 19 November, 1912, when a contract was received from the Admiralty for an experimental fighting biplane, armed with a machine-gun.

After many layouts had been considered, the Vickers designers decided that the only practical one was the pusher biplane with the gunner located in the nose. This marks the beginning of the era of Vickers military aircraft, for the design was later classified as E.F.B.1 (Experimental Fighting

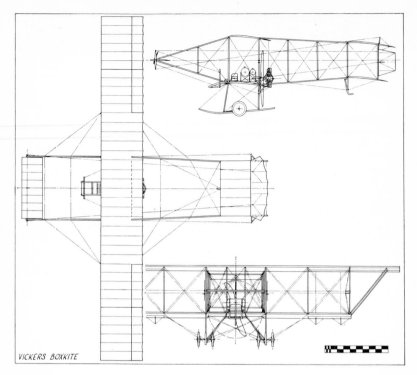

VICKERS BOXKITE

Biplane No. 1) and named *Destroyer*. It was displayed at the Aero Show at Olympia in February 1913, and created great interest as the first gun-carrying aeroplane designed as such. Unfortunately, it crashed on taking-off on its first test flight at Joyce Green. The E.F.B.1 was powered by a 60/80 hp Wolseley eight-cylinder vee engine with water-cooled exhaust valves and air cooling for cylinders and inlets. The curious scimitar-shaped Vickers-Levasseur propeller was fitted.

The armament was a movable Vickers gun, lightened and modified so as to dispense with the water-cooling jackets of the infantry type, to give an unobstructed field of fire. The airframe was nearly all metal, the nacelle being of steel tubes covered with duralumin. The wings were staggered and employed warping for lateral control, as was then general practice.

Flight records the appearance of the E.F.B.1 at the Aero Show of 1913 as follows: 'The 60–80 hp Vickers Biplane. A very interesting machine, not only for the fact that, hitherto, the Vickers organisation have confined their attentions exclusively to monoplane construction, but for the great amount of thought and care that, it is evident, has been spent on its construction and design. Standing before this biplane, the first feature that arrests the attention is that there is a Vickers automatic gun protruding from the front of the neatly rounded Duralumin covered body. Then even the lay mind can arrive at the principal reason why the propeller has been

44

placed at the rear of the machine—it is designed to have that position mainly in order to give an unobstructed range of fire in front of the biplane.

'The body of the machine, which extends forwards from the main planes, is constructed in a precisely similar manner to that of the Vickers monoplane.

'In its interior sits the passenger and, behind him, the pilot, both sheltered

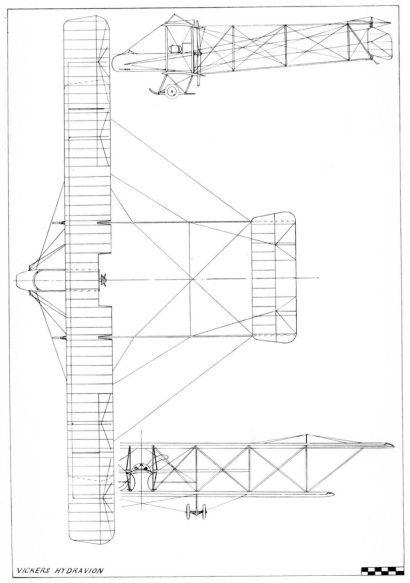

VICKERS HYDRAVION

Vickers original fighting biplane under construction at Erith works only a few weeks before its public premiere at Olympia; on the right is the Wolseley engine, and in the background are B.E.2s being built.

to a great extent from the wind by the neat metallic covering that is fitted over the body. Seated in front, the observer, and he will have to be a gunner too, has a perfectly clear view all around him. The gun before him is arranged to swivel through an angle of 60° in both horizontal and vertical planes, while the ammunition is stored in a box travelling on wires, beneath his seat. When the gun is not in use the ammunition box is in a position just over the centre of pressure of the planes; when it is required to operate it, the box is wound forward on its wire rails and brought within reach of the gunner. As we have remarked, the pilot sits immediately behind him, and he grips a double-handled vertical lever whereby he controls the machine. Still further behind, the motor is mounted, its lugs bolted to the top two members of the fuselage.

'The planes are made on a system which has little difference from that observed in the building of the Vickers monoplane wings. They are

E.F.B.1 *Destroyer* on display at the Aero Show, Olympia, 1913.

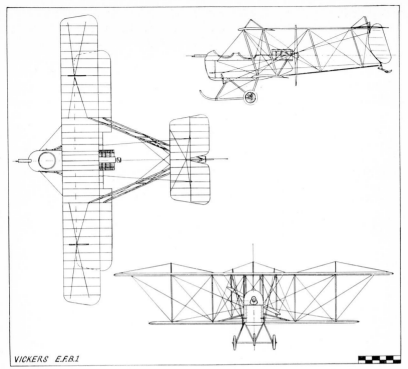

VICKERS E.F.B.1

"staggered". Contrary to the more usual plan of using piano wire for the bracing of the planes, stranded steel cable is employed in this machine. As a matter of fact, all the bracing throughout is of stranded cable, excepting the body, where stout wire is used. The planes are so designed that in a very little time they may be dismantled, leaving only a centre section that is no wider than the body itself. Close examination of this central section of the top plane will reveal that in its interior there is a small petrol tank from which fuel is fed to the motor by gravity. It is supplied from a main tank in the body, under pressure, and the tubes leading to and from it are neatly tucked away behind the wooden filling pieces that are used to "streamline" the tubular cellule spars. By the way, the machine does not carry an oil tank, for sufficient oil is stored in the base-chamber of the motor to last for a six hours' flight.

'The landing chassis is, at first sight, very much like that of the mono-plane. Its flexible suspension, however, will be found to be altogether different. A central hollow skid of ash is joined to the body by two Vs of steel tubing. Two other Vs of tubing extend downwards and outwards from the side of the body, and, in crutches, at their lower extremities, the axles of the landing wheels travel against the tension of the strong rubber springs. Altogether, the chassis is exceptionally light and compact, and, moreover, looks strong enough to bear any ordinary landing strain that

47

it is likely to be subject to. Differing from the monoplane, too, there is no backward extension of the central landing skid. The weight of the tail is carried by a small steel spoon-shaped tail skid, so fixed that it pivots with the rudder and enables the machine to be steered more or less accurately over the ground at slow speeds.

'The tail, level with the top main plane in flight, is attached to the top of the tubular steel tail outriggers. In plan form it is approximately rectangular, and its interior construction is of steel throughout, tubing being used for its outline, while the cambered ribs are of channel section, acetylene-welded in position.'

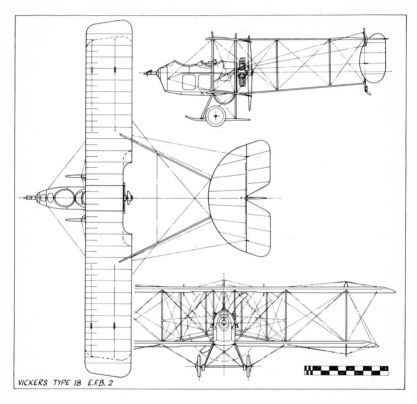

VICKERS TYPE 18 E.F.B. 2

In 1913, Type 18, the E.F.B.2, appeared as an unstaggered biplane with slight overhang on the top wings and with large celluloid windows in the sides of the nacelle. It was flown frequently at Brooklands by Capt Wood and Harold Barnwell during that year, and was powered by a 100 hp Gnome monosoupape rotary engine. E.F.B.3 or No. 18B appeared in December 1913 with the side windows deleted and with ailerons replacing the wing warping. It was shown at the 1914 Olympia Aero Show. An order for six modified No. 18Bs, known as Vickers Type 30s, was placed

E.F.B.2 with Vickers machine-gun in trunnion mounting and clear-view side panels at Brooklands in 1912.

in December 1913 by the Admiralty. However, before delivery was effected the Type 18B design was still further improved; the contract was taken over by the War Office, and this led to the prototype E.F.B.5, which retained the semicircular tailplane characteristic of the early Type 18. When this latest variant went into production the tailplane was made rectangular, and various nacelle configurations necessitated by different armament mountings were tried before the familiar blunt nose of the standard F.B.5 emerged. At this time the F.B.5 was dubbed the Gunbus.

It will be noted at this time that the prefix E, signifying experimental, was dropped. The first F.B.5 Gunbus was delivered to No. 6 Squadron of the Royal Flying Corps at Netheravon in November 1914. In it the lighter

E.F.B.3 with metal-sheathed nacelle at Brooklands in 1913 with Harold Barnwell, Vickers' chief pilot, in rear seat.

49

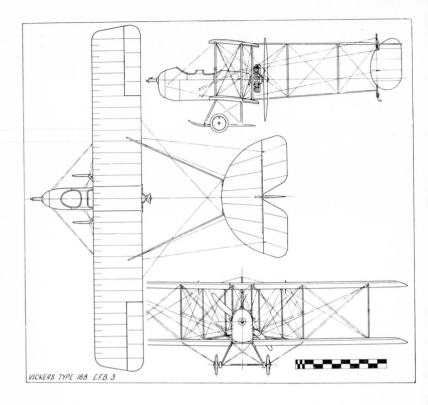

VICKERS TYPE 18B E.F.B. 3

and handier Lewis gun replaced the Vickers gun,* which, however, continued to be used in the air war as a fixed weapon with the whole aeroplane aimed at the target. Before this happened, however, a satisfactory means had to be invented to enable a fixed gun to fire through a revolving tractor propeller. One of the earliest of such devices was, in fact, the Vickers-Challenger interruptor gear. By this time aviation had become an arm of the Services, tentatively at first for reconnaissance and later for air attack.

The Crayford works took over the production of Vickers aircraft in late 1914, and the first F.B.5s were delivered from there. Three aircraft comprised the initial delivery to Netheravon, but two were returned to Joyce Green to create the nucleus of the Air Defence of London. The first recorded use of a Gunbus in action was on Christmas Day 1914, when 2nd Lt M. R. Chidson with Corporal Martin as gunner took-off from Joyce Green to attack a German Taube monoplane and, according to circumstantial evidence, destroyed it. The type went to the Western Front, and the first F.B.5 to arrive there was Chidson's, he having been posted to No. 2 Squadron in France on 7 February, 1915.

* One or two F.B.5s used by the Royal Naval Air Service retained the Vickers gun on a pivot mounting.

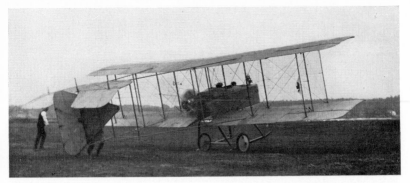

Experimental version of E.F.B.3 with revised fin and rudder and test instrumentation on starboard aileron strut. (*Flight photo.*)

In November 1915, 2nd Lt G. S. M. Insall was awarded the Victoria Cross for gallantry displayed after forcing down a German Aviatik reconnaissance machine while flying a Vickers Gunbus. Compelled by ground fire to land near the front lines of the Allies, Insall repaired the damage to his aeroplane during the night and returned next morning to his squadron. In spite of these and other successes, the Gunbus suffered in company with other Allied aircraft from the unreliability of the rotary engine, largely because servicing and maintenance in the early days were not of the high standard reached later.

Experimental work was carried out with the Gunbus concept, and the E.F.B.6 was a variant flown in 1914 with extended top wing, presumably to obtain more lift for load carrying, but was not proceeded with. Before that, an advanced project following the general configuration of the E.F.B.1 *Destroyer* had been designed under the classification E.F.B.4.

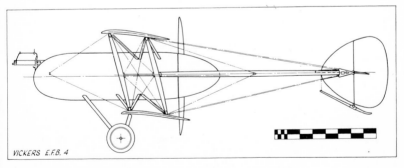

VICKERS E.F.B. 4

The F.B.5A was fitted with the Le Rhône or Clerget engine of 110 hp, and at least four were constructed with armour-plated nacelles. Two F.B.5s were fitted with the experimental Smith static radial air-cooled engine, nominally of 140 hp, while another was equipped with floats for operation off water but before this could be tried was reconverted to standard form and flown back to France.

E.F.B.5 prototype as first flown at Joyce Green, showing progressive development, including wooden interplane struts.

Head-on view of prototype E.F.B.5 revealing Levasseur-type propeller and semicircular stabiliser.

E.F.B.5 prototype in service under serial 664 with gun pylon added—sometimes described as F.B.4, although the E.F.B.4 was a project development of E.F.B.1.

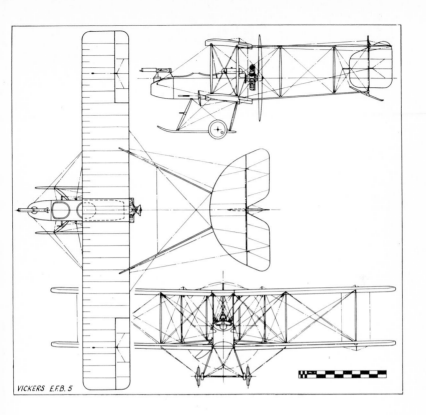

First production F.B.5 at Brooklands for trials before delivery.

One of the first batch of F.B.5s for the Royal Flying Corps presented by the City of Bombay to H.M. Government in 1914; this Gunbus was the pattern for the replica built in 1966.

Last of the line to be made was the F.B.9, which was sufficiently sophisticated to be known as the Streamline Gunbus. A lot of cleaning up had had to be done, the wing tips and tailplane were neatly rounded off, the nacelle was of much better aerodynamic form and the older skid undercarriage (which incidentally had proved very useful on the early primitive landing grounds in France) was replaced by a V type. Streamlined,

One of the F.B.5s used by the Royal Naval Air Service, with modified nose and Vickers machine-gun; for the Admiralty the designation was Vickers Type 32.

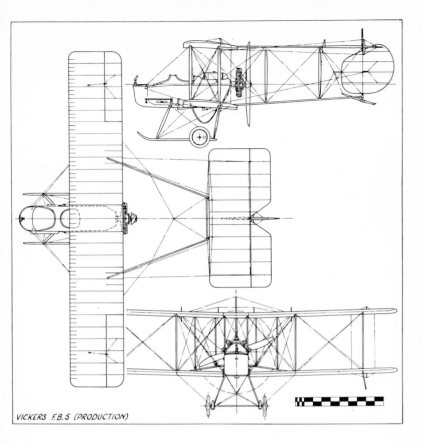

VICKERS F.B.5 (PRODUCTION)

One of the four F.B.5As built at Bexleyheath with an armour-plated nose and V undercarriage; oleo-type undercarriages were also tried.

A Gunbus on the Western Front in 1915 in traditional Christmas conditions.

adjustable Rafwires* had replaced the stranded steel cables and turn-buckles of the earlier machines. Between June 1916 and September 1917, 95 F.B.9s were built and used mostly for training duties at home, as by then the much more powerful F.E.2d with a 250 hp Rolls-Royce Eagle I was available for overseas as a pusher fighter-bomber. One F.B.9 was especially modified as a trench-strafer with an armour-plated nacelle and an oleo undercarriage.

Some F.B.9s were used in the Battle of the Somme which started on 1 July, 1916. From the personal notebook of 2nd Lt Lionel Morris of No.11 Squadron, RFC, it is learned that he and Lt Torre of the same squadron were detailed to collect 'Streamlined Gunbuses' from Villacoublay aero-drome near Paris on 25 June, 1916, as stand-ins for the Squadron's F.E.2bs fitted with the 160 hp Beardmore engine. This engine, which was a more powerful version of the 120 hp standard Beardmore, was giving continual trouble, leading to serious break-up of internal components, just at a time when every aeroplane was needed for the first major offensive of the Allies. It is probable therefore that French-built or French-assembled F.B.9s were used at that time by other RFC squadrons primarily equipped with the higher-powered Beardmore F.E.2bs.

In France, S. A. Darracq of Suresnes in fact made 99 F.B.5s and F.B.9s under licence, but an intention for Vickers' Italian subsidiary, Vickers-Terni, to manufacture the type fell through for political reasons. A further development, the F.B.10, was projected with the Italian 100 hp Isotta-Fraschini engine, but was not proceeded with, as Vickers designers were otherwise engaged in evolving the variety of experimental aircraft as

* External bracing wires invented by the Royal Aircraft Factory. They were rolled, on specially designed machines, from round swaged steel rods to an oval streamline section to reduce drag.

described in the next chapter. In any case, the Gunbus was being out-classed by more advanced designs of fighting aeroplanes.

A side issue of some interest to the Gunbus story was the request from the German Government, made early in 1914, for details of Vickers fighting biplanes. Apparently there was nothing sinister in this approach, which was similar to that made to the Sopwith and other British aircraft companies; Britain was never seriously regarded as a potential enemy by Germany even at that late date, and its interest was doubtless genuine.

In offering the Type 18 series to the Germans, Vickers said, 'What we have at the present moment is a type of machine which is not existent in the German Army, in fact not in Europe except in England. This machine

F.B.6 at Brooklands in 1914 with large overhang on top wing braced by pyramid kingposts.

is intended for offensive action in the air against other planes and dirigibles, consequently it is not equipped with a bomb-dropping apparatus. The light Maxim gun mounted in the nose is so placed as to enable the gunner to have a free field of fire against other aeroplanes. We can carry Pilot, Observer, Barograph, Gun, 300 rounds of ammunition, and fuel for 4 hours. Loaded with this, it can easily attain a height of 800 metres in 15 minutes. The speed of the machine is 105 km/hr instead of 90 required by the German Authorities. We can reduce to 70 km/hr if required.'

This design was not accepted, but in response to a further request from the German Government, three advanced designs for aircraft, called G.F.B.1, G.F.B.2 and G.F.B.3 (German Fighting Biplanes), which resembled in many respects the *Hydravion* projects, were prepared during the early months of 1914. Details of only the last two are now available; these were alike, except that the G.F.B.2 had two 100 hp Gnome monosoupape engines while the G.F.B.3 had two 140/165 hp Austro-Daimlers. The engines were mounted side by side in the fuselage, driving two tractor propellers, and clutches could cut out one or both.

These large three-seat biplane designs had provision for a 37-mm one-pounder gun mounted in the nose, and the pilot and observer were seated in the fuselage behind the engines. Specified equipment included wireless and 50 rounds of ammunition. The upper wings were of greater span than

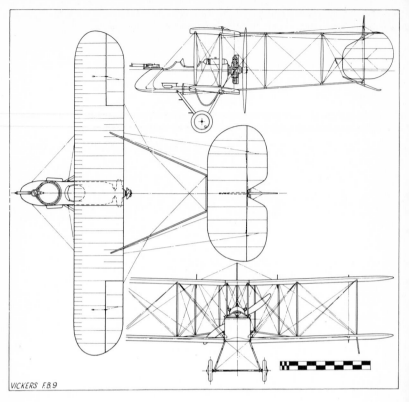

VICKERS F.B.9

the lower, and for hangarage purposes the outer sections of the upper wings could be lowered, thus reducing the span from 72 to 59 ft. The G.F.B.3 was designed for a maximum speed of 72 mph with an endurance of five hours, and the all-up weight was estimated at 4,000 lb. The outbreak of war in August 1914 prevented construction of these interesting designs.

Another Vickers design prepared early in 1914 was the S.B.1 school biplane, based on the E.F.B.3 but with the gunner's cockpit replaced with a pupil's position fitted with dual controls. The engine intended for this development was to have been the 100 hp Anzani static radial.

A replica F.B.5 Gunbus was made by the Vintage Aircraft and Flying Association (Brooklands) in 1966 to celebrate the centenary of the Royal Aeronautical Society. It was fitted with a 100 hp Gnome monosoupape rotary engine rebuilt from two surviving examples found in RAF redundant stores. This aeroplane flew faultlessly at the first attempt, piloted by D. G. Addicott, a Vickers test pilot. Despite its low power, the replica disclosed good handling qualities and is an existing testimony to the excellence of the design for the requirement of its day, which was to provide a steady gun platform for air offence.

An early F.B.9 showing rounded wing tips and tailplane, sharper nose and cleaner lines, leading to the appellation of the Streamline Gunbus.

Scout Biplane—One 100 hp Gnome monosoupape. Accommodation pilot and passenger. Span 25 ft; length 20 ft 7 in; wing area 270 sq ft. Empty weight 600 lb; gross weight 1,200 lb. Max speed at ground level 100 mph; range 350 miles.
Vickers School Biplane—Boxkite—One 50 hp Gnome. Span 51 ft 3 in; length 39 ft; wing area 433 sq ft. Gross weight 835 lb.
Hydravion—One 100 hp Gnome. Accommodation pilot and three passengers. Span 72 ft 8 in; length 43 ft; height 12 ft 2 in; wing area 819 sq ft. Gross weight 2,400 lb. Max speed at ground level 51·5 mph.

Gunbus

	E.F.B.1 (*Destroyer*)	E.F.B.2 Type 18	E.F.B.3 Type 18 B	F.B.5 (Gunbus)	F.B.9
Accommodation:	Pilot and gunner	Pilot and gunner	Pilot and gunner	Pilot and gunner	Pilot and gunner
Engine:	80 hp Wolseley	100 hp Gnome mono-soupape	100 hp Gnome mono-soupape	100 hp Gnome mono-soupape	100 hp Gnome mono-soupape
Span:	40 ft	38 ft 7 in	37 ft 4 in	36 ft 6 in	33 ft 9 in
Length:	27 ft 6 in	29 ft 2 in	27 ft 6 in	27 ft 2 in	28 ft 5½ in
Height:	11 ft 11 in	9 ft 7 in	9 ft 9 in	11 ft	11 ft 6 in
Wing Area:	385 sq ft	380 sq ft	385 sq ft	382 sq ft	340 sq ft
Empty Weight:	1,760 lb	1,050 lb	1,050 lb	1,220 lb	1,029 lb
Gross Weight:	2,660 lb	1,760 lb	1,680 lb	2,050 lb	1,820 lb
Max Speed:	70 mph at ground level (est.)	60 mph at ground level	60 mph at ground level	70 mph at 5,000 ft	82·6 mph at sea level
Service Ceiling:	—	—	—	9,000 ft	11,000 ft
Initial Climb:	450 ft/min*	200 ft/min	300 ft/min	—	—
Climb to:	—	—	—	5,000 ft in 16 min	10,000 ft in 15 min
Range:	4½ hr	150 miles	300 miles	250 miles	250 miles
Armament:	One Vickers	One Vickers	One Vickers	One Lewis	One Lewis

* Estimated

59

The replica Gunbus built by the Vintage Aircraft and Flying Association (Brooklands) on an engine test flight piloted by 'Dizzy' Addicott with Alan Blower as observer. (*Photo R. Palmer.*)

Vickers Designs 1914–18

When war broke out in 1914 there was a serious shortage of British military aircraft compared with those possessed by France and Germany, and various aeronautical experimenters made efforts to remedy this deficiency. Among these private-venture attempts was one by Harold Barnwell, who had been appointed chief test pilot by Vickers after the closing of their flying school at Brooklands. In spare moments from testing production Gunbuses he took upon himself the task of designing and constructing under cover a small high-speed scout, fitted with a Gnome engine spirited out of Vickers' Erith stores.

Barnwell's creation was a tubby little machine with a circular-section streamlined fuselage and stubby unstaggered wings of small span. It soon acquired the name of the Barnwell Bullet. On its first flight early in 1915, in the hands of its designer, it was found to have insufficient control, particularly on the elevators. On landing, its undercarriage collapsed, and the Bullet stood on its nose. This mishap must have revealed its existence to Vickers' management, for R. K. Pierson, a young graduate apprentice then in the drawing office who had also learned to fly at Vickers' Flying School, was given the task of redesigning the Bullet into an experimental scout with the designation of E.S.1, powered with a Gnome monosoupape engine.

E.S.1 redesigned and rebuilt from the original Barnwell Bullet, shown wearing the 1914 Union Jack insignia.

E.S.1 had larger tail surfaces than those of the original Barnwell Bullet and a stronger undercarriage. No armament was carried. After a period of flight testing it was sent to the Central Flying School at Upavon for official trials. Certain disadvantages were disclosed, particularly in the pilot's view upwards as well as downwards over the side of the fat body. There was no drain hole in the engine cowling to jettison surplus oil and petrol vapour centrifuged by the rotary engine.

An improved version was then developed with the 110 hp Clerget rotary engine. A small window of celluloid was inserted in the top centre section to improve the pilot's view upwards, and the fairing was removed from the

E.S.1 bearing Service markings for official trials at the CFS, Upavon.

E.S.2 or E.S.1 Mk II, according to taste, in its war paint ready for Service trials.

underside of the fuselage. In this form the type was known to Vickers as the E.S.2.* Two were made, and one was used for trials of the Vickers-Challenger gun synchronising gear which enabled a fixed machine-gun to be fired through a tractor propeller. This gear was used operationally on the Sopwith One-and-a-half Strutter two-seat fighter. In the summer of 1916 one E.S.2, equipped with a forward-firing fixed Vickers gun and the synchronising gear, was sent to France for operational trials by No. 11 Squadron, RFC, then operating Vickers Gunbuses. There it kept company with a small number of Bristol Scouts, but reports on the Vickers Bullet, as the E.S.2 was known, confirmed the CFS opinion of the E.S.1 that it was too blind from the pilot's point of view. The E.S.2 was also flown before H.M. King George V during a visit to Vickers' Crayford works in September 1915 and demonstrated to a visiting Russian Imperial aviation mission.

* In official documents it appears as E.S.1 Mk. II.

An F.B.19 Mk I being started up at Brooklands with Harold Barnwell in the cockpit and Stan Cockerell leaning against the starboard wing.

A further development of the Bullet appeared in August 1916 as the F.B.19, in an unstaggered version as the Mk I and later in a staggered version, the Mk II. The former had either the 100 hp Gnome monosoupape or 110 hp Le Rhône and the latter the 110 hp Le Rhône or the 110 hp Clerget. About 50 Mk Is and 12 Mk IIs were made at Weybridge and were used in small numbers on the Western Front, in Macedonia and Palestine. A demonstration Mk I was sent to Russia which led to a small batch of Mk IIs being sent to Archangel, but there they remained in their crates when the Revolution intervened, Russia withdrawing from the war, and are believed to have been destroyed by British Forces in 1919.

A Vickers F.B.19 Mk I in service with Soviet forces in company with a Sopwith Triplane.

In 1916 a single-seat fighter to take the Vickers-sponsored Hart radial engine was designed by R. K. Pierson. This was the F.B.16 tractor and was known as the Hart Scout. The Hart engine proved as disappointing as previous power units (such as the Boucier) sponsored by Vickers. After considerable redesign the type reappeared as the F.B.16A with a 150 hp Hispano Suiza, a French-designed water-cooled engine then coming into favour with the British air authorities. Later the more powerful 200 hp Hispano Suiza was substituted, and in this form the aeroplane became the F.B.16D. It earned the unqualified praise of Maj J. B. McCudden, the British air ace, of 56 Squadron, whose book on five years in the RFC remains the classic on air fighting and the technology thereof in the first world war. In this book he describes vividly, as follows, his experiences in flying the all-red F.B.16D at Joyce Green, where he was a constant visitor when on leave from France.

'On 22 June, 1917, I flew the little Vickers tractor, the F.B.16D, which was now fitted with a 200 hp Wolseley-Hispano. I climbed to 10,000 ft in eight minutes and at that height the machine did 136 mph. Whilst flying

A Weybridge-built F.B.19 Mk II Bullet, 1917.

that machine I got some idea of the speed of future machines, for at 10,000 ft it was 30 mph faster at least than anything I had yet flown. Harold Barnwell liked this little machine, although he said it cost him a new pair of trousers every time he flew it, as it always smothered his legs with oil. It has a very deep fuselage rather out of proportion to the size of the machine and Barnwell always alluded to it as "Pot-Belly".'

F.B.16 Hart Scout in its original form with the Hart radial engine.

F.B.16D—known to Barnwell as 'Pot Belly', and the favourite hack of the British ace McCudden; in the centre of the spinner the exit hole for bullets from the engine-mounted machine-gun can be seen.

McCudden was keen to take the F.B.16D with him to his Squadron in France, but it was not the policy to allow pilots, however distinguished, to have, at the Front, personal aircraft which differed from standard equipment. He therefore left the F.B.16D at Joyce Green when he returned to France, where he was killed in an accident to his S.E.5a before reaching his base.

The F.B.16D never went into production because large contracts had been placed for the contemporary S.E.5a, particularly with Vickers at Crayford and Weybridge, and because the engine in the Vickers fighter was inaccessible for servicing and maintenance in the field. But it embodied an unusual feature for a British aeroplane. A Lewis gun was installed between the vee formed by the cylinder blocks and fired through the hollow propeller-shaft which rotated through gearing above the engine crankshaft. How the ammunition drums were changed or whether a belt feed was substituted, or, indeed, how the empty cartridge cases were collected or jettisoned, remains unexplained.

F.B.16E with Lorraine engine being completed in the French works of S. A. Darracq.

A line-up of Vickers experimental aircraft at Joyce Green;
(*left to right*) F.B.12C, F.B.14, F.B.11, F.B.16.

A derivative of the type, the F.B.16E, was made, under licence by S. A. Darracq in France, with larger two-bay wings to cater for the extra weight of the 275 hp Lorraine-Dietrich engine, but it did not go into large-scale production there.

Also in the single-seat fighter class were the two Vickers pusher types, the F.B.12 and the F.B.26. Both had chequered careers. The F.B.12 was also intended for the 150 hp Hart static radial engine, but continual delays with this engine and the shortage of rotaries for experimental work led to the installation of an 80 hp Le Rhône taken from another aeroplane. The F.B.12 flew in June 1916, but, being underpowered, had a most disappointing performance. A 100 hp Gnome monosoupape was then substituted. Even in this guise, as the F.B.12A, it still had only two-thirds the designed power, and so lost any performance advantage it might have had (with the 150 hp promised from the Hart) over the D.H.2 and F.E.8 pusher fighters already in service, but it went to France in December 1916 for operational trials. The F.B.12B with the Hart engine was completed in February 1917, its wing span increased from 26 ft to 29 ft 9 in, but it crashed, thus helping to settle the fate of the Hart engine once and for all. A contract was placed with the Wells Aviation Company of Chelsea for the F.B.12C, and the few examples made were fitted with a variety of engines, including Gnome

F.B.12C re-engined with 100 hp Gnome monosoupape; its distinguishing feature is the excellent pilot's view provided by the raised nacelle.

The prototype F.B.26 with Hispano Suiza engine at Joyce Green, 1917, showing close resemblance to the F.B.12.

monosoupape, Le Rhône and the Anzani static radial, all nominally about 100 hp. The AID report on the first production example, A7351, was so critical, and disclosed a top speed of only 87 mph, that, coupled with the failure of the Hart, it could lead to nothing but a cancellation of the contract.

The later F.B.26 pusher was a more sophisticated design originally intended as a single-seat night-fighter, powered with a 200 hp Hispano Suiza. During an evening test flight on 25 August, 1917, Harold Barnwell spun the prototype into the ground just after take-off at Joyce Green,

F.B.26A Vampire II with Bentley B.R.2 rotary engine and twin machine-guns.

almost at the feet of his devoted mechanic H. J. Kingsnorth, who had just started up the aeroplane and was the only close witness of the fatal accident. The cause of this tragedy with so able a pilot remains a mystery. Writing from New Zealand, whence he emigrated in 1919, Kingsnorth said that he never recovered from the death of his hero Harold Barnwell, who, terse of speech and bluff in manner, had played a great part in the early development of British aviation, as did his brother, Capt Frank Barnwell, of the Bristol Aeroplane Company.

Three modified F.B.26s were built, and under the then recently introduced official nomenclature were named Vampire. One was modified as the F.B.26A, and named Vampire Mk II, with an armoured nacelle for ground attack, power being provided by the 230 hp Bentley B.R.2 rotary engine. But the contracts that were placed for this specialist duty type went to the Sopwith Salamander, a tractor biplane. One of the F.B.26s

Rear view of one of the very few F.B.26 single-seat pusher fighters made, photographed in the winter of 1917/1918, the prototype having crashed in the previous August.

was fitted with the Eeman three-gun universal mounting, designed to increase fire power, but this armament proved unwieldy in practice. The F.B.26A was probably the last of the single-seat pusher fighters of the first world war, but the design philosophy was revived years later in the Vickers COW gun fighter of 1931.

A further development of the Gunbus was projected in the F.B.23 for a pusher fighter of 38-ft span as a replacement for the F.B.9. This failed to materialise, but an unusual development of this design to carry the Crayford rocket gun was built in Vickers' experimental shop at Gravel Hill, Bexleyheath. This was the F.B.25, and the power unit was the 150 hp Hispano Suiza. It was intended as a night-fighter to fill the same requirement as Farnborough's N.E.1, but it was crashed by a Service test pilot in May 1917, after an unflattering flight-test report.

Vickers fared a little better with their excursions into the tractor biplane field for multi-seat aircraft, after a poor start with the F.B.11 designed by Howard Flanders as a Zeppelin airship destroyer, for which purpose it had a fighting top mounted on the centre section of the upper wing. On

The F.B.25 two-seat night fighter of 1917 in modified form, compared with the original design with nose-mounted searchlight. The trial installation of an oleo-pneumatic undercarriage may also be noted, but the outstanding feature was the Crayford rocket gun intended for attacking hostile airships, an operational philosophy revived in Vickers' COW gun fighter of 1931, illustrated on pages 242–6.

a trial flight the F.B.11 proved to be deficient in control, and Harold Barnwell spent five weeks in Crayford hospital as a result. Its sole claim to distinction was that it was the first Vickers aeroplane to be powered with a Rolls-Royce engine, the early Eagle I of 250 hp.

In 1916 Vickers produced the F.B.14 general-purpose single-engined tractor biplane of smaller dimensions than those of the F.B.11, but bearing obvious Flanders influence, such as the single-bay wing cellule with a larger top wing and splayed-out struts. From the F.B.14 descended a lengthy line of tractor biplanes to be described in later chapters. Its

F.B.14 running up for air test in 1916 from AID base then located at Farnborough; later the airframe was submitted to static structural testing at the Royal Aircraft Factory.

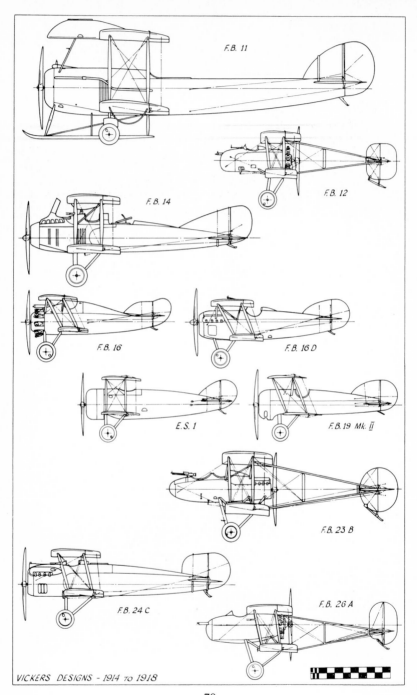

F.B. 11

F.B. 12

F.B. 14

F.B. 16

F.B. 16 D

E.S. 1

F.B. 19 Mk. II

F.B. 23 B

F.B. 24 C

F.B. 26 A

VICKERS DESIGNS - 1914 to 1918

70

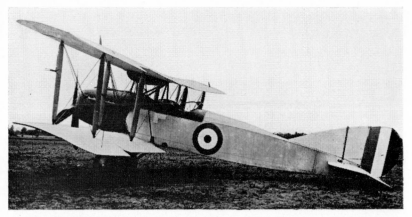

The F.B.14D with Rolls-Royce Eagle engine and two-bay wings, in which Sir Vernon Brown and Sir Melville Jones had an exciting combat in July 1917.

steel-tube fuselage followed the early pattern derived from the R.E.P. type monoplane, and this feature created official interest, and on structural test at Farnborough it disclosed good strength factors. Although intended for the 200 hp B.H.P. engine (later to become the 230 hp Siddeley Puma), the F.B.14 was powered with the 160 hp Beardmore, which itself was proving unreliable enough for it to be replaced by the older 120 hp Beardmore. Thus once more the bogey of underpower appeared, and although 100 airframes were built at Weybridge, only relatively few ever received suitable engines. Intended as replacement for the B.E.2c, B.E.2d or B.E.2e in

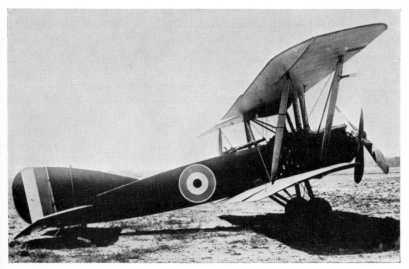

F.B.14F with 150 hp Raf 4a air-cooled engine—an obvious attempt to find an alternative for the unsatisfactory 160 hp Beardmore.

Experimental civil conversion of F.B.14 at Bexleyheath, 1919.

Middle East squadrons, an indefinite number of F.B.14s were reported as sent to Mesopotamia and seven are known to have been used by Home Defence squadrons.

Other variants to materialise were the F.B.14A with a 150 hp Lorraine-Dietrich, the F.B.14D with a 250 hp Rolls-Royce and the F.B.14F with a 150 hp Raf 4a, an air-cooled twelve-cylinder vee engine which was the standard power unit for the R.E.8 general-purpose aeroplane. The F.B.14D with the Rolls engine had increased span with two-bay wings, and on test at the new experimental aerodrome at Martlesham Heath, near Ipswich, it recorded a speed of 111·5 mph. Later it was used for gunnery trials at Orfordness on the Suffolk coast, fitted with a Vickers gun firing forwards and upwards at 45 degrees and two Lewis guns firing rearwards, one under the tail.

With an experimental periscopic gunsight for the pilot, the Orfordness F.B.14D chased a hostile raid back to the Belgian coast in July 1917, and obtained an unconfirmed victory over a Gotha bomber, which was seen to go down in the sea off Zeebrugge.*

The F.B.24 was a straightforward two-seat tractor biplane for fighter

* This account of the incident has been recently verified by Sir Vernon Brown, who was the pilot, and Sir Melville Jones, the observer, who had invented the gunsight. The pilot laid the sight on the target for the gunner to fire the guns. In the device, allowance had been made for relative speeds of the aircraft and for wind velocity.

reconnaissance and comparative with the Bristol Fighter, designed by Capt Frank Barnwell, brother of Vickers' Harold Barnwell. It was yet another design intended for the ill-fated Hart engine and followed the familiar pattern in being fitted with a variety of makeshift power units. The prototype, designated F.B.24A, had the 200 hp Hispano Suiza, as did also the second airframe, the F.B.24B; the F.B.24C was fitted with the 275 hp Lorraine-Dietrich in the French works of S. A. Darracq while the F.B.24D had the 200 hp Hispano Suiza. In the F.B.24E the upper wing was attached directly to the top of the fuselage, to improve the view of the crew. The F.B.24G with the large 375 hp Lorraine was built by Darracq in France and did not fly until some time after the war; it used the wing and fuselage arrangement of the F.B.24E, but was an ungainly aeroplane.

F.B.24 experimental fighter-bomber with Hispano Suiza engine.

Before leaving the experimental Vickers aircraft of the first world war, mention must be made of the continuance of the buried-engine idea in the projected F.B.15, with two Rolls-Royce engines mounted in the fuselage and driving two outboard propellers via shafting and gearing. All these projects were stillborn because of the difficulty of engineering the gearing at that time. The span of the F.B.15 was to have been 80 ft and the length 46 ft; construction of two prototypes was started but soon abandoned.

A smaller aircraft, again with buried engines, reached an advanced stage of construction before being abandoned, most probably for the reason already stated in connection with the gearing. This was the triplane F.T.2 (see drawing on page 482), intended to take two 200 hp Lorraines, with a designed speed of 124 mph and a weight of 2,055 lb as compared with the estimated weight of 3,700 lb for the F.B.15.

These projects were based on the battleplane philosophy of air combat; that is, a large aeroplane bristling with armament covering all blind spots, but in reality easy meat to the highly manoeuvrable fighters of that era.

Between the wars ungainly French aircraft of this class, called *multiplaces de combat*, did emerge, but not until the second world war was the idea ever realised in battle, when the high-flying massed formations of American heavily armed decoy bombers fought in daylight against the Luftwaffe.

The two twin-engined designs, the E.F.B.7 and its derivative the F.B.8, are discussed in the next chapter because they led to the emergence of a really successful aeroplane, the F.B.27 Vimy, last of the wartime designs

F.B.24C with Lorraine-Dietrich engine as built in France.

of 1914–18. It had been a formative period for Vickers' aviation, in which practically the whole range of existing aeroplane design had been covered experimentally. Much had been learned, although little of consequence had emerged. Effort had been bedevilled by the dearth of suitable engines, an experience shared by other private manufacturers but not, as C. G. Grey of *The Aeroplane* so often said, by the Government constructors at Farnborough, at least not until the priorities had been adjusted by the alteration in respective status halfway through the war. Even for the prototype Vimys, Vickers had to search around for engines until the Rolls-Royce Eagle VIIIs became available, when the Vickers Vimy/Rolls-Royce combination proceeded almost immediately to create aviation history.

E.S.1—Barnwell Bullet rebuilt—One 100 hp Gnome monosoupape. Span 24 ft 4½ in; length 20 ft 3 in; height 8 ft; wing area 215 sq ft. Empty weight 843 lb; gross weight 1,295 lb. Max speed 114 mph at 5,000 ft; climb to 10,000 ft—18 min; endurance 3 hr. No armament.

E.S.2—Bullet—One 110 hp Clerget. Span 24 ft 5½ in; length 20 ft 3 in; height 8 ft; wing area 215 sq ft. Empty weight 981 lb; gross weight 1,502 lb. Max speed 112·2 mph at ground level; climb to 10,000 ft—18 min; service ceiling 15,500 ft; initial climb 1,000 ft/min; endurance—2 hr at 8,000 ft. Armament one Vickers gun (synchronised by Vickers Challenger interrupter gear).

F.B.11—One 250 hp Rolls-Royce Eagle I. Span 51 ft; length 43 ft; height 15 ft; wing area 845 sq ft. Empty weight 3,340 lb; gross weight 4,934 lb. Max speed 96 mph at 5,000 ft; climb to 10,000 ft—55 min; service ceiling 11,000 ft; absolute ceiling 12,000 ft; endurance 4½ hr. Armament two Lewis guns.

F.B.12C—One 150 hp Hart. Span 29 ft 9 in, upper, and 26 ft 9 in, lower; length 21 ft 10 in; height 8 ft 7 in; wing area 237 sq ft. Empty weight 927 lb; gross weight 1,447 lb. Max speed 87 mph at 6,500 ft; climb to 10,000 ft—18½ min; service ceiling 14,500 ft; absolute ceiling 15,000 ft; endurance 3¼ hr. Armament one Lewis gun mounted in nose of nacelle.

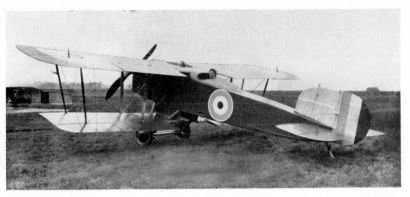

F.B.24E showing direct attachment of upper centre section to top longerons of fuselage
—combat disposition of crew seems a problem, as this example was experimental, with
the pilot in the rear seat.

F.B.14—One 160 hp Beardmore. Span 39 ft 6 in, upper, and 33 ft, lower; length 28 ft 5 in; height 10 ft; wing area 427 sq ft. Empty weight 1,662 lb; gross weight 2,603 lb. Max speed 99·5 mph at ground level; climb to 10,000 ft—40¾ min; service ceiling 10,000 ft; absolute ceiling 10,600 ft; endurance 3¾ hr. Armament one Lewis gun and one Vickers gun.

F.B.14D—One 250 hp Rolls-Royce Eagle IV. Span 42 ft, upper, and 39 ft 6 in, lower; length 30 ft 8 in; height 10 ft 3 in; wing area 485 sq ft. Empty weight 2,289 lb; gross weight 3,308 lb. Max speed 111·5 mph at 6,500 ft; climb to 10,000 ft—15½ min; service ceiling 15,500 ft; endurance 3½ hr. Armament two Lewis guns and one Vickers gun.

F.B.16D—One 200 hp Hispano Suiza. Span 25 ft, upper, and 22 ft 4 in, lower; length 19 ft 6 in; height 8 ft 9 in; wing area 207 sq ft. Empty weight 1,376 lb; gross weight 1,875 lb. Max speed 135 mph at 10,000 ft; climb to 10,000 ft—10½ min; service ceiling 18,500 ft; absolute ceiling 21,000 ft; endurance 2¼ hr. Armament two Lewis guns.

F.B.19—Bullet Mk I—One 110 hp Le Rhône. Span 24 ft; length 18 ft 2 in; height 8 ft 3 in; wing area 215 sq ft. Empty weight 900 lb; gross weight 1,485 lb. Max speed 102 mph at 10,000 ft; climb to 10,000 ft—14 min; service ceiling 15,000 ft; absolute ceiling 17,500 ft; endurance 2¾ hr. Armament one Vickers gun.

F.B.19—Bullet Mk II—One 110 hp Clerget. Span 24 ft; length 18 ft 2 in; height 8 ft 3 in; wing area 215 sq ft. Empty weight 890 lb; gross weight 1,475 lb. Max speed 98 mph at 10,000 ft; climb to 10,000 ft—14½ min; absolute ceiling 16,500 ft; endurance 3 hr. Armament one Vickers gun.

F.B.24E—One 200 hp Hispano Suiza. Span 35 ft 6 in, upper, and 30 ft, lower; length 26 ft; wing area 340 sq ft. Empty weight 1,630 lb; gross weight 2,610 lb. Max speed 122 mph at 5,000 ft; climb to 10,000 ft—15 min; absolute ceiling 16,000 ft; endurance 3 hr. Armament one Vickers gun and one movable Lewis gun.

F.B.25—One 150 hp Hispano Suiza. Span 41 ft 6 in; length 28 ft 1 in; height 10 ft 10 in; wing area 500 sq ft. Empty weight 1,608 lb; gross weight 2,454 lb. Max speed 86 mph at 5,000 ft; climb to 10,000 ft—27¼ min; service ceiling 11,500 ft; absolute ceiling 13,500 ft; endurance 4½ hr. Armament one Vickers Crayford rocket gun.

F.B.26—Vampire Mk I—One 200 hp Hispano Suiza. Span 31 ft 6 in, upper, and 29 ft, lower; length 23 ft 5 in; height 9 ft 5 in; wing area 267 sq ft. Empty weight 1,470 lb; gross weight 2,030 lb. Max speed 121 mph at 5,000 ft; climb to 10,000 ft—10 min; service ceiling 20,500 ft; absolute ceiling 22,500 ft; endurance 3 hr. Armament twin fixed Lewis guns.

F.B.26A—Vampire Mk II—One 230 hp Bentley B.R.2. Span 31 ft 6 in, upper, and 27 ft 6 in, lower; length 22 ft 11 in; height 9 ft 5 in; wing area 267 sq ft. Empty weight 1,870 lb; gross weight 2,438 lb. Max speed 121 mph at ground level; climb to 10,000 ft—12 min; absolute ceiling 19,000 ft; endurance 2 hr. Armament twin fixed Lewis guns.

Prototype F.B.27 with Hispano Suiza engines before its first flight, made by Gordon Bell on 30 November, 1917; the F.B.19 Mk II was presumably one of the first known chase planes.

The Vimy and the Vernon

Shortly after the start of the first world war Vickers engaged Howard Flanders to design a new twin-engined fighting aeroplane to carry a Vickers one-pounder gun. Classified as the E.F.B.7, it was powered with wing-mounted Gnome monosoupape engines, and the pilot was seated behind the wings and the gunner in the nose. It flew some time in August 1915, and thus vied with the comparable French Caudron and other designs for the claim of being the first twin-engined military aircraft to fly successfully.

However, in the E.F.B.7 the distance separating the two-man crew was found unacceptable in practice; in the variant, the E.F.B.7A, the pilot was brought forward of the wings, just behind the gunner. An attempt to re-engine this Flanders-designed machine with two 80 hp air-cooled Renaults (because of the shortage of Gnomes) was unsuccessful, as the loss of some 40 hp meant a serious drop in performance. In consequence, a contract for 11 F.B.7 aircraft being built by Darracq and Company (1905) Ltd of Townmead Road, Fulham, was cancelled.

The E.F.B.8, which appeared in November 1915, powered by two Gnome monosoupapes, was smaller than its predecessor and carried only a single light Lewis gun, which could be accommodated equally well in single-engined types. This redesign was entrusted to Pierson, who stored the knowledge gained and revived it when a new twin-engined bomber was called for from Vickers by the Air Board in 1917, in the following circumstances.

Capt Peter D. Acland, at the time assistant manager in the Aviation Department of Vickers, gave the following account, in 1944, of the inception of the Vimy: 'The initiation of the design of the Vimy by Rex Pierson was the result of a conversation I had with Alec Ogilvie * at the old Hotel Cecil in July 1917. At the time a large number of Hispano engines was

* Holding a position corresponding later to the Director of Technical Development.

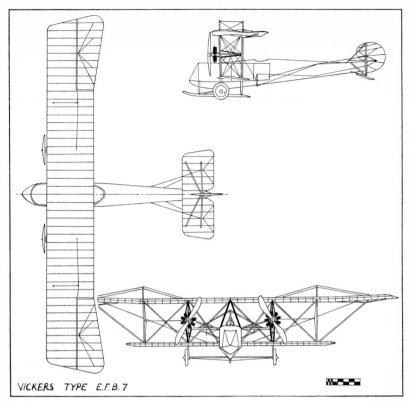

VICKERS TYPE E.F.B.7

surplus to fighter requirements for which they (the Air Board) were seeking a use. At that same time they were not getting sufficient Rolls-Royce Eagles to fulfil all their bombing requirements, and it was suggested to me that

Flanders-designed E.F.B.7 in original form with Gnome monosoupape engines, and pilot behind wings.

77

Pierson development of E.F.B.7 was this E.F.B.8, designed as a twin-engined fighter for the Lewis gun seen parked against the nose; the oil slinger rings around the Gnome rotary engines are also of interest.

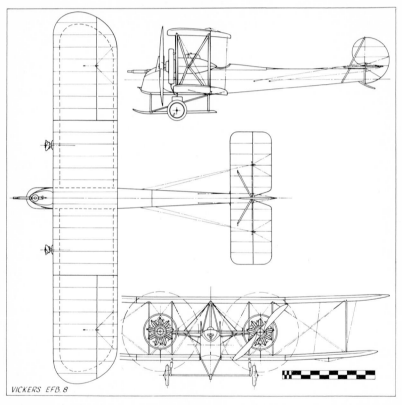

VICKERS EFB. 8

Vickers should attempt to build a bomber around the Hispano engine to the same specification as the Handley Page O/400.

'Pierson rapidly produced general layout designs, and an immediate order for prototypes was given. The first of these was flown by Gordon Bell at Joyce Green on 30 November, 1917. There was a different type of engine fitted into each of the other prototypes, including B.H.P., Fiat, Salmson and, subsequently, the Rolls-Royce Eagle.

'When the time came to place the production orders in April 1918, the Rolls was decided upon. History tells us the rest. The designing, building and flying of the machine in a period of four months was, to my mind, one of the highest spots of co-operative effort I have come across in many years in the industry.'

Pierson had related this story in a broadcast talk in 1942, when he said that with Maj J. C. Buchanan of the Air Board (later Air Ministry) he drew up the outline of the proposed Vickers bomber on a piece of foolscap paper in the Hotel Cecil, the Board's headquarters.

Prototype F.B.27 Vimy under final erection at Joyce Green in 1917; for the roll-out the floor of the hangar had to be recessed to provide height clearance for the completed aeroplane.

The four F.B.27 prototypes were fitted with 200 hp geared Hispano Suizas (later re-engined with 260 hp Salmsons), 260 hp Sunbeam Maoris, 300 hp Fiat A-12 and 360 hp Rolls-Royce Eagle VIIIs. These prototypes were conveniently referred to as Marks I to IV, but surviving Weybridge drawings do not confirm this early nomenclature, and official evidence on the subject seems to be conflicting. The Mark number system was never received with much enthusiasm on the production side until recent history, when it came to mean a lot more than merely airframe or engine modifications.

In the first F.B.27, called Vimy when the official naming of aircraft was introduced in 1918, the Hispanos were changed to Salmsons; the second, with Maoris, was lost soon after trials began because of engine failure; and the third, with the Fiats, also was lost by stalling on take-off at Martlesham and blowing up in the resulting crash as its bombs were armed

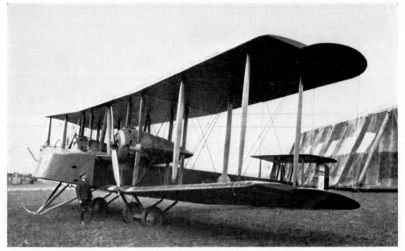

Prototype B9952 as re-engined with Salmson water-cooled radial engines.

(presumably for live practice over the nearby Orfordness armament and bombing ranges). The fourth Vimy prototype, with Eagles, went to Martlesham on 11 October, 1918, and confirmed the impression of exceptional performance for the period earned by the original F.B.27 in the previous January, also under test at Martlesham, the then newly established Aeroplane Experimental Establishment.*

The original Vimy, with its geared Hispanos of dubious reliability, had lifted a greater load than the much larger and more powerful Handley Page O/400. The Eagle-powered Vimy prototype had a speed of 100 mph and endurance of 11 hours with full crew and a load of nearly 5,000 lb (including fuel) out of a take-off weight of 12,500 lb, a remarkable achievement in its day.

Behind the scenes in official quarters a controversy had raged between the protagonists of tactical and strategic bombing. This seems to have been

* Later renamed Aeroplane and Armament Experimental Establishment.

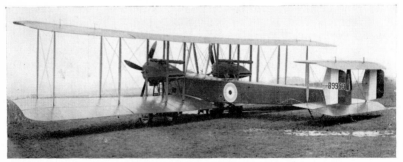

Second prototype Vimy, B9953, with Sunbeam Maori engines, which was written off through an engine failure on flight trials.

Third prototype Vimy, B9954, with Fiat A-12 engines, which also met with disaster at Martlesham Heath.

resolved because of the need to retaliate against the night bombing of targets in Britain by German aeroplanes, which began in September 1917. In consequence, the Vimy was one of the new heavy bombers selected for production. The first contract, for 150, received by Vickers was on 26 March, 1918, and was followed shortly afterwards by another for 200, the first batch to be made at Vickers' Crayford works and the second at Weybridge. With contracts to other firms, the order book reached 1,130, with variations as to the specified power units. Production during 1918 was to be reserved for aircraft for anti-submarine duties (carrying two torpedoes) and subsequent deliveries for night-bombing aircraft.

The urgency of combating the U-boat menace with a more devastating weapon than the Blackburn Kangaroo, then operating, probably dictated the priority for anti-submarine work, but no Vimy was in fact ever used in that rôle.

In October 1918 one Vimy bomber was flown to Nancy, in northeast France, to stand by for a series of long-range raids deep into Germany, including Berlin. The Armistice of 11 November, 1918, cancelled this plan, and consequently the Vimy was not used operationally in the first world war.

The final prototype Vimy, F9569, with Rolls-Royce Eagle VIII engines which ensured the success of the new bomber.

81

A view inside Weybridge new erecting shop early in 1919 showing Vimy bombers under construction, and in the background, on the right, the prototype Vimy Commercial, on the left, the Transatlantic Vimy, less outer planes.

Following the cessation of hostilities, the Government drastically reduced all orders for military aircraft, including those for Vimys, after Crayford had made seven and Weybridge six, but subsequently Weybridge made 99 Vimys for the peacetime Royal Air Force. Components already completed were purchased from certain of the former outside contractors, which aided production, and special aircraft were modified from the military versions to undertake long-distance pioneering flights. Indeed, the first aeroplane to make a trans-oceanic flight non-stop was the now famous Vimy crewed by Capt Jack Alcock * and Lt Arthur Whitten-Brown on 14–15 June, 1919, across the Atlantic.

The production Vimy followed the conventional design trends of its time, having a wire-braced biplane wing structure and stabiliser, also of biplane form, with twin fins and rudders. The front fuselage was of steel tube and the rear fuselage was of wood with steel end-fittings and swaged tie-rod bracing. The rear longerons were hollow spars to the McGruer patent, devised by a Clyde yacht designer and consisting of wrapped shims machined circumferentially from spruce logs. Recently examined by the inventor, the longerons on the transatlantic Vimy now in the Science Museum in London were found to be in perfect condition. Rudders and ailerons were aerodynamically balanced by extensions forward of the hinge points. The whole design was well proportioned, and upon this factor depended its success. Its Rolls-Royce engines were admirably suited to it, which was a new experience as far as Vickers were concerned, for their designers had suffered miserably from the allocation of unsuitable engines for previous aircraft, as has already been emphasised.

The use of Vickers' own wind tunnel at St Albans, the first commercially

* Among his colleagues in the pioneering days of pre-1914 Brooklands, Alcock was known as 'Jack'.

82

owned example anywhere, helped considerably in predicting aerodynamic performance and configuration, and Pierson cleverly exploited the reduction in scale from contemporary designs (as represented by the Handley Page O/400) to reduce structure weight. He also introduced refinements in detail design to achieve maximum strength factors.

Provision was made in the fuselage for part of the bomb load, the rest being carried under the bottom planes, with simple release gear. Two gunners could be carried, one in the nose with a Lewis on a Scarff ring, another similarly armed aft of the wings, with provision for shifting the gun to a pivot mount on the bottom of the fuselage for firing aft under the tail, with side windows for light when changing ammunition drums.

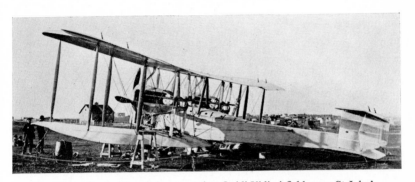

The Transatlantic Vimy being erected at Quidi Vidi airfield, near St John's, Newfoundland—later it was flown to Lester's Field for take-off.

Maximum range was 1,880 miles, and the Vimy was easily capable of carrying what was for its time quite a respectable bomb load to Berlin. Various figures of speed have been quoted, from 98 mph to the 112 mph which Capt Broome, a Vickers pilot, was able to record on one test flight. Climb to 6,000 ft took 18 minutes, and the Vimy's ceiling, when fully loaded, was not more than 12,000 ft. Within this performance envelope, Alcock and Brown had to fly through the weather across the Atlantic. This led them into icing troubles and flying attitudes of the most unfamiliar character, in weather conditions which today's high-flying airliners can usually avoid.

The Ross and Keith Smith brothers' flight to Australia at the end of 1919 in a specially prepared Vimy proved the soundness of the design from another angle. It showed that the aeroplanes of the time could be operated across continents to far distant places and foreshadowed the day when scheduled services would be operated between Europe, the Far East and Australia, just as Alcock and Brown had presaged regular Atlantic air routes. The attempts to reach Cape Town by air by the Vimy of Van Ryneveld and Quintin Brand, and the other, sponsored by *The Times* and flown by Vickers' test pilots, Cockerell and Broome, did not experience complete success. But a far-reaching discovery had been made. Technical

Take-off of Alcock and Brown in Vimy for the first direct Atlantic flight, 14 June, 1919; photographer was H. J. Holloway of St John's, and the copyright was afterwards acquired by Vickers.

progress was needed to overcome the combined effect of high operating temperatures and greater altitudes on engine behaviour and performance, and on improvements in airframes, for wood and fabric and tropical conditions did not agree with one another.

Although the three pioneering flights undertaken by Vimys soon after the first world war have been fully documented, including a book* on Alcock and Brown's Atlantic conquest, the essential details are included here to keep the record complete.

For the Atlantic flight all the military equipment was removed from a standard Vimy† and extra tankage installed in its place, thus increasing the fuel capacity from 516 to 865 gallons to give an optimum range of 2,440 miles. Actually, enough fuel for another 800 miles remained in the tanks after the flight had terminated in the Derrygimla bog at Clifden, County Galway, for the prevailing westerly wind had been of some assistance, as is normal in scheduled operations today. The engines were the standard Rolls-Royce Eagle VIIIs of 360 hp each, and they functioned reliably except for an occasional icing-up of the air intakes. In the twin-engined

* *The Flight of Alcock and Brown*, Graham Wallace (Putnam).
† The 13th airframe off the post-war production line at Weybridge.

configuration it was possible for the crew to see the radiators and air intakes; with a single-engined tractor aeroplane this was not possible, and one theory now advanced for the failure of Hawker to complete the Atlantic flight on the Sopwith single-engined tractor machine was that his radiator shutters were partially closed through a control maladjustment, thus causing the engine temperature to rise. Had he been able to see his engine, this would not have occurred, and some weight is lent to this conjecture by the fact that the Sopwith also had the Rolls-Royce Eagle VIII engine, the type which did so well in the Vimy.

From take-off near St John's, Newfoundland, to landing in Ireland, the Vimy took 16 hr 27 min on the 1,890 mile non-stop flight, which included the night of 14 June. Visibility was too poor most of the time for the navigator to take sights and the weather anything but good for such an adventure virtually into the unknown. Their objective was Galway Bay, the conditions of the *Daily Mail* £10,000 prize having specified 'anywhere in the British Isles' as the terminating point. Whitten-Brown, with his improved nautical methods of navigation, devised while he was a prisoner of war, crossed the Irish coast at Clifden, only a few miles north of his flight plan.

The Vimy was partially wrecked on landing in the bog; had the two airmen but known, the green pasture next to the one they had selected was quite solid, according to eye-witnesses at the time. The omission of the nosewheel in Newfoundland to reduce drag and weight was probably a sound idea, but that wheel might have saved the aircraft from nosing into

End of first direct Atlantic flight in the Derrygimla bog, Clifden, Co. Galway, Ireland, on 15 June, 1919.

85

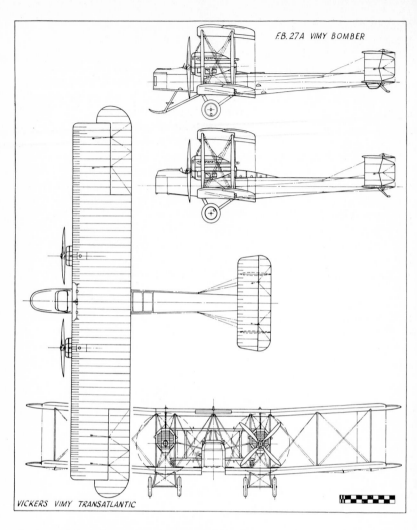

FB.27A VIMY BOMBER

VICKERS VIMY TRANSATLANTIC

the bog. The Vimy was rebuilt at Weybridge after recovery, and now is a treasured exhibit in the Science Museum in London, where one can engage in an interesting exercise in comparing it with modern aircraft, particularly with regard to its primitive navigational aids, and to its structure, now partially exposed to public view.

The next major event which was to concern the Vimy was the offer of a prize of £A10,000 by the Australian Government for the first flight by Australians from Britain to Australia, to be completed within 30 days and before the end of the year 1919. Maxwell-Muller had engineered the Vimy at Weybridge for the Atlantic flight and prepared another for this fresh challenge. It was more or less of the standard military type with few

Crew inspection of Vimy bomber selected for the England–Australia flight—in front, left to right, Capt Ross Smith, Lt Keith Smith and Sgt W. H. Shiers; in rear cockpit, Sgt J. M. Bennett.

Take-off of Vimy for Australia on 12 November, 1919, from the old Hounslow airfield, the site of which was about two miles east of the present London Airport, Heathrow.

changes apart from the provision of additional stores, to cope with tropical flying, in place of the normal military load.

The pilots chosen were the Smith brothers, Ross and Keith, of the Australian Air Force, as were the two mechanics, Sgts W. H. Shiers and J. M. Bennett. A considerable amount of pre-flight planning had to be done, petrol, oil and essential stores laid down at strategic points *en route*, and landing grounds carefully surveyed by agents in advance.

As far as Calcutta the air route was fairly well known, but eastwards from there the flight took on the form of trail blazing. The Vimy, valiantly flown and serviced by its Australian crew, won through, like Sir Francis Drake, 'after many vicissitudes', including vile weather, and reached Darwin from Hounslow in just under 28 days on 10 December, 1919, having covered 11,130 miles in 135 hr 55 min elapsed flying time. The aeroplane, G-EAOU, is now preserved in a memorial hall on the airport at Adelaide, home of the pilots, for the building of which the Australian public subscribed some £A30,000.

Australian Vimy G-EAOU running engines on Singapore racecourse preparatory to resuming flight.

The third great flight attempted by the Vimy was for a flight from England to Cape Town. Several efforts were made, but two Vimys achieved the greatest success. One was a standard military type, called the *Silver Queen*, flown by Lt-Col Pierre Van Ryneveld and Maj C. J. Quintin Brand of the South African Air Force. They left Brooklands on 4 February, 1920, but crashed at Korosko between Cairo and Khartoum a week later, a mishap caused by a leaking radiator. A second Vimy was loaned by the Royal Air Force in Egypt and named *Silver Queen II*. This one reached Bulawayo in Southern Rhodesia. There it failed to lift off from the high-altitude aerodrome in high temperature with a failing engine, caused by dirty oil, and was put out of action. The crew borrowed a D.H.9, completed the flight to Cape Town and were awarded £5,000 each by the South African Government. They were knighted by King George V, as were the Smith brothers and Alcock and Brown, after their respective efforts.

Vimy G-UABA *Silver Queen* on the compass base at Brooklands, being inspected by Van Ryneveld and Quintin Brand before their attempt to fly to Cape Town.

Height and heat also defeated the other attempt by a Vimy, chartered from Vickers by *The Times*, with Dr Chalmers Mitchell as their Press representative on the flight. The aeroplane was the prototype Vimy Commercial G-EAAV (originally K-107). It left Brooklands on 24 January, 1920, and crashed at Tabora, Tanganyika, on 27 February, failing to take-off in tropical conditions. It was found that the water in the cooling system of one of the engines was contaminated. It was clear that further engine and airframe development would be needed to operate in such conditions if the lessons of these African flights were to be fully applied. Judging from the successful use of the Vimy and its family successors in Egypt, the Middle East and India in later years, it seems clear that these troubles in African flying were taken to heart.

G-EAAV Vimy Commercial (originally K-107 prototype) taking off from Brooklands on 24 January, 1920, for an attempt on the Cape flight.

89

G-EAAV on a landing ground in the Sudan during the attempt by Vickers pilots Cockerell and Broome to fly to Cape Town, 1920.

No. 58 Squadron RAF, in Egypt in July 1919, was the first to receive the Vimy bomber, as the Handley Page O/400 replacement, and operated the Vickers type until disbanded in February 1920. Subsequently, the type equipped other Middle East squadrons, and No. 216, with Vimys, ran some of the first mail services between Cairo and Baghdad. No. 7 Squadron at Bircham Newton was equipped with Vimys in June 1923, although 'D' Flight of 100 (the nucleus of 7 Squadron), had previously operated them at Spittlegate. Nos. 9 and 58 home-based Squadrons received Vimys in April 1924, on the re-forming of those units.

After replacement by the larger and more powerful Virginias in 1924 and 1925, the Vimy remained in service with 502 Squadron at Aldergrove, Northern Ireland, until 1929. Subsequent to their withdrawal from first-line service as standard heavy bombers, Vimys were re-engined with air-cooled radials, either Bristol Jupiters or Armstrong Siddeley Jaguars, in

AOC's inspection of 4 FTS equipped with Vimy trainers at Abu Sueir, Egypt, 1930. (*MoD*(*Air*) *photo*.)

Vic flight of Vimy bombers somewhere in Egypt.

Coventry Ordnance Works one-pounder gun mounted on a Vimy bomber—
the complete installation was in adaptable kit form.

A Vimy of an early Weybridge batch converted there as a Jupiter-engined trainer.

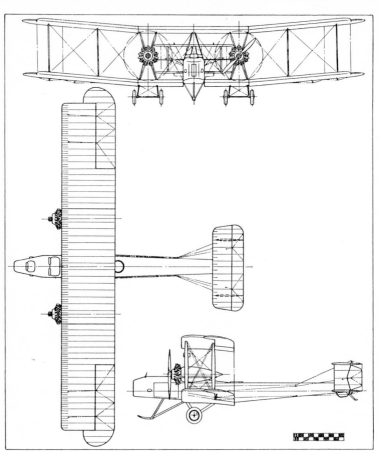

Vickers Vimy Jupiter Trainer

Jupiter-engined Vimys of the RAF Parachute Training School, Henlow.

place of the water-cooled Rolls-Royce Eagles. These were used in flying
training schools such as No. 4 F.T.S. at Abu Sueir, Egypt, and for parachute training at Henlow. From Biggin Hill a night-flying unit equipped
with Vimys operated long after the type had disappeared from the rest of
the Royal Air Force; in fact, the Vimy was used right up to the time of the
Munich crisis in 1938 as target aircraft for the searchlight crews of the
Royal Engineers training at Blackdown, Hants.

After the Armistice of November 1918, and the rapid cancellation of
contracts for military aircraft, the executives of Vickers' aviation started
to look around for aircraft projects which might prove attractive in the
new world of civil aviation, then thought by many to be just round the
corner. Most favoured by Capt Peter Acland, by that time Aviation
Department Manager, and by Pierson, was a civil version of the Vimy
intended as a passenger carrier for the small private-enterprise airlines
about to be formed.

In January 1919 the civil Vimy project, known originally as the Mono-
coq, crystallised into the design of a new fuselage of generous dimensions

A Jaguar-engined Vimy trainer at Abu Sueir. (*MoD(Air) photo.*)

to replace the slender bomber fuselage. A forebody of oval cross-section, completely clear of internal obstructions, such as struts or cross-bracing, was joined to the standard rear fuselage, with light fairings attached top and bottom to produce a reasonably streamlined structure, on which the wing cellule, engine mountings and biplane tail of the standard bomber were mounted.

In the forebody wooden box-formers were located on box longerons (to mate with those in the rear fuselage), and the structure was covered with Consuta copper-sewn plywood, the whole comprising a form of stressed-skin construction in wood. Underfloor tanks carried the fuel, which was lifted to service tanks in the upper wing by Vickers' windmill-driven pumps, mounted outboard on the lower centre sections. The longerons aft were of circular section Vickers-Ryan segmented wood type.

Although externally the effect of this large fuselage was not particularly attractive, internally it embodied a spacious cabin capable of carrying 10 passengers in comfort, seated in unstressed leather-padded or wicker chairs. Passenger steps attached to the inside of the rear door, which was hinged at the bottom, added to the modern aspect of the cabin. Regrettably, Vickers' test pilots at Joyce Green refused to consider the neat enclosed flight deck intended to complement the design, saying that vision would be impaired and that they preferred the fresh air of their open cockpits. So the standard cockpit was incorporated as on the bomber, with the eventual change of the captain's seat from starboard (as on the trans-atlantic Vimy) to port, to comply with the then new air-traffic regulations

The prototype Vimy Commercial being prepared for its first flight at Joyce Green in February 1919.

94

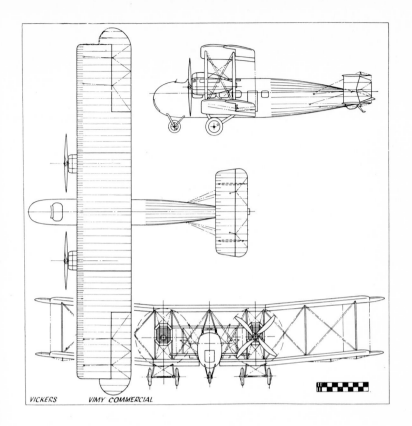

VICKERS   VIMY COMMERCIAL

for left-hand approach circuits as soon as these became mandatory. As in modern practice, by removing the passenger seats, a rear freight space of 300 cu ft could be provided to carry 2,500 lb.

In still air the performance of this Vimy Commercial, as it was eventually named, was slightly in advance of that of the bomber, a bonus probably of carrying stores inside instead of outside; but when adverse winds were encountered its short range was a limiting factor, and with full load a refuelling stop had to be made at a landing strip on the London–Paris route. However, the original concept was sound, and it survived for many years throughout Vickers' range of large military and civil transports up to the Valentia bomber-transport in regular service well into the second world war.

Built in Vickers' aircraft experimental shop at Bexleyheath, the prototype Vimy Commercial first flew on 13 April, 1919, at Joyce Green in the hands of Stan Cockerell. Bearing the interim civil registration K-107, it flew at various presentations of Vickers aircraft, including the ELTA exhibition at Amsterdam. Later as G-EAAV it attempted the flight to the Cape as previously noted.

G-EASI Vimy Commercial in its first livery of S. Instone and Co; later it wore that of Imperial Airways.

In 1919 the Chinese Government ordered 40 Vimy Commercials with 35 VIM trainers (converted from surplus wartime F.E.2ds) and 20 re-conditioned Avro 504Ks from Vickers, to establish civil aviation in China. The financing of this contract proved difficult, and was eventually arranged by the floating of Chinese Vickers bonds in London. In his book *Sagittarius Rising*, Cecil Lewis describes his experiences in China with the assembly and flying of some of these Commercials, but most of them appear to have remained in their crates unused.

A production line of Vimy Commercials was established at Weybridge, No. 41 was registered G-EASI and named *City of London* by its operators,

G-EASI taking off at Croydon for Paris in the very early days of civil air transport.

S. Instone and Co, a shipping line pioneering an airline. G-EASI was in service for five years on various European short-haul routes, being taken over by Imperial Airways, which in a later merger of private airlines absorbed Instone's interests. By 1 April, 1924, it had flown 108,000 miles and carried many thousands of passengers.

A Vimy Commercial, G-EAUL, came second in the large aeroplane class of the Air Ministry competitions for civil aircraft in 1920. Another was bought by the French airline, Grands Express Aériens, for whose service it was engined with Napier Lions and registered F-ADER; but in a modification made at Weybridge later on, it was fitted with 400 hp Lorraine-Dietrich engines.

This Russian photograph of the so-called Vimy Commercial supplied to the USSR in 1922 reveals its true identity as a hybrid Vernon with Lion engines.

A Vimy Commercial was also bought by Soviet Russia at about the same time, but no information exists as to its career, except that it was flown in the Moscow region. It combined features of the Instone G-EASI and the later Royal Air Force Vernon and was powered with Napier Lion engines. On delivery, no registration marks were carried. From S. Davis, Vickers' service engineer who went to Russia with this Vimy Commercial and a Vickers Viking IV amphibian, it was learned that the Russians gave him the impression that the acquisition of these aircraft was to familiarise themselves with the latest Western ideas and practices in aeronautics.

In 1921 a military ambulance version of the Vimy Commercial was produced for the Royal Air Force, to carry four stretcher or eight sitting cases, with two medical staff in attendance, the stretchers being loaded through a door in the nose. This was probably the first instance of nose loading. Five of these Vimy ambulance versions were built, powered with Lions, but overseas they did not give a highly impressive performance.

97

Interior of Vimy Ambulance showing unobstructed cabin typical of the
Commercial series and continued in the Vernon and Victoria.

One Vimy ambulance (J6904) was fitted with extra wing tanks to Vernon
Mark III standard as a reconditioned conversion and others followed.

VERNON. From the Vimy Commercial and the Vimy Ambulance came
the Vernon, originally called a troop transport, but later classified in
official terminology as a bomber-transport, like the Victoria and the
Valentia which followed. In fact, its rôles in service were just that, for the
Vernon was indeed the first aeroplane of the Royal Air Force to be specifically operated as the transport equipment of an emergency fire brigade, to
quell outbreaks of violence in Cyprus and later among the tribes in the
mandated territory of Iraq. This it performed in two ways: it carried small
bodies of infantry with supplies to trouble spots and, secondly, was con-

verted in the field to bombing duties, primarily as a show of strength when the mere dropping of bombs around a village with a hoped-for shattering of morale was judged a sufficient deterrent, although later on it proved necessary to adopt the sterner method of destroying the villages when the Kurdish tribes in Iraq proved especially fractious.

From 1921 onwards the maintenance of law and order in Iraq was made the responsibility of the Royal Air Force, which was capable of carrying out this task over wide areas of territory at small cost, with economy of military power. Thus the Vernon led the way in establishing a military philosophy which still has great value today in the so-called bush-fire wars. But it is in a much more peaceable rôle that the Vernon deserves to be recognised as a true pioneer.

In March 1921 a conference was held at Cairo between the Secretary of State for the Colonies and the Chief of Air Staff, with local Army and RAF commanders, for discussions prior to the formation of the Middle East Department of the Colonial Office. In addition to making the momentous decision about RAF military control of Iraq, the conference made another, which was to open a desert air route between Amman and Ramadi. The objects were to forge a link in the Imperial chain of communications between Europe, India and eventually Australia; to enable aircraft to proceed direct to Iraq; to serve as training in long-distance flying; and to evolve a rapid means of communication for military purposes by running a regular air mail. It is noteworthy that this last idea was later developed into a civil air mail service, carrying the Royal Mail emblem on its aircraft. In fact, after lengthy negotiations with the Postmaster-General, civil mails were carried almost from the start. The air mail telescoped the time that

Vernon over Bridge of Boats, Baghdad—at the end of the mail run.

A line-up of Vernon Is (Eagle engines) of the RAF in the Middle East.

a letter took to reach Baghdad from London from the former 28 days into nine, a significant event in the absence of railways and a portent of things to come. Vernons bore the brunt of the service until 1926, aided by RAF Vimys pressed into duty as mail carriers.

All the objects of the Cairo conference were thus met, and some idea of the conditions of flying the air mail route in those early days as recorded by Sqn Ldr Roderic Hill (later Air Chief Marshal Sir Roderic Hill), then commanding No. 45 Squadron equipped with Vernons, is worth noting. His paper presented to the Royal Aeronautical Society on 1 March, 1928, was entitled *Experiences on the Cairo–Baghdad Air Mail* and contained some interesting observations, amplified by his subsequent book.

Course setting by compass bearing was too risky at the low altitudes and speeds then prevailing, so a *Bradshaw* track was laid across the desert by plough and by wheel marks of the surveying vehicles, later more clearly defined by the tracks of a commercial goods transport service which was established. The distance from Amman to Baghdad was over 500 miles, so the possibility of an aeroplane getting lost in the desert in event of forced landing was very real indeed. Therefore, every 20 miles or so, emergency landing grounds were established, marked and ringed with series letters and numbers, a practice surviving to this day with a different purpose, that of marking the chain of pumping stations on the Middle

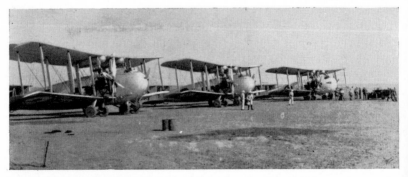

Vernon IIs of the Cairo–Baghdad air mail service at a desert staging post *en route*—under the starboard wing of the nearest aeroplane can be seen the distinctive Flight marking of a Finnish-type swastika. (*MoD(Air) photo.*)

East oil pipe-lines. Radio was essential for communication, and portable transmitting masts were carried for use in the event of forced landing. This was probably one of the first occasions when radio telecommunication was established on a recognised air route of continental status.

As the mail service gained experience, reliability improved and the amount of mail carried in the first sixteen months increased tenfold, according to Roderic Hill. Of the Vernon, he said that with its big 'saloon hull', heavily loaded in hot weather, it had a rather disappointing perform-ance. He wrote, 'To give it a higher performance the 450 hp Napier Lion

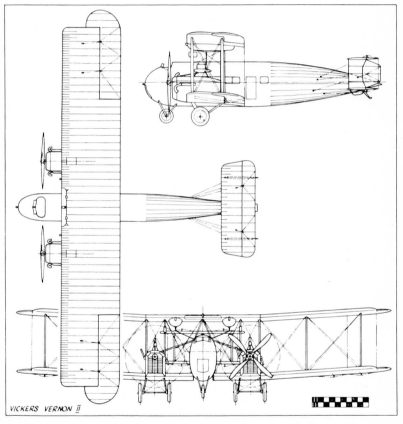

VICKERS VERNON II

was installed in place of the Rolls-Royce Eagle VIII engine and No. 45 Squadron's Eagle Vernons became animated with the fury of Lions. Meanwhile 45 Squadron also captured its big game and took over the mail until early in 1926.' An innovation on the air mail service was the naming of individual aeroplanes, particularly in No. 70 Squadron, whose Vernons were called *Ancaeus, Argo, Aurora, Morpheus, Vagabond, Vaivode, Valkyrie, Venus* and *Vesuvius*, while the name *Pelican* adorned one of No. 70's Vernons.

Another use was made of the Vernons during operations in Kurdistan, Northern Iraq, in 1922, when British troops, who had been stricken with dysentery, were evacuated to base hospitals in Baghdad in a matter of hours, thus saving the days of uncomfortable travel by surface transport which would otherwise have been involved. According to the *Journal of the RAMC* for November 1925, the Royal Air Force moved 161 patients from outlying stations such as Kirkuk, Ramadi and Mosul in 15 months, mostly in Vernons.

On the left is a close-up of the nose of a 45 Squadron Vernon with bomb-aimer's peep hole, and right the bomb-aimer's station keyed as F—bomb sight, K and L—single release toggles, H—head-piece for Gosport speaking tubes, N—winch for W/T trailing aerial, O and G—chart boxes and M—salvo release cable; the 'bowler hat' is a chest cushion.

In an address to the Institute of Transport in 1960, Air Marshal Sir Denis Barnett, then AOC-in-C, Transport Command, said: 'Between the two wars, the thinking generated by the first found its expression, until the second drew near, in the development of that celebrated family of maids-of-all-work, the family of (Vickers) bomber transport aircraft which had their culmination in the Valentia. Any story told during those years would be embellished brightly by the rich diversity and enduring value of the operations of those squadrons. Indeed our modern networks of worldwide air routes owe much more than is customarily remembered today to their imaginative and pioneering exertions.'

At the time the Vernon Mark Is were operating in the Middle East, improved versions were being evolved by Vickers and the lessons learned were being embodied therein. The need for more power, as mentioned by Roderic Hill, was evident, and Vernon J6884 went to Martlesham in January 1922 for evaluation with Lion engines. In the next month Vernon J6879 also went to Martlesham for trial with outboard tanks of 120-gal capacity each, a Vickers oleo-pneumatic undercarriage in place of the former elastic-cord spring type and bomb-release gear.

As a result of these trials, Vickers received a second contract for Vernons to Mark II standards as called for under specification 43/22. Other improvements requested in Middle East Command reports, which arrived regularly every six months, were the provision of long horn-shaped engine

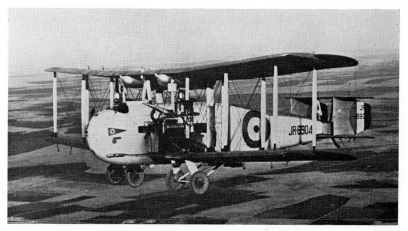

A Vernon Mk III rebuilt from a Vimy Ambulance, hence the serial number JR6904—R meaning reconditioned; note the final deletion of the standard nosewheel in this Mark.

air intakes to prevent the ingress of sand, even at that time regarded as number one enemy in the desert. Similarly, the gauze windows in the cabin let in sand and were eventually replaced with mica or Triplex glass. In March 1923 the AOC Middle East supported the design of a new aeroplane of larger dimensions and capacity with greatly increased range and, with other recommendations on the need for a more powerful bomber than the Vimy, Vickers proceeded to the Virginia/Victoria concept, as will be told later.

Meanwhile, a further improvement of performance was made in the Vernon Mark III for another contract placed in 1924, by the installation of geared high-compression Lion III engines and long-range tanks.

Data for E.F.B.7, E.F.B.8, Vimy and Vernon appear on page 104.

E.F.B.7 and E.F.B.8

	E.F.B.7	E.F.B.8
Accommodation:	Pilot and gunner	Pilot and gunner
Engines:	Two 100 hp Gnome monosoupape	Two 100 hp Gnome monosoupape
Span:	59 ft 6 in upper, 37 ft 6 in lower	38 ft 4 in upper, 36 ft 8 in lower
Length:	36 ft	28 ft 2 in
Height:	—	9 ft 10 in
Wing Area:	640 sq ft	468 sq ft
Empty Weight:	2,136 lb	1,840 lb
Gross Weight:	3,196 lb	2,700 lb
Max Speed at 5,000 *ft:*	75 mph	98 mph
Climb to 5,000 *ft:*	18 min	10 min
Ceiling:	9,000 ft	14,000 ft
Endurance:	2½ hr	3 hr
Armament:	One 1-pdr Vickers gun in nose	One Lewis gun in nose

Vimy and Vernon

	Vimy (F.B.27)	Vimy Mk II (F.B.27A)	Vimy Commercial	Vernon Mk II
Accommodation:	Pilot and 2 gunners	Pilot and 2 gunners	2 crew 10 passengers	3 crew 11 passengers
Engines:	Two 200 hp Hispano Suiza	Two 360 hp Rolls-Royce Eagle VIII	Two 360 hp Rolls-Royce Eagle VIII	Two 450 hp Napier Lion II
Span:	67 ft 2 in	68 ft	68 ft	68 ft
Length:	43 ft 6½ in	43 ft 6½ in	42 ft 8 in	43 ft 8 in
Height:	15 ft 3 in	15 ft 7½ in	15 ft 7½ in	15 ft 3 in
Wing Area:	1,326 sq ft	1,330 sq ft	1,330 sq ft	1,330 sq ft
Empty Weight:	5,420 lb	7,101 lb	7,790 lb	7,890 lb
Gross Weight:	9,120 lb	12,500 lb	12,500 lb	12,500 lb
Max Speed:	87 mph at 5,000 ft	103 mph at ground level	98 mph at ground level	118 mph at ground level
Climb to 5,000 *ft:*	23·5 min	22 min	28 min	13½ min to 6,000 ft
Service Ceiling:	6,500 ft	7,000 ft	—	—
Absolute Ceiling:	9,500 ft	10,500 ft	10,500 ft	11,700 ft
Endurance/Range:	3½ hr	11 hr	450 miles	320 miles at 80 mph
Armament:	Two Lewis guns Eighteen 112-lb and two 230-lb bombs	Two Lewis guns 2,476-lb bomb load	—	—

The Vulcan

Design work was started in February 1921 on an eight-passenger single-engined biplane in the same class as the Airco (de Havilland) 18. It incorporated a fuselage similar in layout to that of the Vimy Commercial, with capacious unobstructed cabin. Low initial and operating cost was a prime consideration, for although airlines were promised a subsidy, this was contingent upon payment by results. By using the war-surplus Rolls-Royce Eagle VIII engine, as marketed by the Aircraft Disposal Company, a price of £2,500 or thereabouts was attained, an appealing figure to the small newly established airlines with limited capital.

Preliminary drawings and data were completed in the following September and circulated to prospective customers, among them S. Instone and Company, the Australian Government and KLM Royal Dutch Airlines. In addition, the Department of Civil Aviation of the Air Ministry had expressed interest as the responsible body for the development of civil air transport, including civil aircraft.

Prototype Vulcan being built in Weybridge works in 1922.

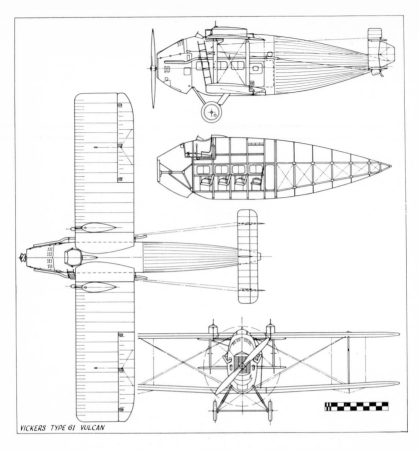

VICKERS TYPE 61 VULCAN

The Vickers project appeared promising. At a mere 45 hp per passenger, an estimated range of 360 miles was offered at 100 mph up to 10,000 ft, then the maximum operating height for civil aircraft. There seemed every prospect for the struggling airline pioneers to show a small profit on the short air routes with this type of aeroplane. In the event, the Vulcan had a chequered career and never matched up to the genuine optimism of its sponsors. Looking back over 40 years, the informed observer will conclude that too little was known then for the establishment of satisfactory parameters in civil aircraft design or, indeed, of the basic principles of air transport operation. Everyone in the business, designers, production engineer and operator, had to learn the hard way, but from those tiny and tortuous beginnings came the vast fund of knowledge of today. From then on civil aviation gradually became a highly specialised industry. If the Vulcan served a useful purpose, then surely it was in throwing into sharp relief the existence of many unsolved problems. For example, the phenomenon of lift loss at the outer panels of low aspect ratio rectangular wings,

106

as used on the Vulcan, was only in the exploratory investigation stage by the Aeronautical Research Committee. The deficiencies of its high-lift T64 aerofoil section could only be exposed by trial and error (as referred to in the chapter on the Viking Amphibian), and the blanketing effect of large fuselage bodies on small tail surfaces, like those of the Vulcan, in certain flight attitudes was not fully appreciated. The reduction of power-loading per passenger to achieve operational efficiency proved not only a fallacy in theory but also expensive in practice.

Consequent on a combination of factors of this character, the Vulcan suffered more than the average number of mishaps during its short life measured in hours flown. Some were attributable to operational inexperience, such as running the engine at too rich a mixture, thereby increasing the fuel consumption and so running short of range. The failure of the Australian Vulcan to meet its contract performance over the Charleville–Cloncurry route of Queensland and Northern Territory Aerial Services (QANTAS) was attributed to loss of engine power caused by the reduced weight of aspired charge in the tropical heat. A similar problem confronted the early Vernons in Iraq.

Structurally, the Vulcan closely followed the lines which had proved sound in the Vimy and its derivatives. The main members of the wings were front and rear spruce box-spars supporting profile ribs of spruce, internally braced with segmented wooden struts and tie-rods. The forebody was built up on wooden box-formers of elliptical shape located on longitudinals with a three-ply wood covering which took a proportion of the stress. The rear fuselage was a trussed wooden structure braced with tie-rods and faired off with light stringers, covered with the conventional linen fabric.

The biplane tail structure favoured by Pierson provided a strong unit at a time when single-cantilever surfaces were unacceptable because of the absence of suitable materials of sufficient strength values. Where the moment arm was long enough, as in the Vimys, and when comparatively

The first Vulcan, G-EBBL, in the livery of Instone Air Line. Later a rectangular fin was fitted centrally above the upper tailplane to improve the yaw characteristics of the type.

unshrouded, such tail surfaces were adequate, but with a short tubby fuselage, as in the Vulcan, their effectiveness was more doubtful.

From the pilot's single-seat cockpit situated just in front of the top leading edge the lines of the nose fell away sharply to the car-type frontal radiator, thus providing good vision in most directions. Some trepidation was expressed about danger to the pilot if the aeroplane turned over on the ground, but no record exists to suggest that this ever happened. The Vulcan had a Vickers oleo-pneumatic undercarriage which was quite efficient if properly serviced and, in any event, this danger was if anything not so apparent as with contemporary low-wing monoplanes with open cockpits.

S. Instone and Company ordered four Vulcans for their airline in December 1921, straight off the drawing board, then a rarity but now conventional. Two were intended for passenger carrying and two for freight, a somewhat optimistic outlook, but nevertheless one indicating the courage of the early operators. The first Vulcan was registered G-EBBL in February 1922 and flew in the following April, late on contract time because of unforeseen circumstances connected with the necessity to keep to the quoted cost. Extra equipment ordered by Instone included air flotation bags, Reid control indicators (early blind flying equipment), Marconi AD2 radio, air-sickness basins and pneumatic safety belts.

G-EBBL was flown by Cockerell to Croydon for demonstration on 8 May, 1922, and there it made an immediate impression, particularly in respect of its short take-off and initial climb. It soon acquired the nickname of the *Flying Pig* allegedly from the staff of Instone Air Line. It was put into service on the London–Paris route on 1 June. It was officially named *City of Antwerp* and was used mainly on the London–Brussels route, together with the two succeeding Vulcans, G-EBDH and G-EBEA, delivered in July.

The fourth Vulcan was ordered by the Air Ministry to specification 12/22 as a freight carrier, mainly to decide whether this type of aeroplane

Vulcan G-EBEK as cargo carrier to Air Ministry order.

108

G-EBEM originally built as cargo carrier, but converted to 8-seat passenger type—note addition of upper central fin to improve directional stability.

could initiate goods carriage by air as a commercial proposition. In consequence, extended trials were carried out at Martlesham under the civil registration G-EBEK. This Vulcan was powered by the Rolls-Royce Eagle IX, a Derby development which maintained power at maximum revolutions more consistently than the old Mk VIII.

No. 5 Vulcan was the second freight carrier, originally ordered for Instone (the other having been converted to passenger carrying), but was converted to the passenger layout and registered G-EBEM. In the name of Douglas Vickers it was flown in the 1922 King's Cup Air Race by Cockerell with several passengers, and was placed seventh, having covered the 810 miles course in 9 hr 24 min flying time.

Nos. 6 and 7 Vulcans were the two intended for QANTAS, but only the second, registered G-EBET, was shipped to Melbourne for route-proving, with the result already mentioned. The other was registered G-EBES, but is believed to have been left uncompleted.

In 1924, when Imperial Airways had absorbed the private airlines, including Instone, interest was revived in the Vulcan but powered with the 450 hp Napier Lion. No doubt it was hoped that this increase of power might solve at least some of the difficulties previously encountered, one of which was inability to carry the specified load of eight passengers in the most adverse operating conditions. Some obligation existed for the manufacturers to implement previous contract terms which had been inherited by Imperial Airways from S. Instone and Company.

Hence, the first Lion-powered Vulcan, G-EBFC, was delivered to Imperial Airways just before Christmas 1924, at a reduced price. It had been a competitor in the 1923 King's Cup Race (like G-EBEM in 1922

Vulcan c/n 7 for Qantas before shipment for Australian trials; note curved aileron trailing edges as on Air Ministry Vulcan.

in the name of Douglas Vickers), but had experienced engine trouble on the first leg of the course. The second Lion Vulcan was delivered in May 1925, registered G-EBLB. This was the ninth and last aeroplane of this design. Both these newer Vulcans were used on Imperial Airways' continental services, principally on the Brussels route but occasionally as far as Cologne, together with the Eagle-powered G-EBEM and G-EBEK, the Air Ministry freighter converted to passenger carrying and loaned or hired out to the airline. In this guise, G-EBEK was on display at the 1925 Empire Exhibition at Wembley as representative of Britain's progress in civil aviation, perhaps—considering all things—not a particularly suitable choice.

Lion-engined Vulcan for Imperial Airways showing starboard exhaust system.

Lion-engined Vulcan for Imperial Airways showing port exhaust system.

The ultimate fate of the remaining Vulcans was that 'FC was withdrawn from service in 1926 after considerable expense in repair and modifications, the Eagle-powered 'EM was sold to Leslie Hamilton for charter work, and 'LB, which had many more flying hours than the other Vulcans, crashed near Purley in July 1928 on a test flight out of Croydon airport.

So ended a chapter of trial and error and tribulation, with little to show but the answers to quite a few unknowns. As said earlier, these answers were to prove invaluable to Vickers' designers and engineers as well as to their opposite numbers in the airline-operating business.

Vulcan

	Type 61	Type 74
Accommodation:	Pilot and 6/8 passengers	Pilot and 6/8 passengers
Engine:	360 hp Rolls-Royce Eagle VIII	450 hp Napier Lion
Span:	49 ft	49 ft
Length:	37 ft 6 in	38 ft
Height:	14 ft 3 in	14 ft 3 in
Wing Area:	840 sq ft	840 sq ft
Empty Weight:	3,775 lb	4,400 lb
Gross Weight:	6,150 lb	6,750 lb
Max Speed at Sea Level:	105 mph	112 mph
Initial Climb:	450 ft/min	500 ft/min
Climb to:	6,000 ft in 14 min	5,000 ft in 13 min
Absolute Ceiling:	9,500 ft	10,500 ft
Range:	360 miles	430 miles

Prototype Viking amphibian in course of construction at Weybridge.

The Viking Amphibian

In December 1918 a project design was drawn up by Pierson for an amphibian flying-boat, to have its engine mounted above the hull deck under the centre section of the top wing. In order to provide crew and passenger accommodation forwards a pusher propeller was essential. This had to be of restricted diameter for hull clearance and, consequently, with wide blades to absorb the power.

To ease production in a class of aeroplane not previously built by Vickers (although they had the experience of S. E. Saunders and Co of Cowes, Isle of Wight, then Vickers' subsidiary, to rely on) and to provide a simple manually retracting land undercarriage, a hull with almost vertical sides was decided upon. This resulted in a narrow-beam planing bottom, as contrasted with the wider beam featured in the Linton Hope type of hull with sponsons, a design successfully exploited by the Supermarine Aviation Company, then a competitor of Vickers in this class. This narrow beam led to a measure of hydrodynamic instability, and various changes were made in the hull design to improve water-planing efficiency, through the various marks of Viking. Only in the last versions, named Vulture and Vanellus, was any serious attempt made to flare the sides of the hull to provide a wider planing bottom. The report of Vickers' water test-tank at St Albans, established in 1912 for testing ship models, disclosed a tendency of the Viking to porpoise, a phenomenon caused by the crests of the waves, formed by the front step, striking the chine aft.

112

The Viking prototype, the Mk I, was built in two months in a Weybridge dance hall, which had been used during the first world war by Vickers as a woodworking shop, and was completed at Brooklands. Female labour was principally employed. The aircraft flew at Brooklands in landplane form in late 1919 and was registered as G-EAOV.

Construction was conventional, with spruce wing members and elm timbers in the hull, which was covered with the patent Saunders Consuta copper-wire sewn plywood. A neat cabin was provided, with dual wheel control, and seats for four passengers. Pierson had studied a Norman Thompson NT2B single-engined flying-boat, exhibited in Harrods of Knightsbridge as a civil aeroplane, and fitted with a cabin. The Vickers design office was then (1918) located at Imperial Court, Basil Street, close to Harrods.

Prototype Viking amphibian, G-EAOV, in readiness for a test flight at Brooklands.

Late in the design stage some difficulty was encountered in choosing a suitable engine. After considering the 200 hp Wolseley-built geared Hispano Suiza, Pierson eventually decided to fit the 275 hp Rolls-Royce Falcon. Apparently one of the problems of the Hispano Suiza was how to embody a satisfactory air intake in a pusher arrangement, although earlier series of the same engine had been installed in the Vickers F.B.26 and the Royal Aircraft Factory's F.E.9 and N.E.1, all pusher propeller aircraft. The greater power of the Falcon was also desirable, and in subsequent marks further increases of engine power were found necessary; the Viking in its earlier versions was underpowered.

On 18 December, 1919, Sir John Alcock, then Vickers' chief pilot, was flying the Viking I, G-EAOV, solo to the Paris Aero Show when he ran into thick fog near Rouen, and in attempting a forced landing he struck a tree in an orchard. The aeroplane was wrecked and Sir John was killed, only a few months after he and Whitten-Brown had created air history by flying across the Atlantic. It was a premature ending to a brilliant flying career which began in the pioneering days at Brooklands aerodrome.

The Mk II Viking appeared later in 1919 and contained a number of

113

Viking II G-EASC at the Aero Show, Olympia, in 1920 behind wings of Vimy Commercial. At the rear is the Short Silver Streak and on the right the Martinsyde Type A Mk II civil transport.

modifications. It was powered by a Rolls-Royce Eagle VIII of 360 hp, mounted independently of the wing structure on a pylon mounting. The wheelbase was widened and undercarriage details improved, with increased-diameter wheels, and the wing area was increased and a third rudder added behind the central fixed fin. To overcome the tendency of the prototype to dig its bows into the water during take-off the nose of the Mk II was made more blunt. The re-entrant curve of the planing bottom between the steps was modified to try to solve the wave crest problem, and behind the rear step an oleo-pneumatic tailskid cum water-rudder was fitted. Stan Cockerell, who had taken the place of Sir John Alcock as chief pilot (later joined by Capt Broome), flew the Viking II, registered G-EASC, at Cowes in June 1920, and it was displayed at the Aero Show in Olympia that year. In August it won the Antwerp Seaplane Trials.

As a result of Cockerell's report, further modifications were made in the Viking Mk III, which was entered for the Air Ministry Competitions for civil aircraft held at Martlesham Heath and Felixstowe in September and October 1920. Registered G-EAUK, the Viking III won the competition for amphibians and the first prize of £10,000. The Supermarine entry was such a close runner-up that the second prize was increased from £5,000 to £8,000. (Later on, in 1928, Vickers acquired the Supermarine Aviation Company.) In the official report of the Competitions was a suggestion that the tendency of the Viking to porpoise might be cured by altering the position or shape of the step, and also that the shape of the bows should be modified to keep down spray and sea. Flown by Cockerell, the performance of the Viking III was assessed as very good, and the judges were obviously impressed with the safety of the boat type of amphibian.

The main differences between the Mks II and III were the fitting of a still more powerful engine, the 450 hp Napier Lion, the lengthening of the

Viking III taxying across Woodbridge–Felixstowe road at Martlesham for
Air Ministry Competition, 1920.

Viking III taxying at Felixstowe during Air Ministry Competition, 1920, in which
it won first prize for amphibians.

G-EAUK Mk III Viking during London–Paris centre-to-centre flights in 1921.

nose while retaining the same shape of bows, a redesigned tailskid cum water-rudder, a further increase in wing area by introducing a slightly wider chord and, to counter greater engine torque, a small rectangular fin was added above the upper tailplane.

On 6 February, 1921, Cockerell began a series of tests with G-EAUK to determine the feasibility of passenger services from the River Thames, in the heart of London, to the River Seine, in Paris. These journeys took only two and a half hours, which bears comparison with elapsed times between the city centres of the two capitals today. Sir Frederick Sykes, Controller of Civil Aviation in Britain, and M. Laurent Eynac, his French opposite number, tested the service for themselves in April 1921. Subsequently, the Viking III went for trials on the aircraft carrier HMS *Argus* for which it was allocated the service number N147. The deck-handling and operating trials were quite satisfactory, the aeroplane taking-off easily and landing with no external aids except the deck-arrester wires.

As a result of these successful tests, covering a wide range of operational use both off the water and from land aerodromes, firm interest was created, and a production line was started at Weybridge of the Viking Mk IV in three main variants: fleet spotter, military and commercial. Some were

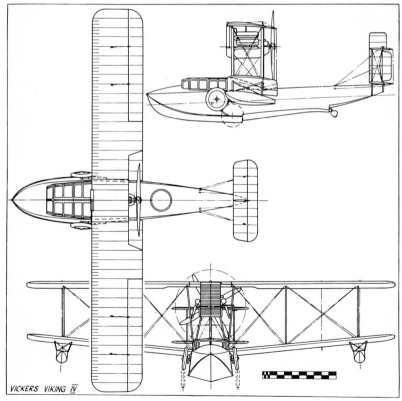

VICKERS VIKING IV

116

fitted with folding wings, notably the fleet-spotter variants, where stowage space was a limiting factor.

The production Viking Mk IVs embodied further improvements from their experimental predecessors. The nose was made even more blunt, the beam of the hull was increased by one foot and the rear step was moved back also by one foot. The wheels were fitted with brakes and the tailskid cum water-rudder assembly again modified. The span was increased by 4 ft to 50 ft overall, and the loaded weight went up from the 4,500 lb of the Mk III to nearly 6,000 lb. Some Mk IVs retained the 46-ft span.

First production Viking amphibians; in centre Type 54 French order, and on outside, Dutch East Indies Type 55s with extended wing span.

To promote quick take-off from restricted water areas a new high-lift wing-section, the T64, was made optional, in place of the Royal Aircraft Factory 15 standard wing-section. This new high-lift section had been developed from propeller design and had a flat undersurface similar to that later known as Clark Y. It had one drawback, a vicious tip stall. This, combined with the couple caused by the high thrust-line and the low drag component of the hull, made the Viking IV with the T64 wing-section a specialist type to fly. With the engine on, it was nose heavy; with the engine off, it was tail heavy. To inexperienced pilots, especially those accustomed to landplanes, the Viking presented quite a problem in avoiding the flat spin which was the bugbear of aircraft of comparatively slow speed. In addition, handling on or near the water in halation approach conditions on a mirror surface sea was then a little-practised technique (when actual height and horizon were difficult for positional assessment by the pilot).

In spite of all these difficulties, the Viking in production form rendered good service throughout the world in greatly differing operating conditions. Twenty-six examples of the Mk IV were sold. The first was the Vickers Type 54 for the French Navy, a commercial version with enclosed cabin but with provision for conversion for military duties 'with minimum of inconvenience', to quote the contract. It bore the French registration F-ADBL and was delivered on 27 September, 1921.

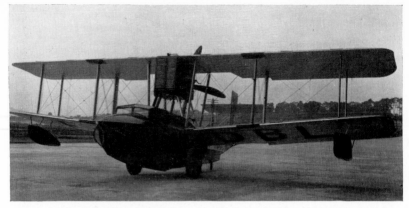

Type 54 Viking F-ADBL as completed for delivery with cabin.

During 1922 the Viking production line was busy with orders for the Dutch Forces in the East Indies (10), the Imperial Japanese Navy (2), the Russian Trade Delegation (1) and Laurentide Air Services (Canada) (1). One was used for demonstration in Spain and registered G-EBED. It was subsequently sold to Capt Leslie Hamilton, who used it on charter to Capt Lowenstein, and also as an air taxi operating from the St Moritz winter sports centre in Switzerland, where it landed in soft snow on the hull and took-off from hard snow or ice with the wheeled undercarriage.

The Dutch Vikings were non-folders with Raf 15 section wings and Consuta-covered hulls. High-compression Napier Lion engines were fitted which ran on a benzol mixture, but reports indicate that some difficulty was experienced in starting, from which peculiarity German high-compression aero engines had also suffered. This was a matter for experienced ground engineering, while the sensitive fore-and-aft trim was a matter for experienced piloting. One of the two crashes of Vikings in Java was attributable to the fact that the pilot had never flown a flying-boat, while the other was caused by faulty maintenance in tropical sea conditions resulting in loss of rigging efficiency in the airframe and corrosion in the metal fittings. With long-range tanks, the range of the Dutch Vikings could be increased to 925 miles.

A Dutch Viking in Java.

118

The Japanese Vikings were test flown by Maj H. G. Brackley off the carrier *Hosho* in March 1933 on acceptance trials. They were ordered as fleet spotters with T64-section wings, but the proposal to fit a 37-mm cannon for anti-submarine patrol was not proceeded with. In this connection both the Swedish and Italian navies considered slinging an 18-in-diameter torpedo aboard the Viking, but this proposal also was not pressed to a decision or an order. The Laurentide Viking for Canada was fitted with a Rolls-Royce Eagle IX and was rather underpowered. It was used for most of its time in Eastern Canada.

The Viking IV for the USSR was delivered in September 1922 and on arrival was sent for service in the Leningrad region. It was one of the

Leslie Hamilton's G-EBED, showing diagonal planking of hull and undercarriage-retracting rack quadrant.

first with a hull planked in SCT plywood made by the Tucker Armoured Plywood Company of Crayford. The initials SCT stood for 'securely cemented together', and the material consisted of two layers of Honduras mahogany board glued diagonally at right angles to each other; whether this produced any technical advantage over the Consuta planking does not seem to have been recorded. G-EBED, the Viking IV bought by Leslie Hamilton, also had the SCT-planked hull and wing-tip floats.

A special Viking IV registered G-EBBZ was prepared for Sir Ross Smith, commander of the Australian Vimy flight of late 1919, for a round-the-world attempt in 1922. It was a non-folder of the commercial version but with open cockpits. Various detail modifications were made, including

Leslie Hamilton's Viking at Pobla, Spain.

some non-corrosive fittings, such as stainless-steel exhaust manifolds, and passenger space was taken up by stores and long-range tanks. After a preliminary test flight by Cockerell, at Brooklands on 13 April, Sir Ross Smith, with his mechanic of the Australian flight, Sgt Bennett, himself took the Viking up. At about 2,000 ft he stalled during a sharp turn and a flat spin developed. Ross Smith opened the engine up and this action seemed to correct the spin. The engine was again shut down and the spin restarted at too low a height to be corrected a second time. The aeroplane crashed into the back of the Byfleet banking of the motor track near

Only photograph of Ross Smith's round-the-world Viking, in erecting shop at Weybridge.

the River Wey and both occupants were killed. Sir Keith Smith, who had been delayed on his train journey from London and had intended to participate in the flight with his brother, was an eye-witness of the accident. The cause was thought to be the pilot's unfamiliarity with the aeroplane, particularly in regard to the engine on/off condition, and the tendency of the T64-section wing to tip stall.

Further orders for Viking IVs were received in 1923. This type of aeroplane seems to have been one of the first, certainly of Vickers design, to which the practice now called custom-built was applied. For example, one fleet spotter, ordered for the United States Navy in 1922 and delivered in February 1923, had the T64 wing section with the original span wing of 46 ft. A Lion engine was fitted in the American Viking, but the two Vikings delivered a week later to the River Plate Aviation Company,

A civil Viking for the Argentine with Eagle engine.

Argentina, were powered with the Rolls-Royce Eagle IX and were of the commercial type, with 50-ft span wings and the gap between the upper and lower wings increased by one foot, as well as having the Raf 15 wing section. One had an enclosed cabin and the other had open cockpits; both were fitted with large service fuel tanks mounted on the top wings. These two Argentine Vikings operated a regular service between Buenos Aires and Montevideo, and the service was so popular that it was difficult for intending passengers to get a seat. A high load factor was therefore obtained, but in spite of this the service had to be subsidised, and eventually the Vikings were withdrawn when financial support from the Argentine Government was cancelled. The only criticisms of the aircraft were that take-off was difficult in calm water conditions and that the wheels and tyres did not stand up to heavy duty. The Viking IV was undoubtedly underpowered with the 360 hp Eagle when loaded to nearly 6,000 lb.

The four Vikings delivered to the Argentine Navy in May 1923 were Lion-powered with full-span T64-section folding wings and were serialled R3, R4, R5 and R6. At the same time the Royal Canadian Air Force took delivery of two Viking IVs with Rolls-Royce Eagles, mainly to be used for starting a forestry fire patrol service and for survey work. Skis were fitted during winter operation. A proposal to fit Leitner-Watts metal propellers to these Vikings was not pursued. As a result of the successful introduction of Vikings for special service in Canada, a batch was made at the Canadian Vickers works in Montreal, and further specialist designs emanated from that source in their own right (see page 489). Canadian Vickers thus became one of the pioneer organisations in aircraft manufacture in Canada.

A Canadian Viking IV flying over typical lake terrain, exemplifying ideal use of amphibian aircraft.

Two other Vikings were delivered in April 1922. These were to an Air Ministry requirement but with the special equipment used in RAF operation, and to comply with conditions laid down in the specification they were classified as Mk Vs. They were given the serial numbers N156 and N157, and were attached to 70 Squadron in Iraq, more or less in an exploratory exercise to determine the utility of amphibian aircraft in areas like the Middle East. Several discoveries were made. One was the frailty of aero wheels and tyres at that time in tropical conditions, although the RAF Viking Vs had oleo-sprung undercarriages, an innovation in the Viking amphibian. A hulled aeroplane with its short undercarriage was found difficult to operate off irregular desert surfaces because of insufficient clearance between the bottom of the hull and the ground, a penalty imposed by the amphibian configuration. In spite of these limitations, the Viking

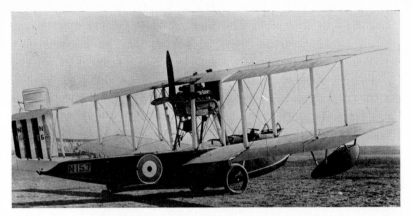

Viking Mk V in Iraq, with uncowled Lion engine.

Vs fulfilled their purpose in adding to the experience being built up by the engineering branch of the Royal Air Force overseas. Particularly there was an awareness of the need for metal-framed aeroplanes to avoid loss of rigging truth inherent in wooden aircraft operating under tropical conditions, a factor encountered already with other Vickers wooden aircraft.

The Viking never seemed to suffer unduly from water soakage in its wooden hull, probably because on the average it spent half its life out of the water, thus allowing the intake of moisture to dry out. This was an unsuspected bonus of the amphibian configuration as compared with the wooden-hulled sea-going flying-boat operated only from marine bases. The design fully justified the ideas which had led to the formation of the original project. Its varied service in many parts of the world was a vindication of its name, Viking.

VULTURE AND VANELLUS. The last variants of the Viking, the Mks VI and VII, were named Vulture and Vanellus respectively. Vulture has not a particularly pleasant connotation; but Vickers usually had to search hard for appropriate aircraft names, and when the Wallis geodetic aircraft came along they must have found relief in the change to the initial letter W for the time being. When the Air Ministry requested a water-fowl name for the military Mk VII, Weybridge proposed Vidgeon, which was promptly rejected as an unrecognised corruption of Widgeon, and Vickers House then suggested Vanellus, which was accepted.

The Vulture had a redesigned wing structure as compared with the previous variants of the Viking. A thicker wing section with deeper and stronger spars was used, which facilitated the introduction for the first time of a single-bay wing structure. The span was reduced slightly, but an increase in the chord resulted in a greater wing area. Balanced ailerons were fitted by setting the hinge pivots back a few inches, a new method at

123

Man-power roll-out of Vulture I from Vickers' flight shed at Brooklands in 1923.

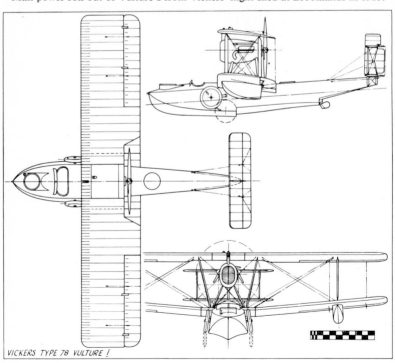

VICKERS TYPE 78 VULTURE I

the time and a better one than putting balance horns on the outer ends, as on the Vimy. There is good reason to suppose that Pierson was introducing an early type of Frise aileron by arrangement with the Bristol Aeroplane Company; Vickers were certainly the first licensed users of the patent on Virginias and Victorias in 1926. Horn balances led to a twisting couple on the surface with loss of aerodynamic efficiency, apart from undesirable torsional stress in the surface. The real purpose was, of course, to relieve the stick force about the roll axis. As the Vulture was a non-folder, advantage was taken to splay the inner struts from the hull, well outboard of the upper centre section, to improve their structural efficiency.

Two Vultures were built as private ventures, the second as a possible military successor to the RAF's Viking Mk V. The Vulture II had the Rolls-Royce Eagle IX engine and provision for Scarff gun mountings, but the rectangular fin above the top stabiliser was deleted. In the accompanying photographs may be seen the wider-beam planing bottom, provided by a distinct slope of the hull sides, to improve water performance. In this respect the Vultures later behaved quite well in heavy seas during Sqn Ldr MacLaren's round-the-world attempt, on which endeavour both Vultures were ultimately employed.

Vulture II in original form with Eagle engine.

For MacLaren's attempt, the Vulture II was converted back to Vulture I standard with the Napier Lion, so that both aircraft were identical, including a new type of oval radiator with neatly faired engine cowling. The rectangular fin was restored, but the Scarff ring deleted. Long-range tanks were fitted, and other stores, needed for such a hazardous flight, filled the spaces originally provided for military or civil equipment.

The Vulture I was registered G-EBGO and the Vulture II G-EBHO. The round-the-world attempt started from the Calshot seaplane base on 25 March, 1924, in G-EBHO with Sqn Ldr A. S. C. MacLaren, the organiser, as navigator, Flg Off W. N. Plenderleith as pilot and Sgt R. Andrews, on loan from the RAF, as flight engineer. The route planned was across the Aegean to the Persian Gulf, over India and Burma to Singapore, thence

G-EBHO Vulture at Calshot at start of round-the-world attempt; in pilot seat is Flg Off Plenderleith with Sqn Ldr MacLaren and in the bows is Sgt Andrews.

Salvaging G-EBHO after its mishap at Akyab, Burma.

Substitute G-EBGO Vulture brought back from Japan to Akyab to resume flight.

via Tokyo to the Bering Sea, Alaska, across Canada and then on the northern short-stage route across the Atlantic. In the event more than half of the projected flight was accomplished.

G-EBGO was shipped to Tokyo as a spare machine, and a spare Lion engine was made available in Montreal for the Atlantic passage. As things went, even more Lions were needed, and it was fortunate that the type was in use in the Middle East and India at the time.

The first misfortune to befall G-EBHO was at Corfu in the Aegean, where a reduction gear failed, and delay occurred in getting an engine replacement. Another engine change had to be made at Parla in India. On reaching Akyab in Burma, the Vulture ran into monsoon conditions with torrential rain for two days, with no cover for the aeroplane, which took its toll on the airframe. In attempting to take-off the machine crashed, an accident attributed to the sogginess of the wings and a mal-adjustment of the tailplane incidence, caused by prolonged exposure to rain at Akyab and by the great heat in India.

Sqn Ldr MacLaren cabled for a new propeller of increased pitch to be provided at a point farther along the route. Meanwhile, the reserve Vulture, G-EBGO, was brought back from Tokyo to Akyab on the US destroyer *William B. Preston*, and the flight was resumed on 25 June. All went well until, in attempting to cross the Bering Sea, MacLaren in the second Vulture encountered thick fog and crashed in heavy seas near Nikolski off the Siberian coast on 2 August, 1924. The hull and engine were salvaged with other valuable parts and returned, in due course, to Weybridge via Vancouver.

Last of Vickers amphibians—the Vanellus or Viking VII.

Although the Air Ministry had rendered great assistance in support of this brave attempt, and *The Times* had partly sponsored the flight in return for exclusive news rights, the Vultures belonged to Vickers. But the expense borne by the constructor was justified by the valuable experience gained and by an experimental order for a development of the Vulture, the Viking VII, later called Vanellus. This was designed to specification

127

46/22, which oddly enough at the outset called for a single-seat fleet-spotter amphibian, but the requirement was changed to a three-seater soon afterwards.

The Vanellus showed progressive development from the Vulture. The main difference was the fitting of a monoplane tail to give a better field of fire for the rear gunner. The front gun-ring was mounted behind the pilot, which must have been disconcerting for him when the gun was fired. The inner interplane strut system was modified from the Vulture arrangement to provide for rearward folding wings, the struts being brought back to the vertical with provision for the insertion of jury struts for the folding operation. The span was reduced to 46 ft, the dimension of some Viking IVs, to enable the aeroplane to be raised or lowered unfolded in the lift

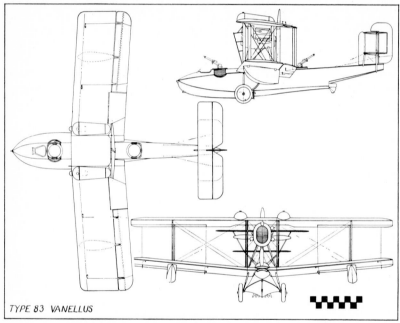

TYPE 83 VANELLUS

Original design of Vanellus as fleet-spotter with biplane tail—
compare with photographs.

of the aircraft carrier *Eagle*, there being a limiting dimension of 50 ft in the lift.

Full-span ailerons on upper and lower wings, balanced by set-back hinges as on the Vulture, were another innovation. This modification may have indicated an attempt to use them as flaps for take-off or landing, as the type was ordered for experimental purposes and, indeed, was delivered to the Royal Aircraft Establishment on 25 March, 1925. The mechanical problems in the control system arising from such use with folding wings would have been difficult to solve, and no record exists that this was, in

Side-view of Vanellus.

fact, the intention. Service tanks were slung under the top wing outboard of the centre section, similar to those later used on the Vixen V for Chile.

Only one Vanellus was constructed, N169, and it went for comparative test with the Supermarine Seagull III on the carrier *Argus*. No further orders were placed, and so the amphibian concept disappeared from Vickers' design, if the later Supermarine types are considered as a separate design family.

In 1925 Vickers at Weybridge were just starting out on the long series of large bombers and military transports and single-engined tractor biplanes, so the termination of their efforts with the Viking series was not material. This individual type left behind many valuable lessons, not the least of which was the experience gained from world-wide use by customers with varied requirements and operating conditions.

Viking Amphibian

	Mk I (G-EAOV)	Mk III (G-EAUK)	Mk IV Type 55	Mk IV Type 69	Mk VI Type 78— Vulture
Engine:	One 270 hp Rolls-Royce Falcon III	One 450 hp Napier Lion	One 450 hp Napier Lion	One 360 hp Rolls-Royce Eagle IX	One 450 hp Napier Lion
Span:	37 ft	46 ft	50 ft	50 ft	49 ft
Length:	30 ft	32 ft	34 ft 2 in	34 ft	38 ft 2 in
Height:	13 ft	13 ft	14 ft	14 ft 2 in	14 ft 6 in
Wing Area:	368 sq ft	585 sq ft	635 sq ft	635 sq ft	828 sq ft
Empty Weight:	2,030 lb	2,740 lb	4,040 lb	4,020 lb	4,530 lb
Gross Weight:	3,600 lb	4,545 lb	5,790 lb	5,650 lb	6,500 lb
Max Speed at sea level:	104 mph	110 mph	113 mph	100 mph	98 mph
Climb to:	6,000 ft/12 min	6,000 ft/5·2 min	3,000 ft/3·2 min	5,000 ft/15 min	5,000 ft/16·3 min
Range:	340 miles at 85 mph	420 miles at 90 mph	925 miles with long-range tanks	—	—

The Virginia Saga

'On 24 April, 1920, you were invited to tender for the design for a long-distance bomber to a general specification. The Air Ministry hope that you will give it full consideration and that a practical proposition will result. . . .'

This extract, from an Air Ministry letter to Vickers, is the starting-point in the design history of a family of night-bomber and bomber-transport aeroplanes—Virginias, Victorias and Valentias—which for some 20 years were operated by the Royal Air Force and had a considerable influence on its operational development.

The first proposal to meet the specification (Long-Distance Bombing Aeroplane (A), DoR Type 4) was based on the Vimy. This project envisaged a stretched Vimy wing of 88-ft span and a biplane tail unit. The finalised design was basically an enlarged Vimy of 86-ft span, powered by two 450 hp Napier Lion engines. Initially, the name Vulcan appears to have been given to the design, but Virginia was officially adopted, probably in accordance with the general policy of naming RAF bombers, flying-boats and transport aircraft after places.

An initial order for two aircraft was placed under contract at a cost of £13,250 each. The first aircraft, J6856, was designated Virginia I, and the second, J6857, was the Virginia II. In official documents the word Mark is conspicuous by its absence, and this numbering referred loosely to prototypes 1 and 2; later they were recognised as Mks I and II.

Virginia J6856 in its original prototype form at Brooklands before its first flight.

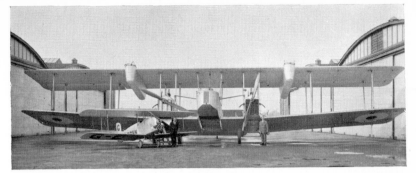

J6856 with fore-and-aft type 'fighting tops' before delivery to Martlesham; in front is the Vickers Viget lightplane.

VIRGINIA I AND II. To clarify the differences between the marks, which have remained obscure for so long, the career of the Virginia I is traced in some detail. This is followed by a description of the changes in succeeding marks, made because of the necessity at the time to stretch the procurement outlay on military aircraft as far as possible on limited budgets. In consequence, many conversions, rebuilds and reconversions were made from the earlier marks. Thus occurs the anomaly in which identical serial numbers are found in photographs showing Virginias obviously of different vintages.

The Virginia I was constructed mainly of wood with fabric covering, the structural design being based on that of the Vimy. The lower planes only had dihedral and there was no sweepback. The two Napier Lion engines were mounted in large flat-sided nacelles, similar to the installation used on the Vernon I, with car-type radiators.

On 24 November, 1922, the prototype, J6856, was flown by Cockerell, taking-off from Brooklands in a gusty 10 mph surface wind. It was quickly airborne, with the engines at about three-quarters throttle, but only a short flight was possible because of excessive vibration in the starboard engine. Lateral and fore-and-aft control was satisfactory, but the two rudders were ineffective. As a result of this flight, several recommendations

J6856 with Condor III engines in original installation which was later modified.

131

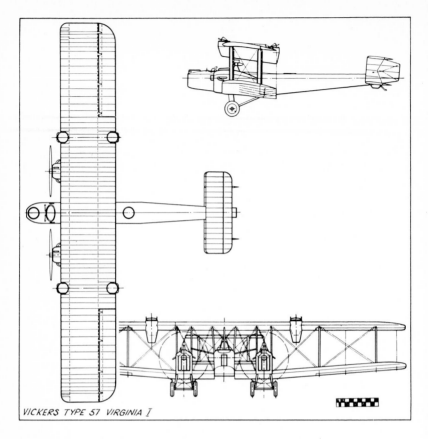

VICKERS TYPE 57 VIRGINIA I

were made by the pilot, including changes in the rudder control, fitting a larger windscreen and cutting back the cockpit fairing by four inches to improve the view.

Further flights with modified fins and rudders were made by Broome on 7 December. On the second flight of the day, made with larger rudders, directional control became effective but heavy. Starboard engine vibration remained a problem on these early flights.

All the manufacturer's trials were made from Brooklands, with the exception of the full-load test, which under the contract had to be made from Martlesham. These trials were satisfactorily completed by 11 December and the aeroplane was delivered to Martlesham, where the full-load trial was completed according to the terms of the contract. After this, continuous flying was carried out by Service pilots, and the Virginia quickly established a good reputation. At this time, J6856 was doing more flying than any other type at Martlesham, and was giving very little trouble, in spite of innovations such as oleo-pneumatic undercarriage struts.

After the completion of contractor's trials a letter was received from the Air Ministry requesting Vickers to design and install gunners' positions in fairings attached under the top mainplanes for experimental trials. These installations, known as 'fighting tops', consisted of four gunners' positions in two nacelles. The modification added 1,033 lb to the all-up weight of the aircraft.

The second Virginia, J6857, was completed on 5 April, 1924, and joined J6856 in the flight-test programme shortly after, This aircraft differed in several important respects from the Virginia I, and a new engine installation incorporating a close-fitting low-drag cowling and a semicircular Lamblin-type radiator, situated between the undercarriage legs, replaced the old Vernon-type nacelle. The new installation was developed in collaboration with Capt Anderton Brown of the Air Ministry. In order to provide the bomb-aimer with greater comfort, the nose was lengthened, and one of the nine internally mounted 112-lb bombs was omitted to allow more leg room. Tailplane incidence could be altered in flight, a hinge joint in the rear fuselage making this possible. After taking part in the development programme, J6857 was delivered to No. 7 (Bombing) Squadron at Bircham Newton for Service trials.

The Virginia I continued armament trials with fighting tops until it was withdrawn from the test programme to have a new engine installation requested by the Air Ministry. The engines to be installed were Rolls-Royce Condor IIIs, and two of these, Nos. 40 and 42, were delivered to Vickers from No. 4 Stores Depot at Ickenham in September 1924. Apart from the new engines, aileron control changes and the incorporation of a third central rudder were the only major modifications to the aircraft.

The first flight with the Rolls-Royce Condors was made on 3 October, 1924. The flight lasted for 25 minutes but the aeroplane was very unstable fore and aft in all conditions and the ailerons were very heavy; rudder control, however, was good. Another flight, of 20 minutes duration, was made on 10 October with additional ballast in the front cockpit and two pilots. The aileron gearing was also modified. Again the Virginia was

J6856 after conversion to Mk VII standard with final arrangement of fighting tops.

unstable fore and aft, although it was neutral with engines off, but aileron control was easy to operate at all speeds. A further flight was made on 13 October with an extra 200 lb of ballast in the front cockpit. Again, the aeroplane was unstable longitudinally with power on.

As a result of these flights the engines were moved forward 25 inches and the radiators were enlarged and placed under the top main planes. The modified aeroplane was flown on 29 December, after which an additional fin was fitted forward of the central rudder. From then on, much flying was done with the Condor III engines at Martlesham, and this included all aspects of performance, including climbs to 13,000 ft, speed in level flight and measured take-off distances. It is interesting to record the minimum and maximum take-off distance of 118 and 185 yards respectively —STOL performance today.

After completing tests at Martlesham and also at Biggin Hill, J6856 was returned to Weybridge for several alterations, including a six-foot extension in the fuselage aft of the wings, a new front fuselage, two and a half degrees dihedral on both main planes and smaller fighting tops mounted aft of the rear spar only. It was also proposed to incorporate two and a half degrees sweepback on the main planes for centre-of-gravity purposes, but there is no evidence to confirm that this was ever done. In its modified form the Virginia was in fact the prototype Mk VIII, but it remained the sole example.

After further test flying the aeroplane was re-engined with Napier Lions and converted to Mk VII standard, including six degrees sweepback on the main planes. It was delivered to Service units, notably Nos. 7 and 10 (Bombing) Squadrons, for trials with fighting tops.

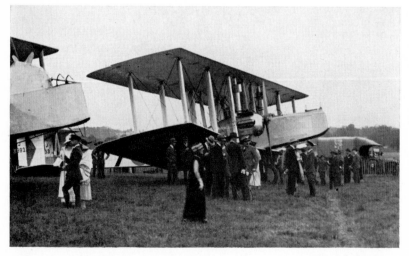

The second Mk III Virginia, J6993, in the new-types park, Hendon Air Pageant, 1923; on left, nose of Handley Page Hyderabad. (*Flight photo.*)

The fifth Mk III in flight from Bircham Newton; this was the first official Mark of the Virginia. (*MoD(Air) photo.*)

At the end of 1928, J6856 was rebuilt to Mk X standard and delivered to 7 (Bombing) Squadron at Worthy Down, as a standard Service aircraft. At the end of 1935, 13 years after its first flight, the aeroplane was still flying, but by that time it bore no resemblance to the original as its airframe had been completely metallised.

The Virginia II, J6857, appears to have spent most of its life as a squadron aircraft. Soon after its initial introduction into 7 (Bombing) Squadron a mid-air engine fire resulted in a forced landing. After repair it was returned to Service use until mid-1927, when it was converted into a Mk VII. Two years later J6857 was reconditioned and fully metallised, as a Mk X. In this form it was on the strength of 58 (Bombing) Squadron at Worthy Down in 1933, nine years after its initial flight.

VIRGINIA MK III. A production contract was placed for Virginia aircraft on 23 October, 1922. This was for the supply of two Virginia Mk III prototypes to specification 1/21. These two aircraft, J6992 and J6993, were basically similar to the Virginia II, differing only in detail. The most important of the changes was the introduction of dual controls. Two under-wing bombs of either 112 lb or 550 lb were introduced, the standard internal load remaining at eight 112-lb bombs. Provision was also made for a downward-firing gun in the front fuselage.

In 1923 an additional four Virginia Mk IIIs were ordered, J7129, J7130, J7131 and J7132. These four aircraft, together with J6992, joined the Virginia II in No. 7 (Bombing) Squadron at Bircham Newton. The Virginia Mk III was powered by two Napier Lion Series II engines, each rated at 468 bhp. The contract speed was 95 mph at 10,000 ft with full load, and 105 mph with half fuel load and without bombs. The maximum bomb load was 1,996 lb.

VIRGINIA MK IV. Ordered under contract to specification 28/23, the Mk IV was identical to the Mk III except for additional electrical equipment,

135

J7275, the second Virginia Mk IV. (*MoD(Air) photo.*)

an increase in the number of R.L. bombs * fitted and their repositioning, and an increase in the under-wing bomb load. There were only three Virginia Mk IVs, J7274, J7275 and J7276. One of these, J7274, was used for the trial installation of an additional centrally mounted rudder. This was flown on 29 July, 1924, with Flt Lt E. R. C. Scholefield (Vickers' chief test pilot, then recently appointed) at the controls, and was very successful. As a check the aircraft was flown again on 31 July in its original form without the centre rudder. The result of the latter flight confirmed the improvement in directional control afforded by the new layout.

VIRGINIA MK V. The introduction of the additional rudder, first flown on J7274, was the major change in the Virginia Mk V, which was otherwise basically a Virginia Mk III. The Virginia Mk V, ordered to specification

* R.L. was the symbol for Woolwich Arsenal products and was the abbreviation of Royal Laboratory.

A Virginia Mk V at Brooklands with the familiar Vickers flight hangar, with flying buttresses, in the background.

12/24, was the first major production version of the aircraft. A total of 22 was built, these being J7418–J7439. With the Mk V came the introduction of the dark green Nivo dope scheme familiar on all inter-war night-bombers, in place of the aluminium finish previously used.

VIRGINIA MK VI. Criticism of the time taken to fold the wings of the Virginia led to the redesign of the folding arrangements. At the same time, one of the Virginia Vs was re-rigged with two and a half degrees dihedral on both top and bottom mainplanes instead of the four degrees dihedral only on the lower planes of the earlier marks. These changes were embodied in the Virginia Mk VI, which was the subject of two orders. The first contract was for 10 aircraft, J7558–J7567, and the second was for 15 aircraft, J7706–J7720. In addition, six Virginia Vs were reconditioned as Mk VIs, these were J7423, J7422, J7418, J7437, J7438 and J7439. Apart from the wing changes, this version was similar to earlier marks. Several squadrons, including No. 58 (Bombing), were equipped with Virginia VIs.

J7438, which was built as a Mk IV, shown as converted to Mk VI.

VIRGINIA MK VII. In May 1925 the second prototype Virginia Mk III, J6993, returned to Weybridge to have a new design of nose fitted for experimental purposes. This was requested by the Air Ministry to improve the pilot's view and to provide access to the front gunner's cockpit from the pilot's compartment. While this modification was being done, a further request was made to have the aeroplane brought up to the then

137

latest standard, which was the Mk VI. Following indications of considerable improvement in lateral control obtainable with the Frise aileron developed by the Bristol Aeroplane Company, it was decided to install ailerons of this type on J6993 for test purposes.

At this time severe criticism of the Virginia's stability was being made by RAF squadrons. Longitudinally, the aeroplane was said to be very unstable, the adjustable tail only trimming-out load dispositions. The Virginia could not be flown hands-off. Laterally, a wing would drop in turbulence, requiring correction by the pilot, and directionally the Virginia was said to yaw as soon as a pilot lost his horizon. As a bomber the aeroplane left much to be desired because of the concentration required by the pilot to keep the Virginia flying straight and level, which left him with little time to make additional bombing corrections. In cloud it was said to be almost impossible to keep course, only the most experienced pilots being able to attempt this, and it was considered inadvisable for any pilot to fly it at night.

In answer to the criticisms, reference was made to the Martlesham report on the Virginia I. In this report stability of the aeroplane was summarised in the following terms:

Longitudinal—satisfactory at all speeds,
Lateral—good at top speed, satisfactory at cruising speed, poor at slow speed,
Directional—normal for this type of aeroplane.

The centre of gravity of the Virginia I was 0·343 mean chord, and the pitching moment records showed definite longitudinal stability; production

J7427, a Virginia Mk VII converted from a Mk V, at Brooklands.

138

Virginias, however, had the c.g. at 0·355 mean chord, due to the additional weight aft caused by the tail incidence gear and downward-firing gun. Vickers concluded that the Virginia I was only just stable; the spring-loaded compensator fitted to the elevator controls gave an impression of considerable stability that was not in fact present. It was necessary to remedy the defect, and accordingly it was proposed to position the c.g. at 0·327 mean chord by sweeping back the main planes two and a half degrees. This was intended to improve the longitudinal stability, while the Frise ailerons would take care of lateral control.

In order to investigate the longitudinal stability problem, and before adopting a definite sweepback angle, J6993 was flown with a six-foot insert in the fuselage, aft of the wings. On its first flight the Virginia was ballasted to represent two and a half degrees sweepback, with c.g. at 0·342 mean chord; on the next, ballast was added to bring the c.g. to 0·315 mean chord, equivalent to 4·9 degrees; a third flight was made with full load, with the c.g. in the same position. From these tests it was obvious that with the c.g. at 0·315 mean chord there was considerable stability.

While these tests were taking place the Air Ministry requested the transfer of the W/T installation and operator to a position aft of the rear spar bulkhead. This transfer of weight aft aggravated the c.g. problem and would have required a wing sweepback angle of seven and a half degrees to bring the c.g. back to the optimum position. As this angle raised severe structural problems, it was decided to adopt six degrees as a compromise, the c.g. then being at 0·332 mean chord. This was incorporated in J6993, and thus the Virginia Mk VII was evolved.

On 28 August, 1925, Flt Lt Markham of 9 (Bombing) Squadron, standing in for Scholefield,* flew the fully modified Mk VII prototype out of Brooklands on its maiden flight of 25 minutes. The weather was fine but bumpy, thus providing a good test of stability. On this flight the Virginia was loaded with 3,000 lb, comprising fuel, ballast and crew, but it lifted easily, with little tendency to swing. There was a complete absence of rolling and wallowing on take-off. In the air the aeroplane turned very naturally, and straight and level could be flown hands and feet off for over a minute without any sign of turning. The general impression after this flight was that this aeroplane was a great improvement on previous Virginias. The new nose was found to be excellent, the view from it being especially good for taxying.

So successful were the trials of the Mk VII that a decision was made to convert earlier marks of the Virginia to the latest type. In addition to the prototype, 38 were converted under three separate contracts. They were J6856, J6857, J6992, J7129–J7132, J7274, J7275, J7419–J7422, J7424–J7436, J7438, J7439, J7559–J7561, J7565, J7566, J7706, J7710–J7713. Eleven production Mk VIIs were built at Weybridge, J8236–J8241, J8326–J8330.

* There was an unofficial practice at that time for Service pilots of exceptional experience to deputise for manufacturer's test pilots if necessary.

Besides their normal duties, Virginia Mk VIIs were employed on numerous test flights. J7436 was used for experimental propeller tests at 12,500 lb weight; J7130 was flown with Napier Lion VB engines, and equipped with either two- or four-bladed propellers; J7131 was flown with the tail-turret installation later adopted for the Mks IX and X; and J7436 and J6857 carried out tests with statically balanced ailerons. Probably most significant of all was the test flying of J7439 with metal planes, fuselage and tail units, which led to the final abandonment of wooden construction and to the last of the production Virginias—the Mk X with all-metal airframe structure. J8236 was used for catapult research.

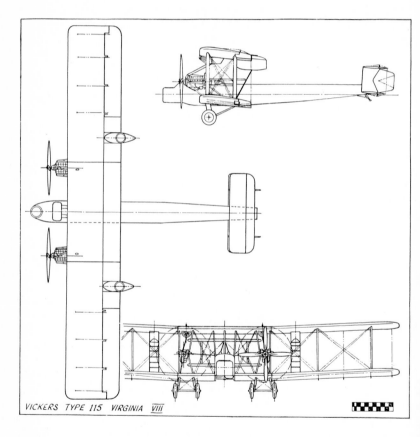

VICKERS TYPE 115 VIRGINIA VIII

VIRGINIA MK VIII. This was a projected version of the Virginia powered with Rolls-Royce Condor III engines of 650 hp each and equipped with fighting tops. J6856, the original prototype, at one stage in its long and varied career acted as the sole example of this mark.

VIRGINIA MK IX. As already related, tests were carried out for some years with fighting tops at the request of the Air Ministry, but Vickers favoured the rear gunner's station aft of the tail as an alternative scheme. There were drawbacks to fighting tops, such as aerodynamic drag penalties and difficulties in heating the crew in intense cold. There was a lack of official enthusiasm for tail-gun positions because of the uncomfortable rides experienced by their occupants in previous experiments with other bombers. Vickers' proposals proved sufficiently acceptable, and a decision was made to have a Virginia VII, J7131, modified for trials.

To counteract increased yawing and pitching moments induced by the weight of the gunner and his equipment, the tailplanes were decreased in chord and increased in span. The elevators were partially balanced, and the fins and rudders set further apart. The increase in weight aft necessitated a longer nose to maintain balance, and also to this end the W/T installation was moved to a bay immediately aft of that of the pilot. The new Virginia was designated Mk IX and was a great success from the start. Fighting tops were abandoned from that moment and 'tail-end Charlies' were born. The Virginia IX was held in such high esteem that the Director of Equipment promised that every Virginia squadron would receive one of the new aeroplanes, although in fact many more were delivered.

A decision was made to convert 27 existing Virginias to the new mark. They were J6993, J7130, J7132, J7274, J7423, J7428, J7435–J7438, J7558, J7561–J7564, J7567, J7707–J7709, J7711, J7715, J7716, J7718–J7720, J8236, J8240. In addition, eight production Mk IXs were built, these being J8907–J8914.

Development of the Virginia continued, and several Mk IXs were used on special trials. Wheel brakes were fitted for the first time on J7436, which flew with No. 7 (Bombing) Squadron on service trials of this equipment. Automatic wing slots were also to have been fitted to this particular aeroplane, but instead were fitted to J7720.

When the wireless operator was repositioned just aft of the pilot's cockpit this brought his compartment in line with the propellers and resulted in considerable discomfort from noise, which had been a continuing cause of complaint in earlier marks, where the pilots were in a similar position; the compartment was therefore sound-proofed with a lining material known as Alva, said to have been made from seaweed. From the Mk IX onwards this became standard on all Virginias. To provide further soundproofing, J7720 was fitted with a transparent canopy over the pilot's cockpit; this was not standardised on the Virginia, but provided useful data for later designs.

The use of automatic slots on the Virginia gave promise of reduced landing speed, so a trial installation was made on J7720. Initial trials disclosed that these slots reduced the minimum speed of the aeroplane and eliminated any wing-dropping near the stall; but they would not close fully until 85–90 mph was reached, consequently there was a severe loss

141

in climb and speed performance. The effect of open slots in normal flight was to make the Virginia tail-heavy between 60 and 70 mph. In stalled flight the aeroplane became increasingly nose-heavy with decreasing speed, but 38–40 mph could be maintained. Lateral control remained effective without any violent tendency to drop a wing. With the engines throttled back and a light load condition, a rate of descent of 600 to 700 ft per minute could be maintained. With slots the landing speed was reduced by 10 mph to about 50 mph. The slot-closing problem was eventually solved by modifying the local geometry of the leading edge in the slot area. Most Virginias from then on were modified to incorporate automatic slots.

In 1927 one of the new types of engine going into production was the Bristol geared Jupiter VIII. The Air Ministry requested, on 12 March, that a pair of these engines should be installed in a Virginia VII for trials.

Mk IX J8236 with Bristol Jupiter engines.

It was intended that engines Nos. 7 and 8 off the line should be allocated. A request by Vickers for earlier engines was declined on the grounds that they were required for more modern types of aircraft, as the demise of the Virginia was considered imminent. (Ten years later a newly-formed expansion scheme squadron, No. 215, received Virginia Mk Xs as front-line equipment until Handley Page Harrows were delivered.)

On 1 December, 1927, the Air Ministry decided to substitute two French-built Gnome Rhône Jupiter VIIIs for the British engines, which disappointed Vickers because the French versions gave less power, to the detriment of performance, but the power loss was taken into account during trials. On 22 June, 1928, a Virginia IX, J8236, was selected for the Jupiter installation in place of the Mk VII originally planned. After completing the light-load test satisfactorily at Brooklands the aeroplane was sent to Martlesham to carry out full-load tests, which were completed by 12 October. The geared Gnome Rhône Jupiters were giving trouble, and on

A Virginia Mk IX being catapulted during RAE experiments at Farnborough
(*Flight photo.*)

one flight the piston in No. 9 cylinder of the port engine broke up and a landing was made on the power of the starboard engine alone. Bristol-built Jupiter IXs were substituted and J8236 continued trials for some time, but was eventually reconverted to a Mk IX with Napier Lions, while the two Jupiters, with their mountings, were transferred to Mk X J7421 for further trials.

VIRGINIA MARK X. Following experience gained from the experimental set of metal wings for a Vimy, which were used for structural investigation in connection with the Vickers Vigilant flying-boat project of 1920, the Air Ministry in due time requested that a set of metal wings be designed for actual flight trials on a Virginia. This policy was in general agreement with the changeover to metal aircraft structures. The reduction in weight and the increase in stiffness and strength promised big improvements in

Virginia Xs of 502(B) Squadron at Aldergrove, Northern Ireland. (*Flight photo.*)

Vic flight of Virginia Xs at the 1935 Hendon Air Display—nose panels hinged forward for bomb sighting. (*Flight photo.*)

load-carrying ability, and some slight increase in performance was expected through reduction in drag brought about by slimmer gap struts. The original wooden wing cellule weighed 2,300 lb, and it was estimated that the metal version would weigh 1,559 lb—a saving of 741 lb. Test specimens were extensively used to prove the structural integrity of the new design. Complete metallisation of the Virginia rear fuselage was already being carried out, at a weight saving of 49 lb on a Mk VII, J7439. Vickers suggested that the metal wings should be test flown on that aeroplane also, to which the Air Ministry agreed. The eventual weight saving was 1,100 lb.

J7439 was flown in its new form towards the end of May 1927, and the main trials with the new wing were carried out at Martlesham. During the latter half of August the incidence wiring in the outer starboard wing bay failed in flight, and the aeroplane had to force-land in a small field, but after a month of repairs to the wing, J7439 was flown out of the field, which provided a ground run of only 140 yards.

Virginia Xs from Henlow for the parachuting demonstration at Hendon in 1935; their overall finish was red.

As the trials progressed, problems developed in control. The ailerons were overbalanced and the Virginia was flying one wing down. These were trimming faults and, once solved, complete metallisation of the wings and fuselage was adopted following the successful completion of the trials. J7439 was found to have a top speed of 99·5 mph at a loaded weight of 17,210 lb when powered by two Napier Lion VB engines.

At this time it was proposed to introduce an experimental installation of a new rudder-control system. Originally a servo rudder-control system was under development, but this was abandoned when it was concluded that the desired improvement in control could be obtained by a simple all-moving balanced twin-rudder design without fins. A fully metallised biplane tail unit incorporating the new rudder system was designed and it was intended to fit this to J7436—then at Brooklands for reconditioning and for the trial installation of wheel brakes. However, severe floods on

Parachute training from a Virginia X at the Home Aircraft Depot, Henlow.

Brooklands aerodrome prevented J7436 from being moved and it was therefore decided to take the new tail unit by road to Martlesham and fit it to J7439. The total metallisation of J7439 was thus completed and, although it was in fact a Mk VII, it may be regarded as the Mk X prototype without the tail gunner's position and the longer nose of the production aeroplane.

Trials of the new rudder system confirmed the expected improvement and it was adopted as standard for future marks. Under an initial Air Ministry contract it was requested that the last six aeroplanes of a batch of 15 Virginias, being reconditioned at Weybridge to Mk IX standard, should be metallised. These were to be known as Virginia Mk IX (metallised) aeroplanes, but with the acceptance of the new rudder system as well they received the designation Virginia Mk X.

The Mk X version of the Virginia was by far the most numerous. Several Air Ministry reconditioning contracts were received by Vickers to cover the conversion of earlier marks, as well as a substantial production order for new aeroplanes. The reconditioned Virginias to Mk X standard were the following: J6856, J6857, J6992, J7129–J7132, J7275, J7419–J7422,

J7424, J7427–J7430, J7433, J7434, J7436–J7439, J7559–J7563, J7565–J7567, J7706, J7708, J7710, J7711, J7715, J7717–J7719, J8237, J8238, J8240, J8241, J8326, J8328–J8330, J8907, J8908, J8910, J8912–J8914, a total of 53 aircraft. Fifty production Mk Xs were built, K2321–K2339 and K2650–K2680, to specification 5/31.

As with earlier marks, the Virginia X was the subject of various trial installations during its long career, and constant improvement in equipment was made to keep the aeroplane in line with technical developments. Hydraulic wheel brakes became standard after trials were successfully completed. Landing lamps, of RAE design, were first installed on K2652, and were subsequently adopted to aid night landings.

Following successful trials with the experimental installation in the Virginia IX J7558, three-axes auto-pilot control became standard equipment on a number of Virginia IXs and Xs. This was instrumental in effecting a great improvement in bombing accuracy in the night-bomber squadrons. The Lawrence Minot Trophy for bombing was won five times by Virginias.

Early standard Virginia Xs were powered by Napier Lion VB engines,

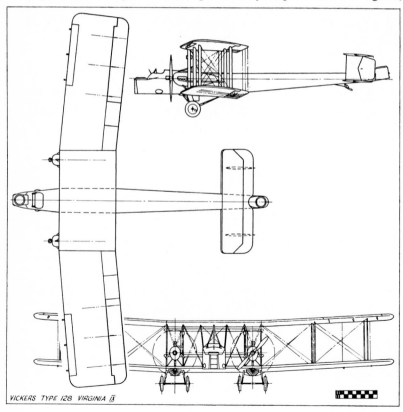

VICKERS TYPE 128 VIRGINIA IX

Tail gunner's station (left) and bomb aimer (sight-panel removed) in a Virginia Mk X.

but it was proposed to make a trial installation of the new Lion XI engine of increased power. J8238 was selected for the conversion, and trials were carried out with a number of different propellers to determine the most efficient design. Initially the increased performance promised by the new engine was not realised, and the propeller tests were conducted to bring the speed as near as possible to the estimate of 113 mph. Eventually the top speed was established as 108 mph, and this applied to the standard Virginia Mk X at full load. Propellers used in the later tests included one of hollow-steel design—later to become standard practice. Following the successful completion of these engine trials the Lion XI was adopted as standard for the Mk X.

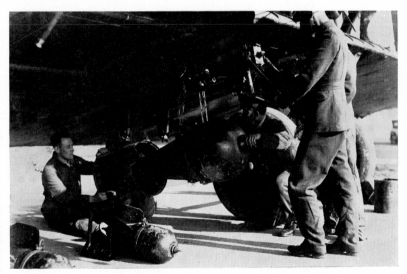

Bombing up a Mk X with underwing 550-lb and 112-lb bombs (for fuselage racks). (*Flight photo.*)

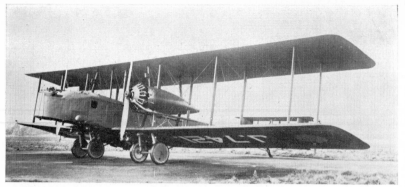
J7421 Mk X for trials with Jupiter engines originally installed in Mk IX J8236.

During test flying with the Lion XI installation J8238 conducted trials with a new silencer (being used successfully on racing cars at Brooklands) which, it was claimed, would increase engine revolutions as well as reducing noise. One of these was fitted to each of the three cylinder banks of one of the Virginia's Lions, and the aeroplane was then flown over ground observers, first on one engine and then on the other, at a height of 800 ft. They reported a slight decrease in the noise of the muffled engine, while the pilot reported a marked change in engine note. The standard Lion exhausts produced a distinct crackle accompanied by a whistle, while the silenced exhausts produced a steadier sound, which was acknowledged to be more comfortable for pilots on very long flights. With only one installation it was not ascertained if the troublesome unsynchronised beat would still be evident. The claim for increased revolutions was not substantiated, and no further development was undertaken. J8238 also carried out tests with a rudder-overload device to prevent pilots overstressing the tail unit during violent rudder movements; this became standard on Virginia Xs.

The trials with Bristol Jupiter engines first installed in the Mk IX J8236 were continued with a Mk X. The entire power units and mountings were transferred from J8236 to J7421 which continued test flying for some time. Various designs of exhaust-collector rings were fitted and test flown during this period. J7421 remained the only Jupiter-engined Virginia, although a similar installation was flown on a Victoria.

In 1933 the Bristol Pegasus IM3 nine-cylinder radial engine became available and numerous new designs were projected with this power unit. Conversions of existing types to take the new engine were, of course, also suggested, and the Virginia was an obvious choice. The increased power gave a big improvement in performance, the cruising speed being about 100 mph. This version of the aeroplane was offered to the Air Ministry as a progressive development, with an ultimate change of mark number.

J7130 was the Mk X chosen for the Pegasus installation, which was the IIM3 version of the engine. The aeroplane was test flown under the conditions imposed by specification B.19/27, the general performance being

Originally a Mk III, J7130 is shown here as an all-metal Mk X with Pegasus engines.

within the figures laid down. Fully loaded the Pegasus-engined Virginia had a top speed of 126 mph.

A number of designs, some of which were built and flown, were submitted by the aircraft industry to meet the specification B. 19/27, which was in reality for a Virginia replacement. The Handley Page Heyford and later the Fairey Hendon were the successful entrants, although in fact they supplemented, rather than replaced, the big Vickers night-bombers.

Although it was unsuccessful in securing more orders, the Pegasus-Virginia had a long and useful career as an armament test aeroplane. Progressive modifications kept J7130 in line with current developments, and in its final form it was equipped with Townend rings, four-bladed propellers, a tailwheel and a vee windscreen.

During early flight-refuelling experiments a Virginia Mk X, J7275, acted as the tanker, passing fuel through a flexible hose to several different types of receiver during many flights, these tests being made from Farnborough and Ford aerodromes. The system was demonstrated at the Hendon Air Display in 1936, with the Virginia as tanker and a Westland Wapiti.

Virginia Mk Xs equipped Nos. 7, 9, 10, 51, 58, 214, 215, 500 and 502 (Bomber) Squadrons of the Royal Air Force and remained in front-line service until late 1937. They were also used for parachute training by the Home Aircraft Depot at Henlow and for other duties by various Service establishments.

At dusk the characteristic, menacing silhouette and the melodious but unsynchronised drone become familiar to many as the big bombers flew

The final development of the Virginia was a Mk X, J7130, shown here on the left along-side a Valentia at Brooklands. It had Pegasus IIM3 engines with Townend rings, four-bladed propellers, a tailwheel and a vee windscreen. In this form the aeroplane was a possible competitor for the B.19/27 specification, which was eventually met by the Fairey Hendon monoplane and the Handley Page Heyford.

Skittle bombing by Virginia Xs of 9(B) Squadron at the 1935 Hendon Air Display.
(*Flight photo.*)

on night exercises. During the heyday of its long career the Virginia appeared before the public at Hendon Air Displays and Empire Air Days, and the highlight of its repertoire at Hendon was the low-level attack on giant skittles with 8-lb practice bombs.

Long after it had been replaced as the standard heavy-bomber in the front-line squadrons, the Virginia continued to render valuable if less spectacular service on vital tasks, and some were still flying as late as 1941. Sadly, not one Virginia has been saved for posterity; only photographs and memories remain of this wonderful old bomber which, more than any other aeroplane, formed the basis of and provided the experience for the emergent RAF Bomber Command.

Virginia

	Mk I—Type 57	Mk VII—Type 112	Mk X—Type 139
Accommodation:	Pilot, navigator, 2 gunners	Pilot, navigator, 2 gunners	Pilot, navigator, 2 gunners
Engines:	Two 450 hp Napier Lion	Two 500 hp Napier Lion V	Two 580 hp Napier Lion VB
Span:	86 ft 6 in	86 ft 6 in	87 ft 8 in
Length:	50 ft 7 in	50 ft 7 in	62 ft 3 in
Height:	17 ft 3 in	16 ft 11 in	18 ft 2 in
Wing Area:	2,166 sq ft	2,166 sq ft	2,178 sq ft
Empty Weight:	9,243 lb	9,243 lb	9,650 lb
Gross Weight:	16,750 lb	16,500 lb	17,600 lb
Max Speed:	97 mph at sea level	104 mph	108 mph at 5,000 ft
Climb to 5,000 ft:	12½ min	12½ min	10 min
Service Ceiling:	8,700 ft	7,420 ft (full load)	15,530 ft
Range:	1,000 miles at 75 mph	980 miles at 100 mph a 5,000 ft	985 miles at 100 mph at 5,000 ft
Armament:	Nine 112-lb bombs	Bomb load: 2,320 lb	One Lewis gun in nose Twin Lewis guns in tail Bomb load: 3,000 lb

The Biplane Transports

On 8 June, 1920, Vickers were asked to tender for the design of a military transport. The specification, known as Troop Carrying Aeroplane (B) D of R Type 12, called for an aeroplane carrying 25 fully armed soldiers at 100 mph for a distance of 400 miles, and overload tankage was to be provided to extend the range to 700 miles without troops. The transport, which could be powered either by two Napier Lions or two Rolls-Royce Condors, had to be capable of flying on one engine if necessary and operate from rough ground when required. The landing speed was stipulated as not more than 50 mph. The wings were to fold, and the height when folded was to be not more than 20 ft, because of hangar dimensions.

J6860, the first Victoria, running up before its first flight from Brooklands.

Vickers at this time were engaged in studies to meet the Long-range Bombing Aeroplane requirement which, as already described, finally resulted in the Virginia. They therefore suggested that they could produce a design to meet the troop-carrier specification, in which many components would be interchangeable with the bomber. The first proposal, as in the case of the bomber, was for a stretched Vimy of 88-ft span—the fuselage in this case being based on that of the Vimy Commercial/Vernon. In one version of this project the wing span was stretched to 100 ft. These initial studies received the unofficial name Viator.

The second project was for a developed Vimy, with a wing of greater chord and a span of 86 ft. This project again followed the bomber design in parallel, and a further development was eventually finalised. In April 1921 the Air Ministry placed an order for two prototypes, J6860 and J6861; they were to be manufactured at the same time as the two Virginia prototypes and cost £13,690 each. They were identical, with the exception of the fuselage and underwing fuel tanks, to the first Virginia prototype.

F   151

The two troop-carrier prototypes differed from each other externally only in respect of the underwing fuel tanks used to give increased range; J6860 had the tanks installed beneath the lower centre section, whereas J6861's were installed in a similar position beneath the upper centre section, and each tank had a capacity of 96 gals. In June 1921 the name Victoria was officially given to the aeroplane.

Construction of the first Victoria proceeded at a leisurely pace, and eventually two Napier Lion IC engines were allocated for the aeroplane. The engines were originally to have been Lion IIIs, but in fact neither these nor the two allocated Lion IC engines were delivered; instead two Lion series IAX engines were installed in J6860.

J6860 during tropical trials in Iraq.

While the construction of the prototypes was in progress an inquiry was received for the supply of 15 heavy freight aeroplanes capable of carrying a crew of two and two tons of cargo in the tropics. The source of the inquiry was never disclosed but, unfortunately, delivery was required within a year, and as at this time neither the Virginia nor the Victoria prototypes had flown, an order could not be met. An aeroplane based on either of these types could have met the specification.

On 22 August, 1922, J6860 (designated Victoria I) took-off from Brooklands with Cockerell at the controls. The weather was hazy with a 5 mph wind and, with a slow throttle opening, the aeroplane was airborne in 10 seconds. The Victoria climbed away very well, but it was soon apparent that it was tail heavy; in the cabin all the ballast was moved right forward, but even then the aeroplane was still slightly tail heavy. It was obviously necessary to put the tailplane up one notch on the tail-trimming device for the next flight. Aileron control was quite effective, and fore and aft control was also good but heavy because of the general tail heaviness. Stability in all planes was good, with little difference with power on or off; rudder control, however, was sluggish. A maximum speed of 106 mph—one mph above the estimate—was recorded on this flight. The landing speed was very low, but as the landing was made when almost dark, no accurate measurements could be taken. The initial impression formed by the pilot after this first flight was that the Victoria would be very satisfactory with little modification.

J6860, the first Victoria, at Farnborough for trials.

All the initial trials were carried out by Cockerell and Broome at Brooklands, but the full-load trials had to be from a smoother airfield. Vickers suggested Martlesham, but the Air Ministry decided that Farnborough should be used, and from there on 25 September, 1922, two flights were made, one at 75 per cent load and the second at full load. On the former flight the take-off was made, of necessity, downwind. In this adverse condition the Victoria was airborne in 15 seconds; the climb, however, was very slow at 65 mph, giving the impression that there was no reserve of power at all. The cruising speed obtained, at 1,900 rpm (one engine had to be throttled back to effect synchronization) was 85 mph, and top speed was 101–102 mph at 1,500 ft. The landing was made at 42 mph. The full-load test take-off was made in 20 seconds, the wind having veered to 90 degrees across the take-off direction. The only difference noticed on this flight was an even slower climb and a slightly higher landing speed, at 45 mph. After these tests the opinion was formed that the Victoria I was underpowered with the existing engines, and would require good weather and large airfields with unobstructed terrain when flying with a full load.

The second aeroplane, J6861 (designated Victoria II), was completed and flown in January 1923, again from Brooklands with Cockerell and Broome. All light-load tests were made there, but the full-load tests were conducted at Martlesham, although the aeroplane certainly made some

J6861 at Martlesham, after redesign of engine nacelles.

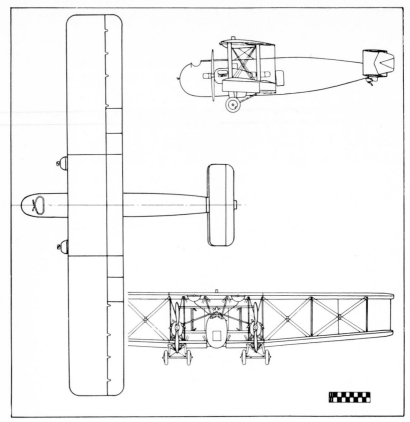

Vickers Victoria Mk II.

flights from Farnborough. After considerable flying trials J6861 had the standard Virginia and Victoria engine cowlings installed in place of the original car-type radiators with flat-sided cowlings, but it is not known whether J6860 was modified in a similar manner.

These aeroplanes were the only straight-winged Victorias and corresponded to the Virginia Mks I to V. No evidence exists to show that dihedral on both outer wings, as on the Virginia Mk VI, was ever applied to either of these prototype aeroplanes.

VICTORIA MARK III. Following extended trials of the two prototypes, J6860 and J6861, covering two and a half years, a production contract for the supply of 15 Victorias was placed in May 1925 to specification 13/25. These aeroplanes bore the serials J7921–J7935 and differed extensively from the prototypes.

During the years of Victoria trials the Virginia bomber had gradually evolved into the then pending production type, the sweptwing Mk VII.

154

Fourth production Victoria Mk III, showing dihedral on upper and lower wings.

The initial production version of the Victoria, designated Mk III, was based on the Virginia Mk VII. The basic components of the wings and tail unit, as well as a substantial part of the rear fuselage structure, were identical in the two types. The engines installed in the Victoria III were initially Napier Lion IIs of 450 hp each. J7921 made its first flight in January 1926, and the fifteenth, J7935, in July of that year. J7921 went to Martlesham for further trials, following the initial tests at Brooklands, and J7933 conducted trials of propellers, the oil-cooling system, and a spare engine carrier slung under the starboard lower centre plane.

Three further contracts for Victoria Mk IIIs were placed. These were for six aeroplanes, J8061–J8066 (delivered 9 July – 26 August, 1926); another 10 aeroplanes, J8226–J8235 (delivered 23 October – 14 December, 1926); and a final contract for 15 aeroplanes, J8915–J8929 (delivered 13 December, 1927 – 8 March, 1928). The 46 Victoria Mk IIIs cost £9,000 each.

Shortly after the production aeroplanes were accepted for service Nos. 70 and 216 (Bomber-Transport) Squadrons were equipped with Victoria Mk IIIs as replacements for Vernons and Vimys—virtually doubling the load-carrying capacity of these squadrons. Both 70 Squadron, based at Hinaidi, and 216 Squadron, at Heliopolis, did extensive flying, and many interesting flights were made.

On 15 September, 1926, two Victorias of 216 Squadron (J7928 and J7929) took-off from Heliopolis, Cairo, on a flight to Aden, arriving on 19 September. J7929 took 27 hr 35 min for the journey and J7928 ten minutes longer, with stops at Wadi Halfa, Atbara, Port Sudan and Massawa. On 23 September the two aeroplanes flew from Aden to Lander in Somaliland in 3 hr 15 min, returning to Aden later that day. They left Aden on 25

September on the return flight, making stops at Assab, Massawa, Kassala, Khartoum, Station 10, Wadi Halfa, Aswan and Assiut. After a flight time of 29 hr 20 min the two Victorias landed back at Heliopolis at 15.25 on 29 September. During these flights J7928 operated at a loaded weight of 17,080 lb and J7929 at 17,240 lb. Each aeroplane carried 400 gals of fuel and 30 gals of oil, with an additional 100 gals of fuel in cans in the cabin. Each aeroplane also carried rations and 18 gals of drinking water as well as desert survival kit.

After many flights in high-temperature conditions unsatisfactory reports were sent to Vickers by squadron pilots. One report was scathing about various aspects of performance and other defects. In particular, the climb and cruise performance, propeller flutter, pilot's view and dope finish came in for criticism. On the Cairo–Aden flight by one of the Victorias the climb to 10,000 ft had taken nearly two hours, and the maximum cruising speed at 1,900 rpm had been 65 mph. In the bumpy air continual propeller flutter had occurred, and the Victoria had apparently felt lifeless, tending to lose height whenever the nose was pulled-up in order to climb. On this flight the aeroplane, with a crew of eight, had a fuel load for only five hours and therefore was much below maximum all-up weight.

These reports were very disturbing, and H. J. Payn of Vickers went to the Middle East for a six weeks fact-finding tour. His investigations showed that while some of the criticism was justified, as in the case of the doping and the propeller flutter, the rest was due to unauthorised squadron modifications or incorrect operating procedure; in general, the Victorias in 70 and 216 Squadrons were giving excellent service and were meeting the specification requirements.

Victoria IIIs in service flying over familiar landmarks.
156

Early spare-engine carriers—a Lion in a Victoria III (*left*) and a Pegasus in a Valentia (*right*). The object protruding from the fuselage is the wind-driven generator, less fan, in retracted position.

The report of poor cruise performance was found to be caused by two major factors. During the excessive heat of the Middle East summer additional engine cooling was necessary, and an auxiliary radiator of Bristol Fighter type was installed on each engine nacelle, with a detrimental effect on the drag of the aeroplane, while 216 Squadron had worsened the case by removing the engine cowlings of their Victorias. The propellers were found to produce flutter in the very bumpy air in these hot climates, restricting the engine revolutions to 1,900 per minute. The combination of these problems reduced the cruising speed from the established 82 mph to a mere 65 mph.

This was a serious reduction, and modifications were introduced to overcome the deficiency. Bigger radiators were provided for installation during the summer months, as well as new propellers, which, after extensive development, allowed the engines to achieve their recommended 2,000 rpm. An improved dope scheme was introduced to give better resistance to the climate. Tests with many different propeller designs established the optimum shape which reduced the tendency to flutter in hot bumpy conditions.

With all these modifications introduced, the type became renowned for its reliability in the very difficult terrain. Many historic flights were made, and it is a little known fact that the Victorias pioneered the air routes for Imperial Airways prior to the introduction of the Handley Page 42 *Hannibal* class.

157

A Victoria IV during the Kabul air lift of 1929.

One of the greatest achievements of the Victorias took place at the end of 1928 and was the world's first major air lift. The Shiamwari tribal uprising against King Amanullah of Afghanistan resulted in the British Legation in Kabul being cut off, and the British Commissioner asked that all women and children should be evacuated. This was only possible by air, and many aircraft of the Royal Air Force were pressed into service. The major part was played by the Victorias, which, with their large capacity, proved ideal for the task. Most of these were Mk IIIs, although some all-metal Mk IVs also took part. Between 23 December, 1928, and 25

Arrival of civilians at Peshawar after air lift from Kabul in a Victoria.

February, 1929, 586 people were flown from Kabul to Peshawar over 10,000-ft mountains in one of the worst winters ever recorded in the region.

Of the operation, *The Times* correspondent wrote: 'In those winter weeks—surely destined to be famous forever in the history of the Air Force—the great aeroplanes went to and fro in all weathers over mountainous country of the most forbidding kind, where landing was practically impossible and any sort of failure in skill or in material must have meant disaster. There was no disaster. In more than seventy journeys, nearly 600 men, women and children were rescued, and not one suffered injury. . . . It is a great thing to have won the Schneider Trophy. It is a greater thing, greater for the country and for the future of travel by air, to have effected the rescues from Kabul.'

VICTORIA MK IV. Metallisation of the Virginia was going through in 1928, and it was obvious that the Victoria structure should also be brought into line, especially in view of the type's service in hot and humid climates where wooden structures were at a disadvantage.

On 9 September, 1927, a contract was placed for an all-metal Victoria fitted with Bristol Jupiter engines. It was given the serial J9250 in May 1928 and was sent to Martlesham for trials in the following October, where it remained until March 1929. It then went to Iraq for Service and tropicalisation trials. Throughout its life it was always referred to as the Victoria Jupiter and it was written off on 29 March, 1931, in a crash. It was replaced in these trials by a Mk V, K2340, with Jupiter XFBM engines, as mentioned below.

At first four existing Mk IIIs were to be converted to have all-metal wing structures for service trials in the East, but this contract was later increased to cover 10 aeroplanes. These were J8916–J8922 and J8924–J8926. Photographic evidence suggests that others were also converted later.

At this time the Virginia Mk X type all-metal tail unit, with finless rudders, was being test flown at Martlesham on a Victoria Mk III; as on the Virginia, this unit provided great improvement in directional control and was adopted for all future marks of the Victoria.

Victoria IIIs converted to the interim metal version Mk IV with metallised outer planes—note Handley Page slots.

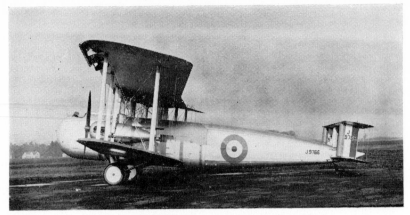

A standard Victoria Mk V, last of the initial order.

Three further conversions of existing airframes to all-metal construction, with the addition of the new tail unit, were ordered. These were designated Victoria Mk IV and were J7921, J7934 and J7935. The Victoria Mk IV was powered by two Napier Lion IIB engines, and some of these aeroplanes were delivered to 70 Squadron and took part in the historic Kabul operations already described.

VICTORIA MARK V. Designed to specification 7/29, the Mk V was the main production type of the fully metallised Victoria airframe, differing from the experimental Mk IV in being powered by two Napier Lion XIB engines.

Initially seven existing airframes were going to be converted and known as Victoria Mk IV (Lion XI) aeroplanes. In the event, it was thought that confusion with the Lion V powered Mk IV would arise, and the new mark

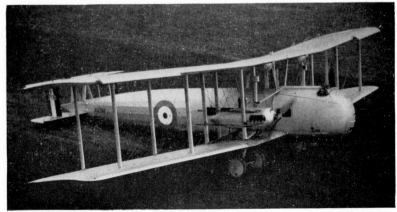

A Victoria V equipped with experimental Leitner-Watts variable-pitch propellers (ground adjustment only).

'Look—no hands!'—Victoria Mk V K2344 used by the Central Flying School for blind flying training.

number was therefore given. With the allocation of Mk V, seven new production aeroplanes were ordered instead of conversions, and these received the serials J9760–J9766 (delivered between 14 September and 14 October, 1929). These were in most respects transport counterparts of the Virginia Mk X, and the seven were followed by K1310–K1315 (delivered between 6 June and 7 October, 1930), while a further six followed, K2340–K2345 were delivered between 10 September and 11 November, 1931. The biggest and final contract for new aeroplanes of this type was for the supply of 18—K2791–K2808 (delivered between 11 July, 1932, and 15 September, 1933). These last 18 aeroplanes were supplied to specification 6/31.

Inside the cabin of K2344 while airborne as in companion picture.

161

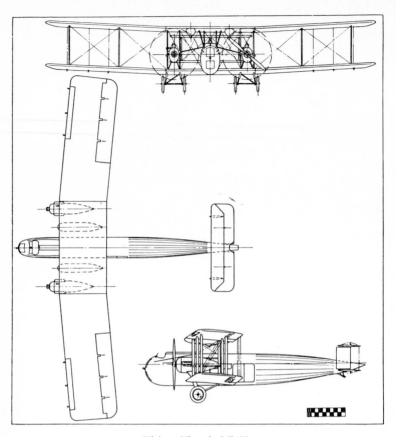

Vickers Victoria Mk V.

The first aeroplane of the third contract, K2340, was powered by two Bristol Jupiter XFBM engines and, although numerically the first contract aeroplane, was in fact completed later—in November 1931—because of the engine changes. Many months of engine test-flying was carried out by K2340, especially in relation to temperature recording, at Martlesham and later in Iraq. A special Mk V, K2344, was used by the Central Flying School for blind-flying instruction, the aeroplane being flown by pupils at controls within the cabin.

The Victoria Mks IV and V were a great improvement on the wooden versions; the cruising speed was 10 mph higher, the climb was better and the fuel consumption 50 gal/hr instead of 60 gal/hr, and ease of handling and crew comfort in the air was much better because of the lighter controls. A projected version of the Victoria V, with Rolls-Royce 'H' (Buzzard) engines, had an estimated top speed of 135 mph at sea level, but was not proceeded with.

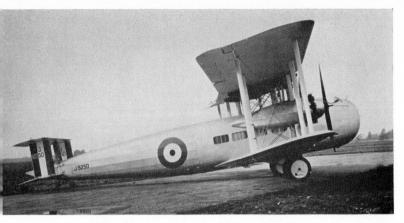

J9250 with first installation of Jupiter engines.

VICTORIA MK VI AND VALENTIA MK I. After a long and faithful career the Napier Lion engine was at the end of its useful life. During its years of arduous service it had earned an enviable reputation for great reliability coupled with higher power. It had performed in the extreme heat and dust of the desert and in the intense cold during climbs through the mountainous region of Northern India. But now the squadrons were looking towards a new engine of greater power to continue the good work.

On 4 November, 1932, Mutt Summers, by then chief test pilot of Vickers, received a letter from an officer of 216 (Bomber Transport) Squadron requesting that the Victorias should be re-engined with the Bristol Pegasus and provided with wheel brakes and a tailwheel. He also suggested that

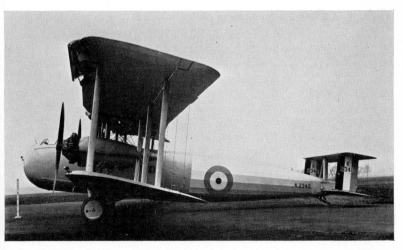

Victoria Mk V with Pegasus IM3 engines, later brought up to Valentia standards.

The first production Mk VI Victoria K3159.

the aeroplanes should be fitted with a swing tail to enable heavy and bulky loads to be loaded easily into the cabin, the fuselage being trestled for the purpose.

Probably unknown to this officer, Vickers had already investigated the possibility of installing the Pegasus in the Victoria V airframe, and K2340 had already been selected for the initial conversion. This aeroplane was in Iraq testing the Bristol Jupiter XFBM engine (predecessor of the Pegasus) with which it was powered, and the conversion to Pegasus power was made there by the Royal Air Force. The Pegasus chosen was the IM3. Later a similar conversion was carried out in England on the last Mk V, K2808.

Following successful trials, the Air Ministry were favourably impressed with the Victoria/Pegasus combination, and therefore ordered 11 new Victorias in this form. They requested that these new aeroplanes should be powered by the IIL3 version of the Pegasus, although Vickers would have preferred the adoption of the Bristol M series engines, which in their opinion were more suited to Middle East conditions.

The existing airframe structure, when powered with the new engine, was stressed to permit flying up to a weight of 18,000 lb—which did not take advantage of the full potential of the increased power available. It was therefore proposed to increase the strength of the wing structure by additional internal bracing. The undercarriage structure, too, was to be

164

K2340, one of the Victoria V Pegasus test-beds, after conversion to Valentia standard.

strengthened to take the new permissible weight of 19,500 lb. Whereas the old undercarriage had been wire-braced, the new design incorporated an additional diagonal bracing strut which dispensed with all wire bracing. Pneumatic wheel brakes and a tailwheel were to be introduced at the same time. The Air Ministry requested that K2808 should be modified to incorporate the new structural improvements, but in the event K2807 was used for the trial installation—being re-engined with Pegasus IIL3s at the same time.

A decision was then made that the introduction of the Pegasus to new and existing Victorias should now be proceeded with extensively. This operation was to take place in two phases, the first with the existing airframe and the second with the structural improvements. At this time the Air Ministry asked that a new name should be given to the big Vickers transport; why, after so many years, the Victoria should be renamed is still a mystery. The new name was to apply only to the improved, weight-increased aeroplane, and there the most likely explanation lies; had the 19,500-lb aeroplane merely been given a new mark number, there could possibly have been confusion, and disaster could have resulted if the earlier type were loaded to the new weight. It therefore seems logical that the adoption of the new name was to prevent this occurrence. Service personnel were probably more inclined to observe instructions if they applied to an apparently new aeroplane.

165

The name favoured by the Air Ministry was Victory, but Vickers did not like this, and at that stage no agreement was reached. Then, in view of the aeroplane's Eastern associations, Vickers suggested the name Vindhya, a mountain range in India; the Air Ministry in their turn rejected this proposal and suggested Vancouver. Vickers agreed with this, but pointed

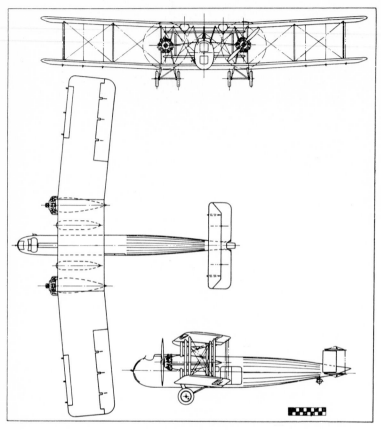

Vickers Valentia.

out that there could be confusion with the flying-boat of that name produced by their Canadian associates, Canadian Vickers. As an alternative, the Air Ministry proposed that Valentia should be used, pointing out that the earlier Vickers flying-boat* of that name was never used by any of the Services. In February 1934 Vickers agreed and the name was finally adopted.

The application of the Pegasus to the basic Victoria Mk V airframe (designated Conversion 1) permitting flying up to a weight of 18,000 lb,

* See drawing on page 478.

166

First production Valentia K3599—distinguishing feature of all Valentias was the tailwheel.

changed its description to Victoria Mk VI, and the structurally improved version (designated Conversion 2), permitting flying up to a weight of 19,500 lb, became the Valentia Mk I.

Contracts for new Valentias were placed, and in all 28 were built at Weybridge, where Victorias K2340, K2344, K2345, K2795–K2797 and K2799–K2807 were also converted to Valentia Mk I standard. Other conversions were undertaken by the RAF in the Middle East, and the time taken to convert a metal Victoria to Valentia standard was recorded by the RAF station at Hinaidi as 8,000 man hours. In all 54 conversions were made.

During flight development at Martlesham with K2807 there was much criticism of the lateral control of the heavier Pegasus version; it was suggested by the Air Ministry that any improvement should be included at the Conversion 2 stage, and improved control was developed and incorporated as suggested.

Several interesting developments of Valentia details and equipment were undertaken at this time. In 1933 the Air Ministry asked for the design of a new spare-engine carrier, instead of the Lion carrier previously used, to transport all the types of Service engines. A trial installation of this type was carried out on K2807 with an Armstrong Siddeley Panther engine in November 1933. Two special Valentias, K4634 and K4635, were powered by two Pegasus IIM3 engines each, to specification 30/34 for trials in India.

For sky-shouting to marauding tribes during air police duties, loud-speaker equipment was fitted to K4632, the weight of this installation, which incorporated four loud-speakers, being 1,430 lb. Previously, a similar public-address system had been used on the Victoria V, K2345.

At the end of September 1935 Vickers were asked to design gun positions, in the nose and amidships, for installation in the Valentia, the Italian invasion of Abyssinia with massive air support having led to the possibility of Valentias being attacked on the frontier regions of that country. The

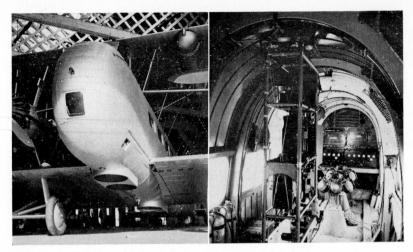

K4632 sky-shouter showing on right the broadcasting equipment.

Air Ministry wanted simple conversions to be carried out by the squadrons in the Middle East, the drawings being speedily despatched by Vickers; at home the trial installation was carried out on K4633 and proved the effectiveness of the scheme. Subsequently, a number of Valentias were converted.

A further, more complicated, scheme was planned which would have utilised the entire rear gunner's position of the Virginia Mk X. Although the attachment to the Valentia fuselage was simple, the Virginia and Valentia basic internal structures being identical, the fuselage fairing proved more difficult. Although the scheme was quite practicable, the Air Ministry decided not to pursue the matter and, as far as is known, no trial installation was ever carried out.

Following successful trials which were currently being conducted with Virginias, it was requested that a Victoria Mk VI, K3168, should be equipped for flight-refuelling. It was emphasised by the Air Ministry that the equipment should be of the simplest form to permit it to be installed by the Royal Air Force using only a small number of unskilled men. The aeroplane was to be fitted with six 50-gal tanks and to act as the tanker. In trials to be conducted at Farnborough it was to supply fuel, in flight, to an Airspeed Courier.

Before K3168 was completed in its new form, it was transformed into a Valentia by the application of Conversion 2. Following these trials at Farnborough, the aeroplane was sent to the Middle East for further test flying. A flight-refuelling conversion set was also sent to the Middle East for installation in a Victoria by the Royal Air Force.

In 1933 Sir Alan Cobham was making preparations, with the collaboration of the Air Ministry, to fly to India in the Airspeed Courier. With his co-pilot, Sqn Ldr Helmore, Sir Alan planned to fly non-stop—with refuelling in flight at four points. The tests at Farnborough with the Valentia tanker were in connection with this flight. Throughout 1933 the tests and preparations continued with such types as Virginias, Handley Page W.10s, a Westland Wapiti and the Middle East Victoria (converted by the RAF with the set despatched by Vickers).

On 22 September, 1934, the Courier took-off from England and was immediately refuelled with 100 gal from a Handley Page W.10; the next day a second W.10 transferred 180 gal to the Courier over Malta. In addition to petrol, the W.10 supplied 19 gal of oil and 2 gal of water to the Courier. During this refuelling petrol was transferred at a rate of 50 gal/min. Unfortunately, shortly after the completion of this operation the throttle linkage of the Courier failed, and a landing at Malta had to be made. The attempt to fly to India non-stop was abandoned; had the flight continued, the Victoria tanker would have transferred fuel over Alexandria, and the final refuelling would have been made over Basra by the Valentia tanker, K3168.

Despite this set-back, the practical application of flight-refuelling had proved satisfactory, and further tests were made with the Victoria, Valentia, Vickers B.19/27 and Virginia tankers—the latter, in particular, undertaking tests and demonstrations of the technique to Imperial Airways, for potential civil applications. The big Vickers biplanes contributed a great deal

Valentia bristling with hostility as converted for readiness during the
Italian–Abyssinian war, 1936.

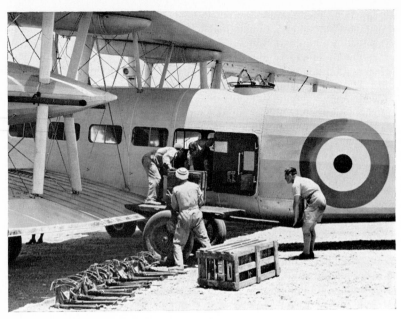

Loading military stores into a Valentia somewhere east of Suez.

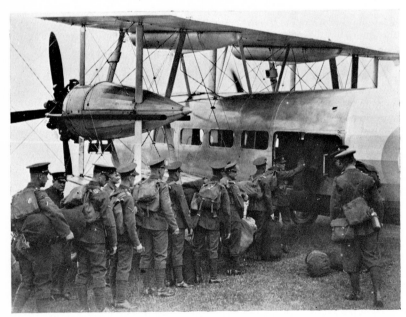

Troops embarking in an RAF Valentia.

to the build-up of flight-refuelling knowledge, and it is fitting that the experience is being employed today by the VC10s of the Royal Air Force—continuing the long association and tradition of Vickers aeroplanes, including the Valiant bomber, and the flight-refuelling technique.

It is interesting to recall that the earliest projects for the Vickers B.9/32 and B.1/35 bombers (which materialised in the Wellington and Warwick) incorporated flight-refuelling equipment, although these aeroplanes in their production form never used this method of extending operational range.

The Central Flying School's special flying classroom, the Victoria Mk V K2344, returned to Vickers for conversion to Valentia standard. Afterwards this aeroplane continued for many years to train the future pilots of the RAF in blind flying and for instruction in autocontrol.

In squadron service the Victoria Mk VIs and Valentias amassed an impressive total of flying hours, keeping open the vital supply lines. They were the pack-horses of the Services, and over the years transported troops and bulky equipment wherever, and whenever, they were required.

The Victorias and Valentias built the foundations of the later RAF Transport Command, and they further developed the civil air routes across the Middle East, originally created by Vernons. In 1940 they added more offensive tasks to their normal rôle in the Western Desert and other theatres of war, making night-bombing attacks. As late as 1943 some were still flying on communications duties. The last Valentia to survive, K3600, was sold to India in July 1944.

VANGUARD. Early in 1921 Vickers initiated the design of a 23-seat commercial transport, following inquiries from the Instone Air Line for a single aeroplane of this type. The design to meet the requirement was, like the Victoria, based on that of the Virginia I. The fuselage of the new aeroplane was similar to that of the Victoria, being an all-wood monocoque structure—but widened to accommodate civil passengers in comfort. The lower centre sections, engine installations, undercarriage, and outer upper and lower mainplanes were identical to those of the Virginia and Victoria, but the upper centre section was widened to take the new fuselage width. The tail unit was also identical to that of the standard Virginia and Victoria of that period. The span of the Vanguard was 88 ft, compared with 86 ft 6 in of the Virginia and Victoria. Power was supplied by two Napier Lion engines of 468 hp each.

As design work proceeded, the Air Ministry became interested in the project and invited Vickers to tender for the design of a 23-seat commercial aeroplane to specification 1/22. The proposals sent to the Air Ministry were accepted, and a contract for the supply of one aeroplane was drawn up. The type name Vanguard, suggested by Vickers, was adopted, and the aeroplane was given both the serial number J6924 and the civil registration G-EBCP during different phases of the test programme.

The Vanguard, which was the largest and most advanced commercial

171

Vanguard biplane in original form with Lion engines and dihedral only on lower wings.

landplane of its day, caused world-wide interest. One proposal from France was for the type to be manufactured under licence, but as a French engine of similar power to the Napier Lion did not then exist, it was suggested that three or four Lorraine or Hispano Suiza engines should be used. The United States Air Attaché to Britain also showed great interest, and at his suggestion Vickers submitted a proposal for a Rolls-Royce Condor variant for his perusal. In the event, neither of these inquiries bore fruit, and there was only one aeroplane of the type.

On 18 July, 1923, the Vanguard was airborne out of Brooklands on its first flight, with Cockerell at the controls. The weather was clear, with a westerly wind blowing at 7 mph across the take-off direction. The aeroplane took-off well in a very short distance. With 400 lb of ballast in the forward fuselage, the machine was still tail heavy, but when this was trimmed-out the handling and stability were good in general; the rudders, however, were ineffective and required additional area. But the flight augured well for the future. The good general behaviour of the Vanguard was to be proved as more flights were undertaken, and during trials from Martlesham, where it was flown by numerous Service pilots, it quickly established the reputation of being a delightful flying machine.

As trials progressed it became obvious that even better performance could be obtained by installing two Rolls-Royce Condor III engines in

Vanguard with Condor engines and dihedral on upper and lower wings.

172

place of the Napier Lions, as had been suggested by the Americans. A Condor installation was being flown at this time in the Virginia I, J6856, and it was therefore a simple task to convert the Vanguard, with its standard Virginia wing structure, to take the more powerful Rolls-Royce engine. The resultant installation was identical to the finalised design used in J6856, the engines remaining uncowled—although a neat streamlined nacelle fairing was eventually to be fitted.

While the engine installation was being revised a change was also made in the wings. Originally, as on the Virginias and Victorias of the period, the lower wings had four degrees dihedral. This was changed to two and a half degrees on both upper and lower planes—conforming to the Virginia Mk VI standard. With the changes completed the Vanguard was ready for service with Imperial Airways (which by then had absorbed the Instone Air Line), operating mainly from Croydon.

Vanguard in Imperial Airways service at Croydon airport. (*Flight photo.*)

The Vanguard was delivered to Imperial Airways in May 1928 for scheduled operations, apparently under a loan arrangement with the Air Ministry whose property it was. One of the first pilots to fly it at Croydon was Capt Jimmy Alger, who had been engaged by Imperial Airways fresh from two and a half years flying on the Cairo–Baghdad air mail route on Vickers Vernons with 45 Squadron, RAF, and from service with No. 58 at Worthy Down on Virginias and Victorias.

Capt Alger writes as follows: 'It was therefore natural, with nearly 1,000 hours on these types, that Maj Brackley, then Air Superintendent of Imperial Airways, decided to give me a big share of the flying on the Vanguard when it came to Croydon in May 1928. After my initial six landings for B licence endorsement, my enthusiasm for the aircraft quickly developed, and from my pilot's log book I see that I was on the job the same day, off to Berck and Paris, and from then on I flew it every time I got the opportunity.

'Imperial Airways decided to operate it firstly to Paris with stops at Berck, to help cope with the spring and summer traffic, but also I believe they thought it wise to keep it near "home base" during the period of early

173

development. It quickly proved itself, however, and gave remarkably little trouble and, from a pilot's point of view, was delightful to fly. The performance in and out of small landing grounds like Berck was excellent.

'After a couple of months on the London–Paris route it was then operated mainly on the London–Brussels–Cologne service, and stayed on that run until it was returned to Brooklands for a trial modification in October

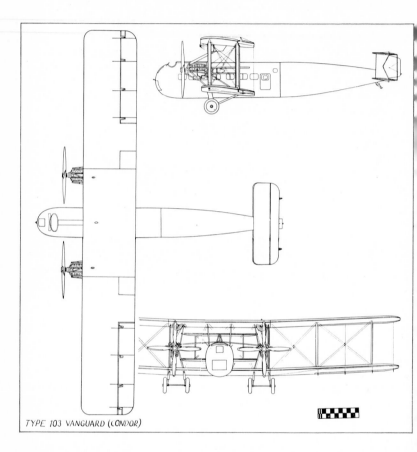

TYPE 103 VANGUARD (CONDOR)

1928. I never did find out why a "mod." had to be carried out, as I was posted to Cairo on 31 October, 1928, but the news of the tragic accident which occurred when Tiny Scholefield took it up on test after the modification came as a great shock to us all.

'To the best of my knowledge there were no untoward incidents while it was operated by us, and except for an engine failure the aircraft gave little trouble that I as a pilot knew about.

'A great pity it ended like that because it was a great advance on the Handley Page W.8, W.8b and W.10 (and the Vulcan of course) then operating on those routes, and I am sure a fleet of Vanguards would have become as popular with everyone as the present day Vanguard is.'

The Vanguard was regrettably the only civil development of the Victoria/Valentia concept which played such a great part in the development of military transport between the wars.

Cabin interior of Vanguard biplane airliner.

Capt Alger's log shows 128 hr 50 min operational flying on the Vanguard, exclusively on the air routes he mentions, between 25 May and 26 September, 1928. London–Paris direct was flown in 2 hr 6 min in the fastest time, and 2 hr 45 min the longest. The London–Brussels–Cologne route was normally flown there and back in the day, the outward flight taking 3 hr 8 min in the fastest time, and the homeward flight averaging just over four hours, largely because of the prevailing headwinds at the low levels then flown.

Circumstantial evidence indicates that the modification referred to by Capt Alger was the fitting of a new tail unit of the Virginia X pattern with all-flying rudders. There had been much success with this unit, as already related in connection with the Virginia, and it is now thought that Tiny Scholefield applied too much rudder force, which caused overstressing. In consequence, later designs fitted with the new tail unit carried a rudder-control compensating device which prevented pilots from inadvertently applying too much angular force. Unfortunately, it seems that no photograph was taken of the Vanguard with the new tail unit before it crashed at Shepperton with the loss of Scholefield and Frank Sharrett, his flight observer.

	Victoria Type 56	Victoria Mk V Type 169	Victoria Mk VI Type 262	Valentia Type 264
Accommodation:	2 crew, 23 fully armed troops	2 crew, 23 fully armed troops	2 crew, 23 fully armed troops	2 crew, 22 fully armed troops
Engines:	Two 450 hp Napier Lion IAX	Two 570 hp Napier Lion XIB	Two 660 hp Bristol Pegasus IIL3	Two 635 hp Bristol Pegasus IIM3
Span:	86 ft 6 in	87 ft 4 in	87 ft 4 in	87 ft 4 in
Length:	51 ft 7 in	59 ft 6 in	59 ft 6 in	59 ft 6 in
Height:	17 ft 3 in	17 ft 9 in	17 ft 9 in	17 ft 9 in
Wing Area:	—	2,178 sq ft	2,178 sq ft	2,178 sq ft
Empty Weight:	10,155 lb	10,030 lb	9,806 lb	10,994 lb
Gross Weight:	18,100 lb	17,760 lb	17,600 lb	19,500 lb
Max Speed:	106 mph at sea level	110 mph at sea level	130 mph at 5,000 ft	120 mph at 5,000 ft
Climb to 5,000 ft:	21·5 min	11 min	8·5 min	11 min (to 6,000 ft)
Ceiling:	—	16,200 ft (service)	18,300 ft (absolute)	16,250 ft (service)
Range:	400 miles	770 miles	800 miles	800 miles

Vanguard—Type 103—Two 650 hp Rolls-Royce Condor III. Accommodation—Two crew and 20 passengers. Span 87 ft 9 in; length 53 ft 10 in; height 17 ft 3 in; wing area 2,182 sq ft. Empty weight 12,040 lb; gross weight 18,500 lb. Max speed 112 mph at sea level; climb to 5,000 ft in 10·5 min; service ceiling 16,400 ft.

The Vixen Family

In 1922 Vickers decided to increase their sales potential by designing a two-seat military tractor biplane as a private venture. With the experience of the wartime F.B.14 on which to base an improved project, Pierson, after an exploratory conference with the Air Ministry, wrote a specification for a fighter-reconnaissance-bomber aeroplane which could be adapted either as a replacement for the Bristol Fighter or for the D.H.9A.

Unlike the F.B.14, which never received the engine for which it was designed (the B.H.P.—later called the Siddeley Puma), the new Type 71 Vixen was more fortunate in that the 450 hp Napier Lion was available, a powerful engine of proven reliability. Retaining a steel-tube fuselage and wooden wings as in the F.B.14, the prototype Vixen was flown in February 1923 by Capt Broome, and soon after went to Martlesham for evaluation. The official testing of private ventures was normal practice, particularly of military types. Indeed, almost complete control was exercised by the Directorate of Research of the Air Ministry, who issued certificates of airworthiness in due course; in such cases the manufacturer paid the cost of official testing, that for the Vixen being £20.

From the basic Vixen I came a number of improvements and variants to form a distinct line of succession extending over nearly 20 years, ending with the Vildebeest and Vincent, both of which saw service in the early

176

Vixen I as flown in January 1923, with short fuselage and frontal car-type radiator.

days of the second world war. There were the various marks of Vixen, the Valparaiso, the Venture, the Vivid, the Valiant, and (as offshoots) the Vendace and the Vespa. At the end of this development of the single-engine tractor biplane, with the Vildebeest and Vincent, the type family had merged in quite a different operational rôle to that originally planned in 1922.

At that time there was little hope of any new type of military aeroplane receiving anything more than token home orders, so small was the Royal Air Force. But countries backward in aviation were trying to make progress. The Vixen attracted attention abroad, and inquiries were received

Vixen II flown in August 1923, with longer fuselage, faired-off nose and cleaner lines than Vixen I.

177

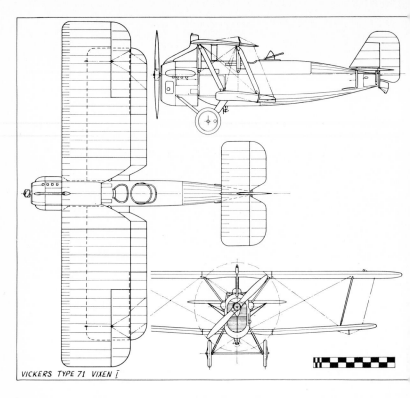

VICKERS TYPE 71 VIXEN I

from Greece, Denmark, Peru, Chile, Portugal, Serbia, Russia and Aus‑
tralia.

At Martlesham the Vixen I with the low-compression Lion I (5·3:1)
climbed to 10,000 ft in just over 10 minutes, where it had a speed of 137
mph; at 15,000 ft, which it reached in 20 minutes, its speed was 129 mph.
Its service ceiling was 19,400 ft. These figures were obtained with full
military load and compared favourably with those of contemporary de‑
signs in the general-purpose class. As a result of this evaluation, the Air
Ministry suggested modification to fit the Vixen for a day bomber rôle
and these were embodied, with classified Service equipment, in a rebuild of
the same airframe, as the Vixen II.

Meanwhile a certificate of airworthiness had been obtained for the type
as the Vixen I, it had received the civil registration G-EBEC on 22 July
1922. The Vixen II flew as the Type 87 at Brooklands on 13 August, 1923.
Vixen II's chief claim to distinction was that it was used for the prototype
trials of a new Vickers machine-gun designed to replace the Lewis. This
led to the subsequent production of Vickers drum-fed guns for airborne
use.

On 6 February, 1924, the Vixen II was flown for one hour at Martlesham
by Flt Lt Orlebar. He reported favourably enough for the Air Ministry

award a development contract for six aircraft of a still further improved Vixen II type to specification 45/23, to fit the two-seat armed reconnaissance rôle.

VENTURE. Difficulty was experienced in offering a name, acceptable to the Air Ministry, for the improved type beginning with the letter V. From the alternatives of Vulpes (common fox), Vortex and Venture, the last was officially adopted.

The military Venture combined Vixen II mainplanes, controls and propeller and Vixen I fuel system and rigging, with Vixen III (then just completed) extended-type fuselage, underslung radiator, tail and chassis. A remarkable thing to note in these days of successive line assemblies is that all six Ventures were completed at the same time, and all but one were delivered in the same week of July 1924. The Ventures were serialled J7277 to J7282, but the first, J7277, was held back for two months for further manufacturer's trials. Its first flight was at Brooklands on 3 June, 1924, and it flew at Martlesham on 17 June, where Service pilots reported a top speed of 135 mph with full operational load, as well as docile handling characteristics.

In spite of this favourable report, in September 1924 Vickers were informed that the Venture was unacceptable as a standard DoR Type 3 for Corps reconnaissance. The reasons given were that the aeroplane was 'too large', the pilot's downward view inadequate, the longitudinal stability insufficiently positive and the landing run too long. Proposals to meet these objections, except that of size, seem to have had no effect, and

Venture at Martlesham showing general similarity to Vixen II.

subsequently the six Ventures were parcelled out to Service stations an establishments for experimental work.

J7277 and J7278 were allocated to the Royal Aircraft Establishment fo various investigations, such as fuel economy trials with the Lion engine the former after a spell with 4 Squadron; J7282 was attached to the A an AEE at Martlesham, and was still there in 1927; J7280 went to the RAI Technical College at Henlow, but was borrowed in February 1925 for demonstration at Brooklands before a Japanese Army mission; the res seem to have been attached to various squadrons and then disappearec

Valparaiso I (Lion engine) in Portuguese service showing mixture of Vixen I and II features.

VALPARAISO. Meanwhile Vickers went ahead with the overseas inquiries and in November 1923 Portugal ordered four Vixen Is with Rolls-Royc Eagle engines and 10 with Napier Lions. In order to distinguish the over seas types from those built for British sales, which carried classified officia equipment, they were renamed Valparaisos. The Lion-engined versior was the Valparaiso I, and the Eagle variant the Valparaiso II. The proto type at first was simply called Vickers V type, but eventually was sold to Chile as a Valparaiso Mk I. It was test flown on 29 August, 1924, and dis closed a performance almost identical to that of the Vixen I, G-EBEC.

At the end of 1924 the Chilean Valparaiso reached 20,000 ft, so beating the existing height record of South America. Without doubt, the per formance of this aeroplane in the hands of Chilean Army pilots led to the subsequent order for Vixen Vs from that quarter.

The Portuguese Valparaisos also rendered good service for a long period The *Diario de Noticias*, a Lisbon newspaper, reported on 28 September 1925, that Lt José Cabral gave a breath-taking performance at an air dis play 'with prodigious ease over an anxious crowd', while at another ai pageant near Lisbon in the following year all the aircraft participating were Vickers Valparaisos except one, an Avro 504K.

In May 1928 two Valparaiso Is, piloted by Capts Ramos and Viegas flew to the Portuguese colonies in Africa, Angola and Mozambique, and back, the outward flight covering 11,500 miles and taking 94 flying hours

Valparaiso II with Eagle engine, in Portugal.

The longest stage was from Vila Luso via Elizabethville and Broken Hill to Zomba, some 1,000 miles across Central Africa. For those days this was a considerable feat in equatorial conditions. There were only two involuntary landings by the two aeroplanes, and the only technical trouble encountered was with the fuel pumps, probably caused by impurities in the fuel supplies obtainable in regions then unaccustomed to aviation standards. The effort was particularly meritorious, as very stormy weather with heavy rain was encountered during the early stages. This was the first attempt to establish contact by air between the homeland and the Portuguese African colonies, and the flight was sponsored by the Commercial Association of Lisbon.

About this time Vickers and the Portuguese military authorities, through agents, were considering the licence construction of the Valparaiso type by their aircraft factory at Alverca do Ribatejo. After the 540 hp Lorraine-Dietrich liquid-cooled engine had been considered it was decided to return a Valparaiso to Weybridge to be rebuilt to take the Gnome Rhône Jupiter VIa air-cooled radial engine. This version was designated the Valparaiso III, and was test flown at Brooklands on 28 July, 1929. To this Mk III standard, with the French-built Jupiters, at least 13 were constructed in Portugal. They gave a good account of themselves in service, according to Portuguese military information, up to as late as 1936. Four of them toured Northern France on a goodwill visit in 1935.

Line-up of Portuguese Valparaiso IIIs with Jupiter engines.

181

Vixen III G-EBIP on compass base at Brooklands with Chilean aviation mission representatives.

VIXEN III. Thus far the original Vixen layout had remained basically unchanged. In detail, the heavy frontal appearance of the Mk I, produced by the car-type nose radiator and the close cowling of the engine, was altered in the Mk II conversion by the provision of a ventral radiator, underslung between the legs of the oleo-pneumatic undercarriage, and a faired nose-cowling behind the propeller. The coolant header tank and faired pipe-line were moved to the starboard side of the upper centre section, since the position in the Mk I, on the aircraft centreline, must have interfered with the pilot's forward vision and threatened him with a hot shower in the event of a water leak.

To improve the pilot's upward view in the Vixen II, the cut-out in the centre section was enlarged. To increase range two additional petrol tanks were fitted on the underside of the upper wings, just outboard of the centre section; the fuselage was lengthened by three feet and faired off to provide more effective tail control and introduce a less portly appearance; and to further improve vision, a fall-away over the nose from the pilot's

Vixen III floatplane at Felixstowe marine base, with over-wing extra fuel tanks.

eye-line was provided. These improvements were made after a close official scrutiny of the Vixen I and to meet the Venture development contract, for which a fuel-pump system feeding a centre-section service tank was a requirement.

In addition to these changes, both the Venture and Valparaiso embodied a rudder horn balance of revised shape, cut at 45 degrees instead of horizontal as on the Vixen I and II and similar shaped elevator horn balances were also introduced, these aerodynamic refinements being intended to relieve control loads.

The Vixen III contained all these improvements, and was, in fact, a Venture with larger wings with area increased by 18 sq ft. It reverted to a cleaned-up version of the nose-radiator layout of the Vixen I with a close-fitting cowling. The Mk III had rounded wing tips for the first time

Tiny Scholefield, Vickers pilot, starting in the 1927 King's Cup Air Race on Vixen III G-EBIP, which averaged 141·6 mph from scratch.

in the Vixen series and, in due course, a modest one and a half degrees dihedral appeared on the top wing, both improvements promoting greater aerodynamic efficiency.

The reason for increasing the wing area in the Vixen III was to improve performance at height with a higher compression (5·5:1) Lion II engine, and many redesigned components were introduced. The Mk III was registered G-EBIP in January 1924 and first flew at Brooklands in the following April. In May it was flown to Martlesham, where it showed the desired improvement in performance and handling characteristics and earned favourable comments from the official pilots. The Vixen III was placed fifth in the 1924 King's Cup Air Race when it was flown by Maj H. J. Payn, technical assistant to Pierson, who shared Vickers' testing at that time with Capt Broome.

Later in the year, G-EBIP was converted to a floatplane, and in December was tested from Avro's base at Hamble, later going to the Marine Aircraft Experimental Establishment at Felixstowe for official seaplane tests. In this form the Mk III had the tailskid removed, and a larger rudder and ventral fin fitted.

As a floatplane, G-EBIP was 15 mph slower, with comparative reductions in other performance figures. Reconverted from its marine guise, it was flown again by Maj Payn in the 1925 King's Cup Air Race. For the 1926 race various refinements were made, including the introduction of the new Napier Lion Mk V high-compression (5·8:1) engine. The cut-out of the wing centre-section was filled, the pilot's position was raised and faired off to a single-seat configuration, and smaller wheels were fitted because of the reduced racing weight of the aeroplane. The upper wing ailerons were discarded, and a cleaner top wing reduced drag. Flown by Flt Lt E. R. C. Scholefield, the 1926 version of the Vixen III came in a very close second in the race on handicap, having started from scratch. In the 1927 King's Cup, G-EBIP was placed third on handicap with an average speed of 141·6 mph, again flown by Scholefield.

VIXEN V. The Valparaiso I in Chile had been doing so well, building up many flying hours in the difficult conditions of that country with its enormous latitudinal range, that in May 1925 the military authorities there placed an order for 12 general-purpose aircraft based on the Vixen III; in July this was amended to 18, and the first three of the order were completed and flown in September by Scholefield at Brooklands. Number four was tested at Martlesham and met the specification agreed on in the contract.

The Mk V's principal alteration from the Mk III was in the tail, which had an asymmetrical fin section to improve yaw characteristics and lighten rudder-bar load, while the rudder itself was reduced in chord. The Lion V of 500 hp with high compression was standardised, as rapid climb was essential because of the peculiar Chilean geography, which consists of a 2,000-mile coastline running north to south with only a narrow width of national territory. To meet any potential attack from the East—the only direction from which it could come—the Chilean Army air arm would have to take-off and climb to height over the Cordillera mountains, only

A Vixen V for Chile, at Brooklands; distinctive features include large service fuel tanks on upper centre section.

Business end of Vixen V for Chile, with wing-mounted bombs.

0 miles distant from Santiago, the capital. A glance at a map will make
iis operational requirement clear.

At that time the only fuel available for high-compression engines was a
iixture in the proportion of two-thirds petrol to one-third benzol. One of
ie service troubles was with burnt-out pistons, rings and valves, and in
outh America this was traced to diluted mixtures, for aviation fuel supply
as difficult. Examination of the Lion engines of the Argentine Navy
iking amphibians disclosed similar troubles at the same time. The
ooden airframe was a further problem in the extreme heat of Northern
hile, causing shrinking of the members and needing constant tightening
p of fittings and rigging, a condition similar to that already encountered
the Middle East by Vickers military aircraft such as the Vimys, Vernons
nd Victorias.

With the Vixen Vs, Chile created a little air force of its own and pub-
cised the fact in rather flamboyant terms in its Press, no doubt to im-
ress its international neighbours on the deterrent principle so familiar
oday. In the Chilean national newspaper *La Nacion* for 17 July, 1925, a
hole page was devoted to a report of the acceptance of the 'formidable'
ritish aeroplanes and to the celebration in the form of a sumptuous
incheon for the Chilean officers and mechanics who had been to England
or training by Vickers. This function was attended by the President of the
hilean Republic, its Minister of War and its Director General of Aviation.

No time was lost in testing out the Vixens under Service conditions
Long-distance flights of several hundred miles were attempted, including
visit by five aircraft to Buenos Aires. The only mishaps to occur durin
this shaking-down period were both attributable to inexperienced piloting
one a landing on an emergency strip at too high a speed with the tail up
and the other caused by an attempt by one crew to take a short cut t
Buenos Aires through a mountain pass, a diversion from the flight plan
In spite of the reservation already made about wooden construction and
the doubtful quality of the local fuel, the Vixen Vs gave good service and
perhaps more important still, were a boost to national morale. It is note
worthy that the next aeroplanes bought by Chile from Vickers were in fac
all-metal Wibault Scouts. When the Valiant biplane, to be described later
was taken to Chile for demonstration Scholefield reported that the Vixen
had all flown over 400 hours, and all had stood on their noses at some tim
or other.

VIXEN IV AND VI. At the end of 1924 the airframe of G-EBEC underwer
another metamorphosis, and was modified to take the 650 hp Rolls-Royc
Condor III direct-drive engine. The fuselage was lengthened as in th
Valparaiso and Venture, and other modifications were made in the light
of experience gained since the debut of the Vixen II. The idea was to offe
this Vixen IV, as it was classified, as a night-flying interceptor. The exper
ment had limited success, and flight trials at Brooklands and Farnboroug
showed the anticipated better performance, but without any startlin
advance over the existing Mks III and V.

Accordingly, some months later a developed version of the Condor II
with geared drive and high compression, was installed, and more airfram
modifications made. These included the greater wing area of the Vixe
III, enlarged rudder and elevator area, and the installation of an engine

G-EBEC as Vixen VI with Condor engine.

driven fuel pump with service tank in the centre section, as in the Venture and the Vixen III. The Vixen IV already had the small amount of top-wing dihedral included, and this was retained, but, in order to submit the still further modified aeroplane for consideration in the general-purpose class, it was called Mk VI.

In this form the Vixen reached 151 mph in operational trim, climbed at 1,000 ft/min up to 20,000 ft and reached 27,500 ft. It underwent official trials at Martlesham in connection with the 1927 general-purpose competition in company with a number of other aircraft, including the Vickers Valiant, a new design with an all-metal airframe and based on the Vixens III and V but powered by the Bristol Jupiter air-cooled radial engine. The official verdict on the Vixen VI was that it could not be considered because the Condor engine was too heavy and too powerful, an interesting commentary on prevailing Service thought at the time. Later on, the Mk VI was considered by the Chilean military mission as a possible replacement for their Mk Vs. The chief claim to fame of G-EBEC was made on 26 August, 1929, when, flown by Mutt Summers and Col Russell of the Irish Air Corps, it carried the first airborne Irish mail, from Galway to London.

VALIANT. A need for the development of all-metal airframes had been foreseen for some time by Vickers as a result of experience with their aircraft in parts of the world subject to extremes of temperature and humidity, conditions which had exposed the limitations of wooden construction. In addition, the lessons learned in this direction by Service units had been noted by the Air Ministry, who, in the later 1920s, issued an edict that, after an interim period, no more wooden aeroplanes would be considered for the award of official contracts.

Valiant biplane equipped with an experimental metal propeller, at Martlesham.

Following Vickers tradition the Vixen series had always embodied metal-frame fuselages, and the next problem was to evolve metal-frame wings and tail surfaces, thus reverting back to the early Vickers monoplanes with their R.E.P. metal-tube construction. In 1926 a Vixen Mk VII was drawn up with this object in view, no doubt to meet the reports already coming back from Chile regarding the wooden-winged Mk Vs.

This project was soon after renamed the Vivid, and at the same time, to meet a military requirement issued for a general-purpose aeroplane, a parallel design was undertaken and known as the Valiant, a name to be resurrected by Vickers in later years. This single-engined tractor biplane was an entrant for the 1927 Air Ministry competition for a general-purpose aeroplane. Held at Martlesham, this contest had been materialising for a long time, the object being to replace the D.H.9A, which had soldiered on since the first world war and had fully justified its general-purpose classification. One of the conditions of the replacement competition was that as many D.H.9A components as possible should be used in the new design, for large stocks, including wooden outer planes, were still held in stores.

A variety of new designs turned up at Martlesham in the spring of 1927, among them the Valiant, one of the few aspiring to an all-metal airframe,

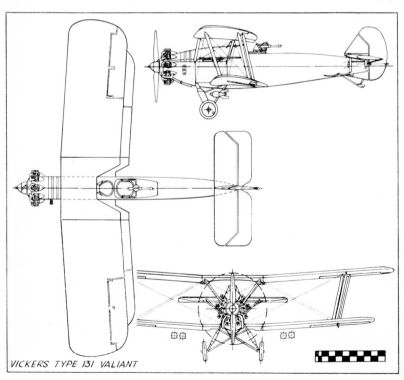

VICKERS TYPE 131 VALIANT

thus obeying that official dictum to the effect that no more wooden aircraft would be accepted for contract. In the event, the Westland Wapiti gained the D.H.9A replacement contract and, in fact, rendered yeoman service, although initially it had been a wooden aeroplane.

The Valiant, with its Bristol Jupiter engine, endeared itself to the official test pilots not so much on account of its generally good performance as for its docile handling characteristics. From a report of an on-the-spot Vickers' service engineer we learn that 'Mr. England* said she is a wizard', which seems to have been one of the earliest recorded uses of this metaphor so familiar later on.

The same report notes that some of the competing types were having trouble with their metal propellers and spinners, and Scholefield did test the Valiant with these, but they were discarded on account of flutter in the thin blades at high flight speeds and spinner trouble; the Valiant therefore went through the tests with the normal wooden propeller.

After the Martlesham tests the Valiant was sent round to certain RAF stations for Service evaluation, to Western Zoyland for bombing and gun firing, to Netheravon for handling and to Spittlegate for handling, speed and climb tests. The short-list of competing aeroplanes was afterwards assembled at Andover for final assessment by the Air Staff with the result already mentioned, the Westland Wapiti being selected as the winner, with the Valiant well up in the marking, particularly on account of its ease of maintenance.

On 11 January, 1928, the Valiant was granted a certificate of airworthiness under the civil registration G-EBVM and was fitted with a split-axle undercarriage in place of the continuous-axle type used for the competition. It was then shipped to Valparaiso for demonstration to the Chilean authorities, on offer as an all-metal replacement for the Vixen Vs in service in Chile. It was flown by Scholefield and put up impressive performances, afterwards being used by Chilean pilots for various missions of long duration, one of eight hours' flying with pilot and two passengers to find a lost Wibault Scout. Although the Valiant G-EBVM appears to have been retained by Chile, no further order materialised.

VIVID. While the Valiant was being constructed, the Vixen III G-EBIP was dismantled and reconstructed with similar metal wings; this all-metal airframe was designated Vixen VII, but shortly afterwards renamed Vivid. A suggestion had been received from Capt Broome, then in Chile looking after the assembly and flying of the Vixen Vs, that an all-metal Vixen might be acceptable there. This was eventually followed up by the despatch of the Valiant after it had completed its trials at Martlesham, as already related. Meanwhile, the Vivid was first flown as a landplane, converted to a floatplane for another official competition and reconverted to a landplane, in which form it had quite an adventurous career.

* A Martlesham test pilot.

The Vivid was registered **G-EBPY** in January 1927, was flown on 27 June by Scholefield and was fitted with the Lion VA engine, which had high compression (5·8:1). Flight trials necessitated the increase of the dihedral from three degrees to four and the fitting of smaller tail surfaces. The new wings, like those of the Valiant, gave complete satisfaction, and set a pattern for Vickers aircraft until the French Wibault construction came along, followed in due course by the Wallis experimental wings.

Vivid under construction at Weybridge in 1926, among various Virginias; its airframe was all-metal.

Briefly, the Vivid and Valiant wings were based on front and rear spars of drawn double T-section booms in light alloy with a laterally corrugated web, also in light alloy, which became known as the wandering web system. Profile ribs were of duralumin tubing, while the compression ribs were similar but with T-section drawn flanges, with tie-rod cross bracing. A strong cruciform structure replaced the tie-rod bracing in the centre section. The rival claims regarding balanced ailerons having been settled, Frise-type ailerons were adopted as on other contemporary Vickers aircraft.

The next step was to equip the Vivid as a floatplane with Short-designed floats on a Vickers oleo-pneumatic chassis, and it was tested in this form at Avro's Hamble seaplane base. In May 1928 it went to Felixstowe for the competition then proceeding for a naval floatplane. It had been re-engined with the 540 hp Napier Lion XI, and the performance proved to be a great improvement not only on the Vivid with the Lion VA but on the older Vixen III, too, when tested as a floatplane. The only other modification made was the fitting of a wooden propeller in place of the Fairey-Reed metal type.

After the Felixstowe trials the Vivid was remounted on a land under-carriage of the split-axle type, and on 6 September, 1928, Scholefield flew it to Bucharest in 10 hours' flying time with intermediate stops at Brussels, Nuremberg and Belgrade. At Bucharest it took part in a competition for a general-purpose aeroplane for the Rumanian air service, but although it put up at least as good a performance as other entries and better than most, no order resulted. The most searching questions were asked about design methods and strength factors, which seemed odd, as British pro-cedure followed by the Air Ministry and the RAE for certification of all aircraft was second to none, and the Vivid had satisfied them completely.

Vivid as floatplane being beached at Hamble.

Subsequently, the Vivid airframe was sold in 1931 to J. R. Chaplin, who, with Capt Neville Stack as pilot, proceeded to set up out-and-back records from the United Kingdom to Berlin, Copenhagen and Warsaw, and made an attempt on the England–Australia record. After this it was acquired by a syndicate including G. R. 'Speedy' Higgs and was destroyed in a fire at Chelmsford aerodrome while in for overhaul and engine change in September 1932.

Vivid in final form with modified aileron control system.

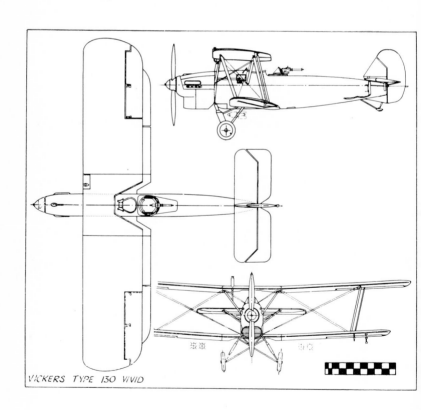

VICKERS TYPE 130 VIVID

Capt Neville Stack (on right), who with J. R. Chaplin set up several out-and-back records to European cities in the Vivid.

Vixen Family

	Vixen I Type 71	Valparaiso I Type 93	Vixen V Type 116	Valiant Type 131	Vivid Seaplane Type 146
Accommoda- *tion:*	Pilot and gun- ner	Pilot and gun- ner	Pilot and gun- ner	Pilot and gun- ner	Pilot and gun- ner
Engine:	One 450 hp Napier Lion I	One 468 hp Napier Lion IA	One 500 hp Napier Lion V	One 455 hp Bristol Jupiter VI	One 540 hp Napier Lion XI
Span:	40 ft upper 34 ft 6 in lower	40 ft upper 34 ft 6 in lower	44 ft upper 38 ft 6 in lower	45 ft 7 in	45 ft 1 in
Length:	29 ft	29 ft	29 ft	34 ft	36 ft 9 in
Height:	13 ft	11 ft 8 in	12 ft	13 ft	14 ft 1 in
Wing Area:	526 sq ft	526 sq ft	590 sq ft	590 sq ft	588 sq ft
Empty *Weight:*	3,098 lb	3,128 lb	3,320 lb	2,973 lb	4,379 lb
Gross Weight:	4,720 lb	4,720 lb	5,080 lb	5,550 lb	6,287 lb
Max Speed at *10,000 ft:*	137 mph	136 mph	133·7 mph at ground level	125 mph at ground level	124 mph
Climb to *10,000 ft:*	10¼ min	10¼ min	25 min/15,000 ft	14 min	16·3 min
Initial Climb:	—	—	1,250 ft/min	940 ft/min	960 ft/min
Ceiling:	19,400 ft (service)	19,500 ft (service)	20,000 ft (absolute)	21,800 ft (absolute)	Report F/34 Felixstowe
Range:	—	550 miles at 110 mph at 10,000 ft	764 miles	—	—
Armament:	Two Vickers guns and one Lewis gun	Two Vickers guns and one Lewis gun	—	—	—

193

Vendace I on first flight at Brooklands in March 1926, with Eric Fernihough's then new garage in the background; note raised seating-position of pilot.

Vendace and Vespa

In October 1924 a specification, 5A/24, was issued for a float seaplane for training purposes. To meet this, Vickers submitted a project design for a tractor biplane with folding wooden wings, wooden tail and a steel-tube fuselage. An ingenious chassis was evolved, sprung by the Vickers oleo-pneumatic system, which could be converted from floats to wheels or vice versa, either operation taking two flight engineers only 10 minutes. The pilot was seated close behind the pupil to facilitate in-flight communication. Power was the 275 hp Rolls-Royce Falcon III engine, and the petrol supply was carried entirely in two gravity tanks of streamline form mounted on the top centre section.

This proposal was accepted, and an order for one aeroplane placed in August 1925. A name of a fish, either freshwater or sea, was requested to comply with the Air Ministry's nomenclature system. Dr Chalmers Mitchell, a naturalist and already known from his participation in the Vimy Commercial flight to Africa in 1920, suggested Vendace (a small freshwater fish), which was accepted. The serial number N208 was allocated in March 1926, and by this time the Vendace, as a landplane, was already undergoing manufacturer's preliminary flight trials with light loads at Brooklands.

On 15 April the Vendace was flown to Coastal Area headquarters at Gosport equipped with arrester hook, as it then flew on to HMS *Furious* for type trials in deck operation. These trials appear to have been eminently

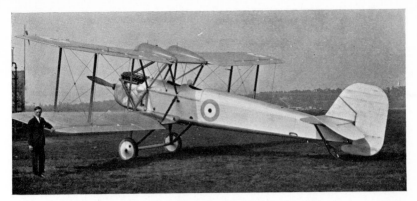

Vendace I before delivery to Martlesham for trials.

satisfactory, as the ensuing report commented on the suitability of the aeroplane for flying instruction, its positive and light controls, its ease of take-off and landing, and its full control down to 42 kt when the nose gently dipped. A top speed of 102 kt was recorded, and climb to 10,000 ft took 15 minutes. That 'its extremely good power of recovery would enable pilots of poor capability to make good deck landings' was another opinion expressed in the report.

A design feature of appeal was the provision for raising the seats for better visibility during take-off and landing; when airborne, the crew could lower them and fly comfortably in well-protected cockpits. Still on its landplane chassis, the Vendace went to Martlesham in August 1926, but returned to Weybridge the following month to have a larger radiator.

By the end of the year the Vendace had completed its official tests as a landplane, and on 25 March, 1927, it was transferred to nearby Felix-stowe, where the floats, as developed by Vickers with the aid of their water test-tank at St Albans, were fitted for its trials as a float seaplane, as

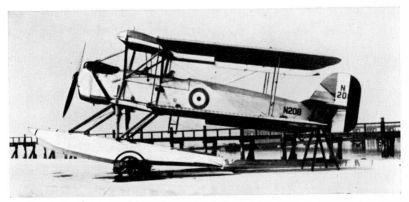

Vendace I in floatplane form, with serial N208, at the Marine Aircraft Experimental Establishment, Felixstowe.

195

originally ordered. The company pilots, Flt Lt Scholefield and Maj Payn, did the flying. For comparison, two different propellers were used. The only trouble experienced was from corrosion in the floats, which were of duralumin; modern protective treatments were then unknown, and adequate maintenance involved constant inspection, draining and painting. Stainless-steel exhaust pipes were fitted.

The Vendace I was kept at Felixstowe for experimental purposes, in company with the varied selection of floatplanes and flying-boats which made flying so interesting there in those days.

VENDACE II. Although no production order materialised from the satisfactory compliance with the official specification, Vickers were sufficiently confident in the design of the Vendace to build a second airframe as a private venture, powered with the 300 hp ADC Nimbus, an inline six-cylinder engine developed from the Siddeley Puma. This second Vendace was intended either as a passenger carrier or as a trainer, and it was registered G-EBPX on 3 January, 1927, and received its C of A soon after, as all the RAE stressing investigations and the official trials had already rubber stamped the type in N208. The new Vendace flew in November 1927, no urgency having been given to it, as Vickers were busy with other contracts, and it was used for demonstration.

As a result of a successful presentation in April 1928, the Aircraft Operating Company bought the Vendace II for aerial survey work and mapping in South America for the Brazilian and other governments. Various modifications were specified in the contract, and these consisted of provision to carry a photographer in the rear cockpit in place of the trainee pilot (the Vendace had always been equipped with dual control), and various photographic and survey sighting equipment. An Eyrie camera was mounted in the fuselage bay immediately behind the photographer, and the fairing under the fuselage was moved rearwards as far as the tail to facilitate oblique photography. A sliding panel covered the lens, and the rest of the rear fuselage underneath was covered-in with fabric attached to the longerons. Slots with remotely controlled shutters were

Vendace II with Nimbus engine before conversion for photographic survey.

Vendace II as a floatplane after conversion for air survey.

provided between the spars of the lower wing roots, and negative lens sights were fitted in the floor of both cockpits, the sides of which were enlarged to provide downward vision for the crew.

Vendace II had been purchased as a convertible landplane or floatplane, and it was flown from Brooklands to Hamble, where it was quickly converted to its latter form and tested by Maj Payn and Capt Holland on 22 May, 1928. The floats were found to be very clean above the hump speed, and everything else was in good trim. It was shipped to Rio de Janeiro and started some of the first aerial mapping in South America.

VENDACE III. On 1 October, 1928, the Bolivian Government placed an order for three Vendace trainers for the air arm it was trying to build up, as the dispute with neighbouring Paraguay over the almost sterile Gran Chaco region between the Pilcomayo and Paraguay rivers had reached the cold-war stage, with the hotter one to come. Later, Bolivia purchased Vespa army co-operation biplanes and 'Bolivian Scouts' (Type 143) from Vickers, but no doubt the Vendace III trainers were the start of life in the air for many Bolivian pilots who between 1932 and 1935 gallantly served their cause in decidedly unpleasant flying conditions.

The Vendace III was powered with the 300 hp Hispano Suiza, which gave an equivalent performance to that of the Air Ministry's Vendace I, N208. In Bolivia the Vendaces were test flown and demonstrated by Vickers' representative, Flg Off H. W. R. Banting, who, in his spare time, also did some flying instruction. He reported enthusiastically on the flying qualities of the Vendace, especially on its aerobatic capabilities, as apparently the Bolivians expected an aerobatic display on every conceivable occasion; the only manoeuvre he was unable to master at once was a spin from the inverted flight attitude, at which most of the Vickers aircraft, including the

197

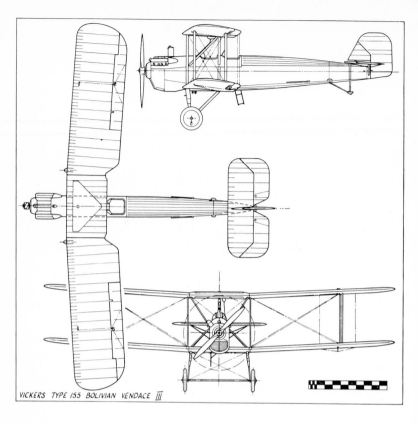

VICKERS TYPE 155 BOLIVIAN VENDACE III

Vespas and the Type 143 Scouts delivered subsequently, seemed particularly apt.

After putting in several hundred hours flying between them, the Vendace IIIs began to experience engine trouble, partly attributable to the extremely dusty conditions during Bolivia's dry season. Spares had to be shipped from France (the Hispano engines being French-built), which took time. Later, one had its wings neatly bisected by the Fairey-Reed metal propeller of a Vespa which taxied into it on the ground, with no damage to the propeller or its Jupiter engine, but with disastrous consequences for the Vendace. Enough has been recounted to indicate that conditions in Bolivia were hardly conducive to the efficient operation of an air force, but in the end it was Bolivian air power in the Gran Chaco war which prevented the Paraguayans from gaining an outright victory with their Pilas native ground forces.

VESPA I AND II. Sandwiched between all other developments at Weybridge in 1925, a new tractor biplane was produced with large lightly-loaded two-bay wings and a slim fuselage suspended between them. A

198

specification had been issued, 30/24, for an army co-operation aeroplane, in which capacity the wartime Bristol Fighter still functioned and indeed continued to serve for some time after. Vickers submitted this Vespa I, as it was named, with a Bristol Jupiter IV engine, as a private venture for consideration in this class, and as such it was given the civil registration G-EBLD.

The Vespa was flown at Brooklands in September 1925 by Scholefield, and he delivered it to Martlesham in the following February. He then reported aileron kick, which was cured by mass balancing. The certificate of airworthiness issued on 8 February precluded aerobatics, as was

Vespa I with wooden wing structure and interplane struts, and rudder extension below sternpost.

customary for civil aircraft unless specially licensed for such manoeuvres, which, incidentally, appear then to have been called acrobatics. As the Vespa obviously was required to depart from a straight course during official testing as a military aeroplane, a compromise wording was agreed upon in the C of A. This incident appears to suggest that civil aircraft were required officially to be stronger than military types if indulging in abrupt changes of attitude.

In spite of the fact that the Vespa was a private-venture aeroplane with a civil registration, it had been entered for a military competition, and consequently was on the secret list at that time. A. H. R. Fedden (later Sir Roy Fedden) had to be reminded of this when he requested a photograph of what his secretary described as the 'Vesper'. He was chief engineer of the engine division of the Bristol Aeroplane Company and was concerned because the in-flight performance of the Jupiter IV appeared to be some 20 hp down on test-bed rating. This led to the substitution of a Jupiter VI after the Vespa had returned to Weybridge from Martlesham.

There may be some interest in detailing the duties demanded at the time from an army co-operation aeroplane. They included various classes of reconnaissance—close, medium, photographic, artillery and night—with attack on ground targets thrown in for good measure. Each duty required different loadings, with variations in the equipment carried and in the fuel and oil capacity, and therefore the official trials required the aeroplane to be flown in each of these categories and tended to become exhaustive and lengthy. The trials were conducted in two parts, 'Type', usually made at Martlesham and occasionally at Farnborough, and 'Service', for which the entrant was flown and examined at one or more RAF Stations.

On a test flight to prepare the Vespa for exhibition in the new-aircraft park at the Royal Air Force Display on 24 June, 1926, Scholefield unfortunately experienced engine trouble, but was able to crash-land the aeroplane without sustaining a complete write-off, no doubt assisted by its gentle approach and slow-landing characteristics. Even more disappointing was the notice received in the same week that Vickers' tender for two aircraft of the type, made the previous November, had been declined.

In spite of these setbacks, opportunity was taken to design and fit a new set of wings of metal construction with fabric covering and to make other small modifications to meet Martlesham criticisms. The Vespa, as rebuilt and designated Mk II, then proceeded for Service trials at Old Sarum and Odiham, during which it completed 64 hours and made 111 landings. Maj F. C. Atkinson, Vickers' chief inspector, examined the new metal wings after the trials and made a very favourable report on their condition and also reported that copal varnish appeared to be a good protection against corrosion in the light-alloy members.

The result of fitting the Jupiter VI engine and metal wings was a small but significant all-round improvement in performance, including an increase of ceiling by 1,400 ft to 21,700 ft. Without doubt the high-lift properties of the Vespa and a high ceiling, together with its STOL characteristics, impressed the Bolivian military mission visiting England, who placed an order for six Vespa IIIs in 1928.

In this form and specially rigged as Vespa II, it participated in the 1927 King's Cup Air Race. Flown by Maj Payn, it was averaging 115·5 mph on the 'round' course when it had to retire through damage in flight caused by a loose Hucks starter claw on the propeller boss.

VESPA III. A detailed report on the improvements made to the Mk III production Vespas for Bolivia contained much of interest, perhaps the most significant being the reduction in loaded weight achieved by the lighter and stiffer metal wings, of similar structural design to those of the Vivid and Valiant. For some time at Vickers, research and development had been in progress on metal construction in association with the structural test departments of the RAE. The three aircraft, Vespa, Vivid and Valiant, represented the first practical applications to complete aeroplanes evolved by Vickers since the early monoplanes.

The performance of the Vespa III was better in maximum speed by 5 mph, rate of climb by 200 ft/min at 10,000 ft, and service ceiling by 2,200 ft, that is, compared with the Vespa I. The cockpits had been improved externally and internally to enhance crew comfort, which was also the reason why an engine-exhaust collector-ring replaced the individual stubs previously fitted. The additional weight of this ring together with that of the heavier engine, 134 lb in all, made possible the moving forward of the c.g. to improve fore-and-aft stability, which was one of the faults discovered in the Vespa I at Martlesham. This rearrangement of weights was eased by 'the difference of 20 lb lighter weight of the new metal tail unit than that of the original wooden unit', to quote the report.

In addition, the undercarriage chassis was increased in height by six inches to give the lower wings greater ground clearance, this also being improved by modifying the contour of the rudder by removing the portion on the Vespa I which protruded below the stern post. The range of tail

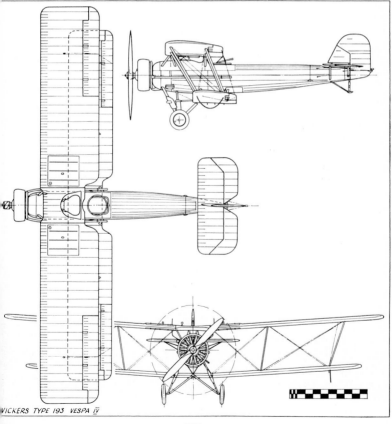

VICKERS TYPE 193 VESPA IV

201

Vespa IV at Brooklands for Irish Air Corps, with metal wings and struts and with rudder extension deleted.

adjustment for trim was insufficient during the type trials of the Mk I, an this also had received attention. A resubmission of the Vespa in this form to the Air Ministry elicited the reply that an additional type of army co operation machine was shelved pending the issue of a new specification when the whole question was to be considered afresh.

The high-flying capability of the type was amply demonstrated by th production Vespa IIIs in Bolivia, with its mountainous terrain. On on occasion Flg Off Banting and a passenger flew from Alto La Paz, the cen tral airfield located at an altitude of 13,000 ft, to Illimani at 24,200 ft, an to Illampu Lake at 25,000 ft, with an unsupercharged Jupiter VI engin and without oxygen. Later, Banting broke the South American heigh record by reaching 27,000 ft. The Bolivian Vespas appear to have bee used largely for training as operational conversion aircraft, following u the *ab initio* Vendaces, but in the Gran Chaco war, which was fought at lo altitude, only one or two are recorded as having been in action. The

Vespa Vs in service with Irish Air Corps at Baldonnel. (*Flight photo.*)

202

was the so-called Vespa Flight, which consisted of a bombed-up Vespa flying with two Vickers 143 Scouts as fighter escort.

VESPA IV AND V. In 1929 the Irish Free State ordered four Vespas fitted with Armstrong Siddeley Jaguar VIC geared radial engines, followed a year later by an order for a further four. The first batch was labelled Mk IV and the second Mk V, as various refinements and improvements were made as dictated by the operation of the earlier variant. Externally the Mk IV was distinguished from the Mk V by the Townend ring around the Jaguar engine. These Irish Vespas rendered good service and were a familiar sight in County Dublin in the middle 1930s, flying from the base of the Army Air Corps at Baldonnel, 10 miles due west of Dublin.

Flg Off H. W. R. Banting with the Vespa VI *en route* for demonstration to Chinese authorities in 1931.

VESPA VI. For an undisclosed reason the rebuilt Vespa II with Mk III improvements received a new registration, G-ABIL, in January 1931, as it was needed for demonstration in China to the Central Government. It was re-engined with a supercharged Jupiter VIIF, which promised a considerable increase in performance. As the Type 210 it also received a new mark number, becoming the Vespa VI. It embodied many components from the Mk IV, which was the designation of the first batch of Vespas supplied to the Irish Army Air Corps, and was fitted with a Fairey-Reed metal propeller. Tested at Brooklands in February 1931, the Vespa VI had a true air speed of 148·5 mph at 10,000 ft, at which height its rate of climb was 1,050 ft/min, the service ceiling was 26,700 ft and the landing speed 49 mph.

The Vespa VI was demonstrated in China before various authorities, including various generals of the Central Government, who, at that period,

Vespa VI with Townend drag-reducing engine ring.

Vespa VII for height record with large-diameter propeller, but without Townend ring.

Vespa VII during height record flown by Capt Cyril Uwins. (*Flight photo*.)

Vespa VII as RAE test aeroplane with variable-pitch propeller.

were conducting an internal struggle with the rival Cantonese Government. Flg Off Banting, who, with the Vickers engineer, C. B. Holmes, had taken charge of the Chinese presentation after returning from Bolivia, had a dreadful time contending with the Shanghai Customs, the heavy rains and flooding at Hungao aerodrome, near Shanghai, and in finding someone with enough authority to permit him to fly the Vespa 200 miles to Nanking for demonstration before the military hierarchy. After many abortive attempts he was finally successful, flying to Nanking and back over 'impossible' terrain—impossible, that is, for a forced landing. The Chinese were more interested in aircraft with a turn of speed with which to frighten the bandits rather than effective air action, and so the enterprise was terminated, somewhat abruptly, as Banting had meanwhile contracted paratyphoid.

In the end, the original basic Vespa, much modified as the Vespa VII, did achieve fame, for, fitted with a Bristol Pegasus 'S' supercharged engine, it captured the World's Height Record on 16 September, 1932, flown by Cyril Uwins, then chief test pilot of the Bristol Aeroplane Company. The altitude reached was 43,976 ft, exceeding the previous record held by a US

The Vespa VII as converted for the height record attempt with Bristol Pegasus S.3 engine, photographed at Filton airfield. (*Photo Bristol Aeroplane Co.*)

Navy pilot by over 800 ft. The effort was a supreme example in the technical sense of the closest collaboration between R. K. Pierson, the aeroplane designer, A. H. R. Fedden, the engine designer, Capt F. S. Barnwell, designer of Bristol aeroplanes, who in his inimitable, methodical way worked out the more abstruse calculations, such as position errors, connected with the flight, and, of course, the pilot, Cyril Uwins. The Vespa had been selected for this effort, as it was the only aeroplane available at that time with the required wing area and high-lift capability at height. It was finally bought by the Air Ministry, given the serial K3588 and used by the RAE for high-altitude research with supercharged engines and variable-pitch propellers.

Vendace

	Mk I—Landplane Type 120	Mk I—Seaplane Type 120	Mk III Type 155
Accommodation:	Pilot and pupil	Pilot and pupil	Pilot and pupil
Engine:	One 270 hp Rolls-Royce Falcon III	One 270 hp Rolls-Royce Falcon III	One 300 hp Hispano Suiza 8F
Span:	44 ft 7 in	44 ft 7 in	44 ft 7 in
Length:	32 ft 3 in	35 ft 2 in	33 ft 3 in
Height:	12 ft 8 in	13 ft 11½ in	12 ft 9 in
Wing Area:	533 sq ft	525 sq ft	533 sq ft
Empty Weight:	2,585 lb	2,960 lb	2,604 lb
Gross Weight:	3,475 lb	3,850 lb	3,270 lb
Max Speed:	117 mph	111 mph	119 mph at 13,000 ft
Initial Climb:	680 ft/min	476 ft/min	720 ft/min
Ceiling:	20,000 ft (absolute)	9,470 ft (service)	25,800 ft (absolute)
Climb:	To 5,000 ft in 5 min	To 5,000 ft in 6¼ min	To 13,000 ft in 16 min

Vespa

	Mk II Type 119	Mk V Type 208	Mk VI Type 210
Accommodation:	Pilot and observer	Pilot and observer	Pilot and observer
Engine:	One 455 hp Bristol Jupiter VI	One 490 hp Armstrong Siddeley Jaguar VIC	One 530 hp Bristol Jupiter VIIF
Span:	50 ft	50 ft	50 ft
Length:	31 ft 3 in	33 ft	32 ft 6 in
Height:	10 ft 3 in	10 ft 6 in	10 ft 6 in
Wing Area:	561 sq ft	576 sq ft	576 sq ft
Empty Weight:	2,468 lb	2,882 lb	2,917 lb
Gross Weight:	3,925 lb	4,370 lb	4,370 lb
Max Speed:	129 mph at 10,000 ft	139 mph at 10,000 ft	148·5 mph at 10,000 ft
Climb to:	13,120 ft in 15 min	15,000 ft in 16 min	15,000 ft in 16 min
Ceiling:	21,700 ft (service)	26,000 ft (absolute)	26,700 ft (service)
Range:	—	580 miles at 116 mph at 15,000 ft	—

The Wibault Family

In a dossier of information prepared for the National Advisory Committee for Aeronautics and the military and naval authorities in the United States in 1926, Vickers made the following claims regarding metal construction:

'From the earliest Vickers designs, the ultimate employment of all-metal construction has been in view, and all-metal components have been incorporated in several types. Thus, the early Gunbus had a metallic nacelle while the later Vimy had the front fuselage entirely composed of steel tubing. In general, the policy has been to incorporate metal where possible and so gradually to work towards the establishment of completely metallised aircraft.

French Wibault 7.C1 from which Vickers Wibault Scout was developed.

'When compared with wooden or wood and metal constructions, the all-metal machine can claim the following advantages—longer life, quicker production, reduced waste of material, improved durability in extremes of climate, requires no expensive housing. The adoption of metal construction should not bring with it any intrinsic defects such as—added difficulties of inspection and repair, increased weight, complication of structure, prohibitive cost.

'The Vickers-Wibault patents and system of construction have been developed with due regard to these points and are considered to surmount the difficulties that exist so far as inspection and repair of metal aircraft are concerned. Maintenance of both civil and military types should be easy and requirements of field equipment kept down to a minimum.'

The statement goes on to say that the system could be adapted to all types of aeroplane, large or small, and that the metal employed throughout was the patented light alloy known as duralumin, which had the strength and hardness of mild steel.

This structural design philosophy undoubtedly reflected the experience gained the hard way with Vickers wooden or part-wooden aircraft in the Middle East and South America.

The Vickers-Wibault system of construction referred to was based on the patents of Michel Wibault, founder of the French aircraft company of Avions Michel Wibault of Billancourt, Seine, whence the earlier R.E.P. patents had emanated. Wibault first became associated with Vickers as a consulting engineer in 1922 and was one of the pioneers of metal construction, his ideas closely following those of the German Junkers and Dornier concerns.

In broad terms, the Wibault structure consisted of fabricated light-alloy components of simple shapes and sections. It avoided costly machining operations and the intricate rolled sections in sheet steel that were becoming fashionable for class one stressed members such as wing spars. The semi-cantilever wing of deep high-lift section (adapted from Eiffel 400) had two box spars with plain booms and plate webs with closely pitched plate ribs, covered with a corrugated light-alloy skin only four-tenths of a millimetre thick. The skin panels were laid chordwise over the ribs, and the deeper corrugations and joints were secured by through rivets so that both heads were visible externally and clenched with a levered hand-riveting tool. Panels could be easily renewed at any time, which justified the claims made for facility of maintenance and inspection.

The fuselage was of box form with L-section longerons and struts with a triangulated system of T-section diagonal members to take shear and torsional loads, all joined by gusset plates riveted to the members. To attach the thin corrugated skin, 'bowler hat' stringers were riveted to the fuselage frame, and these mated internally with the corrugations, and so the skin was secured externally by through rivets in the same manner as the wing panels.

This system provided an all-metal structure to achieve durability and ease of maintenance as claimed in the Vickers dossier, but was not truly stressed-skin. According to J. Bewsher, one of Vickers' senior designers, who afterwards exploited the Wibault system in part in the Jockey and Venom fighters, the very thin skin did lend some measure of torsional rigidity and take a small degree of stress in certain conditions, but that was not the main purpose of the structural theory, which was as stated.

In the Vickers-Wibault wing the heavier chordwise corrugations were the riveted joints, and the lesser chordwise lines the panel stiffeners. The drag loss from skin friction was of small account at the flight speeds then prevailing. The Wibault all-metal system may be regarded as an interesting milestone on the road to the sophisticated light-alloy construction of today.

Vickers Type 121 Wibault Scout under construction at Weybridge.

The Wibault family of Vickers aircraft consisted of the Scout Type, the Vireo single-seat fighter and the Viastra high-wing civil transport, while the Vellore and Vellox transports which followed owed some constructional features to the Wibault influence. In addition, a French-built military two-seat high-wing Wibault monoplane, closely resembling the Scout but larger, was supplied to Air Ministry contract through Vickers in 1928 under the British serial number J9029. Assembled at Weybridge, its 500 hp Hispano Suiza engine was replaced by the Napier Lion XI, and it was tested at Martlesham with varying results, but in particular was dogged by engine-cooling troubles. The French designation was Type 12.C2, but the British equivalent was Vickers-Wibault Type 122—not to be confused with Vickers own type numbers.

WIBAULT SCOUT. In 1925 Vickers placed an order with Avions Michel Wibault for a demonstration model of their single-seat 7.C1 high-wing parasol monoplane to be fitted with a British-built Bristol Jupiter engine, a Vickers oleo-pneumatic undercarriage made at Weybridge, and British instruments and equipment. A speed of 134 mph was promised with a high-compression engine, as was a ceiling of 32,000 ft. No doubt it was this latter characteristic, as well as the claims made for the all-metal construction, that attracted the interest of the Chilean authorities which later materialised into a substantial order.

The 7.C1 was flown from Villacoublay to Weybridge via Croydon early in February 1926 by the Wibault pilot Doucy, after some difficulty in tuning the British Jupiter engine because of a misfitting of the engine controls and the varying composition of the petrol/benzol mixture in France.

The aeroplane bore the French registration F-AHFH, as some objection was made to the issue of a British registration because of the completely

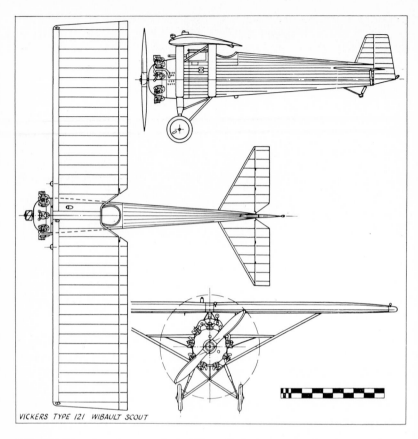

VICKERS TYPE 121 WIBAULT SCOUT

different formulae then employed for calculating strength values in France and England, and was used for demonstration to Col Grove and Maj Aracena of the Chilean Air Mission. Later the original wing struts were replaced by others giving 67 per cent better strength factors.

Eventually, an order was received from Chile for 26 Vickers-Wibault Scouts, and the 7.C1 was returned to Avions Wibault for further demonstrations, one of which was in a Spanish military competition. Over a year later an amusing exchange of correspondence took place between Vickers and the French company regarding the substituted wing struts. For some obscure reason the original French struts had been put back on the 7.C1, and the following is an extract taken from Avions Wibault's letter on the subject:

'We are very sad to be compelled to inform you that the struts presently fitted are the good old French type, as existing before stiffening of C of A requirements. We believe a possible explanation of this somewhat strange fact may be as follows. You have perchance prepared a set of heavier struts for 7.C1, with a perfectly true intention of putting same into place.

Afterwards, for some reason or other, the operation has not been carried off and the poor machine was sent back to us with the old struts, the big new ones remaining sadly neglected in some odd shadowy corner of some obscure shed. . . . If you are lucky enough to discover afresh the pukka struts intended for the machine and care to send them along to us we should be delighted in putting same into place with the utmost possible precision.'

The first Wibault Scout was flown by Scholefield at the end of June 1926. It was also the first time he has taken a parachute with him on such an occasion, and he needed it, for, in attempting to test the spin recovery from inverted flight conditions, the aeroplane slipped into five uncontrollable spins. Tiny Scholefield had to bale out at a height of between 2,000 and 1,500 ft. The aeroplane crashed in the middle of the Vickers' sports ground at Byfleet, which has led to the legend of the old lady who, as a nearby witness of the accident, demanded to know when the next exciting

Wibault Scout for Chile, showing braced parasol configuration.

exhibition was due to take place. Tiny, for all his 15 stone or more, landed quite gently in a back garden, and strolled quietly back to the aerodrome at Brooklands with his parachute slung over his shoulder, with all the factory and neighbourhood out looking for him.

The upshot of the inevitable investigations was that with the parasol configuration and high-lift section, the c.g. position was found to be critical in the inverted flight condition, the tailplane incidence of five degrees positive as set for the initial test flight being excessive. No further trouble was in fact encountered from this cause. Later, in Chile, one Vickers-Wibault lost its wing in the air, apparently caused by some faulty ground engineering. In those days there was no after-sales service as understood today; customers were left to carry on with new types as soon as the initial batch of a few aircraft had been erected by one of the manufacturer's engineers, aided usually by the test pilot and some indigenous semi-skilled assistants.

In the case of the Wibault Scout, all-metal construction was a novelty in

211

South America, although some Junkers aircraft were beginning to appear there. In consequence, the Vickers engineer, J. M. Wyatt, whose main experience was in engine tuning, and Capt Val Baker, the pilot (afterwards of Martin-Baker Aircraft), had no end of a time assembling the unfamiliar components, particularly as a number of ailerons had been damaged in the shipping of the aircraft in packing cases from England to Valparaiso.

In service, the Wibaults appear to have given satisfaction, although, according to contemporary reports, it is doubtful whether all the 26 were erected and flown. Against the undoubted advantage of the all-metal construction, with the corollary of little or no rigging as required in wire-braced biplanes of the period, must be set the unfamiliarity of the repair scheme for the Wibault system. From all accounts there was no attempt at service training for the ground engineers, and information advanced by way of technical publications such as workshop manuals hardly existed.

However, the Vickers-Wibault Scouts, with the Vickers Vixen Vs already in service, must have given Chile quite a formidable air force, judged by South American standards then, while its deterrent effect, joined with that of the equally formidable Chilean Navy, kept that country out of the numerous international squabbles in the southern hemisphere of the New World.

VIREO. On 15 December, 1925, Vickers submitted a tender for the supply of one single-seat fighter ship-plane, to specification 17/25. From the Air Ministry's point of view, this was a dual-purpose experiment to test the efficiency of all-metal construction as exemplified in the Vickers-Wibault system and to explore the operational value of low-powered fighters for carrier-borne use at sea. The engine selected was the supercharged Armstrong Siddeley Lynx IV of 230 hp. The name of a land bird, exclud-

Vireo light fighter in flight, displaying corrugated skin of Wibault concept.

212

Vireo in floatplane form, showing Lynx engine and exhaust collector.

ing birds of prey, was requested, and Vireo was accepted as being the Latin equivalent to greenfinch, the contract for one aircraft meanwhile having been placed.

The Vireo was intended to be used either on a wheeled undercarriage suitable for catapulting at sea or on a float chassis capable of being adapted for the same purpose; in practice it was fitted with each at different times. Apart from its structure, which closely followed that of the Chilean Wibault Scout except that the Vireo was a low-wing monoplane, the fighter was designed to incorporate wing-mounted machine-guns firing outside the propeller disc. There was one in each wing, an arrangement made possible by the deep wing section, and they were of Vickers Auto RC type, then recently developed and known officially as the E type. The cartridge chamber was of the undermounted revolver pattern and was controlled remotely through a linkage system. This appears to have been an early attempt to engineer a satisfactory free-firing weapon arrangement to avoid the limitations imposed by synchronising gear by which the gun fired through the propeller disc. Hitherto, such attempts had been handicapped by the impossibility of burying a gun in existing thin-section wings, such as Raf 15.

Flight tests of the Vireo early in March 1928 disclosed a lower engine power than had been expected, and also that the aeroplane had a better performance with a wooden than with a metal propeller. The reason so much time had elapsed before the first flight was because, since the design was an experimental one, full opportunity had been taken at the RAE to conduct various structural and aerodynamic tests on wings and other parts of the structure, to modify certain items according to the findings and to meet the requirements of the Air Ministry technical officers.

Before delivery of an improved Lynx, the Vireo was sent to Martlesham in April 1928 for land tests, with marine-based tests to follow at Felixstowe.

It was allocated the serial number N211, with service markings painted on the natural metal finish. During the land tests small mishaps occurred, the windscreen shattered in flight, an exhaust branch broke and the rear fuselage longerons and stern post were buckled by several heavy landings during take-off and landing trials. According to the Martlesham report, the Vireo had a tendency to drop suddenly just before touching down.* In

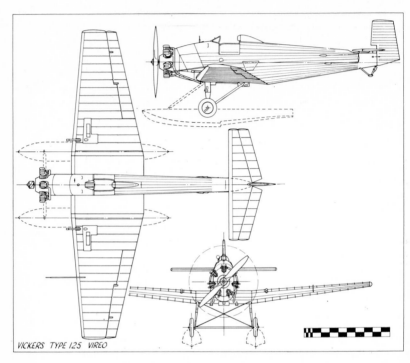

VICKERS TYPE 125 VIREO

the following July the overhauled aeroplane was flown to Gosport preparatory to deck landing on the aircraft carrier HMS *Furious* on July 12 for trials.

As a result of the thorough testing of the Vireo fitted with a wheel undercarriage, the seaplane trials were not proceeded with because, for the purposes of the experimental contract, sufficient information on the lowpowered but rapidly produced small fighter was obtained, as the Vireo proved to be no faster than the contemporary Fairey IIIF, then in service as a multi-purpose ship- or shore-based type. The all-metal structural

* In an article entitled 'Hindsight is always One Hundred Percent' published in the Centenary *Journal of the Royal Aeronautical Society* (January 1966), Beverley Shenstone remarks, 'The Vireo was wrong because of the high drag of the corrugated wing, fuselage and tail, the uncowled engine, the fixed undercarriage and perhaps worst of all, the serious root interference of the highly cambered wing which resulted in unpleasant stalling characteristics.'

Viastra I with three Lynx engines, on Woolston slipway, Southampton.

philosophy had also been probed sufficiently by Vickers to encourage the further development of the system in the subsequent Jockey and Venom fighters.

VIASTRAS. In April 1928 Vickers evaluated a specification for a 10-passenger commercial monoplane powered by one Bristol Jupiter IX engine or three Armstrong Siddeley Lynx IVs. In a market survey accompanying his design study, the opinion was expressed that the best possibilities for such a type would be in regions where surface transport had not reached the efficiency achieved in Europe, and where air transport would be the quickest and most economic means of providing new communications. The provision of subsidies was also examined, and again it was concluded that the right type of aeroplane with a modest subsidy would have appeal in dominion, colonial and other under-developed territories, rather than to the few established European airlines.

Viastra I being towed on lighter to Hamble for test flying.

Two configurations were considered: a low-wing monoplane with two wing-mounted engines and a third mounted in the nose, and a high-wing monoplane with two cabane-mounted engines below the wing and a nose-mounted engine. The first layout followed closely a type already evolved by Wibault, with a special high-lift wing section. Eventually the high- (or shoulder-) wing layout was adopted, and the study then concerned a choice between Wibault's tapered wing with its special W116 section and a rectangular wing of Raf 34 section. After extensive wind-tunnel tests with both aerofoils, at Weybridge, St Cyr and Farnborough, the rectangular Raf 34 wing was chosen. The new Type 160 Viastra was powered by three

Front end of Viastra I in Supermarine Works, Woolston, with tail of Southampton flying-boat in background; the forward luggage compartment is noteworthy.

270 hp Armstrong Siddeley Lynx Major engines, and its all-metal structure was based partly on Vickers' own developments, such as the wandering web spar, with various Wibault adaptations, notably the fuselage construction and the external metal skinning, including the wing. This produced an aeroplane capable of weathering in the open and requiring little maintenance beyond routine servicing. The Viastra was representative of the class of aeroplane then emerging, such as the Fokkers and Junkers, which since have been regarded as a sort of half-way stage to the streamlined cantilever all-metal piston-engined monoplanes which reached their peak in the second world war.

Originally it was intended to build the Viastra I at Vickers' Crayford works; in fact, the fuselage was built there, but the work was transferred to the Supermarine Aviation works at Woolston, Southampton, which had

Cabin structure of Viastra in corrugated light alloy.

just been acquired by Vickers. Although Supermarines were already familiar with metal construction in their own designs, notably hulls for the Southampton II flying-boats, the construction of the Viastra was in the charge of Trevor Westbrook from Weybridge, where production capacity was fully occupied with more pressing commitments, notably for military aircraft.

On completion at Woolston, the Viastra I was towed down the Itchen river and round to Hamble aerodrome on a lighter of similar design to that used for towing the Schneider racing seaplanes, a practical method of transport to be expected of the marine-minded Supermarine organisation, but one which appears to have occasioned some disrespectful comment from landlubbers. Bearing the registration G-AAUB, the Viastra I was then flown at Hamble by Mutt Summers on 1 October, 1930.

Viastra II for Australia taking off for trials.

VIASTRA II. Interest in the Viastra design was created in Australia by Sir Keith Smith, who at that time was managing Vickers' aviation affairs there. Qantas and West Australian Airways were operating internal services, and the latter was looking for suitable replacements for its three-engined D.H.66 Hercules biplanes, and particularly for an all-metal British type capable of satisfying the Australian Government's requirements in respect of the subsidy for the Perth–Adelaide postal and goods service.

As regards passengers, Vickers were able to offer a 12-seat aeroplane with a total payload of nearly 3,000 lb, and a range of 300 miles at a cruising speed of 130 mph. These figures were based on the assumption that the three-engined Viastra I would be required, but after much deliberation by Maj Norman Brearley (later Sir Norman), the managing director of West Australian Airways, and by the Controller of Civil Aviation of the Australian Government, it was decided to order two Viastra II aircraft, each powered with two geared Bristol Jupiter XIF engines, and one Viastra with a single Jupiter XIF, later to be given the series number VI.

In operation on the Perth–Adelaide service the first Viastra II, registered VH-UOO, created a good impression, and proved perfectly airworthy in

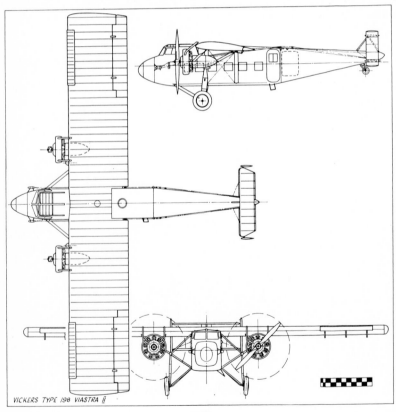

VICKERS TYPE 198 VIASTRA II

Viastra II in service on the Perth–Adelaide route of West Australian Airways.

the violent storms which occasionally blew up on the route and in intense heat conditions over the Nullarbor Plain. The Jupiter XIF geared engines unfortunately did not match up to the advanced conception of the joint effort and proved to be under-developed for operation under the desert conditions. Several in-flight failures occurred, resulting in forced landings, fortunately with no airframe damage of any consequence. Direct-drive Jupiter VIs from the D.H. Hercules were substituted for several flights, and occasionally a Viastra took-off with a geared Jupiter XIF on one side and a direct-drive Jupiter VI on the other. Performance was little affected save that of economic cruising consumption, but the pilots deserve full marks for keeping such an asymmetrically powered aeroplane on course, or perhaps for their skill in manually matching the engine revolutions to that end.

At no time during the operation of the Viastra II in West Australian's service was it possible to fly the aeroplane on one engine under full-load conditions without losing height, and, in response to repeated requests from Maj Brearley, the three-engined configuration was explored later with G-AAUB re-engined with the Jupiter VIFM. This experiment

Viastra VI with one Jupiter engine, built to a requirement of
West Australian Airways but not delivered.

219

confirmed previous calculations that maintaining height on two engines was achieved only at the expense of a certain loss of payload.

Various modifications made to the second Viastra II, VH-UOM, without altering any major components, were improvements such as increasing the gauge of the wing skin panels subjected to buffeting from the slipstream, and improving the tracking of the tailwheel by elastic-cord dampers. Triplex safety-glass windows replaced the Celastoid panels which had quickly proved unsatisfactory in Australia. The two Viastras were popular vehicles with the public at a fare of £A12 between the two capitals, Perth and Adelaide, the interminable railway journey costing £A11 18s. 9d. Passenger amenities such as toilet and wash basin, and with smoking permitted in the cabin, were innovations in those times in Australia.

G-AAUB re-engined with Jaguar VIcs as Viastra III.

VH-UOM was written off in a staging-post landing crash in Western Australia on 11 October, 1933, and VH-UOO was finally retired in 1936 when West Australian Airways was merged into Australian National Airways. The other order for the single-engined Viastra VI had been cancelled some time before this merger, presumably because of the difficulties with higher-duty engines in the Viastra IIs.

VIASTRA III AND VIII. A decision was made in October 1930 to convert the Viastra I with three Lynx engines to a similar layout to the Mk IIs, but with two Armstrong Siddeley Jaguar VIc engines, this conversion being given the new Type number 199 and series number III. The main alterations were those made in the structure and configuration of the tail surfaces. The central fin and auxiliary rudder were replaced by the tubular structure as used in the IIs, and the main rudders were increased slightly in chord to add to their area. Wire bracing was also introduced in the wing cellule; an oddity, for this was the only Viastra ever to use wire bracing of any sort.

In this form, the Viastra III, G-AAUB, was demonstrated at Croydon airport on 25 October to Dominion and Colonial Ministers, in company

Viastra VIII was G-AAUB reverting to the three-engined layout but with Jupiters and Townend rings on the outer engines only.

with the Vickers Vellore freighter G-AASW. In the following May a further change was made, and G-AAUB reverted to the three-engined layout but with Bristol Jupiter VIFM engines, under the new series number VIII. This exercise was inspired undoubtedly by Maj Brearley's repeated requests for a three-engined Viastra able to maintain height with one engine out, which he could not get with the Viastra IIs.

VIASTRA X. At the end of 1932 Sir Robert McLean, then Chairman of Vickers (Aviation) Ltd, intimated that a special twin-engined Viastra was to be built at Southampton, with certain parts made at Weybridge. This was given the type number 259, and ultimately it was disclosed that the modified Viastra was to be for the use of the then Prince of Wales on official flights. A fuselage for a fourth Viastra had, in fact, been built, and this was appropriated for the new series X.

Various refinements were specified and included proper soundproofing—sandbags riveted to the frame had been tried on earlier models—electrical heating in the cabin, safety-glass windows and full instrumentation with blind-flying panel and autopilot. Parachutes were to be provided for crew and passengers, and the wheels were to be enclosed in spats. The cabin interior was to be furnished to what today would be called executive or VIP standards. The engines decided upon were Bristol Pegasus IIL3 type.

The Viastra X was registered G-ACCC on 19 December, 1932, in the name of Flt Lt E. H. Fielden, A.F.C., the Prince of Wales' pilot and later Captain of the King's Flight. It was flown by Mutt Summers at Hamble aerodrome in April 1933 and was tested at Martlesham in May. The only defect of any consequence reported was pulsation in the cabin walls at low noise frequencies, thought to be caused by the proximity of the slipstream. The maximum speed recorded was 144·5 mph at operating height, which was 2,000 ft. The first flight and initial testing was done with Pegasus IM3s. In January 1934 the later IIL3s were temporarily installed.

This special Viastra was not used much as a Royal Barge, and last appeared in that guise at the RAF Display at Hendon in June 1934. The following year it was converted by the Air Ministry for the installation

221

HRH Prince of Wales (later Duke of Windsor) alighting from his Viastra X for an official visit to the RAF Display at Hendon in 1934.

and flight testing of experimental radio, for which it was quite suitable since it had a cabin in which could be carried not only bulky sets and electrical ancillaries but also their operators, seated in comparative comfort. The modifications were all undertaken by Imperial Airways at Croydon, where this last Viastra was dismantled in 1937.

One of the suggestions made by Maj Brearley of West Australian Airways when operating the Viastra IIs was that a lighter wing should be evolved. B. N. Wallis had at that time just joined the Weybridge works as structures designer, from Vickers' airship work, and one of his first tasks was to design a special wing structure for the Viastra. This was duly built and tested for mechanical strength at the RAE Farnborough, but no record exists that it was ever test flown. Arising out of this and other structural research and development, such as that for the M.1/30 torpedo-carrier, he eventually evolved his famous geodetic system for fixed-wing aeroplanes.

The Wibault family of Vickers aircraft may be regarded as an interesting essay in all-metal construction and as an off-shoot of some significance in the family tree, but hardly one of its stronger branches.

Wibault Scout—Type 121—One 455 hp Bristol Jupiter VI. Span 36 ft 1 in; length 23 ft 8 in; height 11 ft 6 in; wing area 237 sq ft. Empty weight 1,920 lb; gross weight 2,970 lb. Max speed 144 mph at 15,700 ft; climb to 17,000 ft in 12 min; service ceiling 23,000 ft; range 300 miles. Armament two machine-guns.

Vireo—Type 125—One 235 hp Armstrong Siddeley Lynx IV. Span 35 ft; length 27 ft 8 in; height 11 ft 5 in; wing area 214 sq ft. Empty weight 1,951 lb; gross weight 2,550 lb. Max speed 120 mph; service ceiling 14,750 ft. Armament two machine-guns.

Viastra II—Type 198—Two 525 hp Bristol Jupiter XIF. Accommodation two pilots, 12 passengers. Span 70 ft; length 45 ft 6 in; height 13 ft 6 in; wing area 745 sq ft. Empty weight 7,880 lb; gross weight 12,350 lb. Max speed at sea level 120 mph; initial climb 970 ft/min; climb to 4,920 ft in 4·5 min; range 535 miles.

Vellore and Vellox

In September 1925 Vickers' design office prepared a memorandum out-lining the leading characteristics of a single-engined tractor biplane to meet specification 34/24 for a civil freight and mail carrier. The idea of a special-ised aeroplane to transport only dead weight for commercial purposes was not new, the Air Ministry's Vickers Vulcan, previously described, probably being one of the first. Only today is this class of aeroplane at last coming into its own, because the trading facilities now available are propitious for the express and exclusive delivery of valuable or perishable merchandise over global distances.

The 1925 project was drawn up as a large, low-speed type with a span of 98 ft and powered by a Rolls-Royce Condor III engine. The perform-ance was not particularly significant because the gain in time, compared with surface transport, over stage lengths of up to 300 miles was still considerably in favour of the air freighter.

A tender was submitted and accepted, and consequently a name for the project was requested, this having to be that of an inland town in the British Empire; Vellore, the name of a town in India, was agreed upon. In May 1926 the Air Ministry asked for the project to be modified to take the Bristol Jupiter VI as power unit. In consequence, a smaller aeroplane was drawn up, with a wing span of 74 ft and with the all-up weight reduced from the 14,000 lb of the Condor-powered scheme to 8,000 lb. In the

Vellore I in original form with Jupiter engine, at the Hendon Air Display in 1928.

223

Vellore I re-engined with a Jaguar, on trials at Brooklands for its Australian flight.

special requirements was a provision for rapid replacement of all major components, including the engine, and a quickly removable covering to the fuselage. The Vellore was therefore offered as an all-metal airframe with fabric covering.

After consideration, the engineering details were settled and the final form embodied a Jupiter IX engine, a span of 76 ft and a total loaded weight of 9,500 lb. The Vellore I flew at Brooklands on 17 May, 1928, in the hands of Scholefield and Payn. As it was built to Air Ministry contract a Service serial number, J8906, was allotted, but shortly afterwards the civil registration G-EBYX was substituted. With the addition of the number 11 in large figures on the fuselage sides, it appeared in this guise at the RAF Display on 30 June, 1928, at Hendon.

After light-load trials at Brooklands, the quadruple rudders were reduced slightly in chord, and on 9 October, 1928, the Vellore went to Martlesham for full trials. There the results exceeded expectations, for at all-up weight the top speed was 111·5 mph, which was 3·5 mph above estimate, and the ceiling was also 1,500 ft above estimate. In addition, the Martlesham report stated that the Vellore was the first aeroplane to go through all its trials without a mechanical failure, which from that source was praise indeed.

The next step concerning the Vellore I was a semi-official proposal to use it for a very-long-range flight, either non-stop or in stages, presumably to test the feasibility of long-distance goods transport by air. The first survey envisaged the use of a Rolls-Royce F.XIVB, but early in 1929 the Vellore was re-engined with a geared Armstrong Siddeley Jaguar VI to fly to Australia, for which effort the aeroplane was loaned to Vickers by its owners, the Air Ministry. The fuel capacity was raised to a maximum of 513 gal by fitting extra tankage in the cabin. The crew were Flt Lt J. Moir and Flg Off H. C. Owen, two Australians who wished to return home.

The Jaguar-Vellore I left Lympne on 18 March with a full load of 5,000 lb largely consisting of fuel, spares and stores, taking-off in 100 yards. The first part of the route was via Marseilles, Rome and Malta to Benghazi, where an engine examination was made because of a bad cough over the Mediterranean. Some 200 miles out from Benghazi the engine again gave

224

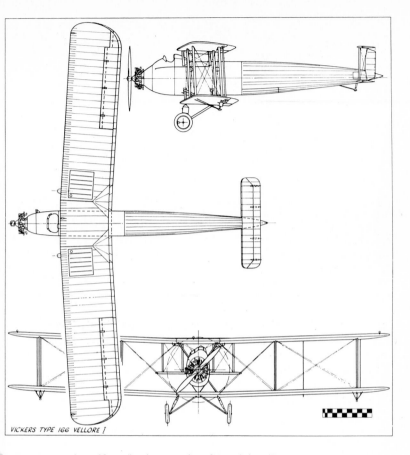

VICKERS TYPE 166 VELLORE 1

indications of malfunctioning, and a forced landing had to be made at Mersa Matruh, during which a wing and the undercarriage were damaged by brushing a house on the approach. New components had to be shipped out and assembled by E. H. C. Tullett, the Vickers service engineer, with the aid of Bedouin labour.

On 28 April the flight was resumed, and continued through the Middle East and India down to South East Asia through all sorts of storms and bad weather. The Vellore rode all these, but on crossing the Timor Sea on the last lap, with the light fading, the engine started to give trouble again about 160 miles from Darwin. The crew clung on, for a chance of survival from a ditching was out of the question, and eventually Moir reached the lighthouse at Cape Don and pancaked the Vellore on some trees in the vicinity. The sea all around was full of sharks, and lagoons inland were abounding with crocodiles! The aeroplane was a write-off, but the crew made a grateful report to Vickers on its excellent handling characteristics and comfort over long distances.

Vellore III leaving Hanworth airfield on first leg of King's Cup Air Race 1930.

VELLORE III. About the same time as the abrupt and only just successfu
ending to the Vellore I's Australian flight, Vickers decided to proceed wit
a development of the type to provide more hold or cabin capacity. Desig
study indicated a twin-engined aeroplane which appealed to the Ai
Ministry as a replacement for their lost Mk I.

Because the Weybridge works were loaded to capacity with military
contracts, the construction of the Vellore Mk III powered by two Bristo
Jupiter XIF engines was undertaken by Vickers' Crayford works. Thi
aeroplane was the last ever to be built there, and so ended a fine record o
aircraft manufacture, the bulk of which was achieved between 1914 and
1918.

Vellore III on Supermarine floats taking off for tests from Southampton Water.

The Vellore III was registered G-AASW in December 1929 and first flown at Brooklands by Mutt Summers on 24 June, 1930. It competed in the King's Cup Air Race on 5 July, but was unplaced, averaging 126·8 mph for the whole course after starting from scratch.

Later on, G-AASW was fitted with Supermarine-designed floats and flown from Southampton Water in March 1932 by Henri Biard, Supermarine's chief test pilot, and Mutt Summers. In the meantime, the Air

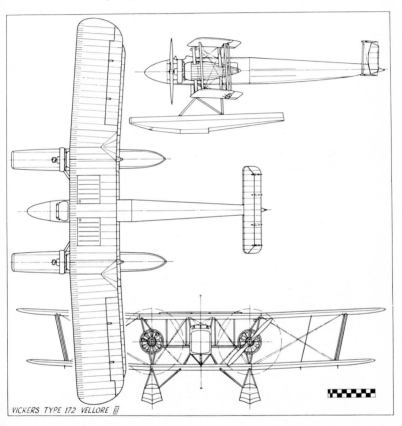

VICKERS TYPE 172 VELLORE III

Ministry had written a specification around the twin Vellore, at that time labelled Mk II, for a civil mail carrier. This was numbered 5/30 and was dated 14 April, 1930. A supplementary specification, GE168, was also issued at the same time for an apparatus for dropping mail bags in flight, for which purpose it was intended that the Vellore should be adapted. In consequence, the second twin-engined Vellore airframe was not required to have the larger fuselage already projected and was in fact a replica of G-AASW.

The engines allocated for this second twin Vellore were Jupiter IXs with a slightly higher compression ratio than the Mk XIs also considered

(5·3:1 against 5·15:1). Extensive ancillary equipment changes had been made as a result of many official conferences, indicating that the project for an all-freight aeroplane was taken quite seriously.

The crew of the second Vellore comprised a pilot and wireless operator mechanic, and 1,000 lb of mail was to be carried in bags of 15 lb/cu ft density. The aeroplane was registered G-ABKC, but in August 1931 a decision was made to complete it as a Service type, which meant that the mail-carrying requirement had once again been pigeon-holed. Also in consequence of this change of duty, the mark number was changed from II to IV. It was originally intended to allot the aeroplane to the RAE, but in fact it spent most of its life at the A and AEE, Martlesham, carrying stores and troops to and fro between that station and the satellite station at Orfordness, a dozen miles only. The Service serial number was K2133. In February 1935 it was replaced by a Vickers Valentia for ferry duties at Martlesham.

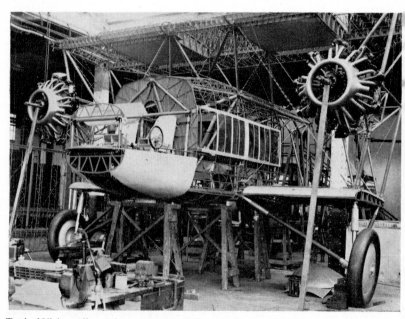

Typical Vickers all-metal construction of the period is shown in this picture of the Vellox, refined version of the Vellore; wandering web spars and alloy tubing ribs had supplanted Wibault concepts at this time, although a corrugated panel cabin front bulkhead survives, while a reversion to a metal-tubed fuselage structure had also been made.

VELLOX. A third twin Vellore was under construction when it was decided to make a fuselage with a larger cabin capacity, as already proposed during the Vellore III design but abandoned when the Air Ministry ordered the mail-carrying Vellore. Using parts from this third Vellore, such as wings and tail, a new type emerged called the Vellox after the suggested name

228

Vellox before delivery to Imperial Airways.

Victrix had been dropped. It was registered in March 1931 as G-ABKY
and was intended for short-haul passenger carrying. An attempt to create
interest in the Vellox with Jupiter XFBM engines, as fitted to the Victoria V,
as a troop carrier to specification C.16/28, was unsuccessful.

Eventually, the type of engine selected for this new civil transport was
the Bristol Pegasus IM3, which had moderate supercharging. There was
provision for carrying a crew of two pilots, a steward and 10 passengers
(or 3,000 lb of freight). One of the claims made for the Vellox was optimum airfield performance, that is, short take-off and landing. It flew on
23 January, 1934, at Brooklands in the hands of Mutt Summers, and on a
second flight the same day carried its full design load. On 25 January it

A fine picture of the Vellox in flight.

was delivered to Martlesham for civil type tests. It is interesting to note that at this time many of the modern conveniences of air travel were being introduced into the Vellox, such as punkah louvre ventilation (from ram air with roof intake), stressed seating with sponge rubber upholstery, sound-proofed and lined cabin walls, full galley and toilet services, as well as engineering refinements, including inertia-type engine starters, electrical instrumentation, pneumatic wheel brakes and experimental de-icing on the leading edges of wings and tail surfaces.

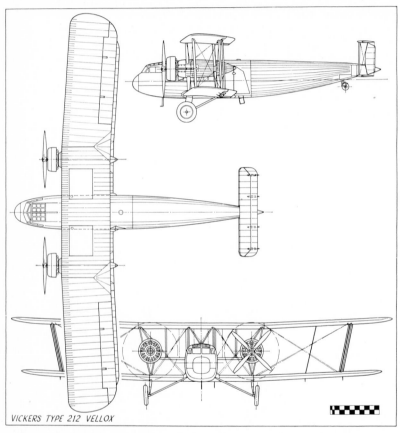

VICKERS TYPE 212 VELLOX

A certain degree of vibration was evident at cruising speeds, and this was cured by fitting four-blade propellers as used on the Supermarine South-ampton X flying-boat. Interest in the Vellox in Australia was somewhat reduced by the choice of engine, and one proposal from that quarter was to fit Rolls-Royce Kestrels. An intriguing inquiry came from Charles Ulm, Kingsford Smith's co-pilot on trans-Pacific record flights, suggesting using the Vellox for a long-distance flight on his own account, but the project fell through. Eventually the Vellox was sold to Imperial Airways and used as a freighter without conspicuous success. The main drawback was a comparatively low cruising speed, and an attempt to improve matters by fitting Pegasus IIL engines proved abortive. Much of the reduction in performance from the original Martlesham figures was thought by Vickers to have been caused by the additional drag and weight of extra equipment fitted by the airline.

Vellore and Vellox

	Vellore Mk I Type 134	Vellore Mk III (Seaplane) Type 172	Vellox Type 212
Accommodation:	Pilot and navigator	Pilot and W/Op. mechanic	2 pilots, steward, 10 passengers
Engine(s):	One 515 hp Bristol Jupiter IX	Two 525 hp Bristol Jupiter XIF	Two 600 hp Bristol Pegasus IM3
Span:	76 ft	76 ft	76 ft
Length:	51 ft 6 in	48 ft	50 ft 6 in
Height:	16 ft 3 in	16 ft 3 in	16 ft 3 in
Wing Area:	1,416 sq ft	1,373 sq ft	1,374 sq ft
Empty Weight:	4,796 lb	7,925 lb	8,150 lb
Gross Weight:	9,500 lb	13,000 lb	13,500 lb
Max Speed:	114 mph at sea level	127 mph at sea level	157 mph at 6,500 ft
Initial Climb:	515 ft/min	850 ft/min	1,230 ft/min
Climb to 5,000 ft:	12½ min	7 min	4·4 min
Range:	350 miles at 80 mph	300 miles	690 miles at 133 mph

Vickers Fighters

At the end of 1925 Vickers aviation department noted that since the S.E.5a of first world war fame, of which the greatest number had been made by Vickers, no new British fighter with a liquid-cooled engine had appeared in service. As Rolls-Royce were engaged in developing an engine of this class suitable for installation in single-seat fighters, the time was thought propitious for Weybridge to start a new design for a fighter with a water-cooled engine. Several projects based on an improved S.E.5a had been designed at Weybridge, one of which is shown on page 483.

Pending the arrival of the new Rolls-Royce engine, a 400-hp twelve-cylinder Hispano Suiza T52 was bought from France, through Vickers' Wibault agency, for £1,200. Design proceeded with this engine, and in March 1926 the new Vickers fighter, the Type 123, was registered G-EBNQ as a private-venture aeroplane. Once again the difficult problem arose of finding a suitable name. Among those considered that had not appeared before were Valour, Vassal, Vandal, Villain and Virago; eventually it was decided to await events to see whether a production series was reached before applying a name, and the aeroplane was known simply by its Vickers type number.

Vickers Type 123 Hispano Scout with duralumin propeller and underslung radiator.

All-metal construction with fabric-covered surfaces was used for the whole of the airframe. This was of fabricated duralumin sections and plates for the spars and duralumin tubes for the wing ribs and fuselage members, with steel tubes for class one stressed members, such as the drag bracing struts in the wings and load-bearing struts in the front fuselage. An item of interest was the forged duralumin propeller with detachable blades which was specially designed for trial in the Type 123.

The Vickers 123 Hispano Scout first flew on 9 November, 1926, and it

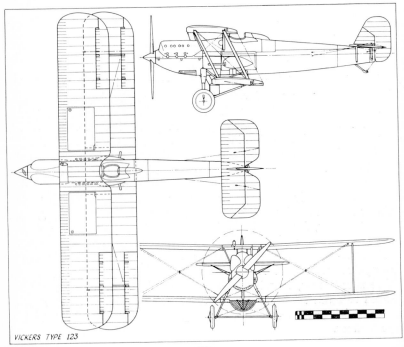

VICKERS TYPE 123

had a better performance than the Weybridge-built Wibault Scout in respect of speed and ceiling, and slightly less speed but a much superior ceiling than the French Wibault 9.C1 fitted with the same type of Hispano engine.

In May 1927 the original intention to fit the aeroplane with the new Rolls-Royce FXI was revived when it became available as a late development of the Falcon range of engines. A reconstruction of the airframe was undertaken, the chief modifications being in the front fuselage—the streamline nose of Type 123 disappeared, as did the peculiar semicircular radiator mounted under the bottom centre section. In the rebuild, known under a new Type number, 141, a blunt nose appeared without a propeller spinner. A retractable radiator of rectangular shape was mounted in the bottom of the front fuselage at the leading edge of the lower wing.

TYPE 141 SCOUT. The Vickers 141 was entered for the single-seat fighter competition at Martlesham in January 1928, in company with other entrants, which included the Armstrong Whitworth Starling, the Avro Avenger, the Blackburn Turcock, the Bristol Bulldog, the Hawker Hawfinch and the Westland Wizard. One of the Martlesham pilots who tested the 141 was Flg Off Mutt Summers, soon after to become Vickers' chief test pilot, who reported that the aeroplane was very light on the controls. Its top speed was 174 mph and its speed range impressive but it failed to gain an order.

After return from Martlesham the shape of the fin and rudder was altered and the civil registration G-EBNQ restored, as on Type 123. Soon after, further modifications were made to Type 141 to suit it for deck-launching and landing trials as a fleet fighter to specification 21/26. A chin radiator in the nose was introduced, and the rear legs of the undercarriage were shortened to enable them to be anchored to the front spar of the

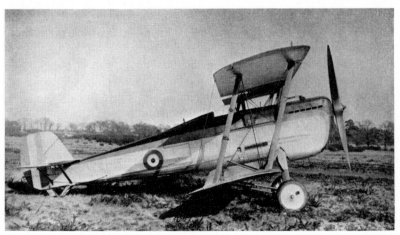

Vickers Type 141 Scout as rebuilt from Type 123 with Rolls-Royce FXI engine.

233

141 Scout with restored civil registration.

bottom centre section. The supercharged Rolls-Royce FXIS was installed. Other changes or innovations for naval operation included quickly detachable wing spar joints, crane lifting attachments in the top-wing centre section, a catapult hook, wheel brakes and interconnected elevators. Later, the dihedral of the lower wings was increased from three to five degrees to improve lateral stability.

In this form the aeroplane went to Martlesham to pass suitability trials as a ship-board type prior to sea trials on HMS *Furious*, which eventually took place in June 1929. These were not as satisfactory as Vickers had hoped, and it was the opinion of eye-witnesses that the naval pilot did not fully exploit the deck-handling capacity of the 141. As a result, the Martlesham and Gosport reports did not fully agree with one another.

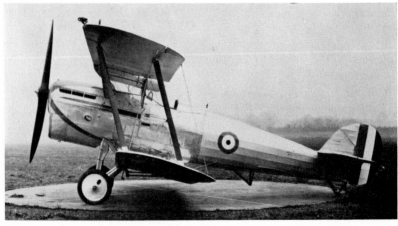

141 Scout in third form as fleet fighter, with chin radiator and arrester gear under fuselage.

Front view of Type 141 with Flg Off J. Summers soon after his appointment as Vickers' chief test pilot.

On its return from sea trials the Vickers 141 was flown from scratch in the 1929 King's Cup Air Race on 5 and 6 July by Summers but retired on reaching the Castle Bromwich check point. In due course it was reduced to scrap, but from its basic design the 143 Bolivian Scout was evolved and also a new ship-board aeroplane, the Type 177.

TYPE 143 BOLIVIAN SCOUT. To complete the organisation of its small air force, in 1929 Bolivia ordered six Vickers fighters based on the Type 141. These were fitted with the 450 hp Bristol Jupiter VIA air-cooled radial engine, an obvious advantage, as the Vickers Vespa IIIs already supplied had the same power unit. The Bolivian Scout was an improved version of Type 141, the major changes being the provision of a split-axle undercarriage, the fitting of a Fairey-Reed metal propeller and the use of an improved and more streamlined fuselage to suit the radial engine.

The five-degree dihedral on the lower wings, as introduced in the final modification to the Type 141, was retained, as were the rounded fin and rudder. A reversion to wing hoop-skids under the interplane struts was made because of the rough airfields in South America at that time, which also accounted for the special robust undercarriage. Type 143 was flown by Mutt Summers on 11 June, 1929, at Brooklands, and this was the first prototype and the first aeroplane of any type he flew for Vickers after being engaged as their chief test pilot. His score of Vickers' prototypes eventually

Type 143 Bolivian Scout with Jupiter engine and split-axle type undercarriage.

amounted to 30, but this included three Supermarine aircraft, one of which was the prototype Spitfire, K5054.

The first Bolivian 143 was tested by Payn at Brooklands with 240 lb overload for contract compliance and had a speed of 150 mph at 11,500 ft, climbing to 4,000 metres (13,123 ft) in 10 minutes and easily reaching the minimum specified height of 15,000 ft.

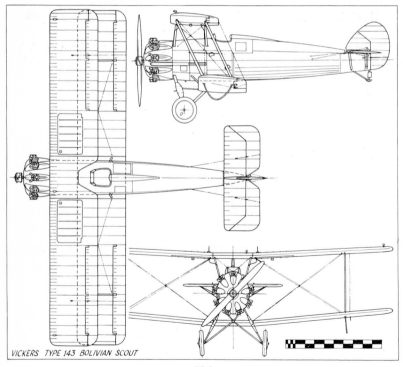

VICKERS TYPE 143 BOLIVIAN SCOUT

236

Four Vickers Bolivian Scouts with (*on left*) three Vickers Vespas at Alto La Paz air base, Bolivia.

The Vickers 143s, the first single-seat fighters in Bolivian service, began to arrive at Alto La Paz in January 1930, and when assembled and flown by Flg Off Banting made a great impression, and even more when the Bolivian pilots themselves started to fly them. Although only six were supplied, because of lack of the necessary finance for additional machines, there is no doubt that they played a great part in familiarising the Bolivian Air Force with air action, as the Gran Chaco war was fast approaching. Some of them were written-off before that event, but three remained to give a good account of themselves in company with the Curtiss Hawks which ultimately replaced them.

The sixth Bolivian 143 was fitted with a Bristol Jupiter VII engine for Air Ministry comparative trials at Martlesham, and when returned to Weybridge was re-engined with the Jupiter VIA before despatch overseas.

TYPE 177. A seventh Type 143 airframe was started with a prospect of submitting it as an improved entry to specification 21/26, which was for a single-seat ship-board fighter. Only the fuselage was completed, and parts of this formed the basis of a redesign embodying a Jupiter XF engine. The new type was given the Vickers number 177, and it was produced entirely as a private venture; in consequence, no Service serial number was allocated.

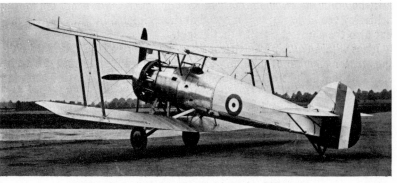

Vickers Type 177 ship-plane with Jupiter XF engine.

The Type 177 was flown by Summers at Brooklands on 26 November, 1929 and was the final development of the Vickers single-seat tractor biplanes. In February it went to Martlesham for type trials, and the only airframe trouble was with the tailskid shoe which kept breaking off,

237

probably because of its small size. On 6 March the engine seized at 20,000 ft, but the Service pilot brought the aeroplane down in a field about four miles from Felixstowe, only the fin and rudder being damaged. On 20 May the aeroplane did its terminal-velocity dive from 20,000 ft and reached a speed of 300 mph.

On 1 June the Type 177 was at Gosport preparatory to undergoing deck-landing trials on HMS *Furious*. None of the pilots could get used to the steerable hydraulic brakes, and, when landing on *Furious* in Torbay on 11 June, one of them put it on its nose through braking too hard, smashing the four-bladed propeller. This was replaced at once by a spare propeller of two-bladed type. Trials were continued without use of the brakes, although with practice no doubt they were an advantage in ship operation. The interchange of two- and four-bladed propellers was apparently the cause of some difficulty in firing the guns properly, as the successful operation of the gun-control gear was dependent on correct and precise timing. In the event, the Type 177 ship-board fighter did not prove acceptable to the authorities, nor did several other contenders for the same requirement. A proposal to fit a more powerful Armstrong Siddeley Panther engine to the Type 177 was considered so as to give a higher performance, but this was not followed up, as Vickers held a Jaguar engine in stock. There is some evidence to show that this Jaguar was fitted, but no record survives of the result.

TYPE 151 JOCKEY I. A decade after the end of the first world war the British defence strategists realised that the prior concern of a British fighter force in a future war would be to intercept enemy bomber attacks on Britain. Thus was born the philosophy of the interceptor fighter, a policy fully vindicated in the Battle of Britain. The race to win the pro-mised contract would be for the swiftest aeroplane, which not only meant achieving the highest possible speed at the estimated height of likely raids but also the shortest time to that height.

Ideas within the Air Ministry at that time, 1927 and 1928, centred on an interceptor capable of climbing to 20,000 ft in under 12 minutes with a speed at that height of more than 200 mph. Three classes of aeroplane were required for comparative tests under these conditions: biplane, high-wing monoplane and low-wing monoplane. Vickers were selected to design a low-wing monoplane and chose an improved form of the Wibault construction principles, with non-structural metal wing covering. For ease of maintenance accessibility it embodied a sideways hinged engine-mounting, all controls, piping and wiring (including the Constantinesco gear) hingeing without disconnection.

The requirement was written up in specification F.20/27 for an 'inter-ception single-seater day fighter' capable of overtaking in the shortest possible time an enemy passing overhead at 20,000 ft at a speed of 150 mph (the average speed of bombers until the advent of the Fairey Fox), with fighting view and manoeuvrability as prime considerations. The engine to

Jockey fighter in original form with Mercury engine.

be fitted was the air-cooled Bristol Mercury IIA radial, rated at 480 bhp at 13,000 ft with supercharging.

Vickers' design to this requirement was given the Type number 151 and the name Jockey. This name did not fall in with the Air Ministry system of nomenclature, and as far as can be ascertained Vickers were not officially asked for one; it was in fact adopted to attract the French, who were using that nickname for single-seat fighters at that time. In official documentation the Type 151 was always referred to as Vickers Interceptor (more often spelt Intercepter) F20/27, although the R.T.O. (Resident Technical Officer) at Weybridge, who at that time was N. E. Rowe, occasionally lapsed into the local description Jockey. The aeroplane was allotted a serial number, J9122, as it was the subject of an experimental contract.

In charge of the design under Pierson was J. Bewsher, who had then recently joined Vickers and was previously a consultant designer of small aeroplanes. Among investigations he had to make, to satisfy the conflicting considerations of performance and the cantilever low-wing structure, was one to select a suitable wing section of high-lift characteristics. He

Jockey with redesigned rear fuselage, Jupiter VIIF engine enclosed by Townend ring, and wheel spats.

239

visited Avions Michel Wibault to obtain particulars of their W116 section, but in fact the Raf 34 was chosen, as it was for the Viastra. One advantage of the thick wing was the elimination of internal and external bracing, thus dispensing entirely with rigging adjustments and reducing the maintenance routine simply to greasing control bearings.

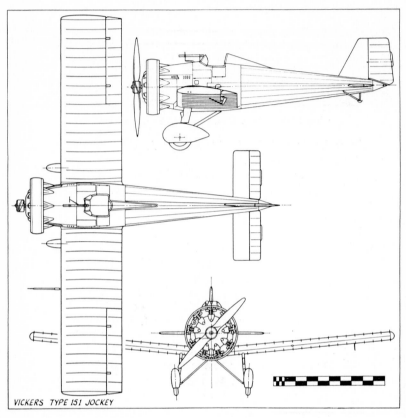

VICKERS TYPE 151 JOCKEY

Somewhat unusually for that period, 1930, when completed the Jockey airframe was taken by road to Martlesham to be test flown for preliminary trials. There it was fitted with a Bristol Mercury IIA engine on loan from the Air Ministry. The flight tests were made by Vickers' pilots, Scholefield and Payn, and a large Service pilot named Pope. Ralph Sorley of the Air Ministry wrote to Pierson to request the fitting of side doors to the cockpit, because if the aircraft were to turn over with Pope in it 'it would be quite hopeless for him to move'.

The first flight tests took place in April 1930 and disclosed defects, in the form of vibration with a lack of torsional rigidity in the rear fuselage. This may have been caused by a lack of strength because of the small cross-section near the tail attachment points and the widely spaced longerons or possibly through slip-stream buffeting. To cure the latter an intermediate modification was made in 1931 by the fitting of leading-edge slots at the wing roots; these were later discarded, which obviously eliminated the buffeting theory for the time being, although it was re-examined later when the RAE conducted an investigation into the flat spin tendency of the Jockey. Drag-reducing wheel spats were fitted.

One improvement made, with a bonus in increased speed, was the fitting of a Townend drag-reducing ring around the Mercury IIA engine, and when a Jupiter VIIF was installed in January 1932 the Townend ring was retained. At the same time the rear fuselage aft of the cockpit was completely redesigned structurally and alterations made to the tail surfaces, the new rear fuselage design being entrusted to B. N. Wallis. Features of his Jockey rear fuselage reflected his previous methods of airship structures, such as triangulated tube trusses inside the metal-skinned semi-monocoque body.

In this form, with the Jupiter, the Jockey went to Martlesham for extended trials. Continual trouble was encountered with the automatic boost control, and eventually this was replaced by a gate throttle control, but caused considerable delay in the test programme. In the meantime some confusion had arisen because estimated performance figures had been published for the Jockey with the Mercury IVS2 supercharged engine, whereas those obtained with the supercharged Jupiter VIIF were not permitted to be published.

The intended installation of the Mercury IVS2 and a new rear fuselage design of more conventional braced structure were, in fact, never undertaken, for in June 1932, during spinning tests at Martlesham, the Jockey developed a flat spin from which it failed to recover. The pilot baled out at 5,000 ft and landed safely, but the aeroplane was wrecked, thus precluding further development. This was unfortunate as the aeroplane was beginning to show real promise.

Shortly afterwards J. L. Nayler, secretary of the Aeronautical Research Committee, wrote to Pierson requesting the loan of a model of the Jockey for aerodynamic investigations by the National Physical Laboratory, and from that point started a chain of research into the theory of the flat spin, which up till then had not been properly evaluated. In 1933 the Royal Aircraft Establishment presented two reports on tests in their free-spinning wind-tunnel of a $\frac{1}{22}$ scale model of the Jockey. The tests sought to reproduce as far as possible the conditions of the spin as described by the pilot, allowing for scale effects. While the conclusions were not decisive, they established the fact that the aeroplane was loath to come out of a flat spin with the elevators depressed even to a small extent, and various cures, such as raising the tailplane or placing it behind the fin and rudder or the provision of a dorsal fin, were suggested. The Jockey was heavily loaded for its day, but this was not thought to be a contributory factor. Later the design was continued to specification F.5/34 as the Jockey II, subsequently and officially named Venom, described later.

Vickers COW gun fighter in skeleton form.

COW GUN FIGHTER. Meanwhile another interesting fighter design was produced to specification F. 29/27, which called for an interceptor to carry the big 37-mm Coventry Ordnance Works (COW) gun capable of firing one-and-a-half-pounder shells. Various attempts had previously been made to mount this type of armament on aircraft in pursuit of the one punch theory of attack.

The basic requirement was the same as in specification 20/27: to overtake in the shortest possible time an enemy flying at 150 mph at 20,000 ft. In addition, steadiness as a gun platform was essential with what was termed dead beat stability at operating speeds. The gun, weighing over

Type 161 COW gun fighter in original form.

200 lb, was to be in a fixed position firing forward at an elevation of at least 45 degrees to the horizontal, and automatic loading of the 50 shells was to be provided, the whole mechanism to be easily accessible to the pilot.

The combat strategy underlying this requirement was to fly up and under an enemy raider, which presupposed that the target would continue on a set course. This thought lends colour to the idea then prevalent that Zeppelin airships of high performance might be used for high-level reconnaissance, and this requirement was to cover such a contingency. There was a top-level scare much later, in the early days of the second world war, but from high-flying Junkers-Ju 86P bombers. Oddly enough, Vickers produced a high-altitude fighter to meet this later F.7/41 requirement which, like the F.29/27, also failed to materialise in production form.

COW gun fighter in final form with altered shape of fin and rudder and additional vertical side fins. (*MoD(Air) photo.*)

Tenders for specification F.29/27 were issued to seven aircraft firms, and some interesting designs were produced not the least of which was that by Vickers. A complete reversion was made to the single-seat pusher fighter configuration which had been the subject of much work on Vickers' part in the F.B.12 and F.B.26 during the first war. The result was a highly sophisticated aeroplane which, after some small problems, one of which was yaw stability, flew extremely well. The gun was fired in armament trials without much noticeable effect on the airframe and performance. However, the gunnery trials pilot must have had quite an interesting time. The gun/aeroplane combination was locked on target through a periscopic sight mounted on the left of the centre of the pilot's dashboard, while the COW gun itself kept him company on the starboard side of the nacelle, complete with its oversize and automatically fed ammunition clips stored in racks.

During preliminary construction a Mercury IIA was fitted to the airframe, but eventually the Jupiter VIIF was installed. Summers took the COW gun fighter for a short flight on 21 January, 1931, after what was

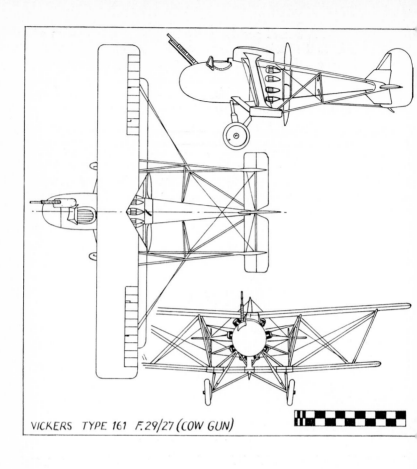

VICKERS TYPE 161 F.29/27 (COW GUN)

supposed to have been a taxying trial, to test the tail structure and tailskid strength. Further flight trials indicated certain modifications, which were a broader-chord rudder, a new tailskid shoe, alterations to the geometry and gearing of the elevator trim tab, and the addition of small fins near the extremities of the tailplane. To improve longitudinal trim, 60 lb of ballast was placed in the nose of the aeroplane, which meant that in practice provision could be made for the carrying of more military load.

The Type 161 Vickers COW gun fighter (J9566) went to Martlesham for evaluation in September 1931. Apart from minor maladjustments, such as a loose propeller fairing and broken bracing wires in the tail-boom structure caused by loose stones thrown up by the rotating propeller, the trials were without incident and the aeroplane was liked by the pilots.

As an experimental type, most of the interest in the COW gun fighter derived from its ingenious structure, which among other fine points embodied concealed control wires carried inside the tubular tail booms. The high-aspect-ratio wings with a duralumin plate and tube structure,

244

fabric covered and of Raf 34 section, were efficient in promoting rapid climb. Interference between upper and lower aerofoils was reduced to a minimum by the wide gap, supported by faired single-tube K struts in a two-bay arrangement. The curious propeller fairing was included to promote directional stability although, in response to a query from the National Physical Laboratory, it was stated that it added a few mph to the speed, as their previous deductions were that spinners or fairings behind pusher propellers reduced their efficiency. The metal monocoque nacelle had a smooth outer skin with a corrugated inner skin riveted directly to it. This was to withstand the severe shocks expected from the big gun, which then was unusual in so small an aeroplane. The Vickers COW gun fighter was probably the first aeroplane to use elevator trim tabs which were adjustable in flight.

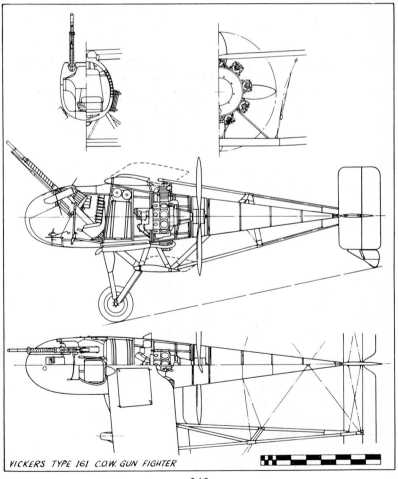

VICKERS TYPE 161 C.O.W. GUN FIGHTER

A frontal view of J9566 giving a good impression of its COW gun trained at fixed elevation. (*MoD(Air) photo.*)

There was no further development of the type, although a big shot fighter of the offensive capability of the Vickers COW gun aeroplane might have been of use in the Battle of Britain, firing upwards at the massed enemy formations. Proximity fuses, as later developed, would have added effectiveness to the fire power of the heavy gun. With the advent of the turbojet, the aft-mounted engine layout with a forward-located pilot and free zone of fire power ahead was revived.

VENOM. At the end of 1934 a new interceptor specification was issued as F.5/34. This had been rendered necessary because the performance of bombers had so improved that the speed margin between them and opposing fighters had narrowed considerably. Engagement height had gone up to 15,000 ft, and bomber speeds well up to the 200 mph mark. Therefore the time to reach combat altitude had been so reduced that an interceptor had only one chance of launching an attack at a decisive range. Striking power was also deemed to be of greater importance, and the specification called for no fewer than eight Browning machine-guns.

Vickers decided to produce a redesigned and improved Jockey to meet the new requirement. The engine chosen was the 625 hp sleeve-valve Bristol Aquila AE-3S, with a long-chord NACA cowling and a hinged mounting for easy access to accessories and to facilitate servicing. This arrangement needed flexible pipe runs and controls, which was not altogether to the liking of the engine designer.

The Vickers F.5/34 embodied many advanced features. It had 90-degree deflection trailing-edge flaps, and at that time was unique in this respect; and it was actually flown on its first test with its full battery of eight

246

Vickers Venom fighter at Brooklands.

Brownings installed in wing mountings, the engineering of which had been facilitated by the use of the deep, high-lift, Raf 34 wing section. The under-carriage was retracted by a worm-drive actuated by electric motors. Electrical power from a 12-volt generator operated gun heating, engine starter, navigation, identification and landing lamps, undercarriage warning horn and reflector-sight illumination, as well as flap and under-carriage retraction, and provision was made for power for the operational radio. The pilot's cockpit was enclosed with a Perspex canopy.

By this time Vickers' system of metal construction had become highly sophisticated, and a smooth exterior had been obtained by a stressed skin of flush light-alloy sheet fixed by countersunk rivets. The fuselage of the F.5/34 was a metal monocoque structure which ensured torsional rigidity, and the aircraft had an estimated speed of 320 mph at 15,000 ft. The Wibault system of metal wing covering had been entirely abandoned because the installation of the Browning guns in the wings ruled out the drag members required with a non-structural metal covering like that of the Wibault. For this reason, as well as for smoothness, a thicker plain

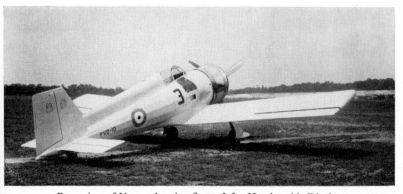

Rear view of Venom bearing figure 3 for Hendon Air Display.

Venom being flown by Vickers test pilot Jeffrey Quill.

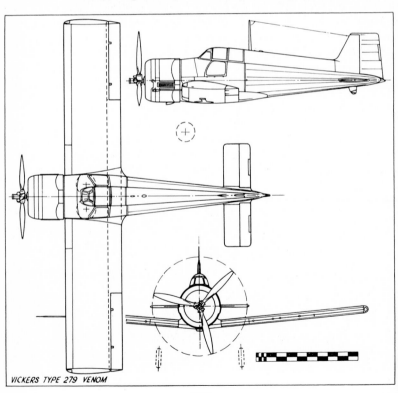

VICKERS TYPE 279 VENOM

sheet-metal skin was used to take the drag loads as well as eliminating the corrugations and projecting rib flanges of the Wibault system. The smooth skin also facilitated the provision of large removable panels to give access to the wing armament.

Mutt Summers flew the aeroplane at Brooklands on 17 June, 1936, nearly three months after he had flown the prototype Spitfire K5054 at Eastleigh. In view of the large difference in the respective powers of the two fighters, this was ominous for the Venom, as Vickers' F.5/34 fighter had by then been renamed. No British air-cooled radial engine of sufficient power, with dimensions compact enough, seemed likely to materialise to keep pace with the development of the liquid-cooled vee Rolls-Royce PV12, soon to become so well known as the Merlin.

So the Venom proceeded to its official trials after a great deal of manufacturer's tests carried out mainly by Flt Lt J. K. Quill, who had joined Vickers' flight test team from the Royal Air Force. To release Brooklands for test flying of production Wellesleys, Vildebeests, Vincents and the prototype B.9/32, many of these flights with the Venom were made by Quill from Eastleigh, which fitted in well with his early test flying of the Spitfire. The Venom was flown at Martlesham fitted with a tail parachute, then a novelty, but installed for spinning tests which were never made, as unserviceability was experienced with the engine and other ancillaries.

Hinged Aquila engine mounting of Venom fighter giving access for easy servicing.

The Venom was a good attempt to design an advanced interceptor around the air-cooled radial engine, and in performance it was indeed little behind its much more powerful contemporaries with liquid-cooled engines. It had the undoubted advantage of superior manoeuvrability in turning-radius and rate of roll, and in fact had its full battery of guns mounted before most of its competitors. It was scrapped in 1939, but its more powerful and later counterparts made their mark in the second world war—the Focke-Wulf Fw 190, the Republic P-47 Thunderbolt, the Mitsubishi Zero-Sen and the Hawker Tempest.

Vickers Type 432 in flight piloted by Tommy Lucke.

TYPE 432. Much later in the time scale, in 1940/41, came Vickers' last fighter design to reach construction; its concept was consequently completely different from its predecessors in all respects. It was a twin-engined monoplane and was the first Vickers type to be built with true stressed-skin construction. The wing design was of interest, being of the interim structural philosophy known as 'lobster claw'. This description derived from the heavy gauge skin which was provided with a thickened section to accommodate the span-wise spar booms, thus in cross-section appearing as a lobster-claw shape for the whole torsion box, including the wing leading edge. In theory, a complete aerofoil could be made on this system without spars or ribs, the thickened spanwise portions of the skin replacing the normal spars, and the complete tube of narrow section being self balancing stresswise, as in a perfect cylinder. The geodetic structure of the Windsor wing was developed at the same time on the same principle, but in the Type 432 fighter the wing structure was a compromise.

The fuselage was a streamlined tube with a flush-riveted skin attached to closely spaced circular frames. Much attention was given to reduction of skin friction drag by flush riveting all over the airframe, and polishing was resorted to later in a quest for higher speeds. The coolant radiators were buried in the wing in a duct, which reduced drag and also offered the advantage of the ram air intake generated by the velocity of the aeroplane.

The requirement to which the Type 432 eventually emerged was for a high-altitude fighter capable of intercepting and destroying the high-flying Junkers bombers in raids which were expected in strength. As the war proceeded these attacks never materialised sufficiently to justify any great urgency being placed on the project, although the Westland Welkin, designed to the same specification F.7/41, went into limited production. The 60 Welkins produced were never used operationally.

The Vickers F.7/41 twin-engined fighter was developed by an evolutionary process through various project designs for twin-engined cannon fighters; one of these was to specification F.22/39 and had a turret similar to that installed in the Wellington II, to carry the Vickers 40-mm gun. After a complete project design had been prepared to specification F.16/40 the requirements were altered, which necessitated restressing throughout. The undercarriage and other major components were redesigned, and certain parts were either discarded or revised to meet the higher strength factors.

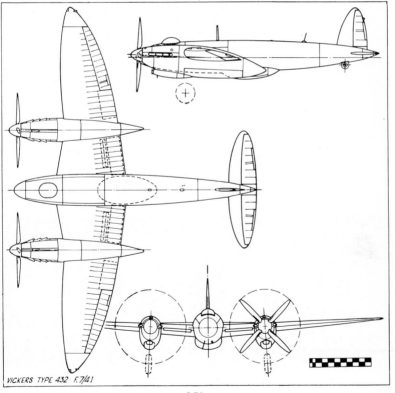

VICKERS TYPE 432 F.7/41

Vickers Type 432 high-altitude fighter nearing completion in the Foxwarren experimental hangar, 1942.

Much of this revision was concerned with the armament, which was the main payload of the aeroplane. This was to be a formidable pack of six 20-mm Hispano cannon carried in a ventral blister; in the event it was never fitted because of the change in Air Staff policy consequent upon the alteration of operational conditions already referred to.

The airframe was built in the prototype hangar at Foxwarren, between Weybridge and Wisley, and the completed fighter was taken to Farnborough for taxying trials and first flight. Some difficulty was experienced in getting the aeroplane to run straight while taxying, and the undercarriage had to be moved back three inches to correct the bad tracking. Tommy Lucke, a Vickers' test pilot, first flew the Vickers F.7/41 on 24 December, 1942, by which time it had received its serial number, DZ217.

Early trials disclosed several defects, notably the impossibility of making a three-point landing, thought to be caused by tailplane stall or ground cushion effect and overbalance on the ailerons, but alteration of tail settings and the replacement of the Irving-type ailerons by Westland-type alleviated these faults.

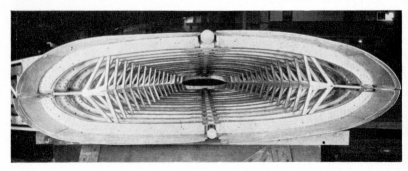

Lobster-claw construction of wing on Vickers high-altitude fighter.

252

The F.7/41's estimated performance of 435 mph at 28,000 ft was never realised, as the Merlin 61 engines would not run satisfactorily above 23,000 ft in this aeroplane, the reasons not being ascertained because of its short flying life. In the two years before the exercise was abandoned, DZ217 made 28 experimental flights, 25 flown by Tommy Lucke and three by other pilots, one of whom was Mutt Summers. He confirmed all the observations on the handling characteristics previously made by Lucke. The highest speed actually reached by DZ217 was 380 mph at 15,000 ft in MS gear and at 20,000 ft in FS gear on 14 May, 1943.

Vickers high-altitude fighter at Farnborough for type test.

The second prototype was not completed, being cancelled on 1 May, 1943, and the whole programme was officially stopped at the end of that year, although DZ217 was retained by Vickers in flying trim till the end of 1944, to carry out control evaluations for the B.3/42 Windsor, particularly in relation to aileron design. The Windsor drawings were in fact held up for a time pending results of these investigations. The aeroplane was a problem for the local observer posts at the time of its test flights in the neighbourhood of Farnborough and Brooklands, since to them it was only an experimental number in the official recognition handbook, AP1480. Usually it was known to post observers as the 'Tin Mossie' from its resemblance, apart from the wing shape, to the Mosquito.

The Vickers F.7/41 indeed reflected some of the design features of the Windsor, notably the elliptical wing shape, the reasons for the selection being discussed in the later description of the Windsor.

No firing tests were ever conducted with the type, and the pressure cabin was not completed. All the test flights were carried out with oxygen supply for the pilot. The airframe was eventually dismantled, leaving Tommy Lucke with the control column as a permanent souvenir of his anxious moments wrestling with heavy ailerons and elevators.

Vickers Fighters

	Type 123	Type 143
Engine:	One 480 hp Hispano Suiza T52	One 450 hp Bristol Jupiter VIA
Span:	34 ft	34 ft
Length:	28 ft 6 in	27 ft 10½ in
Height:	9 ft 4 in	11 ft 3 in
Wing Area:	378 sq ft	336 sq ft
Empty Weight:	2,278 lb	2,246 lb
Gross Weight:	3,300 lb	3,120 lb
Max Speed:	149 mph at 10,000	150 mph at 11,500 ft
Climb:	10,000 ft in 6·6 min	13,100 ft in 10 min
Service Ceiling:	—	20,000 ft
Armament:	Two Vickers machine-guns	Two Vickers machine-guns

F21/26—Type 177—One 540 hp Bristol Jupiter XFS. Span 34 ft 3 in; length 27 ft 6 in; height 11 ft 3 in; wing area 336 sq ft. Empty weight 2,835 lb; gross weight 4,050 lb. Max speed 190 mph at 13,120 ft; climb to 13,100 ft in 9·5 min; absolute ceiling 30,000 ft; range 470 miles at 175 mph at 15,000 ft.

Jockey—Type 171—One 530 hp Bristol Jupiter VIIF. Span 32 ft 6 in; length 23 ft; height 8 ft 3 in; wing area 150 sq ft. Empty weight 2,260 lb; gross weight 3,161 lb. Max speed 218 mph at 10,000 ft; climb to 10,000 ft in 4·8 min; initial climb 1,850 ft/min; absolute ceiling 31,000 ft. Armament two machine-guns.

COW gun fighter—Type 161—One 530 hp Bristol Jupiter VIIF. Span 32 ft; length 23 ft 6 in; height 12 ft 4 in; wing area 270 sq ft. Empty weight 2,381 lb; gross weight 3,350 lb. Max speed 185 mph at 10,000 ft; climb to 10,000 ft in 5·8 min. Armament one 37-mm COW gun.

Venom—Type 279—One 625 hp Bristol Aquila AE-3S. Span 32 ft 9 in; length 24 ft 2 in; height 10 ft 9 in; wing area 146 sq ft. Gross weight 4,156 lb. Max speed 312 mph at 16,250 ft; initial climb 3,000 ft/min; service ceiling 32,000 ft. Armament eight machine-guns.

F7/41—Type 432—Two 1,565 hp Rolls-Royce Merlin 61. Span 56 ft 10½ in; length 40 ft 7½ in; height 13 ft 9 in; wing area 441 sq ft. Empty weight 16,373 lb; gross weight 20,168 lb. Max speed 435 mph at 28,000 ft; initial climb 2,750 ft/min; service ceiling 37,000 ft; range 1,500 miles at 30,000 ft. Armament six 20-mm Hispano cannon. (Performance estimates—see text.)

Experimental Bombers

The Virginia, after seven years of progressive improvement, was beginning to reach its limit of design development in the standard production Mk VII. The metallisation of the airframe was imminent. Although the Virginia was to remain in service for another 14 years, in 1927 Vickers were giving attention to a successor which would embody the lessons and experience gained from its extensive operational experience. The Napier Lion engine, too, was gradually being superseded by newer and more powerful engines, such as the Rolls-Royce FXI and FXIV, and the Bristol radial air-cooled engines, the Jupiter VIII and the Mercury.

Vickers' project ideas on a Virginia replacement were represented by a twin tractor biplane of clean aerodynamic layout, with a crew disposition similar to that of the earlier bomber. The front fuselage of this project was in fact a modified Virginia component, and the newly adopted tail gunner's station was incorporated. The wings, unlike those of the Virginia, were of unequal span but retained the square-cut tips.

B.19/27 bomber in original form in November 1929 with Rolls-Royce FXIV
engines and retractable radiators under the top centre section.

The overall span of this project was 78 ft, compared with the 87 ft 8 in
of the Virginia, and the respective lengths 59 ft 9 in and 62 ft 3 in. The new
bomber had an estimated weight of 14,300 lb, which was 3,270 lb less than
the weight of the latest Virginia at that time, the Mk IX. The engine to be
standardised for the project was the Bristol Jupiter VIII, with the Napier
Lion XI and the Rolls-Royce FXI as alternatives. With the Jupiters an
estimated maximum speed of 135 mph at 5,000 ft was expected, compared with the 99 mph of the Virginia IX with Lions or 108 mph with
Jupiters, at the same height. The design having been finalised, details
were sent to the Air Ministry.

At that time the Air Staff were formulating their own plans for a new
bomber to replace the Virginia, and in consequence, on 17 August, 1927,
the Directorate of Technical Development issued specification B.19/27.
In the light of later events and with knowledge of the contracts subsequently awarded, some of the more important requirements of this specification are of interest today. Under the general section, 15 items were
included, the salient ones being pilot's vision, steadiness for bombing at
night, capability for self-defence and ease of maintenance. The aeroplane
had to be a steady bombing and gun platform in a speed range of 70 per
cent up to maximum, and its basic structure had to be constructed in metal.

In the power unit section of the specification it was stipulated that two
British engines of any approved type should be installed and were to have a
facility for easy removal. Originally, two Bristol Orion engines were to
have been called for, but this proposal was dropped from the specification.
Metal propellers were considered desirable.

The performance required was a maximum speed of not less than 120
mph at 10,000 ft, a service ceiling of 17,000 ft and a landing speed of not
more than 55 mph. The range, with allowance for 30 minutes at maximum
speed at ground level, was to be 920 miles cruising at 115 mph at 10,000 ft.
Load required was to consist of the following alternatives: two 1,000-lb,
four 520 or 550-lb, ten 230 or 250-lb, sixteen 112-lb or four 20-lb bombs for
sighting and practice drops. It is interesting to note that this was a lighter

bomb load than that carried by the Virginias, although when one of the successful entrants in the B.19/27 competition went into service the bomb load had increased to a maximum of 3,500 lb. Defence had to be provided by three Lewis-gun stations. In a wind of not more than 5 mph the aeroplane had to take-off with full load in 200 yds and reach a height of 60 ft within 600 yds. Wheel brakes were required.

Vickers, through a misunderstanding, assumed that their original project would be adopted, but it was pointed out to them that when the B.19/27 specification was issued the intention was to order several designs for competitive flight trials, following which orders would be placed. The original project sent to the Air Ministry was, in most respects, very close to the B.19/27 specification, and with little redesign was brought into line. The result was a biplane of unequal span (upper wing 77 ft 6 in, lower wing 67 ft 6 in) and a length overall, tail down, of 59 ft 6 in. Many of the features of the earlier project design were retained, including the Virginia's forward fuselage components. The engine installation remained as before, with the Bristol Jupiter VIII as the basic power unit.

One major change concerned the tail unit. The all-moving finless rudder system of the then new Virginia Mk X was taken a stage further and was combined with an all-moving tailplane. This tail design became familiar on other Vickers types of that period.

The Vickers B.19/27 had a loaded weight of 13,820 lb when carrying 1,546 lb of bombs. The range at 115 mph cruising speed was estimated at 920 miles, the maximum and landing speeds were 131 mph and 56 mph respectively, while the service ceiling was expected to be 17,700 ft. These figures applied to the Jupiter version, the alternatively powered versions varying slightly in detail.

A second Vickers B.19/27 biplane project was powered by the Bristol Mercury II, with a marked improvement in general performance. This was enhanced when the supercharged, geared version of the engine was considered, particularly in respect of service ceiling, which was increased to 24,200 ft. Top speed was increased to 144 mph at 15,000 ft, that of the direct-drive Bristol Mercury version being 138 mph at the same altitude. Loaded weight of the Mercury-engined version was estimated at 13,840 lb, of which 4,153 lb was basic structure. Vickers considered that only the geared version of the engine would be practical because the direct-drive Mercury produced propeller tip speeds of 1,070 ft/sec, resulting in most unpleasant noise in the cockpit, apart from less obvious disadvantages.

The design team at Weybridge had produced a number of metal monoplanes, still comparatively rare in 1928, and had accumulated quite substantial experience in their construction. As it was the apparent intention of the Air Ministry to order a monoplane as well as several biplane prototypes for comparative tests in the B.19/27 competition, the Weybridge team also projected a monoplane version of their bomber. They had their own experience in mind and were convinced, even at that time, of the eventual ascendency of the monoplane over the biplane.

256

With a similar fuselage and tail unit to the biplane, the monoplane design had a constant-chord, square-cut wing of 100-ft span and, in order to keep a similar wing loading, the area was almost identical to that of the biplane, 1,385 sq ft. In consequence, the great span required led to a thick wing for structural stiffness, and so to an increase in drag. The result was reduced performance and increased weight, which was unfortunate in view of the advanced conception of the project.

When powered with the Bristol Jupiter VIII, the monoplane had an estimated speed of 129 mph at 10,000 ft; service ceiling was 15,800 ft and landing speed 59 mph, neither of which figures met the specification; and loaded weight was 15,550 lb, of which 5,551 lb was structure.

Vickers B.19/27 with 12-degrees sweepback, being readied for the 1930 RAF Display at Hendon.

These Vickers designs were all submitted to the Air Ministry, along with many from other aircraft firms, and from these several were selected for actual construction and entry in the B.19/27 competition. One of Vickers' tenders was accepted, the chosen project being the biplane with the geared Mercury II engines. Construction began in mid-1928, and the serial J9131 was allocated to the aeroplane.

On 2 August, 1928, discussions took place between the Director of Technical Development and representatives of Vickers regarding a possible change of power unit. It was agreed that subject to the aeroplane meeting the specification, Rolls-Royce FXIV liquid-cooled engines could be installed in place of the Mercurys, with promise by Vickers of higher performance. The Air Ministry agreed, and work proceeded on the new installation.

As finalised, the design was still very close to the original project. The length of the fuselage, now entirely redesigned, was 60 ft 6 in; the upper and lower wings were of 76 ft 6 in and 66 ft 6 in span respectively, with chords of 10 ft 6 in and 9 ft 3 in; sweepback was twelve degrees, common incidence six degrees and common dihedral three degrees; and aerofoil section was the Raf 34.

Vickers had doubts about using wing slots and wanted to delete them, but the DTD insisted on their retention, as it was pointed out that Parnalls had successfully flown slotted wings on the Peto, which used the Raf 31 section, closely allied to the Raf 34. Vickers were reassured and slots were retained. The Raf 30 section was used for the tail surfaces, following Vickers practice.

With the Rolls-Royce FXIVs, the B.19/27 weighed 15,400 lb and had a maximum speed of 143 mph at 12,500 ft; at sea level 124 mph was estimated and 130 mph at 20,000 ft; and climbing at 98 mph, the aeroplane was expected to reach 12,500 ft in 19 minutes, the maximum rate of climb at sea level being 814 ft/min. Service ceiling was 23,000 ft and landing speed 55 mph.

Construction of the Vickers prototype proceeded during 1929, and on 8 November a group of Air Ministry representatives visited Weybridge to inspect the completed aeroplane. By 18 November the B.19/27 was cleared for flight and awaiting suitable weather.

On 30 November, 1929, the new bomber was airborne for the first time with Mutt Summers at the controls, this initial flight being of 10 minutes duration. A second flight of 55 minutes was made on 3 December, Summers this time having J. Radcliffe with him as observer. After a period of flying from Brooklands on contractor's trials, the aeroplane went to Martlesham for further flying by Service pilots. The two Rolls-Royce FXIV engines (Nos. 7 and 53) were, at this time, subject to limitations because of the experimental nature of the gears employed. Engine No. 7 was limited to 73 hours and No. 53 to 70·5 hours, this permitting 50 hours flying by Vickers, the rest of the hours on each engine having been taken up by test-bench running. The B.19/27 also flew from Digby, and on 28 June, 1930, it took part in the Hendon Air Display.

The engine cooling system initially employed was a new evaporative type, designed by Rolls-Royce, which featured semi-retractable radiators. Much flying was carried out on cooling tests, but the system was proving difficult and unsatisfactory in operation. The engines became overheated on the ground due to the insufficient cooling airflow, and to cure this larger radiators were installed. While these were satisfactory in rectifying the ground-running trouble, they were 35 per cent oversize in the air under British summer conditions and temperatures; at top speed the engines became too cool to achieve their optimum performance. Even with the radiators retracted, in which only a small area was offered to the airflow, and at a height of 10,000 ft in level flight, the coolant temperature was under 70 deg C. As a result of these tests new, redesigned radiators were ordered.

During one test flight both engines of the bomber failed suddenly, and the forced landing that followed caused considerable damage to the airframe. Extensive tests on the fuel system and its handling technique failed

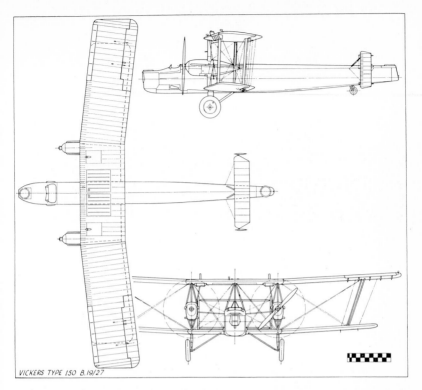

VICKERS TYPE 150 B.19/27

to find any definite reason for the sudden stoppages, and it was generally
believed that fuel contamination was the cause. The B.19/27 was returned
to Weybridge to be rebuilt.

While the rebuilding was taking place a critical report was sent to
Vickers by a Martlesham test pilot, recommending that certain modifications be made during this time to improve the aeroplane. Some of his
proposals were as follows: that the forward fuselage structure be made of
steel tube in place of duralumin tube; smaller radiators be provided; the
pilot's seat be raised to improve the view, and emergency exits provided in
the fuselage. In addition, this pilot made two further points of criticism
which concerned the general stability of the aeroplane and the torsional
rigidity of the rear fuselage. In the case of the former, it was stated that
the bomber tended to wallow in the lateral plane when both engines were
running. Diagnosing this as insufficient dihedral, the pilot recommended
an increase of dihedral angle from 3 to 3·5 degrees, which was duly incorporated in the rebuilding of the bomber. In the second case rear
gunners had complained of much more twisting of the rear fuselage in
flight than in the Virginia Mk IX or X, making the position unpleasant.
To cure this trouble Vickers embodied thicker internal bracing wires, thus
increasing the torsional stiffness of the rear fuselage component. Most of

B.19/27 with Rolls-Royce Kestrel III engines, wheel spats, engine steam condensers (behind V struts) and two degrees sweepback, at Martlesham.

the Martlesham proposals were incorporated, and a further aerodynamic refinement was the introduction of wheel spats.

In order to cure the constant cooling difficulties, a new steam condenser system, employing a header tank, was designed by Rolls-Royce and completed in time to be installed before the aeroplane resumed its flight trials. At the same time Rolls-Royce Kestrel IIIs replaced the original engines.

The rebuilt B.19/27 was weighed on 11 May, 1931, the all-up weight being 15,877 lb. Sir Robert McLean, Vickers Aviation chairman, directed that the type should henceforth be known as the Vickers Vanox; this was Vickers' own name, and the description Vannock, sometimes applied, is a misnomer. Shortly after the weighing, the flight-test programme was resumed, and normal development proceeded, until a further forced landing became necessary. During single-engined flying, the operating engine failed, but luckily no damage occurred during the landing. The cause of this failure was established as excessive boost pressures, and all future flying was restricted to minus $\frac{1}{2}$ lb boost.

On 9 July, 1931, the aeroplane returned to Weybridge for further modification. On this occasion the main wheels were moved back six inches to improve ground behaviour. Two days later, in a further attempt to cure persistent roll instability, the dihedral angle of the wings was reduced from 3·5 to 2 degrees. Troubles with the engine installation continued, which prompted Vickers to design a twin Bristol Jupiter layout as an insurance against the possible failure of the existing installation.

In October 1931, in common with several other Vickers projects, the application of Wallis' newly developed metal structure to the B.19/27 was investigated. The structure was to have been similar to that of the M.1/30, which was based on airship design, and production B.19/27s would have had this type of construction.

Directional instability now became manifest, and to effect a cure wood fairings were fitted to the tailplane struts to provide additional aft area. A similar fault on the Victoria had been cured in this manner. This modification was completed on 22 October, 1931, but during flight trials the following day another engine failure occurred, this time to the port engine, but fortunately this happened just as the aeroplane was landing, and no damage ensued. The cause of this failure was clogged fuel jets in the carburettor.

Martlesham continued to evaluate the various B.19/27 contestants, and at this period sent an unfavourable report to the Air Ministry regarding the Vickers entry. The major complaint was the aeroplane's general instability, both directional and lateral. Under certain conditions of loading the bomber continued to wallow when flying in bumpy weather, and sometimes an improvement was made by not carrying the rear gunner and his equipment. The Martlesham pilots also apparently disliked the spring-balanced controls.

During the early part of November 1931 the Vickers aeroplane was flown in competition with the Handley Page B.19/27 (later known as the Heyford), but stability troubles persisted, and on 26 November a redesigned tail unit was ordered.

The tendency to wallow and general lateral instability were undoubtedly caused by a combination of comparatively high sweepback and dihedral. Today this phenomenon, known as Dutch roll, is clearly understood, but in 1931 the true nature of the trouble was only partially recognised; sufficient was known, however, to suspect that excessive dihedral was to blame, and the angle was therefore changed from two degrees to one-half of a degree. This change did improve the situation, but obviously further investigation was needed. As a result, excessive sweepback became suspect, and on 22 March, 1932, the mainplanes were changed from 12 to 7 degrees sweepback. This time the modification appears to have brought success, for these angles remained unchanged for the rest of the aeroplane's life.

Troubles with the Kestrel engine installation continued and seemed to be insurmountable. Further development with these engines was therefore

B.19/27 after conversion with Bristol Pegasus engines in May 1932.

abandoned, and a new engine installation was ordered by the Air Ministry on 7 May, 1932. The engines chosen for the new design were Bristol Pegasus IM3 air-cooled radials, initially of 554 hp each with standard Vildebeest propellers. In view of the intensive evaluation of the various B.19/27 designs, it was of paramount importance that the modification should be completed as soon as possible, and this was done by 21 May. With a subsequent increase of engine power to 662 bhp at 4,500 ft, a speed of 145 mph was estimated. Service ceiling was 23,000 ft, climbing speed 90–96 mph and landing speed 57 mph. The completed aeroplane was weighed on 23 May, the all-up weight being 16,018 lb. This was later raised to 16,103 lb by an increase of equipment installed. Flight trials were resumed as soon as possible, and by 3 June, 1932, the aeroplane had returned to Martlesham. On 11 June Summers flew the bomber for 1 hr and 20 min, during which time he climbed to 15,000 ft, made level-speed checks, and during the test three landings were also made. On 14 June the aeroplane was twice flown by Flt Lt Richmond during the day—for 1 hr 55 min during the morning and 1 hr and 45 min in the afternoon. The only complaint concerned the lightness of the elevator on backward control movement. The next day a flight was made to 15,000 ft. A special climb to 16,500 ft was made on 18 June, and speed trials were carried out two days later. By 25 June, after intensive flight trials, the B.19/27 was being prepared to go to a Service squadron. After a month of waiting, during which time occasional flights were made, the aeroplane, armed with 112-lb bombs, was prepared for a further series of trials from Martlesham.

After this period of bombing trials the B.19/27 was delivered to Boscombe Down, probably to 9 (Bomber) Squadron. On 19 September, 1932, it was flown to North Coates Fitties, in Lincolnshire, where gunnery and bombing trials were carried out. The gunnery results were very good, but bombing proved to be unpleasant for the bomb-aimer because of slipstream entering the open window. Bombing was carried out from 8,000 and 5,000 ft, at 115 mph, and also at 100 mph in an attempt to lessen the

Side view of the converted B.19/27 with Pegasus engines.

262

B.19/27 in final form with two-bay wings, half a degree dihedral and deep bomb-aimer's window.

wind effects. As a result, a larger bomb-aimer's window was fitted, and this completely cured the trouble. After this, remarkably accurate results were achieved with live bombs from 3,000 ft, and 100 mph, all bombs falling within the target circle. The general performance of the aeroplane greatly impressed the pilots who flew it during these trials. Particularly impressive was the climb to 10,000 ft with full war load in 17 minutes 12 seconds at 80 mph.

On 4 October the bomber returned to Boscombe Down and was handed on to 10 (Bomber) Squadron. Meanwhile the design team at Weybridge were concentrating on improving the performance still further, particularly in respect of range and ceiling. A new set of outer mainplanes was designed and ordered on 5 July, 1932. An additional bay was introduced in the outer sections, increasing the upper and lower wing spans to 85 ft 6 in and 79 ft respectively. An additional 114 gal of fuel was stowed in a new centre section tank. The dismantled bomber returned to Weybridge on 22 December and was completed again on 2 February, 1933. On 10 February the weight of the revised aeroplane was established at 16,007 lb, subsequently increasing to 16,400 lb with equipment additions. The revised B.19/27, known as the Type 255, returned to Martlesham on 14 March.

By this time the contracts for the successful entrants in the B.19/27 competition had been placed. The two designs chosen, the Handley Page Heyford and Fairey Hendon, in part supplemented the Virginia they were designed to replace. Only the Heyford was produced in any numbers, although the Hendon was at one time thought likely to become the main-stay of the night-bomber squadrons.

The Vickers entry continued to spend its days at various establishments, carrying out armament tests. Its final days were spent at the Royal Aircraft Establishment at Farnborough, where it acted as a flight-refuelling tanker. It was last seen at a public display in 1937, when it appeared with an Overstrand in a flight-refuelling demonstration.

263

Type 163 under construction at Weybridge, showing mounting for tandem engines and Raf 34 wing section in typical Vickers wing structure of the time.

TYPE 163. In December 1928 the Air Ministry Directorate of Technical Development invited certain firms to submit designs to meet a newly formulated specification for a troop-carrying landplane.

This specification, C.16/28, was for an aeroplane designed to fulfil the main duty of a troop-transport, carrying 10 soldiers and their equipment over distances up to 1,200 miles. Level speed was to be as high as possible at 10,000 ft, and the maximum ceiling required was 22,000 ft. The landing speed had to be not more than 55 mph. Besides the trooping rôle, the aeroplane had to undertake the additional task of heavy night-bomber, and in this latter form had to carry ten 250-lb and four 20-lb bombs, the latter being used for sighting and practice. Alternative bomb loads were to be provided. Defence against fighters was provided by two Lewis-gun positions, with 12 drums of ammunition. In both forms the aeroplane had to take-off in 200 yds and reach a height of 60 ft in 600 yds in a wind of not more than five mph.

Originally three engines, of approved British type, were specified as the power installation, but at the end of February 1929 this was revised to permit the use of four engines, if this arrangement was more acceptable to designers. A number of projects were submitted by various firms to meet the specification, using both engine layouts.

Vickers' thoughts on the project hardened towards a four-engined aeroplane, the Type 163, closely allied aerodynamically to the then current B.19/27 design. Many design features were common to both types, the Type 163 being fundamentally a slightly scaled-up four-engined version of the twin-engined bomber, although an early layout of the wings favoured a sesquiplane form.

264

In this initial design the upper plane span was 97 ft and the lower 61 ft. Overall length was 67 ft 1 in, and all-up weight 22,850 lb. As required by the specification, two Lewis-gun positions were initially projected, in the nose and extreme tail—although side guns were added later. The engine installation consisted of four Rolls-Royce FXIV engines mounted in tandem pairs, in a similar manner to that employed by the Gloster entry. The front propellers were two-bladed, and the rear, four-bladed; the rear propellers were provided with a brake system to prevent them rotating in the slipstream from the front propellers when the rear engines were shut down for taxying. With these engines a top speed of 170 mph was estimated, which was considerable for a big aeroplane at this period—the fastest fighters reaching only about 215 mph. The landing speed was 60 mph, slightly higher than specified. Maximum range was estimated at the required 1,200 miles.

During the course of project development the wing design was changed to a more conventional arrangement. In this layout the overall span was 90 ft, the overall length was decreased to 66 ft 9 in and the design was finally frozen. The revised Type 163 had the original top speed of 170 mph, a cruising speed of 140 mph and a landing speed of 62 mph. The all-up weight was slightly increased to 23,600 lb, and maximum bomb load consisted of twelve 250-lb and four 20-lb bombs. Maximum range was 1,150 miles, maximum rate-of-climb was 950 ft/min and ceiling, 25,000 ft.

Vickers, convinced of the exceptional qualities of the design and desirous of having an additional entrant in the B.19/27 competition, decided to go ahead with the construction of a prototype without awaiting official decisions on the C.16/28 specification. The Type 163 could meet most of the requirements of specification B.19/27, but carried a much larger bomb

Type 163 in original form with SBAC classification O-2 for Hendon Air Display 1931.

Vickers four-engined bomber at the RAF Air Display 1932, showing steam
condensers over engines. (*Flight photo.*)

load, although the use of four engines was unspecified. In view of the
intended entry in the bomber competition, the aeroplane was completed
in that form and was finished in standard night-bomber Nivo dark green.
As the aeroplane was a private venture, no official serial number was
allotted, but it carried the SBAC prototype number O-2 in white on the
fuselage sides.

A difference of opinion occurred between the Air Ministry and Rolls-
Royce over the engine performance figures, upon which Vickers had based
their calculations for the C.16/28 entry. The Air Ministry team evaluating
the Vickers design reduced the engine horsepower figures considerably
with disastrous effect on the estimated performance of the aeroplane.
Consumption of petrol and oil was also increased in their estimates, to the
detriment of the range, or to the all-up weight if more fuel and oil capacity
became necessary to compensate for the revised figures. Rolls-Royce were
surprised by the Air Ministry's figures, with which they did not agree,
and made strong representations on the subject. After much discussion the
Air Ministry agreed to base their calculations on the figures obtained
during the engine type tests. These were substantially similar to the original estimates, and in fact the subsequent flight testing of the aeroplane
proved the accuracy of the initial calculations.

After considerable evaluations of various projects the Air Ministry sent
a letter to Vickers at the end of August stating that their C.16/28 tender
had not been successful in securing the contract. A four-engined Gloster
biplane and the three-engined Handley Page HP 43 received contracts,
although neither progressed beyond the prototype stage, presumably
because of a change in operational requirements.

Two months after the rejection of their initial tender, Vickers submitted
new proposals to the Air Ministry regarding the use of Type 163 in other
rôles. Emphasis was placed on the deployment of the aeroplane in a new
tactical concept—the battle cruiser. Known as the Vickers Battleplane,
the gun armament was much revised. Single 37-mm COW guns were to be
installed in nose and tail positions, with a third firing downward beneath
the fuselage to ward off attack by fighters like the COW gun interceptors.

266

which were under development at the time. (These fighters were intended to be flown below a bomber or airship to enable the upward-firing COW gun to be aimed at its target.) Three other positions were to be sited amidships, armed with either twin 0·303-in guns or one 0·5-in gun. It was the intention that the Battleplanes should be used singly or in small formations to clear a heavily defended target of fighters, enabling the bombers to attack it without severe losses. It was thought that an aeroplane of this type would be able to establish local air superiority. This was a long-lived operational philosophy dating back to the first world war.

In addition to the heavy fighter rôle, the Battleplane was intended to perform the original duties of heavy night-bomber, day-bomber, long-distance reconnaissance, troop-carrier, supply aeroplane and also for naval reconnaissance, in which form the aeroplane could be equipped with floats and armed with 18- or 21-in torpedoes.

Construction of the prototype Type 163 continued throughout 1929 and 1930. Although the project was financed entirely by Vickers, the Air Ministry retained a close interest in the aeroplane and agreed to the loan of four Rolls-Royce F engines for the project, but originally the Air Ministry was reluctant to release FXIVs from stocks for a private venture. The engines offered were similar in most respects, but of earlier marks, and were fully supercharged. In view of their interest in the Type 163, the Air Ministry later changed their decision and allocated four FXIV engines from stores. Towards the end of the life of the aeroplane, Kestrel IIIAs (developed from the Rolls-Royce F series) were installed.

In order to provide the tandem engine installation with propellers of optimum efficiency, two-blade tractor and four-blade pusher units were chosen. The four-blade propellers were designed to be carved in one piece, and this caused official concern, as these were considered unsuitable for tropical use; two-part four-blade propellers, requiring a long hub, were

Another view of Type 163 at the Display showing prominent wheel spats.
(*Flight photo.*)

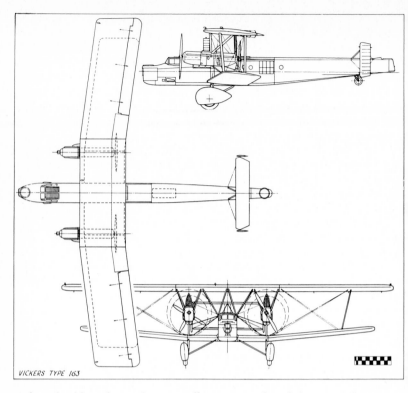

VICKERS TYPE 163

preferred. Also, the pusher propellers were to be of the same diameter as those fitted in the tractor position, which was a fundamental principle of this type of engine installation, and one that precluded the use of larger-diameter two-blade units for the rear engines. It was suggested by the Directorate of Technical Development that the higher-running Rolls-Royce FXI or FXII engines could be used in the aft position, with two-blade propellers, but Vickers had already investigated this possibility and came to the conclusion that the performance loss was unjustified. It was pointed out that the existing installation, of low-running engines and integral propellers, was only temporary—the two-part design used in conjunction with higher-running engines being ultimately used. But as far as can be ascertained, the existing units were used throughout the aeroplane's life, although, at one time, three-blade propellers were considered for the Type 163.

The high all-up weight of the project presented stressing problems, in respect of the large-diameter single main undercarriage wheels which, shortly after flight testing began, were faired by large spats. Although these wheels were cleared for use in the prototype, the strength factor was near the permissible limit, and further aeroplanes of the type would have had a tandem twin-wheel undercarriage in order to spread the weight over

268

a larger number of contact points, in a similar manner to the bogie designs of today.

Early in 1931 the big bomber was completed, and on 12 January Summers, with Radcliffe as observer, flew it for the first time. This flight was of 25 minutes duration and was followed three days later by a flight of 10 minutes. Thereafter, normal contractor trials were carried out. Almost all of these flights were made in the vicinity of Weybridge, although on two occasions the bomber visited Croydon. The Type 163's longest air-borne time during this period was 85 minutes.

Shortly after the flight test programme began, it was decided to install evaporative cooling for the engines, using a similar condenser system to that used on the B.19/27. The installation took a great deal of time, and the aeroplane was on the ground for a long period.

On 15 February, 1932, the Type 163 flew from Brooklands to Martle-sham, in 55 minutes, for full-load trials, and stayed there for 12 days for handling trials by Service pilots. The flight back to Brooklands on 26 February was made in 45 minutes.

As the test programme advanced it became obvious that the Type 163, with its very similar configuration, was suffering from the stability prob-lems which had been so troublesome on the B.19/27. Directional control was in particular difficult, and to improve this a third fin was added on the centreline of the aeroplane. Design changes to the tail unit were also introduced, but the problems were still not overcome. On the B.19/27 the troubles were solved only after drastic alterations to the dihedral and sweepback, but as the Type 163 was a private venture these extreme measures were not undertaken because there was little hope of official finance for the programme, interest in the aeroplane having waned. Orders for the winners of the B.19/27 competition had been placed, and the C.16/28 specification had been abandoned without any production orders.

As in the Vickers B.19/27, the cooling system of the Type 163 was a source of continuous trouble. Serious difficulty was encountered while the aeroplane was at Martlesham in May 1933, and for the following eight months it remained in the hangar while efforts were made to diagnose and rectify the cooling faults. The condensers were eventually found to be the cause, and a new type was ordered and installed. But in the early summer of 1934 the big aeroplane was finally broken up, after having completed some 40 hours of test flying.

During its design life the Type 163 was projected in other forms. As is often the case with a large military design, the possibility of adapting the layout for civil purposes was investigated, and a 37-seat transport version was projected. This, powered by four Kestrel IIIA engines of 510 hp each, had an estimated maximum speed of 145 mph. The loaded weight of this project was 30,970 lb, which included fuel for four hours flying, with commercial reserves. The instruments, lighting and wireless were to the specifications laid down by Imperial Airways, but the project remained a paper aeroplane.

269

An interesting investigation was undertaken in January 1932 into the possible problems involved in flying heavy bombers and transports to the Middle East. Vickers suggested to the Air Ministry that experimental heavy bomber or transport prototypes that had almost completed their test programmes might be used for investigating the problems by undertaking such a flight. Route analyses were made for both the Type 163 and B.19/27. A version of the Type 163, powered by two Rolls-Royce Buzzard engines, and with extended range, was also considered.

Two routes to the Middle East were proposed, one over land and the other completely over water to avoid foreign territory. The point of departure was specified as Boscombe Down, and the main destination was Malta. The direct route to Malta lay across France, the distance being 1,326 statute miles. The second route to Malta was over sea, using flight-refuelling at Gibraltar and, although this route was much longer, covering 2,474 statute miles, it was considered tactically the more desirable. Of the three aeroplanes investigated, the standard four-engined Type 163, with its inherent safety in the event of an engine failure, was found to be the most satisfactory. All three designs could easily have met the demands of such a flight, and the Buzzard-powered Type 163 would have had a maximum range of some 2,000 miles, but no such flights were ever made.

Gloster's big biplane troop-carrier, another entrant in the C.16/28 competition and employing a very similar four-engined configuration, also experienced problems with the rear propellers. When taxying, the two rear

New-types park at Hendon Air Display 27 June, 1931, with Vickers 163 in centre—other aircraft are from Viastra I G-AAUB on the extreme left and in a clockwise direction—Armstrong Whitworth AW XVI Fleet fighter, Handley Page Gugnunc, Cierva Autogiro C19 Mk III, Westland Pterodactyl IV, Hawker Fury I, Hawker Hoopoe II, Gloster SS 19A fighter, Fairey Gordon, Bristol 118 fighter, Short Gurnard II, Avro 626, Westland Wessex and, next to the Viastra, the Saro Cloud. (*MoD(Air) photo*.)

engines were usually shut down and the slipstream of the front propellers caused the rear units to rotate freely. Since this had been solved on the Type 163 by the introduction of propeller brakes, H. P. Folland, the chief designer of Glosters, wrote to Pierson requesting details of the brake system—which had been developed jointly by Rolls-Royce and Vickers. In response to this letter, the details were sent and the system adopted—an example of the free exchange of technical information within the industry.

The Type 163 was one of the many prototypes of the inter-war period which showed promise but never produced in quantity. The aeroplane required further development to realise its true qualities and, as the entire finance for the project was met by Vickers with little hope of future official interest, its full potential was never realised. Although the lack of Air Ministry interest in the later life of the aeroplane seems surprising, their thoughts at this time were rightly concentrated on the new specification for a fast monoplane concept to replace the old biplane formula.

B.19/27 and Vanox

	B.19/27 Type 150	Vanox Type 195
Accommodation:	4 crew	—
Engines:	Two 480 hp Rolls-Royce FXIVS	Two 600 hp Bristol Pegasus IM3
Span:	76 ft 6 in upper, 66 ft 6 in lower	76 ft 6 in upper, 66 ft 6 in lower
Length:	60 ft 6 in	60 ft 4 in
Height:	19 ft 3 in	19 ft 3 in
Wing Area:	1,367 sq ft	1,367 sq ft
Gross Weight:	15,400 lb	16,103 lb
Max Speed:	143 mph at 12,500 ft	135 mph at 5,000 ft
Climb:	12,500 ft in 19 min	10,000 ft in 17 min
Service Ceiling:	23,000 ft	15,000 ft
Armament:	Two Lewis guns	Two Lewis guns

Type 163—Four 480 hp Rolls-Royce FXIVS (Kestrel). Accommodation five crew, and could carry 21 troops. Span 90 ft; length 66 ft 9 in; height 22 ft 4 in; wing area 1,918 sq ft. Gross weight 25,700 lb. Max speed 160 mph; initial climb 950 ft/min; service ceiling 25,000 ft; range 1,150 miles at 140 mph. Armament two Lewis guns; bomb load twelve 250-lb and four 20-lb bombs.

Prototype Vildebeest N230 in original form with Jupiter VIII engine.

Vildebeest and Vincent

In June 1926 Vickers submitted a tender for a torpedo-carrying and bombing landplane to specification 24/25. The project design emerged as a large single-engined tractor biplane with unstaggered wings. It followed developments of the Vixen family and, although larger, resembled the Vendace most closely. The torpedo-bomber was regarded at that time as a front-line weapon for coastal defence, and a replacement was required for the Hawker Horsley, which, although designed as a day-bomber to specification 26/23, had been adapted to the coastal defence rôle.

Vickers' proposals received favourable consideration, and a contract for one experimental airframe was placed by the Air Ministry. The chief requirements were a high ceiling with steadiness at height for precision bombing and, for coastal defence, an alternative arrangement with the greatly increased load imposed by an 18-in torpedo of 2,000 lb weight, with reduced aircraft performance.

The power unit specified was the air-cooled radial Bristol Jupiter VI, with the Bristol Orion planned to follow in supercharged form. The Orion did not materialise, but on 17 November, 1927, sanction was given for the installation of the 460 hp Jupiter VIII, a geared engine on loan from the Air Ministry.

Prototype Vildebeest N230 with Jupiter XF and Townend ring.

The prototype Type 132 was completed at Weybridge in the spring of 1928 with the serial number N230. In April it was flown at Brooklands by Scholefield, and on 14 September it went to Martlesham to begin type trials in competition with the Blackburn Beagle. The Jupiter engine was mounted on the end of a blunt but faired nose with protruding cylinder heads and ram's-horn exhaust stubs. The nose and the fuselage top decking were painted black.

As early as September 1926 the name Vildebeest had been approved, others submitted being Vicuna and Vulpes, the selection having to be from names of mammals. Vildebeest, an Afrikaans word, had been suggested

Prototype Vildebeest bearing civil registration G-ABGE, at Le Bourget for demonstration at Paris Aero Show, 1930.

273

to Vickers by Sir Pierre Van Ryneveld, then acting as their consultant in South Africa, as he thought that the authorities there might be interested in such an aeroplane. The name Vildebeest fitted in nicely with Vickers alliteration; many misspellings subsequently occurred, the usual error being to add a final e, particularly in official documents such as the specification when a development contract was issued in 1931 and the letter from the Air Ministry confirming the name. The spelling error was only cleared up by the Air Ministry in 1934. Another fairly common mistake was the version Vildebeast.

N230 during Martlesham type tests.

After protracted flight trials at Martlesham with N230 it was fitted with a float chassis and tested in seaplane form from the M and AEE at nearby Felixstowe. Great difficulty was experienced, in both landplane and floatplane versions, in attempts to get the engine to run cool, and the addition of a Townend ring around the cylinder heads aggravated rather than cured the trouble, although its main purpose was drag-reduction. Various reasons were advanced for engine over-heating, such as the shape of the nose, and eventually a Jupiter XF replaced the Jupiter VIII without any marked improvement in the cooling problems.

At the end of October 1930 it was decided to present the Vildebeest at the Paris Aero Show, held from 24 November to 5 December, and to give flight demonstrations from Le Bourget, with Air Ministry permission, as the aeroplane was their property. A Jupiter XIF with Townend ring re-

N230 with float chassis, at Weybridge among contemporary Siskin production.

placed the Jupiter XF, and a dummy torpedo, loaded to the correct weight, and full armament were carried in the demonstrations which particularly impressed the Spanish aviation delegation to the Show. For this presentation in another country the civil registration G-ABGE had been granted in lieu of the military serial N230 and was retained on the return of the Vildebeest to Brooklands after the Paris Show, for the resumption of the type trials.

Meanwhile a second Vildebeest had been built in 1930 at Weybridge as a private venture to specification 24/25. First intended to be fitted with a Jupiter XIF engine, it was eventually powered with a geared Armstrong Siddeley Panther IIA, which was also of the air-cooled radial type. It was flown at Brooklands in August 1930 and soon after went to Martlesham under the SBAC symbol O-1, signifying the manufacturer's ownership before application for a civil registration. The PV Vildebeest remained

Private-venture Vildebeest with Panther IIA engine.

Original prototype airframe N230 in third guise as O-3, with Hispano Suiza engine and Supermarine floats for demonstration to Spanish naval mission, from Southampton Water in June 1930.

on test at Martlesham for several months, during which the engine was returned to its makers several times for servicing and overhaul. Compared with the earlier N230, its performance was inferior, and it encountered cooling problems, like N230 and most aircraft at Martlesham at that time.

The object in building this second Vildebeest was to demonstrate it to foreign governments, notably those of Spain and the Argentine. Other countries interested were Rumania, Yugoslavia and Turkey, and, later, Switzerland considered the design, presumably as a tactical bomber. A civil registration, G-ABJK, was issued for the PV Vildebeest, but was later withdrawn because the installation of a Spanish-built 600 hp Hispano Suiza 12Lbr engine (on the suggestion of the Spanish authorities) was transferred to the other Vildebeest.

In January 1931 a development of the Bristol Jupiter engine, known

Puzzle picture at Weybridge—PV Vildebeest with Hispano Suiza engine installed, accompanied by N230—later this operation was countermanded and the Hispano was fitted to N230 for the Spanish demonstration and the marking changed to O-3.

N230 torpedo-bomber during Service trials with 100 Squadron at Donibristle in May 1931.

as the XFBM, was test flown in the first Vildebeest. In due course this engine was replaced by the Pegasus which became, in its various versions, the standard power unit of the RAF Vildebeests. With the advent of this new Jupiter, the cooling troubles vanished. A change to a mineral-based engine lubricant was thought to have contributed to the great improvement in engine performance and behaviour, according to H. Beadle, Vickers' service engineer at Martlesham at the time, an opinion confirmed by engine constructor's tests.

End of the British road for N230—sold to Spain with Hispano engine and delivered with wrong registration—the right one was EC-W11.

The so-called Vickers hangar of Spanish-built Vildebeests at San Janier naval air base; T-25, the last built by CASA, Cadiz, is on the right. (*Spanish Aeronaval official photo.*)

With the XFBM engine, the second Vildebeest, carrying the Service serial N230, was flown on 21 May, 1931, to Donibristle for Service trials with 100 Squadron in the torpedo-dropping rôle and on to Leuchars for firing and bombing. At these RAF stations it passed its trials successfully. All the pilots who flew the aeroplane reported very favourably on its handling qualities, including Wg Cdr G. S. M. Insall, VC (his VC having been won on a Vickers Gunbus in the first world war). After completing its Service trials the Vildebeest was flown to Northolt for inspection by the Chief of Air Staff.

Following the successful type tests and Service trials, a development order for nine Vildebeest torpedo-bombers was placed in October 1931, to a rewritten specification, 22/31. The engine was to be the production version of the XFBM, known as the Pegasus IM3. Certain Service modifi-

Spanish Vildebeest floatplane at San Janier. (*Spanish Aeronaval official photo.*)

278

cations were needed, and of some interest was a requirement for smoke-screen-laying apparatus or target-towing gear.

For the original airframe the former civil registration G-ABGE was retained under approval from the Air Ministry, but the SBAC symbol O-3 was also applied initially. The aeroplane appeared in this guise fitted with the 600 hp Hispano Suiza 12Lbr engine and mounted on Supermarine-designed floats and chassis. The formalities needed to gain approval for flying a Spanish-built engine in a British aeroplane were protracted, but after a short while a French-built version of the same engine was substituted and the engine type approval was easier.

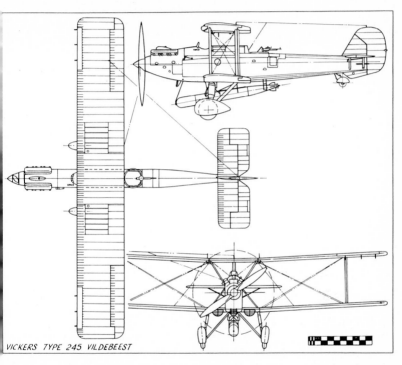

VICKERS TYPE 245 VILDEBEEST

The Vildebeest in seaplane form with the Hispano Suiza engine was flown in June 1930 from Southampton Water by Henri Biard, chief test pilot of the Supermarine Company, then a subsidiary of Vickers. Soon after, it was demonstrated at Hythe seaplane base to an aviation mission from the Spanish Ministry of Marine and was chosen by them for Spanish naval service in preference to the Blackburn Ripon, which was also under their scrutiny. In 1932 a licence was negotiated for the construction of 25 Hispano-engined Vildebeest torpedo-bombers for the Spanish Navy by Construcciones Aeronauticas SA of Cadiz.

On 20 September, 1931, G-ABGE, in the same seaplane form with the Hispano engine, left Southampton on a demonstration tour to Baltic

K2916, the first Vildebeest Mk II, being tested at the MAEE, Felixstowe, as a
floatplane with new style fin and rudder.

ports, flown by Biard. It called at Amsterdam, Copenhagen, Kalmar,
Stockholm, Helsinki, Riga and Memel, from whence it was shipped back
to London. Between Riga and Memel it ran into a most violent storm,
including heavy snow, and Biard had to put the Vildebeest down in a small
creek running into a forest, where it remained for five days tied up to a
tree. Its adventures were not over on reaching England, for, on being
towed back to Weybridge on a land chassis, it met with a road accident
when crossing Putney Common. It was repaired, sold to Spain with
components for a second Vildebeest and ferried in March 1932 to Seville
by H. W. R. Banting. The comedy did not end there, for it flew under the
wrong Spanish registration, EC-WLL, which should have been painted on
as EC-W11. Modified by many engine changes and new components of
later design, the original Vildebeest N230 had as colourful a career in four
years as any other airframe in its generation. The PV O-1 was retained by
the Air Ministry and was written off in a crash at Farnborough.

This complicated story of the two experimental Vildebeest prototypes
was matched by the involved numbering system used by Vickers in identi-
fying the changes made in these aeroplanes, and three others modified
from RAF Vildebeests. Various type and series numbers* were used,
but the real mark numbers of Vildebeests were those built to Air Ministry
contracts for the RAF and consisted only of I, II, III and IV.

The nine Mk I Vildebeests on the first order were S1707 to S1715; one,
S1713, was delivered to No. 100 (torpedo-bomber) Squadron at Donibristle in 1932 for familiarisation. This squadron later moved to Singapore
and established an association between that base and the Vildebeest which
lasted until the Japanese invasion of 1941. In February and March 193..
twelve Vildebeests of 100 Squadron accomplished a round trip of 6,500

* See Type List in Appendix II.

280

Mk II Vildebeests of 100 Squadron in line-abreast formation; note ventral fin initially retained in Mk II. (*MoD(Air) photo.*)

miles from Singapore through Burma and India, calling at 14 places; only one aeroplane of the 12 failed to complete the entire course back to base.

In 1933 the 635 hp Pegasus IIM3 engine became available, and this type was fitted to the Mk II Vildebeest ordered in December of that year.

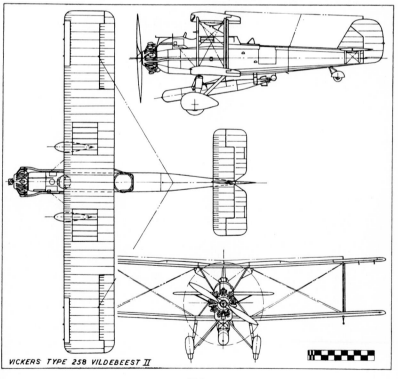

VICKERS TYPE 258 VILDEBEEST II

281

K2814, one of the first batch of Mk I Vildebeests converted to Mk III standard with Pegasus IIM3 engine and three-seat configuration.

S1715 Mk I converted to night bomber rôle.

Mk III Vildebeest of 36 Squadron over Singapore in 1936. (*MoD(Air) photo.*)

Various detail improvements were made to the airframe, including modified tail surfaces. The small ventral fin, a distinctive feature of earlier but not all versions of the Vildebeest, was finally deleted, and the fin and rudder adopted the characteristic square-cut appearance of most Pegasus-engined Vildebeests, the Perseus-engined Mk IV and the Vincent. The first Mk II, K2916, was fitted with a float chassis and tested as a seaplane at M and AEE, Felixstowe, for possible sales to the Latvian Government. It was subsequently converted back to landplane form for trials at the RAE at Farnborough.

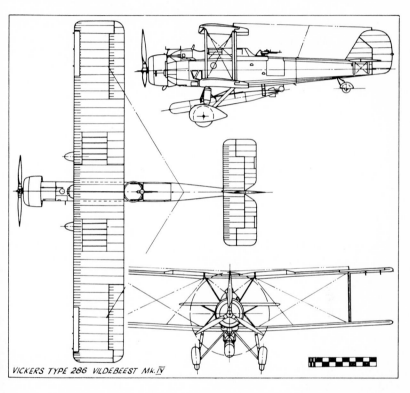

VICKERS TYPE 286 VILDEBEEST Mk. IV

When 30 Mk II Vildebeests had been completed the Air Ministry requested the addition of a third crew member in a redesigned rear cockpit. With this modification the airframe became the Mk III, to specification 15/34. This new requirement arose through service experience with the Vildebeest, which called for a more precise operational technique in the torpedo-dropping rôle. Much trial-and-error experience was being gained in practice with the Vildebeest over the Stokes Bay torpedo range at Gosport. The pattern of torpedo-dropping from aircraft was developed in these exercises and led to a perfection of the art to be used with great effect in the second world war, notably with the Fairey Swordfish.

Vildebeest Mk III flown by solo pilot round RAF stations on Empire Air Day, 1937, from Gosport. (*MoD(Air) photo.*)

The Mk III Vildebeests were delivered to No. 36 Squadron in 1934 and to 22 Squadron in 1935, both torpedo-bomber units. Also in 1935 the New Zealand Government evaluated the aeroplanes and bought 12 Mk IIIs for the Royal New Zealand Air Force; later they acquired another 15 Mk IIIs from the Air Ministry contract, and the RAF serial numbers were changed to NZ numbers. One difference in the New Zealand Vildebeests was the provision of folding wings.

Continuous improvements and developments in the Bristol range of air-cooled radial engines led to the introduction of the 825 hp Perseus sleeve-valve type. This new engine was installed in a Mk III Vildebeest, K4164, as a flying test-bed. This aeroplane had been at the disposal of the

Mk III Vildebeests of 100 Squadron refuelling at Kuala Lumpur. (*MoD(Air) photo.*)

Directorate of Technical Development since October 1934 for experimental use at the RAE and elsewhere. The prototype Perseus PRE-4M engine was mounted in K4164 as a power-egg complete with accessories and with a Bristol-NACA long-chord cowling. A Rotol three-blade variable-pitch propeller was fitted as a further refinement.

Vildebeest production in 1932, with Type 163 bomber.

The first sleeve-valve radial engine to enter service, civil or military, the production Bristol Perseus VIII, led later to the Hercules and Centaurus, both widely used in the second world war and after. With the increased power available from the Perseus, the performance of the Mk IV Vildebeest was greatly improved compared with previous marks. Top speed was 156 mph and initial climb 840 ft/min. Reversion was made to a two-man crew, the third cockpit of the Mk III being covered by a hatch. Two airframes were converted in 1936 from Mk III to Mk IV, the test-bed K4164 and, oddly, K4614. Vickers' records show 18 Mk IVs built at Weybridge, K6408–K6414 and K8078–K8088. Other figures of Mk IVs produced may refer to conversions made outside the factory.

Of the original nine Mk Is, the last three were converted for evaluating the suitability of the Vildebeest for rôles other than torpedo-bomber. S1713 was adapted as a three-seat TSR (torpedo-spotter-reconnaissance) type, S1714 as a general-purpose aeroplane as the prototype Vincent, and S1715 was modified as a night-bomber.

A Mk II airframe was converted at Weybridge as Type 252 for demonstration and submission to TSR specifications S9/30 and M1/30. Carrying no serial number, it flew first under the SBAC denomination O-7. Later

Prototype Mk IV Vildebeest converted from Mk III, with Perseus engine in long-chord cowling, and wheel spats.

it obtained the civil registration G-ACYV. For the M.1/30 submission, it was fitted with a Pegasus IIIM3, but was also tested with the Pegasus IIM3 and IIL3 for comparison. It was similar in appearance to the Perseus-engined Mk IV with long-chord cowling and wheel spats. It failed to win an order, but undoubtedly set a pattern for later TSR shipboard aircraft. Meanwhile Vickers had prepared a Wallis design also for the M1/30 specification, and its short career is traced in the next section.

Perseus sleeve-valve engine installation in Vildebeest Mk IV.

Mk II Vildebeest airframe completed at Weybridge for submission to TSR specifications and later used for demonstration under registration G-ACYV—note long-chord cowling for Pegasus engine, and wheel spats.

VINCENT. On 21 December, 1932, the converted Mk I Vildebeest, S1714, was sent on an extended tour of Royal Air Force stations in the Middle East, the Sudan and East Africa, on trials as a general-purpose aeroplane. Later, the Air Ministry issued specification 21/33 for this class, and the satisfactory completion of the tour by S1714 and flight tests at Martlesham led to an initial order for 51 GP Vildebeests on 8 December, 1933. A new name was requested, as the rôle was quite different from that of the torpedo-bomber Vildebeests. An historical association was desired, and from a number of names submitted, which included Vortigeon and Verulam, that of Vincent was selected, presumably from Admiral Rodney's victory over the Spanish fleet at Cape St Vincent in 1780.

S1714 Mk I Vildebeest converted to prototype Vincent with long-range tank between undercarriage legs.

287

The first production Vincent, K4105, at Martlesham for Type test, without long-range tank but with wing-mounted bombs.

The Vincent replaced the Wapitis and Fairey IIIFs which had served overseas for so long. The rugged airframe of the Vildebeest/Vincent class with the robust and reliable Bristol Pegasus IIM3 air-cooled radial engine fitted the requirement admirably. The Vincent was a three-seat type with an auxiliary fuel tank underslung between the undercarriage legs in place of the torpedo of the Vildebeest. This external tank was the one distinguishing feature of the Vincent, and with it the range was extended to 1,250 miles. Maximum disposable load was about 4,000 lb, and specific bomb load was 1,000 lb. Comprehensive tropical equipment was provided, and specific military equipment included message pick-up gear for Army co-

Vincent in full war paint on active service. (*Photo R. J. Hobbs.*)

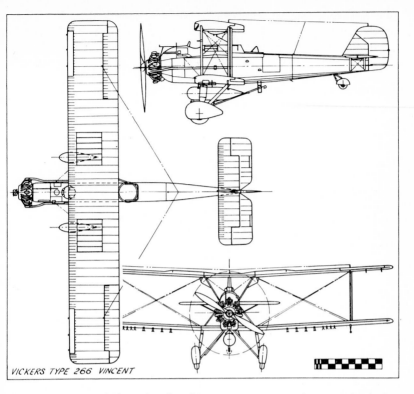

VICKERS TYPE 266 VINCENT

operation, pyrotechnics, sleeping bags, emergency rations, and wireless
telegraphy and telephone with collapsible masts for ground operation.

The first Vincent was a converted Vildebeest Mk II, K4105, type-tested
at Martlesham to the revised GP specification 16/34, and it appeared in
the RAF Display of 1935. There was a large conversion of Vildebeests to
Vincents and considerable production of new airframes, the total operating
as Vincents being 197.

Vincents became operational at the end of 1934 with No. 8 Squadron at
Aden replacing Fairey IIIFs, and superseded the Wapitis of Nos. 55 and
84 Squadrons in Iraq and of 31 Squadron in India. In 1937 a flight of five
Vincents of 47 Squadron with two Vickers Valentias of 216 Squadron flew
from Khartoum to West Africa and back, thus confirming the suitability
of the Vincent for long-range operation in tropical conditions.

At the beginning of the second world war Vildebeests and Vincents had
to stand in for later aircraft not available immediately for service. The
Vildebeest was the only torpedo-bomber of RAF Coastal Command, and
Vincents were in action in East Africa in 1940–41 and in Iraq in 1941.
The two Vildebeest Squadrons, 36 and 100, were left to face the Japanese
invasion of Singapore in 1941, but as this was overland, their resistance,
however gallant, was unavailing and their losses heavy. Two Vildebeests

289

of 36 Squadron continued the fight in Java, but were lost in Sumatra when trying to reach Burma.

Although ungainly by modern standards, with their square-cut outlines, Vildebeests and Vincents were endeared to the RAF more for their stout construction, which stood up well in the trying heat and dust in Iraq, India and the Sudan, than for any startling performance. The family represented a typical Pierson design, no doubt influenced by the production team, which disliked curves and streamlines difficult and costly in manufacture. The Vincent was the last to use the Vickers metal-framed construction, with a tubular fuselage and tail, and wings of steel spars with double tubular booms and wandering webs, with light-alloy tubular ribs. How this structural pattern was to change into the geodetic airframe of Wallis conception is related in the next section.

Vildebeest

	Type 132 (N230)	Type 209	Type 216 (Landplane)
Accommodation:	Pilot and observer	Pilot and observer	Pilot and observer
Engine:	One 460 hp Bristol Jupiter VIII	One 525 hp Bristol Jupiter XIF	One 600 hp Hispano Suiza 12Lbr
Span:	49 ft	49 ft	49 ft
Length:	36 ft 8 in	36 ft 8 in	38 ft 6 in
Height:	14 ft 8 in	14 ft 6 in	14 ft 8 in
Wing Area:	728 sq ft	728 sq ft	728 sq ft
Empty Weight:	3,990 lb	3,571 lb	4,702 lb
Gross Weight:	7,527 lb	7,529 lb	8,500 lb
Max Speed:	115 mph at 15,000 ft	123 mph at 10,000 ft	155 mph at 10,000 ft
Initial Climb:	345 ft/min	605 ft/min	650 ft/min
Climb to 5,000 ft:	18·1 min	9·5 min	7 min
Absolute Ceiling:	16,700 ft	15,000 ft	26,500 ft
Range:	—	—	1,120 miles at 148 mph
Armament:	One Vickers gun, one Lewis gun One torpedo or 1,100-lb bomb load	One Vickers gun, one Lewis gun One torpedo or 1,100-lb bomb load	One Vickers gun, one Lewis gun One torpedo or 1,100-lb bomb load

	Type 244 Mk I—Landplane	Type 267 Mk III—Landplane	Type 286 Mk IV—Landplane
Accommodation:	Pilot and observer	Pilot, observer and gunner	Pilot and observer
Engine:	One 600 hp Bristol Pegasus IM3	One 635 hp Bristol Pegasus IIM3	One 825 hp Bristol Perseus VIII
Span:	49 ft	49 ft	49 ft
Length:	36 ft 8 in	36 ft 8 in	37 ft 8 in
Height:	14 ft 8 in	14 ft 8 in	14 ft 8 in
Wing Area:	728 sq ft	728 sq ft	728 sq ft
Empty Weight:	4,229 lb	4,773 lb	4,724 lb
Gross Weight:	8,100 lb	8,500 lb	8,500 lb
Max Speed:	140 mph at 10,000 ft	143 mph	156 mph at 5,000 ft
Initial Climb:	630 ft/min	630 ft/min	840 ft/min
Climb to 5,000 ft:	7·5 min	7·5 min	6 min
Absolute Ceiling:	19,000 ft	19,000 ft	19,000 ft
Range:	1,250 miles at 122 mph	1,250 miles at 122 mph	1,625 miles at 133 mph
Armament:	One Vickers gun, one Lewis gun 1,100-lb bomb load	One Vickers gun, one Lewis gun 1,100-lb bomb load	One Vickers gun, one Lewis gun 1,100-lb bomb load

Vincent—Type 266—One 635 hp Bristol Pegasus IIM3. Accommodation—Pilot, observer and gunner. Span 49 ft; length 36 ft 8 in; height 17 ft 9 in; wing area 728 sq ft. Empty weight 4,229 lb; gross weight 8,100 lb. Max speed 142 mph at 5,000 ft; initial climb 765 ft/min; absolute ceiling 19,000 ft; range 1,250 miles at 133 mph. Armament—one Vickers gun, one Lewis gun, 1,000-lb bomb load.

M.1/30, G.4/31 and the Wellesley

When the airship construction programme was abandoned by the British Government after the R.101 disaster in October 1930, Vickers' subsidiary, the Airship Guarantee Company, was liquidated. Consequently, all the leading executives and technicians concerned in the design and construction of the Vickers' airship R.100 were released for other work. B. N. Wallis, the designer of R.100, joined Pierson at Weybridge as chief structures designer. There he proceeded at once to apply his considerable knowledge of light-alloy stressed members, gained from airship structures, to airframe design for aeroplanes.

In March 1930 a specification had been issued for a torpedo-bomber ship-plane replacement for the 450 hp Napier Lion powered Blackburn Ripon, to provide an improved all-round performance. Obviously, one of the later British engines of much greater power was needed for its successor, and for their tender Vickers chose the 825 hp Rolls-Royce H10 engine, later named the Buzzard IIIMS, which was geared and moderately supercharged. A special development of the Buzzard known as the Rolls-Royce R enabled the Supermarine S6 and S6B to win the Schneider Trophy international seaplane races of 1929 and 1931 respectively. Much later still, the

M.1/30 being assembled at Weybridge; its close structural affinity to airship practice may be seen in the wing spars.

291

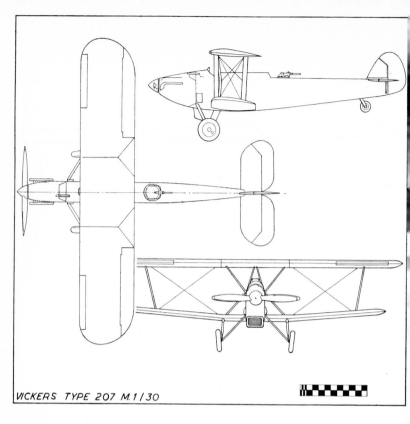

Rolls-Royce Griffon was of the same cubic capacity and configuration as the Buzzard and the R. The H of the engine type designation referred to the series and not to the configuration, which was of typical Rolls-Royce design, that is, of the upright vee twelve-cylinder liquid-cooled type.

To this new specification, M.1/30, Vickers prepared a massive and purposeful design of the conventional single-engined tractor biplane type, with a single-bay wing cellule. In response to official requirements, comprehensive Service equipment was included, such as radio, electrical services, wheel brakes, arrester hook and hoisting-gear attachments. Handley Page slots and Frise ailerons were fitted, while the control surfaces were mass balanced. Servo control was applied to the elevators by aerodynamic means, consisting of mounting the movement lever direct on the trailing-edge tab so that when the tab was moved angularly up or down into the air flow it would move the elevator up or down, but in the opposite direction, thus relieving the pilot of stick load. The wings folded backwards to facilitate carrier stowage.

Structurally, Vickers M.1/30—it was never named—was highly interesting. In the tender an unusual lightness was claimed 'by the incorporation of structural methods similar to those recently used so successfully on HMA R.100'. The wing spars were double duralumin tubular booms with W type webs built up from lightened diagonal channels, as in airship members. The heavier drag ribs also had diagonal webs of similar design. Adapted from a Wallis invention for airship construction, the longerons were riveted lengthwise from two halves of pressed duralumin, and were made in sections between the bulkheads or frames, joined with special lightweight screwed fittings in a complex arrangement which also provided anchorages for the fuselage struts and cross bracings. The fuselage struts were built-up duralumin girders, and the complete structure was stabilised by angle-section longitudinal stringers which supported the fabric-covering. The interplane struts were steel tubes, encased with massive fairings.

The undercarriage, with Vickers oleo-pneumatic springing, was of the split-axle type, to accommodate the torpedo between the legs. Provision was made for ground adjustment of the angle of incidence of the torpedo, to provide differential water-running characteristics. As a bomber, the M.1/30 could carry, in the torpedo position, one 2,000- or one 1,000-lb bomb, or four 500-lb bombs under the lower inner planes, or variations on these arrangements.

At one stage during the project design a proposal to use steam evaporative engine cooling was examined, as some difficulty was encountered in designing an aesthetically pleasing underslung radiator—because of the torpedo or bomb position. Evaporative cooling had been tried on Vickers' contemporary B.19/27 bomber, but had been found to need more experimental development, and so was discarded on the M.1/30.

The Vickers M.1/30, S1641, was first flown at Brooklands on 11 January, 1933, by Mutt Summers, with John Radcliffe as his flight observer. During the next few months 24 flights were made, some of only short duration, but some of up to an hour. Various modifications were made, such as

M.1/30 running up at Brooklands before its first test flight. (*Rolls-Royce photo.*)

adjusting the positioning of the control surface mass balances. The only major change was the introduction of a two-degree dihedral on the hitherto flat top plane to improve lateral stability.

Nearly all the test flying was done by Summers and Radcliffe. On 23 November, 1933, they took-off to carry out ceiling and level speed trials at full load, including an unarmed torpedo, as required by the official acceptance type tests, which the M.1/30 was shortly to undergo at Martlesham. As the engine was running a little rough, Mutt Summers decided to break off his original flight plan and to proceed direct to the next stage, which was the high-speed dive. In his flight test report, John Radcliffe continues the story: 'The nose was put down gently to an angle of about 45 degrees and the air speed rose to about 200 knots. After a further slight increase of speed the nose came up slightly which change of attitude was accompanied by a small pressure on the seat. Then things began to happen. Simultaneously there was a sharp shock from the direction of the starboard wing, an alteration in the appearance of the starboard wing structure and a very violent and uncontrolled half-roll to the right, accompanied by a continuous noise of breaking structure.'

In the inverted position a very large force occurred, detaching the fuselage from the rest of the aeroplane and throwing out the pilot, whose parachute opened at once. Radcliffe's safety belt was released or broken, and he found himself suspended by his parachute back-strap from the machine-gun on the starboard side of his cockpit. In this position he noticed that the tail unit was properly in position, with pieces of fabric caught up on the tailplane. After some seconds he became detached and he then released his parachute.

G.4/31 biplane during erection with early geodetic-type fuselage and conventional Vickers wing structure.

'The fuselage was seen to be falling without wings and portions of fabric and structure were falling on all sides,' continued Radcliffe, an observation confirmed by eye-witnesses on the ground. The crew landed safely. The unarmed torpedo was found in a local churchyard.

This was the first time the M.1/30 had been dived at speed, and the accident was later thought to have been caused by a distorted tailplane incidence jack. Certainly the incident caused much investigation into tail stiffness factors by the RAE. The excessive bending moment on the wings could have been produced either by a maladjustment or a misalignment of the tail surfaces, probably the latter, as Radcliffe saw the tailplane in one piece during his suspension in mid-air. One result of the accident was a complete rewriting and reassessment of tail structure stress formulae in the official publication A.P.970 on design calculations.

Lesser men than Wallis might have been discouraged from probing further into theories of lightweight structures. But he proceeded to evolve the unique geodetic form of construction with its multiple members and its exceptional strength/weight ratio.

G.4/31 biplane in flight at Brooklands; the pilot's position with all-round view is noteworthy.

G.4/31. An opportunity to utilise the talents of Wallis came when, in November 1931, Vickers submitted a tender to specification G.4/31 for a general-purpose bombing and torpedo aeroplane. A preference was expressed in this specification for an air-cooled engine, and the Bristol Pegasus IM3 type was selected. Vickers wrote up project design data around three separate paper aircraft. The first was a low-wing monoplane with open cockpits and trousered fixed undercarriage, and a Pegasus IM3 engine mounted in a pointed, streamlined nose; the second was a similar monoplane but with the Rolls-Royce Kestrel IIIMS water-cooled engine mounted in a pointed nose with an underslung radiator; and the third was for a wide-span Pegasus-engined biplane, reminiscent of the earlier Vespa, and again with a trousered undercarriage.

These proposals were examined by the Air Ministry; the third alternative was accepted, and a contract placed in April 1932. Design speed was 162 mph at 4,500 ft, and the torpedo version was to weigh approximately the same as the M.1/30 torpedo-carrier. Drawing-office and production work proceeded on the biplane, but, in parallel, a private-venture monoplane designed to the same specification was being engineered by Wallis on a fully geodetic system as already embodied in embryo form in the biplane fuselage.

In its concept this biplane incorporated a Wallis-designed fuselage structure consisting of four light-alloy longerons made in sections with lightweight screwed joints, as in the M.1/30, but simpler. Around these longerons were wrapped spiral channel members in opposing directions, clockwise and anti-clockwise, to form a type of multiple lattice structure with curved members.

This breakaway from the established structural design practice in airframes, which had persisted since the first world war, was a direct result of

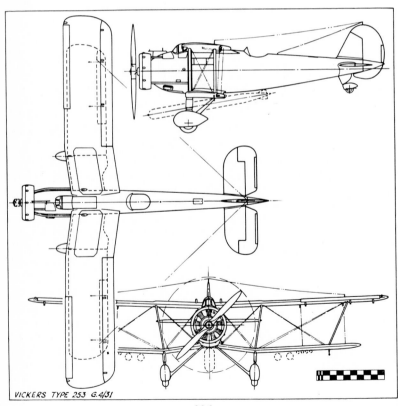

VICKERS TYPE 253 G.4/31

Vickers G.4/31 biplane and monoplane together at the Hendon Air Display of 1935.

the experience Wallis had gained from airships. He sought to dispense with the primary and secondary members by substituting a lattice work system of main members only, but with dual purpose, an idea he derived from the wire netting containing the gas bags of R.100. If such a system could be perfected, then there would be a great saving in weight, which would introduce startling new strength/weight factors in fabric-covered aeroplanes. This was eventually achieved, but the G.4/31 biplane fuselage represented only a mid-way stage between the M.1/30 exploratory structure and the full geodetic private-venture monoplane later to achieve fame as the Wellesley.

A geodetic line is the shortest line between two points on a sphere and is known in global navigation as a great-circle route. Applied to airframes, the theory had advantages, in that load transfer from member to member was by the shortest possible route and a multiplicity of redundant members combined to form almost a perfect fail-safe system. In the Wallis lattice-work pattern if one series of members was in tension the opposite members were in compression, thus the system was stress-balanced in all directions. Cut-outs for cockpits, gun turrets and bomb compartments needed special reinforced frames.

An attempt was made to design a single-spar wing system for the G.4/31 biplane with what were termed co-planar struts, which meant simply single-strut outer bays with self-balancing torsional bracing by an inverted V pyramid of two struts to the inner bays. This design was based on the Raf 34 wing section as used by the M.1/30; but a proposal to revert to the well-established Raf 15 section in a two-spar wing with two struts to each bay, with a thickened centre section to accommodate the fuel tanks (as on the Vildebeest), was accepted by the Air Ministry in August 1933. The reason given was that the Raf 34 characteristics were too little known at that stage, particularly in relation to the effects on the stabilising behaviour of tail surfaces, with the M.1/30 experience in mind, and Vickers preferred to rely on the time-proven Raf 15 in conventional biplane wings.

In this form and powered with a Pegasus IIM3 engine, the G.4/31 biplane, K2771, was flown solo by Summers from Brooklands on 16 August, 1934. Subsequently it was flown with various experimental modifications at Brooklands, by the RAE at Farnborough and on official trials at Martlesham. In February 1935 the engine was changed for a Pegasus IIIM3. Meanwhile the Vickers PV monoplane was approaching completion. It was flown by Summers for the first time at Brooklands on 19 June, 1935, and on the following day he made another flight with Wallis as his passenger.

Comparative trials of the two Vickers G.4/31 designs showed such disparity in their respective performances that the Air Ministry were placed in a dilemma, as 150 biplanes had been ordered. This was evident at the RAF Display at Hendon in June 1935 when, from the few particulars released about them, as revealed on a display board in the new-types park, it could be deduced that the PV monoplane (designated O-9) had a better all-round performance at a greater all-up weight, which meant a better

Prototype G.4/31 monoplane under construction at Weybridge, showing complete geodetic structure; in background G.4/31 biplane and, on left, Pegasus engine and former for B.9/32 mock-up.

The prototype G.4/31 Wellesley private-venture monoplane.

payload, since its airframe was lighter with the same engine, the Pegasus IIIM3. A reappraisal of the two types was unavoidable, and in the event the prototype G.4/31 biplane survived as the only example, being retained by Bristol Aeroplane Company at Filton until the war as a flying test-bed.

WELLESLEY. Strong representations were made by Sir Robert McLean, chairman of Vickers (Aviation) Ltd, to the Air Ministry about the relative merits of the two G.4/31 designs. In consequence, the biplane contract was cancelled, and on 10 September, 1935, a new contract was placed to a rewritten specification, 22/35, for 96 monoplanes, with the type name Wellesley. Much of the performance advantage of the monoplane as a much cleaner aeroplane was gained from reduction of drag, and also from its high-aspect-ratio wing, of nine to one with excellent lift/drag ratio, made possible by its geodetic construction.

On 23 July, 1935, the G.4/31 prototype monoplane crashed on landing at Brooklands. One leg of the manually operated retractable undercarriage was damaged on being raised after take-off, by the flight observer R. C. Handasyde, because of mechanical misalignment. The port wing was extensively damaged, being pierced by the loose wheel and leg in the crash.

Pre-production Wellesley K7556 at Brooklands in January 1937.

299

First production Wellesley, K7713.

It had been flying with a prototype variable-pitch propeller, as later developed and fitted to the long-range Wellesleys.

The reconstructed aeroplane underwent extensive modification. In its new form, as the pre-production Wellesley, it was given the serial number K7556. Enclosed cockpits with sliding hoods were fitted, a hydraulically-operated undercarriage replaced the original manual type, a broader-chord rudder was incorporated and panniers were suspended below the wings on pylon struts to serve as bomb containers. At that time it was thought inadvisable to break the continuity of the geodetic structure of the fuselage to provide a bomb-bay. Later, this problem was satisfactorily solved in the Wellington. One point of some import was that the Wellesley had been ordered as a medium bomber—the general-purpose and torpedo-carrying requirements of the specification apparently having been dropped, although the latter duty was to be re-assessed at a later date. K7556 was powered with the later Pegasus X engine, which was fitted with the Bristol-Townend ring and integral exhaust collector as used on O-9. The propeller was of fixed-pitch Fairey-Reed type with three duralumin blades. In March 1936, K7556 went to Martlesham, where it remained for a time on type and development trials.

Much evolutionary work was put in hand on this aircraft with production

Wellesley production at Weybridge works.

Pilot's cockpit of prototype Wellesley.

type wings fitted. The hydraulic system, in addition to operating the undercarriage, was also applied to the Schrenk-type flaps and to the bomb slips.
Comprehensive electrical services were introduced for the various forms

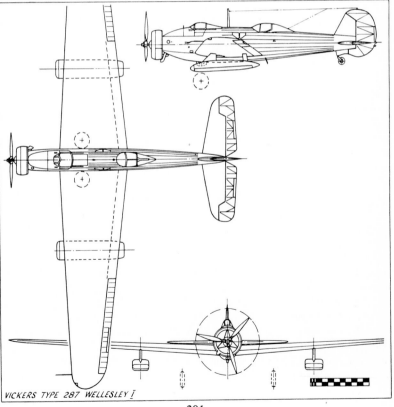

VICKERS TYPE 287 WELLESLEY I

Wellesleys of 45 Squadron airborne in Egypt. (*MoD*(*Air*) *photo*.)

of lighting, gun heating, bomb-gear control, chassis and flap indicators, petrol gauges and camera actuation. A new type of tailwheel was introduced. In fact, the Wellesley was beginning to take on the more refined and somewhat sophisticated look of a modern aeroplane, which was later to be enhanced when the time came to embody the latest Service equipment.

There is little doubt that the Wellesley was responsible for the great technical advance in Vickers design taking place in the middle 'thirties, to be absorbed into the B.9/32 bomber project and so leading to the production Wellington. So much new development work was going on at Weybridge at that time that a promising design for a dive-bomber with a Rolls-Royce engine to specification O.27/34 * had to be dropped after metal had been cut.

Much engineering development was necessary because of the unusual form of the individual members of the Wellesley structure. In addition, metallurgical research was needed, and various structural test rigs were installed to prove the strength of the airframe design. These requirements led to the sophisticated aircraft laboratory and systems test equipment at Weybridge today. A great stirring was evident then in the aircraft industry, fortunately, because the Royal Air Force expansion scheme was imminent.

One problem was how to devise a satisfactory method of fabricating the multiplicity of curved geodetic channels. From an elementary hand-operated forming machine, evolved for making light-gauge components in older Vickers types such as the Vellore and the Vildebeest, power-driven machinery was developed which was able to produce members in quantity at a rate which solved the problem of production time and removed doubts in the minds of the Ministry's technical officers as to the efficacy of the airframe system evolved by Wallis. And the equipment devised for forming curvilinear channels has been used ever since, as highly developed

* See drawing on page 485.

machinery, to produce fuselage frames and similar members for the succession of post-war Vickers aircraft up to the VC10.

It has been said that Vickers might have gone straight into stressed-skin construction at that time, and so short-circuited a great deal of development effort; but true stressed-skin was then in an exploratory stage only, particularly in British aircraft design, and still required a considerable amount of research and test. Wallis's geodetics set a new high in strength factors which other structural systems did not match for a considerable time, particularly in high-aspect-ratio wings.

In August 1936 the contract for Wellesleys was amended to include the Bristol Pegasus XX engine for standard production, to provide a maximum speed of 213 mph. At the same time talks were started on the use of the Wellesley as a Hercules test-bed, this engine being the latest development of the air-cooled type with sleeve valves. It subsequently became one of the power plants which played a notable part in second world war aircraft.

The first production Wellesley, K7713, was flown at Brooklands by Summers on 30 January, 1937. It was delivered on 18 March, and was immediately flown to Martlesham for type tests by Flg Off J. K. Quill, of Vickers' flight-test staff. The second production Wellesley, K7714, was delivered to 76 (Bomber) Squadron at Finningley for Service trials. The first squadron to be re-equipped with Wellesleys was in fact No. 76 (B), and within a year other bomber squadrons to receive Wellesleys as new equipment were Nos. 35 and 207 (Worthy Down), 77 (Honington) and 148 (Scampton). Shortly afterwards the Middle East Squadrons 14, 45 and 223 also received Wellesleys.

In March 1938, at a conference held to consider bringing the Wellesley medium bomber up to operational readiness standards, it was reported that 176 of the type were in service, 57 of these being home-based. Among the more important items considered were the provision of a third crew member amidships at a navigating station, and detail improvements in the prone bombing position. K7748 was selected for trial modifications under Type 402. This may have incorporated an inter-cockpit glazed canopy as referred to later, but no mention is made of this in Vickers' records.

After the first eight Wellesleys had been delivered, a speed limitation of

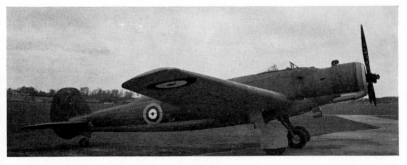

Wellesley K7772 as Hercules engine test-bed for Bristol Aeroplane Company.

303

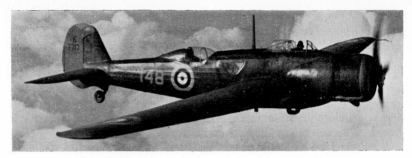

K7717, trial Wellesley for the Long Range Development Flight.

200 mph was imposed until they had been returned to the manufacturers to have the wings strengthened to a standard to which all later Wellesleys were built, after which the maximum permissible speed was raised to 264 mph. Some vibration was experienced when diving with the bomb-container doors open. This was overcome partly by cutting back the leading edges of the doors and wholly by deleting them altogether, without much influence on drag.

An operational requirement just beginning to receive serious attention was the jettisoning of fuel. There had been provision for off-loading some of the fuel of the long-range Wellesleys specially modified for the Long Range Development Unit of the RAF, which had been formed at Upper Heyford in January 1938. Any malfunctioning in the early stages of a long-distance flight, thereby necessitating a forced landing, might make it desirable to reduce the landing weight for safety, especially when carrying a large fuel load.

K7717, the fifth production Wellesley, had an interesting career. After being allocated to 45(B) Squadron in Egypt, it was there fitted temporarily with a Pegasus XVIII for tropical engine trials, and then returned to the United Kingdom for use as a trial horse for the long-range conversions,

Wellesley K7744 jettisoning fuel during experiments at RAE; the long glazed canopy between the cockpits led to the unrecognised designation Mk II.

with the later strengthened wing, and as a flying test-bed for the special Pegasus XXII engine also being developed for the long-range Wellesleys. It also served to prove fuel jettisoning as a practical emergency procedure, an exercise later continued at the RAE by K7744. The latter had the inter-cockpit glazed canopy, which has led to the designation of Wellesley Mk II, although Vickers' documents do not contain any such identification.

A great deal of thought and effort was put into the development of special Wellesleys and engines for the long-range flights to explore the limits of extreme range with a Service type aeroplane, and with the ultimate objective of an attempt on the world record for distance in a straight line, at that time held by the USSR. This enterprise was officially inspired and sponsored, and was most ably supported by the engine makers, the Bristol Aeroplane Company.

The special version of the Pegasus, the Mk XXII, was prepared with a slightly higher compression than the standard Mk XX as fitted to the Service Wellesleys, and with a smaller supercharger, as the operational height for the long-range flights was fixed at 10,000 ft. The planned objective was to attain the optimum economical cruising fuel consumption. That more notice was not taken of this significant, and indeed ominous, achievement seems in these days surprising. Perhaps the atmosphere was clouded by international events contemporary with the capturing of the world record by the Wellesleys, events which culminated in the notorious Munich Agreement, when everyone relaxed—a short-lived breather. It was little realised that before long the national existence would depend in part upon long-range load-carrying military aircraft.

In quite a different way, the success of the long-range flights was of equal merit and portent to the winning of the Schneider Trophy races by the Supermarine seaplanes which led to the evolution of the Spitfire. The Wellesleys showed the way to the sorties of extreme duration which became part of operational flying in the war, destined, unhappily, to follow within a year of their flying non-stop from Ismailia, Egypt, to Darwin, northern Australia, some 7,158 miles, early in November 1938.

Indicative of the advanced techniques used for the record flight of the three Wellesleys of the Long Range Development Unit was the introduction of automatic boost and mixture control for the Pegasus XXII engines, thus ensuring that the pilots neither wasted fuel by faulty manual control nor damaged the engines by using an extremely weak mixture. This device was later applied to operational aircraft generally, and was of great value.

Five standard Wellesleys, apart from K7717, were converted for the Long Range Development Unit which had been formed under the command of Wg Cdr O. R. Gayford, DFC, AFC, who, as a Sqn Ldr, with Flt Lt G. E. Nicholetts had flown from Cranwell to Walvis Bay, S.W. Africa, in 1933 in a special Fairey monoplane.

The five Wellesleys were L2637, L2638, L2639, L2680 and L2681. The

Flt Lt Hogan's Wellesley at Ismailia, being rolled out for the attempt on the world distance record by the RAF Long Range Flight.

Sqn Ldr Kellett landing at Ross Smith airfield, Darwin, after breaking the world distance record with Flt Lt Combe.

RAF Long Range Flight of three Wellesleys during tour of Australia after record flight.

changes made to them were the substitution of the Rotol constant-speed propeller for the standard de Havilland-Hamilton two-pitch type, deletion of all military equipment, the introduction of the Mk IV automatic pilot, increase of the fuel (100-octane leadless petrol) capacity to 1,255 gal (later increased to 1,290 gal by the sacrifice of the crews' personal baggage), oil tankage increased to 60 gal with a tropical oil radiator, a rest position for the third man and a strengthened undercarriage with heavier tyres. Various additional engine accessories included an engine-driven vacuum pump for instrument actuation and an additional hydraulic pump for undercarriage actuation (the other being diverted to the propeller operation gear) driven from the rear of the engine by carden shaft. The NACA type long-chord cowling was developed on K7717 by Bristols to reduce drag and promote cooling, baffles being added between the cylinders. The front fuselage monocoque was faired into a circular section to mate with the special cowling. K7717 was used at Filton as a test-bed for the Pegasus XXII and was flown by Capt Cyril Uwins, Bristols' chief test pilot, on 21 January, 1938. On 25 January he completed a seven-hours test flight, and flight development on economical cruising consumption proceeded.

On 7 July, 1938, a flight of four long-range Wellesleys, L2638, L2639, L2680 and L2681, under the command of Sqn Ldr R. Kellett, flew 4,300 miles in 32 hours, from Cranwell, Lincolnshire, to the Persian Gulf, doubling back and landing at Ismailia, Egypt. Later they returned to Upper Heyford, home base of the Long Range Development Unit, to prepare for the attempt on the world distance record.

On 5 November the Wellesleys L2638 (Sqn Ldr Kellett), L2639 (Flt Lt H. A. V. Hogan) and L2680 (Flt Lt A. N. Combe) took off from Ismailia's 3,600-ft runway and set out for Australia. Take-off weight was 18,400 lb, and the operating height of 10,000 ft was reached in 45 minutes as planned. It had been hoped to get help from favourable winds, which was one reason the route had been selected. After 12 hours' flying they became adverse, and over the Bay of Bengal the weather deteriorated. Flying conditions became still worse over the South China Sea, with cloud, heavy rain and lightning. The existing record held by the USSR was surpassed by all three aircraft after passing Macassar on the island of Celebes, but it became evident on reaching the Dutch East Indies (now Indonesia) that L2639 might not have enough fuel to get to Darwin, the terminal point. By mutual agreement between the commanders of the three Wellesleys (fitted with short-range R/T as well as two-way wireless equipment), Flt Lt Hogan landed at Kupang, Timor, continuing his flight after refuelling.

Sqn Ldr Kellett and Flt Lt Combe crossed the Timor Sea and, after 48 hours in the air, landed at Darwin at the airfield named after Ross Smith, commander of the first flight from England to Australia in the Vickers Vimy 19 years earlier. L2638 had 44 gal of fuel left and L2680 had 17, a marginal residue indeed, but due to adverse winds over much of the flight. The world distance record created by the Wellesleys was homologated by the FAI as 7,157·7 miles and stood for eight years until 1946.

Wellesley in raid on Keren during Italian East African campaign in 1940.

In a personal letter to Vickers' sales manager, then Tommy Broome, the former test pilot, Sqn Ldr Kellett wrote from Australia: 'The planes are in awfully good shape, the fabric bare and torn in places from rain, otherwise as new and very clean. Two broken valve springs the only engine defect found, apart from routine adjustments. The automatics behaved splendidly in them all.' The automatics referred to were three-axes automatic pilot control system as first developed by the RAE and test flown in Virginias.

Wellesleys were replaced in RAF Bomber Command in 1939 by Hampdens, Whitleys and Wellingtons; they were transferred to Middle East Command and continued to render signal service and featured in the early stages of the second world war. They were used in the Italian East African campaign and in the air attack launched from Aden on Italian Somaliland, as well as in the desert war in North Africa. Meanwhile the B.9/32 medium-bomber project, which had run parallel with Wellesley production at Weybridge, had blossomed into the Wellington, which from then on occupied most of Vickers' attention.

M.1/30—Type 207—One 825 hp Rolls-Royce Buzzard IIIMS. Accommodation pilot and observer. Span 50 ft; length 43 ft 7 in; height 14 ft 5 in; wing area 724 sq ft. Empty weight 5,200 lb; gross weight 9,600 lb. Max speed 159 mph at 4,000 ft; climb to 4,000 ft in 5 min; service ceiling 16,000 ft. Armament one Vickers gun, 2,000-lb bomb load.

G.4/31 Biplane—Type 253—One 635 hp Bristol Pegasus IIM3. Accommodation pilot and observer. Span 52 ft 7 in; length 37 ft; height 12 ft 6 in; wing area 579 sq ft; empty weight 4,500 lb; gross weight 8,350 lb. Max speed 161 mph at 4,500 ft. Armament two Lewis machine-guns.

Wellesley—Type 287—One 925 hp Bristol Pegasus XX. Accommodation pilot and observer. Span 74 ft 7 in; length 39 ft 3 in; height 12 ft 4 in; wing area 630 sq ft. Empty weight 6,369 lb; gross weight 11,100 lb. Max speed 264 mph; initial climb 1,200 ft/min; climb to 19,680 ft in $17\frac{1}{2}$ min; service ceiling 33,000 ft; absolute ceiling 35,250 ft; range 2,590 miles at 188 mph at 15,000 ft. Armament two Vickers guns, 2,000-lb bomb load.

308

A familiar scene during the early period of the Bomber Command offensive against German targets; Wellingtons taxying out for take-off at dusk from a base in Britain.
(*IWM photo.*)

The Wellington Bomber

In October 1932 Vickers tendered for a twin-engined medium day-bomber to specification B.9/32. In the design study submitted for this new type a special feature was made of the geodetic construction that had been so successfully introduced in the Wellesley. Structural tests of the Wellesley airframe at the RAE, Farnborough, had produced remarkable results. A strength factor of 11 was reached without any sign of failure, which was far in advance of the mandatory figure of six. When the detail design of the B.9/32 came to be undertaken, further development of the geodetic concept led to a reduction in the size of the individual members, which were formed into standard sections, of simpler and lighter construction than those of the Wellesley.

Although great progress had been made in aircraft and engine design since the end of the first world war, it had become obvious to designers and engineers in the industry that the mandatory requirements of the official specifications had become out of step with the advances achieved in aerodynamics, structures, metallurgy and motive-power efficiencies. In previous tenders for new designs, insistence was placed on the requirement that the tare weight of the aeroplane as laid down by the specification should be adhered to, an obligation which restricted the designer by limiting the structural weight, and hence the weight and power of the engine.

Pierson of Vickers and Volkert * of Handley Page, who were both tendering to the same B.9/32 specification (the Handley Page submission became the Hampden) made representations to the Air Ministry about this handicap, which undoubtedly tended to produce slow and inefficient weight-carrying aircraft. Pierson and Wallis were convinced that the new Vickers bomber should be equipped with the most powerful engines available, irrespective of the influence of their weight on the tare weight of the

* G. R. Volkert was chief designer of Handley Page Ltd at that time.

K4049 B.9/32 prototype being rolled across the River Wey at Brooklands over the bridge, at that time on private property; the landowner used to charge a toll for all aircraft except those bearing roundels, signifying Ministry ownership.

aeroplane. During the period between the submission of the B.9/32 tender in 1933 and the completion of the prototype in 1936 the tare weight of the Vickers bomber rose from 6,300 lb to 11,508 lb. This meant in effect that the Air Ministry had accepted the advice of the aircraft designer and had removed the crippling terms of the specification.

While design of the B.9/32 was in progress the political and military climate of Europe was changing rapidly. The threats of the German and Italian dictators began to exert pressure on the British Government to make a reappraisal of the strength of its armed forces, especially that of the Royal Air Force.

The potential offered by the B.9/32 design was the subject of new concepts of bomber policy. From 1933 onwards its bomb load and range were being constantly revised. As early as November 1935, the Air Staff were inquiring about the possibilities of using the aeroplane at an all-up weight of 30,500 lb with assisted take-off—a very high figure for a medium-bomber of those days.

By 1936 it was realised that the priority requirement was to provide the largest number of bombers—the spearhead of attack—in the shortest possible time, to form the nucleus of the new Bomber Command of the Royal Air Force. In fact, an initial order for 180 Wellingtons was placed in August 1936, before the first meeting to decide the details of the production aircraft.

The following year, 1937, was crucial for Vickers. Besides the pilot order to the parent company, a contract was placed during October with the Gloster Aircraft Company for 100 Mk 1 Wellingtons with Bristol Pegasus engines, to be followed by another 100 Mk IIs with Rolls-Royce Merlin Xs.

Some time later an order for 64 Wellingtons was placed with Sir W. G. Armstrong Whitworth Aircraft of Coventry. In the event, these orders were eventually transferred to the Chester and Blackpool works of Vickers Armstrongs when the shadow factory scheme was introduced.

With production of the Wellington assured, Vickers were faced with the problem of making the manufacturing process as simple as possible. They responded by announcing their target of one aeroplane per day; an actual exercise was undertaken when a complete Wellington airframe was assembled in 24 hours. This feat had never before been attempted in metal construction and with so large an aeroplane by a British aircraft manufacturer.

Critics of the geodetic form of construction, while accepting its high strength/weight ratio and its ingenuity, condemned it on the grounds that for quantity production it was impracticable and would take too much production time. But Wallis, whose baby it was, together with the Weybridge production team valiantly led by Trevor Westbrook backed up by the toolroom and the draw-bench shop, devised the necessary tools and methods for producing the numerous parts which went together to make

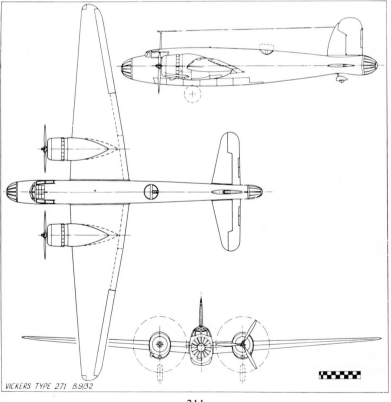

VICKERS TYPE 271 B.9/32

up the complete airframe. The real proof of the essential simplicity of the Wellington structure, not obvious from a cursory inspection, was proved by its subsequent extensive production in the factories at Blackpool and Chester, which between them produced 8,946 airframes with a minimum of key personnel, the bulk being semi-skilled workers new to aircraft construction.

The prototype B.9/32 participating in a demonstration of Vickers aircraft at Eastleigh airfield, Southampton, on 18 June, 1936, three days after its first flight at Brooklands; the Spitfire prototype, as a Vickers-Supermarine product, also took part.

A civil version of the Wellington was prepared as a design study for Nigel Norman, of Airwork, in May 1939, and in September of that year two representatives of British Airways (the pre-war airline eventually merged with Imperial Airways to form BOAC) visited Weybridge to discuss a civil version for use on the West African route, with the possibility of an extension across the South Atlantic. Another study was submitted to the Air Ministry for a transport version, providing for a maximum of 13 troops but no navigator or, alternatively, 11 troops plus a navigator. At that time, too, New Zealand was re-equipping its Air Force, and ordered 18 Wellingtons.

With the higher cruising speeds of the Wellington, it was realised that the old type of exposed or semi-exposed gun mounting would have to give way to a totally enclosed turret; more important still, such a turret would have to be power-operated if it were to be effective against opposing fighters moving in at high speed and capable of rapid positional manoeuvres.

These turrets caused some hard thinking and absorbed many man-hours in design. Vickers, like other aircraft manufacturers, were convinced that with their long experience of aircraft hydraulics they were capable of designing turrets themselves. But the more the basic problems were gone into, the more evident it became that gun turrets were a specialised subject

312

which required undivided attention. The Air Ministry then insisted that they were to be ancillary equipment, designed and supplied by independent manufacturers. This decision relieved the airframe designer of a large amount of detail design work and also led to a certain degree of standardisation between British bombers.

During 1935 the shadow group of Government-sponsored factories was proposed for the quantity production of airframes and aero-engines in the event of war. Their function was to produce in quantity any type of airframe or engine that had been officially frozen in design. This in turn allowed the parent firm to develop new or improved types and, in time, to place them with the shadow factories for production. So, it was hoped, there would be a continuing technical advance, keeping the production of military aircraft abreast of operational requirements.

With the Wellington there is no doubt the system proved eminently successful, for more of the type were produced than any other British bomber, and its diversity of operational rôle was wider. Wellingtons, in fact, served in all flying commands except Fighter, and the massive support in production rendered by Vickers' factories at Chester and Blackpool proved, in the event, of the greatest value to the parent works at Weybridge, particularly after the disruptive enemy action there in September 1940.

Just recognition must be made here of the notable contribution that Barnes Wallis's unique system of geodetic construction made to the war effort of Britain. Many an aircrew, including those who were later to hold important commands in the Royal Air Force, survived to tell the tale of the apparent invulnerability of the Wellington. The engineering term fail-safe is a more recent introduction, but never had it been more justified and earned than by the Wellington.

The invitation to submit a design study to specification B.9/32 came from the Air Ministry on 20 October, 1932. In the following December the

Front fuselage of B.9/32 prototype bomber, without fabric covering, disclosing detail of geodetic construction and cupola-type windshield for front gunner.

313

RAF personnel inspecting the internals of a Wellington wing at Vickers' Squires Gate Blackpool works; this was one of the 'shadow' factories set up by the Government fo the RAF expansion scheme in the late 1930s.

estimated tare weight of this bomber project was increased from 6,300 t 6,500 lb. A comparison of the respective performance details of the Bristo Pegasus IS2 or IIS2 and the Armstrong Siddeley Tiger engines resulted i the choice of the Pegasus, that is, for the air-cooled engine version of th bomber; for the liquid-cooled engine variant of the basic project the Rolls Royce Goshawk I was selected.

These two versions were submitted in tender designs in February 193 and in the following September the Air Ministry placed a pilot contrac for a bomber with Goshawk engines. Meanwhile the tare weight had re mained at 6,500 lb.

By this time the revised specification included front, rear and midshi

Wellington X, HE239, after return from Duisburg raid, April 1943.

314

gun mountings with wind protection. The proposed aeroplane was also altered from a high- to a mid-wing configuration, to give a better view to pilots flying in formation, a change which also improved the aerodynamic characteristics. The revised specification also called for the modification of bomb undershields and the incorporation of spring-loaded bomb doors. The oil system was also revised. Permission to raise the tare weight to 5,798 lb was requested, and this increased weight was accepted in principle.

So the detail design proceeded, while the ancillary installations became progressively more complicated as a result of production and operational requirements. The fixed-weight penalty became apparent, and by June 1934 the Air Ministry had cancelled the prohibitive tare weight limit of 6,500 lb.

Typical aircrew of Wellington posing in front of Frazer-Nash rear turret.

In August 1934 Vickers submitted proposals for using the more powerful Bristol Pegasus or Perseus air-cooled engine in place of the Goshawk, promising considerable improvement in speed, climb, ceiling, and ability to fly on one engine, without a correspondingly serious increase in all-up weight. It was also hoped that the delivery date of the first aircraft could be brought forward. The Air Ministry quickly accepted these proposals, and took the opportunity to increase the fuel load to provide a range of 1,500 miles at 213 mph at 15,000 ft. The Pegasus engines were to be fitted with variable-pitch propellers, and, following wind-tunnel tests, Vickers' nose and tail turrets were also accepted. The loaded weight by this time was mounting rapidly, following the removal of the restrictive fixed tare weight.

The first flight of the prototype B.9/32, K4049, was made at Brooklands on 15 June, 1936, by Mutt Summers, accompanied by Wallis and Westbrook. K4049 was powered by two 915 hp Bristol Pegasus X engines giving a speed of 250 mph at 8,000 ft at an all-up weight of 21,000 lb. Of interest in design was the borrowing of the profile shape of the Vickers-Supermarine Stranraer fin and rudder, to save time in design hours.

A crew of four was provided for, with allowances for one supernumerary for special duties. The bomb load was nine 500-lb bombs or nine of 250 lb for long-range operations. Nose- and tail-gun stations were fitted for single guns in each. These cupolas were hand-operated, but there was provision for a third gun with a retractable shield to be mounted in a dorsal position halfway along the fuselage.

The Vickers B.9/32 was rightly regarded at that time as the most advanced design of its day, and its subsequent flying trials proved beyond doubt that it was of exceptional merit and that a production order would follow as a matter of course. But before its trials were fully completed it met with an unfortunate accident while undergoing Service tests in April 1937. The horn balance of the elevator was of the type which was shielded at small angles of trim but was exposed to the slipstream at full travel; in this condition, excessive load caused the failure of the horn balance and the aeroplane turned on to its back. The pilot was thrown through the roof of the cockpit and escaped by parachute, but the flight engineer, unable to get free, was killed in the crash, the aeroplane being completely destroyed.

The name Crecy was originally chosen for the B.9/32 in June 1936, just before it was publicly shown in the new-types park at the Royal Air Force Display at Hendon; but in September the name was changed to Wellington. In a later explanation Pierson said that it had been correctly named after a town according to Air Ministry nomenclature, but the name Wellington also perpetuated the memory of the Iron Duke, and followed tradition in that its geodetic predecessor bore the Duke's family name, Wellesley. Moreover, it established the practice of using the initial letter W for Vickers aircraft with Wallis geodetic structures.

MK I. At the first meeting to discuss production-design requirements, the main details were decided for the Mk I Wellington. The engines selected were Pegasus XVIIIs, with allowance for Pegasus XXs in the event of delays in developing the two-speed supercharger intended for the Mk XVIII. The fuel capacity was fixed at 696 gal maximum, and the maximum bomb load at 4,500 lb, while the all-up weight was estimated at 21,000 lb.

Defensive armament comprised bow and stern power-operated turrets

Wellington Mk I prototype, L4212, on the apron at Brooklands before the first flight.

Wellington I fuselages in the erecting shop at Weybridge in 1939 showing typical 'basket weave' geodetic construction.

plus a ventral retractable turret midships, all mounting two 0·303-in Browning guns. These turrets were of Vickers design, but the Air Ministry asked that the Frazer-Nash control unit should be used, as it was being developed to a highly satisfactory degree at that stage. Provision was made for 600 rounds of ammunition for the front-turret guns and for 1,000 rounds for each of the mid and rear turrets.

There was provision for cockpit heating and for de-icing, and it was agreed that cabin heating should be developed and introduced at a later stage. De-icing was classified as ancillary equipment and was also to be installed as development proceeded.

The propellers initially fitted were of the de Havilland-Hamilton two-pitch type, but the possible development of the constant-speed type with increases of up to 20 degrees pitch was to be kept in mind and fitted when available. Dual-control conversion sets were stipulated, indicating that dual training was to be a priority with the first aircraft to be delivered to the Royal Air Force.

A special discussion on the fuel system took place at Weybridge in December 1936. The geodetic construction of the wing offered a then unique method of stowing the fuel, the unobstructed space between the front and rear spars being available outboard of the engine nacelles, and containing three separate tanks in each wing. Each tank was piped independently to a collector box in the bottom of the fuselage, the pipe entering through a non-return valve so as to isolate each tank.

As a result of the flying experience gained with the B.9/32 while it existed,

317

Prototype Wellington Mk I, L4212, taking off for its first flight from Brooklands on 23 December, 1937; the wooded St George's Hill in the background consists mainly of coniferous trees.

a new specification, 29/36, was issued in February 1937 to cover the production version of the Wellington. This specification could be described as an interim measure to speed the provision of aircraft for the rapidly expanding Royal Air Force.

The production Wellington Mk I was a complete redesign, and went hand in hand with the detail design of the larger and heavier B.1/35 (Warwick) twin-engined bomber. As a result, large portions of the two aeroplanes were common to one another, an engineering operation made easier by the singular features of the geodetic structure with its special member-forming machinery. This parallel detail design suited the Wellington admirably, for a deeper fuselage emerged which nicely accommodated the specified larger bomb load and associated equipment. It also provided better disposition for the regular aircrew, who were increased to five.

The nose was lengthened to accommodate the revised gun turret and bomb-aimer's position. The waisting on the B.9/32 in the rear fuselage forward of the tail unit was deleted in the redesign and replaced by a straight

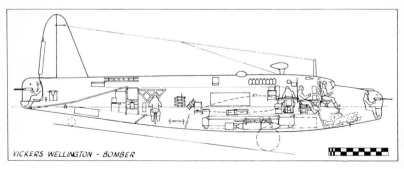

VICKERS WELLINGTON - BOMBER

318

taper, which in effect deepened the rear end. Accordingly, advantage was taken to raise the tailplane by six inches to give a better position on the deeper fuselage. The redesigned horizontal tail unit of high aspect ratio also allowed the deletion of the horn balances of the B.9/32. This unit, with the deep fuselage and tapered wings of high aspect ratio and the tall single fin and rudder assembly, became a characteristic feature of the Wellington—which perhaps was just as well in view of the elementary state of aircraft recognition early in the war. Constant-speed propellers were introduced, and another feature introduced at that time was the fitting of a retractable tailwheel.

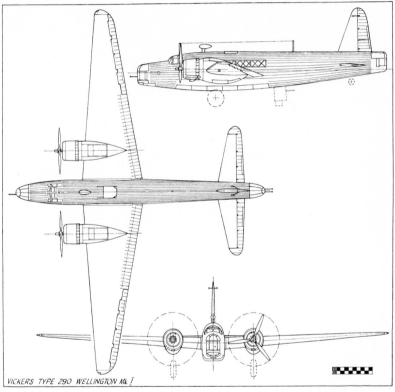

VICKERS TYPE 290 WELLINGTON Mk I

Meanwhile, Frazer-Nash turrets had made further progress during the redesign of the Wellington, and the Air Ministry requested the replacement of the Vickers ventral midships turret with one of Frazer-Nash design. This was heavier than the Vickers type, and there was consternation when Pierson produced data showing that the aeroplane c.g. position with this alternative turret was extremely critical. The outcome was a decision to fit the Frazer-Nash turret to the first production aircraft only, compensating by ballast to obtain the required flying characteristics during handling trials.

319

The first Mk I, L4212, first flown by Summers on 23 December, 1937, at Brooklands, was powered by Bristol Pegasus XXs—the Mk XVIIIs had not then completed type trials. An intensive flight programme followed, unfortunately held up during February and March 1938 by an under-carriage failure caused by the misalignment of a toggle strut. While repairs were being made the Pegasus XVIII became available and was installed, the whole repair and engine change being completed by 12 April, when test flying was resumed.

Production Wellington Mk I on test near Weybridge; note upper surface of wing revealing geodetic-member pattern. (*Flight photo.*)

During the flight trials with K4049 the basic aeroplane had been found to be aerodynamically stable and to possess considerable self-righting properties. Therefore it seemed fairly safe to assume that the production Wellington I would have similar characteristics, but when conducting diving trials on L4212 it was discovered that the aeroplane was nose heavy in the dive. This was a serious matter. An immediate investigation was held and the trouble traced to the elevator arrangement. In place of the horn balance of the B.9/32, the elevator had been redesigned, balancing being effected by tabs plus a reserve tab for trimming. Vickers and the RAE could not agree on the solution, Vickers wishing to return to the horn balance, and the RAE recommending the inset-hinge arrangement. Con-sequently, a decision was made to experiment with both systems.

A new horn-balanced elevator was fitted and flown on L4213 on 9 September, 1938. Then followed a series of modifications involving a small increase in horn balance and trim-tab areas, the latter mass-balanced, while the chord of the flaps was decreased. The flaps were also inter-connected with the elevator tabs. The modifications provided acceptable handling qualities at that stage.

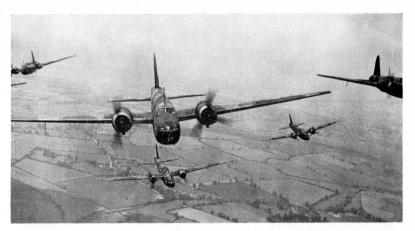

Wellington Mk Is of No. 9 Squadron, which took part in the second raid of the war, in formation.

In the meantime engine availability determined the next developments of the Wellington. The Mk II (supplementary specification Wellington 2P1) was to be fitted with Rolls-Royce Merlin Xs, and the Mk III (3P1) with Bristol Hercules IIIs. As some time was obviously to elapse before these two types of engine could be available in production form, a decision was made to anticipate some improvements intended for the two later marks by introducing these in variants designated IA, IB and IC.

MK IA. In the supplementary specification written for this variant (Wellington IAP1) it was stated that the design was to be in accordance with that of the Mk II. Therefore, the IA was based in fact on the then

A Wellesley and a line-up of Wellington Mk Is seen under the starboard wing of the Wellington Mk II prototype at Brooklands before airfield dispersal was necessitated by the outbreak of war.

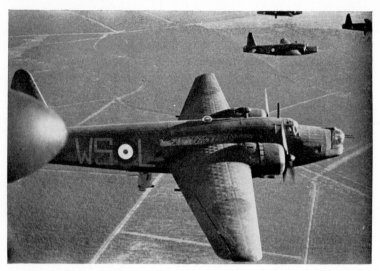

Wellington Mk IA R3000 of 9 Squadron flying over Honington early in 1941, with its ventral mid-turret lowered to combat position. (*Photo Tim Mason.*)

unborn Mk II; not on the Mk I. Another interesting fact was that the engines were to be interchangeable, Pegasus or Merlin, but this scheme was never pursued, the Pegasus X being fitted exclusively.

Salient features of the Wellington IA included Frazer-Nash turrets in the nose, midship and stern positions, an airframe stressed at the all-up weight, 28,000 lb, of the Mk II, and a strengthened undercarriage to allow for the increase in all-up weight. The wheels were increased in diameter and the chassis was also moved forward slightly to improve the centre-of-gravity characteristics of the aeroplane. The bomb gear and oxygen supply were also redesigned as in the system for the Mk II.

MK IB. A Wellington IB was proposed as a result of difficulties experienced with the armament. The Vickers' nose and stern turrets gave considerable trouble during firing and other operational trials. These difficulties, combined with the c.g. problems caused by the Frazer-Nash ventral turret, added up to a situation in which the Wellington was defensively weak, a condition which could not be tolerated; consequently, with the deletion of the ventral turret on all Wellington variants and the general introduction of the Frazer-Nash nose and stern turrets, the Mk IB, intended as an armament trial-horse, was to all intents and purposes identical with the IA, and so never appeared in Vickers production records. Some doubt exists as to whether any IBs were, in fact, ever completed; if so, they must have been quickly reclassified as IAs.

MK IC. In the Mk IC variant all the development experience that had been acquired up to that time was incorporated. A redesigned hydraulic system was introduced using VSG pumps, together with a 24-volt electrical system required to operate the DR (directional radio) compass. The engineering evolution of the Wellington IC was one of those examples of ingenuity which have always characterised the British aircraft industry. The merits of combining new hydraulic and electrical systems, demanded by the rising standard of operational requirements, in one variant instead of two was due to the initiative of Westbrook, then in executive control of production at Weybridge. In consequence of this independent action, approved at a local technical committee meeting, type records had to be written up some time later to put the designation IC in order and to remove the embarrassment of a variant that officially did not exist.

One of the most important modifications introduced on the Mk IC, and subsequently incorporated on all marks, was the substitution of beam guns in the midship position for the unsatisfactory ventral turret. The whole Wellington I sub-type position was finally cleared up by this modification, and on 19 August, 1940, the Air Ministry issued a directive which said, 'Mk IA and IC aircraft on which the mid-turret has not been fitted are to be considered as the standard aircraft for their respective types.' It is significant that the proposed IB was not mentioned.

Wellington Mk IC P9249, equipped with Frazer-Nash turrets, built at Weybridge and delivered in January 1940.

Beam guns of Vickers K type were installed on the Wellington Mk IA P9211, which was flown to Boscombe Down for trials, where the Aeroplane and Armament Experimental Establishment had been moved from Martlesham. The A and AEE recommended, as a result of firing trials, that Browning 0·303-in guns should be used instead of K guns and that the beam gun position should be moved farther aft. Some IA and IC aircraft had provision for either type: the Vickers K mounted above the cabin window, or the Browning within the window itself.

The Wellington IC with the Pegasus XVIII was a most successful bomber,

323

Chester-built Wellington Mk ICs of 311 Squadron with the modified roundels of late 1940.

and 2,685 were built. Its airframe and systems in general formed the basis for later marks. In the Mk IC the Royal Air Force had initially an aeroplane in which the engineering was geared to the exigencies of the time.

By the time the Mk IC entered service in force the strategy of day-bombing had changed into one of formation night-bombing only. Operational experience had dictated the futility of attempting daylight raids at medium heights by unescorted large bombers, even though comparatively heavily armed. The failure of the reconnaissance and bombing sortie by 24 Wellington Is over the Schillig Roads and Wilhelmshaven on 18 December, 1939, with the loss of over half the formation, drove this lesson home forcibly.

For as the Wellington had set the pace in bomber design and development prior to the second world war, so it measured up to the tactical plans and preconceived theories of the air offensive against Germany when hostilities began on 3 September, 1939. No. 3 Group of Bomber Command, equipped with Wellington Mk Is and IAs, was based in East Anglia on that date and comprised 8, 9, 37, 38, 99, 115 and 149 Squadrons and the two Reserve Squadrons, 214 and 215.

On 4 September, 14 Wellingtons of 9 and 149 Squadrons raided Brunsbüttel, where two German warships had been reported by air reconnaissance. Bad weather and heavy anti-aircraft fire interfered with the action, and two aircraft, which had penetrated the harbour, were lost. Others failed to locate the target, while the bombs which did score hits were ineffective. In addition, there was an embargo imposed by the War

The Wellington Mk IC production line at Weybridge which was the target of a low-level
daylight raid by Junkers-Ju 88s on 4 September, 1940; the large number of casualties
led to the rapid extemporising of a wide dispersal of component production in small
units throughout the locality, the main assembly remaining at Brooklands.

Cabinet on attacks on other than strictly military targets, which precluded
the bombing of enemy ships in harbours, for fear of injuring civilians in
the vicinity.

On 3 December a force of 24 Wellingtons from 38, 114 and 147 Squadrons, based at Mildenhall and Marham, attacked units of the German
fleet moored at Heligoland, from high level in cloud, with almost negative
results on either side. This action was taken to confirm that Wellingtons,
with their turrets and strong geodetic construction, and flying in close
formation, could penetrate strongly defended areas. But this confidence
was shaken on 14 December, when 12 Wellingtons of 99 Squadron penetrated the Schillig Roads near Wilhelmshaven at low level, under heavy
fire from warships, flak-ships and fighters which came up to join the fight.
The Wellingtons maintained formation and shot it out, but five were lost
and one crashed when almost home, against the loss of one enemy fighter.

Four days later, on 18 December, the 24 Wellingtons from 9, 37 and
149 Squadrons, attempted an attack, as mentioned earlier, on the German
fleet and naval bases in the Schillig Roads and Wilhelmshaven. Alerted
by radar, German fighters pounced on them near Heligoland, and they
were under continuous fighter attack until 80 miles from home on the
return flight, except when engaged by anti-aircraft guns of the naval bases.
Although they covered the whole target area, the Wellingtons were unable
to drop their bombs, as all vessels were in harbour, where bombing might
have endangered civilians. Over half the force was lost in one way or
another against four German fighters destroyed.

Typical scene on a wartime Bomber Command station; a Wellington Mk IC of
149 Squadron bombing up and refuelling.

Unescorted day-bombing was thereafter abandoned, and the Wellington
force of Bomber Command was gradually built up into a weapon of attack
on German industrial and communication targets by means of night raids.
Lessons learned from the Wellington's early daylight raids were that the
Vickers-designed turrets had insufficient traverse; that the dustbin ventral
turret was useless against beam attacks from above; and that self-sealing
fuel tanks were essential to avoid disastrous fires caused by bullets punc-
turing the tanks and allowing the petrol to spill out near the engines.

MK II. In accordance with the change of official policy regarding the
choice of the most powerful engines available for any class of aeroplane
rather than specifying tare weight as the criterion, the design of the Wellington Mk II was begun in January 1938, with the Rolls-Royce Merlin as an
alternative power plant. This action had the additional advantage of
unbroken supply in the event of delay in the production of air-cooled
engines.

Although the Mk II was primarily an engine-change modification, some
redesign was undertaken, based on experience gained from the Mk I.
Because of delay in the production of the Merlin X, the prototype Mk II,
L4250, did not fly until 3 March, 1939.

At the first weighing it was discovered that the engine packs were 403 lb
heavier than the original weight allowed; this was a very undesirable feature, for it resulted in a forward shift of the c.g., with detrimental effect on
both flight characteristics and ground handling. An adjustment for flying
trim was therefore made by the addition of ballast at the aft-turret position.
Corrections for ground handling were made by moving the main chassis
legs and wheels slightly forward in the down position by introducing longer
backstays, an innovation later used to overcome similar problems when
overload conditions had to be accepted.

326

Prototype Wellington Mk II, L4250, before its first flight on 3 March, 1939.

The main changes in the Mk II were the introduction of Frazer-Nash turrets at the nose, midship and stern positions, and the installation of a 24-volt electrical system for the aircraft and radio services. The oxygen supply was also modified to suit the Frazer-Nash turrets, while the hydraulic system incorporated VSG type pumps to provide a 1,000 lb/sq in power supply for aircraft services, the turrets being powered by a secondary system at 300 lb/sq in. Cabin heating was installed and an astrodome fitted.

After the first test flight the engine gear ratio was changed from 0·477:1 to 0·42:1, with the propeller blade setting increased to suit. An ice guard was fitted to the fuselage in the disc plane of the propeller, because at altitude these tended to throw ice. During the second test flight it became apparent that the Mk II was unstable fore and aft, and that the performance was below the estimated design figures. To overcome this instability, about 40 sq in were added to the horn balances of the elevators, which type had after all been reinstated; this modification proved ineffective, and the eventual solution was to enlarge the tailplane by increasing the chord by one foot.

Another contributory cause of instability was the opposite rotation of

Wellington Mk II W5461 of No. 104 Squadron, which received this Mark in April 1941.

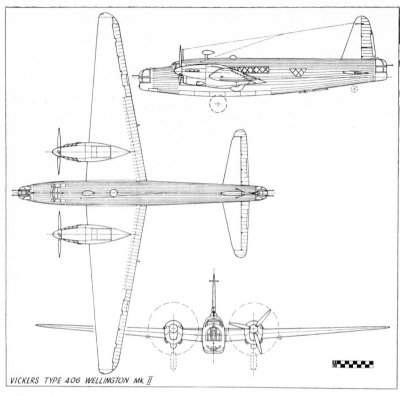

VICKERS TYPE 406 WELLINGTON Mk. II

the Merlin-propeller combination to that of the Bristol-engined marks, and also the difference in shape of the Merlin nacelles. When the Pegasus was exchanged on the same aeroplane as a trial the original flying qualities were restored. The Rotol propellers were changed to a de Havilland type and at a high-level conference on 1 May, 1939, the changes on the Merlin-powered Mk II were approved. For production, the larger tailplane was to be fitted, and, in addition, a stronger undercarriage with larger-diameter wheels was required.

The Mk II prototype, L4250, was then delivered to Rolls-Royce at Hucknall for further tests on drag reduction, and after exhaustive tests the all-round performance was raised to much higher figures. As can be imagined, these difficulties involved an enormous amount of test flying, most of which was carried out by Summers and R. C. Handasyde.

Production of the Mk II was planned to begin in June, and the first serial numbers were to be P2515 and P2533. But on 16 October, 1939, the Air Ministry stopped work on the series under a revised scheme of engine production and allocation, caused by war exigencies. Despite this hold-up, the majority of the modifications were implemented, and by the end of 1939 the performance of the Mk II was superior to that of the Mk IC.

328

Another Wellington Mk II of 104 Squadron, W5437, EP-Q; based at Driffield with 4 Group for the night-bombing offensive in the European theatre until the Squadron moved to the Middle East.

Take-off and maximum speed were better, and with the increased power developed by the Merlins, a higher all-up weight could be achieved. Consequently, a greater load of bombs could be carried, or range could be increased by carrying more fuel. With a higher ceiling and cruising speed as well, the Mk II possessed factors taken into consideration when it was chosen for further developments, namely the first 4,000-lb bomb installation, the 40-mm heavy gun experiment, the high-altitude Mk V Wellington and later the Whittle turbojet test-beds. In these matters the power available for take-off was particularly attractive.

By the end of February 1940 the Air Ministry were again ready to proceed with the production of the Mk II, and Vickers were instructed to allot a IC airframe, R3221, for conversion to Mk II standard. About this time data was sought for the Wellington fitted with Rolls-Royce Griffon engines, but the promise of the Bristol Hercules 7SM ruled this out.

A Wellington Mk II of 305 (Ziemia Wielkopolska) Polish Squadron being rolled out for an operational sortie.

Loading an F.24 camera in its crate into the bomb bay of an operational Wellington; a little-known duty in the massive air raids was to bring back photographic records of ground strikes—on the left is the photographic section officer with distinguishing star on lapel.

Despite the work already done on pitch stability, the tail unit was still a subject of experiment and modification at this time, but the instability was now confined to the single-engine case; this situation had to be fully resolved because of the number of aircraft that would have to return in this condition from sorties over enemy territory.

On 1 May, 1940, the production order for Mk II Wellingtons was increased to 200, and with modifications introducing the 4,000-lb bomb, tropicalisation, long-range tanks and so on, the all-up weight was increased to 33,000 lb. Take-off data was based on the use of 100 octane fuel, with engines at 3,000 rpm and 9 lb boost, and flaps at 18 degrees. During tests at these figures the pilot reported that take-off was straightforward apart from a swing to starboard below 40 mph, corrected by partially closing the starboard engine throttle, after which the swing could be checked by rudder alone. Distance to clear the 50-ft screen was about 1,450 yd.

In a letter to Vickers from the Deputy Director Operational Requirements, dated 8 August 1940, was this comment: 'Mr. Wallis turned up to a meeting I held yesterday on the subject of big bombs, and I am interested in his proposals for carrying a 4,000-lb bomb in a Wellington. . . .' Thus the installation began in a rather casual manner, but led to a special contract and instructions to proceed in the following October.

A Wellington Mk II, W5389, was selected for the conversion. To effect this, the normal bomb beams and the intermediate bomb doors were removed, and special vertical members were inserted in the centre-section spar bracing, with fittings on the forward frame to suit the suspension of

330

he 4,000-lb bomb. The aeroplane was weighed on 20 January, 1941, and flown shortly afterwards. W5389 and W5399, similarly converted, were despatched to the Royal Air Force for trials, and, later, W5400 followed. These trials proceeded normally until March, when two incidents occurred almost simultaneously which confirmed the value of preliminary flight trials before the operational introduction of major advances.

The pilot of W5399 reported that after about five and a half hours flying violent vibrations suddenly started in the bomb beam; until then everything had been normal. The vibrations became so intense that the pilot was apprehensive of serious damage to the aeroplane, which was losing height. He therefore decided to jettison the bomb, cruising around for a quarter of an hour looking for a suitable dumping ground, and did so in a flooded area near Stoney Stratford by means of the manual toggle release. In the case involving the second Wellington, W5400, the pilot reported again that after about five and a half hours flying, and while passing over Newmarket airfield, very violent and sudden vibrations of the bomb beam occurred, lasting from five to ten seconds and then stopping as the 4,000-lb bomb released itself and fell away. The incidents were immediately investigated and the following conclusions reached.

The bomb was of the type which was steadied and controlled in descent by parachute, at that time commonly called a land-mine when employed by the enemy and a block-buster when used against the enemy. In both

A Wellington Mk II was used for dropping trials of prototype models of the Wallis spinning bomb off Herne Bay during the secret preparations for the famous raid on the Ruhr dams by 617 Squadron in May 1943; in this picture the models and the carrying and release gear can be seen.

tests the vibrations were first set up by the parachute-casing giving way after about five hours flying, thereby releasing the parachute. In W5399 the electro-magnetic unit was properly locked, and the bomb could not release itself, despite 15 minutes of severe vibration, and so had to be jettisoned by hand; in W5400 the same unit was inadvertently left unlocked, and this in turn left the bomb-slip in a semi-locked condition which allowed the parachute to pull the bomb away from the aeroplane, this accounting for the short period of the vibrations in this case.

These faults were soon remedied and the trials satisfactorily completed. In consequence, the 4,000-lb bomb was approved by the Ministry of Aircraft Production in March 1941, for installation initially in the following aircraft: Wellington IC, II and later marks, Manchester, Lancaster, Halifax, Stirling and Warwick. This installation did not entail allocation of a new mark for the Wellington, but was incorporated as a modification on existing variants, and added to later marks as required.

MK III. Instructions to proceed with the Wellingtons Mk II and III had been issued simultaneously. It was originally intended to use the 10th and 11th airframe of the first production run for these two types, but neither the Merlin nor the Hercules engine was available in time. Such was the production of the airframes that eventually the 38th and 39th were selected as the prototypes for these two marks (L4250 as the Mk II and L4251 as the Mk III).

The detail design of the Mk III began in 1938, and the first prototype flew on 19 May, 1939, with Summers as pilot and Handasyde and Wg Cdr Rider-Young as crew. The engines were the Bristol Hercules HEISM two-stage supercharged type, fitted with de Havilland constant-speed propellers of 12 ft 6 in diameter. The all-up weight for the first flight was 21,400 lb. The preliminary flying trials were soon completed successfully, but engine performance was below expectation, and the aeroplane was sent to Bristol for intensive development work and trials to improve the power.

It was hoped that the Wellington III would be a substantial advance over the Mk I and its variants in load-carrying capacity and performance.

The prototype Wellington Mk III, L4251, with Hercules HEISM engines.

332

A Wellington Mk III in flight; there was little discernible difference from the later Mk X. (*Aeroplane photo.*)

The delay caused by the poor engine performance became a serious matter indeed, as the Mk III was regarded as the main strike weapon of Bomber Command until the introduction of the four-engined heavy bombers. In due course the engine development improved and Hercules production became assured. The Air Ministry requested that a second Mk IC airframe be converted to take the Hercules III, then the most up-to-date engine of the Hercules family. The airframe chosen was P9238, and the engine was fitted with a Rotol electric propeller of 12 ft 9 in diameter. Incidentally, this engine was built as a pack unit, that is, the engine mounting, cowling, auxiliary drive and gearbox were assembled as a power-plant unit by Bristols. This became a standard installation on the majority of production aircraft used during the later stages of the war. P9238 first flew in January 1941, and became the first production Mk III.

The delay in engine production had its compensations, as during this time Wellingtons were gaining operational experience over enemy-occupied Europe; from the lessons learned, many improvements and modifications were introduced into the Mk III. For example, the armour plating fitted at the outbreak of hostilities was faulty or inadequate and was modified to suit active-service requirements, and at the same time all fuel tanks were fitted with bullet proofing. Barrage-balloon wire-cutters were also fitted to the leading edges of the wing.

The Mk III was also intended for duties in the Middle East and in the tropics, so that full tropicalisation was also required. Flying these Wellingtons out to the East over the extra-long ranges meant the installation of longer-range fuel tanks; on the other hand, flying in European conditions

333

dictated de-icing on all Wellingtons. Provision for a direct-vision windscreen and wipers also became a standard fitment on the Wellington III and all subsequent aircraft of Bomber Command.

Another weakness exposed during operations was the inadequate counter fire power from the rear turret and beam guns when under attack, and a number of suggestions were made to overcome this problem. They were the fitting of a 20-mm Hispano cannon rear turret or of a turret with four 0·303-in guns, and the installation of a low-drag Frazer-Nash 21A ventral turret at the midship position. The Hispano cannon turret involved a weight penalty of just over 200 lb, which meant a deficiency of that weight in bomb or fuel load, and because of this its use was abandoned. The Frazer-Nash 21A ventral turret was also abandoned, and it was finally resolved to fit the four-gun Frazer-Nash 20A rear turret and to return to the beam guns. The first Frazer-Nash 20A was fitted to L4251 in March 1940, and trials proved that the installation was satisfactory. There was some delay in the production of these Frazer-Nash 20A turrets, and as a temporary measure a number of the first Mk IIIs were fitted with the Frazer-Nash 4 turret.

As the production run of the Wellington III got under way, modifications were introduced to provide for other rôles. They were glider- and fighter-towing apparatus, torpedo installations and long-range fuel supply to the far-flung theatres of war. In addition, the decision to form airborne divisions in the British Army threw an additional load on the already over-worked Royal Air Force. The gliders were to be piloted by Army pilots, but the responsibilities of towing fell on the RAF. Much of the training for glider-towing was carried out by obsolescent aircraft such as the Whitley; nevertheless, provision had to be made for the most up-to-date aircraft to be available should the need arise for any full-scale operation. Hence the Wellington III was cleared, after suitability trials with X3268 at Ringway in March 1942, for towing Hotspur, Hadrian and Horsa troop-carrying gliders. Of interest is the towing speed of 147 mph and the all-up weight of the largest glider, the Horsa, at 15,750 lb. The take-off weight of the Wellington III in the towing rôle was 30,993 lb with 10 paratroops and four 350 lb equipment containers.

Another obscure duty which fell to the lot of the Wellington III was the rôle of fighter tug. Little seems to be known about this scheme, probably because the operations were conducted under cover. Spitfires were to be towed from Gibraltar until within range of Malta. They were then to be cast-off and flown in, on their own full tank capacity, to reinforce the island. Whether Wellingtons were, in fact, used in this operation remains unconfirmed, although they were seen practising over Salisbury Plain towing Spitfires, first from two hooks on the leading edge of the fighter's wing and later from one attachment.

The modifications and provisions in a single airframe for the various rôles called for the utmost ingenuity in design, in an effort to keep the weight to a minimum. Just how important this was is shown by the following table, which indicates how the all-up weight escalated during the design period up to the Mk III.

Description	Tare Weight	All-up Weight
Original design (Mk I)	19,200 lb	28,000 lb
First increase in all-up weight	—	30,000 lb
Second ,, ,, ,, ,,	—	33,000 lb
Final ,, ,, ,, ,,	21,160 lb	34,500 lb

At the final figure the design parameters of the Wellington airframe were at their limit. How provision was made for yet a further increase in all-up weight and the fitting of more powerful engines is described later, in the section dealing with the Mk X and all subsequent marks.

The Mk III entered service during 1942 and was Bomber Command's mainstay until the arrival of the four-engined bombers. But such was the rate of development at that time that the Mk III became, like the IA and IC, an interim type that reached finality in the Mk X. The total of Mk IIIs built was 1,519; 780 being produced at Blackpool, 737 at Chester and two prototypes at Weybridge.

A Wellington Mk III of the Desert Air Force; the need for engine air filters to prevent the intake of sand is evident, and one may be seen beneath the starboard engine cowling.

MK IV. At the outbreak of war in 1939 two factors arose which determined the next mark of Wellington. The first was that the production of the Wellington was now well in its stride, and it became apparent that airframe output was outstripping that of engines at the time and that other sources of power units were required. The second factor was that the majority of liquid-cooled engines being produced were required for aircraft of Fighter Command. This was also instrumental in reducing the number of Mk II Wellingtons being produced. The American aircraft industry was the first choice, but the Italian firm of Alfa Romeo was also considered as a possible source, although the latter proposition was soon dropped in view of the then prevailing anti-British attitude of the Italian Government.

Wellington Mk IV, R1220, converted from a Chester-built Mk IC to take the Twin Wasp engine.

A decision was taken to install the US Pratt & Whitney Twin Wasp SC3-9, and a contract was placed on 9 September, 1939, for a Wellington prototype fitted with two of these engines. This installation was progressing satisfactorily until February 1940, when the United States Government gave permission for the most up-to-date version of the Wasp, the R-2800, to be made available for use in the Wellington. This engine, although heavier, gave a similar performance to that of the projected Hercules installation, and Pierson requested a decision from the Air Ministry on the suitability of the Wasp. In their reply they stated that, after a review of the intended arrangements, it had been decided to cancel the Wasp installation entirely. The Wright Cyclone GR-1820/C2054 engine was also considered in September 1940, but very little work was done, and this installation was also cancelled.

After the serious military reverses sustained in the spring of 1940, and with Britain believing it faced imminent invasion, the question of using American engines was again proposed, and at a meeting held at Weybridge on 27 July, 1940, it was decided to proceed once more with the Twin Wasp installation, using the R-1830 version.

The Wasp Wellington installation was designated Mk IV, and the first prototype flew early in December 1940, about four months after the instructions to proceed had been received. This was a notable achievement in view of the amount of adaptation required for use of an American engine with British counterpart equipment.

This Mk IV was produced at the Chester works, with the serial number R1220. The first flight report made by the pilot, Mike Hare, referred to the excessive level of noise at high revolutions. The first attempt to cure this was to crop the propeller blades from 12 ft diameter to 11 ft 6 in, but at a later date a Curtiss electric propeller was fitted which gave much better results. The lowering of the noise level was entirely attributed to the fitting of cuffs at the roots of the blades and also to the fact that the centreline of the blades was slightly farther forward than that of the Hamilton propellers as first fitted.

At that time it was intended to tropicalise the Mk IV in a similar manner

336

to the IC, II and III. But production was limited, and the engine lubricating system was giving considerable trouble and causing heavy oil losses and high cylinder temperatures at maximum revolutions; it was therefore decided not to operate the Mk IVs with Wasps under tropical conditions.

The prototype, R1220, crashed at Addlestone, near Weybridge, soon after arriving from Chester for tests, but production was such that a replacement was available immediately and with it the test flying continued. The rapid rate of production of Mk IVs enabled nine to be sent to Boscombe Down for official development purposes. Among these was Z1248, which during 1941 underwent tests, at an all-up weight of 31,000 lb, in engine cooling and general handling.

Z1260 carried out oil-system and flame-damping tests, while Z1320 was used for cabin-heating and crew-space contamination effects. Fuel-consumption trials were carried out by R1515 and Z1288. The latter aeroplane made an endurance flight at a take-off weight of 31,504 lb and flew 1,420 miles at 15,000 ft in $7\frac{1}{4}$ hours, with a bomb load of 2,400 lb.

Another Mk IV, Z1244, fitted with the Lindholme air-sea rescue gear, was used on tests over the Clyde during September 1942. Although the tests were successful, air-sea rescue never became a rôle of the Wellington, but from the experience gained on the Mk IV, Lindholme gear was installed with great success on the Warwick, as described in the relevant chapter.

One Mk IV, R1653, designated Wellington Special, was allocated to the Telecommunications Research Establishment at Swanage for the installation of special radio. The main points of identification were aerials mounted on the top of the fin and two azimuth aerials mounted on the underside of the rear fuselage similar to those on the Wellington Mk VIII. The two aerials consisting of copper foil were inserted between the structure and the fabric covering of the elevator surfaces. This involved modifying the elevators to correct for aerodynamic balance.

Because of the greater power of the Wasp, Coastal Command asked for complete performance data for this mark in the ASV–Leigh Light and torpedo rôles, for comparison with the Hercules-engined family of Wellingtons. Although a slightly better all-round performance was predicted, the matter was not pursued any further. The Mk IV was a Chester works product—25 being completed against the first contract and 195 against the second.

MK X. As far as reserve-strength factors were concerned, the original Wellington airframe had reached its maximum loading in the Mk III. To increase the all-up weight any further was impossible, but developments in light alloys produced a new range equal in strength to former mild-steel specifications, and with the use of one of these, DTD646, the Wellington received a new lease of life. The advantage was two-fold. Very little redesign was needed, and the modification was simply one of change in the structure material. An increase in all-up weight was possible with little

A Blackpool-built Wellington, X3595, completed as a prototype Mk X bomber with Hercules VI engines.

A Wellington T.Mk X of Flying Training Command.

The interior of a Wellington T.Mk X equipped as a navigational trainer; through the bulkhead door is the second pilot's control column, on the bulkhead is the Marconi 1154/5 transmitter-receiver, to its left and behind the air-vent duct is the radar aid to navigation, probably Rebecca/Eureka, in the foreground is the chart table and above it on the left of picture is the variable controller for the compass (cylindrical object), while the square box is the air-position indicator; the rolled-up blinds above the windows were let down during navigation instruction.

338

addition to the basic airframe weight, and the installation of the higher-powered Hercules VI or XVI engines, instead of the Hercules XI of the Wellington Mk III, became possible.

For engine performance evaluation, a Blackpool-built Mk III, X3374, was selected by the MAP for trials as the Mk X prototype with the Hercules VI. The first production Mk X, DF609, was from Blackpool, and was weighed on 30 July, 1942, about a month behind schedule. Mk X production was shared between Blackpool and Chester, the first airframe from Chester being HE147.

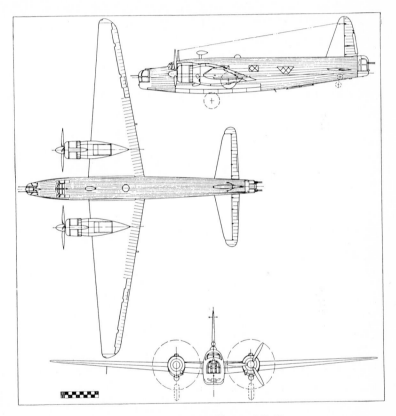

Vickers Type 440 Wellington Mk X

The Wellington Mk X filled all the rôles of the Mk III, but with improved performance, particularly in load, and was the most efficient and numerous of all the Wellingtons. When Bomber Command began to use four-engined aircraft over Europe in 1943 the Mk X remained for general duties in that theatre of war but retained its bomber rôle in the Middle East and India, and played a most prominent part in the North African campaign.

Flying test-bed Wellington Mk X, LN715, taking off at Wisley in 1948, with Rolls-Royce Dart propeller-turbine engines destined for the Viscount.

The bomber version was the B.Mk X and the trainer version the T.Mk X, the latter having the front and rear turrets removed and fairings substituted. The T.Mk X was the last of the Wellingtons to survive, and this was in the Air Navigation School, where it was eventually to be replaced by the Valetta T.3, and at 201 Advanced Flying School at Swinderby, where it was replaced by the Varsity. The Mk X airframe was used as a test-bed for numerous engine developments, including that of the Rolls-Royce Dart propeller-turbine, which subsequently powered the Viscount civil transport.

Wellington

	Mk I Type 290	Mk IC Type 415	Mk II Type 406	Mk X Type 440
Accommodation:	Pilot and 4 crew	Pilot and 4/5 crew	Pilot and 4 crew	Pilot and 4/5 crew
Engines:	Two 1,050 hp Bristol Pegasus XVIII	Two 1,050 hp Bristol Pegasus XVIII	Two 1,145 hp Rolls-Royce Merlin X	Two 1,675 hp Bristol Hercules VI/XVI
Span:	86 ft	86 ft 2 in	86 ft 2 in	86 ft 2 in
Length:	61 ft 3 in	64 ft 7 in	64 ft 7 in	64 ft 7 in
Height:	17 ft 5 in	17 ft 5 in	17 ft 5 in	17 ft 6 in
Wing Area:	840 sq ft	840 sq ft	840 sq ft	840 sq ft
Empty Weight:	18,000 lb	18,556 lb	20,258 lb	22,474 lb
Gross Weight:	24,850 lb	28,500 lb	33,000 lb	36,500 lb
Max Speed:	245 mph at 15,000 ft	235 mph at 15,500 ft	254 mph at 17,500 ft	255 mph
Initial Climb:	1,120 ft/min	1,120 ft/min	670 ft/min	—
Climb to:	15,000 ft in 18 min	—	—	15,000 ft in 27·7 min
Service Ceiling:	21,600 ft	18,000 ft	23,500 ft	22,000 ft
Range:	3,200 miles at 180 mph at 15,000 ft	2,550 miles at 180 mph at 15,000 ft	2,200 miles at 180 mph at 15,000 ft	1,885 miles at 180 mph with 1,500 lb bomb load
Armament:	Forward and ventral one- (later twin-) gun turrets Bomb load 4,500 lb	Twin-gun nose and tail turrets, two beam guns Bomb load 4,500 lb	Twin-gun nose turret, four-gun rear turret, two beam guns Bomb load 4,000 lb	As Type 406

Coastal Command Wellington Mk XIIIs operating out of Gibraltar during the second world war—compare picture of BEA Viscount on page 421.

The Wellington in other Rôles

A characteristic of all the famous aircraft of the second world war was their ability to fulfil any rôle allocated to them, and the Wellington was no exception. In fact, it probably operated in as many rôles as any other type. The first opportunity to extend its utility came late in 1939 when the magnetic mine appeared as Hitler's much vaunted secret weapon and confronted the naval authorities with a critical situation. The Luftwaffe began laying these mines around the coasts of Britain, particularly in estuaries and other regular seaways, to the peril of Allied shipping. They were detonated by the magnetic field created by ships passing over them. The German Command regarded them as immune to any possible antidote. But thanks initially to the Wellington, specially converted to deal with the emergency, and to wider measures subsequently adopted, within a few months the secret weapon had become a normal hazard of war.

Early in the attack by the mine-laying enemy aircraft, one unexploded mine was fortuitously recovered and its secrets revealed by courageous naval specialists. Work was undertaken immediately to find out whether

Converted Mk I, HX682, operated as a magnetic mine destroyer under the designation Wellington DWI Mk I.

this type of mine could be destroyed where it lay on the shallow sea-bed, by an aeroplane carrying its own magnetic field and flying over the mine at a reasonably safe height. The preliminary investigation was made by the Admiralty Research Laboratory and the Royal Aircraft Establishment, and the decision was reached that such counter-action was feasible. Accordingly, a Wellington IA, P2516, was taken off the production line at Weybridge and adapted for an emergency programme.

This Wellington was fitted with special equipment comprising a large magnetic coil 48 ft in diameter attached to the underside of the nose, tail and outer planes. It was fed with electrical power from a 35 kW Maudesley generator driven by a Ford V8 engine, both mounted within the fuselage. When the Ford company was asked by Vickers for technical data it sent a motorist's handbook, but when the true nature of the request was confidentially disclosed Fords reacted swiftly and co-operated to the fullest extent. This installation provided the first successful means of defeating the magnetic mine. The narrow margin of safety was accurately assessed by the theoretical calculations of Dr C. S. Hudson of the RAE, in determining the height at which the Wellington could fly above the mine in relation to the timing of the explosion and the menace of the resultant water spout behind the aeroplane.

Four Mk IAs were converted for this duty, which had been undertaken at the request of the Admiralty and with the knowledge of the Air Ministry. Overall approval was then given, but a proposal made to equip other types of older and obsolescent aircraft for anti-magnetic mine work was not proceeded with. The first conversion was made at Weybridge and involved many hours work without a halt, including the whole of the Christmas period of 1939, under the direction of G. R. Edwards.

As one result of Dr Hudson's calculations, it was soon realised that advantage could be gained by amplifying the magnetic field without increasing the hazards to the aeroplane, and a 50 per cent increase in magnetic force was achieved by raising the power output to 90 kW through an English Electric generator driven by a de Havilland Gipsy Six air-cooled aero-engine. Some reduction in the total weight of the equipment was also achieved. The coil was cooled by air circulating within the light-alloy streamlined casing, via scoops at the front and outlets at the sides and rear.

The first four IAs converted to take the Ford auxiliary power unit were allocated Vickers' designation Type 418 and known as the DWI Mk I. These were later equipped with the Gipsy Six auxiliary power units and, together with 11 Wellington Mk Is withdrawn from service for conversion, were classified as Type 419s and known as DWI Mk IIs. DWI was an abbreviation for 'directional wireless installation' deliberately intended to

A magnetic mine-sweeping Wellington DWI at work over Tripoli harbour, Libya, North Africa.

mislead the enemy as to the real purpose of the special Wellingtons. One of these, fitted with long-range tanks, was flown out to the North African theatre of war, the magnetic gear being transported separately. It was used with great effect for sweeping the Suez Canal and Mediterranean harbours then in Allied occupation, and in due course other Wellingtons were converted for DWI duties in the Near East.

By that time degaussing gear had been fitted to ships, enabling them to pass safely over magnetic mines. Mine-sweepers, so neutralised, began the systematic destruction of magnetic mines in a wide area grid pattern by towing charged electrodes behind them. The degaussing gear comprised in its elements an anti-magnetic field generator.

The use of an auxiliary engine coupled to an electrical generator in an aeroplane was later to prove of value when airborne searchlights were introduced by Coastal Command in the battle against enemy submarines. The sub-type designation DWI Mk III referred to this further duty and not to the original magnetic-mine destroyer requirement.

Wellington Mk II, L4250, with the 40-mm Vickers cannon installation and single fin.

MK II WITH 40-MM GUN. As with the Wellington Mk I series, the Mk II proved the versatility of the basic aeroplane in accepting an unusual rôle for experimental work leading to a technical breakthrough in offensive capability. The Mk II was selected for the installation of a 40-mm dorsal gun, the heaviest weapon fitted to an aeroplane at that time, and this proved to be a remarkable piece of work and an exercise that involved all the resources of Vickers-Armstrongs Ltd * and certain of its associated companies. In addition, it was a further demonstration of the flexibility and strength of the geodetic airframe.

Proposals to fit the big gun in the Wellington originated in 1938, and in June of that year the Crayford works began experimenting with a flexible form of ammunition link that would enable the stowage and feed to be contained within the dimensional limits of the Wellington fuselage. As initially this was purely an armament matter, instructions to proceed were given to Vickers-Armstrongs on 11 February, 1939. The scheme was divided into three parts, a Vickers self-loading 40-mm gun, a predictor unit and a turret with sight. The airframe was also selected at this time, and it was indeed convenient that Vickers should have the Mk II Wellington so eminently suited to the job.

This combination would today be called a weapons system. The predictor unit, gun turret and sight were to be interconnected in such a manner that the combination of all three constituted a mechanism whereby the gun was correctly and automatically traversed and elevated by the action of the gunner keeping the sight on the target.

The complete installation was assembled at Weybridge under the supervision of Capt Naninni of Vickers House. The Variable Speed Gear Company of Elswick, a Vickers subsidiary, designed and produced the hydraulic engines (a combination of electrically driven pumps). The gun was designed and manufactured at Vickers' Crayford works, and Weybridge was responsible for the turret and details, sharing the construction of the predictor and sight evolved by Capt Naninni with Cooke, Troughton and

* The full name of the operating company is used here to attribute the credit for the development to the armament division of Vickers Ltd, the parent company.

344

L4250 in twin-fin layout for 40-mm cannon flight and firing trials.

Simms, another Vickers subsidiary. The whole operation was conducted with great enthusiasm and attention to detail, the gun being sent for trials to the Swanley range, Kent, late in 1939, passing them successfully.

While all this was going on, the flying and engine trials on the Mk II Wellington prototype, L4250, were completed in 1940, and this aircraft was allocated to receive the 40-mm gun installation. The centre fuselage was modified to take a stressed-skin section to accommodate the turret assembly, which comprised the turntable, gun cradle and gunner's seat, predictor, photo-electric cells, ejector system, hydraulic engines, and cupola and range finder. With 25 rounds of 40-mm ammunition and 516 gal of fuel, the all-up weight of the aeroplane was 25,367 lb.

An exciting first flight ensued. The eccentric mounting of the turret, with its large proportions, rotating through 360 degrees, caused severe tail vibrations and made control difficult. A decision was then made to replace the normal Wellington central fin and rudder with twin fins and rudders fitted outboard on the tailplane in line with the propeller slipstream. With this new twin-fin arrangement, firing trials were conducted over Lyme Bay, Dorset, on 8 March, 1942, and consisted of three shots at maximum and minimum elevation at each of the eight cardinal positions of the turret relative to the aircraft axis. Twenty-six shots were in fact fired, including one misfire, and while firing across the engine nacelles on both sides the blast seriously damaged the fabric covering on the wings. Further trials, however, proved satisfactory, and in October 1944 the installation was officially named VA 40-mm gun class 5 Mk I.

Later, L4250 was the subject of another armament installation, a special mid-upper turret carrying four 0·50-in guns, intended for the Short R.14/40 flying-boat. The 40-mm weapon was removed and sent to the RAE for further development, while, after the 0·50-in gun battery experiment, L4250 itself was scrapped at the end of 1942.

Another Mk II, Z8416, was used as a test-bed for trials of a nose-mounted 40-mm gun as Type 439. This exercise was conducted in connection with a Vickers' tender for a twin-engined fighter to specification F.22/39, which was intended to carry such a forward-firing gun. Only general handling of the gun and its system was carried out and eventually the nose-gun installation and the project specification were abandoned.

345

One of the two prototype Wellington Mk V high-altitude bombers.

MK V. In the autumn of 1938 the Air Staff requested Vickers to investigate the possibilities of using the Wellington as a high-altitude bomber to operate at 35,000 ft with a maximum ceiling of 40,000 ft, using a pressurised cabin. This meant marrying a pressure vessel to the geodetic airframe, which was theoretically a contradiction in terms. However, it was carried out most successfully, the cabin being attached by means of integral feet anchored to the nodal point of the geodetic structure. This scheme allowed the cabin to expand and contract independently of the rest of the structure. The standard Wellington fuselage was modified by the addition of the cabin forward, suitably faired on the underbelly into the normal fuselage shape aft.

This requirement meant starting from scratch, with very little previous experience to call upon, although the Air Ministry suggested that Vickers should co-operate with the Short and Fairey companies, who had been experimenting with pressure cabins for civil passenger-carrying. But the investigations of these two companies were directed to physiological standards rather than to the engineering strength requirements of the cabin. The civil cabins were to operate at $2\frac{1}{2}$ lb/sq in, whereas the cabin on the Wellington was to be maintained to the equivalent altitude of 10,000 ft, which meant a pressure of 7 lb/sq in.

Installation of pressure cabin in geodetic fuselage of high-altitude Wellington.

The operation of the aeroplane as envisaged at that time was that it should climb to 15,000 ft and fly towards the objective at that level until nearing the target zone. The aeroplane would then climb to its operational ceiling to carry out its particular mission, reversing this process when returning to base. It was also intended that there would be free passage to and from the pressure cabin when flying at lower altitudes. The preliminary requirements were a crew of three, a bomb load of 1,000 lb, and an endurance of 9·6 hours at an all-up weight of 30,000 lb.

Delay occurred in the delivery of the intended Hercules HE8MS engine; it was therefore decided, in June 1940, to install the Hercules III by accepting its limited performance. Considering the amount of research and complex test requirements of the numerous installations, such as the operation

The Bristol Hercules VIII installation with exhaust-driven supercharger on the Wellington Mk V.

of flying and engine controls, the airframe progress was comparatively good. But with the fall of France and the Low Countries in the spring of 1940 it became of paramount importance that actual flying experience at high altitudes be gained, a point that Lord Beaverbrook was quick to point out when he became the first Minister of Aircraft Production. He placed the Wellington Mk V high on his list of priorities. 1 August was the original date for completion, but this date could not be met, and the certification of design memorandum was not dated until 31 August, 1940. Pilots' log books fail to show the exact date of the first test flight, but, in consequence of the enemy air attack on Weybridge works in September 1940, the MAP instructed Vickers to take dispersal action with all experimental types, and the first prototype, R3298, was flown to Blackpool on 25 September, 1940.

On arrival at Blackpool a number of tests still had to be made. Not until 21 October, 1940, was the first high-altitude flight attempted. An altitude of 20,000 ft was reached before ice on the pilot's canopy dome and the prone bomb-aimer's windows caused the flight to be curtailed. On 29 October the second and third flights were made up to 23,000 ft, when ice on the inside of the pilot's dome prevented higher altitudes being reached. On 31 October 30,000 ft was reached for the first time, icing troubles having been reduced by the introduction of warm air blowing over the glazing. Every test flight brought its problems, and the following report submitted after one of these flights is a good indication of their nature:

Interior of Wellington high-altitude pressure cabin showing pilot's position.

'During yesterday's flight, which lasted over three hours, we reached 30,000 ft. The outside temperature was minus 44 deg C. After a bit at this height we heard a series of bangs on the port side, and a little later, a lump of material like hard grease appeared on the wireless operator's window. As we came down this thawed to oil, and when we landed we found a row of holes in the fabric opposite the port airscrew apparently punched through by lumps of solidified oil. The engines are being overhauled today in consequence, they were covered in oil when we got down.'

At an acceptance conference held on 15 November, 1940, some of these difficulties were resolved and requirements were finalised. Among details proposed were that the rear gun turret could not be expected to be workable under all conditions by a rear gunner. So the rear turrets were fixed and operated by an electro-magnetic firing control from the pressure cabin, a periscope being installed to provide observation of the rear hemisphere.

The second prototype, R3299, was fitted with the Hercules VIII engine in November 1940. Its power was below expectations, and the required

348

ceiling was not realised. It now became apparent that the Hercules engine and its variants were unable to provide the necessary power for altitude, and already the installation of the Merlin 60 was being considered. The estimated performance with the Merlin offered a better ceiling and cruise performance at height. From this time the Mk VI, as the Merlin-engined version was designated, became the target.

The design and flying trials of the prototype Wellington Vs, R3298 and R3299, provided the basis for all pressure-cabin installation in this country, the Supermarine Spitfire and the Westland Welkin being the first in which the experience was applied. The enormous amount of work and ingenuity expended in overcoming all the problems encountered should not go unrecorded. Even the Americans, who had been conducting their own experiments with pressure cabins during that time, requested data, and a set of drawings of the Mark V pressure cabin was despatched to them as a result of a Government request. Although not a direct exchange, it is interesting to note that the American Sperry bomb sight was used on the Mk V and Mk VI—a good example of co-operation between the Allies at that time. As this cabin was one of the first serious attempts at pressurisation for high-altitude flying, a description in some detail appears in the section dealing with the Wellington VI.

Although the Mk V never reached its estimated performance, a small production order of 30 aircraft was started in the dispersed Weybridge units. Before completion the change-over to Merlin power units reduced these numbers to nine airframes completed, and these were written off at a later date.

MK VI. Before flying trials had begun on the Mk V, Rolls-Royce were developing the Merlin REISM engine, the prototype of the Merlin 60 series, which was fitted with a two-speed two-stage supercharger suitable for high-altitude flying. Later in 1941 the MAP issued instructions to Vickers to proceed with the installation of the power-egg units (then becoming standard practice for power plants). Further, the Merlin version was to have priority over the Mk V production then under way.

Airframe W5795 was removed from the line, fitted with the Merlin power plants and designated Type 431. The certificate of design was dated 28 October, 1941, and recorded that the engine change was the chief modification. Vickers were required to undertake a minimum of testing, simply a climb to 30,000 ft to carry out handling trials, operation of cabin blowers and the recording of oil and cabin temperatures and pressures. After its first flight W5795 was flown to Boscombe Down for evaluation and, finally, to Rolls-Royce at Hucknall for further development trials.

The Mk VI was designed and equipped for high-altitude bombing, the pressure cabin housing the entire crew, pilot, navigator, bomb-aimer and wireless operator. Estimated service ceiling was over 40,000 ft, and the range was 1,590 miles with a 4,500-lb bomb load or 2,275 miles with 1,500 lb of bombs. The pilot only was protected by armour plating.

Wellington Mk VI DR484 with Merlin 60 engines, in high-altitude finish.

The armament was to have been a pressurised Frazer-Nash 70 rear turret with four 0·303-in guns, but it was not available in time, and a Frazer-Nash 20A type was substituted, being locked in position at altitude (as in the Mk V), and operated from the pressure cabin by remote control on the electro-magnetic principle. The sighting on the aft underside of the fuselage was accomplished by using a periscope. Other requirements included the American Sperry bomb sight and automatic-flying controls. Provision was also made for cameras and for full tropicalisation.

As previously stated, the pressure cabin was supported on the geodetic structure, and in this way was relieved of the ordinary fuselage loads, the cabin mainly having to sustain the load due to pressurising, which reached the figure of 7·5 lb/sq in during flight. The cabin was proof-tested to 15 lb/sq in, and its shape was cylindrical with a hemispherical rear, and a nose approximately ellipsoidal. The diameter was 65 in, length 18 ft 3 in, and volume 320 cu ft. The entry door, of 3 ft 2 in diameter, had in its centre a large hand-operated valve to release the internal pressure before the door could be opened. There was a device guarding against the external air pressure exceeding that inside the cabin, as might have occurred in a quick descent caused by engine or blower failures.

The pilot's view was obtained through a plastic dome, which could be tilted to afford a clear view through the gap under its forward edge on take-off or landing or in the event of mist or rain on the outside. An optically-flat double window for the bomb-aimer was situated below the

Front view of Merlin-powered Wellington VI high-altitude bomber.

nose of the cabin and was inclined at about 30 degrees to the line of flight. It was tested to 50 lb/sq in without breaking, even with one face being fed with hot water while the other was kept cold with solid carbon dioxide 'ice'.

There were rectangular windows along the top of the cabin to enable the navigator to obtain sextant readings. All windows and the pilot's dome were prevented from misting and frosting internally by an additional inner pane of Perspex, and a supply of hot air was passed between the panes. With the exception of the pilot's dome, the inner panels could be removed and cleaned during flight.

No sealing compound was used during construction of the cabin. It was applied after riveting the seams on the interior. When the cabin underwent its proof-testing the air pressure had the effect of forcing the compound into the seams, thus completing the seal. The method of testing for leakage rate was to time it for the pressure to drop from 8 to 7 lb/sq in; with the air supply cut off in this way the rate of leakage could be assessed. Compression of the cabin air was the only source of heat, and its proper conservation was therefore of great importance. Consequently, the cabin was lagged thoroughly with carded noil, a material which resembled cotton-wool in appearance.

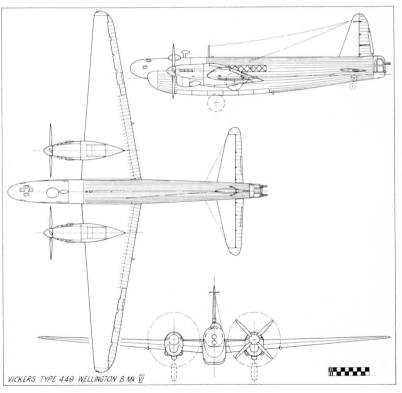

VICKERS TYPE 449 WELLINGTON B Mk VI

The air to the blower units was drawn from inside the unpressurised portion of the fuselage aft of the pressure cabin. After passing through an air filter the intake piping ran through the inner planes to the engine nacelles, where the blowers were situated. The reason for taking the air from the inside of the fuselage was to minimise the ingress of foreign and undesirable materials, and to avoid icing troubles. The compressed air was returned to the fuselage by 2-in diameter piping with thick noil lagging, and then fed to the various windows and installations that required temperature maintenance control.

Most of the hydraulic system was external to the pressurisation, and was therefore exposed to the intense cold of the upper atmosphere. With ordinary hydraulic fluid, trouble was experienced and caused sluggishness and immobility of the system by the thickening of the fluid when very cold. This was overcome by using a mixture of equal parts of paraffin and a non-freezing oil. Similar expedients were used to liquefy the bearing oil of the control surface hinges, as a marked tendency was experienced at great heights towards freezing of controls.

Wellington VI W5798 on flight trials from Boscombe Down experimental station.

There were no special features in the oil system, and there were no long runs of exposed pipes which required lagging. Pressurisation of the oil tank was considered as a stimulant to the oil flow if necessary, but this was never installed. The oxygen system was a fixed installation as for bombers, and a portable oxygen set was provided for each member of the crew for use in the event of parachute descents being necessary.

To avoid vapour locks in the fuel system, the fuel pumps were of the submerged type fitted directly below the tank outlets, and the problem of fuel boiling, due to reduction of atmospheric pressure combined with the retention of ground temperature, was investigated but no action was considered necessary.

Changes in Air Staff policy caused by the rapidly changing pattern of war operations, particularly in the air, led to an indecisive attitude towards high-flying aircraft in 1941 and 1942. This affected the proposed produc-

Flying test-bed Wellington Mk II, T2545, originally intended as a Mk VII but converted at Hucknall by Rolls-Royce to test the Merlin 60 series engine.
(*Rolls-Royce photo.*)

...ion programmes for the Wellington V and VI. While Vickers were involved in all these changes of policy, intensive flying with the two high-altitude Wellingtons continued at Boscombe Down. Meanwhile, the requirement for high-level bombing was being adequately filled by developments of the Mosquito, which, with oxygen equipment but without a pressure cabin, could outmatch the performance of the Wellington at height.

Except for aid extended to the Supermarine company in developing a pressure cabin for the PRU (photographic reconnaissance unit) Spitfires, the work on the high-altitude Wellingtons was of little immediate avail. But the techniques evolved to meet the stringent requirements of the pressure cabin in the Wellington V and VI were later of great value to Vickers when the post-war pressurised aircraft such as the Viscount and Valiant were produced.

MKS VII AND VIII. In May 1941 an order for 150 Mk VII Wellingtons was placed but cancelled in the following September, presumably because the specified Merlin XX engine was required for more urgent use, the Hercules being by that time well established as the Wellington power unit. This Mk VII was intended as an improved version of the Mk II.

The Mk VIII, which followed in numerical order, was quite a different proposition. Indeed, it was one which eventually had great impact on the course of the war at sea, and re-established the Wellington as a front-line weapon after it has been replaced in Bomber Command by the four-engined heavies.

Several obscure points, hitherto unrecorded, concerning the development of the Mk VIII and its derivatives in Coastal Command are worth mentioning. The Mk VIII contained one of the first integrated weapons systems fitted into an aeroplane. This began as an improvisation, was developed into a major weapon for use against the U-boat and was one

353

Weybridge-built Wellington Mk VIII, HX419, with the early form of ASV antennae, and retracted Leigh light just visible underneath fuselage.

of the prime factors in securing victory in the Battle of the Atlantic. This early weapons system was the combination of Leigh light and ASV (air-to-surface vessel) radar, synchronised with the actual dropping of bombs, depth charges or torpedo on the target.

The idea of illuminating the target from an aeroplane fitted with a searchlight was not new, but previously this method had suffered from the handicap of revealing the attacker's position to the hunted adversary if the light was not aimed directly on the target. It had been shelved for some time as of doubtful operational utility, but with the arrival of ASV radar it became possible to track a vessel at sea in complete darkness and, at the critical moment, expose it to the attacking aeroplane by means of a powerful light directed straight at the target. This concept combined two most valuable weapons in war, surprise and confusion. The follow-up of depth charges to accomplish the destruction of the submarine made this system an almost perfect weapon, if conducted in the correct manner from a steady airborne platform such as the Wellington.

Airborne searchlight installation had been in the minds of two members of the Royal Air Force at that time, Sqn Ldr Helmore at the Air Ministry and Sqn Ldr Leigh on the personnel staff of Coastal Command. Both officers had grasped the potentialities of ASV for search purposes, but their ideas of illumination of the target differed. Helmore had directed his efforts to the

Wellington Mk VIII, W5674, completed at Weybridge as prototype with Pegasus XVIII engines, for trials of ASV radar.

354

detection and destruction of enemy aircraft, and favoured a short burst of widely diffused light over sufficient area to expose the enemy; Leigh approached the problem from his own Command's point of view, which was the illumination of a vessel at sea. He proposed a concentrated beam of light projected on to the target, relying on the accuracy of the ASV to pin-point it.

Coastal Command had used the magnetic-mine destroyer Wellington DWI in 1940, and it occurred to Leigh that its source of auxiliary power could be used for the operation of a searchlight. Through Air Chief Marshal Sir Frederick Bowhill, C-in-C Coastal Command, a DWI Wellington was acquired for this purpose. Two meetings, tabled by coin-

Wellington fuselages on the Blackpool production line, destined for Coastal Command variants.

cidence on the same day, one official and the other a freelance enterprise,* were held by the same Service staff quite independently, and concerned the introduction of ASV search radar and the replacement of the DWI magnetic ring by a searchlight. In the latter meeting Vickers were involved. Quite naturally, these two proposals merged into one, and the DWI Wellington, P9223, was allotted for the dual installation at the end of February 1941. This aeroplane was referred to as DWI Mk III, a designation used to conceal the real identity of the exercise.

The modifications comprised replacement of the nose fairing by a Mk I nose to house the searchlight operator, the searchlight itself being mounted

* These unofficial conferences were not unusual during the second world war and were of great value in the expression of third opinions to civil and military authorities on vital operational problems. As a technical journalist at the time, the author was involved in more than one of such meetings.

Wellington Mk VIII converted at Weybridge from Mk IC as T2977 to mount the Helmore wide-beam light in the nose.

in an adapted Frazer-Nash 25A turret. The Ford auxiliary engine ai ducts were modified to clear the searchlight beam. Little flying wa done by Vickers on P9223, and it was despatched to Coastal Comman for operational trials. About two months after the converted DWI ha flown, Wellington T2977 was selected to take the rival Helmore wide-bean light in the nose behind a curved transparent panel, with its operator locate in the mid-turret position and the bomb-aimer in a clear vision blister.

While the merits of the two rival searchlights systems were being resolved the installation of ASV had proceeded in a more straightforward manner At a meeting in December 1940 Vickers offered the Wellington IC fo interim development to operate at an all-up weight of 30,000 lb with range of 2,000 miles. A crew of five for night operations and six for da duties was specified, and Frazer-Nash 7A front and rear turrets, each wit two Browning guns, were fitted. Attack weapons were two 420-lb dept charges.

When the searchlight was fitted, the Wellington IC conversion wa officially called the Mk VIII with Leigh light. In May 1941 Coastal Com mand asked for a further 100 sets of Leigh lights and ASV equipment fo installation on the Wellington IC production line then running at Wey bridge. Meanwhile, the two searchlights had been evaluated, and the onl part of the Helmore system to be adopted was the main engine-generate electrical supply to the searchlight through storage batteries. This replace the auxiliary power unit of the DWI, as first proposed.

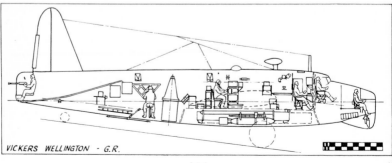

VICKERS WELLINGTON - G.R.

356

Blackpool assembly line of Coastal Command Wellingtons.

As the initial requirements of Coastal Command were satisfied, the next step was to achieve an all-round increase in performance. This was done by using the basic Mk X airframe with the Hercules engine which was capable of providing more power for specific duties. Upon the choice of different versions of this engine depended some of the remaining variants of the Wellington used by Coastal Command.

Later, torpedoes were substituted, as required, for depth charges or bombs. Of some interest is the fact that full tropicalisation and long-range fuel tankage in some Wellingtons coincided with the extension to the runway at Gibraltar, so that it could serve as a staging post for aircraft being ferried out East.

A Coastal Command Wellington during convoy protection duties in tropical conditions; the crew member on the left is signalling with an Aldis lamp, the Browning beam guns are parked—note the stripping of panels of fabric each side superseding earlier type windows.

357

Blackpool-built Mk XIII, JA144, with ASV radar and carrying torpedoes for day duties in Coastal Command.

Wellington Mk XIII with chin-mounted ASV radar.

The subsequent development of Coastal Command Wellingtons became complicated through changes in engine and ASV production and Air Staff requirements being delayed or revised. The official variants with their chief differences are tabulated here.

> Mk XI—Coastal Command, Mk X airframe, Hercules VI and Mk VIII equipment, i.e. ASV Mk II.
>
> Mk XII—Coastal Command, Mk X airframe, Hercules VI, ASV Mk II and Leigh light for night duties.
>
> Mk XIII—Coastal Command, Mk X airframe, Hercules XVII, ASV Mk III and torpedoes for day duties.
>
> Mk XIV—Coastal Command, Mk X airframe, Hercules XVII, ASV Mk III and Leigh light for night duties.

In the autumn of 1944 a number of Mk XI and Mk XIII aircraft were converted for training purposes as Mk XVII and XVIII respectively.

> Mk XVII—As Mk XI, but with portion of the Mosquito nose modified to house radar scanner, used for training night-fighter crews.

Conversions were carried out by Service engineering units.

> Mk XVIII—As Mk XIII, but with radio operator and navigator's compartment redesigned to accommodate four pupils, instructor and radar equipment, with Mosquito nose and scanner as Mk XVII.

358

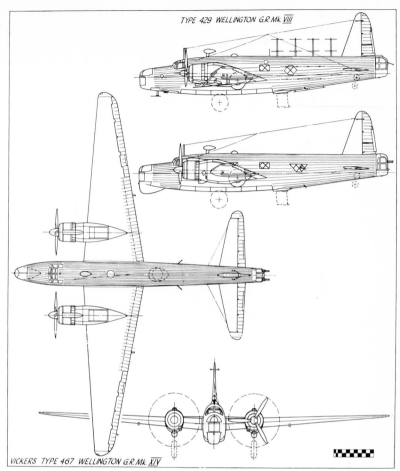

TYPE 429 WELLINGTON G.R.Mk. VIII

VICKERS TYPE 467 WELLINGTON G.R.Mk. XIV

Blackpool-built Wellington T.Mk XVIII with Mosquito nose, modified to house radar scanner for training night-fighter crews.

As in Bomber Command, the requirements of Coastal Command were changing from day to day and, accordingly, Wellingtons were frequently modified to accommodate different service equipment. In this process the all-up weight was sometimes up to 36,500 lb, and RATOG (rocket assisted take-off gear) was experimented with.

MK. XIX. In 1946 a number of Mk X airframes were adapted to incorporate the results of all the operational experience accumulated during the war years, together with new equipment that had been developed at the same time. The last variant of the Wellington, which embodied all these improvements and provided a basic training aeroplane for a number of years, was the Mk XIX.

A Wellington Mk XIX, converted by the RAF from Mk X NA851 in 1946, at 24 MU Stoke Heath to provide a basic trainer; precursor of the Valetta and Varsity trainers to follow in Flying Training Command. (*N. C. Parker photo*.)

Among the vast number of project installations of special equipment which were proposed for the Wellington as an airborne test-bed, one worthy of mention which did materialise was the AGP (auxiliary generator plant or power) in Type 451. This was the installation of a mid-upper turret mounting four 0·5-in guns being developed by Frazer-Nash for the Short R.14/40 flying-boat. These power units and control systems, designed by different manufacturers, were tested in turn from Staverton aerodrome, near Cheltenham, in a Wellington Mk IA, N2963, converted by fitting a wooden floor to receive the unit through the mid-upper turret aperture. The Frazer-Nash 36 turret was abandoned in 1947, but tests with various AGP units continued.

TROOPER, FREIGHTER AND CIVIL WELLINGTONS. As previously stated, the possibility of using the Wellington as a civil transport had been visualised early in its design, but although several schemes had been proposed prior to the war, none materialised. Wellington Is were used for passenger-carrying early in the war on various Service missions, but not until 1941 were Vickers asked to prepare data for troop- and freight-carrying versions.

A Wellington C.Mk IA in use as a transport aeroplane by BOAC during the war and named *Duke of Rutland*.

An urgent request was received from RAF Middle East Command during May 1941 for transport aircraft to provide greater mobility in that theatre. Originally the requirement was a simple Wellington conversion for the transport of troops and equipment by removing all military equipment, including oxygen, and installing seats of the old Vickers Valentia pattern. Later, this turned into a major transport rôle, including the air lift of fuel and oil stores, and finally for passenger-carrying at home and abroad.

Mks IC, II, III and IV were allocated for conversion in *ad hoc* fashion at various places at home and abroad; consequently, the exact number so converted is not known. The accommodation provided was austerely practical, the sole purpose being the transport of troops on operational duties. The requirements were all certified as Type 437 Wellington Mk IX. At various full loadings according to the original marks the IXs could carry 18 fully equipped troops or any equivalent military load over a minimum range of 1,000 miles or a maximum of 2,200 miles.

During 1943 the call for transport aircraft became a priority. As Wellingtons were then available in some quantity, having been replaced in Bomber Command, Vickers were asked to convert numbers of Mk I, IA and IC, no fewer than 100 of the ICs being required. The prefix letter C was used

A Wellington Mk IX transport bearing civil registration.

361

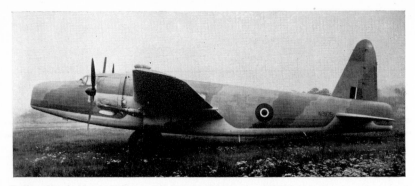

Built at Weybridge in 1939 as a Mk IA, this Wellington, N2875, is depicted as a transport aeroplane in 1944 as a Mk XVI, at first designated C.Mk IA; the engines were Bristol Pegasus.

at first to identify these conversions as C.Mk IA and C.Mk IC, but in service, with further modifications, they were reclassified as Mk XV and Mk XVI respectively. With these two variants the whole Wellington range from Mk I to XIX was completed. It represented a versatility probably unsurpassed in operational application on active service.

Before leaving this impressive record of the technical and operational development of the Wellington, a brief mention must be made of its use as an airborne test-bed for the early Whittle jet engines. This exercise, which pioneered the rear-mounted jet-engine installation, started on 8 May, 1942, with a request for Vickers to attend a meeting for the forming of a small committee to develop the turbojet engine. Under conditions of strict security, a Whittle unit was installed at Weybridge in a Wellington Mk II, Z8570, which flew in July 1942, with Merlin Xs as the main engines. Later, Merlin XXs were substituted, and in March 1943 the Rover-Whittle unit was installed.

For the further development of experimental turbojets, two hybrid Wellingtons were allocated, W5389 and W5518. They had Mk II fuselages,

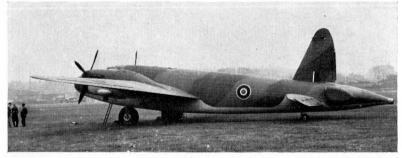

A hybrid Wellington, with Merlin 62 engines, as the flying test-bed for the pioneer Whittle jet engine mounted in the tail of the fuselage—the first instance of a rear-mounted jet.

362

Mk VI wings and Merlin 62 engines. The selection of the Mk VI wings and these particular engines was in order to achieve high-altitude flights for testing the jets at their proper and most efficient operating height. Between 1944 and 1945 at least 15 types of jet engines were evaluated in these high-flying test-bed Wellingtons, and a total of 512 hours was completed in 366 separate flights.

So ends the involved story of the Wellington, as absorbing to the student of technological development as to the military historian. The grand total of 11,461 Wellingtons means more than simply being the largest number of any British bomber ever produced; it represents a massive effort on the part of all concerned in the Wellington's design, development, production and, indeed, operation. Without it the course of the second world war might have taken quite a different turn.

Wellington (other rôles)

	Mk VI Type 442	Mk VIII Type 429	Mk XIII Type 466
Accommodation:	Pilot and 3 crew	Pilot and 5/6 crew	Pilot and 5/6 crew
Engines:	Two 1,600 hp Rolls-Royce Merlin 60	Two 1,050 hp Bristol Pegasus XVIII	Two 1,735 hp Bristol Hercules XVII
Span:	86 ft 2 in	86 ft 2 in	86 ft 2 in
Length:	61 ft 9 in	64 ft 7 in	64 ft 7 in
Height:	17 ft 8 in	17 ft 8 in	17 ft 8 in
Wing Area:	840 sq ft	840 sq ft	840 sq ft
Empty Weight:	20,280 lb	21,118 lb	21,988 lb
Gross Weight:	30,450 lb	30,000 lb	31,000 lb
Max Speed:	300 mph	235 mph	250 mph
Service Ceiling:	38,500 ft	19,000 ft	16,000 ft
Range:	2,275 miles with 15,000-lb bomb load	2,550 miles at 144 mph	1,750 miles
Armament:	Remote control four-gun rear turret	Front and rear two-gun turrets	Two-gun front turret and four-gun rear turret
	Max bomb load 4,500 lb	Two 420-lb depth charges or two torpedoes	Torpedoes and ASV Mk III
		Leigh light	

First prototype B.1/35, K8178, with Rolls-Royce Vulture II engines.

Warwick and Windsor

In 1935 great hopes were held for engines of high power which had been planned for future development as propulsive units for heavy-bombers. In the previous chapter the technical career of the ubiquitous Wellington has been traced in detail, and the inevitable conclusion of the historian is that its design and subsequent development represented an unqualified success. For a number of reasons the parallel design to the Wellington in the heavy-bomber class, the Warwick, was much less satisfactory. One reason was the inability of the high-power engine designs to match up to their early promise within the time scale allotted for their introduction into service. In consequence, the Warwick failed to get the power plants for which it was designed in time for it to play any outstanding part in the war in the air. Subsequent events accelerated the arrival of the four-engined heavies, by which time the twin-engined Warwick was having to employ power units of lower output than those which its progressive development demanded.

One misapprehension must be removed from the record, which is that the Warwick was designed as a replacement for the Wellington; the two designs were intended by the Air Staff to be complementary, and the B.9/32 and B.1/35 structural details had much in common. In fact, the first Wellington Mk I was, in its main essentials, a cut down B.1/35 Warwick.

Specification B.1/35 was written for a heavy-bomber of under 100-ft span,* with a speed of not less than 195 mph at 15,000 ft, and a range of 1,500 miles carrying 2,000 lb of bombs, an interesting requirement being

* Span of large military landplanes was still limited by existing hangar dimensions at RAF bases.

Front view of B.1/35, K8178, with Rolls-Royce Vulture engines.

flight refuelling. The engines were to be two units of 1,000 hp each fitted with variable-pitch propellers. To this specification Vickers submitted a tender on 2 July, 1935, for an aeroplane powered by two Bristol Hercules HEISM engines of 1,300 hp each, with an estimated speed of 261 mph at 15,000 ft and a time to that height of 10 minutes at an all-up weight of 23,500 lb. These figures improved upon those of the specification by a good margin.

The B.1/35 project was a completely new design with only a slight resemblance to the B.9/32, which had then still to fly. It could be considered, however, as a heavy-bomber version of the smaller type, and a major mock-up for it was at first considered unnecessary. After a preliminary contract had been placed on 7 October, 1935, the situation was reconsidered, and a complete mock-up was ordered on 14 March, 1936, largely because of design changes. The B.1/35 type number was 284, and the redesign of the B.9/32, which became the Wellington I, was the Type 285.

Thus, the close association of the two aircraft, Wellington and Warwick, was at once established. In detail, the similarity of the respective airframes was evident in both wings and fuselage. There were seven fewer stations in each inner plane of the Wellington and 12 fewer stations in its fuselage, while the Warwick had, in addition, an extension to the nose consisting of five extra stations. Most of the geodetic members were, therefore, common to both, which was a great asset in production.

By July 1936 the all-up weight of the B.1/35 had risen to 30,370 lb; the weight of the prototype was still rising by January 1937, when a set of

Second prototype B.1/35, L9704, with Bristol Centaurus engines.

365

alternative mountings was requested by the Air Ministry for the Rolls-Royce Vulture, one of the higher-power engines under development. In 1937 an interesting suggestion was made for a nosewheel undercarriage which, using brakes, promised a shorter landing run, but this did not materialise.

On 2 July, 1937, a second B.1/35 prototype was ordered under the serial L9704, the first prototype being K8178. On 28 October an investigation was requested into balloon-barrage cable resistance; and in November 1937 a requirement was issued for consideration of the Napier Sabre, another of the higher-power engines. Supplementary specification P.13/36 was issued to cover aircraft powered with the Vulture or Sabre, including the B.1/35.

Second prototype B.1/35, L9704, with mid-upper turret added and rudder balance changed from horn to mass type as shown.

Following this supplementary specification, the Air Ministry amended the Vickers contract for the B.1/35 to provide for the fitting of Vultures to the first prototype, and Sabres to the second, with alternative Vulture mountings. At this time the engine situation was becoming critical, and of all the project designs submitted to specification P.13/36, only the B.1/35 and Avro Manchester survived as twin-engined types in the heavy bomber class.

On 16 December, 1937, the Bristol Centaurus was added to the list of higher-power engines to be considered for the B.1/35. Common bulkhead attachment points were agreed upon by the respective engine manufacturers, by the adoption of the Vulture standard, to achieve interchangeability of power units. Revised requirements were issued at this time showing considerable advances on the general performance and bomb load originally envisaged.

By March 1938 the design was completely different from the tender submitted in July 1935, although the dimensions were much the same. As with the Wellington, the initial design of gun turrets proved a major problem. By 1938 Frazer-Nash turrets had replaced those of Vickers design, and the B.1/35 prototypes were then to be fitted with F-N 5 nose, F-N 9 midship and F-N 10 tail types, all with two Browning guns in each. Propellers were also receiving much attention at this time, as the aeroplane's all-up weight and maximum speed had changed; the latter was now 332 mph, with Rolls-Royce Vulture S engines driving propellers of 14 ft 6 in diameter.

Because development of the Sabre engine lagged behind estimates, the Air Ministry substituted the Centaurus in L9704, with the Sabre still the alternative for K8178. De Havilland propellers were ordered for the Centaurus and Sabre, and constant-speed Rotol propellers for the Vulture-powered aeroplane. Estimated delivery dates for the respective engines were given as: Vultures by the end of January 1939, and Centaurus and Sabres by the end of March. At the same time, December 1938, there was official doubt about the geodetic construction of the B.1/35, and work was stopped on the jigs and tools. Later, a resubmission at high level of data relating to specification P.13/36, with the three engines alternatively in-

L9704, with fin stripes added, disclosing original horn-balanced rudder.

stalled in the aeroplane, led to production being resumed at the end of June.

In the meantime, Vulture engines had been delivered, as well as Rotol constant-speed propellers, with de Havilland Hydromatic propellers as alternatives. The aeroplane was weighed on 6 July, 1939, tare weight being 26,000 lb but rising to 27,032 lb with the Rotol propellers, armour plating and other additions. All-up weight was calculated at 42,182 lb, which included 7,500 lb of bombs, 700 gal of fuel and 40 gal of oil, a military load of 1,040 lb and a crew of five. The design certificate for flight trials was issued for K8178 to fly at a light load of 30,000 lb from Brooklands, which it did on 13 August, 1939, in the hands of Summers, accompanied by Westbrook as observer. Some trouble was experienced with the carburettor linkage, and K8178 was airborne for minutes only. With a Vickers-designed linkage it flew again on 19 August and trials continued.

The second prototype, L9704, was by then nearing completion, and the two Centaurus CEISM engines were delivered in December 1939, the de Havilland constant-speed propellers following in January. L9704 was intended for use as a flying test-bed for the Centaurus engines for at least 25 hours. A comparison made at this time between the standard 0·303-in and 0·5-in machine-gun armament specified the disposition of the Frazer-Nash turrets as nose, mid-upper, mid-lower and stern.

K8178 was slowly adding to its flying hours, and various modifications were made to improve its handling characteristics, including alterations to the elevator dimensions. L9704 was flown for the first time, by Summers, from Brooklands, on 5 April, 1940, at a weight of 29,015 lb. Both aircraft were flown on the same afternoon, and a fair comparison was therefore possible, L9704 with the Centaurus showing marked improvement.

In April 1940 the decision to fit Sabres in K8178, as the Type 400, was cancelled because these engines were needed for fighters. Delays in getting the other engines into production led to a high-level discussion on 12 July, 1940, when a proposition to fit four Merlin XXs was abandoned because of a serious decrease in bomb load and range. From statements made at the meeting, it could be discerned that if the B.1/35 was to go into production other suitable engines would have to be found. A suggestion was made to obtain two Wright engines from the United States.

Design estimates were also made for the B.1/35 with Pratt & Whitney Double Wasp R-2800 engines. The performance proved to be very similar to that of the Wellington III with Hercules III engines, but with double the bomb load over a 2,000 mile range. On 24 July, 1940, two Double Wasps were allocated for installation in L9704 under the Type number 422.

Meanwhile, with the Centaurus, L9704 had carried out handling trials at Boscombe Down. Elevators and rudder were found to be heavy, there was control-column vibration and too much noise in the crew compartments. New elevators and rudder were proposed, and it was thought that the fitting of the Double Wasps would help solve the other troubles.

K8178 had gone to Rolls-Royce at Hucknall for engine-development flying, and there it was fitted with two production Vulture II engines. On 24 November, 1940, it jumped a chock during engine runs and damaged a propeller; some delay ensued before another was fitted in January 1941, when it was flown to Blackpool, where the Vultures were removed and stored by Rolls-Royce. The aeroplane was then allocated to Bristol for flight testing the Centaurus power-egg.

In October 1940, L9704 was the subject of flight tests with different Frazer-Nash mid-upper turrets, but, more significantly, modifications were made which included the fitting of a Wellington I fin and rudder in an attempt to improve yaw stability.

Although far too much time had been lost to ensure a success for the B.1/35 to match that of the Wellington, in December 1940 Vickers proposed that a batch of five should be constructed to take Pratt & Whitney Double Wasp engines. The design still had much promise despite its lateness, and apparently the Ministry thought so too, for a contract was placed for 250 airframes on 3 January, 1941, to be built at Weybridge, split into 150 Mk Is and 100 Mk IIs, deliveries to commence in November 1941.

Now that an order had been placed for the B.1/35, the Air Ministry decided that the time had come to give it a name. From a list of 119 names

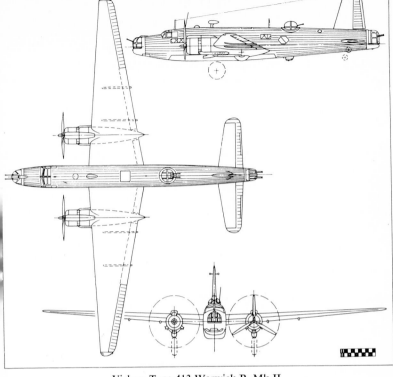

Vickers Type 413 Warwick B. Mk II.

of towns beginning with W, Warwick was finally chosen in January 1941. At the same time the proposed production versions were designated Warwick B. Mk I with the Double Wasps (Type 422) and Warwick B. Mk II with the Centaurus (Type 413).

During February 1941 Vickers prepared designs for a special high-altitude Warwick comparative with the Wellingtons V and VI. The estimated ceiling of 40,000 ft was higher than that of any contemporary fighter. The engines proposed were two modified Bristol Centaurus CE5MASMs or four Rolls-Royce Merlin RM6SMs. At all-up weights of 45,000 lb and 49,982 lb, respectively, 7,500 lb of bombs could be carried over respective ranges of 1,926 and 1,481 miles, at cruising speeds (maximum altitude) of 284/322 mph and 300/337 mph, out and back. On the homeward flight the mean service ceiling was 44,000 ft.

The interesting features of this study was that the four-Merlin project crystallised into the Warwick Mk III (Type 433) and was renamed the Windsor, dealt with later. In this developed design the span was increased to 117 ft and the wing area to 1,209 sq ft.

Meanwhile the Warwick II prototype, L9704, was having a stormy passage with the unsuitable engine gear ratio offered with unmatched propellers of various vintages. Delays occurred because the Double Wasps were despatched by sea, and the propeller situation was finally resolved by selecting 14-ft diameter Hamilton Hydromatic fully-feathering types to match the engine gear ratio of 0·5. The production Warwick IIs were to have a 0·4 engine gear ratio with Hamilton Hydromatic fully-feathering propellers of 15-ft diameter.

Although the works order for installing the Double Wasp R-2800 S1A4-G engines was issued in February 1941, the flying programme with the Centaurus was still proceeding with L9704, with particular attention to a revised tail unit. This consisted of a new servo balance tab and a modified servo trim tab to the elevators with the borrowed tailplane of K8178 which had a thin section. Summers flew L9704 at Blackpool on 1 May 1941, and the thin-section tailplane proved much superior aerodynamically and even gave a small increase of $1\frac{1}{2}$ mph over the former thick section. The pilot was completely satisfied with the handling characteristics.

The conversion of L9704 to take the Double Wasps was finally accomplished in July 1941. The aeroplane was weighed on 19 July, coming out at 26,183 lb tare. Shortly after, it went to Boscombe Down for trials and, on return, was fitted with production engines and Hamilton Hydromatic propellers of 15-ft diameter. After returning to Boscombe with the new engines considerable difficulty was experienced in starting, and the booster coils eventually had to be replaced with another type. At a mean gross weight of 38,500 lb the performance under ICAN conditions included a maximum speed of 256 mph at 15,000 ft, a maximum weak mixture cruise of 216 mph and an initial rate of climb of 550 ft/min.

Then followed a bewildering multiplicity of designs, specifications and amendments to meet the Ministry's desire to fit the Warwick into a number of possible operational rôles, but the description that follows is related to the actual aircraft produced, using the mark numbers as the main guide.

WARWICK B. MARK I. Of the 150 Warwick B. Mk Is ordered to specification Warwick 1/P1, only 16 were actually built. This was due in part to the shortage of high-power engines and partly to the continually changing policies. When the first production aeroplane, BV214, was being rolled out the requirement for a Warwick bomber no longer existed, because other aircraft that were faster and could carry a heavier bomb load over the same range were being produced. BV214 was weighed at Weybridge on 19 April, 1942, at 28,450 lb tare. After initial flight trials at Brooklands it went to the A and AEE at Boscombe Down on 3 July for Service acceptance trials, and was flown at an all-up weight of 36,900 lb. These trials disclosed a need for control-surface adjustments and attention to single-engine performance in maintaining height.

These matters having been attended to, trials proceeded, but the life of BV214 was very short. On 28 August, 1942, it crashed and was burnt out, an accident caused by fabric panel attachments on the wings coming loose.

The first production Warwick—a B.1—BV214, with Double Wasp engines, photographed in May 1942.

A standard panel was taken from production for pressure testing, and all other Warwick aircraft had their outer planes checked.

Trials were continued on BV215 with particular reference to single-engine performance. The Warwick could fly on either engine, but there was a great difference between the two engines as regards maximum cruising speed and directional control. Experiments were made with rudder horn balances and spring tabs, but, while on test at Farnborough, BV215's starboard engine caught fire on the ground after restarting for a further flight, and the aeroplane was destroyed. Tommy Lucke, Vickers' test pilot, escaped in a hurry from the cockpit.

Stability tests were continued on BV217. A new bulged rudder was introduced and increased rudder trim movement tried, while a new elevator was fitted with reduced horn balance and servo tab, with the tail-plane adjusted to suit. With these and other control modifications, the single-engine performance was nearly the same with either engine out.

Further tests with the Warwick B.Is, BV217, BV218 and BV224, were conducted at Farnborough and Boscombe. BV217 was used for engine-cooling tests and, late in 1944, for evaluating rudder characteristics for the VC1 (Viking) airliner project.

The first production Warwick B.1 bomber, BV214, in May 1942, by then outmoded by better types.

Warwick C.1 freighter at Brooklands in 1943.

The Warwick B. Mk I was little used as a bomber, but provided useful service in some technical investigations. BV224, for example, conducted navigational-equipment tests at Boscombe in 1943, and position-error, fuel-consumption and engine-cooling trials in 1944; BV228 was used for the trial installation of an airborne lifeboat; BV224 and BV295 were tried at the RAE for carbon monoxide contamination at the various cabin crew stations, and both passed the tests; BV296 was converted to ASR standard to give air-sea rescue and, additionally, clearance for transport versions of the Warwick; and BV230 was intended for type trials as a glider-tug, but was actually delivered to the A and AEE at Boscombe.

WARWICK C. MK I. Early in the development of the Warwick it was apparent that its ultimate service would be in the troop-carrying and general transport rôles, so much had engine difficulties and operational policy changes delayed its appearance as a first-line bomber. In 1942 the design to fulfil transport needs reached finality with an order for 14 Warwicks for the British Overseas Airways Corporation.

The BOAC Warwicks were needed to carry mail, freight and passengers, in that order of importance, across Africa from Bathurst to Cairo, flying boats being used from England to Bathurst. The intention was to have the Warwicks ready by the end of 1942, and they were to be converted from B. Mk Is. This time-scale was optimistic. Major modifications were needed, which included deletion of all military equipment and ancillaries, and their replacement by such civil details as cabin windows, freight floor

The prototype converted C.1 Warwick for BOAC, as flight tested by
R. C. Handasyde at Brooklands on 22 February, 1943.

Warwick C.1, G-AGFA, in BOAC service, with Double Wasp engines.

exhaust flame dampers for night-flying concealment and provision of extra-long-range fuel tanks. Despite the magnitude of this conversion, the first aeroplane, BV243, was fully modified by 29 January, 1943, and flew on 5 February. Royal Navy representatives looked at this civil aeroplane for the possible supply of 30 to 50 as naval air transports, but apparently preferred the RAF Transport Command Warwick project then envisaged.

The 14 Warwicks for BOAC were taken straight off the Weybridge production line and were originally BV243 to BV256 inclusive, but were allotted civil registrations G-AGEX to G-AGFK. Payload was 9,600 lb and, with a crew of four, 1,010 gal of fuel and 50 gal of oil, the take-off weight was 41,996 lb. The engines were Double Wasp R-2800-S1A4-Gs. Various trimming changes were made to the rudder.

On 22 February, 1943, G-AGEX was flown by Handasyde for level-speed tests at an all-up weight of 31,500 lb, with normal passenger seating installed. The speed obtained was 251 mph IAS at 6,050 ft and 2,600 rpm at plus 7·75 lb boost. Vickers-type short air-intakes were originally fitted, but in April the long Vokes air-filter types, suitably modified, were substituted. The last test flight by Vickers was carried out by Lucke, at an all-up weight of 40,000 lb in asymmetric engine trials, when port and starboard were nearly matched as regards aircraft speed at approximately 5,000 ft. G-AGEX was then delivered to Boscombe for single-engine performance and handling trials.

Warwick C.1, BV256, with Double Wasps in October 1944.

The Warwick C. Mk I was used by BOAC on their Middle East routes, and a report dated 4 January, 1944, complained of 'quilting of the wing fabric in flight', a phenomenon already experienced by them with their Wellingtons, which Pierson had explained as normal with a geodetic structure. The airline did not keep the Warwicks long before they were transferred to 167 Squadron, RAF, and finally to 525 Squadron of Transport Command at Lyneham. All reverted to their Service serial numbers on being taken over by the RAF.

WARWICK ASR. Early in 1943 the Air Staff decided that the Warwick I and II would not be used as bombers, but for air-sea rescue and freighting. This meant that the aircraft had to be modified to carry Lindholme life-saving equipment or an airborne lifeboat. In the latter case the requirements were a range of 1,800 miles at the most economical cruising speed while carrying a lifeboat. The Mk I lifeboat or, alternatively, two sets of Lindholme rescue equipment, consisting of 10 containers, had to be successfully dropped at speeds between 100 and 130 mph. A crew of seven was specified, and no oxygen equipment was to be carried.

Vickers prepared designs for an ASR Warwick under Type 462. In May 1943 an order was placed for 100 ASR and 100 freighter Warwicks, these superseding previous orders. BV228 was selected to take the first lifeboat; but as airframe modifications were necessary and as time was needed to select a suitable boat, interim aircraft were modified to take the Lindholme equipment only, designated Warwick Bomber/ASR, and 40 were so converted. As some had already been delivered as B. Mk Is, they were returned to Weybridge for this purpose. BV297 was the first conversion and had provision for two sets of Lindholme gear; it had no ASV radar and no lifeboat suspension gear.

WARWICK ASR (STAGES A AND B). The airborne lifeboat was designed and built by Uffa Fox, and was complete with engines, rocket gear and parachutes, the total weight with ASR equipment being over 1,630 lb. Wind-tunnel dropping tests were carried out at the RAE on a $\frac{1}{13}$ scale model, and proved satisfactory without any airflow stabilising fin.

Handling tests on BV228 with a production lifeboat having also proved satisfactory, the next steps led to the first production Warwick ASRs,

Warwick ASR I, HF971, with Double Wasp engines, in tropical finish.

Warwick ASR (Stage A) carrying airborne lifeboat Mk I.

which were referred to as ASR (Stage A). It should be stated here that dropping trials with lifeboats for air-sea rescue had previously been done off Cowes, in 1943, from a Hudson III converted specially for the purpose by Cunliffe Owen Aircraft. Early results had in all cases proved satisfactory, and the trials proved the feasibility of the system.

The first Warwick ASR (Stage A), equipped for the carriage of the airborne lifeboat Mk I and Lindholme gear, was BV298. Nine others followed, and all had bomb doors cut away to accommodate the boat. Intensive trials at Boscombe Down were carried out with BV242 and BV298, for a total flying time of 183 hr 40 min. The measured maximum speed of BV301 carrying the boat at 43,200-lb all-up weight was 235 mph at 4,000 ft, with 2,600 rpm and plus 8·75 lb boost. After sea trials with the first production boat the whole exercise was regarded as satisfactory, and the first squadron to receive Warwick ASRs was 280 at Langham, in Norfolk. Three aircraft were delivered in August 1943: BV282, BV284 and BV286.

While the Stage A ASR Warwicks carried only the Mk I lifeboat and two sets of Lindholme gear, Stage B versions had provision for ASV radar with wing and front fuselage aerials and the F-N 120A tail turret, while the F24 camera-mounting was omitted. There were 20 Stage B aircraft converted as such.

Front view of air-sea rescue Warwick IA with Double Wasp engines and de Havilland electric propellers, at Brooklands; in the background is a white Wellington XIII, and behind port wing tip of Warwick is a parked barrage balloon.

WARWICK ASR MK I. The Stage C was the finalised version, later designated Warwick ASR Mk I, of which 204 were built. It embodied all the
equipment previously mentioned and could be operated in four configurations: with Mk I lifeboat at 42,924 lb, with Lindholme gear only at
41,534 lb, with Mk II lifeboat at 44,764 lb and with extra tankage for
reinforcing ASR units at a minimum range of 2,000 miles, at 41,984 lb all-
up weight. The range of the first three of these configurations was 1,500
miles.

Uffa Fox was not completely satisfied with the Mk I lifeboat fitted to
the Warwick ASR Mk I, and he supplied a modified version Mk IA at
about the same weight. Eventually, a Mk II boat was produced at a weight
of 3,600 lb, which meant that when this was carried no Lindholme gear
could be accommodated. Wind-tunnel dropping tests of a $\frac{1}{13}$ scale model
of the Mk II lifeboat by the RAE were satisfactory, the boat being directionally stable in the air without tail fins and showing no tendency to roll
over.

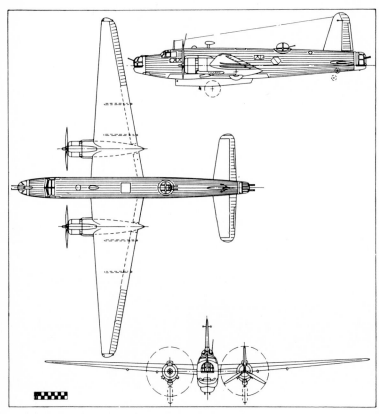

Vickers Type 462 Warwick ASR Mk I (Stage A).

376

Warwick ASR Mk I carrying airborne lifeboat Mk II.

Handling trials with the Mk II lifeboat fitted to BV228 were undertaken t Brooklands by Sqn Ldr Longbottom in October 1943. Heavy-load trials ere continued at Farnborough, and a satisfactory drop was accomplished y the RAE before the series of trials was completed by 1 November, 1943. ervice trials at Boscombe Down were made with BV403 during which a inge of 1,255 miles at a cruising speed of 125 kt IAS, and an all-up weight f 45,000 lb was obtained while carrying the Mk II lifeboat.

Warwick air-sea rescue aircraft made many sorties in the later part of ie war, dropping lifeboats and rescue equipment to Allied aircrews own in the sea. One outstanding example was the dropping of a lifeboat) the crew of a Mosquito which had ditched in the southern part of the ay of Biscay; they took four days to return, but return they did.

WARWICK ASR MK VI. A further batch of ASR Warwicks was produced nder the designation Mk VI, but of the 94 built, only two of the last 25, N828 and PN862, actually went into squadron service; the others nished up in RAF Maintenance units, presumably being held in reserve

Warwick ASR pressed into service in Burma campaign to fly in supplies during the siege of Imphal. (*Photo Peter Almack.*)

for the anticipated extension of the war in the Pacific which never materia
ised. The main difference from their predecessors was that they wer
fitted with the Double Wasp R-2800-2SBG engines instead of the R-2800
S1A4-Gs. The first ASR Mk VI was BV296, which was, in fact, the flyin
test-bed for the 2SBG engine at Boscombe Down.

WARWICK B MK II. Under the Vickers Type 413, a contract was awarde
in 1940 for one Bristol Centaurus engined prototype. Design had bee
proceeding since December 1937, and the first tentative speed estimate wa
quoted in January 1938 as 348 mph at 17,500 ft. As the Centaurus de
veloped, the mark of the engine changed, but it was finally settled that
was to be the IV, and on 16 October, 1941, BV216 was selected to be cor
verted from a B. Mk I into the B. Mk II prototype. Rotol four-blad
propellers of 14 ft 9 in diameter were to be fitted.

The aeroplane was weighed at the end of June 1943 at a tare weight c
29,174 lb and flew shortly after. There was much development flying b
Bristol at Filton, and in 1944 they changed the engines to Centaurus VIII
BV216 finally going to 45 MU in October 1945. No other B. Mk IIs wer
built because of the shortage of engines and the reduced need for bomber
Maximum speed recorded by Weybridge before delivery of the B. Mk
was 290 mph at 20,000 ft at 47,500 lb all-up weight. This increase in weigh
had been achieved through the greater power then available.

WARWICK GR MK II. In 1943, when the Centaurus engines were becomin
available, the Mark II was given another rôle, that of general reconnai
sance. A new type number was allocated, 469, and the power unit was th
Centaurus CE7SM. Two versions were planned, one to be a torpedo
carrier with three 18-in or two 24-in weapons, or 12,250 lb of bombs, an
the other a Leigh light variant carrying 15,250 lb of bombs. Productic
was split into 75 per cent torpedo-carriers and 25 per cent Leigh ligl
carriers.

In May 1943, the Leigh light was deleted and 12 to 15 depth charges sul
stituted for bombs, in some configurations, as well as provision for 1

Warwick GR II, HG348, with Centaurus engines.

378

ocket projectiles on early production aircraft. Some difficulty was experienced with the mid-upper turret in providing sufficient defensive fire-power for daylight operations, according to tests at the A and AEE carried out with Warwick GR Mk II HG343.

The directional stability of the Warwick was also in doubt at this time, and was the cause of three accidents within a few days early in 1945, one of which happened to Mutt Summers in HG364, from which he and his flight observer, Jimmy Green, escaped without serious injury. Another accident was experienced by Maurice Summers, Mutt's brother, on PN777, and in this the flight observer, G. F. Hemsley, broke his leg. In the third, Sqn Ldr Shorty Longbottom was killed. Lucke experienced the same trouble on two occasions, but was able to apply rudder correction before the situation became catastrophic. The cause was rudder aerodynamic overbalance and was corrected in the later GR Mk V and retrospectively to other marks, mainly by the addition of a dorsal fin.

WARWICK GR MK II MET. At the end of 1944 it was decided to use the GR Mk II for meteorological duties and for training crews in high-altitude navigation. In consequence, operation of the engines in FS gear was required, and oxygen equipment was to be fitted. Various modifications included the removal of all bomb gear and associated equipment and the replacement of the nose armament by a wide-vision nose window, the mid-upper turret being removed in the long-range version only. The prototype GR Mk II Met Warwick was HG362, converted from GR Mk II standards with temporary oxygen equipment and S blower controls. The production order was for 90 Warwick GR Mk II Met aircraft, but only 14 were actually built, and none went into squadron service.

Various trainer versions of the GR Mk II were mooted but few materialised, except those converted by the RAF. Two of these were HG 349 and HG350 at Wing, Buckinghamshire. The crew of 12 comprised two pilots, two bomb-aimers, two W/T operators, three navigators and three gunners.

WARWICK C. MK III. While the original Warwick Mk III was developed into the Windsor, as stated earlier, under the Air Ministry mark number system the Warwick Mk I was the B. Mk I with Double Wasp engines, the Mk II was the B. Mk II with Centaurus; but the Mk III was a transport/freighter version designated C. Mk III, Vickers Type 460.

A comparison made in August 1942 between the Wellington X, with the Hercules VI, and the Warwick I, with the Double Wasp, for a transport aeroplane showed that the latter could carry 30 troops and their equipment 250 miles farther, at a slightly higher ME cruising speed, compared with the Wellington with 12 troops. Operational requirements for a Warwick I transport were issued shortly after to specification CS16588. These requirements were that as a troop-transport it should be able to carry 26 fully equipped troops or 20 paratroops; as a freighter, aero-engines or military cargo; as an air ambulance, six stretcher patients and two medical

Warwick C III, HG248, with Sabre engines, in the transport/freighter rôle, wit
Mk GR V dorsal fin, added retrospectively, and ventral pannier replacing bomb doo
of bomber versions.

orderlies; or be used as a glider-tug. A crew of four was specified. N
elaborate modifications were needed, and special equipment had to t
capable of being fitted within 24 hours. In the event, the order for 1C
C. Mk IIIs was completed, the first production aeroplane being HG21
Performance requirements included a still-air range of 2,500 miles at M
cruise speed at 15,000 ft, and single-engine flight up to 8,000 ft at 37,000 l
loaded weight.

The actual design of the C. Mk III was developed from the B. Mk I wit
some components identical to those of BOAC's C. Mk I aircraft. Mod
fications included removal of all armament and armour, and their assoc
ated hydraulics and electrics, with the ventral-turret aperture then adapte
as the paratroop exit. The entrance door was resited aft, and the freighte
stretcher entrance located on the starboard side of the fuselage, with prov
sion for light-freight compartments in lieu of nose and tail turrets. A larg
ventral freight-pannier was added in place of the bomb doors to hou
four 125-gal fuel tanks. At this time the C. Mk III was also considered as
flying fuel-carrier to lift 920 gal in drums, obviously for reinforcing ove
seas fuel supplies as, with 700 gal of fuel, the range was 1,200 miles with
crew of three.

For development trials, the first C. Mk III was flown at Boscombe ;
43,000 lb instead of the normal 45,000 lb to avoid the necessity for fu
jettison. In October 1944 various configurations for different rôles wer
evaluated at differential all-up loadings, from between 40,000 lb for th
ambulance version to 45,000 lb for the freighter, which could accommoda
11,600 lb. HG218 was given trooping as its rôle, but in April 1945 it re
ceived a somewhat unfavourable report from the Airborne Forces Exper
mental Establishment at Beaulieu, in the New Forest, on its capabilities ;
a paratroop transport.

A great deal of experimental work was done with Warwick C. Mk II
at the A and AEE concerning performances, cabin heating and ventilatio
ambulance trials and carbon monoxide contamination tests. Meanwhil
Vickers were interested in a design for a civil transport based on th

Warwick for continental passenger operations. This project proceeded as far as a $\frac{1}{18}$ scale wind-tunnel model.

The first squadron to receive Warwick C. Mk IIIs was No. 525 at Lyneham, the first aircraft, HG219, being delivered on 24 June, 1944. Eleven more were delivered up to 14 July. The next squadron to receive them was 165, followed by 301 (P) and 304. No. 525 Squadron experienced considerable trouble in handling caused by stiff elevator trim tabs and the difficulty of filling and off-loading the overload fuel tanks on mission change. These were matters which could receive attention and be improved; but one fault of all Warwicks reappeared, fabric lifting off the elevator and other upper surfaces. In the Far East the heat cracked the top surface fabric, and complete recovering was the only sound answer. The C. Mk IIIs were considered unsuitable for use in the Far East, and so were used on the United Kingdom–Middle East runs until they were all withdrawn from service before March 1946.

To complete the history of the Warwick C. Mk III, mention must be

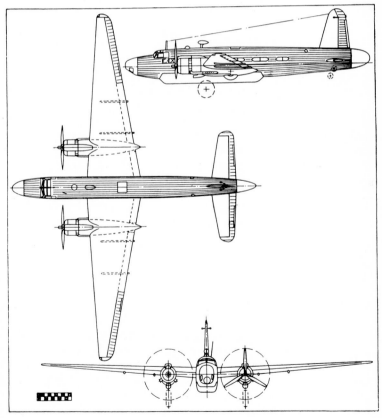

Vickers Type 460 Warwick C. Mk III.

381

made of the subsequent careers of HG252 and HG330. HG252 was fitted with a Warwick Mk V tail unit and tested at A and AEE in October 1944 to investigate the poor handling qualities reported by RAF Transport Command. First it was dived up to 280 mph (IAS) and then, on 31 October, 1944, up to 330 mph (IAS) at an all-up weight of 42,300 lb, so the results with the new tail must have been satisfactory.

Later, HG252 was tested with a Mk IV auto-control installation, also with satisfactory results. HG330 was also tested with auto-control at the RAE, and with a Mark V tailplane. Finally, in April 1945 the new Warwick V fin and dorsal fin were added and tested, following which other C. Mk IIIs were similarly converted.

WARWICK GR MK V. The C. Mk IV was a transport version of the Warwick II to fulfil the same rôles as the C. Mk III with Centaurus engines, but only one conversion was completed. Shortly after the GR

Warwick GR V, PN697, with Centaurus VII engines, at Boscombe Down for cooling and performance trials.

Mk II was given the go-ahead the Leigh light was reintroduced into Warwicks, and Vickers drew up fresh specifications under their type number 474 and with the official designation of GR Mk V. This development was almost identical to the GR Mk II, except that two beam guns replaced the mid-upper gun turret, leading to a saving of weight and a decrease in drag, with a consequent increase in range of 170 nautical miles.

The Leigh-light turrets were not ready at the end of October 1943, so the first GR Mk Vs built had the Leigh light installed at a fixed inclination of seven degrees. The first GR Mk V was PN697, and the initial production called for 100 aircraft. Differences which eventually emerged between the GR Mk II and the GR Mk V included a new nose flooring, Leigh-light equipment in place of the mid-upper turret but lowered through the floor, and bomb gear increased to 20 slips. Armament of the GR Mk V was revised to one 0·5-in gun in the nose, two 0·5-in beam guns, and four 0·303s in the rear turret with no RP (rocket projectile) installations. The all-up

Another view of PN697 at the A and AEE, Boscombe Down.

weight was increased to 49,000 lb, the landing weight remaining at 43,000 lb. The engines were Centaurus VIIIs.

The first GR Mk V, PN697, was flown in April 1944, at Brooklands, and underwent manufacturer's trials there before proceeding to Boscombe for type trials. Service trials were conducted at RAF Hullavington with PN701 and PN702, while PN703 was supplied to BOAC with no armament or Leigh light.

In August 1944 the all-up weight was increased to 50,000 lb, and in October to 51,250 lb. In November the GR Mk V was cleared for operational duties in temperate and tropical climates at 50,000 lb all-up weight and a maximum dive speed of 285 kt. But Boscombe found that the bomb gear needed more development.

Despite all the progress made with the last of the Warwick production series, directional instability was still being encountered. Warwick GR Mk Vs, PN761, PN765, PN775 and PN777, were all used to solve the problem once and for all in February 1945, and a dorsal fin was fitted on PN710 at the instigation of the RAE. Flight trials of PN710 were conducted above 10,000 ft for safety reasons, and the aeroplane was put into the same evolutions that Summers had done with dire effects on the GR Mk IIs. It was violently yawed, but there was now no locking over of the rudder, and success was at last achieved. Even the single-engine performance was now symmetrical, being 130 kt at 3,000 ft on either engine.

A Coastal Command Warwick GR V, showing ventral ASV blister and flat panel-type transparent nose with single gun.

383

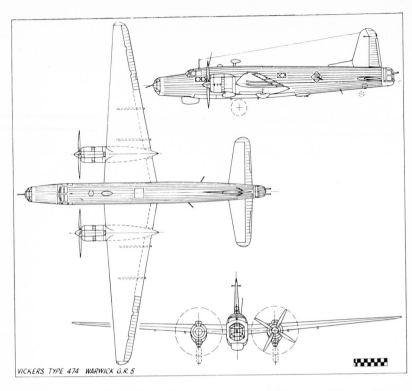

VICKERS TYPE 474 WARWICK G.R. 5

The rudder overbalance, main cause of the preceding accidents at large angles of sideslip, was finally cured by adding the dorsal fin, by limiting the rudder travel to port and starboard and by reducing chord and gearing of the balance tab. These modifications were made retrospective for all Warwicks in service. Thus, at the end of the road the Warwick, as the GR Mk V, emerged as a perfectly satisfactory aeroplane with powerful and reliable engines, almost 10 years after the design had first been projected as a heavy bomber.

Warwick GR Mk Vs were issued to 179 Squadron of Coastal Command at St Eval in Cornwall in the spring of 1945. Had the Pacific war continued, it would have rendered valuable service indeed; in fact, it remained in service for only a short period after the cessation of hostilities.

The only civil GR Mk V was PN703 to which the registration G-AGLD was allotted, and it was used by BOAC for experience in the operation of the Centaurus engine. It first flew at Brooklands on 25 August, 1944, received a civil certificate of airworthiness on 17 October and then went to the BOAC Development Flight at Hurn as a test-bed for the Centaurus VII. After making a flight to South Africa in October 1945, it was eventually broken up at Wisley.

Other Warwicks were allocated as test-beds for various purposes, such

384

Warwick, HG248, as converted from a C.Mk III by the Napier Co at Luton as an engine test-bed for the Sabre VI—long after the original design was intended to have Sabres as standard engines—a dramatic picture. (*Flight photo.*)

as engine-development flying with later versions of the Bristol Centaurus and Napier Sabre, as detailed in the Appendices. One airframe, HG336, was selected for the high-altitude testing of the Pratt & Whitney R-2800-S7 with GEC turbo-blower, an engine of 2,800 hp. Warwick Type 606 was earmarked for use in experimental flying by Flight Refuelling Ltd, but the most notable of all Warwick test-beds was the second prototype, L9704, which became involved in the development of remotely controlled armament for the Windsor.

The second prototype B.1/35 Warwick, L9704, converted to carry two aft-firing nacelle barbettes, controlled from the rear gunner's station, as a trial horse for Windsor armament.

So ends the story of the Warwick with its chequered career. Technical progress is not achieved without such examples, and from the experience with the Warwick and its various power plants emerged a fund of knowledge which was applied later to solve problems in design and development in both civil and military aircraft at Weybridge, where all Warwicks were built. One of the lessons driven home was that engine development takes time—usually far longer than the sanguine expectations of powerplant designers.

WINDSOR. Following the success achieved by Roy Chadwick, chief designer of A. V. Roe and Company, in converting his twin-engined Manchester bomber into the four-engined Lancaster, it was natural to assume that Pierson, who had always been a champion of the large multi-engined aeroplane, should attempt a similar conversion of the Warwick. Both the Manchester and the Warwick had indeed suffered from the initial failure of the high-power piston-engine programme on which bomber policy had been based in the years before Munich.

The story of the Windsor, however, started long before the emergence of the Lancaster. To exploit the physical characteristics of the geodetic concept to the full it was necessary to go to very large sizes of aeroplane, and Pierson did enter a design to the B.12/36 specification for a four-engined long-range bomber, the same requirement to which R. J. Mitchell of the Supermarine Company produced his highly promising and, regrettably, last design.

Mitchell chose a low-aspect-ratio wing, with high induced drag and comprising a massive structure which contained a large part of the bomb load, whereas Pierson chose a wing of high aspect ratio and low induced drag, oddly enough of elliptical planform resembling that of Mitchell's Spitfire. In the event, the contract for B.12/36 went to the Short Stirling, which, with its low-aspect wing and high loadings, exposed the effect on performance of such a configuration. Vickers were aware of the advantage that wings of very wide span had at the aircraft performances then prevailing, and a specimen geodetic wing had been built of this type for a proposed enlarged B.1/35 (Warwick).

First prototype Windsor, DW506, at Farnborough in October 1943.

386

Windsor DW506 in flight during early trials.

Vickers' tender to B.12/36 being unsuccessful, another was entered to specification B.1/39 for a heavy bomber with a range of 2,500 miles carrying a 9,000-lb bomb load at a cruising speed of 280 mph, with four Bristol Hercules or four Rolls-Royce Griffons, then emergent engines. This tender also met with no success, but in 1941 a further specification was issued, B.5/41, for a high-altitude heavy bomber to be equipped with a pressure cabin and have a speed of 345 mph at 31,000 ft. Pierson submitted a design for a modified Warwick III under type number 433 with either four Centaurus or four Merlins, and again embodying an elliptical wing planform, of high aspect ratio.

The project extended the wing span of the Warwick by 20 ft and the fuselage by 4 ft. On this basis, a contract was placed for two prototypes to B.5/41 under the serials DW506 and DW512, with four Rolls-Royce Merlin 60 engines. From the place-names Worcester, Wentworth and Windsor, the last was selected for the new design. The original layout specified a two-wheel main undercarriage, but in September this was

Another view of DW506 in the air, showing distinctive chin-type radiator housings.

changed to a lateral four-wheel layout with one wheel and leg assembly in each engine nacelle. This unusual arrangement led to some criticism of the likelihood of high drag on take-off and approach in the event of engine failure, but this did not prove valid in practice.

One of the requirements originally intended was that the Vickers B.5/41 should have a pressure cabin and cockpit similar to that of the Wellington VI, but this provision was eventually abandoned, so a new specification, B.3/42, was drawn up to cover the revised design of the Windsor, Type 447. The new requirements included four Merlin 61 engines, later amended to Merlin 65s, nose turret to have two 0·303-in Browning guns, take-off weight 55,000 lb and landing weight 42,500 lb, with a maximum speed of 350 mph.

By December 1942 the take-off weight had risen to 68,000 lb, carrying 12,000 lb of bombs. At this time there was a survey of the Windsor as a possible Coastal Command type with ASV and Leigh light. In February 1943 it was decided that the first Windsor was to be completed with bearded radiators and cowlings, and the second with the more refined off-

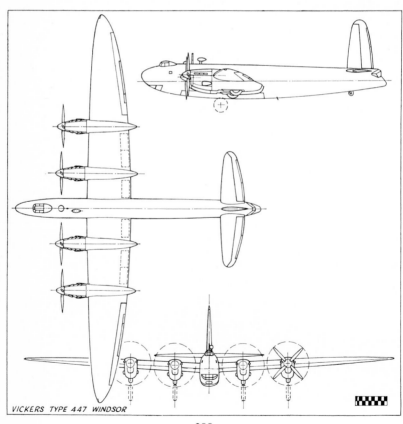

VICKERS TYPE 447 WINDSOR

Windsor NK136 without outer nacelle barbettes.

centre annular radiator and cowling assembly, with either the Merlin 65s or the Rolls-Royce 14SMs (Griffons), depending on the progress of the latter engines. The type number of this second Windsor was 457. Both were equipped with oxygen equipment in place of the originally proposed pressure cabin.

At a meeting held at the Ministry of Aircraft Production on 15 February, 1943, it was decided to equip the Windsor with remotely controlled defensive armament to satisfy an Air Staff requirement. Of four alternatives considered, that comprising rearward-firing nacelle barbettes with a tail-sighting gunner's station was adopted. The second Warwick prototype, L9704, was converted to carry two aft-firing nacelle barbettes, each with two 0·5-in guns, remotely controlled from the tail gunner's position; one of these was demonstrated to MAP, and it was then decided to place the Windsor barbettes in the two outboard nacelles. Firing trials of the Warwick experimental barbette armament were held at Vickers' gun range at Eskmeals, north of Barrow on the Westmorland coast, in July 1943, and a year later similar trials were held there of the Windsor barbette with Hispano cannon. All the armament design and development had been carried out by the Crayford and Dartford works, under the technical supervision of Capt Nannini of Vickers House.

The completed prototype barbettes were installed in Warwick L9704 which was ready to fly in February 1944. Proof trials on the ground were

Windsor NK136 at Wisley airfield, with barbettes installed.

389

made at Boscombe Down in March, and in April the Warwick was flown to Pembrey and Angle in South Wales for further ground firing. The air-firing trials which followed were made over Freshwater Bay, Isle of Wight, against a target drogue towed by an Anson. In September 1944 it was decided that enough had been learned, and the barbettes were taken out of L9704, which was then dismantled. The barbettes were taken back to Vickers to serve as models for the Windsor installation.

Close-up of Windsor barbette with twin 20-mm Hispano cannon.

Other technical investigations being conducted at that time included proposals for a second sighting station in the astrodome and a third to enable the pilot to fire the nacelle guns dead aft. The promising development of AGLT (automatic gun laying and tracking) also made this a possibility for installation in the Windsor. Other proposals were for self-sealing fuel tanks, hot-air de-icing through exhaust heat exchangers, H2S radar and alternative engines.

Windsor DW506 was first flown from Farnborough by Summers on 23 October, 1943, it having been assembled there in a specially built hangar later used by the Empire Test Pilots' School. Summers reported that the handling characteristics were satisfactory and were maintained when the all-up weight was increased later to 54,000 lb. At its first take-off weight of 46,000 lb the speed was 302 mph at 25,000 ft. It was flown purely as an aerodynamic test-bed with ballast in place of armament and bomb gear, with no automatic control or other Service equipment beyond oxygen. Two of the four-bladed propellers were those formerly used on the Wellington VI.

After a total flying time of 33 hr 45 min, DW506 force-landed on Grove airfield, Wantage, on 2 March, 1944, breaking its back. This mishap was caused by a piece of metal getting into the constant-speed unit of the starboard inner propeller, making feathering impossible. The airframe was

S. Walsh, Vickers design engineer for armament installations, examining Windsor barbette.

dismantled, the outer mainplanes being used to test their vulnerability to gunfire, and the rudder was taken later for the second Windsor prototype, DW512, in which the only visible change was the annular engine installation.

DW512 was heavier than its predecessor because of armour plating and minor modifications. It was first flown from Wisley on 15 February, 1944, by Maurice Summers and disclosed a performance almost the same as DW506. During a subsequent test flight, DW512 was put into a dive, and it was observed when pulling out that the fabric on the upper surfaces of the wings was ballooning. A distinct wrinkling of the same surfaces had been noticed previously on DW506. As flying time increased, deformation of the fabric-covering became worse and had a severe effect on the stalling behaviour of the aeroplane. Matters became crucial when a bird struck the underside of the starboard wing between the engines on one flight; on landing, it was discovered that about 10 sq ft of the fabric covering was missing.

Modifications included re-covering the wings with a thin glasscloth-backed fabric, the fitting of the DW506 rudder, a modified tailwheel and an increase of tailplane incidence. Very promising results were obtained, and DW512 was used for stability tests and to determine the actual twist of the airframe in flight because of a possible influence on the angular deflection of the guns in relation to the remotely controlled gunsights, but in fact the

391

twist was negligible. DW512 was notified for disposal on 28 June, 1946 and was broken up.

The only other Windsor to fly was NK136, which first flew on 11 July 1944, without barbettes. Its normal all-up weight was 60,000 lb, although it was stressed to 70,000 lb, and the landing weight was 50,000 lb. There were no speed restrictions, as had been applied to its predecessors. In two months it had flown 21 times and accumulated 32 hours. A wiremesh backed heavyweight fabric replaced the lightweight material of the two previous Windsors, and the wings were left unsealed to reduce the wrinkle and billowings, resulting in a considerable improvement.

Another difference of NK136 was that it had a four-longeron fuselage instead of the three-longeron one used for the earlier Windsors. This was to ensure that there was no lateral displacement of the tail in flight, particularly when the barbettes were fitted. Another type of structural deflection was the pronounced droop of the wings when the aeroplane was on the ground compared with the flexing upwards of the outer wings when in flight, an aeroelastic phenomenon now familiar, but disconcerting to pilots at the time.

The geodetics of the wing structure were so arranged that, outboard, the criss-cross of members was set at 45 degrees for maximum torsional stiffness, while further inboard the angles became more acute, the dense structure so obtained absorbing the greater bending moments towards the wing roots. The wings were sparless, but spacer struts were set vertically between the surfaces at wide intervals, and between these the flexible fuel tanks were housed.

Like DW512, the second prototype, NK136, was powered with Merlin 85 engines in annular cowlings, and its performance in early trials was disappointing, being some 25 mph slower at recorded heights; an attempt to improve this by polishing the surfaces made little difference.

The armament division of Vickers had a major engineering task with the Windsor barbettes. Like the Warwick types, they were designed and made by the Crayford and Dartford works. Each housed two 20-mm cannon

Windsor NK136 in flight during firing trials with barbette armament; the port guns are trained at extreme elevation, but the starboard guns have not been switched on by the gunner in the extreme tail.

Silhouetted outlines of Windsor showing distinctive tail.

nd their installation and trials followed closely the pattern of the Warwick
arbettes.

On 4 and 5 April, 1945, NK136, complete with its novel defensive armament, was shown to foreign representatives at Farnborough, with other
xhibits including a Lancaster also equipped with remotely controlled
)-mm cannon. Ground-firing trials were held at Pembrey and Angle, and
r-firing took place over Lyme Bay, Dorset, at different heights and speeds,
ith both tilting and non-tilting mountings. Tests continued for another
) months until the whole programme was cancelled on 15 March, 1946.
K136 was flown to Manby, Lincolnshire, to serve for a while as a ground
struction aircraft with the serial 6222M.

A fourth Windsor, NN670, Type 471, was almost finished, only 50 per
nt of the radio and 5 per cent of the other services remaining to be com-
leted, when it was also cancelled in March 1946. During its brief life
N670 was reclassified as Type 483 and was to have had an ultimate
nge of 4,000 miles.

Type 483 production B. Mk 1 Windsors were intended to have various
pes of Rolls-Royce engine, the Merlin 100, the Griffon and the RB39,
hich eventually became the Clyde propeller-turbine. With the Clyde,
hich had an equivalent horsepower of 3,000 at sea level, a maximum
eed for the Type 601, Windsor B. Mk II, was 409 mph at 28,000 ft, and as
very-long-range bomber it would have made a distinct impact on Far
ast operations had the Japanese war gone on. Progressive cancellations
me a few months after the end of the war and included the propeller-
rbine engines and the proposed civil Windsor projects. The abandoning
f this enterprise was unfortunate, notably because of the experience that
uld have been gained by the operation of a long-range propeller-turbine
roplane.

As early as November 1943 Vickers proposed two civil adaptations of
e Windsor. The first was a non-pressurised version as a continental 40
ater or as a 24-seat or 18-sleeper Empire route aeroplane, and the
cond a transatlantic type with 24-day or 18-night passengers. In January

1944 two more pressurised versions were proposed for long-range civ
operation. One had a stressed-skin fuselage and the other a new type o
covering for a geodetic structure known as Geosteel, which consisted o
steel strips 1,000th-in thick and 2-in wide, woven into a homogeneous shee
The pressure cabin was to be a flexible rubberised bag contained within th
main structure. The maximum range of these later projects was 4,00
miles, with a speed of 220–225 mph at 20,000 ft.

All these Windsor projects were prepared under the type number 48:
but by June 1945 they were superseded by other concepts in the civ
field, notably the VC1 interim short-haul airliner for European operatio
and the VC2 short/medium-haul airliner with propeller-turbine power.

Warwick

	Mk II Type 413	Mk C. III Type 460	ASR Mk I Type 462	GR Mk II Type 473
Accommodation:	Pilot and 5 crew	Pilot and 3 crew	Pilot and 6 crew	Pilot and 5 crew
Engines:	Two 2,000 hp Bristol Centaurus IV	Two 1,850 hp Pratt & Whitney Double Wasp R-2800-S1A4-G	Two 1,850 hp Pratt & Whitney Double Wasp R-2800-S1A4-G	Two 2,500 hp Bris Centaurus VI
Span:	96 ft 8½ in	96 ft 8½ in	96 ft 8½ in	96 ft 8½ in
Length:	70 ft	70 ft 6 in	72 ft 3 in	68 ft 6 in
Height:	18 ft 6 in	18 ft 6 in	18 ft 6 in	18 ft 6 in
Wing Area:	1,019 sq ft	1,006 sq ft	1,006 sq ft	1,006 sq ft
Empty Weight:	—	29,162 lb	28,154 lb	31,125 lb
Gross Weight:	45,000 lb	46,000 lb	45,000 lb	51,250 lb
Max Speed:	300 mph at 20,000 ft	260 mph at 5,000 ft	224 mph at 3,600 ft	262 mph at 2,000 f
Initial Climb:	—	675 ft/min	660 ft/min	—
Climb to:	—	10,000 ft in 10·1 min	10,000 ft in 16·1 min	10,000 ft in 9·5 mi
Service Ceiling:	28,200 ft	15,000 ft	21,500 ft	19,000 ft
Range:	2,075 miles at 185 mph at 15,000 ft	2,150 miles at 180 mph at 15,000 ft with 6,170 lb cargo or 24 troops	2,300 miles at 150 mph at 5,000 ft	3,050 miles at 1 mph at 5,000 ft
Armament:	Front and mid-upper twin-gun turrets, four-gun rear turret. Bomb load 8,000 lb	Nil	Gun turrets as Mk II Fitted with Mk II lifeboat	Gun turrets as Mk Leigh light an 15,250-lb bor load

Windsor—Type 447—Four 1,635 hp Rolls-Royce Merlin 65. Span 117 ft 2 in; length 76 ft 10 in; height 23
wing area 1,248 sq ft. Empty weight 38,606 lb; gross weight 54,000 lb. Max speed 317 mph at 23,000
initial climb 1,250 ft/min; ceiling 27,250 ft; range 2,890 miles with 8,000-lb bomb load.

Prototype Viking after roll-out at Wisley.

Viking, Valetta and Varsity

Sometime before the end of the second world war it became clear that the immediate post-war period would be one of great progress in a restored and revitalised civil aviation. Since 1939 the performance of aeroplanes had greatly improved under the urgency to attain battle superiority. Speed, climb, range and payload had all shown considerable advances, and those were the very factors that would consolidate air transport. To apply the advances in military aircraft to new civil types would be a logical step. At the same time it was also clear that a breathing space would be needed before all the improved and, indeed, new techniques, such as the gas-turbine engine, could be deployed in the designing of new civil aircraft. Britain had to concentrate almost exclusively on military types throughout the whole of the war, whereas the United States had been able to develop transport aircraft which could be adapted to civil needs immediately hostilities ceased.

Viking prototype G-AGOK running-up before its first flight from Wisley airfield on 22 June, 1945; on the right is a Warwick GR V.

One need was for Britain to produce, without delay, an interim type of transport aeroplane for short-haul work, particularly for the European routes. In 1944 Vickers directed attention to three civil designs, known initially as the Windsor Empire, the Warwick Continental and the Wellington Continental. The most promising of these, as an interim type, was a civil Wellington to meet the immediate short-haul requirement to supplement the ubiquitous DC-3 but offering a better payload. Designated VC1 (Vickers Commercial One) and later named the Viking (thus repeating a type name previously used for Vickers' first complete post-first world war design), this aeroplane borrowed the Wellington configuration, with basic Warwick V tail surfaces but with a new stressed-skin fuselage, embodying

Production line at Weybridge of Vikings in immediate post-war period.

a capacious passenger cabin and underfloor freight holds. Thus the new aeroplane combined the virtues of the Wellington wing and the Bristol Hercules sleeve-valve engine, both well-proven features. The pattern was similar to that after the first world war, when the Vimy Commercial combined the wings of the Vimy bomber design and the Rolls-Royce Eagle engine of established reliability.

This was the start of a new era in the story of Vickers aircraft, for, although notable attempts had been made in civil aviation, as recounted in previous pages, not until after the second world war, when the demand for military aircraft shrank rapidly, did Vickers attempt to concentrate a large proportion of effort on civil types. The assault was led not only in design but, later, also on the business side, by George Edwards, who had become chief designer when Pierson was appointed the company's chief engineer in 1945. George Edwards (later Sir George) had held the responsible post of experimental manager during the vital and burdensome war years, and was therefore closely associated with the Wellington Transport Aircraft as the VC1 was originally called by the Ministry of Aircraft Production.

Loading export radio sets on BEA Viking G-AIVP *Vimy*, bearing the red Key emblem, at Northolt.

The Brabazon Committee, originally appointed at the end of 1942 to make recommendations for the post-war development of civil transport aircraft, made no provision for stop-gap types. As it was apparent that most of the proposed Brabazon types could not be in service much before the 1950s, the Government decided to sponsor a number of interim types, one of which was the VC1 as a Wellington civil conversion. A specification,

A typical scene at Northolt airport showing passengers embarking on a Viking.

Viking Type 610 named originally by BEA as *Virginia*, later renamed
Sir Bertram Ramsay.

17/44, was issued in October 1944, with the provisional serial numbers
TT194, TT197 and TT181 allocated to three prototypes, for which the civil
registrations G-AGOK, G-AGOL and G-AGOM were substituted later.

On 20 December, 1944, Pierson gave technical information on the VC1
to the Brabazon Committee, which had expressed interest in the design,
although it did not come strictly within their terms of reference. He stated
that the Bristol Hercules 10M engine had been chosen, for, compared with
the equivalent civil Merlin, it showed a better single-engine performance
for the purpose because of superior take-off power. In addition, the
Hercules 100, which was the basic production version of the 10M, had
flown 100 hours experimentally in a Wellington bomber, LN718, engine
test-bed to establish performance characteristics, particularly in cruising
conditions.

The way was now clear for material progress with the VC1 Viking, as the
Type 491 had by then been named, and the lead time (period from inception
to production) was cut by using many Wellington and some Warwick
components. The various details of the Wellington, which from operational experience had proved to be in need of attention, were analysed and
improved, notably in the wing structure.

From the outset, Vickers' design team had a fully stressed-skin aeroplane in mind, but at first they proceeded only with a stressed-skin fuselage and a fabric-covered geodetic wing. This combination had advantages
over a converted Wellington geodetic structure adapted to passenger transport. Valuable experience had been acquired by the operation of
Wellington and Warwick transport variants, as recounted earlier.

As a result of the contraction of design and production time by the
adoption of an existing airframe as a basis, the Vickers VC1 prototype,
G-AGOK, was first flown by Summers from Wisley airfield on 22 June,
1945, little more than a year after first thoughts on the Wellington Continental had crystallised, the VC1 Viking thus becoming Britain's first
post-war airliner to fly. The three prototypes ordered by the Ministry
were allocated to development flying, and a thorough assessment of their

performance characteristics was made during the 160 hours accumulated by the end of the year.

Much of the interest in the Viking lay in the evolution by Vickers' designers for the first time of a completely stressed-skin civil aeroplane. The only previous Vickers type with this construction was the F7/41 Type 432 fighter, but the operational requirements were so different from those of the Viking that there could be little structural design in common. There was good reason to proceed with the stress-skinning, because the potential operator, the newly formed British European Airways, was not keen to accept fabric covering, since it would have increased the problems and complexity of their maintenance engineering. As it happened, the change from fabric-covered Vikings to the all stressed-skin versions took place after 19 of the former had been produced.

The inner plane of the geodetic wing was retained. Between the wing roots and the engine mountings and cowlings, the exposed surface of the inner plane was skin-plated instead of fabric-covered. The outer planes were based on a continuation of the single main spar system of the Wellington, with auxiliary spars for attachment of the leading edge and, at the rear, the split flaps, ailerons and falsework.

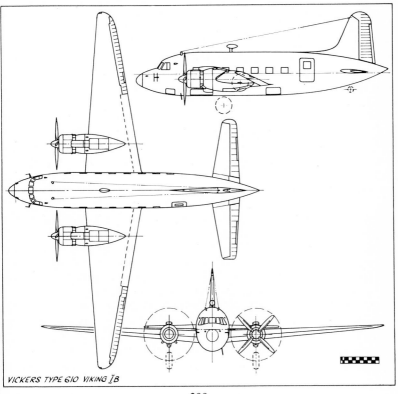

VICKERS TYPE 610 VIKING 1B

The tubular booms, with Warren web bracing, of the centre section and inner plane main spar, which floated in the tunnel through the bottom of the fuselage, were pinned to the new machined and fabricated outer main spar of I-section through massive links located at the outboard sides of the engine mountings. The stressed-skin of the outer planes was riveted to chordwise stringers, with the load-carrying stiff ribs interspaced at wide intervals across the span. The tail unit of the all-metal Viking was constructed on a similar stressed-skin pattern.

As the Viking was intended for medium-altitude operation only, that is, not much above 15,000 ft, its cabin was unpressurised, and consequently was not stressed for pulsating fatigue. A feature of note in the fuselage structure, which was retained in later Vickers aircraft, was the attachment of the longitudinal skin-carrying stringers to the lateral hoop-frames (of a cross-section derived from geodetic members) by small angle brackets known as shear cleats. This method avoided notching the frames, and both stringers and frames were therefore continuous. Keel strength was obtained from the substantial floor of the cargo-hold by means of heavy longitudinal channels. An improved Wellington/Warwick tailwheel undercarriage was fitted, principally to avoid the time lag had a nosewheel type been adopted, which would have involved the redesign and the re-stressing of the front fuselage.

The furnishing and appointments of the Viking passenger cabin needed fresh thinking because the exigencies of war had enforced a concentration on Service requirements, and the Wellington and Warwick civil variants produced during the war had of necessity been equipped with utility passenger facilities. The new approach in the designing of the passenger accommodation in the Viking revealed innovations later to become standard practice. The first requirement was adequate sound-proofing of the cabin walls and ceiling, and this was accomplished by a thick blanketing of cellulose material, the walls being finished by a covering of moquette and pleated leather. The cabin, although unpressurised, was controlled for temperature and ventilation, and there were individual cold-air vents. The floor was fully carpeted, now commonplace in airliners. The passenger seats had all the modern amenities, such as steward call-buttons, neatly inset in the left-hand arm-rest, and an ashtray, inset in the right arm-rest. These Vickers-designed seats were upholstered in soft moquette and embodied adjustable headrests which incorporated reading lamps. Adjustable or fixed seats were optional, as were passenger tables. The large square windows, conveniently positioned in relation to the seating, had concertina-type blinds. The ramp across the cabin interior necessitated by the spar tunnel, a legacy from the Wellington, was used as the division between the fore and aft cabins, and at the partition was a large doorway. The electrically-equipped galley, the toilet and a vestibule for hats and coats were at the rear near the entrance door.

Much thought was given to the design of a functional flight deck, with a central console carrying throttles, trim wheels, fuel-cock controls and an

First Viking Type 604 for Indian National Airways, named *Jumna*.

Type 632 Viking for Air-India.

South⁻African Airways Viking Type 635 named *Cathkin Peak*.

First Viking for charter operator, Airwork Type 627.

instrument-panel display in the modern manner. Wide-angle-vision front and side windscreen panels were included and set a new standard for flight crews, which was continued in later Vickers aircraft up to the VC10.

The Viking was the first post-war design to comply with the then new international (ICAO) regulations for take-off with asymmetric power, and it was notable for the ease with which it could be handled on one engine. Some modifications had to be made to the elevator aerodynamic horn balances to offset asymmetric slipstream effects caused by the large propellers absorbing relatively high power. This was a phenomenon not previously encountered in this form in Vickers aircraft, although a similar problem had been experienced with the Warwick.

Meanwhile, European air routes were being re-established by the European Division of BOAC, largely with DC-3s, and operations clearly revealed a need for new equipment. A production order for 50 Vikings was placed by the Ministry of Aircraft Production on 5 April, 1946, and the certificate of airworthiness was granted on 24 April. On 1 September the new British European Airways Corporation, which had been formed under the Civil Aviation Act, 1946, a month before, operated its first Viking service from Northolt, then serving as London's Continental airport, to Kastrup, Copenhagen, with G-AHOP *Valerie*, commanded by Capt L. G. James, and services to Stavanger, Oslo and Amsterdam started the following day.

The successful introduction of the Viking into scheduled service followed handling trials of the third prototype, G-AGOM, and the first production aeroplane, G-AGON, by BOAC's development flight at Hurn, and a complete investigation into other aspects of its operational suitability was made. G-AGON was later used by the airlines' aircrew training school, then at Aldermaston.

One advantage of providing BEA with a new type of aeroplane of predictable behaviour, based on a successful predecessor, was that the airline itself was developing, virtually from scratch, its own operating methods and route network. The Viking therefore developed along with BEA, and the various phases and aspects of its life must be viewed in that light.

In December 1946 an icing problem of some magnitude appeared. This consisted of accretions on the leading edge of the tailplane of the all-metal Mk 1, causing overbalanced elevators. Post-war civil aircraft were flying higher in winter conditions than pre-war types, and scheduled services were expected to operate to predetermined timetables precluding cancellations except in extreme circumstances. BEA grounded their Viking fleet of 12 aircraft on eight European routes while an intensive programme of icing research was undertaken jointly by BEA and Vickers' flight test and technical teams.

Satisfactory solutions to both elevator overbalance and ice build-up were found, the former by altering the asymmetrical horn balance areas of

Type 634 Aer Lingus Viking EI-ADI.

both elevators, and the latter by increasing the flow rate of the de-icing fluid. This incident serves to emphasise the growing co-operation between manufacturer and operator which has been a notable feature of post-war civil aviation.

Viking services were resumed by BEA in April 1947, when the later Mk 1Bs began to replace DC-3s on the main routes of the airline. The Mk 1B was 28 in longer in the front fuselage, which allowed the passenger capacity to be increased from 21 to 24 seats and later further increased to 27. This version of the Viking was usually known as the long-nose type, and was of all-metal stressed-skin construction like the Mk 1. The earlier Viking with geodetic wings and tail, fabric covered, was then designated Mk 1A. Of the 19 Mk 1As produced, only 11 went into regular service with BEA, who gave them V class names. G-AGON, the first production Viking to fly, went to the RAF for trials as a military transport under the serial number VW214, with G-AGRM and G-AGRN as VW215 and VW216 respectively, together with the prototypes. Five of the original Mk 1A Vikings (Type 498) were re-equipped internally for service in Trinidad with British West Indian Airways after being converted to Mk 1 stressed-skin standard under the type number 657. Most of the geodetic Mk 1A Vikings were converted to Mk 1 stressed-skin standard.

A demonstration Viking 1B, G-AJJN, Type 636, flew to New Zealand in April 1947, returning in June, a total distance of 40,000 miles. It was then used to initiate a communications flight at Wisley, subsequently being sold to BEA.

The history of the Viking variants from then on became complicated; the summary of production and original customers to be found in the Appendices is the clearest way of recording it. The tailoring of basic types of civil aeroplanes to airlines' requirements led to the practice of allocating a new type number to each, a method which was also followed with new designs which succeeded the Viking. This practice of embodying individual operators' selective modifications and equipment, such as flight instrumentation, cabin furnishing, radio and so on, reached its peak in Vickers aircraft with the Viscount. But it was the Viking which enabled Vickers to establish vital contacts with world airlines and accumulate valuable civil air transport experience.

When the Vikings resumed regular service with BEA after the icing troubles the airline was beginning to expand its route network, as radio and navigational aids, as well as airports throughout Europe, were by then assuming a more modern pattern. With the Viking, BEA began a series of proving flights in which airport facilities, diversionary airfields and all operating procedures were explored before the new scheduled services were implemented.

On 13 April, 1950, on a flight over the English Channel, a saboteur's bomb exploded in the rear toilet of BEA Viking *Vigilant*, severely damag-the rear fuselage and tail unit. The commander, Capt I. R. Harvey, successfully brought the aeroplane with its 28 passengers back to Northolt, making a safe landing after an overshoot. This remarkable achievement testified both to the airmanship of the pilot and to the sturdy airframe of the Viking, and Capt Harvey was later awarded the George Medal. One result of this incident was the complete reconstruction of that particular airframe as the first of BEA's new Admiral class, with the seating capacity raised to 36 and the all-up weight increased to 36,712 lb, the new class going into service on 1 October, 1952. When BEA's Vikings were eventually replaced by Viscounts in 1954 the type had flown nearly half a million hours and carried three million passengers.

Overseas airlines which ordered and operated Vikings were British West Indian Airways, Aer Lingus, Indian National Airways, DDL (Danish Air Lines), Iraqi Airways, Central African Airways, South African Airways and Sudair International Airways, while other regular operators included Airwork, Eagle Aviation, Hunting Air Travel and the Argentine Government; some were commissioned as executive-class types, notably in the VIP range exemplified by the Royal Vikings. Thus Vikings materially assisted in establishing and consolidating many airline networks in the formative post-war period in civil aviation. Subsequently, many Vikings found their way into various independent airlines and changed hands on numerous occasions.

404

Viking Type 649 for Pakistan Air Force, serialled J750.

The official interest in the inception of the Viking was maintained by the Air Ministry and the Ministry of Supply when eight Mk 2s were ordered for RAF Transport Command in 1946. The three prototypes, with three production Mk 1As, had been thoroughly evaluated by the Royal Air Force.

In addition to these Service requirements, four Mk 1 Vikings were ordered for the King's Flight, initially for use on the Royal tour of South Africa, which began in March 1947. The Vikings were specially prepared for their distinguished task, with spacious interiors in the two Royal aircraft, VL246 and VL247; VL245 was a 21-seat staff aeroplane, and VL248 was equipped as a flying maintenance unit with full workshop facilities. Engineering modifications included flexible-bag fuel tanks and the replacement of saddle fuel tanks in the Hercules 134 engine nacelles by dinghies.

Their Majesties King George VI and Queen Elizabeth flew separately in the two VIP Vikings, which had similar internal appointments. There were two main lounge compartments, each fitted with four specially designed adjustable chairs, stressed to 25g, two facing forward and two aft. The colour scheme was light blue seating and pleated side walls, with light beige for upper walls and ceiling. The doors were covered in dark beige leather, while the carpet was dark blue. An electric refrigerator and electric

Viking C.2, VL 230, furnished to VIP standards and re-engined with Hercules 634.

405

Royal Flight of Vikings VL245, 246 and 247 about to embark Royal party at Bloemfontein airport for a flight to the Orange Free State game reserve on 13 March, 1947.

heaters were fitted in the pantry. Other refinements included an intercom switchboard in the office of the Flight Captain (Air Commodore E. H. Fielden) for communication between the aircraft. Each Royal aircraft carried a crew of six; two pilots, navigator, wireless operator and two stewards. Vickers were not unfamiliar with these VIP requirements, for they had previously fitted out the Viastra used by the then Prince of Wales on official journeys before the war, as already mentioned. The experience gained there was useful when the call came for executive-class variants in other Vikings and Viscounts. These special Vikings remained in the Royal Flight for some years, and one was used by H.M. Queen Elizabeth, later the Queen Mother, during her State visit to Nigeria in 1951.

A highlight in the career of the Viking was the conversion of the Ministry-owned VX856 to take Rolls-Royce Nene turbojets in place of the civil standard Hercules 634 piston engines. This Type 618 was given the civil registration G-AJPH and was the world's first pure-jet transport aeroplane. Variations from standard included heavier skin-plating on the main and tail surfaces, with metal-covered elevators, and different engine mountings in underslung nacelles. The undercarriage was redesigned with twinwheel units to absorb higher landing weights and speeds.

The objects of this conversion were part of the policy of flight testing new types of power plants and to conduct research into high-altitude flight by civil aircraft. The Nene-Viking was flown for the first time by Summers from Wisley on 6 April, 1948. On 25 July he flew it from London Airport to Villacoublay, Paris, in 34 min 7 sec, at a mean speed of 384 mph, an elapsed time comparing favourably with that of today's jets. Much of the

Nene-Viking Type 618 registered G-AJPH; this was a converted
Ministry of Supply aeroplane.

test flying of the Nene-Viking was done by Flt Lt G. R. Bryce, who had
joined Vickers from the RAF, and later succeeded Mutt Summers as
Vickers' chief test pilot.

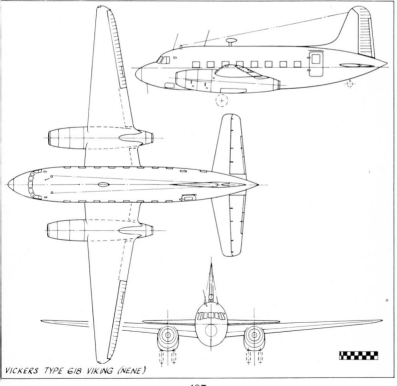

VICKERS TYPE 618 VIKING (NENE)

Subsequently this aeroplane was converted back to freighter Mk 1B standard with a large loading door, for Eagle Aviation. Eagle's fleet of Viking freighters were unofficially labelled Mk 3s, but in Vickers' records this designation was reserved for the new military transport version of the Viking, which design was later named the Valetta.

Military Viking Type 607 completed as Valetta prototype VL249; type tested at Airborne Forces Experimental Establishment, Beaulieu.

THE VALETTA. As a result of the successful trials of the Viking and its operation by the Royal Air Force in Transport Command, a new version was evolved, specially adapted to military requirements as contained in specification C.9/46. The time had come to replace the transport Dakotas which had soldiered on since the end of the war as troopers, freighters, glider-tugs and so on. One requirement was for an aeroplane capable of rapid conversion to fulfil a number of different rôles; troop carrier, military freighter, ambulance, glider-tug, paratroop transport and for supply dropping. These duties led to the Valetta C. Mk 1 acquiring the description of 'five aeroplanes in one'. Thus, the concept of all-round air transport utility, born many years before in the Middle East and India with Vernons, Victorias and Valentias, at last received official recognition. Later on, the multi-rôle military aeroplane was greatly developed in the VC10s for RAF Transport Command (renamed Air Support Command in 1967).

New features embodied in the Valetta, as compared with the Viking 1B and 2, were a stronger cabin floor permitting a contact wheel-loading of 1,500 lb anywhere on the structure and the cutting of a large aperture in the side of the fuselage between the wings and the tail for loading and off-loading bulky military equipment. The double door in this structurally reinforced aperture had a smaller door inserted in it for personnel access and for use as a paratroop exit. Lashing points were provided in the fuselage floor and on the side walls for anchoring cargo. Various types of seats, according to rôle, oxygen cylinders, vehicle ramps, a loading winch, roller runways on the floor and over the spar box in the cabin, glider-towing attachments, stretchers and sound-proof side walls (in the ambulance version), comprised the quickly removable aircraft equipment.

A Valetta—the work-horse of airborne combined operations.

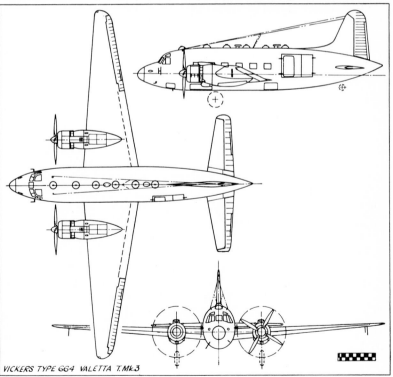

VICKERS TYPE 664 VALETTA T.Mk.3

Paratroops embarking in a Valetta C.1. for an exercise drop.

As a troop transport, the Valetta could carry 34 soldiers with full equipment; as an ambulance, it had provision for 20 stretcher cases with two medical orderlies; as a paratrooper, 20 troops with nine 350-lb containers of fighting equipment and supplies carried externally on twin racks under the centre fuselage could be accommodated; and for glider-towing, a heavy pyramid structure was attached within the rear fuselage, for connection of the hook and release gear. In the prototype and the VIP C.Mk 2, the extreme tail of the fuselage carried a neatly faired cone, but normally the Valetta had a blunt rear end.

Second production Valetta in service as paratrooper.

With these military features, the Valetta's all-up weight was 36,500 lb. Hercules 230 engines were installed to cater for this increase of some 2,000 lb over the all-up weight of the Viking 1B, each providing 2,000 hp for take-off. Other design changes included flexible-bag fuel tanks, as used on the Royal Vikings, and stronger oleo undercarriage legs with longer stroke to cope with the rougher conditions of military operational landings. The prototype Valetta, VL249, first flew on 30 June, 1947, at Brooklands in the hands of Summers.

On active service, the Valetta took part in a number of operations, notably in the Suez Canal zone, in Malaya and in Kuwait. Meanwhile, and apart from maid-of-all-work duties with Transport Command and the Airborne Forces, other versions were produced of the Valetta which still further extended its utility and several remained in service at the time of writing.

Prototype Valetta VL249 during test of vehicle-loading capability at AFEE, Beaulieu.

One C.Mk 2, WJ504, was built with up to 15 seats for high-ranking personnel, and carried 116 lb extra fuel to increase range by reinstating the Viking-type nacelle saddle tanks. A flying navigational classroom variant, to specification T.1/49, was produced, with 10 student training positions built into the cabin; the external distinguishing feature of these T.Mk 3s was the row of plastic astrodomes along the top of the fuselage; they were used by the Air Navigation Schools and by the RAF College, Cranwell.

Valetta T.Mk 3 at the Air Navigation School, Hullavington; the row of transparent astrodomes can just be seen on top of fuselage.

Eighteen T.Mk 3s were converted to the T.Mk 4 variant for radar training and were distinguished by their longer nose, which accommodated the radar scanner and comprehensive equipment.

Experimental work undertaken by Vickers with the Valetta included undercarriage research, with four-wheel and eight-wheel bogies, to explore their characteristics for soft landings. VL275, the ninth Type 645 production aircraft, was used in taxying, take-off and landing tests at Wisley, at Hurn where the concrete runway was used, and at Christchurch airfields. Little ground-handling difference was observed between the bogie and standard type undercarriages.

THE VARSITY. Although the Wellington T.Mk 10 and the Valettas T.Mk 3 and T.Mk 4 were rendering valuable service in aircrew training in the immediate post-war period, it became necessary to re-equip Flying Training Command with a more modern type which could completely satisfy all multi-engined needs. Specification T.13/48 was written to cover this requirement, and Vickers submitted a specialised design as a development of the Viking and Valetta family.

This Valetta-type training aeroplane, which in the event was the last of Vickers aeroplanes to use the piston engine (Bristol Hercules 264) as prime mover, was appropriately named the Varsity T.1 in November 1949. It was somewhat larger than the Valetta, with a 6-ft wider span and an all-up weight increased by 1,000 lb. Appreciable improvement was made in performance, cruising speed, climb, ceiling and range, compared with the performance of the Valetta. In this development the Varsity design benefitted considerably from the emerging concept of the VC2 Viscount at that time.

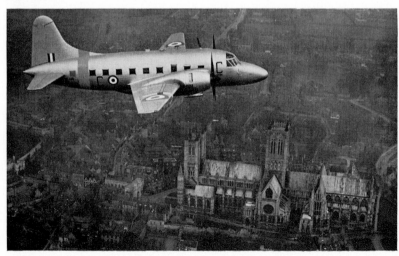

Varsity Type 668, serial WF380, flying over Lincoln Cathedral, from the nearby 201 Advanced Flying School, Swinderby. (*Flight photo.*)

Varsity WJ945 with Signals Command of the RAF; note characteristic protuberance of under-belly as on standard Varsities.

Most notable feature of the Varsity was the use of a Viscount-type nose-wheel undercarriage of the modern pattern, as contrasted with the nose-wheels fitted to the 1919 VIM trainer and Vimy Commercial, which merely acted as fenders in nose-heavy landings. Another distinguishing feature was the fixed ventral pannier accommodating the bomb-aimer's prone position forward and his 24 practice bombs of 25 lb each aft, this external

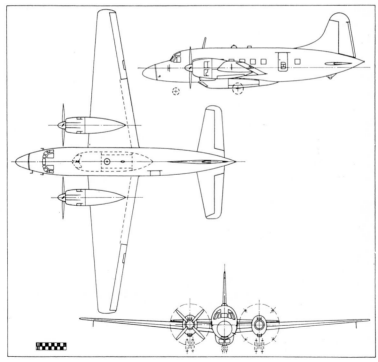

Vickers Type 668 Varsity T.1.

appendage leading to a somewhat undignified name for the Varsity. One practical problem had to be solved, and that was the clouding of the bomb-sighting window by mud or dust thrown up by the twin nosewheels; neat mudguards overcame this trouble.

Engineering development was evident in the Varsity design. Clam-shell low-drag engine cowlings were fitted to promote quick accessibility to the engine controls, services and accessories. Other details for servicing and maintenance set a new note of efficiency which continued on into the propeller-turbine and turbojet aircraft which followed.

Ministry-owned Varsity WF387 converted as G-ARFP for Smiths Aviation autoland research.

Summers flew the Varsity prototype VX828 on 17 July, 1949, from Wisley, with Bryce as co-pilot. A second prototype, VX835, followed on 29 January, 1950, and the first deliveries were made to replace Wellingtons in No. 201 Advanced Flying School at Swinderby at the end of 1951. Varsities were used by Flying Training Command for pilots converting to multi-engined aircraft before proceeding to Hastings, Washingtons, Shackletons and Britannias, and for advanced instruction to navigators and bomb-aimers, continuing in service until the late 1960s and reducing the wastage rate of this command by 50 per cent. By virtue of its ultimate range of 2,600 miles, the Varsity was ideal for long-distance navigational training and also as a stand-in bomber during operational exercises of the RAF. Latterly, the Varsity was put into service by RAF Signals Command.

Varsities WF 412, 417 and WL665 have been used in the lengthy research conducted by the Royal Aircraft Establishment into automatic landing systems for aircraft. This investigation was started in 1949 by the Blind Landing Experimental Unit, first at Martlesham and then at Bedford, although as early as 1923 a Vickers Vimy bomber was used by the RAE for the experimental trials of an automatic landing device based on a mechanical trip system.

For their particular contribution to the development of automatic landing, Smiths Aviation Division used Varsity G-ARFP, which was converted by the College of Aeronautics at Cranfield for this purpose. The ventral blister was removed, reinforced steel spars were fitted to ensure adequate fatigue life, a dual braking system was introduced and the interior of the cabin was rebuilt to accommodate the specialised equipment racks. The Decca Co used Varsity G-APAZ for development work with their navigational system, but this aeroplane was written off in a crash unconnected with the work in hand.

One Varsity, WF416, was converted by Eagle as a personal transport for King Hussein of Jordan, and the ventral bomb-aimer's pannier was removed, adding a few knots to the cruising speed. The Air Ministry sold one to the Royal Swedish Air Force under designation Tp 82; one was used as a flying test-bed for the Napier Eland propeller-turbine later installed in Convair-Liner conversions. Seventeen Varsities, including the two prototypes, were Weybridge-built, and the other 146 were made at Vickers' factory at Hurn, Bournemouth, which was established in 1951 to relieve Weybridge of production load because of the parallel large-scale output there of Viscounts and Valiants.

A civil version of the Varsity was projected under the class designation of VC3. It was intended as a conventional airliner for short-to-medium

Varsity WF416 converted for the Royal Jordanian Air Force as VK-501; note deletion of under-belly bombs and bomb aimer's excrescence.

haul operations as a replacement for older aircraft in the DC-3 class and as an improved Viking. Meanwhile, the VC2 Viscount was on the threshold of unparalleled success, and the VC3 project was dropped.

The Viking family was notable because it covered so many duties and rôles, civil and military. Some 20 years after its inception, the Viking was still in service on charter work, and its derivatives, Valetta and Varsity, following the Wellington T.Mk X and other Wellington trainers, provided the basis upon which was built the post-war Flying Training Command of the RAF. BEA Vikings flew $68\frac{1}{2}$ million miles before being superseded by later aircraft, notably Viscounts. The production figures of 163 Vikings, 263 Valettas and 163 Varsities represented a great deal of experience and effort.

	Type 491 Mk IA–G-AGOK	Type 610 Mk IB
Accommodation:	3 crew, steward, 21 passengers	3 crew, steward, 24/27 passengers
Engines:	Two 1,675 hp Bristol Hercules 130	Two 1,690 hp Bristol Hercules 634
Span:	89 ft 3 in	89 ft 3 in
Length:	62 ft 10 in	65 ft 2 in
Height:	19 ft 7 in (tail down)	19 ft 7 in (tail down)
Wing Area:	882 sq ft	882 sq ft
Empty Weight:	22,116 lb	23,000 lb
Gross Weight:	33,500 lb	34,000 lb
Max Speed:	210 mph at 10,000 ft	263 mph at 10,000 ft
Initial Climb:	1,000 ft/min	1,500 ft/min
Service Ceiling:	22,500 ft	25,000 ft
Range:	1,500 miles at 190 mph	1,700 miles at 210 mph

Valetta C.1—Type 637—Two 2,000 hp Bristol Hercules 230. Accommodation various (see text). Span 89 ft 3 in; length 62 ft 11 in; height 19 ft 7 in (tail down); wing area 882 sq ft. Empty weight 24,980 lb; gross weight 36,500 lb. Max speed 258 mph at 10,000 ft; initial climb 1,275 ft/min; service ceiling 21,500 ft; range 1,460 miles at 211 mph at 10,000 ft.

Varsity T.1—Type 668—Two 1,950 hp Bristol Hercules 264. Accommodation various (see text). Span 95 ft 7 in; length 67 ft 6 in; height 23 ft 11 in; wing area 974 sq ft. Empty weight 27,040 lb; gross weight 37,500 lb. Max speed 288 mph at 10,000 ft; initial climb 1,400 ft/min; service ceiling 28,700 ft; range 2,648 miles at 239 mph.

The Viscount

The Vickers Viscount will always be regarded as one of the milestones in civil air transport. It was the first gas-turbine powered aeroplane to operate a revenue passenger service. It soon established the potential and reliability of the then revolutionary power plant at a time when pure-jet transports were experiencing setbacks in their operational development. The Viscount was the first British airliner to be sold in quantity in North America and it went into service with airlines all over the world in many varying climates and differing operational patterns.

When Pierson met the Brabazon Committee on 20 December, 1944, he not only presented details of the VC1 project but also discussed with them a follow-up replacement for it when that contingency arose. As was his habit, he went straight back to Weybridge to organise a design study to meet this possible future requirement. Although not alone in this respect, he was the sort of designer who had only to get a whisper of a new specification in the corridors of official places to be ready in a few days to submit an outline proposal to meet it, whether invited or not. His reputation was such that his methods were never questioned.

The Weybridge design team came to the conclusion that a propeller-turbine aeroplane offered greater promise then as a Viking replacement

Viscount prototype 630 during first flight on 16 July, 1948, in plain metal externals.

than a pure-jet type, and the Brabazon Committee eventually reached a similar view, after considering two short-haul transports of 30,000 lb gross weight, one with two Merlins and the other with two Rolls-Royce RB41 turbojets. The germ of the idea grew into the positive outline of a 24-seat short-to-medium-haul transport suitable for European routes and powered by propeller-turbines. Lord Brabazon, as chairman of the Committee, wrote to Lord Swinton, Minister of Civil Aviation, early in 1945, recommending the starting of the development of such an aeroplane, the future need for which had become evident.

Further deliberations between the Committee and the Ministry of Civil Aviation led to the framing of a requirement known as Brabazon IIB for this new type; Brabazon IIA being allocated for a similar aeroplane with piston engines, which in due course materialised as the Airspeed Ambassador. On 14 March, 1945, a joint meeting between representatives of the Ministries of Aircraft Production and Civil Aviation and certain scheduled operators (mainly from BOAC and Railway Air Services) was held, and Sir Ralph Sorley, Controller of Research and Development at MAP, said there that the contract for the Brabazon IIB would probably be given to Vickers.

Shortly after this meeting, Pierson submitted to MAP a brochure containing proposals for variations on the same theme, two for a 24-seat

Viscount prototype 630 flying in Vickers livery under registration G-AHRF.

417

aeroplane, pressurised or unpressurised, and the third for a larger 27-seat unpressurised aeroplane, all of 1,000 miles range in still air. The first defined an aircraft with four propeller-turbines, of 34,000-lb gross weight and a cruising speed of 296 mph at 20,000 ft. These proposals were considered by the Ministries, and formal acceptance of the Brabazon Committee's recommendations was conveyed to Sir Archibald Rowlands, Permanent Secretary of MAP, by W. P. Hildred (later Sir William Hildred), who was then Director General of the Ministry of Civil Aviation. On 19 April, 1945, Sir Ralph Sorley instructed his Director of Technical Development at MAP, N. E. Rowe, to arrange for Vickers to proceed with the development of a Brabazon IIB aeroplane. Four prototypes were to be

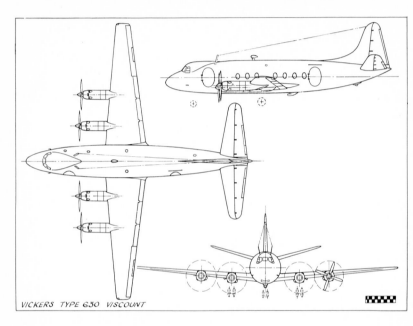

VICKERS TYPE 630 VISCOUNT

planned, closely spaced in time. A discussion on the relative merits of pressurisation or otherwise was settled by a study sent by Pierson to Rowe, stating in detail the case in favour of a pressurised aeroplane.

All these negotiations between the different interested parties might appear complicated, but the system did work, for it led to Vickers submitting firm proposals for the VC2 to comply with detailed users' requirements as issued by the Ministry of Civil Aviation. The end justified the means and contrasted sharply with later procurement decisions, which failed because of vacillations of official policy.

As presented by Pierson, the VC2 was envisaged as a civil transport carrying 7,500 lb payload over a 1,040 mile range at a cruising speed of 297 mph at 20,000 ft. It was to have a double-bubble fuselage with cabin

Type 663 Viscount with Rolls-Royce Tay turbojet engines as VX217 used as flying test-bed for the engines and later by Boulton Paul for powered flying control trials.

accommodation for 24 passengers. Of significance was the choice, from various power units, of four Rolls-Royce Dart propeller-turbines, each of 1,130 ehp. This project, as with the three earlier proposals, was prepared under Vickers' type number 453. In the event of the Rolls-Royce Darts not developing satisfactorily, alternative power was to be Armstrong Siddeley Mamba or Napier Naiad propeller-turbines, but by October 1945 Vickers were firmly convinced that the Darts would finally be chosen.

In the previous month, September, an important event occurred at Weybridge which, without doubt, influenced the ultimate destiny of the VC2 design. Pierson was appointed chief engineer with group executive technical authority and was succeeded as chief designer by George Edwards. Regrettably, Pierson died early in 1948. Edwards thus assumed all technical design responsibility and became completely identified with the VC2 project. His drive and practical approach proved to be the deciding factor in the birth of the Viscount, as the VC2 was eventually

Prototype Viscount 700 as G-AMAV, in tropical surroundings during England–New Zealand Air Race of 1953.

Viscount Type 701, G-AMOG, *Robert Falcon Scott*, of BEA Discovery class.

named. He decided on the Dart engine 'on the grounds of the rugged reliability of the centrifugal compressor and the fact that at that time practically the whole turbine experience had been with this type of engine', to quote his own words.

After a detailed survey of both the double-bubble and circular-section fuselages, Vickers' design team favoured the latter. A development contract for an aeroplane with a circular-section fuselage was placed with

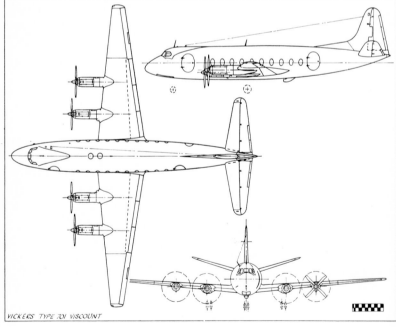

VICKERS TYPE 701 VISCOUNT

Vickers on 9 March, 1946, by the Ministry of Supply, which had absorbed the functions of the former MAP. As an insurance against the failure of the VC2, the MoS also ordered two Armstrong Whitworth AW.55 Apollo aircraft to the Brabazon IIB requirement, powered with four Mambas; these were eventually completed and flown, but the type did not go into production.

On 17 April, 1946, the MoS issued specification 8/46 to Vickers for a Brabazon IIB aeroplane. Its main provisions were for four turbine engines, 24 seats with a possible conversion to 32, cabin air differential pressure of

A BEA Viscount taking off on a scheduled flight from Gibraltar; compare illustration on page 341.

$6\frac{1}{2}$ lb/sq in, cabin noise level of 60 decibels and freight capacity of 275 cu ft. Refinements called for included cabin humidity control, cold air supply to passengers and definitive passenger-floor loadings. The required payload was 7,500 lb, to be carried for a range of 700 miles, with a cruising speed of 240 kt at 20,000 ft. Take-off (with one engine cut) and landing runs were both 1,200 yds. Stalling speed was 70 kt with flaps and undercarriage down.

These requirements are interesting, for they disclose the state of the art at the beginning of the post-war expansion of civil air transport when the VC2 was pioneering a new era of turbine propulsion. Also notable in the specification was the call for a pressure cabin in a British aeroplane, a feature with which Vickers had had experience in the high-altitude Wellingtons V and VI. Operating costs, based on the specification, were estimated at nearly 6d. per capacity ton-mile, assuming a 3,000-hour annual utilisation. About this time the VC2 project was named Viceroy.

Trans-Australia Airlines Type 756 Viscount, VH-TVH, *George Bass*, flying over the outback somewhere in Australia.

When the development contract was issued by MoS the original conception of four prototypes was reduced to two, while Vickers were themselves to finance a third. These were to specification 8/46 and were allocated the type number 609. Work started on them in December 1946. The Ministry's proposed power unit at that time was the Armstrong Siddeley Mamba, as it was showing greater development progress than the Dart. Compared with the original proposals, the gross weight had gone up to 38,170 lb and later to 39,500 lb, the wing span to 89 ft, the wing area to 885 sq ft and the fuselage length to 74 ft 6 in (an increase of 9 ft) to accommodate 32 passengers. One of the facts that emerges from any review of the technical assumptions made during the advent of post-war civil aviation was the continual underestimating of aircraft capacity. Further stretching of the VC2 concept was indeed found essential before it could be accepted for service.

These increases were made to meet the requirements of the then newly formed British European Airways, who were primarily interested in the

Hurn production line of 700 series Viscounts with Type 757 for Trans-Canada Air Lines in foreground.

TCA Viscount Type 724, CF-TGI, at Bluie West 1, Greenland staging post in first delivery flight to North America.

VC2 as a follow-up to the VC1 Viking. The airline and its antecedent, the European Division of BOAC, had closely studied the Viceroy project, and R. C. Morgan, its chief project and development engineer, had made himself fully conversant with the design since its inception. His department subsequently conducted much development work to fit the VC2 into the route pattern, passenger requirements and engineering procedures of BEA. The thoroughness with which this ground was prepared bore fruit later in the consolidation of the airline, following its establishment with the Vickers VC1 Viking, as detailed in the previous chapter.

Although BEA apparently had different ideas at that time, the Ministry notified Vickers on 27 August, 1947, that the Dart installation should be

Inauguration of TCA's triangular service Eastern and Western Canada and New York in the spring of 1955 by Viscounts is illustrated by their Fleet No. 604, CF-TGL, flying over New York.

423

proceeded with, as the engine had been improved. Thus emerged the VC2 Type 630 with the Rolls-Royce Dart RDa1 propeller-turbine as its power unit. The aeroplane had been renamed Viscount, because the Imperial office of Viceroy had disappeared, India having by then become an independent state within the Commonwealth.

Despite the complications of the negotiations between the interested parties, the Viscount project seemed to stand a reasonable chance of getting off the ground. But in the autumn of 1947 BEA expressed doubts about the operating economics of the aeroplane. Various studies were made with alternative power plants, the most important conclusion being that, to use propeller-turbines, the design would have to be stretched. In addition, the Airspeed Ambassador with two Bristol Centaurus piston engines had flown in prototype form, and BEA and the Ministries concerned were under pressure to place an order for it. This decision was made more difficult because a study for the VC2 as a 40-seat type with two Bristol Centaurus piston engines showed similar operating characteristics. Eventually BEA were prevailed upon by Government pressure to confirm an order for 20 Ambassadors instead of buying the Viscount. This was a major setback for Vickers, and their interest waned with existing commitments. Thus the Viscount project remained in jeopardy for some months. Construction of the second Viscount prototype was slowed and the third stopped. Work on the first airframe at Foxwarren continued largely because of the faith of George Edwards in the concept, strongly supported by Sir Hew Kilner, then managing director of the aircraft division of Vickers.

On 16 July, 1948, Summers, accompanied by Bryce as co-pilot, flew the

Cabin *décor* of the executive suite of Viscount Type 737 for the Canadian Department of Transport.

Viscount Type 744, serial XR801, of the Empire Test Pilots' School.

completed Viscount 630 prototype from Wisley for 10 minutes. Subsequent test flights proved without doubt that the aeroplane was an exceptional design, that it possessed excellent handling characteristics and would offer a completely new experience of comfort in passenger travel with its smooth operation. Those early flights did much to revive Vickers' depressed spirits and to sway opinion back in favour of the Viscount and its turbines with their undoubted advantages. Meanwhile the Ambassador had been delayed by structural problems in its wing design, and proposals from Rolls-Royce for an up-rated Dart RDa3 of over 1,500 ehp had made a stretched 630 Viscount a practical proposition.

With larger wings and body, the gross weight could be raised from the 38,650 lb of the Type 630 to 45,000 lb, with accommodation for 43 passengers in higher-density seating, and the cruising speed could be increased at normal loadings to 333 mph. Framed in conjunction with BEA, a new Vickers' specification outlined the design details and operational data of an aeroplane that became the Type 700 Viscount. On 24 February, 1949, the Ministry of Supply placed an order for one prototype, an action largely inspired by Sir Alec Coryton, Controller of Supplies (Air) and Cyril Musgrave, Under Secretary (Air). The MoS specification for the Type 700 was 21/49, dated 19 April, 1949.

Meanwhile the second prototype Type 609, originally ordered by the MoS and originally allotted the civil registration G-AHRG, was converted into a flying test-bed for the Rolls-Royce Tay turbojet engine as Type 663 to specification 4/49. Under the Service serial number VX217,

425

Vickers Type 745 demonstrator G-APLX used to show local service characteristics to various North American operators; in background is one of the erecting shops of the Hurn factory.

it first flew on 15 March, 1950. Subsequently, it was used by Boulton Paul for power-control trials, notably for the Vickers Valiant four-jet bomber.

Vickers had also made parts for the third Type 609, being built as a private venture, and these were diverted to the construction of the proto-type Type 700, thus materially assisting in reducing the time taken to produce it to 18 months. It was first flown by Bryce on 28 August, 1950, at Brooklands and delivered to Wisley for test-flying. Wing span was some 5 ft greater than the Type 630, and it was 7 ft 4 in longer. Registered G-AMAV, the prototype 700 was subsequently flown by BEA in the England–New Zealand Air Race of 1953, taking-off in the tropics at weights

Hurn production line of Viscounts for Capital Airlines.

426

up to 65,000 lb, as compared with its designed weight of 48,000 lb. It flew the 12,500-mile course in 40 hr 45 min, including a non-stop stage from the Cocos Islands to Melbourne, a distance of 3,530 miles, in 10 hr 16 min at an average speed of 343 mph. Later the operational gross weight of the Type 700 was raised to 50,000 lb, with accommodation for up to 53 passengers, and the cruising speed was 310 mph.

The enthusiasm of BEA for the stretched Viscount was natural, for it embodied all the advantages the airline had advocated a year before. In addition, just a month before the first flight of the Type 700, BEA had operated the world's first scheduled commercial passenger service with a turbine-powered aeroplane. On 29 July, 1950, the Type 630 Viscount,

Distinctive red and white livery of Capital Airlines Viscount.

registered G-AHRF, and with a special certificate of airworthiness granted two days before, flew from London to Paris with Capts R. Rymer and W. J. Wakelin and a complement of fare-paying passengers. Capt Rymer was the world's first holder of a pilot's licence for a civil turbine-powered air transport and later became a senior Vickers test pilot. The Paris service continued for two weeks and then, from 15 August until 23 August, the period of the Edinburgh Festival, G-AHRF flew a London–Edinburgh service, 1,815 passengers being carried on the two operations, in a total of 127 flying hours.

Thus the Viscount had amply demonstrated its attractions to the air traveller and the airline operator and had vindicated the conviction of Peter Masefield, then chief executive of BEA, supported and encouraged by Lord Douglas of Kirtleside, his Chairman, that it was indeed the right aeroplane to consolidate the airline. In consequence, BEA signed an order on 3 August, 1950, for 20 (later increased to 26) Type 701 Viscounts, which were a slightly refined version of the 700, which was about to fly. Gross weight was to be 53,000 lb, with accommodation for 47 passengers in five-abreast seating, and underfloor holds for increased freight capacity.

Indian Airlines last Type 768 Viscount, VT-DJC.

The first production Viscount 701, G-ALWE, flew on 20 August, 1952, and was delivered to BEA as the first of their Discovery class, on 3 January, 1953, after completing its trials and acceptance tests. With Rolls-Royce Dart 505 engines it cruised at 302 mph at 23,000 ft and had a gross weight of 56,000 lb, later increased to 57,000 lb. The certificate of airworthiness for the Type 701 was granted on 17 April, 1953, and the following day Viscount G-AMNY, RMA *Sir Ernest Shackleton*, with Capts A. S. Johnson and A. Wilson, began the first sustained propeller-turbine airline service in the world on the route London–Rome–Athens–Nicosia.

So in just over eight years from the forming of the Brabazon IIB requirement, the VC2 Viscount had become a reality as one of the leading airliners in the world. This lengthy period can be attributed to the uncertainty regarding the development of aircraft gas-turbines in the beginning and to early doubts on the potentiality of the turbine-powered civil aeroplane. A better measure of progress was the two years and eight months which elapsed between the placing of the BEA order and the Viscount going into service. In the event, the Viscount, together with the de Havilland Comet, had indeed led a revolution in aircraft power plants by pioneering the gas-turbine into civil aviation.

The airframe structure of the Viscount followed the constructional pattern of the stressed-skin Viking, with a single-spar wing and a fuselage with unbroken hoop frames. But new problems were posed by the requirement for a pressurised cabin and flight deck. Variations from the optimum cylindrical cross-section had to be made to provide for openings such as doors and windows, pilots' hood, and bulkheads and floors subject to pressure loads. To cater for the stresses set up by major cut-outs in a cabin of circular section, a theory was evolved mathematically by Basil Stephenson of Vickers and confirmed by physical testing, whereby an elliptical neutral hole was adopted in which the edge member was relieved of bending loads caused by pressure effects on the surrounding skin. The so-called catenary floor of the flight deck in the Viscount was designed on elastic-membrane principles to allow for an unpressurised nosewheel bay underneath.

After the first order from BEA for Viscounts in August 1950, another 15 months elapsed before more orders materialised. Almost simultaneously these arrived in November 1951, from other European airlines, Air France contracting for 12 Type 708s and Aer Lingus for four Type 707s. The Irish airline showed commendable courage in choosing the Viscount at a time when gas-turbine powered civil aircraft, although no longer a novelty, had still to prove themselves in airline service.

Another seven months went by before a significant order came from Trans-Australia Airlines for six Type 720s. This not only reflected world opinion on the appeal of the Viscount but also displayed the operator's confidence in relying on a manufacturer 12,000 miles away. With the Viscount, equipped with slipper-type long-range fuel tanks, TAA were able to fly the Adelaide–Perth route non-stop, that long haul of 1,300 miles that had caused the Viastra IIs so much hard grind in short stages in the early 1930s.

An even more notable breakthrough came in November 1952, when Trans-Canada Air Lines (now Air Canada) ordered 15 Type 724 Viscounts, thus introducing turbine air travel to North America. This contract involved considerable detail redesign to fit the aeroplane into the American operational pattern, including a two-pilot flight crew, and automatic instrumentation and flight control systems. The interior décor of the cabin was styled to TCA's requirements by Charles Butler, a leading American designer. In February 1953 the prototype Viscount 700 G-AMAV became the first propeller-turbine aeroplane to cross the North Atlantic, when it flew to Canada via the Northern route for cold-weather trials.

In the same month, February 1953, BEA ordered a larger Viscount, the Type 801, to carry 86 tourist class passengers. This was to have the Rolls-Royce Dart RDa5 engines of 1,690 ehp each and be 13 ft 3 in longer than BEA's Viscount 701s. Although this particular type did not materialise, it led the way to the Type 802 for BEA and the later Type 810 series of Viscounts with increased gross weights and higher output engines. It will be noticed in this connection that the Vickers type numbering system had by this time been modified to cover the tailoring of different Viscounts to operators' individual requirements, for what have come to be known as

Alitalia Type 785 Viscount, I-LIZT, one of a large fleet operated by the airline.

Viscount 800 series production line in B.1 shop, built on the site of the old Brooklands sewage farm to accommodate Viscount production.

custom-built aircraft. In consequence, new designs or major modifications involving large structural changes in established designs were allocated a new basic type number with a block of following numbers to cater for each customer variant compared with the time-honoured Vickers system of random numbering.

Thus the appearance of even larger Viscounts was heralded by the allocation of Type 800 series to the new range. The changes in the Vickers type numbering method throughout the years will be clear by reference to the table given in Appendix III.

In May 1953, soon after the introduction of the Viscount into regular service by BEA, the first order was placed by an independent operator, Hunting-Clan, for three Type 732s. Two Vickers Viking operators, British West Indian Airways and Iraqi Airways, ordered Type 700 series Viscounts in the summer of 1953, and the Indian Air Force ordered two in November of that year.

The next month, December, a second production line of Viscounts was started at Vickers factory at Hurn, where the Varsity production had by then been completed. This facility was to prove its value when Viscount output began to assume large proportions. The Hurn site had been originally leased from the Government, owners of Hurn airport, to accept the flight testing of the Valiant bombers pending the construction of a hard runway at Wisley, and then it became responsible for Varsity production. Subsequently, it developed into a complete aircraft factory, with design, flight test and all other relevant facilities. Of the 445 Viscounts built, 279 were produced at Hurn, and at its peak period it was producing them at a rate of six a month. All 60 Viscounts for the United States operator, Capital Airlines, were produced at Hurn.

There was no doubt that BEA had achieved a signal success in introducing smooth and quiet turbine air travel. The passenger appeal the Viscount had fostered was also confirmed in reports from its other early operators, Air France, Aer Lingus and Trans-Australia Airlines. All endorsed the attractions of Viscount travel, and these were reflected in substantial traffic increases, the best of all indexes to an airline operator. By November 1954 most of Air France's European routes were being flown by their Viscount 708s.

Meanwhile, development of the Rolls-Royce Dart engine was continuing, and in April 1954 BEA substituted a tentative order for the Type 801 with a firm one for 12 Type 802s to an amended specification, which included Dart 510 engines of 1,740 ehp. The fuselage was 3 ft 10 in longer than that of the BEA Viscount 701, but the cabin was 9 ft 3 in longer by moving the rear pressure bulkhead farther aft, and it accommodated 57 passengers in normal density seating, or up to 65 in higher densities. An

A familiar sight at London Airport, Heathrow—passengers disembarking from a BEA Viscount.

innovation in the 800 series Viscounts was the introduction of large rectangular doors of the parallel-link hinge type, in place of the original oval doors of the 700 series, to cater for the expansion of alternative passenger or freight transport. Following the order for the BEA 802s, one was received from KLM (Royal Dutch Airlines) for nine Type 803s to a similar specification. This was a notable breakthrough for British aircraft for an airline normally preferring American types.

In July 1954 Central African Airways ordered four Viscounts in the

431

PH-VIA, a Type 803 Viscount of KLM Royal Dutch Airlines.

Viscount G-AOYF, the prototype of the 806 and 810 series, the first of which was for Continental Airlines.

The Type 807 Viscount ZK-BRE *City of Auckland* of New Zealand National Airways, which was specially fitted out in **VIP** *décor* and furnishing for H.M. The Queen during her visit to New Zealand in 1963; in the picture it is flying over Mount Cook, South Island.

700D series which was powered by the more powerful Dart 510 engines as specified for BEA's Viscount 802s. Under the definitive type number 748, the African Viscounts initially had a gross weight of 60,000 lb, which was raised in 1958 to 64,590 lb, and they had a cruising speed of 325 mph.

All Viscounts in the later 700 series were fitted with the Dart 510, while most of the earlier ones were re-engined with the Dart 506 in place of the original Dart 505. A trial order by Capital Airlines of Washington for three Type 744s with the Dart 506 was followed in August 1954 by a substantial order for 37 Type 745s with the Dart 510. In the following December a further 20 were ordered, and the total of 60 Viscounts became the largest production run for one operator. This breakthrough into the American civil airliner market was hailed as a major triumph for the British aircraft industry. Never before had a non-American manufacturer been able to loosen the grip the American constructors had on their own market, the vast network of internal airlines in the United States. It certainly had a salutary effect.

The value of Capital's order was $67 million, the largest British dollar export up to that time. Before the Viscount could enter American service an immense programme of detail adjustment had to be undertaken by Vickers to comply with the 26 additional special requirements of the CAA (later Federal Aviation Agency). These were additional to the British certificate of airworthiness requirements, but all were satisfactorily fulfilled in due course. At that time the CAA had no code of their own for turbine-powered aircraft. Most notable of these requirements were change-overs to American flight instrumentation, navigational and radio aids and other flight equipment. Cold and warm air systems and air stairs were other refinements. The work already done on the Canadian Viscounts was particularly helpful when it came to the larger problem of tailoring the Capital Viscounts, as 19 of the 26 special conditions had already been satisfied.

Following the Canadian and American contracts for Viscounts came the North Atlantic ferry operation for delivery via Prestwick, Iceland, Greenland and Goose Bay, bearing in mind that the Viscount was in fact a short/medium-haul aeroplane. This became a shuttle of visible exports to dollar countries and provided an impressive morale booster for British industry at a crucial time.

So by mid-1958 the order book for Viscounts had reached the 400 mark, and over 300 had been delivered to operators in many countries throughout the world. With an order for 19 Type 806s with the Dart RDa7/520 of 1,700 shp (a derated three-stage turbine engine), BEA, the first Viscount operator, had 77 Viscounts in 1958, and the positive results of their operation were reflected in the profits of the airline. Scheduled airlines and independent operators had discovered a money spinner in the Viscount, passenger load factors averaging 80 per cent being consistently recorded.

While numerous though minor structural improvements had been progressively incorporated during the service life of the Viscount, changes

Viscount Type 812s for Continental Airlines, Colorado, in production at Weybridge.

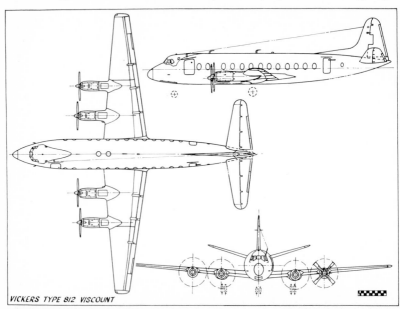

VICKERS TYPE 812 VISCOUNT

D-ANUN, a Viscount Type 814 for Lufthansa.

434

Ansett-ANA Type 832 Viscount, VH-RMI.

made to establish a Type 810, with the developed Dart 525 engine, to meet even higher design weights and speeds, involved the first major modifications in structural strength.

Continental Airlines of Denver, Colorado, ordered 15 Type 812s with the Dart 525. Continental's route network covered a large area of the central and southern part of the United States, where high-altitude and high-temperature take-off performance was a criterion. Gross weight for take-off was 67,500 lb, and cruising speed was 365 mph, while payload was 15,000 lb over stages of up to 1,100 st miles with reserves.

This sale of the first Viscounts in the 810 series was followed by others to All Nippon Airways, Ansett-ANA (Australia), Austrian Airlines, Cubana, Ghana Airways, Lufthansa, Pakistan International Airlines, South African Airways, Trans-Australia Airlines (already operating 720s), VASP (Brazil) and several independent operators.

The 400 mph Viscount promised in the 840 series, to be powered by the Dart 541 of 2,395 shp and with a gross weight of 69,000 lb, did not materialise, but it led directly to the Viscount Major 850 project and later to the 870, from which came the second-generation propeller-turbine airliner, the Vickers Vanguard.

The 810 demonstrator rigged for Vanguard fin de-icing tests.

435

The total value of the 445 Viscounts sold, including spares, was £177 million, of which £147 million was for overseas sales. The 147 Viscounts for North American operators realised £58·6 million. Over 60 operators in some 40 countries acquired Viscounts first hand, including 48 airlines operating scheduled services, and five governments and seven private operators also purchased the type.

The Viscount was unique, as it was the only aeroplane in its class available to potential operators. With its achievements must be bracketed the Rolls-Royce Dart propeller-turbine, one of the pioneers of a completely new era of aircraft propulsion.

Viscount

	Type 630	Type 720	Type 810
Accommodation:	3 crew, steward, 32 passengers	3 crew, 2 stewards, 43 passengers	3 crew, 2 stewards, 57/65 passengers
Engines:	Four 1,380 ehp Rolls-Royce Dart R.Da.1 Mk 502	Four 1,740 ehp Rolls-Royce Dart R.Da.3 Mk 506	Four 1,990 ehp Rolls-Royce Dart R.Da.7/1 Mk 525
Span:	88 ft 11 in	93 ft 8½ in	93 ft 8½ in
Length:	74 ft 6 in	81 ft 10 in	85 ft 8 in
Height:	26 ft 3 in	26 ft 9 in	26 ft 9 in
Wing Area:	885 sq ft	963 sq ft	963 sq ft
Empty Weight:	29,060 lb	38,358 lb	43,500 lb
Gross Weight:	38,650 lb	64,500 lb	72,500 lb
Max Speed:	332 mph at 20,000 ft	380 mph* at 20,000 ft	357 mph† at 20,000 ft
Max Range:	1,380 miles at 277 mph at 20,000 ft	2,000 miles at 317 mph (T.A.S.) at 21,000 ft	1,610 miles at 333 mph (T.A.S.) at 25,000 ft
Range with Max Payload:	—	1,730 miles at 317 mph (T.A.S.) and 11,600 lb payload	1,587 miles at 333 mph (T.A.S.) and 14,000 lb payload

* Cruising speed   † Max cruising speed

The Valiant

At the end of the second world war Bomber Command of the Royal Air Force was due to be completely re-equipped with the B.14/43 Avro Lincoln and the B.3/42 Vickers Windsor. Only the Lincoln went into production, and the prevailing operational philosophy, which included heavy defensive armament and unpressurised crew accommodation, remained static. In the meantime the arrival of the turbojet engine and the nuclear bomb completely altered the picture. Their influence on Air Staff requirements was profound.

If a single weapon could do the work of a thousand-bomber raid of the war there was no longer the need to maintain a large bomber force. Very high speeds could be attained with the steep rise in power output obtainable from the jet engine, and very high operational ceilings could be reached by the introduction of pressure cabins, first explored and developed by Vickers in the Wellingtons V and VI. No defensive armament would

Prototype Valiant, WB210, with straight-slot engine air intakes in wing roots and short jet pipes.

be needed in a high-speed, high-altitude bomber, and electronic equipment would provide precision bombing at elevated speeds and heights.

Therefore the proposition for a completely re-equipped bomber force was becoming reality. Bomber Command would then comprise a small number of high-performance aeroplanes designed to carry any type of bomb, including the nuclear deterrent, at heights of not less than 50,000 ft and at speeds approaching Mach 1. This prospect was of appeal to British political and military philosophy. Because of the high cost of a single bomber, exchequer resources limited the numbers it was possible to build, in a period when the restoration of the national economy after the war was still a priority matter.

On the other hand, international incidents such as the Berlin blockade and air lift lent urgency to the weighty and vital task of the complete and revolutionary re-equipment of British air forces, notably Bomber Command. In other words, the general consensus of public thinking in Britain favoured the policy of rebuilding British military strength through the rearmament drive.

Thus the V-bomber force was born. It would have the task of accurately delivering a rapier-like thrust at lightning speed, if ever that unfortunate duty became necessary. Although the English Electric Canberra was the first jet bomber to go into service with the RAF, its scope of operations was largely tactical, while the new V-bombers would fill the strategic rôle.

Consequently, an Air Staff requirement of 1947 led to the projecting of advanced designs for new jet bombers embodying wings of some 35 degrees sweepback on which the results from theoretical research were available.

437

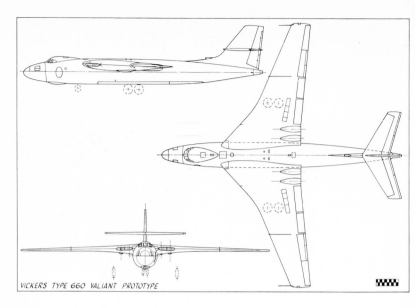

VICKERS TYPE 660 VALIANT PROTOTYPE

Such a configuration of wing plan delayed compressibility effects at Mach numbers approaching the speed of sound, and this technical consideration eventually led to two decisions. One was to seek an aerodynamically advanced form with better performance characteristics and high development potential, and the other was to order a less radical design with inferior performance to that of the more advanced types. This latter conception in fact materialised as the Short Sperrin prototype, which was designed and constructed as an insurance against the possible failure of the more ambitious designs.

Vickers submitted a tender for the high-performance bomber competition and, although at first this was not accepted, later study disclosed that it could meet the original specification in almost all requirements except that of range. While being less advanced aerodynamically than other submissions, such as the Avro Vulcan and Handley Page Victor, it could on that account be available at an earlier date, an attractive proposition at that time.

Air Ministry specification B.9/48 was drawn up around the Vickers design which was allocated the number 660 in Vickers' type list. The prototypes were ordered by contract on 2 February, 1949, the first to have four Rolls-Royce Avon RA3 turbojets, and the second prototype, as Type 667, to be powered with four Armstrong Siddeley Sapphire turbojets.

Design proceeded in 1949, and in 1950 components were being made into complete assemblies at the Foxwarren experimental shop under the direction of A. W. E. (Charlie) Houghton, then manager responsible for prototypes. Although the bomber was ordered off the drawing board in the modern manner, prototypes were still required at the time the B.9/48

438

An early production Valiant, WZ365, in grey finish and with extended jet pipes.

bomber was designed, probably because the concept of the project was then largely exploratory.

Final assembly of the new bomber began early in 1951 at Wisley, and the first flight was made by Summers, accompanied by Bryce, from the grass airfield there on 18 May, 1951. This flight was a short one, and only three more were made from Wisley before flight trials were transferred to Hurn, while a paved runway was being constructed at Wisley. The proto-

Valiant production at Weybridge.

Valiant B(K)1, XD875, taking off at Marham, with main undercarriage just starting retraction; note long-range wing tanks.

type Type 660 bore the serial number WB210, and in June 1951 the bomber was officially called the Valiant, a repetition of the name used for Vickers Type 131 of 1931, a single-engined military tractor biplane.

Flight testing of WB210 continued until 12 January, 1952, when the aeroplane had to be abandoned in flight because of a fire in the port wing during engine shut downs and relights in the air, as part of internal noise-level tests. All the flight crew except one, Sqn Ldr Foster, the co-pilot, escaped safely. Modifications to the atmospheric balance in the fuel system cured the fault which led to a wet start and the fire.

Early flight trials of WB210 had given sufficient indication of the promise of the design to satisfy the Air Staff. Completion of the second prototype, Type 667, was near, so the loss of WB210 was not as serious as it might have been in the absence of the original orders for three prototypes. This second Valiant, WB215, flew on 11 April, 1952, at Wisley, with RA7 Avons and not with Sapphires as originally planned.

An initial order for 25 Valiant B.1s had been placed in April 1951. The production of so large and complex an aeroplane involved a considerable planning effort with a large amount of sub-contracting. Eight major sub-contractors were chosen, with Saunders-Roe responsible for the largest item, the pressurised crew-compartment. Because of the shortage of suitable steel sections, pre-stressed concrete was employed for the interchangeable jig pillars, bolted to the shop floor.

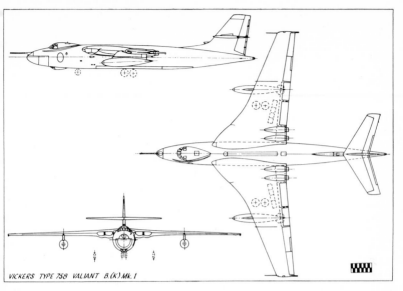

VICKERS TYPE 758 VALIANT B.(K)Mk.1

New production methods were developed and introduced to meet design requirements. Powered stretching and forming tools were used for leading-edge and fuselage panels, fuselage frames and spar sections. Sculpture milling was introduced for the first time by Vickers to manufacture the centre-section spar web plates. Synthetic bonding was applied to doubling plates on control surfaces. A special glasscloth-plastic bonding shop was started to fabricate various dielectric components, such as the nose radome and suppressed aerials, as well as ducting for the air system.

The Valiant was a shoulder-wing aeroplane with compound sweep on the leading edge. The four Avon turbojets were buried in the inner wing, as was British practice at the time of design, contrasted with the contemporary American practice of engine pods slung below the wing. In the

Valiant B(K)1 XD823 with flight-refuelling probe.

441

first prototype the intakes were long rectangular slots extending outboard from the wing-root leading edge. Before the first flight, vertical airflow straighteners were added in the mouths of the intakes, but in subsequent Valiants the familiar spectacle type entries were adopted to provide for a larger mass flow of intake air to feed the higher-power RA7, RA14 and RA28 Avons.

With the shoulder-wing configuration, a cavernous bomb-bay was provided in the circular-section fuselage, and so the Valiant became in due course the first of the V-bombers capable of accommodating the Blue Steel stand-off weapon. The tailplane was mounted part-way up the vertical fin to keep it well clear of the jet efflux.

With a large wing, and consequently a comparatively low loading, the requirements for short take-off and long-range were adequately met by the Valiant. A broad chord inboard enabled the root thickness to be no more than 12 per cent, although embodying sufficient depth to accommodate the power units with their ancillary systems and accessories. In addition this wide root chord facilitated a more acute angle of sweepback at the inner third of the wing span, and so raised the local critical Mach number in an area where the airflow accelerating around the fuselage nose met the wings. The amount of sweepback was decided by the need to achieve a wing aerodynamic centre coincident with the centre of gravity, thus promoting stability and using a smaller variable-incidence tailplane.

A massive backbone member running along the top of the fuselage down the centreline, with two branches at right-angles on each side linking up

Complete Valiant team of aircrew, ground engineers and support equipment and stores.

442

with the main outer wing spars, formed the primary Valiant structure. Bomb loads or other stores were hung from this keel beam, the side members only taking the lift loads from the wings. These side members were in fact the main spars of the centre section, joined at the fuselage centreline, bifurcated and reinforced around the engines. Outer plane spars were heavy channel-section booms tapering towards the wingtips. The stressed-skin wing was constructed on a system of spanwise stringers and built-up ribs. Fuel tanks in the outer planes were of the flexible-bag type.

The Valiant fuselage followed the general pattern of high-tensile light-alloy stressed-skin construction and embodied Vickers' traditional system of flush-riveted skin attached to the longitudinal stringers only, the circular frames being inside the stringers to which they were cleated. The pressurised egg which housed the crew had a concave diaphragm bulkhead forward, with radial stiffening beams, and the aft bulkhead was an unstiffened convex shell. The neutral hole theory as developed in the first Viscounts was applied to the canopy, oval side windows and oval door, starboard emergency exit hatch, roof sextant dome and floor bomb-aimer's compartment. The door was provided with a wind shield to assist crew exit in emergency—only the two pilots had ejector seats.

Aft of the cabin the main part of the fuselage, with the keel beam and associated primary structures, also included the nosewheel bay, the services bay (known as the organ loft), rear equipment bay, bomb-bay and air deflector. This last item comprised a portion of the underside of the fuselage just aft of the bomb-bay; it moved up as far as the top rear of the bay to blank off the airflow into the fuselage when the bomb doors opened, as these travelled upwards on an electrically-driven mechanism inside the fuselage to avoid increasing the drag.

The Valiant systems were almost entirely electrical. The one hydraulic system in the aeroplane was for brakes and steering gear, but even its pumps were driven by electric motors. The main control surfaces were power operated but capable of selective reversion to manual control. A high-voltage 112-volt DC system was chosen because the 28-volt was heavier; at the time of design the AC system was insufficiently advanced in development for this purpose. The sideways and outwards retracting undercarriage, consisting of dual legs and wheels arranged in tandem, was operated by an electrical actuator through worm gearing. The undercarriage assembly stowed into wells in the wing between the fuselage and engine mountings and, when retracted, was enclosed by large doors.

Four types of Valiant entered service. Type 706 was the B.Mk 1 bomber, Type 710 was B(PR) Mk 1 bomber or photographic-reconnaissance, Type 758 was B(K) Mk 1 flight-refuelling receiver aircraft (bomber or tanker rôle), and Type 733 B.PR (K) Mk 1—FR receiver for bomber, photographic reconnaissance or tanker rôles. In addition, a number of indefinite variants of the basic B.Mk 1 were evolved for a variety of special rôles, as will be evident from the short account which follows of the Valiant's Service career.

Valiant B.2 low-level bomber, WJ954, the only example constructed; the distinctive features were the undercarriage housings under the wings.

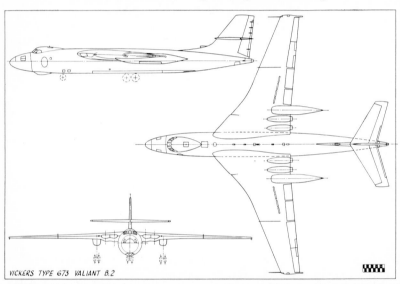

VICKERS TYPE 673 VALIANT B.2

Head-on view of Valiant B.2, showing wheel housings outboard of jet pipes.

444

One other mark number was required, and that was for the B.Mk 2 low-level pathfinder bomber (Vickers Type 673), which, after its appearance at the SBAC show of 1954, was named the 'black bomber' because of its night paint. The distinctive difference from all other Valiants was the underslung pods into which the bogie undercarriage retracted backwards. As the intended rôle for this version was at low level, the main stress-bearing structure had to be considerably strengthened, involving the use of the standard wheel-well spaces for this purpose.

The Valiant B.2 was the last prototype to be built at the Foxwarren experimental shop and was moved in large assemblies along the Portsmouth Road to Wisley, where it was completed and then flown by Bryce, with Brian Trubshaw as co-pilot, on 4 September, 1953. Throughout, its construction had been supervised by A. W. E. Houghton; to him and his team should be attributed the remarkable speed with which the whole Valiant programme was engineered through to the successful production of 104 modern bombers of high complexity, efficiency and performance, in service in well under ten years from the start of project design.

Confronted by what was virtually a new-deal aeroplane, and charged with the task of creating the nucleus of Britain's deterrent force of fast, high-altitude bombers carrying nuclear weapons over great distances with accurate delivery, Bomber Command formed an Operational Conversion Unit (232) at Gaydon. This was to train V-force squadrons in the operation and maintenance of Valiants.

To assist this training a Valiant servicing school was established at Gaydon in the latter half of 1954 after instructors had attended lengthy courses at Vickers' own servicing school at Weybridge, and also those of Rolls-Royce and Boulton Paul to study engine and power control systems respectively.

The first squadron to receive Valiants was 138 at Gaydon, Warwickshire, commanded by Wg Cdr R. G. W. Oakley, who had spent three years as Bomber Command's liaison officer with Vickers. On 5 September, 1955, two Valiants under the command of Sqn Ldr R. G. Wilson, left Wittering on proving trials from 138 Squadron. Operation 'Too Right', as it was called, carried the flag of Britain's first V-bomber to Singapore, Australia and New Zealand. There it was seen and flown by the RAAF and RNZAF to their complete satisfaction. No major unserviceability was encountered throughout a tour in which the two Valiants totalled almost 146 flying hours. Also in September 1955 there was a fly-past of six pairs of Valiants from Wittering and Gaydon at the SBAC flying display at Farnborough. The final test of the capabilities of the aircraft, apart from air exercises and detailed assessment of specialised equipment, was carried out in the spring of 1956, when No. 138 Squadron flew four Valiants for 1,000 hours.

In June 1956 the Valiant was flown with Super Sprite high-test peroxide motors for rocket-assisted take-off. Water-methanol injection was fitted as standard to all Valiants for use on take-off and for extra power boost in high ambient temperatures and in other operational conditions. During

Valiant with Super Sprite rocket-assisted take-off climbs away at the Farnborough Air Show, 1956.

the following winter the Valiant was tested in Canada on winterisation trials. Meanwhile, in July 1956, HM the Queen inspected Bomber Command units at Marham, where there was an impressive concentration of Valiants.

Events crowded in on the Valiant. On 11 October, 1956, No. 49 Squadron participated in radiation and other tests during the dropping of Britain's A-bomb at Maralinga, Australia, by a Valiant commanded by Sqn Ldr E. J. G. Flavell. Almost simultaneously Nos. 138, 148, 207 and 214 Squadrons moved to Luqa, Malta, from which base their Valiants went into action in the Suez campaign, thus becoming the first and only bomber of the V-force to drop bombs in anger. On 15 May, 1957, a Valiant, again of 49 Squadron, under the command of Wg Cdr K. G. Hubbard, was selected to drop Britain's first H bomb in the Christmas Island Operation 'Grapple'.

Valiant, WZ366, which dropped Britain's first atomic bomb, at Maralinga, Australia, on 11 October, 1956.

446

Valiant XD818 which dropped Britain's first H bomb, at Christmas Island on 15 May, 1957.

In a more peaceful arena Valiants represented 3 Group, Bomber Command, in the Strategic Air Command's bombing, navigation and reconnaissance competition held at Pinecastle, Florida, at the end of October 1957. The Valiant Wing was placed 27th out of 45 Wings competing, Sqn Ldr R. W. Payne, of 214 Squadron, and his crew being placed 11th out of the 90 competing crews.

The following year's competition at March Air Force Base, California, saw the RAF 'B' team of Valiants in 7th place in combined bombing and navigation out of 41 participating wings. An individual crew, led by Sqn Ldr R. W. Richardson of 148 Squadron, achieved the high distinction of the 9th place out of 164 competing crews. These efforts were a remarkable testimony to the efficiency of both aircraft and crew, as the RAF, with their comparatively small number of competing aircraft, had the odds against them.

Other operations undertaken by Valiants included 'Snow Trip', a survey of the DEW (distant early warning) radar chain across the Canadian Arctic border; 'Dectra', a comparative test of many sorties of Decca and VOR/DME navigation systems over the North Atlantic (Boscombe Down Valiant WP210); and 'Lone Ranger', which consisted of routine flights by single RAF aircraft overseas.

For some years a large force of RAF Canberras had been allocated to

Valiant at readiness for Suez campaign, 1956, at Luqa airbase, Malta.

Valiant tanker XD812 refuelling receiver Valiant WZ390.

the Supreme Allied Commander Europe as part of Britain's contribution to NATO Forces, but later the decision was taken to replace them by a force of Valiants, thus they not only formed part of Britain's V-force but also augmented the striking power of NATO.

Early in 1959 No. 214 Squadron, based at Marham, started a series of operational trials of the flight-refuelling system, which proved satisfactory and gave the V-bomber force greater flexibility and radius of action and

Complete refuelling equipment being fitted in a Valiant tanker of 214 Squadron.

448

The last Valiant, XD875, taking-off from Brooklands for delivery to the Royal Air Force.

fortified its strategic dispositions. The accompanying list of the principal non-stop flights made in 1959 and 1960 by No. 214 Squadron, some of which were unofficial records, show that the flight-refuelling system, devised and developed by Flight Refuelling under Sir Alan Cobham, was eminently suitable for application to modern military aircraft. These flights also proved that the Valiant was an adaptable aircraft, and its many achievements during its operational service with the Royal Air Force underlined the wisdom of Sir George Edwards when he decided to offer the Service an 'unfunny' aircraft, to use his own description, in the shortest possible time.

Flight	Distance, st miles	Time, hr min	Speed, mph	Aircraft captain
Marham–Nairobi	4,350	07·40	562	Flt Lt B. E. Fern
Marham–Salisbury	5,320	09·42	548	Sqn Ldr J. H. Garstin
Marham–Johannesburg	5,845	11·03	529	Wg Cdr M. J. Beetham
O/h L.A.P.–Cape Town	6,060	11·28	530	,, ,, ,,
Cape Town–O/h L.A.P.	6,060	12·20	492	,, ,, ,,
Marham–Offutt	4,336	09·30	461	,, ,, ,,
Offutt–St Mawgan	4,400	09·03	488	,, ,, ,,
Marham–around U.K.	8,500	18·05	—	Sqn Ldr J. H. Garstin
Marham–Changi	8,110	15·35	523	,, ,, ,,
Butterworth–Marham	7,770	16·16·5	476	,, ,, ,,
Marham–Vancouver	5,007	10·28	481	⌠ Air Vice Marshal
Vancouver–Marham	5,007	09·35	523	⌡ M. H. Dwyer

The Vickers Valiant was, in fact, ordered in November 1948, the prototype flew in May 1951 and the first production aircraft flew in December 1953 and was delivered to the RAF in January 1955. From the sixth aeroplane, the programmed delivery dates were maintained from 1955 onwards. The steady flow of Valiants was greatly assisted by the co-operation of the many sub-contractors in meeting their target dates.

The Valiant proved extremely easy to service, despite its original features and electrical systems. No major snags emerged that could not be

449

Valiant XD818 preserved at Marham in low-level camouflage and destined for the RAF Museum.

quickly overcome, and in Bomber Command the aeroplane remained constantly in readiness on dispersal bases.

The principal stations which operated Valiants were Marham and Honington (strike and tanker aircraft), Wyton (reconnaissance) and Gaydon (OCU). A proportion of the aircraft operated from Marham were those assigned to NATO.

The Valiant, in common with the other V-bombers, assumed a low-level operational rôle early in 1964, officially declared by the Air Minister in February 1964 at RAF Wittering. Low-level operations followed the reassessment of potential enemy defence effectiveness, which showed that high-level operations at subsonic speeds were too dangerous. To reduce the likelihood of visual detection, low-level Valiants were repainted in a camouflage colour scheme similar to that used in the second world war.

Valiants were officially withdrawn from service at the end of January 1965, after investigation had shown that the main wing spars of all aircraft were suffering from metal fatigue. Although repair schemes were feasible, it was decided, for reasons of economy, not to proceed with them, and the force was scrapped. One of the historic aircraft concerned in the British atomic bomb tests was reserved for the RAF museum.

Valiant B.(K) Mk I—Type 758—Four 10,000 lb s.t. Rolls-Royce Avon RA 28. Accommodation two pilots, two navigators, one electronics engineer; two extra crew in tanker rôle. Span 114 ft 4 in; length 108 ft 3 in; height 32 ft 2 in; wing area 2,362 sq ft. Empty weight 75,881 lb; gross weight 140,000 lb. Max speed 567 mph at 30,000 ft; initial climb 4,000 ft/min; service ceiling 54,000 ft; range (with underwing tanks) 4,500 miles. Military load one 10,000-lb bomb or twenty-one 1,000-lb bombs or two fuel tanks in bomb bay of 1,615 Imp gal each.

450

Vanguard G-AOYW, Vickers' demonstrator, without dorsal fin.

The Vanguard

Soon after the Viscount had gone into service with British European Airways in April 1953 discussions began between the airline and Vickers for a successor to be ready in 1959. This was to have 10 per cent better economics than those of the Viscount 806 and to be faster over all its stages. Consideration had been given earlier by BEA to the development of a Type 701 Discovery class replacement. Their survey had ranged over a variety of pure-jet and propeller-turbine propositions, but, despite some hesitancy over the commercial aspects, it became obvious that a larger aeroplane with a larger payload would eventually emerge.

On 15 April, 1953, the chief executive of BEA, Peter Masefield, wrote to Vickers, outlining the airline's requirements. Coincidentally on the same day, Trans-Canada Air Lines issued a brief outline of requirements for a transcontinental Viscount-type aeroplane to carry 60 passengers at a gross load of 72,000 lb.

Meanwhile, BEA had examined the proposals for the Viscount Major, Type 850, which were based on a lengthened fuselage of 95 ft and the Rolls-Royce Dart RDa8 engine of 2,500 hp, as then projected. The airline's specific requirements, which were a cruising speed of 370 kt, a 1,000 st mile stage with 350 mile fuel reserve, accommodation for 100 passengers, and with preferably a high-wing layout, could not be met in the Viscount 850, so attention was then directed to the new Type 870 project.

On 14 May, 1953, at a meeting between Vickers and Rolls-Royce, a

Vanguard G-AOYW at Wisley airfield during early trials.

decision was made to use a new Rolls-Royce propeller-turbine, the RB109, in the Type 870; at that time this type of engine was showing better operating cost figures than the turbojet. A study made in November 1953 of a Type 870 with turbojets, described then as baby Conways, disclosed inferior characteristics compared with those of an equivalent propeller-turbine type over the shorter ranges.

Vickers project design work was consequently concentrated on a development of the 870. Turbojets had been ruled out, as had a swept wing, which had been considered during the 60 or so project studies examined by Vickers; the swept wing would indeed have shown no significant advantages at the estimated 400 mph cruising speed and would have adversely affected the approach speed.

The other matter at issue was the high- or low-wing question. In this the views of the two airlines concerned, BEA and TCA, were somewhat at

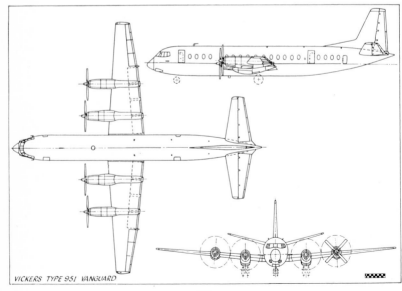

VICKERS TYPE 951 VANGUARD

variance. In their original specification, BEA preferred the high wing because of favourable reaction from passengers to the Ambassador with its unrestricted view from all seats, and the low loading height of the underslung fuselage was also regarded as an asset. TCA, on the other hand, who had taken an interest in the 870 project, cited a number of reasons why a low wing was preferable; the principal ones were that it offered easier refuelling and servicing, and the ability to see the top of the wing from inside the aeroplane during take-off in heavy snow. In addition, the ditching capabilities of low-wing aircraft were known to be superior to those of high-wing types.

Vanguard G-APEB *Bellerophon* of BEA's Vanguard Fleet.

One other factor which mitigated against the choice of the high wing was the difficulty of stowing the undercarriage. Had the inner engine nacelles been utilised for stowage, as in the final form of the design, the hinges of the main legs would have been some 10 ft from the ground and the main undercarriage would have been of greater size and weight than was desirable. Attachment of the main gear directly to the fuselage or to a low stub-wing was considered, but discarded because of the narrow track obtained with this arrangement and the undesirability of attaching the main undercarriage directly to a pressurised fuselage.

The dilemma of the high wing versus low was finally resolved by the need of BEA to carry a high proportion of payload as freight. If this was carried on the same floor as the passenger cabin, an unacceptably long fuselage would be needed. In addition, the tumble-home of the cabin walls in such a configuration would pose problems in providing accommodation of sufficient width. On the other hand, a double-bubble fuselage would provide a considerable depth for low-slung freight holds beneath the passenger cabin and promised an ease of freight loading which could not have been bettered by the high-wing layout.

453

As BEA had specified a working height of between 4 ft and 4 ft 6 in in these freight holds, the more the project design was considered, the more it became clear that the double-bubble was the only possible solution. The final scheme combined with the low wing was also the most attractive structurally.

On 13 April, 1955, the range of design studies had been narrowed down to five, and these were considered at a joint meeting between BEA and Vickers at Weybridge, the airline team being led by Peter Masefield and Beverley Shenstone (then BEA's chief engineer) and the Vickers team by Sir George Edwards and Basil Stephenson (then chief designer). The optimum design showing the greatest capacity, versatility and payload was the double-bubble fuselage with a low wing, and agreement was reached on this point.

The specification of this aeroplane—Type 870 Scheme 16a—included a gross weight of 110,300 lb, a design payload of 20,000 lb, accommodation for 88 passengers and a speed of 420 mph at 25,000 ft. Although BEA had originally required a stage length of 1,000 miles, they were primarily interested in their bread and butter range of 500 miles. Vickers had been stretching the range steadily to meet the requirements of TCA and other potential operators, so that with the integral wing tankage of 5,100 Imp gal, the ultimate range had become 2,600 miles.

The scheme had by this time become the basic Type 900, the BEA version being the 901. As finally agreed, the payload was 21,000 lb, which included accommodation for 93 passengers. The floor area for up to 100 passengers decided the freight volume, so that the latter, with a generous depth of 4 ft 3 in, gave a total capacity of 1,360 cu ft, rather more than the air freight promoters desired at that time but which would be able to meet the expected growth in that sector of air transport.

BEA Vanguard G-APEE *Euryalus* at Punta Raisi airport, Palermo. (*BEA photo.*)

BEA Vanguard landing at Luqa airport, Malta. (*Malta Tourist Board photo*.)

Eventually a gross weight of 135,000 lb was arrived at through the maximum payload/range figure which Vickers thought necessary for world requirements. This involved the acceptance of a small weight penalty by BEA in respect of modified undercarriage and wing structure. Thus the basic type became 950, and the BEA version 951.

At this stage BEA made an announcement regarding the Vanguard, a name selected by them for the Viscount successor, when they spoke of negotiations for a fleet of these aircraft to be in service in 1960 and a contract for 20 was completed on 20 July, 1956. The Vanguard was a private venture; the Government was at no time involved. The name itself was given to G-APEA, flagship of the Vanguard class of the BEA fleet; individual aircraft took the names of famous warships, as detailed in Appendix III.

Thus the initial customer was obtained, with firm intent to press forward with the deal. As a result, the interest previously displayed by TCA intensified, but the basic 950 did not fully meet Canadian requirements. With a full passenger complement and full tanks, the available freight capacity was insufficient. In view of the longer hauls flown by TCA and the Canadian Government requirement to give priority to mail rather than passengers on certain of their routes, a greater payload with the maximum range performance was needed. At the same time the possibility arose of carrying 139 passengers six-abreast in high-density seating, usually referred to as coach-class.

These new considerations led to the Type 952 Vanguard, in which the payload went up to 24,000 lb and, with a strengthened airframe for higher cruising speed at lower altitudes, the gross weight to 141,000 lb. After one of the most exhaustive evaluations ever made by an airline up to that time, not only of the Vanguard but also of other strong contenders, an order for 20 Type 952s was announced by TCA early in January 1957. Later this order became Britain's largest single dollar export order of the post-war period when TCA ordered a further three Vanguard 952s.

455

BEA G-APEA *Vanguard*, flagship of the Vanguard Fleet, emplaning passengers at Nutts Corner, Belfast. (*BEA photo.*)

While this investigation was proceeding between Vickers and the two airlines most intimately concerned with the project, Rolls-Royce, the engine designers, had also been making striking progress with the RB109 propeller-turbine, which had by this time been designated RTy1 Tyne. From the 2,750 shp of the RB109, the RTy1 engine was now required to have an output of at least 4,000 shp, while a power slightly in excess of 4,500 shp was promised for TCA's fleet of Type 952 Vanguards, operating at a higher gross weight. An intensive programme had been undertaken by BEA, in conjunction with Rolls-Royce, in development flying with the Tyne engine in two Airspeed Ambassadors. A total of 1,600 hours was achieved with four individual engines, but most of the work was done by one, which completed over 1,200 hours.

Production was well under way at Weybridge when BEA realised that, were the maximum range not required, they could introduce economy class travel without sacrificing the flexibility of mixed freight and passenger loads originally offered. This suited their operational philosophy then, because the growing threat from pure-jet competitors over the longest European routes caused BEA to consider the introduction of later versions of the Comet.

In consequence, Vickers announced the Type 953 Vanguard on 23 July, 1958, with a 29,000-lb payload at a gross weight of 141,000 lb (the same as TCA's 952 at smaller payload with longer range). The low operating cost appeared so attractive to BEA that they amended their original order to six Type 951s and 14 Type 953s, as production had gone too far to alter the flow of the former type.

First flight of the Vanguard took place on 20 January, 1959, when Bryce

456

took-off from Brooklands' short and then very wet runway, accompanied by Brian Trubshaw as co-pilot. This was the first Type 950 aircraft, built by Vickers for flight test evaluation and registered G-AOYW. The large fin was faired into the top of the fuselage with a small fillet, but later a pronounced dorsal fin was added to check slight rudder hunting at small angles of deflection.

From the design aspect, aerodynamically and structurally, the Vanguard represented orthodox design. Compromise between wing drag and wing loading resulted in an area of 1,527 sq ft with an aspect ratio of nine—at one time, as in the case of the Wellesley, thought to be exceptionally high. The modified NACA 63 aerofoil section was chosen to combine docile stalling with a comparatively high Mach number while keeping the compressibility factor well above the ultimate design cruising speed. The tail unit followed the pattern of the Viscount, with a dihedral angle for the horizontal stabiliser to clear the jet residue efflux and to aid directional and longitudinal stability. The flying controls were designed to be manually operated with aerodynamic balancing. The overall structural concept was based on the fail-safe multi-load-path principles.

The Vanguard fuselage structure closely followed the pattern evolved for the Viking and Viscount, with longitudinal stringers attached to hoop frames with the familiar shear cleat brackets. The skin was flush riveted to the longitudinals. The large elliptical windows were identical to those of the Viscount to equalise the periphery stress on the neutral hole design philosophy mentioned previously.

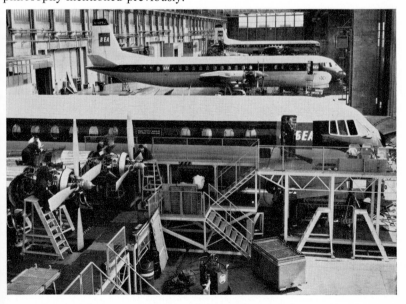

Vanguards under maintenance at the engineering base of BEA at London Airport, Heathrow. (*BEA photo.*)

Only in the wing structure was a departure made from existing practice Skin panels were machined from solid billets of light alloy to incorporate integral spanwise stiffeners, a method promoting strength and reducing manufacturing time and cost. The avoidance of concentrated stress, as represented by the Viscount single-spar wing, was engineered by the introduction of three spanwise shear webs, with the profile of the wing maintained by closely spaced ribs. As those ribs also acted as link members between the integrally machined skins and the webs, the whole structure became a homogeneous torsion box. The whole torsion-box structure, outboard of the centre section, was, in fact, sealed as an integral fuel-tank system.

Other features of note when the Vanguard was designed were the spacious flight deck and the 28-volt DC electrical system, providing a veritable power-station in comparison with electrical systems in earlier aircraft. This became evident with the Vanguard in service, when it was able to rely on its own battery starting power in the absence of starter trolleys on some European airfields.

After the first flight of G-AOYW, which occupied 18 minutes and ended at Wisley flight test centre, there began the programme of initial handling assessment, system checks, tropical performance and route proving. The Vanguard was demonstrated to prospective customers, and G-APEA, the second aircraft, and the first in BEA livery, flew to Hamburg on 6 March 1959, and subsequently to Brussels and Rome.

At the end of June G-APEA was flown to Canada for demonstrations to TCA, the overall time on the return journey being 8 hr 15 min, the Gander-Wisley leg taking only 5 hr 30 min. Later a transatlantic demonstration flight, to Bermuda and Trinidad, was made for the benefit of British West Indian Airways, the only technical hitch being caused by contaminated fuel.

Vanguards in production at Weybridge for Trans-Canada Air Lines (now Air Canada) in 1960.

TCA Vanguard at the Farnborough Air Display of 1960.

A team of training captains from BEA were instructed in the techni-
calities of the aeroplane at Vickers' ground training school at Weybridge,
and on the Tyne engine at Rolls-Royce, Derby. Then, in February 1960,
route-proving started with flights from London to Paris and Brussels.
These proceeded smoothly until the last week of the trials when, on the
Athens route, various troubles ensued which indicated that the aeroplane
could not enter service immediately because the power unit needed further
development. This setback was unfortunate for all concerned, and particularly for BEA, who had banked on the Vanguard going into service at
the start of their peak traffic period on 1 July. The engine problem was
eventually resolved by metallurgical reappraisal of the compressor rotor,
and with the revised engines a 200-hour simulated route-proving exercise
was conducted from Wisley.

G-APEE was allocated for intensive BEA crew training at Stansted on
2 December, and in the Christmas period Vanguards were used to augment
BEA's extra services. Finally, the first Vanguard 951s went into regular
service with BEA on 1 March, 1961, and the first Type 952 with TCA on
1 February, 1961.

Although orders for Vanguards stopped at 43, the type proved to be a
most versatile aeroplane. Its economic advantages were most prominent
on sectors of up to 500 miles, and its use in the coach class with high-
density passenger-seating, was acceptable to the majority of air travellers.
Nowhere has this been more evident than on the Malta run with night
tourist flights consistently carrying full loads of passengers and freight.

The ready acceptance of pure-jet travel by the public and the striking

Vanguard CF-TKA, first of Trans-Canada Air Lines Vanguard fleet.

advance of the turbojet engine in economical cruising fuel consumption, together with the rear-engine configurations since developed (making for quieter cabins), tended in the long run to affect the potentialities of propeller-turbine aircraft such as the Vanguard. The second-generation propeller-turbine aircraft could possibly have been by-passed, but it is easy to be wise after the event. Meanwhile the existing Vanguards proceeded to fly on with their load-lifting duties over long- and short-haul routes, usually with cabins filled to capacity, particularly in the peak holiday season.

In 1966 Air Canada converted one of its Type 952 Vanguards, CF-TKK, to all-freight configuration by removing all passenger accommodation from its cabin and refurbishing it for cargo carriage. In this form the Vanguard freighter, known as the Cargoliner, could carry 42,000 lb of cargo between cities on Air Canada's routes previously served only by the

Vanguard CF-TKP in the livery of Air Canada, introduced in 1964 when Trans-Canada Air Lines changed their name.

fill-up freight capacity of passenger Vanguards and Viscounts. Further developments intended were the incorporation of large freight doors and the installation of rollers in the cabin floor for the loading of standard pallets. It was Air Canada's ultimate intention to convert all their Vanguard fleet to freighters, and BEA have since also decided to convert their fleet of Vanguards to freighters with the marketing name of *Merchantman*.

Vanguard

	Type 951	Type 952	Type 953
Accommodation:	3 crew, 2 stewards, 126 passengers	3 crew, 2 stewards, 139 passengers	3 crew, 2 stewards, 135 passengers
Engines:	Four 4,985 ehp Rolls-Royce Tyne RTy1 Mk 506	Four 5,545 ehp Rolls-Royce Tyne RTy11 Mk 512	Four 4,985 ehp Rolls-Royce Tyne RTy1 Mk 506
Span:	118 ft	118 ft	118 ft
Length:	122 ft 10½ in	122 ft 10½ in	122 ft 10½ in
Height:	34 ft 11 in	34 ft 11 in	34 ft 11 in
Wing Area:	1,527 sq ft	1,527 sq ft	1,527 sq ft
Empty Weight:	84,000 lb	85,000 lb	85,000 lb
Gross Weight:	135,000 lb	141,000 lb	141,000 lb
Max Speed:	400 mph	400 mph	425 mph
Max Range:	—	3,130 miles at 412 mph at 20,000 ft	3,015 miles at 412 mph at 20,000 ft
Range with max payload:	1,550 miles at 380 mph at 21,000 ft	1,830 miles at 412 mph at 20,000 ft	2,070 miles at 412 mph at 20,000 ft

The VC10

When the first VC10 took-off from Brooklands on 29 June, 1962, Vickers had already completed half a century of aviation history. All the knowledge and experience that had been accumulated over the years, often through sweat and tears, had been built into this big jet, latest of the long-range subsonic airliners. The VC10 embodied all the aerodynamic and engineering sophistication that had advanced aeronautics to the threshold of knowledge at the time of its design. Further progress would project air transport into the supersonic band of speed. But the task of evolving the new race of airliners flying beyond the speed of sound was to fall to a new and larger organisation, in fact an international consortium. It would draw inspiration from the impressive record of achievement represented by the names of its constituent aircraft constructors. One such name was Vickers.

Since the end of the second world war Vickers had led the way, with the Viscount in gas-turbine power for civil aircraft, as has been recorded in these pages, and had produced the first British four-jet bomber, the Valiant. Despite these achievements, they had been profoundly disappointed when their Type 1000, generally known as the V1000, was cancelled in 1955. This concept was primarily a development of the Valiant design, and there were to be parallel military and civil transport versions,

Vickers V1000 in advanced stage of construction in 1955 at Wisley.

In the civil sector the ambition was to compete for the lucrative North Atlantic traffic. Subsequent events have proved that this was an aspiration which, had it been accomplished, might have placed British civil aviation in an advantageous position internationally. The V1000 was scheduled to fly in the early months of 1956, and the prototype had reached an advanced stage of construction when the whole project was cancelled by the Ministry of Supply as the Government agency and as the chief guarantors of the scheme.

Although it failed to materialise, the Type 1000 did play a significant part in moulding the approach to later projects. In detail design it contained features later incorporated and developed in the VC10. These in-

First VC10 approaching completion in 1962 at Weybridge in 'Cathedral' flight hangar, specially built for VC10 assembly.

462

cluded integrally machined wing members with supporting fuselage hoop-frames, a variable-incidence tailplane, power-operated flying-control surfaces (divided into segments for fail-safe reasons and moved through electro-hydraulic units) and a split AC electrical system.

One of the first design objectives of the Type 1000 was short airfield performance to meet the requirements of RAF Transport Command with its world-wide operation. An almost identical requirement was specified by the British Overseas Airways Corporation when it ordered the VC10 for its Empire air routes. The Type 1000 also pioneered the cabin width for six-abreast passenger seating.

G-ARTA, first VC10, lifting off Brooklands runway on 29 June, 1962, for its first flight. (*Photo D. Wanstell.*)

Between the time which had elapsed when the Type 1000 was abandoned and the VC10 became a definite project in 1957, the Vanguard had been developed, with the integral machining technique exploited throughout its wing. Other important engineering improvements had also been introduced, resulting from operational experience and testing of the Viscount.

Having successfully introduced the Vanguard, Vickers started a project study on a jet Viscount replacement in May 1956. The first approach was based on the philosophy of producing a cheap pure-jet transport, with a first cost of £750,000. This resulted in a concept using four Rolls-Royce Nenes mounted in pairs under a Vanguard-type wing. Little progress was possible with this specific objective because of the lack of a really suitable engine.

During further studies Vickers became interested in the rear-engine configuration, for it became clear that with thinner wings and the larger diameter of the emerging family of turbo-fan engines, the buried-engine layout as chosen for the Valiant and Type 1000 would be incompatible. Rear-mounted engines, first used in civil aircraft for the Sud-Aviation Caravelle, had been selected by Vickers in 1951 for a military project known as the SP2 short-range expendable bomber, in which the engines were to

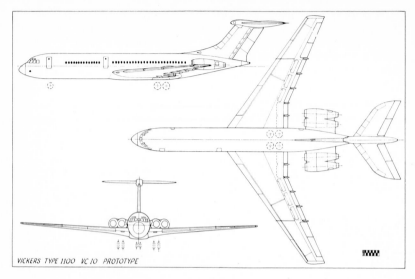

VICKERS TYPE 1100 VC 10 PROTOTYPE

be mounted on the tips of the aft-disposed fins. It is of interest to recall that in 1942 the early Whittle jet engine had been mounted in the rear end of the fuselage of the Wellington flying test-bed.

During the following few months Vickers' intensive project studies grew into a larger aeroplane for short-to-medium-range operation. The resulting design became known as the Vanjet, as it was based on a Vanguard fuselage with three rear-mounted engines. It was to meet the prevailing BEA requirement and was the first of a series of such projects from competing manufacturers. Variations of this Vanjet theme were evaluated which used adaptations of the wing forms of Vickers contemporary high-speed military aircraft, the Valiant bomber and the Supermarine Scimitar naval fighter. During this work a comparative study was made using four jet engines mounted in pods under the wings as in American practice—the proposed engines were to be Bristol BE47s of equivalent thrust to the three Rolls-Royce Avons in the rear-engined layout.

By October 1956 the last-named configuration, by then based on three Rolls-Royce Conway by-pass jets, was clearly superior in meeting an emerging BOAC requirement, which had become the primary objective of the project work after a short spell of trying to meet the requirements of both BEA and BOAC in a single design. During the detailed investigation which followed, it was apparent that the rear-engined configuration provided the good airfield performance so essential in complying with the BOAC route conditions. The growth in size of the aeroplane, now based on four rear-mounted Conways instead of three, had meant that the airfield performance was of over-riding importance, and the uncluttered wing became a vital part in achieving this primary design objective. Better aerodynamic characteristics of the clean wing were obtained with this

464

arrangement, although the rear-engine layout was accompanied by a higher basic weight.

Therefore, the advantages claimed for rear-mounted engines could be outlined as follows: improved airfield performance, giving higher payload and better economy; greater flexibility of operation for an airline like BOAC, with its world-wide network embracing every kind of operational problem; lower approach speeds and improved control characteristics; and last, but not least, a new standard of passenger comfort derived from the drastic reduction of cabin noise level and vibration. Other gains which accrued from this installation were: reduced fire hazards in a crash landing because the engines were well isolated from the fuel tanks; excellent ditching characteristics; structure surfaces less likely to incur fatigue failure from the effects of jet efflux; and a reduced risk of damage to engines by runway debris.

VC10 fuselage side structure incorporating large machined panel with integral window and escape exit apertures.

In March 1957 BOAC issued a specification outlining requirements for an aeroplane to operate on routes to Africa and Australia, carrying a pay-load of about 35,000 lb nearly 4,000 miles in still air. From that time on the design was tailored to BOAC's requirements alone. The airfields on their routes included some of the most exacting in the world, combining high temperature with high altitude and relatively short runways. Their notoriety in this respect was the reason for the flying-boat operations over many of the overseas routes of Imperial Airways in the inter-war years, and the severity of African conditions had been exposed by those pioneering flights of the Vimys in 1920. The critical factors in designing for these

465

G-ARTA during a test flight in original configuration.

conditions were the airfields of Kano, Nairobi and Johannesburg and the routes from Singapore to Karachi (2,600 n miles) and from Kano to London (2,514 n miles).

By April 1957 the design had developed into an aeroplane with a wing area of 2,600 sq ft. In May BOAC signed a letter of intent for 35 aircraft with an option on a further 20, an undertaking considered to be the minimum order needed before proceeding with the project. By then it had become known as the VC10, following the series of post-war civil designations instituted by Vickers with the VC1 Viking. No name was given to the VC10, thus putting an end to a practice that had existed since the official introduction of aircraft nomenclature in 1918.

At this stage the aeroplane was powered by four Rolls-Royce RCo10 Conway engines of 16,500 lb thrust each, had a wing area of 2,700 sq ft, maximum take-off weight of 247,000 lb and maximum payload 38,000 lb. The fuel capacity was 120,000 lb, although only 107,000 lb was needed for the most severe route. Later, when the fuselage cross-section was increased to provide six-abreast seating (as first planned for the Type 1000), the take-off weight was increased to 260,000 lb.

From this specification it was realised that comparatively small changes

VC10 G-ASIW of British United Airways with first large freight door.

G-ARVB over Johannesburg during tropicalisation trials in Africa, showing beaver-tail inter-nacelle fairings, one of the modifications made from G-ARTA.

would be required to give the VC10 transatlantic capability. These changes were incorporated in the design during 1957, and they consisted of increasing the sweepback of the wings from 31 to 32·5 degrees, and an increase in the wing area to 2,800 sq ft and in the wing span to 140 ft, with a resulting increase of 16,000 lb in fuel capacity. For transatlantic operation the gross weight was increased to 299,000 lb, and at this stage the design was based on Conway RCo15 engines rated at 18,500 lb thrust each, which additional power largely offset the effect of the increased weight as regards airfield performance, and, in any case, lengthened runways were becoming available at the major Atlantic terminals. On BOAC's other routes the airfield performance remained unimpaired and the aircraft-mile costs showed only a slight increase over the original version without transatlantic capability.

Although the VC10 was therefore not designed specifically for trans-

VC10 9G-ABO, first for Ghana Airways.

467

Underneath view of a VC10, disclosing flap, undercarriage, rear engine mounting and other details.

atlantic operation, it could now function economically throughout the whole route network of BOAC, and it was on this basis that the airline signed the contract for 35 VC10s on 14 January, 1958, with an option to buy another 20. In March 1960 the specification of the VC10 differed from the requirements of the contract in only one major feature, the engines were changed from the Conway RCo15s to RCo42/1s of 21,000 lb thrust each.

BOAC VC10 G-ARVM taking off at Brooklands for Wisley flight-test airfield; the B.1 and 'Cathedral' buildings in the background cover the site of the old sewage farm of immortal memory.

By the end of the flight development period and at the introduction into service in April 1964, the main particulars were a maximum take-off weight of 312,000 lb; maximum landing weight of 212,000 lb; maximum zero fuel weight of 187,400 lb; and a gross wing area of 2,932 sq ft, which included a leading-edge extension and other modifications resulting from flight development.

The clean wing was the key to the achievement of the high speed and exceptional airfield performance of the VC10. The geometry of this wing and its aerodynamic characteristics, including its aerofoil section, were determined in conjunction with the National Physical Laboratory and the RAE. The common aim was to achieve a competitive high subsonic cruising speed with good long-range cruising economy. These deliberations resulted in the use of a negative camber at the wing roots, changing to a progressively more positive camber at the tips through four changes across the span.

A BOAC VC10 being prepared for a scheduled flight at London Airport, Heathrow —a typical night scene.

To reap the greatest benefit from the clean wing at low speeds, high-lift devices were introduced which resulted in approach and landing speeds and take-off and landing distances comparable with those of propeller-driven transports, and in superb handling near the ground. The highly effective leading-edge slats stretched from just outboard of the wing roots to the tips. Fowler trailing-edge flaps, stretching outboard from the fuselage sides to 65 per cent of the span, were chosen in preference to the double-slotted type because of the superior take-off performance they provided.

The optimum tailplane position had to be decided once the rear-engine, clean-wing layout, had been chosen. Wind-tunnel tests showed that only the highest and lowest positions would avoid the unfavourable effects of the wake over the wings at the operating range of incidence. As the lowest position was well below the fuselage, the obvious place was at the top of the tall fin. This setting had the additional advantage of giving a maximum tail arm with minimum tailplane area and drag and also increased the efficiency of the fin by providing a strong end-plate effect. Both fin and tailplane had

BOAC captains on the flight deck during a proving flight of the VC10.
(*Aeroplane photo.*)

more sweep than the wing to ensure that the control characteristics did not deteriorate at a lower Mach number than those of the wing.

Although the aerodynamic noise generated by the speed of the VC10 did not differ significantly from that of similar aircraft, the rear-engined layout conferred great benefits to passengers. The advance in cabin environment and comfort was as significant as that provided by the turbine-powered Viscount when it entered service in 1953.

In the VC10, Vickers greatly developed the integral structural machining technique as first exploited in the wing panels of the Vanguard, with sculpture milling for other members. The fuselage hoop-frames and inner-

Take-off of first Super VC10, G-ASGA, from Brooklands on 7 May, 1965.
(*Photo D. Wanstell.*)

wing members, as first introduced in the Type 1000, were repeated in the VC10, and the window and door side panels of the fuselage, as well as the skin panels of the tail surfaces, were also integrally machined. Steel beams of spectacle form, machined from forgings and linked across by steel tie beams, supported the engines on each side of the rear fuselage. The four-wheel bogie-type main undercarriage was designed by Vickers, the main supporting legs being machined from massive steel forgings.

Fuel was carried in the whole interior of the wing torque-box, including the centre section of the under fuselage. The fuselage shell was typical of Vickers' post-war structural philosophy, as first evolved for the Viking and developed through the later aircraft.

Super VC10 at Farnborough Air Show 1964.

In October 1960 the first centre-section torque-box was removed from its jig and the first fuselage left its assembly jig in May 1961. The completed VC10, registered G-ARTA, was rolled out at Brooklands on 15 April, 1962, and after a period of ground testing, which included extensive systems checks, resonance tests and engine running, the first flight was made from there on 29 June, 1962. The pilot was Jock Bryce, with Brian Trubshaw as co-pilot and Bill Cairns, a Vickers pilot, acting as flight engineer. Three flight-test observers completed the crew, and after a short flight the aeroplane was delivered to Wisley for the extensive flight-development testing which followed.

While the benefits in take-off and landing performance promised by the clean wing of the VC10 soon became apparent, it also became clear from early flight tests that the cruising performance was not up to specification. This deficiency was discovered sufficiently early for compensating modifications to be made to satisfy the performance guarantee without delaying the completion of the overall acceptance of the aeroplane. In fact, only in this part of the programme were any significant changes made to the

Q   471

First Super VC10, G-ASGA, with spare engine pod, at Wisley.

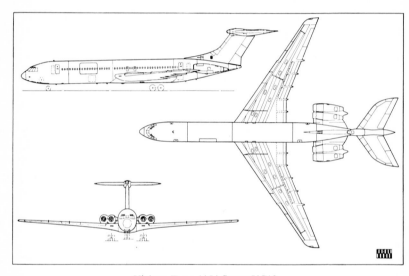

Vickers Type 1154 Super VC10.

G-ASGG Super VC10 landing at Wisley during autoland development trials.

472

VC10. One of these consisted of extending the chord of the leading-edge slats by 4 per cent and slightly drooping their nose. Another improvement was in the addition of Küchemann wing tips, a familiar method of increasing the aspect ratio and hence reducing the drag due to lift. On the RAF VC10s and on the Super VC10, the engine nacelles were given three degrees of incidence and their stand-off distance from the rear fuselage was increased by 11 in. On all VC10s a beaver-tail fairing was added betweeen the inboard and outboard nacelles. The common effect of all these modifications in the wing and around the tail of the VC10 was to minimise the drag and increase the range of the aeroplane. The inter-nacelle fairings also overcame the buffet onset in that area which had appeared with the original design.

Super VC10 5X-UVA in East African Airways resplendent livery.

The VC10 received its certificate of airworthiness on 23 April, 1964, and BOAC introduced it on regular passenger service on 29 April on their route from London to Lagos. It then began to take over the services to other parts of Africa and to the Middle and Far East.

The first major development of the standard VC10 was the Super VC10. This was developed to meet the need of BOAC to provide greater capacity and lower seat-mile costs, particularly on the North Atlantic routes, by making use of the longer runways which existed at the major airports, thereby permitting higher take-off weights than those of the basic aeroplane. A further development of the Conway, the RCo43, increased the thrust available from each engine to 22,500 lb, and these were installed in the Super VC10, in which the fuel capacity was increased to 154,000 lb by adding an integral tank in the fin torque box. The fuselage was lengthened by 13 ft to increase the economy-class passenger capacity from 135 to 163. BOAC introduced the Super VC10 on the London–New York route on 1 April, 1965.

In June 1960 British United Airways, who had ordered two VC10s, specified that they should have large side-loading freight doors in the forward fuselage for convertible passenger/freight operation, thus showing

Take-off of XR808 from Brooklands, one of the 14 VC10s ordered in 1961 and 1962 for the Royal Air Force.

commendable foresight, for their lead was followed by Ghana Airways for one of its two standard VC10s, by RAF Transport Command when it came to order 11 and by East African Airways for its three Super VC10s.

A feature of VC10 operation has been the leasing of some by airlines with a shortage of capacity from airlines with a surplus capacity. Nigeria Airways and Air Ceylon have leased VC10s from BOAC, and Middle East Airlines have leased one from Ghana Airways and one from Laker Airways. The latter aeroplane was formerly G-ARTA, the first VC10 made and subsequently rebuilt at Weybridge for Laker Airways.

The first order for the RAF VC10s was placed in September 1961 for five, and this was increased to 11 in August 1962, all to be of the basic standard with military modifications. Specification C239 was issued in 1960 by the Ministry of Aviation around the civil VC10 as a strategic jet transport to meet an Air Staff requirement. In July 1964 three Super VC10 positions reserved for BOAC were made over by Government action to RAF Transport Command, but to the same specification as the other 11 aircraft. All 14 RAF VC10s were therefore to the same standard.

This standard called for world-wide operation as troop transport, freighter and for aero-medical evacuation; flight-refuelling facility was also required. All the equipment necessary for these various duties had to be capable of easy installation and removal. Despite these particular requirements, the whole RAF VC10 programme was very similar to that for a commercial operator. With a standard VC10 fuselage, the RAF version, known as the VC10 C.Mk 1, had the more powerful Conway 43 engines and the extra fuel capacity as provided in the fin of the Super VC10. The side-loading freight doors of BUA-type were also incorporated, and certain local structural strengthening was included throughout the airframe to achieve the required design weights, maximum take-off weight being increased to 323,000 lb.

In the military transport rôle the RAF VC10, with rearward-facing seats, carries up to 150 troops and their equipment some 4,000 miles non-stop. As the intention was to use the type for carrying Service men's families as well, the cabin was designed to airline standards, including fittings and furnishings, except where lashing points for freighting were located. As a freighter the RAF VC10 could carry a service load of 59,000

474

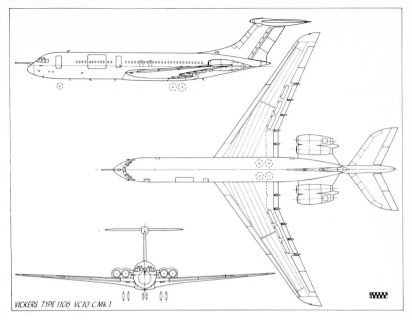

VICKERS TYPE 1106 VC10 C.Mk.1

lb in a total freight volume of 7,032 cu ft. In the casualty-evacuation rôle up to 78 stretcher cases could be accommodated, with six medical attendants, two quartermasters and medical kit.

A smaller edition of the VC10, the VC11, of similar four rear-jet configuration, was planned as a Vanguard replacement for medium-range operation, and this type attracted the interest of certain airlines, but with the formation in February 1960 of the British Aircraft Corporation, which absorbed Vickers' interests in aircraft, this project was superseded by the BAC One-Eleven, which again followed the rear-engine concept. Thus the VC10 became the last aeroplane designed and constructed solely by Vickers.

VC10

	Type 1101 Standard VC10	Type 1151 Super VC10	Type 1106 RAF VC10 C.Mk 1
Accommodation:	5 crew, 5 stewards, 115 mixed class passengers or 135 economy class	5 crew, 7 stewards, 139 mixed class passengers or 163 economy class	5 crew, 150 troops or up to 78 stretcher cases
Engines:	Four 21,000 lb s.t. Rolls-Royce Conway RCo42	Four 22,500 lb s.t. Rolls-Royce Conway RCo43	Four 22,500 lb s.t. Rolls-Royce Conway RCo43
Span:	146 ft 2 in	146 ft 2 in	146 ft 2 in
Length:	158 ft 8 in	171 ft 8 in	158 ft 8 in
Height:	39 ft 6 in	39 ft 6 in	39 ft 6 in
Wing Area:	2,932 sq ft	2,932 sq ft	2,932 sq ft
Empty Weight:	139,505 lb	146,962 lb	142,220 lb
Gross Weight:	312,000 lb	335,000 lb	322,000 lb
Max Cruising Speed:	580 mph	580 mph	580 mph
Service Ceiling:	38,000 ft	38,000 ft	38,000 ft
Max Range:	5,850 n. miles	5,960 n. miles	6,260 n. miles

Miscellany

To complete the history of Vickers aircraft, mention must be made of four types which do not fit into any particular design pattern. These were the VIM training aeroplane of 1919, the Valentia flying-boat of 1922 and the Viget and Vagabond light aeroplanes of 1923 and 1924 respectively.

A batch of 35 VIM (Vickers Instructional Machine) trainers was ordered by the Chinese Government in 1919 from Vickers together with 40 Vimy Commercials and 20 reconditioned Avro 504Ks. The aim was to establish a civil aviation complex in China, but results fell far short of expectations, probably because of Chinese political instability.

The VIM was built from surplus F.E.2d components with a completely redesigned nacelle, seating the pupil in front of the instructor with dual control. Fitted with a surplus Rolls-Royce Eagle VIII engine purchased from the Aircraft Disposal Co, the VIM was a good bargain as an advanced trainer to follow the *ab initio* 504Ks and to familiarise ground and air crews with the Eagle engine as installed in the Vimy Commercials.

The Valentia flying-boat was intended as a replacement for the Porte-Felixstowe F.5, which had not shown the desired advance on the earlier

VIM trainer supplied to China in 1920 was a rebuilt F.E.2d with Eagle VIII engine and redesigned dual-control nacelle.

476

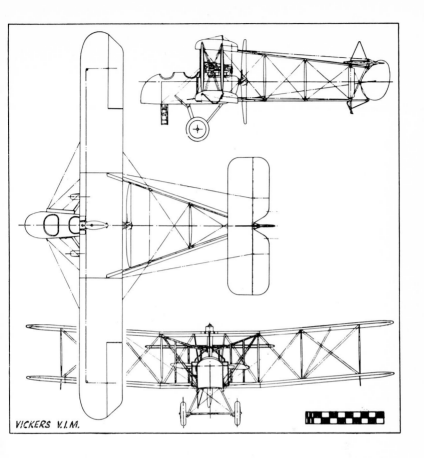

VICKERS V.I.M.

Felixstowe F.3. The Phoenix P.5 Cork was another flying-boat built as an
F.5 replacement, but neither it nor the Valentia was adopted because of
the numbers of F.3s and F.5s in service and on grounds of national
economy.

In May 1918 the Air Board placed a contract with Vickers for three
flying-boats, to be built at Barrow, based on F.5 configuration but with
slab sides for the hull in place of the Linton-Hope sponsons. Some design
work was also done on the wing structure at Weybridge with the familiar
Pierson-type biplane tail. By that time Vickers had acquired S. E. Saunders
and Co of Cowes, Isle of Wight, and the design and construction of one
prototype was completed by the subsidiary. S. E. Saunders had considerable
experience of building marine craft and aircraft and had developed a
stronger and more durable form of plywood known as Consuta, the main
feature of which was its copper wire reinforcement sewn longitudinally
through the plys. The material was particularly suitable for skinning
flying-boat hulls and was first used for this purpose in the Valentia, which

477

Valentia flying-boat, with Vickers superstructure and Saunders hull, moored at Cowes; Vickers bought a controlling interest in S. E. Saunders and Co in 1918, but sold out in 1921, the concern eventually becoming Saunders-Roe Ltd.

underwent flying and seaworthiness trials in the Solent by Stan Cockerell in 1921, the engines were Condors and serial No. was N126.

Following the qualified success of the *Daily Mail* Gliding Competition at Itford Hill, Sussex, in 1922, another competition was held during October 1923, at Lympne aerodrome in Kent for what were termed 'motor gliders', that is, light aeroplanes with low-powered engines. These little power units were selected for economy of operation and to give the machines enough thrust to maintain them in flight or promote a modest rate of climb. Vickers entered a small biplane called the Viget designed by R. K. Pierson. It was of conventional construction and flew quite well in the

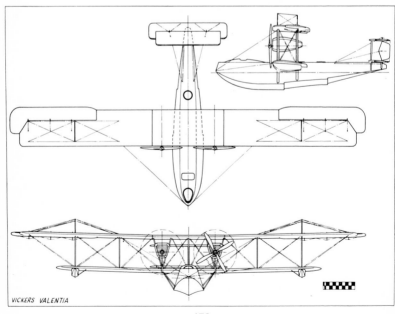

VICKERS VALENTIA

478

Vickers Viget Type 89 G-EBHN single-seat entry for 1923 Lympne light aeroplane
competitions, with 750 cc Douglas flat-twin engine.

hands of Cockerell. Various prizes were offered for greatest aggregate
mileage, lowest specific fuel consumption and so on, but the Viget, while
failing to appear among the winners, probably achieved the greatest
notoriety of all the competitors.

A 750 cc Douglas motor cycle engine provided the power for the Viget,

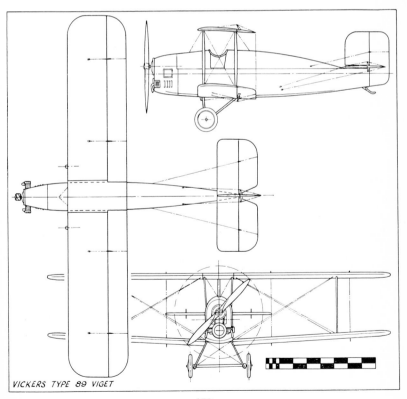

VICKERS TYPE 89 VIGET

Vickers Vagabond Type 98 G-EBJF two-seat entry for the 1924 light aeroplane
competitions at Lympne, with 1,095 cc Blackburne 3-cylinder engine.

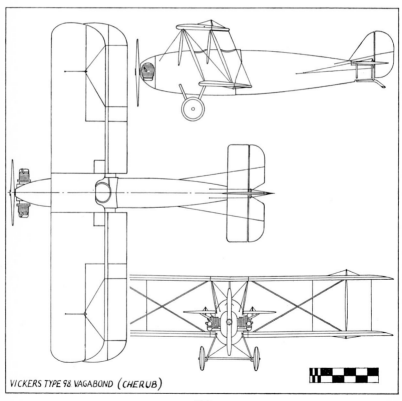

VICKERS TYPE 98 VAGABOND (CHERUB)

and on one flight a rocker arm broke. Cockerell made a successful forced landing at Brabourne about six miles from Lympne aerodrome. The aeroplane had folding wings so Cockerell folded them and proceeded to push it along the road back to base, stopping *en route* for suitable refreshment. *The Aeroplane* reported that on coming out of the pub he was asked by people waiting outside when the next performance was going to start, under the mistaken impression that the folded Viget was a travelling Punch and Judy show.

Such was the success of the Itford Hill and Lympne competitions that in 1924 the Air Ministry decided to organise one for two-seat light aeroplanes in order to foster private flying and encourage the formation of flying clubs, with some State assistance. Official and private money prizes were offered.

The 1924 Competition was held at Lympne from 29 September to 4 October. Vickers entered a design called the Vagabond, larger and heavier than the Viget and powered with a Bristol Cherub. Like the Viget, the Vagabond had folding wings with hinged flaps inboard of the ailerons to facilitate the folding operation. The tail trimming was novel, for the rear fuselage was hinged behind the rear cockpit and wing incidence was controlled by a handwheel between the two cockpits to increase drag on landing, by winding the tail fully up.

In the competition, the Vagabond was flown by H. J. Payn, who as mentioned on other pages, was technical assistant to R. K. Pierson, the designer, and acted from time to time as a Vickers test pilot. Although Vickers entry flew well after some attention to the rigidity of the engine mounting, it was eliminated in the preliminary trials.

VIM—One 360 hp Rolls-Royce Eagle VIII. Span 47 ft 8 in; length 32 ft 4 in. Empty weight 2,950 lb; loaded weight 3,645 lb. Max speed 100 mph.
Valentia—Two 650 hp Rolls-Royce Condor. Span 112 ft; length 58 ft. Empty weight 10,000 lb; loaded weight 21,300 lb. Max speed 105 mph.
Viget—One 750 cc Douglas. Span 25 ft; length 17 ft 4 in; wing area 200 sq ft. Empty weight 390 lb; loaded weight 570 lb. Max speed 58·1 mph.
Vagabond—One 32 hp Bristol Cherub. Span 28 ft; length 21 ft 10 in; wing area 235 sq ft. Empty weight 527 lb; loaded weight 887 lb. Max speed 77 mph.

Some Vickers Design Projects

One of the more interesting features of aircraft design is the large number of projects that were schemed but never became airborne. Only a few of Vickers ideas for new types can be outlined here, but they will serve to indicate a wide range of ingenuity. Some of these projects were proposed developments of existing types like the improved S.E.5a. Some were scaled-up versions of successful types to meet greater operational demands like the enlarged Vimy DoR Type 4. In many cases alternative schemes were submitted on paper in tenders to official specifications; an example was the B.19/27 monoplane.

Some projects even reached the prototype stage and were partly built. Of those selected for illustration here, the F.T.2 triplane of 1916 was abandoned because of engineering difficulties with the engine installation and propeller-drive gearing. The giant Vigilant flying-boat of 1920 and the V1000 of 1955 were both cancelled by H.M. Government when in sight of a breakthrough for British civil aviation. There were others.

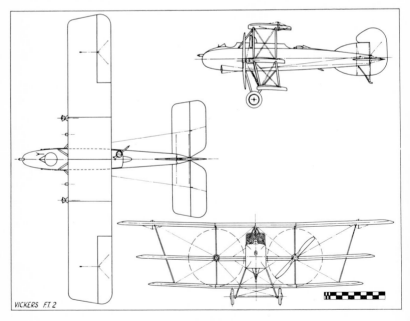

VICKERS F.T.2

F.T.2 fighter-bomber of 1916 with two coupled Lorraines in the fuselage driving opposite handed propellers through shafts and bevel gears.

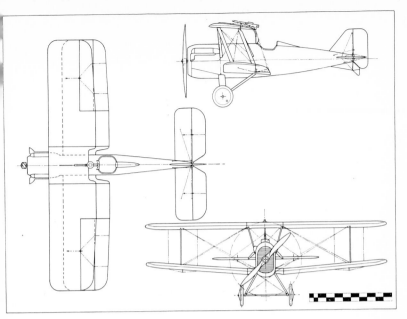

Vickers S.E.5a development of 1921 with Wolseley Viper, Vixen-type radiator, oleo undercarriage and dihedral on bottom wing only.

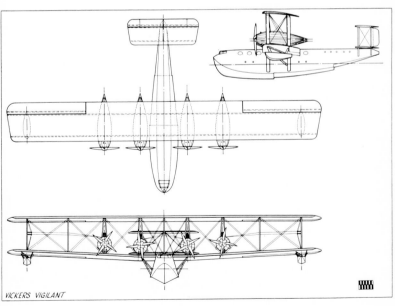

VICKERS VIGILANT

Vigilant flying-boat of 1920 with eight coupled R-R Condors. Span 220 ft; max weight 49 tons; max range 2,000 miles; structure: all duralumin.

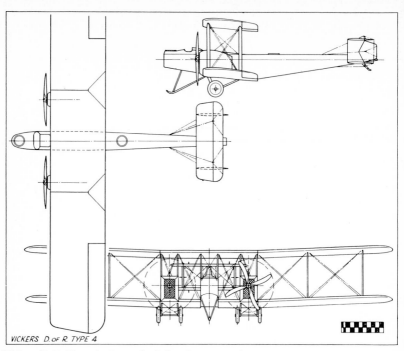

Vickers DoR Type 4—first submission for Long Distance Bombing Aeroplane (A) in 1920 as enlarged Vimy with Napier Lions.

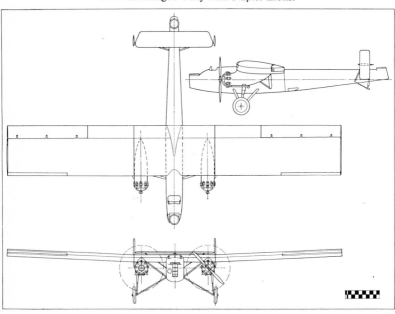

B.19/27 monoplane of 1928 with Jupiter VIIIs submitted as alternative design for Virginia replacement competition; span 100 ft.

484

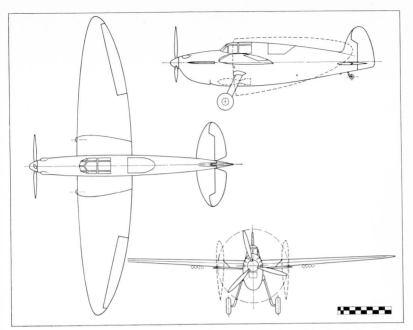

Type 280 O.27/34 of 1936 with R-R Merlin I—dive-bomber with alternative carrier operation capability—comparable to Junkers-Ju-87 Stuka.

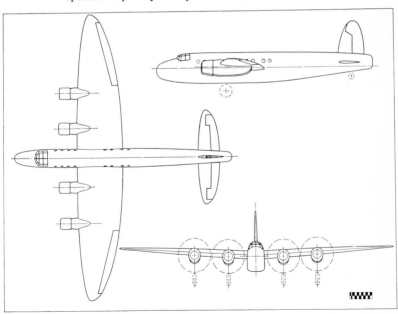

B.12/36 submission for heavy-bomber with four Taurus and geodetic structure.

485

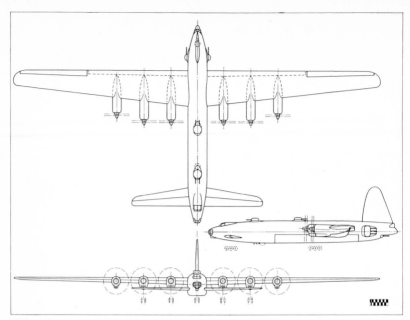

1942 design study for very large bomber of canard (tail-first) configuration with six turbo-supercharged Centaurus; max weight 178,000 lb.

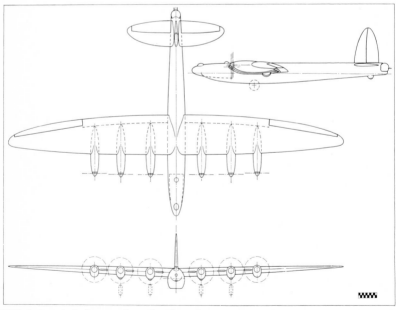

1942 design study for very large bomber of conventional configuration with six turbo-supercharged Centaurus; max weight 168,000 lb.

486

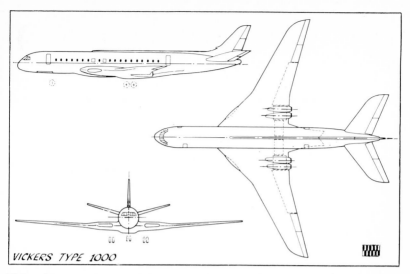

VICKERS TYPE 1000

Vickers Type 1000 was designed to specification C132 for a long-range military jet transport with four Rolls-Royce Conway bypass engines. A parallel requirement for BOAC (VC7) existing at the time of design was not pursued nor was the original order for six military V1000s. It had a strong family resemblance to the smaller Valiant bomber. Its gross weight was estimated at 225,000 lb.

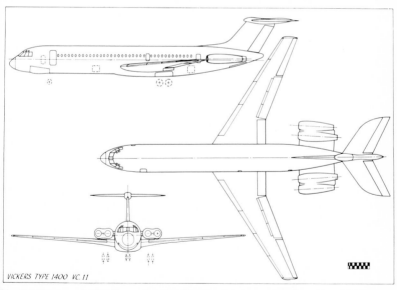

VICKERS TYPE 1400 VC.11

The VC11 was a design for a short/medium-haul jet transport for the mid-1960s. It was to have had a capacity of up to 138 passengers. Its configuration was similar to that of the VC10, and its maximum gross weight was 170,000 lb. The design payload was 28,500 lb, and its power was four Rolls-Royce RB163 (Speys). The high cruising speed was 600 mph and maximum range was 2,000 miles.

487

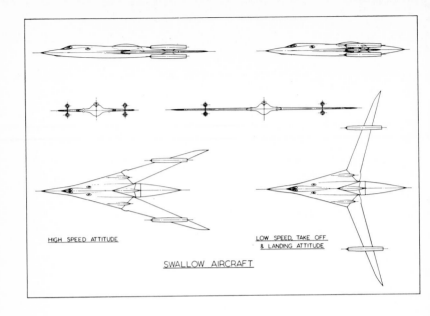

HIGH SPEED ATTITUDE

LOW SPEED, TAKE OFF
& LANDING ATTITUDE

SWALLOW AIRCRAFT

Much of the earlier work in original design of B. N. Wallis has been covered in these pages. At the time when the Wellington with its Wallis geodetic structure was the spearhead of Bomber Command of the Royal Air Force in the first years of the second World War, Wallis was devising novel means of attacking the Axis powers. Harnessing his considerable knowledge of aerodynamic streamlining to ballistic problems, he produced the 12,000 lb Tallboy and the 10-ton Grand Slam bombs with enormous explosive power allied to a positive penetrative force achieved by a terminal velocity of 3,600 ft per sec. The successful attack on the Mohne and Eder reservoir dams in the Ruhr basin by 617 Squadron, RAF, with the Wallis spinning bombs in May, 1943, has been recorded in the history books as a decisive action.

Towards the end of the War, Wallis turned his attention to variable geometry as a means of achieving supersonic flight at the most economical cost in fuel, thereby attaining the greatest possible range. Practical confirmation of his theories was obtained by flying large models of tail-less aeroplanes with variable sweep wings of vee planform. These concepts were known as the Wild Goose and the Swallow, and the experiments, which used radio control, were carried out in secret from Predannack airfield in Cornwall. Wallis used a slender delta wing with every part behind the high density air of the Mach cone and cut away the back to eliminate unwanted drag. He envisaged an airliner of this type flying non-stop from Europe to Australia with a return journey time of 10 hours.

488

Canadian Vickers Aircraft

Canadian Vickers was a subsidiary of Vickers established in 1911 at Montreal as a general engineering and shipbuilding enterprise. In 1922 an aircraft division was formed which successfully tendered to supply the Canadian Air Force with its first native aircraft, eight Viking amphibians, two built at Weybridge and six in Montreal. As a result of Canadian experience with the Laurentide Air Services Viking amphibian, a smaller aeroplane was proposed to suit the special conditions encountered in forestry patrol and in photographic missions for air survey; air reconnaissance being ideal for the rapid spotting and fighting of forest fires. A quick take-off and better climb were needed while providing accommodation for three people.

The result of these deliberations was the design and construction of a small flying-boat known as the Vedette. Its design was started at Weybridge and completed at Montreal by W. T. Reid, who had been appointed by Canadian Vickers as chief designer, having previously held that position

Viking IV Type 85—first complete aeroplane built at the St Hubert works of Canadian Vickers, with staff of aviation division; six Vikings were made there for the Canadian Air Force (later RCAF).

Vedette Mk I in 1925 with Wright Whirlwind J4 engine and production-type balanced ailerons; span 42 ft, length 32 ft 10 in, loaded weight, 3,155 lb, max speed 98 mph, initial climb 650 ft/min, duration 5 hr, crew 3; 61 Vedettes built in all Marks.

for a short while with the British and Colonial Aeroplane Co of Bristol. The first flight of the Vedette was made, with a Rolls-Royce Falcon III as engine, by Flg Off W. N. Plenderleith on 4 November, 1924. Of Weybridge flight test staff, he was the pilot of the round-the-world attempt by Mac-laren, as described elsewhere in this book. The Vedette proved a successful type, and 61 were made, through several variants. Some remained in service until the second world war.

Following the Vedette, Canadian Vickers designed and built other types, and these are recorded pictorially, following this brief history. Leading particulars are appended as compiled with the help of K. M. Molson, Curator of the National Aviation Musuem, Ottawa.

During its subsequent history, Canadian Vickers built under licence Fairchild, Fokker and Northrop aircraft. In the second world war it or its associates produced Hampden fuselages for the British Government, 40 Vickers-Supermarine Stranraer flying-boats for the RCAF, over 300

Vedette Mk V amphibian with undercarriage of Viking type, and Wright Whirlwind J5 engine; G-CAUU was the first of six supplied to Chile. (*RCAF photo*.)

490

Vedette Mk VI with Wright Whirlwind J6 engine, Handley Page slots and metal hull; span 42 ft 2¾ in, length 35 ft 2 in, loaded weight, 4,000 lb, max speed 111 mph, initial climb 680 ft/min, duration 5 hr, crew 3; one built. (*National Aviation Museum photo*.)

Catalinas and Cansos and 600 PBY hulls. Two Stranraers survived the war in civil air transport with Queen Charlotte Airlines (later Pacific Western Airlines) of Vancouver. In 1941 Canadian Vickers took over Canadian Associated Aircraft, and in 1942 it transferred its aircraft activities to a Government factory at Cartierville. In 1944 the aircraft division of Canadian Vickers was transferred to a Crown company known as Canadair Ltd, which itself became a subsidiary of the Electric Boat Co of New London, now the General Dynamics Corporation.

Varuna Mk I twin-engined flying-boat of 1927 with Wright Whirlwind J6 engines; data for Varuna Mk II with Armstrong Siddeley Lynx engines—span overall 55 ft 2½ in, length 38 ft 3 in, loaded weight 5,299 lb, max speed 94 mph, initial climb 600 ft/min, duration 5 hr, crew 3; eight Varunas built

Vista single-seat flying-boat of 1927 with Armstrong Siddeley Genet engine; span 29 ft 6 in, length 23 ft 9 in, loaded weight 1,005 lb, max speed 90 mph, initial climb 650 ft/min, duration 4½ hr; one built. (*National Aviation Museum photo.*)

Vanessa floatplane of 1927 with Wright J5 engine; span 35 ft 3 in, length 30 ft, loaded weight 3,400 lb, max speed 103 mph, climb 550 ft/min, duration 4½ hr, one crew with up to four passengers; one built. (*National Aviation Museum photo.*)

Velos floatplane intended for air survey, with two Pratt & Whitney Wasp engines; span overall 68 ft, length 44 ft, loaded weight 7,918 lb, speed attained 85 mph, initial climb 250 ft/min; one built—trials abandoned; also in picture Fokker Universal and Fokker Super Universal. (*RCAF photo.*)

Vigil single-seat sesquiplane of 1928 with Armstrong Siddeley Lynx; span overall 35 ft 3 in, length (on wheels) 27 ft, loaded weight 2,250 lb, max speed (estimated) 110 mph; one built. (*RCAF photo*.)

Vigil on ski undercarriage; note good downwards view for pilot.

Vancouver Mk I with Armstrong Siddeley Lynx IV engines; span 55 ft, length 37 ft 6 in, loaded weight 6,310 lb, max speed 101 mph; Varuna replacement prototype.

493

Vancouver Mk II with Armstrong Siddeley Lynx geared IVC engines; span 55 ft, length 37 ft 6 in, loaded weight 7,600 lb, max speed 102 mph, initial climb 570 ft/min, duration 4½ hr, crew 3; five built. (*RCAF photo.*)

Vancouver II/SW with Service type Wright Whirlwind J6 engines; span 55 ft, length 37 ft 6 in, loaded weight 7,600 lb, max speed 120 mph, initial climb 750 ft/min, duration 4½ hr, crew 3 to 5; conversion for RCAF coastal patrol—with this exception all Canadian Vickers designs were intended for forestry patrol and associated services, such as fire suppression and air survey; the Vedette was the most successful. (*RCAF photo.*)

The photographs of the Vigil on skis and the Vancouver Mk I on page 493 are by courtesy of the National Aviation Museum.

List of Abbreviations

A & AEE	Aeroplane and Armament Experimental Establishment
ADC	Aircraft Disposal Co
AFEE	Airborne Forces Experimental Establishment
AM	Air Ministry
ANA	Australian National Airways
ANS	Air Navigation School
A-S	Armstrong Siddeley
ASR	Air Sea Rescue
BEA	British European Airways Corporation
BKS	BKS Air Transport
BOAC	British Overseas Airways Corporation
Br	Bristol
BSAAC	British South American Airways Corporation
BUA	British United Airways
BWIA	British West Indian Airways
CAA	Central African Airways Corporation
CAA	Civil Aeronautics Authority
CAAC	Central Aviation Administration of China
CFS	Central Flying School
CI	Channel Islands
CNS	Central Navigation School
DDL	Det Danske Luftfartselskab (Danish Air Lines)
DOT	Canadian Department of Transport
EAA	East African Airways Corporation
ETPS	Empire Test Pilots School
FAMA	Flota Aérea Mercante Argentina
FS	Full supercharge
FTS	Flying Training School
GP	General-purpose
G-R	Gnome-Rhône
GR	General-reconnaissance
IAC	Indian Airlines Corporation
KLM	Koninklijke Luchtvaart Maatschappij (Royal Dutch Airlines)

LAI	Linee Aeree Italiane
LANICA	Lineas Aereas de Nicaragua
LAV	Linea Aeropostal Venezolana
LOT	Polskie Linie Lotnicze (Polish Air Lines)
MAP	Ministry of Aircraft Production
MCA	Ministry of Civil Aviation
ME	Most economical cruising speed
MEA	Middle East Airlines
MoD	Ministry of Defence
MoS	Ministry of Supply
Np	Napier
NZNAC	New Zealand National Airways Corporation
OCU	Operational Conversion Unit
OTU	Operational Training Unit
PAL	Philippine Air Lines
PLUNA	Primeras Lineas Uruguayas de Navigacion Aerea
P & W	Pratt & Whitney
RAAF	Royal Australian Air Force
RAE	Royal Aircraft Establishment
RAF	Royal Air Force
Raf	Royal Aircraft Factory
RCAF	Royal Canadian Air Force
REP	Robert Esnault Pelterie
RFC	Royal Flying Corps
RNAS	Royal Naval Air Service
R-R	Rolls-Royce
SAAF	South African Air Force
SAS	Scandinavian Airlines System
SAS	Special Air Service
TAA	Trans-Australia Airlines
TACA	TACA International Airlines
TB	Torpedo-bomber
TCA	Trans-Canada Air Lines
TDU	Torpedo Development Unit
TSR	Torpedo-Spotter-Reconnaissance
UAL	United Air Lines
US	United States of America
VASP	Viação Aérea São Paulo
VC	Vickers Commercial

Vickers Types

1911–19

Type	Name and Mark	Engine(s)	Details
No. 1	Vickers-REP	60 hp REP	
2	,,	,, ,,	Later Boucier engine
3	Monoplane	,, ,,	
4	,,	,, ,,	Later Viale engine
5	,,	,, ,,	,, ,,
6	Military Trials 'Sociable'	70 hp Viale	Later 70 hp Gnome
7	Monoplane	100 hp Gnome	
8	,,	80 hp Gnome	1913 Olympia Show
	Tractor Biplane	,, ,,	Crashed Long Reach, Thames
	,, ,,	100 hp Gnome	1914 Olympia Show
	Blériot Monoplane	50 hp Gnome	Purchased ex Gustav Hamel, May 1913
	Improved Blériot	70 hp Gnome	No. 22 project
	Boxkites	50 hp Gnome	Nos. 19, 20 and 21 ex Hewlett and Blondeau
	Pumpkin	50 hp Boucier	No. 26—later 70 hp Gnome
	Hydravion	100 hp Gnome	No. 14 and associated projects
E.F.B.1	*Destroyer*	80 hp Wolseley	1913 Olympia Show
2		100 hp Gnome mono	No. 18 and 18A modification
3		,, ,, ,,	No. 18B 1914 Olympia Show—order for 6
4		,, ,, ,,	Improved Destroyer project—not built
5	Gunbus	,, ,, ,,	Prototype
F.B.5	,,	,, ,, ,,	Production
5A	,,	,, ,, ,,	Minor modifications
6	,,	,, ,, ,,	Extended top wing, prototype only
E.F.B.7		Two 100 hp Gnome	1616 and 1617
7A		,, 80 hp Renault	5717
8		,, 100 hp Gnome	—
F.B.9	Streamline Gunbus	100 hp Gnome	Production

Type	Name and Mark	Engines(s)	Details
S.B.1	School Biplane	100 hp Anzani	Trainer version of 18 series—construction doubtful
G.F.B.1/2/3		Various incl. Gnome and Austro–Daimler	Projects for Germany pre-WWI
F.T.1/2/3	Fighting Triplane	(F.T.2) Two Lorraine	Projects, only F.T.2 part constructed
E.S.1	Barnwell Bullet	100 hp Gnome mono	7509 redesign of PV type
E.S.2	,, ,,	110 hp Clerget	7759 and 7760—officially classified as E.S.1 Mark II
F.B.10	Gunbus	160 hp Isotta-Fraschini	Project development
11		250 hp R-R Eagle I	A4814 and A4815
12		80 hp Le Rhône	Later 80 hp Gnome
12A		100 hp Gnome mono	F.B. 12 re-engined
12B		110 hp Le Rhône	
12C		160 hp Hart	A7351—50 ordered
14		160 hp Beardmore	150 ordered
14A		150 hp Lorraine	Later civil conversion
14B		250 hp Beardmore	Project
14C		200 hp BHP	,,
14D		275 hp R-R Eagle IV	C4547
14F		150 hp Raf 4a	A8391
14G		350 hp Lorraine	Project
15		Two R-R Eagle	Two ordered not completed
16	Hart Scout	150 hp Hart	Prototype
16A		180 hp Hispano Suiza	Few built—2nd A8963
16B		200 hp ,, ,,	
16C		200 hp Lorraine	Project
16D		200 hp Wolseley-Hispano	A8963 conversion
16E		275 hp Lorraine	
16F/H		300 hp Hispano Suiza	Projects, construction doubtful
19	Bullet Mk I	100 hp Gnome mono	Production
	,, II	130 hp Clerget	,,
23	Improved Gunbus	150 hp Salmson	Project
23A		150 hp Hart	,,
23B		200 hp Hispano Suiza	,,
24		150 hp Hart	,,
24A		200 hp Hispano Suiza	Prototype
24B		,, ,, ,,	2nd airframe
24C		275 hp Lorraine	French built
24D		200 hp Hispano Suiza	Probably 3rd airframe
24E		,, ,, ,,	Redesign
24G		375 hp Lorraine	French-built

.B.25		150 hp Hispano Suiza	With Crayford rocket gun, crashed
26		200 hp Hispano Suiza	Prototype, crashed
26	Vampire I	,, ,, ,,	B1484–B1489 ordered
26A	,, II	230 hp Bentley B.R.2	B1485 conversion
27	Vimy (I)	Two 200 hp Hispano Suiza	Prototype B9952—later two 260 hp Salmson
	,, (II)	,, 260 hp Sunbeam Maori	B9953—crashed
	,, (III)	,, 260 hp Fiat A-12	B9954—crashed
	,, (IV)	,, 360 hp R-R Eagle VIII	F9569
27A	Vimy Mk II	,, 360 hp R-R Eagle VIII	Production

Name and Mark	Engine(s)	Details
Vimy Commercial	Two 360 hp R-R Eagle VIII	Prototype K-107 later G-EAAV
,, ,,	,, ,, ,, ,,	G-EASI, G-EAUL, F-ADER
,, ,,	,, ,, ,, ,,	Production for China
,, ,,	,, 450 hp Napier Lion	One prototype Ambulance/Vernon series
,, Transatlantic	,, 360 hp R-R Eagle VIII	13th production—bomber conversion
,, Australian	,, ,, ,, ,,	Bomber conversion for Ross Smith flight
,, South African	,, ,, ,, ,,	*Silver Queen I*
,, Ambulance	,, 450 hp Napier Lion	Five built, 1st J6855
Vernon Mk I	,, 360 hp R-R Eagle VIII	Production
,, II	,, 450 hp Napier Lion	,,
,, III	,, ,, ,, ,,	,,
VIM	360 hp R-R Eagle VIII	X41–X75—F.E.2d trainers for China
Valentia	Two 650 hp R-R Condor	Flying-boat with Saunders hull
Valkyrie	,, ,, ,,	Project flying-boat with Saunders hull
Vigilant	Eight 650 hp R-R Condor	Transatlantic civil and military project—Weybridge and Barrow consortium design
Viking I	270 hp R-R Falcon III	Prototype G-EAOV—crashed
,, II	360 hp R-R Eagle VIII	G-EASC—Winner Antwerp Seaplane Trials, 1920
,, III	450 hp Napier Lion	G-EAUK/N147—Winner Air Ministry Competition, 1920, for amphibians

Vickers Types 1920–63

Vickers type number and drawings system was clarified and codified by Paul Wyand, chief draughtsman at Weybridge in 1919. Until then identification of types was varied by the diversity of designs, as the foregoing list discloses. No complete and authentic record has survived of the

53 types which preceded Type 54, with which Wyand started his new list

Type numbers omitted from the list which follows are accounted for by those allocated to miscellaneous drawings for alternative projects, major components, etc.; those allocated to the Supermarine division (after 1928) those reserved for guided weapons (not dealt with in this book), and projects subject to military or commercial security.

Mark numbers quoted are from Vickers technical office records Brackets around others indicate numbers quoted from contemporary publications or official records but not used by the makers. Vickers often used Type series numbers, which in the course of time have been confused with Mark numbers, which strictly should apply only to military designations issued by Government bodies.

Type	Name and Mark	Engine(s)	Details
54	Viking IV	Lion II	F-ABDL
55	,,	,,	Dutch order
56	Victoria I	Two Lion IAX	J6860
57	Virginia I	,, II	J6856
58	Viking IV	Lion II	USA, Japan
59	,, V	,,	N156 and N157
60	,, IV	,,	G-EBBZ
61	Vulcan	Eagle VIII	G-EBBL
62	Vanguard	Two Lion	G-EBCP/J6924
63	Vulcan	Eagle VIII	G-EBEK
64	Viking IV	Lion II	USSR
66	Vimy Commercial	Two Eagle VIII	G-EASI
67	Viking IV	Lion	G-EBED
68	Vulcan	Eagle VIII	Project—Colonial
69	Viking IV	Eagle IX	Laurentide
70	,,	Lion	Stock civil (nil)
71	Vixen I	Lion I	G-EBEC
72	Viking IV	Lion	Stock military (nil)
73	,,	Eagle IX	Argentine
74	Vulcan	Lion	G-EBFC and G-EBLB
75	,,	Eagle VIII	Stock (fuselages)
76	Virginia II	Two Lion II	J6857
77	Viking IV	Lion	2nd Argentine (nil)
78	Vulture (Viking VI)	,,	G-EBGO
79	Virginia III	Two Lion II	Initial production
81	Victoria II	,, IC	J6861
82	Vanellus (Viking VIII)	Eagle	Civil project
83	,, (,, VII)	Lion	N169
84	Viking IV	,,	Argentine Navy R3–6
85	,,	Eagle VIII	RCAF
86	Vulcan	,,	All-metal project
87	Vixen II	Lion I	G-EBEC conversion
88	Vulture	Eagle VIII	Project for Rolls-Royce
89	Viget	Douglas	G-EBHN
91	Vixen III	Lion II	G-EBIP

92	Valparaiso II	Eagle VIII	Portugal
93	,, I	Lion IA	,,
94	Venture I	,, I	J7277 to J7282
95	Vulture II	Eagle IX	G-EBHO—later Lion
96	Virginia	Two Condor III	J6856 re-engined
97	Vagrant	Br Cherub III	Monoplane project of Type 98
98	Vagabond	Cherub III or Blackburne Thrush	G-EBJF
99	Virginia IV	Two Lion II	J7274, J7275
100	Virginia V	,, V	Production
102	Valparaiso	Lion	Chile
103	Vanguard	Two Condor III	G-EBCP re-engined
104	Venture II	Lion	Project improvement
105	Vixen IV	Condor III	G-EBEC re-engined and converted
106	Vixen III	Lion V	G-EBIP for King's Cup
107	Mailplane	—	Project
108	Virginia VI	Two Lion II	25 plus six conversions from Mark V
111	,, VI	,, ,, V	J7439 metal wings
112	,, VII	,, ,, V	J6993 conversion
113	Vespa I	Br Jupiter IV	G-EBLD
114	,,	A-S Jaguar	All-metal project
115	Virginia VIII	Two Condor III	J6856 conversion
116	Vixen V	Lion V	Chile
117	Victoria III	Two Lion II	Production
119	Vespa II	Jupiter VI	G-EBLD, metal wings
120	Vendace I	Falcon III	N208
121	Wibault Scout	Jupiter VI	Chile
122	Virginia VII	Two Lion V	11 plus 40 conversions
123	Scout	Hispano Suiza T52	G-EBNQ
124	Vixen VI	Condor IIIA	G-EBEC re-engined
125	Vireo	A-S Lynx IV	N211
127	Wibault Scout	Lion XI	J9029
128	Virginia IX	Two Lion V	J7131 conversion
129	Virginia VIII	,, ,, V	J6856 re-engined
130	Vivid (Vixen VII)	Lion VA	G-EBPY ex G-EBIP
131	Valiant	Jupiter VI	DH 9A replacement
132	Vildebeest	Jupiter VIII	N230/G-ABGE/EC-W11
133	Vendace II	ADC Nimbus	G-EBPX
134	Vellore I	Jupiter IX	G-EBYX/J8906
135	Venture III	Lion	Project
137	Virginia IX	Two G-R Jupiter VIII	J8236
138	Victoria III	Two Lion II	Metal wings
139	Virginia X	,, VB	Production
140	,,	,, XI	J8238
141	F.21/26	R-R FXI	G-EBNQ conversion
142	Vivid	Lion XI	G-EBPY re-engined
143	Bolivian Scout	Jupiter VIA	Bolivia

Type	Name and Mark	Engine(s)	Details
144	Vimy	Two Jupiter IV	Trainer conversions
145	Victoria	,, IX	J9250
146	Vivid	Lion XI	Military project
147	Valiant	Jupiter XI	G-EBVM for Chile
148	Vixen III	Lion V	Raf 30 wing
149	Vespa III	Jupiter VI	Bolivia
150	B.19/27	Two R-R FXIV	J9131
151	F.20/27 Jockey	Br Mercury IIA	J9122
155	Vendace III	Hispano Suiza	Bolivia
156	Vimy	Two Jaguar	Trainer conversions
157	Vendace II	ADC Nimbus II	G-EBPX air survey
158	Victoria IV	Two Lion IIB or V	Mk III conversions
159	Vimy	,, Jupiter VI	Trainer conversions
160	Viastra I	Three Lynx Major	G-AAUB
161	F.29/27	Mercury IIA	J9566
162	Virginia X	Two Lion V or XI	Slots
163	PV Bomber	Four R-R FXIV	O-2
164	Trooper	,, ,,	Project from Type 163
165	Vellore	—	Commercial project
166	Vellore I	Jaguar VI	G-EBYX for Australian flight
167	Virginia X	Two Jupiter IX	J7421
168	Valparaiso III	G-R Jupiter VIA	Portuguese production
169	Victoria V	Two Lion XI	Production
170	Vanguard	Two Condor III	G-EBCP conversion
171	F.20/27 Jockey	Jupiter VIIF	J9122
172	Vellore III	Two Jupiter XIF	G-AASW
173	,, IV	Two Jupiter IX	G-ABKC/K2133
174	,, V	,, ,,	Project
175	,, VI	,, ,,	,,
176	,, VII	,, ,,	,,
177	F.21/26	Jupiter XFS	Improved Type 143 re-engined
191	Scout	,, VIIF	Type 143 for Martlesham test
192	Vildebeest	Jupiter XF	Type 132 conversion
193	Vespa IV	Jaguar VIC	Irish Free State
194	,,	,, XIF	Project
195	B.19/27 Vanox	Two Br Pegasus IM3	Type 150 converted
196	Jockey	Jupiter VIIF	G-AAWG not built
198	Viastra II	Two Jupiter XIF	VH-UOM and VH-UOO
199	,, III	,, Jaguar VIC	G-AAUB re-engined
200	,, IV	,, Jupiter XIF	Project—Wallis wing
202	,, V	,, A-S Panther IIA	Geared-engine project
203	,, VI	Jupiter IXF	N-1, O-6
204	PV Vildebeest	Panther IIA	O-1
205	Scout	,,	Proposed re-engined Type 177
206	Vildebeest	,,	Type 204, tailwheel

207	M.1/30	R-R Buzzard IIIMS	S1641
208	Vespa V	Jaguar VIC	Irish Free State
209	Vildebeest	Jupiter XI	G-ABGE Paris Show
210	Vespa VI	Jupiter VIIF	G-ABIL/K3588
212	Vellox	Two Pegasus IM3	G-ABKY
213	Victoria III	,, Lion XI	Type 138 re-engined
214	Vildebeest (IV)	Jupiter XFBM	N230 re-engined
215	Vivid	—	Project
216	Vildebeest	Hispano Suiza 12Lbr	O-3
217	Vildebeest (PV)	Jupiter XIF or Hispano Suiza 12Lbr	G-ABJK allocated not used
218	S.9/30	—	Project-TSR
219	Viastra VII	Jupiter XIF	Project
220	,, VIII	Three Jupiter VIFM	G-AAUB conversion
241	Victoria V	Two Jupiter XFBM	K2340
242	Viastra IX	,, IXF	Underslung engines
244	Vildebeest Mk I	Pegasus IM3	Production
245	,,	Hispano Suiza 12Lbr	Spanish licence
246	G.4/31 PV monoplane	Pegasus IIIM3	O-9
248	Victoria V	Two Pegasus IM3	K2340 and K2808
250	Vespa VII	Pegasus S3	K3588 Height Record
251	Vildebeest (X)	,, IM3	S1714 G.P.
252	,, (XI)	,, IIL3	G-ACYV
253	G.4/31 Biplane	,, IIM3	K2771
255	B.19/27 Vanox	Two Pegasus IM3	J9131—conversion of Type 195
256	Viastra	—	Geodetic project
257	Vildebeest (XII)	Pegasus IM3	S1715—night bomber
258	Vildebeest Mk II	Pegasus IIM3	Production
259	Viastra X	Two Pegasus IIL3	G-ACCC/L6102
260	Victoria VI	,, ,,	K2807
261	,, V	Two Lion XI	K2344 auto control
262	,, VI	,, Pegasus IIL3	Production
263	Vildebeest	Pegasus IM3	S1713-TSR
264	Valentia	Two Pegasus IIM3	Production
266	Vincent	Pegasus IIM3	,,
267	Vildebeest Mk III	,, ,,	,,
268	Virginia X	Two Pegasus IIM3	J7130
269	Victoria	,, IIL3	With Herzmark pump
271	B.9/32	,, X	K4049
272	Vellox	,, VII	Project—metal cabin
273	Vellox	,, VII	Project—long range
274	Victoria	Two Lion XI	K2344
276	Valentia	,, Pegasus IIM3	Indian trials
277	Vildebeest	Pegasus IIM3	New Zealand
278	Valentia	Two Pegasus IIM3	K2344 re-engined
279	F.5/34 Venom	Br Aquila AE3S	O-10
280	O.27/34	R-R Goshawk or Griffon	Project—dive-bomber
281	Wellesley	Pegasus X	K7556—Type 246 conversion

Type	Name and Mark	Engine(s)	Details
282	Valentia	Two Pegasus IIM3	K4632—sky shouter
283	,,	,, ,,	K4633—cabin gun
284	B.1/35	Two R-R Vulture II	K8178—prototype
285	Wellington I	,, Pegasus XVIII	L4212— ,,
286	Vildebeest Mk IV	Br Perseus VIII	Production
287	Wellesley	Pegasus XX	,,
288	Vildebeest Mk IV	Perseus PRE-4M	K4614—prototype
289	Wellesley	Br Hercules HE-15	K7772—Hercules test
290	Wellington I	Two Pegasus XVIII	Production
291	Wellesley	Pegasus XX	Blind flying
292	,,	,, XXII	World distance record
293	B.12/36	—	Project for four-engined bomber
294	Wellesley	Pegasus XX	Strengthened wing
295	Wellington	Two Pegasus XVIII	Transposition of W/T and nav. stations
296	,,	,, ,,	Tender for trooper
297	,,	,, ,,	Scheme for VSG hydraulics
298	,, II	Two R-R Merlin X	L4250—prototype
299	,, III	,, Hercules HEISM	L4251—prototype
400	B.1/35	,, Np Sabre	Schemed for K8178
401	,,	,, Br Centaurus CEISM	L9704
402	Wellesley	Pegasus XX	3-seat experimental
403	Wellington	,, XVIII	New Zealand—original order
405	B.1/39	Four Hercules or Griffon	4-engined bomber project
406	Wellington II	Two Merlin X	Production
407	,, V	,, Hercules VIII	R3299 2nd prototype
408	,, IA	Two Pegasus XVIII	Production
409	,, IB	,, ,,	Scheme
410	,, IV	Two P & W Twin Wasp R-1830	R1220
411	B.1/35	Two Vulture II	Production (design only)
412	Wellington IA	,, Pegasus XVIII	N.Z. production
413	B.1/35 (Warwick II)	,, Centaurus IV	BV216
414	F.22/39	—	Project to Type 432
415	Wellington IC	,, Pegasus XVIII	Production
416	Wellington II	,, Merlin X	L4250 (40 mm gun)
417	Wellington III	,, Hercules III	Production
418	Wellington DWI Mk I	Two Pegasus XVIII	P2516
419	Wellington DWI Mk II	,, ,,	L4356
420	F.16/40	—	Project to Type 432
421	Wellington V	Two Hercules III	R3298 1st prototype
422	Warwick II	,, P & W Double Wasp R-2800-S1A4-G	Proposed production
423	Wellington (all Marks to carry 4,000 lb bomb)		Conversion

424	Wellington IV	Two Twin Wasp R-1830-S3C4-G	Production
426	Wellington V	,, Hercules VIII	
427	Warwick I	,, Double Wasp R-2800-S1C4-G	L9704 conversion
428	Wellington DWI Mk III	Hercules XI	P9223
429	Wellington VIII	Pegasus XVIII	Production
430	,, VII	Two Merlin XX	T2545—Cancelled
431	,, VI	,, ,, RMISM	W5795 prototype
432	F.7/41	,, ,, 61	DZ217
433	Warwick III	Four Merlin 60	B.5/41 Windsor project
434	Wellington	Two Pegasus XVIII	Special (SAS no details)
435	,,	,, ,,	T2977 Turbinlite
436	Wellington V	Two Hercules XI	R3298 with turbo-blowers
437	,, IX	,, ,, XVI	P2522 transport
438	Warwick IV	Two Double Wasp	Transport project
439	Wellington II	,, Merlin X	Z8416 40-mm nose gun
440	Wellington X	,, Hercules VI/XVI	Production
441	Boeing B-29	Four Wright Cyclone	Proposal for licence prodn.
442	Wellington VI	Two Merlin 60	Production
443	,, V	,, Hercules VIII	W5816 engine test-bed
445	,, II	,, Merlin X	Z8570/G Whittle W2b/23
447	Windsor	Four Merlin 65	DW506
448	Wellington	Two Hercules 38	Single turbo-blower
449	,, VIG	,, Merlin 60	Production Type 431 modified
450	,, II	,, Merlin X	Whittle W2b cancelled
451	,, IA	Two Pegasus XVIII	N2963 AGP test-bed
452	,, III	,, Hercules III	BJ895 minelayer
453	VC2	Four R-R Dart	Project
454	Wellington XI	Two Hercules VI/XVI	MP502 ASV Mk II
455	,, XII	,, ,,	Leigh light and ASV Mk III
456	Warwick C Mk I	Two Double Wasp R-2800-S1A4-G	BOAC
457	Windsor	Four Merlin 85	DW512
458	Wellington XI	Two Hercules VI/XVI	Production ASV Mk III
459	,,	,, ,,	MP545 with ASV Mk III trial
460	Warwick C Mk III	Two Double Wasp R-2800-S1A4-G	Production
461	Windsor	Four Merlin 85	Project
462	Warwick IA ASR	Two Double Wasp R-2800-S1A4-G	Production
463	Mosquito 'Highball'	,, Merlin 21	DZ471/G prototype conversion
464	Lancaster 'Upkeep'	Four Merlin 20	22 conversions
465	Mosquito 'Highball'	Two Merlin 21	33 conversions

Type	Name and Mark	Engine(s)	Details
466	Wellington GR XIII	Two Hercules XVI	Production
467	Wellington GR XIV	,, ,,	,,
468	Warwick I	Two Double Wasp R-2800-S1A4-G	L9704 with nacelle gun
469	,, GR II	,, Centaurus VII	Production
470	Wellington II	,, Merlin 62	W5389/G Whittle W2b
471	Windsor	Four Merlin 85	NN670 not completed
472	Warwick C1	Two Double Wasp R-2800-S1A4-G	Interim freighter
473	Warwick GR II	Two Centaurus VII	Coastal day
474	Warwick GR V	,, ,,	Coastal night
476	Windsor	Four Merlin 100	Project
478	Wellington X	Two Hercules 100	LN718
479	Windsor	Four Hercules	Project
480	,,	Four Merlin 85	NK136
482	,,	,, RM14SM	Transport project
483	,, B.1	,, 100	First production—cancelled
484	Warwick C IV	Two Centaurus IV	Prototype conversion
485	,, ASR VI	,, Double Wasp 2SBG	Production
486	Wellington II	,, Merlin X	W5518 with W2/700
487	,, XVII	,, Hercules XVII	Service conversions
488	Mosquito 'Highball'	,, Merlin 21	DZ471/G with air turbine
490	Wellington XVIII	Two Hercules XVI	Mk XI converted
491	VC1 Viking	,, 630	G-AGOK
493	Viking	Two R-R Nene 1	Study for Type 618
494	Windsor B.1	Four Merlin 100	Production long range cancelled
495	Viking	Two Hercules 630	G-AGOL
496	,,	,, ,,	G-AGOM
497	Warwick T.3	Two Hercules VI	Interim Trainer
498	Viking 1A	,, 634	Production
499	,, 1	,, 630	All-stressed skin
600	Warwick	Two Centaurus 12	HG341 and 345 test-beds
601	Windsor B.2	Four R-R Clyde 1	NN673 not completed
602	Wellington	Two R-R Dart	LN715 test-bed
603	,,	Two Hercules 630	Test-bed for Viking
604	Viking IB	,, 634	INA
605	Warwick	Two Centaurus	Post-war trainer
606	,,	,, ,,	Flight Refuelling
607	Viking	Two Hercules 230	VL249 prototype Valetta
608	Wellington	Two A-S Mamba	Project
609	VC2 Viceroy	Four ,,	To Type 630
610	Viking IB	Two Hercules 634	BEA
611	Warwick GR II	,, Centaurus VII	Meteorological
613	Viking	Two Hercules	Fuel transport project

614	Viking I	Two Hercules 630	BEA
615	,,	,, 634	Argentine
616	,,	,, ,,	CAA
618	,,	Two Nene 1	G-AJPH/VX856
619	Wellington T.10	Two Hercules 17	Ex T.XIX
620	Viking 1	,, 630	LV-XEN
621	Viking C.2	,, 130	Short nose
623	,,	Two Hercules 134	VL246–247
624	,,	,, ,,	VL245
626	,,	,, ,,	VL248
627	Viking 1B	Two Hercules 634	Airwork
628	,,	,, ,,	DDL
629	,,	,, ,,	BEA
630	Viscount	Four Dart 502	G-AHRF/VX211
631	Viking	Two Hercules 634	34-seat project
632	Viking 1B	,, ,,	Tata (Air-India)
634	,,	,, ,,	Aer Lingus
635	,,	,, ,,	SAA
636	,,	,, ,,	G-AJJN demonstrator
637	,,	Two Hercules 230	Valettas VL262–263
638	Wellington	,, Naiad	NA857
639	Viking 1	,, Hercules 630	Hunting
640	Viscount	Four Naiad	G-AJZW not completed
641	Viking 1A	Two Hercules 630	CAA
643	Viking 1	,, ,,	ZS-BSB
644	Viking 1B	Two Hercules 634	Iraq
645	Valetta C.1	,, 230	Initial production
647	Viking 1B	,, 634	LV-XFM
648	Varsity	,, 264	VX828 and 835
649	Viking 1B	,, 634	J750
651	Valetta C.1	,, 230	Production
652	Viscount	Four Hercules	Project
653	,,	,, Dart	Project-stretched
654	Valetta	Two Hercules 230	Meteorological
656	Viking 1	,, 630	Suppressed aerials
657	Viking 1A	,, 634	BSAA converted 498
658	Valetta C.1	,, 230	Winterisation trials
659	,, C.2	,, ,,	VIP production
660	Valiant	Four Avon RA3	WB210
661	Viking C.2	Two Hercules 130 or 634	VL230, 232 and 233
662	,,	,, ,, 630	RAE Instrument Dev.
663	Viscount	Two Tay RTa1	VX217
664	Valetta T.3	Two Hercules 230	Production
665	Valetta C.1	,, ,,	VL264 for BTH
666	,,	,, ,,	Smiths Aviation
667	Valiant B.1	Four Avon RA7	WB215
668	Varsity T.1	Two Hercules 264	Production
669	Valetta Exp.	Two Hercules 230	VL275—8-wheel chassis
670	,,	,, ,,	VL275—4-wheel chassis
671	,,	,, ,,	Bicycle chassis

Type	Name and Mark	Engine(s)	Details
672	Valetta Exp.	Two Hercules 230	Sperry
673	Valiant B.2	Four Avon RA14	WJ954
674	,, B.1	,, ,,	WP199–203
700	Viscount	Four Dart RDa3/505	G-AMAV
701	,,	DartRDa3/506	BEA
701C	,,	,, ,,	,,
702	,,	,, ,,	BWIA
703	,,	,, ,,	53-seat project
704	VC3	Two Hercules	Civil Varsity project
705	Valiant	Four A-S Sapphires	WB210 proposed conversion
706	Valiant B.1	,, Avon RA28	Production
707	Viscount	,, Dart RDa3/505	Aer Lingus
708	,,	,, Dart RDa3/506	Air France
709	Valiant	,, Avon RA8	WB215 for NZ Air Race
710	Valiant B(PR)1	,, Avon RA28	Production
712	Valiant Exp.	Four Conway RCo3	WJ954 proposed conversion
716	—	—	Studies for Type 1000
718	Valiant	Four Conway RCo2	Project
720	Viscount	Four Dart RDa3/506	TAA
723	,,	,, ,,	IU683
724	,,	,, ,,	TCA
730	,,	,, ,,	IU684
732	,,	,, ,,	Hunting-Clan
733	Valiant B(PR)K1	Four Avon RA28	Production
734	Viscount	Four Dart RDa3/506	J751
735	,,	,, ,,	Iraq
736	,,	,, ,,	Olsen
737	,,	,, ,,	CF-GXK
739	,,	,, ,,	Misrair
739A	,,	,, ,,	,,
739B	,,	,, ,,	,,
742	,,	,, ,,	FAB-2100
743	Valetta T.4	Two Hercules 234	WG256
744	Viscount	Four Dart RDa3/506	Capital
745	,,	Four Dart RDa6/510	,,
745D	,,	,, ,,	,,
747	,,	,, ,,	G-ANXV and G-ANYH
748	,,	,, ,,	CAA
749	,,	Four Dart RDa3/506	LAV
754	,,	Four Dart RDa6/510	MEA
755	,,	,, ,,	Cubana
756	,,	,, ,,	TAA
757	,,	Four Dart RDa3/506	TCA
758	Valiant B(K)1	,, Avon RA28	Production
759	Viscount	Four Dart RDa6/510	Hunting-Clan
760	,,	,, ,,	Hong Kong

761	Viscount	Four Dart RDa6/510	Burma
763	,,	,, ,,	YS-09C
764	,,	,, ,,	US Steel
765	,,	,, ,,	N306
768	,,	,, ,,	IAC
769	,,	,, ,,	Pluna
772	,,	,, ,,	BWIA
773	,,	,, ,,	YI-ACU
776	,,	,, ,,	G-APNF conversion
779	,,	,, ,,	Olsen
780	,,	,, ,,	Basic 700D VIP
781	,,	,, ,,	South Africa
782	,,	,, ,,	Persia
784	,,	,, ,,	Philippine
785	,,	,, ,,	LAI-Alitalia
786	,,	,, ,,	Colombia and Lanica
789	,,	,, ,,	FAB2101
790	,,	Four Dart RDa3/506	Basic local service
793	,,	Four Dart RDa6/510	CF-RBC
794	,,	,, ,,	THY
797	,,	,, ,,	Type 745 conversion
798	,,	,, ,,	Northeast
800	,,	,, ,,	Basic
801	,,	Four Dart RDa6	Revised to Type 802
802	,,	Four Dart RDa6/510	BEA
803	,,	,, ,,	KLM
804	,,	,, ,,	Transair
805	,,	,, ,,	Eagle
806	,,	Four Dart RDa7/520	BEA
806A	,,	,, ,,	G-AOYF
807	,,	Four Dart RDa6/570	NZNAC
808	,,	,, ,,	Aer Lingus
810	,,	Four Dart RDa7/525	G-AOYV
812	,,	,, ,,	Continental
813	,,	,, ,,	South Africa
814	,,	,, ,,	Lufthansa
815	,,	,, ,,	Pakistan
816	,,	,, ,,	TAA
818	,,	,, ,,	Cubana and Lufthansa
827	,,	,, ,,	VASP
828	,,	,, ,,	All Nippon
831	,,	,, ,,	Airwork and Sudan
832	,,	,, ,,	Ansett-ANA
833	,,	,, ,,	Hunting-Clan
835	,,	,, ,,	CU-T-624
836	,,	,, ,,	N40N conversion for Union Carbide
837	,,	,, ,,	Austria
838	,,	,, ,,	Ghana
840	,,	Four Dart RDa11/541	Basic

Type	Name and Mark	Engine(s)	Details
843	Viscount	Four Dart RDa7/525	China
850	Viscount Major	,, RDa8	Project
860	Viscount	,, RDa7/525	Basic
870	,,	—	Viscount jet project
950*	Vanguard	Four Tyne RTy1/506	Basic
951	,,	,, ,,	BEA
952	,,	Four Tyne RTy11/512	TCA (Air Canada)
953	,,	Four Tyne RTy1/506	BEA
1000	Military Transport	Four Conway RCo/5	Ex Type 716
1001	,, ,,	,, ,,	Planned production
1002	Civil Transport	,, ,,	For BOAC
1003	,, ,,	,, ,,	For other airlines
1004	VC7 Transport	,, ,,	Project
1100	VC10	Four Conway RCo/42	G-ARTA
1101	,,	Four Conway RCo/42	BOAC
1102	,,	,, ,,	Ghana
1103	,,	Four Conway RCo/43	BUA
1105	,,	Four Conway RCo/43D	RAF to Type 1106
1106	,, C.Mk1	,, ,,	RAF production
1150	Super VC10	Four Conway RCo/43	Basic
1151	,, ,,	,, ,,	BOAC
1152	,, ,,	,, ,,	All-freight project
1153	,, ,,	,, ,,	EAA
1400	VC11	Four R-R RB163/11 (Spey)	Project

* Preliminary studies Types 900 and 901.

Production of Vickers Aircraft

F.B.5 and F.B.9

1. Prototypes—One Type 18 Admiralty contract CP O.3330/12/53661, 19 November, 1912; one Type 18A and one Type 18B War Office contract A2033, 1913; six Type 18B War Office contract A2321, 18 December, 1913; known serials 32 (RNAS), 648, 664 (prototype F.B.5) and 681.

2. F.B.5—Four, 861–864, to Admiralty contract CP O.2132/14/X (A), 14 August, 1914; nine, 2340–2347 and 4736, to War Office contract A2978, 14 August, 1914; 12, 1616–1627, to War Office contract A2614, 19 September, 1914; 12, 1628–1639, to War Office contract A2705, 2 November, 1914; 12, 1640–1651, to War Office contract A2866 26 November, 1914; 14, 2870–2883, to War Office contract A2974, 30 January, 1915; four, 2865–2868, to War Office contract 87/4621, 23 April, 1915; two with Smith static radial engine, 1534–1535, to Admiralty contract CP 4.7886/X, 20 May, 1915; 50, 5618–5623, 5449–5692, to War Office 87/A/107, 20 September, 1915: total 119 (115 Crayford, four Bexleyheath)—99 built under licence by S. A. Darracq et Cie, Suresnes, France, but some believed completed as F.B.9—probable Darracq serials 3595–3606, 5074–5075, 5078–5079, 5083–5084, 5454–5503.

3. Six known built by A/S Nielson and Winthers, Copenhagen as single-seaters for the Danish Army with Thulin engines, serials N–W 1–6—licence from Vickers was for 12 and others believed completed as two-seaters.

4. F.B.9—20, 5271–5290, to War Office contract 87/A/341, 2 March, 1916; 50, A1411–1460, to War Office contract 87/A/485, 19 June, 1916; 25, A8601–8625, to War Office contract 87/A/485, 2 February, 1917: total 95 (45 Crayford, 50 Weybridge)—probable Darracq serials 7812–7835.

Service: F.B.5—*RFC Squadrons* 2, 5, 6, 7, 11, 18, 41; *Reserve* 10 and 19, *RNAS* Eastchurch and Dunkirk. F.B.9—*RFC Squadrons* 2, 5, 7, 11, 15, 16, 18; *Reserve training* 6 and 10.

F.B.12C

50, A7351–7400, ordered under contract 87/A/997 in November 1916 from Weybridge, but only 18, A7351–7368, built by Wells Aviation Co.

F.B.14

100, A678–777, ordered under contract 87/A/453 in May 1916 from Weybridge, but only 50 built, A678–727, and delivered to Islington store less engines; 150, A8341–8490, ordered under contract 87/A/994 from Weybridge but only 50, A8341–8390, built and delivered as first batch; at least seven used by Home Defence Squadrons, others in Mesopotamia.

F.B.19

Mk I. 53 ordered under contract 87/A/536 in September 1916, only known serials A2992–2122; all built at Weybridge—at least 36 used by RFC Squadrons, a number in Palestine and Macedonia.

Mk II. 12, 5225–5236, ordered under contract 87/A/1345 in December 1916—some sent to Middle East for 50 and 111 Squadrons in Palestine and 11, 17 and 47 Squadrons in Macedonia—12 F.B.19s shipped to Archangel for Imperial Russian Air Service in 1917 but not used.

F.B.26

Six, B1484–1489, ordered under contract AS27055/1 in 1917, but only three built at Bexleyheath, B1484–1486, one used by 141 Squadron; B1485 modified as F.B.26A Vampire II with Bentley rotary engine.

Vimy

The total of Vimys ordered under 18 contracts from nine manufacturing companies was 1,130; after the Armistice of November 1918 most of these were cancelled, and records of those actually built are incomplete, the most accurate figure available is 232, including the three prototypes and 30 post-war aircraft. The following list includes known serials:

1. Three prototypes, B9952–9954, ordered under contract AS22689/1/1917 on 16 August, 1917; built at Bexleyheath.

2. 150, F701–850, ordered under contract 35A/532/C412 on 26 March, 1918, from Vickers, Crayford; seven completed by December 1918, believed 12 built in all.

3. 30, F2915–2944, ordered under contract 35A/1029/C834 in May 1918 from Royal Aircraft Factory; first two completed with Fiat engines; F2917–2920 also built, F2919 became H656, F2920 became H657.

4. 100, F2996–3095, ordered under contract 35A/1030/C835 from Clayton and Shuttleworth—cancelled.

5. 50, F3146–3195, ordered under contract 35A/1032/C837 from Morgan and Co, Leighton Buzzard; 40 possibly built up to F3185: including F3151, 3168, 3171, 3172, 3175, 3180, 3181, 3184, 3185; F3175 and F3185 reconditioned later as FR3175 and FR3185.

6. 50, F8596–8645, ordered under contract 35A/1257/C1166 from Vickers, Weybridge; six completed by December 1918; F8610, 8616, 8619, 8623, 8625, 8630, 8631, 8632, 8633, 8634, 8635, 8637, 8638, 8641, 8642, 8643 are known serials.

7. 150, F9146–9295, ordered under contract 35A/1784/C1895 from Vickers, Weybridge; 50 delivered, F9146–9195—26 later reconditioned and 17 converted to dual control, all at Weybridge; conversions to Jupiter engines F9147, 9168, 9176, 9178.

8. One, F9569, built at Weybridge under contract 35A/3872/C4532 as prototype Mk II with Eagle VIII engines.

9. 20, H651–670, ordered under contract 35A/2057/C2334 from Royal Aircraft Establishment; only 10 confirmed as built: H651, 652, 653, 654, 655, 656 (from F2919), H657 (from F2920), 658, 659, 660.

10. 150, H4046–4195, ordered under contract 35A/2295/C2592 from Boulton and Paul—cancelled.

11. 20, H4196–4215, ordered from Kingsbury Aviation—cancelled.

12. 100, H4725–4824, ordered from Metropolitan Wagon Co—cancelled.

13. 75, H5065–5139, ordered under contract 35A/2388/2689 from Westland Aircraft—approximately 25 built—only two known serials, H5081 and H5089—later reconditioned as HR5089.

14. 100, H9413–9512, ordered under contract 35A/2938/C3353 from Ransomes, Sims and Jeffries—cancelled.

15. One, H9963, built by Vickers, Weybridge.

16. 50, J251–300, ordered under contract 35A/2978/C3411 from Clayton and Shuttleworth—cancelled.

17. 50, J1941–1990, ordered from Morgan and Co—cancelled.

18. 10, J7238–7247, ordered under contract 459943/23 from Vickers, Weybridge at £4,750 each—first post-war aircraft; all built and delivered.

19. 15, J7440–7454, ordered under contract 493802/24 from Vickers, Weybridge—all built and delivered.

20. 5, J7701–7705, ordered under contract 571171/25 from Vickers, Weybridge—all built and delivered.

Vimy Service

Squadrons: 7, 9, 45, 58, 70, 99, 100, 216, 502.
Other Units: 4 FTS; Parachute Training Unit, Henlow; Night Flying Flight, Biggin Hill.

Vimy (Civil)

1. Transatlantic—c/n 13 from post-war production—no registration or other markings —rebuilt after recovery from Clifden for Science Museum.

2. C-105, Vickers owned, allocated G-EAAR but not used.

3. G-EAOL, formerly F8625, flown to Spain and did not return.

4. G-EAOU, formerly F8630, Smith flight to Australia, where it was allotted A5-1 but not used—partly rebuilt after fire in transit to exhibition hall at Smith Airport, Adelaide, 1958.

5. G-UABA, *Silver Queen*, Van Ryneveld and Quintin Brand flight to Cape, crashed at Korosko, Upper Egypt.

6. *Silver Queen II*, replacement for Cape flight from RAF, Heliopolis, with engines and instruments from G-UABA, crashed on take-off at Bulawayo, Rhodesia—flight completed in DH9.

Vimy Commercial

1. Prototype K-107 demonstration, later G-EAAV for Broome and Cockerell attempt on Cape flight.

2. c/n 1–40 built for China between April 1920 and February 1921 and delivered by sea; started Peking to Tsinan air post on 1 July, 1921—known names *Ta Peng* and *Chengku*; financed by issue of Chinese Vickers bonds in London; c/n 39 allotted G-EAUY but not used, c/n 40 as G-EAUL was runner-up in 1920 Air Ministry Competition for civil transports and later shipped for China.

3. c/n 41 G-EASI *City of London* for S. Instone and Co, later to Imperial Airways.

4. c/n 42 F-ADER for Grands Express Aériens.

5. c/n 43 for USSR, delivered in September 1922, loaned to Russian airline Dobrolet by Red Air Fleet in 1924; virtually prototype Vernon with high-lift wings and Lion engines.

Vimy Ambulance

Five built: J6855 to contract 222245/20; J6904–6905 to contract 195542/21 for £6,500 each; J7143–7144 to contract 428716/23 for £6,300 each; all used in Middle East for casualty evacuation; later converted to Vernon standard and used by 45 and 70 Squadrons.

Vernon

1. Mk I. 30, J6864–6893, ordered under contract 121877/21 at £6,000 each; last 10, J6884–6893, delivered as Mk II to specification 43/22.

2. Mk II. Five, J6976–6980, ordered under contract 375419/22.

3. Mk II. 10, J7133–7142, ordered under contract 424489/23.

4. Mk III. 10, J7539–7548, ordered under contract 511657/24 at £6,200 each. Vernons were used in Middle East by 45 and 70 Squadrons.

Viking Amphibian

1. Prototype, G-EAOV, built at Weybridge; first flew November 1919.

2. Mk II, G-EASC, first flown at Cowes in June 1920; won first prize in Antwerp Seaplane Trials, August 1920.

3. Mk III, G-EAUK, for 1920 Air Ministry Amphibian Competition; won first prize and bought by AM under contract 356700/20 as N147 for £8,000; delivered 2 February, 1921.

4. Mk IV, Type 54 F-ADBL for French *Section Technique* at £4,130; delivered 27 September, 1921.

5. Mk IV, Type 55—8 for Royal Netherlands Indies Air Arm; delivered January/February 1922, but two written off and replacements delivered 22 January, 1923; all ten at £5,750 each.

6. Mk IV, Type 58—two for Imperial Japanese Navy at £7,680 each; delivered 16 May, 1921—one for U.S. Government at £6,630; delivered 14 February, 1923.

7. Mk V, Type 59—two, N156–157, ordered under contract 267995/21 at £4,500 each; delivered 17 April, 1922, and attached to 70 Squadron, Iraq, for tropical trials; N156 cannibalised to service N157 at Hinaidi in 1923.

8. Mk IV, Type 60—two, G-EBBZ and G-EBED, built for Ross Smith round-world flight; G-EBBZ crashed 13 April, 1922, at Brooklands with Sir Ross Smith and Sgt Bennett; G-EBED sold for winter sports service Croydon to St Moritz and Nice, 1926.

9. Mk IV, Type 64—one ordered under contract LK220S for Russian Trade Delegation (Reval) for £6,500; delivered 8 September, 1922.

10. Mk IV, Type 67—G-EBED modified for sales demonstration in Spain, but sold as under Type 60.

11. Mk IV, Type 69—one built for Laurentide Air Services, Canada, at £5,200; delivered 12 May, 1922.

12. Mk IV, Type 73, two for River Plate Aviation Co at £5,200 (quoted price amended to net cost price); delivered 21 February, 1923, for Buenos Aires–Montevideo passenger service.

13. Mk VI, Type 78, Vulture I built for MacLaren round-world flight, 1924, G-EBGO.

14. Mk VII, Type 83, Vanellus N169 ordered under contract 402420/23 to specification 46/22; delivered to RAE 25 August, 1925; comparative trials with Supermarine Seagull III on HMS *Argus*.

15. Mk IV, Type 84, four for Argentine Navy R3 to R6 at £6,000 each; delivered 1 May, 1923.

16. Mk IV, Type 85, two for Royal Canadian Air Force at £3,250 each; delivered 9 May, 1923; conducted aerial survey Northern Canada in 1924; six others built by Canadian Vickers, Montreal.

17. Mk VI, Type 95, Vulture II private venture; converted to Vulture I standard as first aircraft for MacLaren round-world attempt, G-EBHO.

Total Production: 31 Viking; two Vulture; one Vanellus.

Vulcan

1. Type 61: prototype G-EBBL c/n 1 built for Instone Air Line for £1,800 and delivered 30 May, 1922; c/n 2 G-EBDH for Instone at £2,500, delivered 15 July, 1922; c/n 3 G-EBEA for Instone at £2,500, delivered 22 July, 1922; c/n 5 G-EBEM built as cargo carrier, but converted to 8-seat transport for 1922 King's Cup Air Race and sold for charter work in 1926 at £1,000; c/n 6 G-EBES for Qantas not completed; c/n 7 G-EBET for Qantas; sent to Australia for acceptance trials, but returned as specification not met.

2. Type 63: c/n 4 G-EBEK cargo carrier ordered under contract 314976/21 to specification 12/22 for £3,200 and delivered 30 October, 1922, with Eagle IX engine.

3. Type 74: c/n 8 G-EBFC for Imperial Airways at reduced price and delivered 22 December, 1924; c/n 9 G-EBLB for Imperial Airways at £2,000, delivered 12 May, 1925.

Vanguard (Biplane)

Type 72: one only, J6924, ordered under contract 156988/21 to specification 1/22 for £14,200 with Lion engines and delivered March 1925; modified to Type 103 with Condor III engines under contract 547689/24 as J6924, but flown as G-EBCP by Imperial Airways; further modifications as Type 170 under contract 700835/26; world load-carrying record 6 July, 1928.

Virginia

1. Two prototypes, J6856–6857, ordered under contract 302897/20 at £13,250 each; J6856, Type 57 delivered 15 December, 1922; J6857, Type 76 delivered 5 April, 1924.

2. Mk III. Two Type 79, J6992–6993, ordered under contract 369333/22 to specification 1/21 on 23 October, 1922.

3. Mk III. Four Type 79, J7129–7132, ordered under contract 429978/23 all delivered to 7 Squadron between 7 and 30 July, 1924.

4. Mk IV. Two Type 99, J7274–7275, ordered under contract 53931/23 to specification 28/23.

5. Mk V. 22 Type 100, J7418–7439, ordered under contract 515990/24 to specification 12/24 delivered between 29 November, 1924, and 7 March, 1925, mainly to 7, 9, 58 Squadrons and RAE.

6. Mk VI. 10 Type 108, J7558–7567, ordered under contract 547527/24 delivered between 21 May and 15 September, 1925, mainly to 7, 9, 58 Squadrons and A and AEE and RAE.

7. Mk VI. 15 Type 108, J7706–7720, ordered under contract 571413/25 delivered between 21 August and 28 November, 1925, mainly to 7, 9 and 58 Squadrons.

8. Mk VII. 11 Type 112, J8236–8241, J8326–8330, ordered under contract 698878/26 delivered between 29 January and 22 March, 1927, mainly to 7, 9 and 58 Squadrons and RAE; with 500 Squadron J8240 was named *Isle of Thanet*.

9. Mk IX. Eight Type 128, J8907–8914, ordered under contract 748566/27 delivered between 24 September and 25 October, 1927, mainly to 7, 9 and 58 Squadrons; 27 conversions listed in Virginia chapter.

10. Mk X. 19 Type 139, K2321–2339, ordered under contract 101683/31 to specification 5/31 delivered between 9 September and 17 December, 1931.

11. Mk X. 31 Type 139, K2650–2680, ordered under contract 141161/31 delivered between 4 July and 20 December, 1932; 53 conversions to Mk X listed in Virginia chapter.

Virginias mainly used by 7, 9, 58, 214, 215. 500 and 502 Squadrons.

Total Production: 126.

Victoria

1. Two prototypes, J6860–6861, ordered under contract 306082/20 at £13,690 each; J6860, Type 56 delivered 30 October, 1922; J6861, Type 81 delivered 23 February, 1923.

2. Mk III. 15 Type 117, J7921–7935, ordered under contract 612920/25 at £9,800 each; delivered between 23 February and 26 July, 1926; conversions—to Mk IV, J7921, 7934 and 7935, to Valentia J7921.

3. Mk III. Six, J8061–8066, ordered under contract 673289/26 at £9,000 each; conversions—to Mk V, J8062, to Mk VI, J8062 and J8065, to Valentia, J8062, 8063, 8065.

4. Mk III. 10, J8226–8235, ordered under contract 707156/26; delivered between 23 October and 14 December, 1926; conversions—to Mk VI, J8231, J8232, to Valentia, J8230–8232.

5. Mk III. 15, J8915–8929, ordered under contract 765521/27; delivered between 13 December, 1927, and 8 March, 1928; conversions—to Mk IV (interim metal), J8916–8922, 8924–8926, to Mk VI, J8916, 8920, 8921, 8922, 8926, to Valentia, J8916, 8919, 8921.

6. Mk IV Jupiter prototype J9250, Type 145 ordered under contract 752716/27; delivered 13 October, 1928.

7. Mk V. Seven Type 169, J9760–9766, ordered under contract 921962/29; delivered between 14 September and 14 October, 1929; conversions—to Mk VI, J9760, 9762, 9763, 9765, to Valentia, J9760, 9762, 9764–9766.

8. Mk V. Six, K1310–1315, ordered under contract 2666/30; delivered between 6 June and 7 October, 1930; conversions—to Mk VI, K1311, 1312, 1314, 1315, to Valentia, K1311–1314.

9. Mk V. Six, K2340–2345, ordered under contract 101677/31; delivered between 10 September and 30 October, 1931; conversions—to Mk VI, K2342, 2343, to Valentia, K2340–2345.

10. Mk V. 18, K2791–2808, ordered under contract 170929/32; delivered between 11 July and 31 October, 1932; conversions—to Mk VI, K2798, 2806–2808, to Valentia, K2791–2808.

11. Mk VI. 11 Type 262, K3159–3169, ordered under contract 170929/32; delivered between 30 September and 22 December, 1933; all converted to Valentia.

Total Production: 97.

Squadrons: 9, 48, 53, 58, 70, 216.

Other Units: C.F.S., RAE, Air Pilotage School, Andover, and Communications Flight, Habbaniya.

Valentia

1. Type 264. 16, K3599–3614, ordered under contract 259487/33; delivered between 15 May and 2 November, 1934.

2. Six, K4630–4635, ordered under contract 338740/34; delivered between 10 July and 3 December, 1935.

3. One, K5605, ordered November 1934 under contract 402241/35; delivered 14 February, 1936.

4. Five, K8848–8852, ordered May 1936 under contract 402241/35; delivered between 6 March and 29 May, 1936.

Total built: 28; 54 conversions, many by RAF in Middle East.

Squadrons: 70, 216—other units SAAF, RAE, C.F.S., Communications Flight, Habbaniya, and 202 Group HQ.

Vixen

Mk I, Type 71, G-EBEC; Mk II, Type 87, G-EBEC modified; Mk III, Type 91, G-EBIP —later converted to G-EBPY as Vivid; Mk IV, Type 105, G-EBEC further modified to take Condor engine; Mk V, Type 116, 18 delivered to Chile between 9 October, 1925, and 9 January, 1926; Mk VI, Type 126, G-EBEC again modified with Condor for general-purpose competition at Martlesham in 1927; Type 148—G-EBIP modified for trials with Raf 30 wings and no top-plane tanks.

Venture

Mk I, Type 94, six, J7277–7282, ordered under contract 483332/24 to specification 45/23 at £2,700 each; J7277 to 4 Squadron for service trials and then to RAE, on 27 March, 1925; J7278 delivered 5 July, 1924, used by RAE; J7279 delivered 4 July, 1924, and J7280–7282 on 9 July; J7280 used by RAF, Henlow, and RAE; J7282 reconditioned in May 1927; J7280 demonstrated to Japanese Army Mission in February 1925; at least one Venture (serial not known) with 2 Squadron.

Valparaiso

Mk I, Type 93, 10 built for Portugal; Mk II, Type 92, four built for Portugal at £5,070 each and delivered 29 July, 1924; one Mk I, Type 102, modified and supplied to Chilean Navy Air Base at Quintero, Valparaiso; Mk III, Type 168, one prototype modified at Weybridge from contract aircraft to take Gnome-Rhône Jupiter; at least 13 licence-built in Portugal by OGMA (General Aeronautical Material Workshops at Alverca do Ribatajo); 20 Valparaisos were with the Grupo de Esquadrilhas de Aviacao Republica in 1934.

Valiant (Biplane)

Type 131—private venture for 1927 AM general-purpose competition, registered G-EBVM for demonstration in Chile, retained there.

Vivid

Type 130—Vixen VII renamed as G-EBPY, rebuilt from G-EBIP as private venture, flown in landplane and floatplane form, sold to J. R. Chaplin on 31 March, 1931, for £300.

Vespa

Mk I, Type 113, G-EBLD private venture to specification 30/24 for Army co-operation; Mk II, Type 119, G-EBLD converted; Mk III, Type 149—six for Bolivia delivered between 9 April and 25 July, 1929; Mk IV, Type 193, four for Irish Air Corps, serials V1 to V4, delivered 14 April, 1930; Mk V, Type 208, four for Irish Air Corps, serials V5 to V8, two delivered 27 March and two 31 March, 1931; Mk VI, Type 210, G-ABIL rebuilt and converted from G-EBLD for Chinese presentation and for world height record after adaptation by Bristol Aeroplane Co for Pegasus S.3 engine; Mk VII, Type 250, G-ABIL converted under contract 241948/33, delivered to RAE on 4 May, 1933, as K3588, later to 4 Squadron and finally as 1051M at 15 School of Technical Training on 15 June, 1938.

Vendace

Mk I, Type 120, N208 ordered under contract 615049/25 to specification 5/24 for float-plane trainer at £3,225; Mk II, Type 133, G-EBPX, private-venture demonstration landplane and seaplane; Mk III, Type 155, three for Bolivia delivered 1 October, 1928; Mk II, Type 157, G-EBPX converted with Nimbus engine and sold to Aircraft Operating Co on 1 June, 1928, for £2,750, despatched by SS *Andora* to Rio de Janeiro for photographic survey.

517

Wibault

1. Wibault Scout, Type 121, 26 built for Chile under licence at £3,700 each, delivered between 16 September and 27 November, 1926, to El Bosque, Santiago.

2. Vireo Mk I, Type 125, N211 ordered under contract 693444/26 to specification 17/25 at £6,053.

3. Wibault 12.C2, Type 127, J9029, French-built aeroplane bought by Vickers, converted to take Lion XI engine and sold to Air Ministry under contract 786338/37 for £4,750.

4. Viastra I, Type 160, G-AAUB built at Supermarine Works, Southampton, but fuselage constructed at Crayford Works.

5. Viastra II, Type 198, two, VH-UOM and VH-UOO, built at Supermarine Works and shipped to West Australian Airways, VH-UOO arrived Fremantle 16 February, 1931, first service Perth–Adelaide on 3 March, 1931.

6. Viastra III, Type 199, G-AAUB conversion.

7. Viastra VI, Type 203, VH-UON built at Supermarine Works for West Australian Airways, but not delivered, flew to Brooklands as N-1, allotted G-ABVM, but flown as O-6.

8. Viastra VIII, Type 220, G-AAUB further conversion.

9. Viastra IX, Type 242, VH-UOM modified for West Australian Airways by lowering engines 15 in on redesigned mountings, reconverted to Type 198.

10. Viastra-Wallis, Type 256, special version. Wallis-designed wings to Experiment 212, delivered to RAE.

11. Viastra X, Type 259, G-ACCC VIP version for then H.R.H. Prince of Wales, based at Hendon with Royal Flight, later as L6102 at Croydon for radio and icing tests.

Vickers Fighters

1. Type 123—G-EBNQ built as private venture in 1926.

2. Type 141—G-EBNQ modified to specification N.21/26.

3. Type 143—Bolivian Scout—six delivered between 3 September and 17 December, 1929.

4. Type 151—Jockey—J9122 ordered under contract 813868/27 to specification F.20/27; delivered on 11 March, 1929, at £6,393.

5. Type 161—F.29/27—J9566 ordered under contract 881544/28 to specification F.29/27; delivered 3 September, 1931, for £7,020.

6. Type 171—Jockey—J9122 modified by installation of Jupiter VIIF engine under contract 979/30; delivered 15 January, 1932; crashed during spin tests at Martlesham June 1932.

7. Type 177 Scout—seventh Type 143 airframe modified initially to specification F.21/26 for AM Deck Landing Competition as private venture.

8. Type 196 Jockey civil project—G-AAWG allotted, but aeroplane not completed.

9. Type 279—Venom—PVO-10 built as private venture to specification F.5/34, airframe scrapped after contracts placed for Hurricane and Spitfire.

10. Type 432—F.7/41—DZ217 and DZ223 ordered to specification F.7/41, DZ217 only completed.

Vellore

Mk I, Type 134, J8906 ordered under contract 812095/25; delivered 9 October, 1928, to Air Ministry for Imperial Airways; Mk II, Type 166, J8906, modified with Jaguar engine and registered as G-EBYX, exchanged with AM for Mk IV, K2133, and flown to Australia in 1929; Mk III, Type 172, G-AASW built as landplane at Crayford works, tested on floats as O-4; Mk IV, Type 173, K2133 ordered under contract 38677/30 to specification 5/30 and delivered to AM as replacement for J8906, registered G-ABKC, but used by A & AEE for ferry and stores carrying until 1935 under military serial.

Vellox

Type 212—G-ABKY developed from Vellore and sold to Imperial Airways in May 1936.

Experimental Bombers

1. Type 150—J9131 ordered under contract 819856/28 as Virginia replacement to specification B.19/27.

2. Type 163—O-2 private venture built to specification C.16/28, but completed to specification B.19/27.

3. Type 195—J9131 rebuilt under contract 63600/30 for A & AEE for trials, re-engined with Pegasus under contract 181512/32 and re-delivered to A & AEE, later to 9 and 10 Squadrons.

4. Type 255—J9131 reconstructed with new outer wings under contract 285256/33 and other modifications and named Vanox (not Vannock) by Vickers, used by RAE for flight-refuelling experiments.

5. Type 207—M.1/30 ordered under contract 55827/30 to specification M.1/30 for torpedo-bomber.

6. Type 253—K2771 biplane ordered under contract 174761/32 to specification G.4/31; delivered 13 April, 1932; contract for production cancelled in favour of Wellesley monoplane.

Vildebeest

Type 132—prototype built at Weybridge under contract 693542/26 as N230 and delivered to Martlesham Heath on 17 September, 1928; demonstrated before Spanish delegations at Brooklands on 22 July, 1929.

Type 192—Series II, N230 modified with Jupiter XF engine.

Type 194—Series III, N230 modified with Jupiter XIF engine; registered G-ABGE and C of A issued 1 December, 1930.

Type 204—Series IV O-1, second prototype, built for private-venture demonstration; to Martlesham Heath 22 August, 1930, and returned to Weybridge in March 1931; to Air Ministry in lieu of Type 132 and crashed at Farnborough in 1932.

Type 209—Series V, G-ABGE/N230 converted to take the Jupiter XIF.

Type 214—Series VI, G-ABGE converted for Jupiter XFBM.

Type 216—Series VII, G-ABGE converted to take the Hispano Suiza 12Lbr engine; later flown as O-3 and also on floats.

Type 217—Series VII, G-ABJK allocated and to have been O-1 converted.

1. (a) Nine Mk I, S1707–1715, ordered contract 131305/31 to specification 22/31 and delivered between 24 September, 1932, and 22 March, 1933, as Type 244; S1707 used by A and AEE for trial modifications and allotted maintenance serial 1623M, eventually to RAF Henlow; S1708 used by 22 Squadron, crashed into sea 22 July, 1935; S1709 used by A Flight, Gosport; S1710 used by A Flight, Gosport, and later to 4 School of Technical Training as 1187M; S1711 used by A Flight, Gosport, and later allotted 720M; S1712 used by A Flight, Gosport; S1713 used by 100 Squadron at Singapore during 1932—later modified as the Type 263; S1714 contract changed in 1932 to 218286/32 and completed as a general-purpose aircraft under Type 258. S1715 contract changed in 1932 to 216891/32 and completed as a night bomber; carried out trials at the RAE by 7 Squadron and at Martlesham; was the Vincent prototype; eventually to 1121M at RAF Cosford.

(*b*) 13 Mk I, K2810–2822, ordered under contract 131305/31 and delivered between 9 January and 29 March, 1933, to 100 (TB) Squadron, except K2810, which went to the RAE and K2816 to Martlesham; K2813 used also by Experimental Development Flight at Gosport, later allotted 1381M; K2816 flown with a float undercarriage; K2817 allotted 969M and to No. 1 School of Technical Training; K2818 modified to Mk II standard 18 January, 1934; K2819 fitted Pegasus IIM3 and Curtiss variable-pitch propeller and tested at A & AEE and RAE, later allotted 2451M; K2821 modified to Mk III standard 6 September, 1935; allotted 1891M, but instead sold to New Zealand as NZ135.

2. 30 Mk II, Type 258, K2916–2945, ordered under contract 131305/31 and delivered between 21 July and 22 December, 1933; K2916 fitted Pegasus IIM3 engine and floats and tested at Felixstowe, allotted maintenance serial 1178M; K2917–2944 all used by 100 (TB) Squadron; K2940 modified to Mk III; four, K2921, 2926, 2936 and 2937, given to Malay Trade Schools; K2945 converted to Vincent by 20 February, 1935, allotted 1093M 7 June, 1938.

3. 84 Mk III, Type 267, K4105–4188, ordered under contract 279218/33: K4105–4155 completed as Vincent under contract 279521/33; K4156–4163 delivered initially to Cardington Storage Unit between 4 February and 4 March, 1935; all to the Far East except K4157 and K4163 used by Gosport; K4157 later converted to Vincent; K4164–4166 used by DTD, K4164 later to Mk IV prototype; K4167–4186 delivered to 36 (TB) Squadron between 30 November, 1934, and 5 February, 1935; K4186 later sold to New Zealand on 23 March, 1940; K4187 used by 22 Squadron and later to New Zealand as NZ117 and used by RNZAF 2 (GR) Squadron; K4188 delivered to Cardington initially and later sent to Singapore.

4. 12 Mk III, Type 277, NZ101–112, ordered under contract 295151/33 and delivered between 1 March and 9 May, 1935; used by the New Zealand Flying Training School at Wigram; NZ101 as B-7/B-8, NZ103 as B-9, NZ104 as B-7/B-8, NZ105 as B-2, NZ106 as B-3, NZ107 as B-4, NZ109 as B-1, NZ112 as B-3 and NZ108 as A-5, most of the above were later transferred to No. 2 FTS at Woodbourne.

5. 27 Mk III, K4588–4614, ordered under contract 327476/34 and delivered between 20 July and 5 September, 1935: K4588–4610 delivered to Cardington Storage Unit; K4611–4614 delivered to 22 Squadron; also used by 22 Squadron were K4588–4592, K4602–4607 and 4610; 42 Squadron flew the following: K4589, 4590, 4595, 4597 and 4612; 36 Squadron flew K4599–4601; nine went to New Zealand—K4589 as NZ131, K4591 as NZ118, K4592 as NZ116, K4593 as NZ128, K4595 as NZ130, K4596 as NZ115, K4597 as NZ134, K4598 as NZ114 and K4612 as NZ113.

6. 39 Mk III, K6369–6407, ordered under contract 406943/35 and delivered between 4 July and 28 August, 1936: K6369–6394 delivered to a packing depot for the Far East and 100 (TB) Squadron; K6395–6407 delivered into store; four to New Zealand—K6395 as NZ133, K6396 as NZ132, K6397 as NZ120 and K6401 as NZ119.

7. Seven Mk IV Type 286, K6408–6414, ordered under contract 470821/35 and delivered 31 March to 7 May, 1937: K6408 to Martlesham, later to Development Flight, Gosport; K6410 to Farnborough; K6409 and K6411–6414 to 42 Squadron; four to New Zealand—K6409 as NZ137, K6410 as NZ121, K6413 as NZ122 and K6414 as NZ123.

8. 11 Mk IV, K8078–8088, ordered under contract 470821/35 and delivered between 24 May and November 1937 to 42 Squadron; eight to New Zealand—K8078 as NZ136, K8079 as NZ129, K8080 as NZ124, K8081 as NZ125, K8083 as NZ126, K8084 as NZ138, K8085 as NZ139 and K8086 as NZ127.

9. 25 Type 245, Series IX, built under licence in Spain for the Spanish Naval Air

Service as T1–25; another was assembled from parts purchased from Weybridge; with EC-W11 (Ex. N230/G-ABGE) sold and ferried to Spain there were 27 Spanish Vildebeests in all.

Total Vildebeest Production

Two prototypes, 22 Mk I, 30 Mk II, 111 Mk III, 18 Mk IV and 26 Spanish: 209.

Vincent

The prototype was S1714, converted Vildebeest Mk I.

1. 51 Type 266, K4105–4155, ordered under contract 279521/33 after the original contract had specified Vildebeest IIs, delivered between 18 July, 1934, and 21 June, 1935: K4105 tested at Martlesham Heath and RAE, later allotted 2285M; K4106–4126 to 84 Squadron; K4127—4150 to 8 Squadron, except K4135, which went to the RAE; K4151–4155 were delivered into stores as spares; four were sold to New Zealand— K4110, 4122, 4125 and 4151; one, K4152, was sold to Iraq.

2. (*a*) Five, K4615–4619, ordered under contract 327201/34 and delivered between 12 and 25 February, 1936, into store; K4617 later to New Zealand as NZ321.

(*b*) 95, K4656–4750, ordered under contract 327201/34 and delivered between 7 September, 1935, and 6 February, 1936. K4656–4686 delivered initially into store; K4687–4710 to 47 Squadron; K4711–4727 to 84 Squadron; K4728–4750 into store; 17 sold to New Zealand—K4660, 4676, 4680, 4710, 4717–4722, 4734, 4739, 4743, 4744 and 4748–4750; three sold to Iraq—K4730, 4735 and 4737.

(*c*) Three, K4883–4885, ordered under contract 327201/34; K4883 delivered 15 June, 1936, to packing depot for Aden and to 9 Squadron; K4884 delivered 19 June, 1936, to packing depot for Aden and to 9 Squadron; K4885 delivered 22 June, 1936, to 3 ASU and to Iraq.

3. 43, K6326–6368, ordered under contract 405119/35 and delivered between 1 September and 30 October, 1936, into packing depot for the Middle East: K6326–6361 formed the initial equipment of 55 Squadron.

Total built: 197.

Wellesley

Prototype built by Vickers as a private venture, Type 246, to specification G.4/31, and flown with temporary SBAC registration O-9; sold to the Air Ministry under contract 436980/35 in September 1935 and given serial K7556; retained by Vickers for trials until it went to the RAE Farnborough on 2 April, 1936, for service trials. 96 ordered under contract 435442/35, to specification 22/35, in two batches, K7713–7791 (79) and K8520–8536 (17): K7713 to Martlesham for evaluation on 4 March, 1937; K7714–7720, 7722, 7725–7726, 7730–7731, 7740–7744 and 7746 as initial issue to 76 Squadron: K7715 first delivered on 22 March, 1937; K7746 last delivered on 30 July, 1937: K7729 to A & AEE 14 June, 1937; K7772 to Bristol Aeroplane Co at Filton.

Squadrons and individual aircraft: 35—K7736, 7738 and 7739 delivered 15 July, 1937, K7745, 7747–7755; 76—see above; 148—K7723 first delivered 5 July, 1937, K7727– 7728, 7732–7735 and 7771; 207—K7756 and 7757 delivered 31 August, 1937, K7758– 7766; remainder to packing depot or to Cardington Storage Unit, except K7791, retained by Vickers from 30 October, 1937, for manufacturer's trials: K7728 and K7735 sold to Egypt in February 1940.

Second batch: K8522 first delivered to Cardington on 4 October, 1937; K8536 last delivered to 77 Squadron on 17 November, 1937.

Squadrons and individual aircraft: 35, Worthy Down—K8526 and 8529–8530; 76, Honington—K8527–8528; 77, Honington—K8524–8525 and 8535–8536; 207, Worthy Down—K8531–8534; K8531 sold to Egypt in February 1940.

Third batch: 80 ordered under contract 537135/36, L2637–2716: L2641 first delivered to RAE Farnborough 26 January, 1938; L2716 last delivered to Vickers DTD 30 May, 1938.

Squadrons and individual aircraft: Long Range Development Flight—L2637–2639, 2680–2681, 2683 and 2697; 14—L2643–2646, 2649–2659, 2692–2696 and 2698–2700; 35—L2688; 45—L2675–2678, 2684–2687, and 2710–2715; 76—L2689–2690; 77—L2647–2648; 148—L2679 and 2691; 207—L2682; 223—L2660–2674 and 2701–2709.

Experimental aircraft. K7717 experimental work for long range; K7772 test-bed for Bristol Hercules engine. L2641–2642 experiments at RAE on de-icing equipment; L2716 experiments at RAE on armoured leading edges; L2679 and 2682 experiments at RAE on de-icing equipment.

Total built: 177.

Wellington

1. Prototype, K4049, first flew 15 June, 1936; ordered to specification B.9/32; Type 271.

2. 180 ordered to specification B.29/36 on 15 August, 1936, Wellington Mk I as L4212–4311 and L4317–4391 under contract 549268/36, also R2699–2703; L4212 built as Type 285 with Pegasus X engines later converted to Type 290 with Pegasus XVIII engines; remainder built as Type 290, also R2699–2703—total 180; L4250 converted to Type 298, Mk II prototype (interim); L4251 converted to Type 299, Mk III prototype (interim); L4311, 4330, 4340, 4350, 4355 and 4360 originally ordered for RNZAF as Type 403 and NZ300–305 but not delivered; conversions to DWI—L4212, 4221, 4227, 4356 and 4358.

The following Squadrons received initial aircraft as listed in chronological order of reception: 99—L4215–4218, 4220, 4222, 4224–4225, 4227–4229, 4232, 4244, 4246–4247, first delivered 10 October, 1938, last 12 January, 1939; 38—L4230–4231, 4234–4243, 4245, 4248, 4295–4296, first delivered 24 November, 1938, last delivered 30 March, 1939; 149—L4249, 4252–4259, 4263–4266, 4270–4272, first delivered 20 January, last delivered 17 February, 1939; 9—L4260–4262, 4258–4269, 4273–4279, 4286–4288, 4320, 4322, first delivered 31 January, last delivered 2 May, 1939; 148—L4280–4284, 4289–4294, 4303–4304, 4308, first delivered 4 March, last delivered 19 April, 1939; 115—L4299–4301, 4305–4307, 4317–4319, 4321, 4323–4325, 4333–4334, first delivered 30 March, last delivered 16 May, 1939; 37—L4325–4329, 4331–4332, 4335–4339, 4347–4349, 4351–4354, first delivered 6 May, last delivered 15 June, 1939; 75—L4330, 4340, 4355, 4360, 4366–4373, first delivered May 1939, last delivered 11 July, 1939; 214—L4341–4346, 4354, 4356–4359, 4361–4365, first delivered in May, last delivered 28 June, 1939; 215—L4375–4390, first delivered 12 July, last delivered 1 August, 1939; L4255 converted for ambulance duties by Air Transport Auxiliary at White Waltham.

3. 100 Mk I ordered from Chester, as L7770–7819, 7840–7874, 7885–7899 under contract B.992424/39, and completed as three Mk I, 17 Mk IA and 80 Mk IC—L7770–7772, Mk I; L7773–7789, Mk IA; L7790–7899, Mk IC; most delivered direct into store at Maintenance Units for modification and future delivery to operational units; all delivered between 4 August, 1939, and 27 June, 1940; L7776 converted later to transport as C XV.

4. 100 Mk IC, built at Chester under contract B.124362/40 as N2735–2784, 2800–2829, 2840–2859; all delivered initially to Maintenance Units between 2 July and 22 August, 1940; conversions to Mk XVI—N2755, 2801, 2856, 2857.

522

5. 120 Mk IA built at Weybridge under contract 549268/36 as N2865–2914, 2935–2964, 2980–3019—12, (NZ306–317), N2874–2879 and N2937–2942 originally allocated to the RNZAF but not delivered. Conversions to Mk XV: N2867, 2871, 2875, 2877, 2880, 2886, 2887, 2909, 2944, 2947, 2954, 2955, 2958—all delivered between 3 November and 27 December, 1939.

6. 100 built at Weybridge under contract 549268/36 as P2515–2532, P9205–9250, P9265–9300—built as 50 Mk IA and 50 Mk IC from P9237; conversions to DWI—P2516—prototype conversion, also P2518, 2521, 2511, 9223 as Type 418; conversion to Mk III—P9238; conversions to Mk XV—P2519, 2521, 2528, 9209, 9222, 9231; conversion to Mk XVI—P9289—all delivered between 8 January and 11 April, 1940.

7. 550 Mk IC ordered from Chester under contract 992424/39 as R1000–1049, 1060–1099, 1135–1184, 1210–1254, 1265–1299, 1320–1349, 1354–1414, 1435–1474, 1490–1539, 1585–1629, 1640–1669, 1695–1729, 1757–1806—all built as IC except 25 converted to Mk IV as follows: R1220, 1390, 1490, 1510, 1515, 1520, 1525, 1530, 1535, 1585, 1590, 1610, 1615, 1620, 1625, 1650, 1655, 1695, 1705, 1715, 1725, 1765, 1775, 1785, 1795; conversions to Mk XVI—R1032, 1144, 1172, 1409, 1452, 1521, 1531, 1600, 1605, 1659, 1659, 1700, 1710–1711 and 1720—all delivered between 22 August, 1940, and June 1941.

8. 100 Mk IC ordered from Weybridge under contract B.3913/39 as R3150–3179, 3195–3239, 3275–3299, but built as 97 Mk IC and three conversions on the production line; conversion to Mk II—R3221; conversions to Mk V—R3298–3299; other conversions to Mk XVI later were R3217, 3225, 3234 and 3237—all delivered between 12 April and 9 June, 1940.

9. 300 Mk IC ordered from Weybridge under contract B.39600/39 as T2458–2477, 2501–2520, 2541–2580, 2606–2625, 2701–2750, 2801–2850, 2873–2922, 2951–3000, but built as follows: 293 Mk IC and conversions on line were: to Mk II—T2545; to Mk VIII —T2919, 2977, 2979, 2982, 2988, 2998—all delivered between 10 June, 1940, and 7 February, 1941; conversions later to Mk XVI—T2850, 2920, 2969.

10. 300 Mk II ordered from Weybridge under contract B.71441/40 as W5352–5401, 5414–5463, 5476–5500, 5513–5537, 5550–5598, 5611–5631, 5644–5690 and 5703–5735, built as 74 Mk IC, 199 Mk II and 27 Mk VIII; W5352, built as Mk IC; T2545, Mk II, built to replace W6352; Mk IC from W5612 except for the Mk VIIIs, which were W5615, 5619, 5623, 5631, 5645, 5647, 5649, 5651, 5653, 5655, 5657, 5659, 5661–5662, 5671–5672, 5674, 5676, 5678, 5725, 5628, 5730–5735; Mk II, W5352–5611, in blocks as above; conversions to Mk XVI—W5686 and 5709; special aircraft were W5389/G with Merlin 60 and wings from Mk VI aircraft fitted with Rover-Whittle W2B jet in tail in place of tail turret, maximum altitude reached was 33,000 ft; W5518/G fitted W2/700 jet in tail, maximum altitude reached 36,000 ft, most delivered to Maintenance Units between 7 October, 1940, and 4 May, 1941.

11. 30 Mk V and VI ordered from Weybridge under contract 67578/40/C.4 (c) as W5795–5824. Only 21 built: 9 Mk V, W5816–5824, cancelled. W5795 prototype, Mk VI, Type 431, reached 40,000 ft; W5796, Mk V, Type 426; W5797–5815, Mk VIA, Type 442, delivered between 28 October, 1941, and 27 May, 1942—two, W5801 and W5802, served for a time in 109 squadron.

12. 500 Mk IC ordered from Blackpool under contract B.92439/40/C.4(c) as X3160–3179, 3192–3226, 3275–3289, 3304–3313, 3330–3374, 3387–3426, 3445–3489, 3538–3567, 3584–3608, 3633–3577, 3594–3728, 3741–3754, 3784–3823, 3855–3890, 3923–3957, 3984–4003; only 50 Mk IC produced, X3160–3179 and 3192–3221, rest were Mk III; the Mk ICs were delivered straight to Maintenance Units between 8 August, 1940, and 6 July, 1942; conversions to—Mk XVI—X3193 and X3935; to Mk X—X3374 and X3595.

13. 750 ordered as: X5330–5359, 5372–5421, 5445–5490, 5523–5547, 5596–5630,

5657–5701, 5726–5775, 5810–5844, 5859–5903, 5920–5964, 5985–6004, 6023–6062, 6079–6128, 6153–6202, 6245–6294, 6311–6355, 6380–6419, 6468–6517, but all cancelled later.

14. 710 Mk IC ordered from Chester under contract 124362/40 as X9600–9644, 9658–9707, 9733–9757, 9784–9834, 9871–9890, 9905–9954, 9974–9993, Z1040–1054, 1066–1115, 1139–1183, 1202–1221, 1243–1292, 1311–1345, 1375–1424, 1459–1496, 1562–1578, 1592–1626, 1648–1697, 1717–1751; only 378 built as Mk IC X9600–Z1181, 195 Mk IV, Z1182–1496; and 137 Mk III, Z1562–1751; all delivered initially to Maintenance Units between 10 May, 1941, and 28 May, 1942; conversions to Mk XVI; X9663, 9678, Z1071, 1150; first delivered was X9600 10 May, 1941; last Mk IC delivered was Z1181 *Gorakhpur* on 9 March, 1942.

15. 200 Mk II built by Weybridge under contract B.71441/40 as Z8328–8377, 8397–8441, 8489–8538, 8567–8601, 8643–8662: all initially delivered to Maintenance Units between 14 July, 1941, and 30 June, 1942. Special aircraft were: Z8416/G fitted with 40 mm 'S' gun in nose; Z8570/G fitted with BTH W2B jet in place of tail turret.

16. 250 Mk IC ordered from Weybridge under contract B.71441/40 as Z8702–8736, 8761–8810, 8827–8871, 8891–8910, 8942–8991, 9016–9045, 9095–9114: conversions to Mk VIII—Z8702–8703, 8705–8708, 8710, 8712–8713, 8715, 8717, 8719, 8721, 8723, 8725, 8727, 8892, 8895, 8898, 8902, 8906—all initially delivered to Maintenance Units between 7 May, 1941, and 30 November, 1941; three subsequent conversions to Mk XVI—Z8709, 8831, 8850.

17. 50 Mk IC built by Weybridge under contract B.71441/40 as AD589–608 and AD624–653: AD646 torpedo-bomber prototype tested by TDU at Gosport—all delivered to Maintenance Units (41 of them subsequently going to the Middle East for 37, 40, 70, 108 and 148 Squadrons)—between 6 December, 1941, and 5 January, 1942.

18. 150 Mk IC ordered from Weybridge under contract B.71441/40 as BB455–484, 497–541, 566–600, 617–656: only 50 delivered, BB455–484 and BB497–516 as 43 Mk IC and 7 Mk VIII (BB461, 466, 571, 476, 481, 503, 513), rest cancelled; all delivered initially to Maintenance Units between 6 January and 11 February, 1942.

19. 600 Mk III built by Chester under contract 124352/40 as BJ581–625, 642–675, 688–730, 753–801, 818–847, 876–922, 958–991, BK123–166, 179–214, 234–281, 295–315, 330–358, 385–408, 425–471, 489–517, 534–564; the majority delivered direct to Maintenance Units between 30 May and 2 December, 1942.

20. 400 Mk III ordered from Blackpool under contract B92439/40/C.4(c) as DF542–579, 594–642, 664–709, 727–776, 794–832, 857–900, 921–956, 975–999, DG112–134 and DG148–197; only 150 built (DF542–743) as 145 Mk III and 5 Mk X (DF609, 686, 701, 730 and 740); all delivered initially to Maintenance Units between 5 August, 1942, and 25 September, 1942. The rest, 250, were cancelled.

21. 100 Mk VI ordered from Weybridge under contract 67578/40 with Merlin LX engines as DR471–504, 519–549, 566–600; only 44 completed (DR471–528), rest cancelled 1 July, 1942; DR471–479 delivered as Mk VIA Type 442 and DR480–504 and 519–528 as Mk VIG Type 449, all serials followed by 'G', i.e. DR471/G, first delivered 27 May, 1942, last on 31 March, 1943.

22. 415 Mk IC built by Chester under contract 124362/40 as DV411–458, 473–522, 536–579, 593–624, 638, 678, 694–740, 757–786, 799–846, 864–898, 914–953; all initially delivered to Maintenance Units between 11 November, 1941, and 13 June, 1942: conversions to Mk XVI; DV491, 594, 617, 704, 738, 761–762, 822, 886, 920–921, 924, 942.

23. 16 Mk IC built at Weybridge under contract B.71441/40 as ES980–995 with ES986 converted to a Mk VIII with a Leigh light: all delivered initially to Maintenance Units between 10 and 19 February, 1942.

24. 1,124 Mk IC ordered from Chester under contract 124362/40/C4(*c*) as: HD942–991, HE101–134, 136–184, 197–244, 258–306, 318–353, 365–398, 410–447, 459–508, 513–556, 568–615, 627–667, 679–715, 727–772, 784–833, 845–873, 898–931, 946–995, HF113–155, 167–208, 220–252, 264–312, 329–363, 381–422, 446–495, 513–545, 567–606; produced as follows; 85 Mk IC, 789 Mk X, 8 Mk XII and 242 Mk IV; Mk ICs were HD942 to HE146; Mk Xs were HD147–995 and HF452–606; Mk XIIs were HF113–120; Mk XIVs were HF121–451 : first was delivered 13 June, 1942, last delivered 7 June, 1943.

25. 153 built by Blackpool under contract B.92439/40/C.4(*c*) as HF609–650, 666–703, 718–764, 791–816: delivered as 123 Mk III, 27 Mk X and three Mk XI; Mk Xs were HF614, 622, 626, 630, 634, 638, 642, 646, 650, 669, 723, 725, 729, 732, 735, 739, 743, 747, 751, 755, 759, 763, 793, 797, 805, 808 and 811; Mk XIs were HF720 and HF803–804; rest were Mk IIIs; delivered between 25 September, 1942, and 3 February, 1943.

26. 84 built by Weybridge under contract B.71441/40 as HF828–869, 881–922, with 62 Mk IC and 22 Mk VIII as follows: HF828, 838, 850, 854, 857, 860, 863, 866, 869, 883, 886, 889, 892, 895, 901, 904, 907, 910, 913, 916, 919 and 922; all delivered to Maintenance Units between 19 February and 11 April, 1942.

27. 300 built at Weybridge under contract B.71441/40 as HX364–403, 417–452, 466–489, 504–538, 558–606, 625–656, 670–690, 709–751, 767–786 with 124 Mk IC and 176 Mk VIII; all Mk IC delivered initially to Maintenance Units between 12 April and 18 September, 1942; Mk ICs as follows: HX364–371, 373–375, 377–378, 380, 382, 384–385, 387, 389–390, 392–393, 395, 397, 399–400, 402, 417, 421, 423, 425, 429, 431, 433, 435, 438, 440, 442, 445–447, 449, 451, 468, 470, 472, 475, 478, 480, 483–484, 486, 488, 506, 508, 510, 514, 516, 518, 521, 523, 525, 527, 529, 533, 536, 558, 560, 564, 567, 569, 571, 573, 577, 580, 583, 585, 589, 591, 594, 597, 601, 603, 606, 627, 631, 633, 635, 637, 639, 643, 645, 648, 651, 655, 670, 673, 676, 680, 682, 685, 688, 710, 712, 714, 716, 718, 722, 724, 727, 730, 734, 736, 739, 742, 746, 748, 750, 767, 769, 773, 775, 778, 781, 785.

28. 850 built by Blackpool under contract B.92439/40/C.4(*c*) as: HZ102–150, 173–209, 242–284, 299–315, 351–378, 394–439, 467–487, 513–554, 570–604, 633–660, 689–727, 752–770, 793–820, 862–897, 937–981, JA104–151, 176–210, 256–273, 295–318, 337–363, 378–426, 442–481, 497–539, 561–585, 618–645 with 62 Mk III, 301 Mk X, 72 Mk XI and 415 Mk XIII. Mk IIIs were HZ103–104, 106–107, 109–110, 112–113, 115–116, 118–119, 121–122, 124–125, 127–128, 130–131, 133–134, 136–137, 139–140, 145–156, 148–150, 173–174, 176–177, 179–180, 182–183, 185–186, 188–189, 191–192, 194–195, 197–198, 200–201, 203–204, 206–207, 209, 242, 244–245, 247–248, 250; Mk Xs were HZ102, 105, 108, 111, 114, 117, 120, 123, 125, 129, 132, 135, 138, 141, 144, 147, 175, 181, 187, 193, 199, 205, 243, 249, 255–273, 277–282, 300–305, 309–314, 353–358, 362–367, 371–376, 398–403, 410–415, 422–427, 434–439, 457–487, 513–521, 528–533, 540–545, 552–554, 570–572, 579–582, 713–720, 809–818, 941–950, JA111–140, 185–194, 341–352, 448–481, 497–512, 519–534; Mk XIs were HZ142–143, 178, 184, 190, 196, 202, 208, 246, 251–254, 274–276, 283–284, 299, 306–308, 315, 351–352, 359–351, 368–370, 377–378, 394–397, 404–409, 416–421, 428–433, 522–527, 534–539, 546–550: Mk XIIIs were HZ551, 573–578, 583–604, 633–660, 689–712, 721–727, 752–770, 793–808, 819–820, 862–897, 937–940, 951–981, JA104–110, 141–151, 176–184, 195–210, 256–318, 337–340, 353–363, 378–426, 442–447, 513–518, 525–539, 561–585, 618–645; production commenced with Hercules VI, but later aircraft fitted with Hercules XVI; most delivered initially to Maintenance Units between 20 December, 1942, and 20 December, 1943.

29. 150 Built at Weybridge under contract B.71441/40 as LA964–998, LB110–156, LB169–197 and LB213–251 of which 16 were Mk IC as follows: LA965, 968, 973, 978, 984, 988, 994, LB110, 116, 120, 126, 131, 141, 148, 152, 174; the remaining 134 aircraft were Mk VIII, delivered to Maintenance Units from 19 September to 31 October, 1942.

30. 1,382 Mk X Type 440, ordered under contract 124362/40/C.4(c) with Bristol Hercules XVI engines and built at Chester as follows: LN157–189, 221–248, 261–303, 317–353, 369–509, 423–458, 481–516, 529–571, 583–622, 633–676, 689–723, 736–778, 791–823, 836–879, 893–936, 948–989, LP113–156, 169–213, 226–268, 281–314, 328–369, 381–415, 428–469, 483–526, 539–581, 595–628, 640–686, 699–733, 748–788, 802–849, 863–889, 901–930, 943–986, LR110–142, 156–164, 168–183, 195–210, delivered between 15 September, 1943, and 18 January, 1945; LN718 with Hercules 100.

31. 600 ordered as Mk X Type 440 on 28 May, 1942, under contract B.92439/40/C.4(c) with Hercules XVI engines and built at Blackpool as 299 Mk X, 297 Mk XIII and 4 Mk XIV as; ME870–914, 926–960, 972–999; MF113–156, 170–213, 226–267, 279–320, 335–377, 389–424, 439–480, 493–538, 550–596, 614–659, 672–713, 725–742: Mk Xs were ME870–883, 951–960, 972–999; MF113–124, 131–144, 193–202, 236–249, 281–288, 311–316, 346–351, 367–372, 299–404, 421–424, 439–441, 452–459, 468–479, 500–538, 550–572, 583–596, 614–615, 624–635, 644–655, 676–687, 695–706, 728–739: Mk XIVs were MF450–451, 726–727; rest were Mk XIII; delivered between 10 December, 1943, and June 1944: six to Royal Hellenic Air Force in April 1946 were ME890, 907, 940; MF190, 466, 643.

32. 250 built at Weybridge under contract AIR/2312 as MP502–549, 562, 601, 615–656, 679–724, 738–774, 789–825, delivered as 105 Mk XI, 50 Mk XII, 42 Mk XIII and 53 Mk XIV; Mk XIs were MP502, 504, 516–535, 543–549, 562–574, 576–577, 579–580, 582–583, 585–586, 588–589, 591–592, 594–595, 597–598, 600–601, 616–617, 619, 621, 623, 625, 627, 629, 631, 633, 635, 637, 639, 649, 651, 653, 655, 679, 681, 683, 685, 687, 689, 691–703. Mk XIIs were MP503, 505–515, 536–542, 575, 578, 581, 584, 587, 590, 593, 596, 599, 615, 618, 620, 622, 624, 626, 628, 630, 632, 634, 636, 638, 650, 652, 654, 656, 680, 682, 684, 686, 688, 690: Mk XIIs were MP704–709, 711, 713, 175, 171, 719, 721, 723, 738, 740, 742–749, 751, 753, 755, 757, 759, 761–762, 764–765, 767–768, 770–771, 773, 790, 793, 796, 800, 804: Mk XIVs were MP710, 712, 714, 716, 718, 720, 722, 724, 739, 741, 750, 752, 754, 756, 758, 760, 763, 766, 769, 772, 774, 789, 791–792, 794–795, 797–799, 801–803, 805–825, delivered between 5 December, 1942, and 18 September, 1943: conversions to Mk XVII; MP518, 520, 522, 526, 529, 531–533, 548: aircraft sold to France in 1946 included MP623, 741, 756, 771, 774, 818 and 825.

33. 27 Mk X built by Blackpool under contract B.92439/40/C.4(c) as MS470–496 and delivered between 3 February and 4 April, 1943.

34. 750 Mk X ordered from Chester under contract B.124362/40 as; NA710–754, 766–811, 823–870, 893–937, 949–997; NB110–155, 167–213, 225–269, 282–329, 341–385, 398–443, 456–502, 514–556, 569–613, 625–670, 684–714, 739–766: only 263 delivered between 2 August, 1944, and 5 July, 1945, the rest being cancelled (from NB140 to 766): NA857 scheduled to have been fitted with Napier Naiad engines, but not converted.

35. 441 Mk XIV ordered from Chester under contract B.124362/40/C.4(c) as NB767–787, 796–841, 853–896, 908–952, 964–999; NC112–160, 164–209, 222–268, 280–327, 339–387, 399–408. Only 296 produced, the following being cancelled: NB784–787; NC235–268, 280–327, 339–387, 399–408, delivered between April 1944 and 8 July, 1945; aircraft sold to France in 1946 included NB796, 812, 826, 876, 913, 919, 927, 942–943, 945, 947, 971, 975, 977, 980, 983, 998, NC122–124.

36. 500 Mk X, Type 440, ordered from Blackpool under contract B.92439/40/C.4(c) with Hercules XVI as NC414–459, 471–517, 529–576, 588–632, 644–692, 706–750, 766–813, 825–870, 883–929, 942–990 and ND104–133; produced as 296 Mk X, 90 Mk XIII, 84 Mk XIV and 30 Mk XVIII; Mk XIIIs were NC414–418, 433, 440, 453–459, 471, 482–489, 503, 510, 534–541, 555–562, 571–576, 588–589, 602–609, 626–631, 656–663, 741–747; Mk XIVs were NC419–420, 441–442, 490–493, 511–513, 542–544, 490–591, 610–

613, 622–625, 632, 644–647, 672–677, 771–776, 785–788, 797–800, 828–835, 848–855, 870, 883–889, 902–907 and ND129–133; Mk XVIIIs were NC868–869, 926–928 and ND104–128, delivered between June and 10 November, 1944; aircraft sold to Royal Hellenic Air Force were NC418, 433; aircraft sold to France included NC492, 647, 922 in 1946.

37. 400 Mk X, Type 440, ordered from Blackpool under contract B.92439/40/C.4(c) with Hercules XVI as PF820–866, 879–915, 927–968, 979–999, PG112–157, 170–215, 227–269, 282–326, 338–379, 392–422; produced as 208 Mk X, 162 Mk XIV and 30 Mk XVIII; Mk XIVs were PF820–822, 831–838, 847–854, 863–866, 879–882, 889–893, 902–911, 931–940, 949–958, 967–968, 979–986, 995–999; PG112–116, 125–134, 139–148, 153–157, 170–174, 183–192, 197–206, 211–215, 227–231, 240–245, 266–269, 282–285, 298–303; Mk XVIIIs were PG236–239, 246–249, 254–257, 349, 356, 367–370, 395–400: delivered between November 1944 and April 1945; aircraft sold to France in 1946 included PF837, 996–997, PG181, 183, 230, 290–291, 316.

38. 600 ordered November 1943 from Blackpool as 200 Mk X and 400 Mk XIII under contract B.92439/40/C.4(c) with Bristol Hercules XVI engines as RP312–358, 373–415, 428–469, 483–526, 538–561, 565–606, 619–663, 677–718, 735–778, 791–835, 848–889, 903–947, 959–999, RR113–156, 169–178; only 226 produced up to RP590, rest were cancelled; produced as 206 Mk X and 20 Mk XVIII; Mk XVIIIs were RP330–335, 348–351, 392–395, 412–415, 428–429 delivered between 7 May, 1945, and the last Wellington delivered was RP590, on 25 October, 1945; RP468 fitted with tail boom radar device at Langley, allotted civil registration G-ALUH, on 22 July, 1949.

39. 402 Mk X ordered from Blackpool under contract B.92439/40/C.4(c) with Bristol Hercules XVI engines as TH450–496, 521–560, 574–598, 612–647, 661–706, 719–757, 771–815, 829–869, 883–927, 937–974, all cancelled.

40. 150 Mk XIV ordered from Blackpool July 1944 under contract B.92439/40/C.4(c) as TN250–289, 310–324, 340–363, 380–427, 440–462, all cancelled.

Squadrons: 8, 9, 12, 14, 15, 18, 24, 35, 38, 40, 57, 69, 70, 75, 93, 99, 100, 101, 103, 104, 105, 108, 109, 115, 142, 148, 149, 150, 156, 158, 161, 162, 166, 172, 179, 192, 196, 199, 203, 211, 214, 215, 218, 221, 227, 232, 244, 280, 282, 283, 294, 299, 300, 301, 304, 305, 311, 326, 355, 403, 405, 407, 415, 419, 420, 424, 425, 426, 427, 428, 429, 431, 432, 458, 459, 460, 461, 466, 467, 524, 544, 547, 567, 612, 614, 621 and 625.

Operational Training Units: 1, 3, 5, 6, 7, 9, 10, 11, 12, 14, 15, 16, 17, 18, 19, 20, 21, 22, 23, 24, 25, 26, 27, 28, 29, 30, 32, 51, 54, 62, 63, 76, 77, 78, 81, 82, 83, 84, 85, 86, 101, 102, 104, 105, 107, 109, 111 and 132.

Flights: Beam Approach Training—3, 9, 10, 1504 and 1505; 3 Group Training—1418, 1429, 1443, 1446, 1473, 1474, 1481; Target Towing—1483, 1485, 1503, 1508, 1689; Aden Communications; Chivenor Radar Training; Christchurch Special Duty; Malta Special Duties; Northolt Station Flight.

Other Units: A & AEE; No. 1 Armament School; 201 Advanced Flying School; 202 Advanced Flying School; Air Fighting Development Unit; 21(P) Advanced Flying Unit; Air Gunners' Schools 1, 2, 3, 10, 11 and 12; Air Navigation Schools 1, 2, 5, 6, 7 and 10; 40 Armament Practice Unit, Air-Sea Warfare Development Unit; Bomber Command Instructors' School; Central Gunnery School; Central Navigation and Control School; Central Navigation School; 202 Conversion Training Unit; Conversion Units 1380, 1381 and 1665; Ferry Training Units 301, 303, 304, 310 and 311; Ferry Units 1, 11 and 18; Gunnery Research Units 1, 2 and 3; 228 Operational Conversion Unit; 7 Service Flying Training School; Signals Flying Unit; 1 Torpedo Training Unit (Abbotsinch); the RAE.

Some of these Units were solely for ferrying, and not all were completely equipped with Wellingtons; some of the OTUs had differing types of aircraft.

Wellington Production Analysis 1938–45

	I	IA	DWI	IC	II	III	IV	V	VI	VIII	TOR VIII	TT VIII	Leigh VIII	X	XI	Spe XI	Trop XI	XII	Trop XII	XIII	Trop XIII	XIV	XVIII	Total
Weybridge 1938	34	—	—	—	—	—	—	—	—	—	—	—	—	—	—	—	—	—	—	—	—	—	—	34
1939	144	124	1	—	1	1	—	—	—	—	—	—	—	—	—	—	—	—	—	—	—	—	—	271
1940	—	42	3	422	36	1	—	—	—	2	—	—	—	—	—	—	—	—	—	—	—	—	—	506
1941	—	—	—	362	305	—	—	2	—	52	—	—	—	—	—	—	—	—	—	—	—	—	—	721
1942	—	—	—	268	59	—	—	1	53	11	47	176	54	—	2	—	—	8	—	—	—	—	—	679
1943	—	—	—	—	—	—	—	—	11	—	21	27	4	—	1	30	72	32	10	1	41	53	—	303
Total	178	166	4	1,052	401	2	—	3	64	65	68	203	58	—	3	30	72	40	10	1	41	53	—	2,514
Chester 1939	3	—	—	—	—	—	—	—	—	—	—	—	—	—	—	—	—	—	—	—	—	—	—	3
1940	—	17	—	469	—	—	1	—	—	—	—	—	—	—	—	—	—	—	—	—	—	—	—	487
1941	—	—	—	711	—	13	173	—	—	—	—	—	—	—	—	—	—	—	—	—	—	—	—	897
1942	—	—	—	403	—	724	46	—	—	—	—	—	—	183	—	—	—	—	—	—	—	—	—	1,356
1943–44	—	—	—	—	—	—	—	—	—	—	—	—	—	2,251	—	—	—	—	8	—	—	538	—	2,797
Total	3	17	—	1,583	—	737	220	—	—	—	—	—	—	2,434	—	—	—	—	8	—	—	538	—	5,540
Blackpool 1940	—	—	—	8	—	—	—	—	—	—	—	—	—	—	—	—	—	—	—	—	—	—	—	8
1941	—	—	—	42	—	157	—	—	—	—	—	—	—	—	—	—	—	—	—	—	—	—	—	199
1942	—	—	—	—	—	572	—	—	—	—	—	—	—	42	1	—	—	—	—	—	—	—	—	615
1943–45	—	—	—	—	—	51	—	—	—	—	—	—	—	1,327	74	—	—	—	—	802	—	250	80	2,584
Total	—	—	—	50	—	780	—	—	—	—	—	—	—	1,369	75	—	—	—	—	802	—	250	80	3,406
Total	181	183	4	2,685	401	1,519	220	3	64	65	68	203	58	3,803	78	30	72	40	18	803	41	841	80	11,460

Including the prototype B.9/32 this makes a grand total of 11,461 actually built from a total of 14,182 ordered.
Abbreviations: TOR—Torpedo; TT—Tropicalised torpedo; Spe—Special; Trop—Tropical.

1. Prototype K8178, ordered 7 October, 1935, to contract 441973/35 as Type 284 to specification B.1/35.

2. Second prototype B.1/35, L9704, ordered 2 July, 1937, under amended contract 441973/35 and further amended 25 February, 1938, to have Napier Sabres as Type 400.

3. 250 ordered 28 December, 1940, under contract AIR/494/C.4(c) and specification Warwick I/P.1, as follows: BV214–256, 269–316, 332–370, 384–421, 436–484, 499–531, as 150 B.I and 100 B.II. Contract amended in October 1941 so that BV216 was built as B.II prototype under contract B.104882/40/C.4(c); contract further amended 28 August, 1942, so that 14 were converted for BOAC, BV243–256, under contract AIR/2534/C.4(c): Air Staff decided on 21 January, 1943, Warwick I and II bombers would be used for ASR duties and freight; production of B.I limited to BV214–215, 217–222, 224, 228–230, 291, 293, 295–296(16); all used for trials, tests and investigations by Vickers, RAE and A & AEE; BV217 used for engine-cooling tests and initial investigation into the rudder characteristics for the Type 491, Viking, late 1944; BV228 used for trial installation of the airborne lifeboat; BV229 and 291 eventually ended up at 5(c) OTU at Turnbury; BV296 converted for ASR and with Double Wasp and transport clearance.

C.I, Type 456: 14, BV243–256, converted and given civil registrations G-AGEX–G-AGFK inclusive; G-AGFJ and FK had different cabin windows; all delivered to BOAC between 6 May and the 1 November, 1943, and used on the North Africa and Mediterranean routes; later all transferred to 167 Squadron at Holmesley South with military serials and to 525 Squadron at Lyneham in 1944; all were withdrawn from overseas service on 27 April, 1944.

ASR: 40—BV223, 225–227, 231–241, 269–281, 283, 285, 287, 289, 297, 299–300, 305, 310, 315–316, 332. *Squadrons and Individual Aircraft:* 279—BV233, 287, 305, 310, 316; 283—BV235–236, 240–241, 280, 289, 297; 293—BV225, 227, 238, 297.

ASR A: 10 aircraft only, BV298, 242, 282, 284, 286, 301–303, 333 and 334; all had modified bomb doors for carrying the Mk I lifeboat and two sets of Lindholme gear. *Squadrons and Individual Aircraft:* 280—BV282 and 284 delivered 18 August, 1943, also 286, 26 August; 281—BV284, 303. *Other Units:* 5(c) OTU BV286, 302, 333–334.

ASR Stage B: 20—BV288, 290, 306–309, 311–314, 335–341, 351–352; BV304 first converted. All could carry the Mk I lifeboat, two sets of Lindholme gear, ASV and F-N120A tail turret. *Squadrons and Individual Aircraft:* 281—BV304, 308, 309, 311, 335, 337; 282—BV288; to Middle East—BV341, 382; 5(c) OTU—BV311, 313.

ASR Stage C—later called ASRI Type 462: 149 built or converted as follows: BV292, 294, 296, 342–350, 353–370, 384–421, 436–484, 499–531. *Squadrons and Individual Aircraft:* 269—BV483, 499, 507–508, 519; 276—BV479, 527, 530–531; 277—BV527; 278—BV528–529; 279—BV392, 516, 518; 280—BV346, 349, 386, 414; 281—BV345, 367, 384, 386, 392, 401, 404, 409–411, 413–414, 417–419, 438–440; 282—BV477, HF944, 960, 952, 959, 961–964, 967, 969, 974; 283—BV441, 450, 472, 504, 526; 292—BV394, 452–453, 456, 463; 293—BV365, 415, 420, 449, 457, 464, 502, 505; 5(c) OTU—BV348, 355, 391, 393, 406, 412, 470, 506, 511, 518; 6 OTU—BV512, 531.

4. 440 ordered under contract AIR/494/C.4(c) as HF938–987, HG114–156, 169–193, 207–256, 271–307, 320–365, 384–414, 435–459, 476–525, 538–585, 599–633, but 82 cancelled, HG538, 540–585 and 599–633, so 358 built as follows:

(a) ASRI: 56—HF938–982, HG124–134. *Squadrons and Individual Aircraft:* 269—HF938 and 940; 276—HF938, 940 and 960; 277—HF938, 940 and 960; 278—HF961–962, 967–968, 976; 279—HF948, 961, 963–964, 978, 981; 280—HF947, 962–963, 967, 976–977, 979; 282—HF976–980; 283—HF966, HG134; 292—HF954, 966, 970, 972,

HG133; 293—HF955, 958, HG131–132; 5(c) OTU—HF939, 946; 6 OTU—HF938, 940, 946, 960, 981.

(b) ASR VI: 69—HF983–987, HG114–123, 135–140, 142–156, 169–193, 207–214 and HG141 test bed. *Squadrons and Individual Aircraft:* 251—HG174, 179, 184; 268—HG136, 138, 142, 148, 156, 171, 174, 179, 192; 279—HF983, 986–986, HG118, 142, 144, 151, 169–171, 173, 176–177, 180–181, 189, 193, 207, 209–210, 212, 214; 280—HF984–987, HG114–115, 119, 121, 123, 136–138, 140, 142, 144–156, 170–171, 173–176, 178, 180, 182, 187–188, 190, 192, 208, 211, 214; 281—HF985–986 HG116–119, 121, 136, 144, 151, 169–170, 172, 176, 183, 193, 213; 282—HG114, 120, 135–136, 155; 520—HG114, 122, 135, 139, 155, 179, 185–186; 5(c) OTU—HF984, 987, HG115–117, 121–123, 190; 6 OTU—HG115, 117, 121–122, 173, 177, 181. HG141, second Warwick to use Centaurus VII as test bed.

(c) GR.II: 118—HG341–365, 384–414, 435–459, 476–525, 539. *Squadrons and Individual Aircraft:* Test Beds: HG341, fitted Centaurus 130 engines for Airspeed Ambassador; HG342, fitted Centaurus XII engines; HG343, fitted Centaurus VII and Centaurus 57 engines for Short Shetland; HG344, engine trials at Bristols; HG345, fitted Centaurus 12SM by Bristols; 6 OTU—HG402, 442–443, 446–448, 460–451, 453, 481–483, 487; 26 OTU—HG349–350; 524—HG348; EANS—HG347; EAAS—HG347; no record of others to units.

(d) GR.II Met: 14, HG513–525 and 539 only. Squadrons—Nil.

(e) C.III: 100—HG215–256, 271–307, 320–340. *Squadrons and Individual Aircraft:* 167—HG219–221, 227–231, 234–235, 237, 278–280, 282–297, 301–302, 305, 320–321, 323, 325, 327; 297—HG277; 301(P)—HG225–226, 236, 275–276, 281, 289, 293–299, 322; 304—HG231, 233, 246, 273, 282, 292, 294–295; 297—298, 300, 306–307, 324, 326, 329–332, 334–340; 525—HG219–220, 223–224, 226–233; CRD and A & AEE—HG215, 217–218, 252; Test Beds: HG248 fitted with Sabre VI engines by Napier.

5. 225 ordered, LM769–803, 817–858, 870–913, 927–968, 980–997 and LN110–153, under contract AIR/494/C.4(c); only 108, GR.V LM777–803, 817–858, 870–900, 902–909 produced, the remainder being cancelled; first, LM777, issued to CRD at Defford 26 May, 1945; most into store but some to MAAF and the following to 179 Squadron: LM791 to 797 between 22 November and 11 December, 1945; LM855 used by the RAE; LM818 fitted with meteorological nose scanner and clear Perspex radome.

6. 300 ordered, PN623–667, 681–696, 697–725, 739–782, 796–839, 853–898, 910–952 and 964–996 under contract AIR/494/C.4(c). Only 127, PN697–725, 739–782, 796–839 and 853–862 actually built as 102 GRV and 25 ASR VI: GRV. *Squadrons and Individual Aircraft:* A & AEE—PN697, 698, 701, 707, 710, 760; 17 (SAAF)—PN704, 706, 723, 741, 742, 755, 757, 766, 767, 782; 27 (SAAF)—PN704, 723, 741, 742, 751, 753–756, 758–759, 761; 179—PN709, 711–712, 715–717, 721–722, 739, 743, 747–750; GR VI: 269—PN862; 280—PN852; 520—PN828; of the remainder PN829–861 were delivered into store: 17 and 27 Squadrons (SAAF), on return to South Africa took 16 aircraft each with them; PN697 Centaurus VII used on cooling and performance trials; PN700 Vickers' trials and installation of Mk VIII auto controls and revised installation of F-N77 Mk II gun turret; PN699 and 776 at RAE for trials of Mk VIII auto controls; PN710 carried out rudder trials with new type fin; PN760, application of beam guns; PN796, application of large nose scanner; GRV Civil: one PN703 registered G-AGLD as cargo carrier for BOAC.

Warwick Production

845 Warwicks of all marks were produced at Weybridge as follows: two prototypes, 16 B.I, 14 C.I for BOAC, 40 ASR bombers, 10 ASR Stage As, 20 ASR Stage Bs, 205 ASR I, 94 ASR VI (the RAF still referred to these as ASR I), one prototype B.II, 118 GR.IIs, 14 GR.II Met, 100 C.III, 210 GR.V and one experimental.

Windsor

Two prototypes, DW506 and DW512, ordered under contract AIR/1153/C.4(*c*) dated 15 July, 1941, to specification B.5/41 and as Type 433 Warwick Mk III for a pressure-cabin development of the Warwick with four Merlin 60s; specification changed to B.3/42 on 16 September, 1942, with four Merlin 61s.

Type 447—prototype DW506 built with Merlin 61s, later fitted with Merlin 65s and first flew on 20 October, 1943.

Type 457—second prototype DW512 fitted Merlin 85s with circular engine cowlings and first flew in February 1944.

Type 461—NK136 ordered 17 December, 1942, to the same contract as above; first flew on 11 July, 1944, with no armament as Type 480, remote-controlled inner nacelle barbettes fitted by April 1945; to Pembrey for armament trials during 1945 and to Manby for ground instruction as 6222M in 1946.

Type 471—first pre-production ordered under contract AIR/1153/C.4(*c*) as NN670 and to be fitted with Merlin 85s; scheduled to go to A and AEE for performance trials, but construction cancelled on 15 March, 1946, when almost complete; to have been fitted later with Merlin 100 engines as Type 483.

Type 476—second pre-production and fifth aircraft ordered under original contract as NN673; scheduled to fly initially with Merlin 100s, but order changed on 27 February, 1945, for fitting of Rolls-Royce Clyde propeller-turbine as the Type 601, cancelled on 16 January, 1946, when 65 per cent complete.

Type 483—300 ordered on 24 June, 1943, under contract AIR/2999/C.4(*c*) to be built at Weybridge as follows: PE510–535, 565–606, 618–658, 671–615, 727–769, 782–826 and 839–878: all to be as the Type 483 B.I, with the first scheduled to fly in February 1945; on 19 June, 1945, the contract was cut to 40 aircraft fitted with Clydes and designated B.II; on 23 November, 1945, all were cancelled.

Viking

Total built—163

C/n	Type	Registration or Serial	Initial Operator, and name	Subsequent Operators
1*	491	G-AGOK	Ministry of Supply	Allotted TT194 not used
2	495	G-AGOL	,,	Allotted TT197 not used, also VX238 to RAF St Athan as 7215M
3	496	G-AGOM	BOAC (BEA Division)	Originally allotted TT181 not used, also VX141 to BLEU
4	498	G-AGON	,, ,,	To RAF as VW214, Eagle, BKS
5	498	G-AGRM	,, ,,	To RAF as VW215
6	498	G-AGRN	,, ,,	To RAF as VW216
7	498	G-AGRO	,, ,,	Fields
8	498	G-AGRP	,, ,,	Fields, Hunting Air Transport, Kuwait Oil Co, Hunting-Clan, Airline Air Spares, Overseas Aviation (CI)
9	498	G-AGRR	,, ,,	Britavia, Mexico XB-QEX, Eagle, Lufttransport D-AIDA, D-BETA, Aero Transport (Austria) OE-FAT

* C/ns 1–9 later changed to 101–109.

110	498	G-AGRS	BOAC (BEA Division)	BSAA, BWIA VP-TAV, Independent Air Travel, Eagle, Orion, Air Safaris, United Dominions Trust (Commercial)
111	498	G-AGRT	,, ,,	BSAA, BWIA VP-TAW *Grenada*, Independent Air Travel, Eagle
112	498	G-AGRU	BEA *Vagrant*	BSAA, BWIA VP-TAX *Barbados*, British International Air Lines, East Anglian Flying Services, Channel
113	620	LV-XEN	Argentine Government	T-1 Argentine Air Force
114	498	G-AGRV	BEA *Value*	Hunting Air Transport, Tradair
115	498	G-AGRW	,, *Vagabond*	Hunting Air Transport, Overseas Aviation (CI), Autair International Airways
116	498	G-AHON	,, *Valentine*	Transworld Charter, Crewsair, Airwork
117	498	G-AHOP	,, *Valerie*	Crewsair, Lep Airservices, Airwork, Guinness Breweries, Marconi, United Airways
118	498	G-AHOR	,, *Valet*	Transworld Charter, Crewsair, Eagle, Airwork, Air Safaris, Trek Airways ZS-DNU
119	498	G-AHOS	,, *Valiant*	BSAA, BWIA VP-TAT *Trinidad*, Independent Air Travel, Eagle, Orion, Air Safaris
120	604	VT-AZA	Indian National Airways *Jumna*	IAC
121	498	G-AHOT	BEA *Valkyrie*	Transworld Charter, Eagle, Crewsair, Airwork, Meredith Air Transport, Trek Airways ZS-DKH, Protea Airways
122	498	G-AHOU	,, *Valley*	BSAA, BWIA VP-TAU *Antigua*, Independent Air Travel, Overseas Aviation (CI), Swiss Universal Air Charter
123	498	G-AHOV	,, *Valour*	Crewsair
124	498	G-AHOW	,, *Vanessa*	Transworld Charter, Crewsair, Eagle and Airwork XD636, Trek Airways ZS-DKI, African Air Safaris, Air Safaris, Eros, Air Ferry, Invicta Airways
125	614	G-AHOX	,, *Vanguard*	To MoS as VW218
126	604	VT-AZB	Indian National Airways *Indus*	IAC
127	621	VL226	RAF	King's Flight, BEA G-AIJE, Independent Air Travel
128	614	G-AHOY	BEA *Vanity*	Hunting Air Transport, Eagle, Pegasus, Autair, Claydon Aviation, Invicta

129	614	G-AHOZ	BEA *Vantage*	BWIA VP-TAZ *British Honduras*, CAA VP-YJA *Hunyani*, Eagle, Channel, East Anglian Flying Services
130	614	G-AHPA	,, *Varlet*	To RAF as VW217
131	621	VL227	Ministry of Supply	BKS G-AIKN, Continental Air Services
132	614	G-AHPB	BEA *Variety*	Hunting Air Transport, Tradair, Overseas Aviation (CI), Autair
133	614	G-AHPC	,, *Vassal*	Hunting Air Transport, Tradair, Air Safaris
134	614	G-AHPD	,, *Vampire*	Hunting Air Transport
135	615	LV-XEQ	Argentine Government	T-2 Argentine Air Force
136	621	VL228	Ministry of Supply	Used at A & AEE and RAE
137	614	G-AHPE	BEA *Vandal*	Aviation Traders, Bond Air Services, BWIA VP-TBB *Bahamas*, Independent Air Travel, Continental Air Services, Overseas Aviation (CI)
138	614	G-AHPF	,, *Vedette*	Aviation Traders, BWIA VP-TBC *British Guiana*, CAA VP-YJB *Luapula*, Eagle, Aero Transport (Austria) OE-FAE
139	641	VP-YHJ	CAA *Sabi*	President Motors ZS-DDO, Independent Air Travel, Falcon Airways, Canopus Airways, Air Sud Kasa, Lux International
140	621	VL229	Ministry of Supply	English Electric, Tradair G-APWS
141	643	ZS-BSB	Suidair International *Rex*	CAA VP-YIR *Luanga*, Eagle, East Anglian Flying Services, Channel
142	639	G-AHPI	Hunting Air Travel *Greta*	
143	604	VT-CEJ	Indian National Airways *Ganges*	
144	624	VL245	RAF	King's Flight
145	621	VL230	,,	Field Aircraft Services G-ANZK, Hunting-Clan
146	616	VP-YEW	CAA *Zambezi*	Eagle
147	639	G-AHPJ	Hunting Air Travel	Overseas Aviation (CI), Autair, Aero Sahara F-OCEH, European Aero Services
148	610	G-AHPK	BEA *Veracity*	
149	610	G-AHPL	,, *Verdant* and *Lord Anson*	Eagle Aviation, CAA VP-YKK *Lundi*, Claydon Aviation, Pegasus, Autair, Invicta

150	621	VL231	RAF	ETPS, RAAF, Lufttransport D-AMOR, D-BONA, Air Ferry, Invicta Airways
151	615	LV-XER	Argentine Government	T-3 for Argentine Air Force
152	610	G-AHPM	BEA *Verderer* and *Lord Rodney*	Eagle
153	621	VL232	RAF	King's Flight, Eagle G-APAT, Orion, Air Safaris
154	604	VT-CEK	Indian National Airways *Tista*	IAC
155	610	G-AHPN	BEA *Ventnor* and *Lord St Vincent*	
156	621	VL233	Ministry of Supply	King's Flight, Tradair G-APOO, Channel
157	610	G-AHPO	BEA *Venture* and *Lord Dundonald*	Eagle
158	607	VL249	—	Military Viking and prototype Valetta
159	616	VP-YEX	CAA *Kafue*	
160	610	G-AHPP	BEA *Venus* and *Sir Charles Saunders*	Aero-Express, Eagle, Transportes Aereos da Indias Portugesas CR-IAC
161	615	LV-XES	Argentine Government	T-4 Argentine Air Force
162	637	VL262	—	Valetta C.1
163	615	LV-XET	Argentine Government	T-9 Argentine Air Force
164	610	G-AHPR	BEA *Verily* and *Prince Rupert*	Field Aircraft Services, Eagle, Independent Air Travel, Maitland Drewery Aviation, Bembridge Car Hire, Air Safaris
165	637	VL263	—	Valetta C.1, to Decca
166	604	VT-CEL	Indian National Airways *Jhelum*	IAC
167	610	G-AHPS	BEA *Verity* and *Sir Doveton Sturdee*	BKS, Deutsche Flug Dienst D-ABOM, D-BORA, Lufthansa, Condor
168	616	VP-YEY	CAA *Shangani*	
169	621	VL237⎤		
170	621	VL238⎟		
171	621	VL239⎟		
172	621	VL240⎬ Ordered by Ministry of		
173	621	VL241⎟ Supply, but cancelled		
174	621	VL242⎟		
175	621	VL243⎟		
176	621	VL244⎦		
177	623	VL246	RAF	King's Flight, Tradair G-APOP, Channel
178	623	VL247	,,	King's Flight later Queen's Flight, Tradair G-APOR, Channel

534

179	626	VL248	RAF	King's Flight later Queen's Flight, Pasquel XB-FIP, Air Couriers G-AOBY
180	615	LV-XEU	Argentine Government	T-6 Argentine Air Force
181	615	LV-XEV	,,	T-5 ,, ,,
182	615	LV-XEW	,,	T-7 ,, ,,
183	615	LV-XEX	,,	T-8 ,, ,,
184	615	LV-XEY	,,	T-184 ,, ,,
185	615	LV-XEZ	,,	T-185 Argentine Air Force later T-76 and LV-AEV
186	604	VT-CEM	Indian National Airways *Sutlej*	IAC
187	615	LV-XFD	Argentine Government	T-10 Argentine Air Force
188	615	LV-XFE	,,	T-11 ,, ,,
189	615	LV-XFF	,,	T-13 ,, ,,
190	615	LV-XFG	,,	T-12 ,, ,,
191	615	LV-XFH	,,	To LV-AFF, Fama
192	615	LV-XFI	,,	
193	615	LV-XFJ	,,	T-80 Argentine Air Force
194	615	LV-XFM	,,	
195	628	OY-DLA	DDL *Tor Viking*	Misrair SU-AGO *Amoun*
196	628	OY-DLE	,, *Torleif Viking*	,, SU-AGN *Seity I*
197	628	OY-DLI	,, *Torulf Viking*	
198	628	OY-DLO	,, *Tormund Viking*	Misrair SU-AGM *Amenhetop*
199	628	OY-DLU	,, *Torlak Viking*	
200	615	LV-XFL	Argentine Government	Re-registered LV-AFU, T-88 Argentine Air Force
201	632	VT-CIY	Air-India	IAC
202	632	VT-CIZ	,,	,,
203	632	VT-CKW	,,	,,
204	632	VT-CKX	,,	,,
205	632	VT-CLY	,,	,,
206	632	VT-CLZ	,,	,,
207	618	G-AJPH	Vickers	Fitted two Nene 1, as VX856, converted to Standard 1B for Eagle
208	634	EI-ADF	Aer Lingus *St Ronan*	Airwork G-AKTV, Channel Airways
209	634	EI-ADG	,, *St Senan*	Misrair SU-AFN *Khoafa*
210	634	EI-ADH	,, *St Celsus*	Misrair SU-AFM, Field Aircraft Services G-AMNK, Hunting-Clan, Don Everall
211	634	EI-ADI	,, *St Mel*	Airwork G-AKTU, Air Safaris
212	634	EI-ADJ	,, *St Flannan*	Misrair SU-AFO
213	634	EI-ADK	,, *St Jarlath*	Misrair SU-AFK
214	634	EI-ADL	,, *St Felim*	Misrair SU-AFL *Rameses*, Autair G-ASBE
215	610	G-AIVB	BEA *Vernal* and *Robert Blake*	Eagle, First Air Trading Co, Transportes Aereos da Indias Portugesas CR-IAD

216	610	G-AIVC	BEA	*Vernon* and *Lord Collingwood*	Eagle, First Air Trading, Karl Herfurtner D-ADEN, D-BEPO, Airnautic F-BJER
217	610	G-AIVD	,,	*Veteran* and *Lord Duncan*	Aero-Express D-ADAM, Lufttransport, Balair HB-AAR, Air Ferry, Invicta Airways
218	610	G-AIVE	,,	*Vestal*	
219	610	G-AIVF	,,	*Vibrant* and *Sir James Somerville*	BKS, Aero-Express, Deutsche Flugdienst D-AGIL, D-BARI, Balair HB-AAN, Air Ferry, Invicta Airways
220	610	G-AIVG	,,	*Viceroy* and *Sir George Rooke*	
221	610	G-AIVH	,,	*Vicinity* and *Lord Howe*	Eagle
222	610	G-AIVI	,,	*Victor* and *Viking*	First Air Trading Co, Lufttransport D-ABEL, D-BALI
223	610	G-AIVJ	,,	*Victoria* and *Lord Jellicoe*	Aviameer OO-EEN, Overseas Aviation, Lufttransport D-ABIR, D-BABY, Air Ferry
224	610	G-AIVK	,,	*Victory* and *Lord Keyes*	British International Air Lines, Kuwait Oil Co, Overseas Aviation, Air Ferry
225	610	G-AIVL	,,	*Vigilant* and *Lord Hawke*	Eagle, Overseas Aviation
226	610	G-AIVM	,,	*Vigorous* and *George Monck*	Aero-Express D-CADA, D-ADEL
227	610	G-AIVN	,,	*Violet* and *Edward Boscawen*	CAA VP-YMO *Rukuru*
228	610	G-AIVO	,,	*Villain* and *Edward Vernon*	Eagle
229	610	G-AIVP	,,	*Vimy*	
230	644	YI-ABP	Iraqi Airways	*Al Mahfouthah*	
231	644	YI-ABQ	,,	*Al Mamounah*	
232	644	YI-ABR	,,	*Al Mahroosa*	
233	627	G-AIXR	Airwork		Tradair, Channel Airways
234	627	G-AIXS	,,		Tradair
235	627	G-AJFP	,,		Indian National Airways VT-DAP, IAC
236	627	G-AJFR	,,		Iraq Petroleum Transport Co, Tradair, Channel, Eros
237	627	G-AJFS	,,		Tradair, Channel
238	627	G-AJFT	,,		Air Safaris, Tradair
239	610	G-AJBM	BEA	*Vincent* and *Charles Watson*	T-29 Argentine Air Force
240	610	G-AJBN	,,	*Vindictive* and *Lord Nelson*	Eagle, First Air Trading Co
241	610	G-AJBO	,,	*Vintage* and *John Benbow*	Eagle

536

242	610	G-AJBP	BEA *Vintner* and *Sir Edward Spragge*	Eagle, BKS, First Air Trading, Airnautic F-BJAH
243	610	G-AJBR	,, *Virginia* and *Sir Bertram Ramsey*	BKS, Deutsche Flugdienst D-AHAF, D-BONE, Condor
244	610	G-AJBS	,, *Virgo* and *Sir Cloudesley Shovel*	T-93 Argentine Air Force
245	610	G-AJBT	,, *Viper* and *Sir Thomas Troubridge*	CAA VP-YNF *Mazoe*, Claydon Aviation, Pegasus Airlines, Autair
246	610	G-AJBU	,, *Virtue* and *Lord Bridport*	Field Aircraft Services, Independent Air Travel, Fieldair, Bembridge Car Hire
247	610	G-AJBV	,, *Viscount* and *Sir Henry Morgan*	Eagle, Iraqi Airways YI-ACJ
248	610	G-AJBW	,, *Vista* and *Sir William Cornwallis*	Eagle, Airnautic F-BFDN
249	610	G-AJBX	,, *Vital* and *Sir Edward Hughes*	Eagle, Arabian Desert Airlines, Karl Herfurtner D-AFIX, D-BABA, Air Safaris, Continental Air Services, Maitland Drewery, Eros, Air Ferry
250	610	G-AJBY	,, *Vitality* and *Lord Torrington*	BKS, Deutsche Flugdienst D-AFUS, D-BELA, Lufthansa
251	632	VT-CRB	Air-India	IAC
252	610	G-AJCA	BEA *Vixen* and *Sir John Leake*	Misrair SU-AIF, Air Safaris
253	632	VT-CRC	Air-India	IAC
254	632	VT-CSP	,,	,,
255	610	G-AJCD	BEA *Vizor* and *Lord Barham*	Eagle
256	610	G-AJCE	,, *Vivacious* and *Lord Exmouth*	Eagle, Svenska Aero AB, Independent Air Travel, Bembridge Car Hire, Continental
257	616	VP-YHT	CAA *Shiré*	Alfons Amann D-BLYK, Airnautic F-BJES, Europe Aero Service
258	610	G-AJDI	BEA *Volatile* and *Lord Keith*	T-91 Argentine Air Force
259	610	G-AJDJ	,, *Volley* and *Lord Beatty*	Misrair SU-AIG
260	610	G-AJDK	,, *Volunteer* and *Richard Kempenfelt*	Eagle, Jordan Air Force VK-500
261	649	J750	Pakistan Air Force	Executive
262	610	G-AJDL	BEA *Vortex* and *Lord St Vincent*	Eagle
263	610	G-AKBG	,, *Votary* and *Sir Thomas Hardy*	Hunting-Clan, Don Everall, Air Safaris, Fields
264	610	G-AKBH	,, *Voyager* and *Lord Hood*	Eagle, Airnautic F-BJRS
265–288		Not Built		

289	636	G-AJJN	Vickers demonstrator	BEA *Vulcan*, BKS Channel, Continental Air Services
290	635	ZS-BNE	South African Airways *Simonsberg*	BEA G-AMGG *Sir Robert Calder*, Eagle
291	635	ZS-BNF	South African Airways *Cathkin Peak*	BEA G-AMNR *Lord Charles Beresford*, Eagle, Independent Air Travel, Bembridge Car Hire
292	635	ZS-BNG	South African Airways *Mont-aux-Sources*	BEA G-AMNX *Sir Philip Broke*, Eagle
293	635	ZS-BNH	South African Airways *Gulakop*	BEA G-AMGH *Sir John Duck-worth*, Transavia Flug D-BOBY, Karl Herfurtner, Continental Air Services, Kay Rings, Transworld Leasing
294	635	ZS-BNI	South African Airways *Devil's Peak*	BEA G-AMNS *Sir Dudley Pound*, Argentine Air Force as T-90
295	635	ZS-BNJ	South African Airways *Signal Hill*	BEA G-AMGJ *Sir John Warren*, Eagle, Karl Herfurtner, Airnautic F-BIPT
296	635	ZS-BNK	South African Airways *Leeukap*	BEA G-AMNJ *Lord Fisher*, Karl Herfurtner, Airnautic F-BIUQ
297	635	ZS-BNL	South African Airways *Mount Prospect*	BEA G-AMGI *Sir Henry Har-wood*, Eagle
298	643	ZS-BWT	President Finance and Acceptance Corpn *Rex* for Sudair International	CAA VP-YIE *Limpopo*, Columbus Luftreederei D-ALUP, D-ACUG, Airnautic F-BJEQ

Valetta

Total built—263

1. One prototype, VL249, ordered to specification C.9/46 and contract AIR/5587/C.B. 6(*b*) as Type 607: evaluated at AFEE.

2. 21 C.1 ordered, VL262–282, under contract AIR/5587/C.B.6(*b*) as Type 637 VL262–266 (VL262 first flew 28 January, 1948), Type 645 VL267–282: A & AEE VL265, 267, 271; RAE VL268; Bristol, Filton, VL269; first, VL262, delivered 30 March, 1948; last, VL281, delivered 25 November, 1948.

3. 53 C.1 ordered, VW140–165, 180–206, under contract 6/AIR/495/C.B.6(*b*) as Type 651: first, VW140, delivered to A & AEE 23 September, 1948; last two, VW203 and 204, delivered 3 May, 1949.

4. 60 C.1 ordered, VW802–851, 855–864 under contract 6/AIR/1489/C.B.6(*b*) as Type 651; first three, VW803–805, delivered to Little Rissington 2 May, 1949; last VW862, delivered to North Luffenham 5 December, 1949.

5. 64 C.1 ordered under contract 6/AIR/2472/C.B.6(*b*) but delivered as: C.1 Type 651 VX483–485, 490–499, 506–515, 521–530, 537–546 and 555–563; T.3 Type 664 VX564; C.2 Type 659 VX571–580: first delivered, VX483, to Manby 4 January, 1950: VX491 and 492 to Little Rissington same day: T.3 carried out Service trials with 1 ANS at Hullavington during 1952 and 1953: last two delivered were VX579 and 580 3 April, 1950, to Little Rissington and Kirkbride respectively: VX500 deleted from contract and delivered to the Royal Swedish Air Force.

6. 73 C.1 ordered under contract 6/AIR/3659/C.B.6(b) as Type 651 and delivered as WD157–171, 58 cancelled: first two, WD157–158, delivered 2 October, 1950, to Kirkbride; last delivered, WD171, to RAE 7 February, 1951.

7. 12 T.3 ordered under contract 6/AIR/5199/C.B.6(b) WG256–267 as Type 664: first two, WG256–257, delivered 21 August, 1951; last delivered, WG267, 4 January, 1952: WG256 converted to T.4.

8. 27 T.3 ordered under contract 6/AIR/5930/C.B.6(b) WJ461–487 as Type 664: first, WJ463, delivered 21 January, 1952, to RAE, last, WJ487, delivered 29 September, 1952, to Little Rissington.

9. 10 C.1 ordered under contract 6/AIR/5929/C.B.6(b) WJ491–499 and 504 as Type 651: WJ504 to C.2 Type 659 before completion: first, WJ491, delivered 3 May, 1951, to Defford; last two, WJ498–499, delivered 9 January, 1952, to Little Rissington: WJ504 to 30 Squadron at Abingdon 9 July, 1951.

Civil registrations G-APII ex VL275 not proceeded with, G-APIJ ex WD162, G-APKR ex VW802, G-APKS ex VL263.

Squadrons—24, 30, 48, 52, 70, 78, 84, 110, 114, 165, 167, 204, 214, 215, 216 and 622.

Units—1 ANS, 2 ANS and 6 ANS FCS, College of Air Warfare and CNCS 228, 238, 240 and 242 OCU.

Varsity

Total built—163 (17 at Weybridge—146 at Hurn)

1. Prototypes VX828 and 835 to specification T.13/48 contract 6/AIR/2489/C.B.6(b), Type 648: VX835 Napier engine test-bed, Napier Eland NE16 fitted in starboard wing.

2. Production Type 668: 60 ordered under contract 6/AIR/4816/C.B.6(b) WF324–335, 369–394, 408–429: first delivered 31 August, 1951, last delivered 18 September, 1952: WF379 used by RRE and fitted radar nose: WF416 converted for King Hussein of Jordan as VK-501.

3. 50 ordered under contract 6/AIR/5 946/C.B.6(c): WJ886–921, 937–950; WJ900 to Royal Swedish Air Force as Tp82 and serial 82001: first delivered, WJ886, 889, 890, and 891, 4 November, 1952; last, WJ950, delivered 25 March, 1953.

4. 67 ordered under contract 6/AIR/6125/C.B.6(a), but 17 cancelled: WL621–642, 665–692; first, WL621, delivered 7 April, 1953; last, WL692, delivered 24 February, 1954.

5. XD366 replacement for WJ900 to Sweden: 33 ordered under contract 6/AIR/7079/ C.B.6(b) but cancelled; 17 to 6/AIR/6125/C.B.6(b)—cancelled; 33 to 6/AIR/7079/ C.B.6(b)—cancelled.

First Varsity, WF328, delivered to 201 Advanced Flying School at Swinderby 1 October, 1951, followed by WF327–335, 372–378, WJ890, WL626 and others.

Other Units equipped AES WF328, 374, 418, WJ896, 897, 909, etc. 1 ANS WJ895, 903, 920, 921, 937, 943, WL626, 627, 669, etc. 2 ANS WF325, 377, 409, 418, 424, 425, WJ891, WL630, 636, etc. 5 ANS WJ916 and BCBS WF334, WJ912, 949, WL627, 675, etc. BLEU WF412, 417, WL665 CFS WJ886, 899, 949, WL666, 671, XD366, etc. CNCS WF335, 370, 422, WJ915, 918, 929, 944, WL628, 629, etc. ETPS WF381, WL667, 674, 679, etc. 1 E & WS WF408, 410, 419, WJ893, 941, etc. 4 FTS WJ917, 921, 939, WL623, 629, etc. 5 FTS WF326, 375, 376, 392, WJ912, 920, WL630, 631, 670, WL676, etc. 11 FTS WF371, 377, 394, WJ937, WL638, etc. 115 Squadron WL621, 622, 636, 678, 684, 688, 691, 692, etc. School of Air Warfare WJ905.

Civil conversions: WF387 to G-ARFP as automatic landing research aircraft with Smiths Aviation Division; WF415 to G-APAZ for radar and navigation system research with Decca.

Total built—445 (166 at Weybridge, 279 at Hurn)

C/n	Type	Initial Registration	Initial Operator and name	Subsequent Operators
1	630	G-AHRF	Prototype	First flew as G-AHRF: trials as VX211
2	663	VX217	2nd prototype	Ex type 609 with Tays, allocated G-AHRG but not used
—	640	G-AJZW	3rd prototype	For Naiads, but parts into G-AMAV
3	700	G-AMAV	Ministry of Supply	As *Enterprise* in England—New Zealand Air Race October 1953
4	701	G-ALWE	BEA *Discovery*	
5	701	G-ALWF	,, *Sir John Franklin*	Channel, Tradair, Eagle *City of Exeter*, Cambrian
6	701	G-AMNY	,, *Sir Ernest Shackleton*	
7	701	G-AMOG	,, *Robert Falcon Scott*	Cambrian
8	708	F-BGNK	Air France	
9	701	G-AMOA	BEA *Sir George Vancouver*	Tradair, Channel, Eagle, Cambrian
10	708	F-BGNL	Air France	Maitland Drewery G-ARBY, BKS, BUA, Air Inter
11	701	G-AMOB	BEA *William Baffin*	VASP PP-SRI
12	708	F-BGNM	Air France	Maitland Drewery G-ARER, BKS, BUA, Air Inter
13	701	G-AMOC	BEA *Richard Chancellor*	Channel, Starways, Eagle *City of Glasgow*, Bahamas VP-BCH, Cambrian
14	708	F-BGNN	Air France	Maitland Drewery, BKS, BUA, Air Inter F-BOEB
15	701	G-AMOD	BEA *John Davis*	VASP PP-SRJ
16	708	F-BGNO	Air France	Air Inter
17	701	G-AMOE	BEA *Sir Edward Parry*	Channel, Starways, Eagle *City of Manchester*, Cambrian
18	708	F-BGNP	Air France	Air Inter
19	701	G-AMOF	BEA *Sir Martin Frobisher*	VASP PP-SRM
20	701	G-AMNZ	,, *James Cook*	Cambrian
21	701	G-AMOH	,, *Henry Hudson*	Channel, Starways *City of Liverpool*, Eagle, Cambrian
22	701	G-AMOI	,, *Sir Hugh Willoughby*	VASP PP-SRL
23	701	G-AMOJ	,, *Sir James Ross*	Channel, Tradair, Cambrian
24	701	G-AMOK	,, *Sir Humphrey Gilbert*	LAV YV-C-AMB
25	701	G-AMOL	,, *David Livingstone*	Cambrian
26	701	G-AMOM	,, *James Bruce*	
27	701	G-AMON	,, *Thomas Cavendish*	Cambrian
28	701	G-AMOO	,, *John Oxenham*	Channel, Starways, Eagle *City of Birmingham*, Cambrian

29	701	G-AMOP	BEA *Mungo Park*	Cambrian
30	707	EI-AFV	Aer Lingus *St Patrick*	Tradair G-APZB, Starways, Eagle *City of Newcastle*, Channel
31	707	EI-AFW	„ *St Brigid*	Eagle (Bermuda) VR-BBJ, Bahamas Airways VP-BCF
32	707	EI-AFY	„ *St Brendan*	Eagle (Bermuda) VR-BBH, Bahamas Airways VP-BCE
33	708	F-BGNQ	Air France	Air Inter
34	707	EI-AGI	Aer Lingus *St Laurence O'Toole*	Tradair G-APZC, Kuwait, Channel
35	708	F-BGNR	Air France	Air Inter
36	708	F-BGNS	„	Starways G-ARIR, Air Inter F-BLHI
37	708	F-BGNT	„	Air Vietnam, Air Inter
38	708	F-BGNU	„	„ „
39	708	F-BGNV	„	Air Inter
40	724	CF-TGI	TCA Fleet 601	Transair
41	724	CF-TGJ	„ „ 602	Air Transport Leasing Corp N117H, Mercer Trucking
42	724	CF-TGK	„ „ 603	
43	724	CF-TGL	„ „ 604	
44	720	VH-TVA	TAA *John Batman*	
45	720	VH-TVB	„ *Gregory Blackland*	Ansett-ANA VH-RMQ
46	720	VH-TVC	„ *John Oxley*	
47	720	VH-TVD	„ *Hamilton Hume*	
48	720	VH-TVE	„ *Charles Sturt*	Ansett-ANA
49	720	VH-TVF	„ *Ernest Giles*	„
50	724	CF-TGM	TCA Fleet 605	Air Inter F-BMCH
51	724	CF-TGN	„ „ 606	Schenley Distillery N744W, Kearney and Trucker N898M
52	724	CF-TGO	„ „ 607	Air Inter F-BMCG
53	724	CF-TGP	„ „ 608	
54	724	CF-TGQ	„ „ 609	Air Inter F-BMCF
55	724	CF-TGR	„ „ 610	World Inc N911H, Air Inter F-BNAX
56	724	CF-TGS	„ „ 611	
57	724	CF-TGT	„ „ 612	
58	724	CF-TGU	„ „ 613	
59	724	CF-TGV	„ „ 614	
60	724	CF-TGW	„ „ 615	
61	701	G-ANHA	BEA *Anthony Jenkinson*	VASP PP-SRP
62	701	G-ANHB	„ *Sir Henry Stanley*	VASP PP-SRN
63	701	G-ANHC	„ *Sir Leopold McClintock*	
64	701C	G-ANHD	„ *William Dampier*	VASP PP-SRO
65	701C	G-ANHE	„ *Gino Watkins*	VASP PP-SRQ
66	701C	G-ANHF	„ *Matthew Flinders*	VASP PP-SRR
67	735	YI-ACK	Iraqi Airways *Ibn Fernas*	
68	735	YI-ACL	„ *Sinbad*	

69	735	YI-ACM	Iraqi Airways *Ibn Battootah*	
70	737	CF-GXK	Canadian Dept of Transport	Executive
71	702	VP-TBK	BWIA	Kuwait Airways G-APTA, Bahamas VP-BBW, Channel
72	702	VP-TBL		Kuwait Airways G-APOW, Bahamas VP-BCD
73	702	VP-TBM	,,	Kuwait Airways G-APPX, Bahamas VP-BBV
74	732	G-ANRR	Hunting-Clan Air Transport	MEA OD-ACF
75	732	G-ANRS	Hunting-Clan Air Transport	MEA OD-ACH, Misrair SU-AKY, Eagle *City of Newcastle*
76	732	G-ANRT	Hunting-Clan Air Transport	MEA OD-ACG, Iraqi YI-ADM, Misrair SU-AKX
77	736	LN-FOF	Fred Olsen Air Transport	BEA G-AODG *Fridtjof Nansen*, MEA OD-ACR, Airwork, Transair, British Midland
78	736	LN-FOL	,, ,, ,,	BEA G-AODH *Roald Amundsen*, BWIA VP-TBY, Airwork, BOAC, BUA
79	723	IU683	Indian Air Force	Indian Airlines Corporation
80	730	IU684	Indian Air Force *Raj Humsa*	,, ,, ,,
81	702	VP-TBN	BWIA	Bahamas VP-BCI, re-registered 9Y-TBN
82	763	YS-O9C	TACA	
83	734	J751	Pakistan Air Force	President
84	720	VH-TVG	TAA *William Hovell*	
85	739	SU-AIC	Misrair	
86	739	SU-AID	,,	
87	739	SU-AIE	,,	Eagle G-ATDV *City of Liverpool*
88	744	N7402	Capital Airlines Fleet 321	All Nippon
89	744	N7403	,, ,, 322	,, ETPS as XR801
90	744	N7404	,, ,, 323	
91	755	CU-T603	Cubana	
92	755	CU-T604	,,	Starways G-AOCB, Eagle *City of Edinburgh*
93	755	CU-T605	,,	Starways G-AOCC, Eagle *City of Belfast*
94	749	YV-C-AMV	LAV	
95	749	YV-C-AMX	,,	
96	749	YV-C-AMZ	,,	
97	747	G-ANXV	Vickers	Butler VH-BAT *Warral*, Ansett-ANA VH-RMO
98	748	VP-YNA	CAA *Malvern*	Air Malawi, Air Rhodesia, Zambia Airways
99	748	VP-YNB	,, *Motopos*	Air Malawi, Air Rhodesia, Zambia Airways
100	748	VP-YNC	,, *Mlanje*	Air Malawi, Air Rhodesia, Zambia Airways

101	748	VP-YND	CAA *Mweru*		Air Malawi, Air Rhodesia, Zambia Airways
102	748	VP-YNE	,, *Mpika*		
103	745	N7405	Capital Airlines Fleet	324	UAL
104	745	N7406	,, ,,	325	,,
105	745	N7407	,, ,,	326	,,
106	745	N7408	,, ,,	327	,,
107	745	N7409	,, ,,	328	,,
108	745	N7410	,, ,,	329	
109	745	N7411	,, ,,	330	UAL
110	745	N7412	,, ,,	331	,,
111	745	N7413	,, ,,	332	,,
112	745	N7414	,, ,,	333	Austrian OE-LAN *Johannes Brahms*, Aloha N7414
113	745	N7415	,, ,,	334	Austrian OE-LAO *Franz Lehar*, Aloha N7415
114	745	N7416	,, ,,	335	Alitalia I-LIRC
115	745	N7417	,, ,,	336	UAL
116	745	N7418	,, ,,	337	Alitalia I-LIRE, G-AWGV
117	745	N7419	,, ,,	338	UAL
118	745	N7420	,, ,,	339	PAL PI-C773, Hawaiian N745HA, Alitalia I-LIRT
119	745	N7421	,, ,,	340	Alitalia I-LITZ
120	745	N7422	,, ,,	341	UAL
121	745	N7423	,, ,,	342	,,
122	745	N7424	,, ,,	343	,,
123	745	N7425	,, ,,	344	,,
124	745	N7426	,, ,,	345	,, BKS G-ATTA
125	745	N7427	,, ,,	346	,,
126	745	N7428	,, ,,	347	,,
127	745	N7429	,, ,,	348	,,
128	745	N7430	,, ,,	349	,,
129	745	N7431	,, ,,	350	,,
130	745	N7432	,, ,,	351	Alitalia I-LIFS
131	745	N7433	,, ,,	352	,, I-LINS
132	745	N7434	,, ,,	353	UAL
133	745	N7435	,, ,,	354	,,
134	745	N7436	,, ,,	355	,,
135	745	N7437	,, ,,	356	
136	745	N7438	,, ,,	357	UAL
137	745	N7439	,, ,,	358	,,
138	745	N7440	,, ,,	359	,,
139	745	N7441	,, ,,	360	,,
140	759	G-AOGG	Hunting-Clan Air Transport		Icelandair TF-ISN *Gullfaxi*
141	742	FAB-2100	Brazilian Air Force		To C92-2100
142	757	CF-TGX	TCA Fleet 616		
143	757	CF-TGY	,, 617		
144	757	CF-TGZ	,, 618		

145	747	G-ANYH	Vickers	Butler VH-BUT, Ansett-ANA VH-RMP
146	756	VH-TVH	TAA *George Bass*	
147	756	VH-TVI	,, *Matthew Flinders*	
148	756	VH-TVJ	,, *John Forrest* and *Ernest Giles*	
149	759	G-AOGH	Hunting-Clan Air Transport	Icelandair TF-ISU *Hrinfaxi*
150	802	G-AOJA	BEA *Sir Samuel White Baker*	
151	802	G-AOJB	,, *Stephen Borough*	
152	802	G-AOJC	,, *Robert O'Hara Burke*	
153	802	G-AOJD	,, *Sebastian Cabot*	
154	802	G-AOJE	,, *Sir Alexander Mackenzie*	
155	802	G-AOJF	,, *Sir George Somers*	
156	802	G-AOHG	,, *Richard Hakluyt*	
157	802	G-AOHH	,, *Sir Robert McClure*	
158	802	G-AOHI	,, *Charles Montagu Doughty*	
159	802	G-AOHJ	,, *Sir John Mandeville*	
160	802	G-AOHK	,, *John Hanning Speke*	
161	802	G-AOHL	,, *Charles Sturt*	
162	802	G-AOHM	,, *Robert Machin*	
163	802	G-AOHN	,, *Alexander Gordon Laing*	
164	802	G-AOHO	,, *Samuel Wallis*	
165	802	G-AOHP	,, *James Weddel*	
166	802	G-AOHR	,, *Sir Richard Burton*	
167	802	G-AOHS	,, *Robert Thorne*	
168	802	G-AOHT	,, *Ralph Fitch*	
169	802	G-AOHU	,, *Sir George Strong Naves*	
170	802	G-AOHV	,, *Sir John Barrow*	
171	802	G-AORD	,, *Arthur Philipp*	
172	803	PH-VIA	KLM *Sir Sefton Brancker*	Aer Lingus EI-AOG
173	803	PH-VIB	,, *Louis Blériot*	,, EI-AOJ
174	803	PH-VIC	,, *J. C. Ellehammer*	,, EI-APD
175	803	PH-VID	,, *Otto Lilienthal*	,, EI-AOL
176	803	PH-VIE	,, *Jan Olieslagers*	,, EI-AOF
177	803	PH-VIF	,, *Leonardo da Vinci*	,, EI-AOE
178	803	PH-VIG	,, *Sir Charles E. Kingsford Smith*	,, EI-AOM
179	803	PH-VIH	,, *Wright Bros*	,, EI-AOI
180	803	PH-VII	,, *Daedalus*	,, EI-AOH
181	756	VH-TVK	TAA *Thomas Mitchell*	
182	701	G-AOFX	BEA *Sir Joseph Banks*	VASP PP-SRS
183	764	N905	US Steel Corporation	Union Steel Corporation
184	764	N906	,, ,,	,, ,,
185	764	N907	,, ,,	,, ,,

186	760	VR-HFI	Hong Kong Airways		Malayan Airways 9M-ALY, Aden Airways VR-AAW
187	760	VR-HFJ	,, ,,		Malayan Airways 9M-AMS, Aden Airways VR-AAV
188	761	XY-ADF	Union of Burma Airways		
189	761	XY-ADG	,, ,, ,,		
190	761	XY-ADH	,, ,, ,,		Kuwait G-APZN and 9K-ACD, MEA
191	765	N306	Standard Oil Co		
192	768	VT-DIO	Indian Airlines (IAC)		
193	768	VT-DIF	Indian Airlines (IAC)		
194	768	VT-DIG	Indian Airlines (IAC)		
195	768	VT-DIH	Indian Airlines (IAC)		
196	768	VT-DII	Indian Airlines (IAC)		
197	756	VH-TVL	TAA *James Cook* and *George Evans*		
198	745	N7442	Capital Airlines Fleet 361		ETPS XP802
199	745	N7443	,, ,,	362	UAL
200	745	N7444	,, ,,	363	,,
201	745	N7445	,, ,,	364	,,
202	745	N7446	,, ,,	365	,,
203	745	N7447	,, ,,	366	,,
204	745	N7448	,, ,,	367	,,
205	745	N7449	,, ,,	368	,,
206	745	N7450	,, ,,	369	,,
207	745	N7451	,, ,,	370	,,
208	745	N7452	,, ,,	371	,,
209	745	N7454	,, ,,	372	,,
210	745	N7455	,, ,,	373	,,
211	745	N7456	,, ,,	374	,,
212	745	N7457	,, ,,	375	,,
213	745	N7458	,, ,,	376	,,
214	745	N7459	,, ,,	377	,,
215	745	N7460	,, ,,	378	,,
216	745	N7461	,, ,,	379	,,
217	745	N7462	,, ,,	380	
218	757	CF-THA	TCA Fleet 619		Warnock Hersey
219	757	CF-THB	,,	620	
220	757	CF-THC	,,	621	
221	757	CF-THD	,,	622	
222	757	CF-THE	,,	623	
223	757	CF-THF	,,	624	
224	757	CF-THG	,,	625	
225	745	G-16-4	Vickers		Aer Lingus EI-AJW, BEA G-APNF *Philip Carterat*, Kuwait Oil Co, BOAC Associated Companies, British International, Kuwait 9K-ACD, BKS
226	798	G-APBH	,,		Northeast N6599C, Essex Wire Corpn N1298

227	784	VH-TVO	TAA *David Lindsay*	PAL PI-C772, Falcon Airways of Sweden
228	745	G-16-3	Vickers	Aer Lingus EI-AJV, BEA G-APNG *James Lancaster*, Kuwait, Royal Bank of Canada CF-RBC, Canadian Breweries, S. J. Grooves N505W
229	797	G-APFR	,,	Canadian Dept of Transport CF-DTA
230	745	G-APLX	,,	Northeast N6595C, Continental Oil Drilling N776M
231	745	N7465	Capital Airlines	UAL
232	798	N6590C	Northeast Airlines	Aloha N7416
233	798	N6591C	,,	Blaw Knox N820BK
234	798	N6592C	,,	
235	772	VP-TBS	BWIA	Re-registered 9Y-TBS
236	772	VP-TBT	,,	,, 9Y-TBT
237	772	VP-TBU	,,	,, 9Y-TBU
238	772	VP-TBX	,,	,, 9Y-TBX
239	754	OD-ACT	MEA	Kuwait
240	754	OD-ACU	,,	Jordanian JY-ACI
241	754	OD-ACV	,,	CAA VP-YTE *Zambezi*
242	754	OD-ACW	,,	Kuwait, Aloha N7410
243	754	OD-ADD	,,	Jordanian JY-ACK
244	754	OD-ADE	,,	
245	754	OD-ACX	,,	
246	794	TC-SEC	Türk Hava Yollari	
247	779	LN-FOM	Fred Olsen Air Transport	Austrian OE-LAE, BEA G-ARBW, SAS, IAC VT-DOD
248	804	G-AOXU	Transair	BUA, LOT SP-LVC, NZNAC ZK-NAI
249	804	G-AOXV	,,	BUA, LOT SP-LVA
250	779	LN-FOH	Fred Olsen Air Transport	Austrian OE-LAB, BEA G-APZP, SAS, IAC VT-DOE
251	779	LN-FOI	,, ,, ,,	Austrian OE-LAC, SAS, IAC VT-DOH
252	779	LN-FOK	,, ,, ,,	Austrian OE-LAD, SAS, IAC VT-DOI
253	802	G-AOHW	BEA *Sir Francis Young-husband*	Originally registered G-AORC
254	802	G-AORC	,, *Richard Lander*	Originally registered G-AORD
255	806A	G-AOYF	Vickers	
256	806	G-AOYG	BEA *Charles Darwin*	
257	806	G-AOYI	,, *Sir Humphry Davy*	Originally registered G-AOYH
258	805	G-APDW	Eagle Aviation	Originally registered G-AOYI, Eagle Aviation (Bermuda) VR-BAX, Maritime Central Airways CF-MCJ, Aer Lingus EI-AMA

259	806	G-AOYJ	BEA *Edward Jenner*	Cyprus Airways
260	806	G-AOYK	,, *Edmund Cartwright*	,,
261	806	G-AOYL	,, *Lord Joseph Lister*	BKS Air Transport
262	806	G-AOYM	,, *John Loudon Mc-Adam*	
263	806	G-AOYN	,, *Sir Isaac Newton*	
264	806	G-AOYO	,, *Adam Smith*	BKS Air Transport
265	806	G-AOYP	,, *John Napier*	
266	806	G-AOYR	,, *Sir Richard Arkwright*	
267	806	G-AOYS	,, *George Stephenson*	
268	806	G-AOYT	,, *James Watt*	
269	757	CF-THH	TCA Fleet 626	
270	757	CF-THI	,, 627	
271	757	CF-THK	,, 629	
272	757	CF-THL	,, 630	
273	757	CF-THM	,, 631	
274	757	CF-THN	,, 632	
275	757	CF-THO	,, 633	
276	757	CF-THP	,, 634	
277	757	CF-THQ	,, 635	
278	757	CF-THR	,, 636	
279	757	CF-THS	,, 637	
280	781	150	South African Air Force	
281	807	ZK-BRD	NZNAC *City of Wellington*	
282	807	ZK-BRE	,, *City of Auckland*	
283	807	ZK-BRF	,, *City of Christchurch*	
284	798	N6594C	Northeast Airlines	Alitalia I-LIRG
285	745	N7464	Capital	UAL
286	798	N6593C	Northeast Airlines	Hawaiian N7464HA, TACA YS-O7C, BKS G-AVED
287	745	N7463	Capital Fleet 381	
288	798	N6596C	Northeast Airlines	Alitalia I-LIRM
289	808	EI-AJI	Aer Lingus *St Gall (Gall)*	
290	808	EI-AJJ	,, *St Columban (Columban)*	
291	808	EI-AJK	,, *St Kilian (Cillian)*	
292	768	VT-DIX	Indian Airlines (IAC) *Bengal*	
293	768	VT-DIZ	Indian Airlines (IAC) *Rajasthan*	
294	768	VT-DJA	Indian Airlines (IAC) *Andra Pradesh*	
295	768	VT-DJB	Indian Airlines (IAC) *Bihar*	
296	768	VT-DJC	Indian Airlines (IAC) *Kashmir*	
297	782	EP-AHA	Persian Government	CAA VP-WAS

298	782	EP-AHB	Persian Government	CAA VP-WAT
299	782	EP-AHC	,, ,,	
300	784	PI-C770	Philippine Airlines	Falcon Airways SE-CNL
301	757	CF-THJ	TCA Fleet 628	
302	757	CF-THT	,, 638	
303	757	CF-THU	,, 639	
304	757	CF-THV	,, 640	
305	757	CF-THW	,, 641	
306	757	CF-THX	,, 642	
307	757	CF-THY	,, 643	
308	757	CF-THZ	,, 644	
309	757	CF-TIA	,, 645	
310	757	CF-TIB	,, 646	
311	806	G-AOYH	BEA *William Harvey*	
312	805	G-APDX	Eagle Aviation	Eagle Aviation (Bermuda) VR-BAY *Good Fortune*, Aer Lingus EI-ALG
316	810	G-AOYV	Vickers prototype	VASP PP-SRH
317	818	CU-T621	Cubana	South African Airways ZS-CVA
318	818	CU-T622	,,	TAA VH-TVR
319	818	CU-T623	,,	Ansett-ANA VH-RML
320	818	N500T	Tennessee Gas Transmission Co	Washington Square Methodist Church
321	769	CX-AQN	PLUNA	
322	769	CX-AQO	,,	
323	769	CX-AQP	,,	
324	784	PI-C771	Philippine Airlines	Falcon Airways of Sweden
325	785	I-LIFE	LAI (to Alitalia)	
326	785	I-LIFT	,, ,,	
327	785	I-LILI	,, ,,	
328	785	I-LAKE	,, ,,	
329	785	I-LARK	,, ,,	
330	785	I-LOTT	,, ,,	
331	773	YI-ACU	Iraqi Airways *Ibn Turaik*	
332	786	HK-943X	Lloyd Aereo Colombiano *Santa Margarita*	TACA YS-08C
333	786	AN-AKP	Lanica *Nicarao* later *Bolivar*	TACA YS-011C, BKS G-AVIY
334	786	AN-AKQ	,, *Ruben Dario*	H. H. May N200Q
335	815	AP-AJC	Pakistan Int Airlines *City of Karachi*	
336	815	AP-AJD	Pakistan Int Airlines *City of Lahore*	G-AVJA
337	815	AP-AJE	Pakistan Int Airlines *City of Dacca*	
338	814	D-ANUN	Lufthansa	Condor Flugdienst
339	814	D-ANOL	,,	,, ,,
340	814	D-ANAD	,,	
341	814	D-ANIP	,,	Condor Flugdienst
342	814	D-ANUR	,,	,, ,,

343	814	D-ANEF	Lufthansa	
344	814	D-ANIZ	,,	
345	789	FAB-2101	Brazilian Air Force	
346	813	ZS-CDT	South African Airways *Blesbok*	
347	813	ZS-CDU	South African Airways *Bosbok*	
348	813	ZS-CDV	South African Airways *Waterbok*	
349	813	ZS-CDW	South African Airways *Rooibok*	
350	813	ZS-CDX	South African Airways *Wildebees*	
351	813	ZS-CDY	South African Airways *Gemsbok*	
352	813	ZS-CDZ	South African Airways *Hartbees*	
353	812	N240V	Continental Airlines	Tennessee Gas N501T, Matman Corp
354	812	N243V	,, ,,	
355	812	N241V	,, ,,	Ansett -ANA VH-RMK
356	812	N242V	,, ,,	
357	812	N244V	,, ,,	Channel G-ATUE
358	812	N245V	,, ,,	,,
359	812	N246V	,, ,,	,,
360	812	N248V	,, ,,	,,
361	812	N249V	,, ,,	,,
362	812	N250V	,, ,,	,,
363	812	N251V	,, ,,	,,
364	812	N252V	,, ,,	,,
365	812	N253V	,, ,,	,, G-ATVR, Treffield International
366	812	N254V	,, ,,	,, G-ATVE, Treffield International
368	814	D-ANAM	Lufthansa	
369	814	D-ANAB	,,	
370	814	D-ANAC	,,	
371	838	9G-AAV	Ghana Airways	MoA XT661
372	838	9G-AAW	,,	
373	756	VH-TVM	TAA *John Fawkner*	
374	756	VH-TVN	,, *William Dampier*	
375	815	AP-AJF	Pakistan Int Airlines *City of Karachi*	G-AVJB
376	815	AP-AJG	Pakistan Int Airlines *City of Dacca*	Luxair LX-LGC
377	785	I-LIRS	Alitalia	
378	785	I-LIZT	,,	
379	785	I-LIRP	,,	
380	785	I-LIZO	,,	
381	806	G-APEX	BEA *John Harrison*	
382	806	G-APEY	,, *William Murdoch*	

383	757	CF-TIC	TCA Fleet 647	
384	757	CF-TID	,,　　648	
385	757	CF-TIE	,,　　649	
386	757	CF-TIF	,,　　650	
387	757	CF-TIG	,,　　651	
389	812	N247V	Continental Airlines	Channel G-AVJL
391	798	N6597C	Northeast Airlines	Victor Comptometer N8989
392	798	N6598C	,,　　　　,,	Potash Co of America
393	739A	SU-AKN	Misrair	Eagle G-ATDR *City of Glasgow*
394	739A	SU-AKO	,,	,,　G-ATFN *City of Truro*
395	804	G-APKG	Transair	BUA, LOT SP-LVB
396	806	G-APKF	BEA *Michael Faraday*	
397	827	PP-SRC	Vasp	
398	827	PP-SRD	,,	
399	827	PP-SRE	,,	
400	827	PP-SRF	,,	
401	827	PP-SRG	,,	
402	831	G-APND	Airwork	BUA, Jordan JY-ADB
403	831	G-APNE	,,	,, , Br. Midland, Jordan JY-ADA
412	806	G-APIM	BEA *Robert Boyle*	
413	806	G-APJU	,,　*Sir Gilbert Blane*	
414	832	VH-RMG	Ansett-ANA	
415	832	VH-RMH	,,	
416	832	VH-RMI	,,	
417	832	VH-RMJ	,,	
418	806	G-APOX	BEA *Isambard Brunel*	
419	831	ST-AAN	Sudan Airways	BUA　　G-ASED,　Aviaco EC-AZK, British Midland
421	808	EI-AKJ	Aer Lingus *St Colman* (*Colman*)	Re-registered EI-AKO
422	808	EI-AKK	,,　　*St Aidan* (*Aodhan*)	
423	808	EI-AKL	,,　　*St Colmcille* (*Colmcille*)	
424	833	G-APTB	Hunting-Clan Air Transport	BUA
425	833	G-APTC	Hunting-Clan Air Transport	,,
426	833	G-APTD	Hunting-Clan Air Transport	,,
427	739B	SU-AKW	Misrair	Jordan JY-ADC, BUA G-APTD
428	807	ZK-BWO	NZNAC *City of Dunedin*	
429	794	TC-SEV	Türk Hava Yollari	
430	794	TC-SEL	,,　　　　,,	
431	794	TC-SES	,,　　　　,,	
432	794	TC-SET	,,　　　　,,	
433	816	VH-TVP	TAA *John Gould*	
434	816	VH-TVQ	,,　*McDouall Stuart*	
435	836	N40N	Union Carbide	Re-registered　N140N,　RAAF A6-435

436	816	EP-MRS	Iran Government	Iranair, RAAF A6-436
437	837	OE-LAF	Austrian Airlines	
438	837	OE-LAG	Austrian Airlines *Franz Schubert*	RAF XT575
439	837	OE-LAH	Austrian Airlines *Anton Bruckner*	
440	837	OE-LAK	Austrian Airlines *Johann Strauss*	
441	837	OE-LAL	Austrian Airlines *W. A. Mozart*	
442	837	OE-LAM	Austrian Airlines *Ludwig v. Beethoven*	Re-registered OE-IAM
443	828	JA-8201	All Nippon Airways	
444	828	JA-8202	,, ,,	
445	828	JA-8203	,, ,,	
446	838	9G-AAU	Ghana Airways	
447	818	D-ANAF	Lufthansa	
448	828	JA-8204	All Nippon Airways	
449	828	JA-8205	,, ,,	
450	828	JA-8206	,, ,,	
451	843	G-ASDP	CAAC (China)	British registration for delivery
452	843	G-ASDR	,, ,,	,, ,, ,,
453	843	G-ASDS	,, ,,	,, ,, ,,
454	843	G-ASDT	,, ,,	,, ,, ,,
455	843	G-ASDU	,, ,,	,, ,, ,,
456	843	G-ASDV	,, ,,	,, ,, ,,
457	828	JA-8208	All Nippon Airways	
458	828	JA-8209	,, ,,	
459	828	JA-8210	,, ,,	

Valiant

1. Prototype WB210 Type 660 ordered to specification B.9/48 with Avon RA3 engines on 2 February, 1949.

2. Second prototype WB215 Type 667 ordered to specification B9.9/48 with AS Sapphire engines but flew with Avon RA7s.

3. Prototype B.2 WJ954 Type 673—low-level sortie.

4. 25 WP199–223 ordered under contract 6/Air/6313/CB6(c) April 1951; delivered as B.1 Type 674—WP199–203; B.1 Type 706—WP204, 206–216, 218, 220, and 222; B(PR)1 Type 710—WP205, 217, 219, 221 and 223; all delivered between 18 December, 1954, and 20 July, 1955.

5. 24 WZ361–384 ordered under contract 6/Air/7375/CB6(c); delivered as B.1 Type 706—WZ361–375 and 377; B(PR)1, Type 710—WZ376, 378–379, 381, 383–384; B(PR)K1 Type 733—WZ380 and 382; all delivered between 12 August, 1955, and 2 March, 1956.

6. 17 WZ389–405 ordered under contract 6/Air/7376/CB6(c); delivered as B(PR)K1 Type 733—WZ389–399; B(K)1 Type 758—WZ400–405; all delivered between 24 March and 17 July, 1956.

7. 56 XD812–830, 857–893 ordered under contract 6/Air/9446/CB6(c), but only 38 delivered as B(K)1 Type 758—XD812–830, 857–875; last Valiant delivered XD875 27 August, 1957—total built 107 including prototypes.

Squadrons: 7, 18, 49, 90, 138, 148, 199, 207, 214, 543 also 232 OCU.

Vanguard

Total built—44 (including prototype)

C/n	Registration	Type	Operator	Name or Fleet Number
701		950	Test Fuselage	
702		950	,,	
703	G-AOYW	950	Trials and Demonstrator	
704	G-APEA	951	BEA	*Vanguard*
705	G-APEB	951	,,	*Bellerophon*
706	G-APEC	951	,,	*Sirius*
707	G-APED	951	,,	*Defiance*
708	G-APEE	951	,,	*Euryalus*
709	G-APEF	951	,,	*Victory*
710	G-APEG	953	,,	*Arethusa*
711	G-APEH	953	,,	*Audacious*
712	G-APEI	953	,,	*Indefatigable*
713	G-APEJ	953	,,	*Ajax*
714	G-APEK	953	,,	*Dreadnought*
715	G-APEL	953	,,	*Leander*
716	G-APEM	953	,,	*Agamemnon*
717	G-APEN	953	,,	*Valiant*
718	G-APEO	953	,,	*Orion*
719	G-APEP	953	,,	*Superb*
720	G-APER	953	,,	*Amethyst*
721	G-APES	953	,,	*Swiftsure*
722	G-APET	953	,,	*Temaraire*
723	G-APEU	953	,,	*Undaunted*
724	CF-TKA	952	TCA (Air Canada)	901
725	CF-TKB	952	,, ,,	902
726	CF-TKC	952	,, ,,	903
727	CF-TKD	952	,, ,,	904
728	CF-TKE	952	,, ,,	905
729	CF-TKF	952	,, ,,	906
730	CF-TKG	952	,, ,,	907
731	CF-TKH	952	,, ,,	908
732	CF-TKI	952	,, ,,	909
733	CF-TKJ	952	,, ,,	910
734	CF-TKK	952	,, ,,	911
735	CF-TKL	952	,, ,,	912
736	CF-TKM	952	,, ,,	913
737	CF-TKN	952	,, ,,	914
738	CF-TKO	952	,, ,,	915
739	CF-TKP	952	,, ,,	916
740	CF-TKQ	952	,, ,,	917
741	CF-TKR	952	,, ,,	918
742	CF-TKS	952	,, ,,	919
743	CF-TKT	952	,, ,,	920
744	CF-TKU	952	,, ,,	921
745	CF-TKV	952	,, ,,	922
746	CF-TKW	952	,, ,,	923

VC10

C/n	Type	Registration	Operator	Remarks
801 802	Static test fuselages			
803	1100	G-ARTA	Vickers	To Laker Airways, MEA
804	1101	G-ARVA	BOAC	
805	1101	G-ARVB	,,	
806	1101	G-ARVC	,,	To Nigeria Airways
807	1101	G-ARVE	,,	
808	1101	G-ARVF	,,	
809	1101	G-ARVG	,,	
810	1101	G-ARVH	,,	
811	1101	G-ARVI	,,	
812	1101	G-ARVJ	,,	
813	1101	G-ARVK	,,	
814	1101	G-ARVL	,,	
815	1101	G-ARVM	,,	
816	1101			Nos. 13–15 for BOAC—
817	1101			cancelled
818	1101			
819	1103	G-ASIW	BUA	First with cabin-level freight door
820	1103	G-ASIX	,,	
821				cancelled
822				
823	1102	9G-ABO	Ghana Airways	
824	1102	9G-ABP	,,	
825	1103	G-ATDJ	BUA	Ex Ghana 9G-ABQ Type 1102 not delivered
826	1106	XR806	RAF Air Support Command	
827	1106	XR807	,, ,, ,,	
828	1106	XR808	,, ,, ,,	
829	1106	XR809	,, ,, ,,	
830	1106	XR810	,, ,, ,,	
831	1106	XV101	,, ,, ,,	
832	1106	XV102	,, ,, ,,	
833	1106	XV103	,, ,, ,,	
834	1106	XV104	,, ,, ,,	
835	1106	XV105	,, ,,	
836	1106	XV106	,, ,, ,,	
837	1106	XV107	,, ,, ,,	
838	1106	XV108	,, ,, ,,	
839	1106	XV109		
840	1102	9G-ABU	Ghana Airways	
851	1151	G-ASGA	BOAC	First Super VC10
852	1151	G-ASGB		First with under wing spare engine pod
853	1151	G-ASGC	,,	
854	1151	G-ASGD	,,	
855	1151	G-ASGE	,,	

C/n	Type	Registration	Operator	Remarks
856	1151	G-ASGF	BOAC	
857	1151	G-ASGG	,,	Used for autoland development
858	1151	G-ASGH	,,	
859	1151	G-ASGI	,,	
860	1151	G-ASGJ	,,	
861	1151	G-ASGK	,,	Used for autoland development
862	1151	G-ASGL	,,	
863	1151	G-ASGM	,,	
864	1151	G-ASGN	,,	
865	1151	G-ASGO	,,	
866	1151	G-ASGP	,,	
867	1151	G-ASGR	,,	
868–875		G-ASGS to G-ASGZ		Cancelled
881	1154	5X-UVA	East African Airways	
882	1154	5H-MMT	,, ,,	
883	1154	5Y-ADA	,, ,,	
884	1154	—	,, ,,	

APPENDIX IV

Other Aircraft Built by Vickers

1. B.E.2/2a–31 ordered by War Office under contracts A1147 (4); A2044 (5); A2159 (17); A2291 (1)—with four others contract not known—all 31 built at Erith works prior to 1914 at £840 each.

2. B.E.2c—103 built by Vickers at Erith (12), Crayford (16) Weybridge (75) all between 1914 and 1916 at £975 each.

3. B.E.8/8a—35 built in 1914–15 at Dartford works (four B.E.8s), rest at Erith, all at £796 each.

4. F.E.8—50 built in 1916 at Weybridge at £680 each—serials 7595–7644.

5. Sopwith 1½ Strutter—150 built in 1916–17 at Crayford at £848 each—serials A1054–1153, A8744–8793.

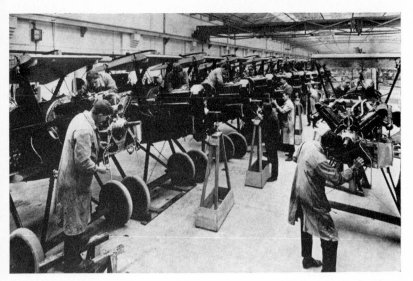

S.E.5a fighter production in the first world war at the Birmingham works of Wolseley Motors, then a Vickers subsidiary.

6. S.E.5a—2,165 built—515 at Crayford, 1650 at Weybridge with an additional 431 by Wolseley Motors, Vickers subsidiary. Weybridge serials: B501–700, C9486–9635, D201–300, D3426–3575, D5951–6200, E1251–1400, E3904–4103, F5449–5698, F8946–9145. Crayford serials: C5301–5450, D301–450, D8431–8580, F551–615. Wolseley serials: C6351–6500, D6851–7000, F851–950, F7751–7800 (only 31 built of last batch).

7. Armstrong Whitworth Siskin IIIA—27 J9353–9379 ordered under contract 855124/28 delivered between 16 March and 15 May, 1929, nearly

S.E.5a production at Weybridge in the first world war; 1,650 were made there, by far the highest total in the country.

Production of Hawker Harts and Hart Trainers at Weybridge in 1933;
in background Vildebeests and Type 163 bomber.

all at £2,079 each; 25 J9872–9896 ordered under contract 937776/29
delivered between 9 January and 7 March, 1930, at £1,750 each; 65 Siskins
later reconditioned or rebuilt at Weybridge.

8. Hawker Hart—50 K2424–2473 ordered under contract 117876/31;
65, K2966–3030, ordered under contract 198868/32; 47, K3808–3854,
ordered under contract 262680/33; all delivered between 18 February,
1932, and 13 March, 1934.

9. Hawker Hart Trainer—114 K5784–5897 ordered under contract
410420/35 delivered between 14 February and 28 May, 1936.

10. Avro Lancaster B.1—500 ordered only 235 built under contract
2791—PA158–198, 214–239, 252–288, 303–351, 365–396, 410–452, 473–
478 and PA509—all delivered between June 1944 and September 1945
from Chester works; further 240 Lancaster B.2—order cancelled.

The Maxim Flying Machine

Although Vickers were not directly concerned with the flying machine invented by Hiram S. Maxim, an American living in England, a short note is presented here of his pioneering efforts in aeronautics, because of his subsequent association with Vickers, Sons and Maxim Ltd. His firm, Maxim Nordenfelt Guns and Ammunition Co Ltd was acquired by Vickers Sons and Co Ltd in 1897, and his original Maxim machine-gun was developed into the Vickers gun, which was widely used in military aircraft.

Maxim's aeroplane was an ungainly structure with five sets of wings, the three centre pairs of which could be removed to vary the wing area from 5,400 to 4,000 sq ft. The total weight of the machine was about 4,000 lb, and it was powered with two compound steam engines fed by a water-tube boiler. They developed 363 hp each and drove a propeller of 17 ft 10-in diameter at 375 rpm. The weight of each engine was about 320 lb, but the boiler added some 800 lb. This boiler was mounted on a midships platform which also carried the crew of three, with the controls and water tanks. The overall span was 125 ft and the length was 104 ft.

The Maxim machine was tested by its inventor in Baldwyn's Park, Bexley, Kent, in July 1894. It was mounted on a specially constructed railway track of 9-ft gauge, with a secondary wooden track of 35-ft gauge on the outside inverted to prevent the machine rising more than a few inches for the preliminary experiments.

As with other early attempts to fly a heavier-than-air craft, evidence was obtained that Maxim's machine did rise off the ground. But the uncontrollability common to all attempts prior to the Wright brothers became catastrophic during the first trials and the machine was wrecked, without injury to Maxim and his assistants. It had cost Maxim over £20,000. Later he became a British citizen and was knighted.

Hiram Maxim's flying machine after its crash.

INDEX—GENERAL

(For Aircraft and Engines see p. 565)

559

Saunders, S. E. and Co, 19, 21, 112, 440
Salisbury Plain, 334
Schillig Roads, 324, 325
Scholefield, E. R. C. 'Tiny', 8, 136, 175, 184, 189, 190, 196, 200, 211
Schrenk flaps, 301
Science Museum, 82, 86
Scott, Maj G. H., 32
Sharrett, Frank, 175
Shenstone, Beverley, 214, 454
Shiers, Sgt W. H., 88
Short Bros, 19, 190
Shute, Nevil, 30, 32
Signals Command, 413, 414
Silver Queen, 88, 89
Singapore, 88, 280–282, 289
Smith, Sir Keith, 6, 83, 88, 121
—, Sir Ross, 6, 83, 88, 119, 307
Smiths Aviation Division, 414
Somme, Battle of, 56
Sorley, Sir Ralph, 240, 417
South Africa, 88, 274, 384, 401, 405
— America, 185, 196, 197, 202, 212
Southampton, 10, 14, 221
— Water, 226, 227, 276
Spain, 120, 277–280
Sperry bomb sight, 349
Spitfire, 14
Spittlegate, 90, 189
Stack, Neville, 191, 193
Stansted, 459
SCT plywood, 119
Strategic Air Command (US), 447
Stavanger, 402
Stephenson, Basil, 428, 454
Stewart, Oliver, 7
Stockholm, 280
Stokes Bay, 283
Stoney Stratford, 331
St Albans water tank, 112, 195
— — wind tunnel, 82
— Cyr, 216
— George's Hill, 41
— John's (Newfoundland), 83, 85
— Moritz, 118
— Vincent, Cape of, 287
Sudan, 90
Sueter, Murray, Capt, 1, 19
Suez Canal, 343
Sumatra, 290
Summers, Maurice, 379, 391
—, 'Mutt', 11, 12, 15, 163, 187, 217, 221, 227, 229, 235, 237, 249, 253, 258, 269, 293–295, 315, 320, 332, 379, 390, 398, 411, 414, 424, 439
Supermarine works, 4, 10, 14, 112, 114, 129, 216, 217, 226, 227, 279, 353, 386
Super Sprite, 445, 446
Supreme Command Europe, 448
Suresnes, 56
Swanage, 337
Swanley range, 345
Swedish Air Force, Royal, 415

Swinderby, 340, 412, 414
Swinton, Lord, 417
Switzerland, 118
Sykes, Sir Frederick, 116

Tabora, 89
Tanganyika, 89
Teed, Maj P. L., 30
Thames, River, 35
Thomson, Lord, 30, 33
Times, The, 83, 89, 127, 159
Timor Sea, 225
Townend ring, 149, 204, 205, 241
Tokyo, 127
Transport Command, 102, 171, 374, 405, 408, 463
—, Institute of, 102
TRE Malvern, 337
Trinidad, 458
Tripoli, 343
Trubshaw, E. Brian, 15, 457, 471
Tullett, E. H. C., 225
Turkey, 276

U-boat, 353
Uffa Fox, 374, 376
Ulm, Charles, 230
Upavon, 3
Upper Heyford, 304, 307
US Air Attaché, 172
— Government, 336
— Navy, 121
Uwins, Cyril, 9, 204–206, 307

Vancouver, 127
Van Ryneveld, Sir Pierre, 6, 83, 88, 89, 274
Vickers-Challenger gun gear, 50, 62
Vickers, Douglas, 109, 110
— Flying School, 2–4, 35, 41, 60
— House, 1, 43, 123
— -Ryan longeron, 94
— 40-mm gun, 344, 345
Vintage Aircraft Association (Brooklands), 58, 60
Vokes air filter, 373
Volkert, G. R., 309
VSG hydraulic power, 344

Wakelin, Capt W. J., 427
Wallis, Sir Barnes, 11, 12, 21, 25, 33, 190, 222, 241, 291, 302, 309, 311, 313, 330, 488
— bombs, 331
Walney Island, 21, 22, 25
Walvis Bay, 305
Wantage, 391
War Office, 2, 37, 49, 218
Washington, 433
Wells Aviation Co, 66
Wembley Exhibition, 110
West Africa, 289
— Australian Airways, 10, 218–220
Westbrook, Trevor, 13, 15, 311, 323

563

INDEX—AIRCRAFT AND ENGINES